Comparative Income Taxation

Kluwer Law International

Comparative Income Taxation

A Structural Analysis

Third Edition

Principal Authors

Hugh J. Ault, Boston College Law School
Brian J. Arnold, Professor of Tax Law, emeritus; Tax consultant

Contributing Authors

Guy Gest, University of Paris II
Peter Harris, University of Cambridge
Peter Melz, Stockholm University
Minoru Nakazato, University of Tokyo
Yasutaka Nishikori, Nishimura & Partners, Tokyo
James Repetti, Boston College Law School
Wolfgang Schön, Max Planck Institute, Munich
John Tiley, University of Cambridge
Richard J. Vann, University of Sydney
Kees van Raad, University of Leiden

Wolters Kluwer
Law & Business

AUSTIN BOSTON CHICAGO NEW YORK THE NETHERLANDS

Published by:
Kluwer Law International
PO Box 316
2400 AH Alphen aan den Rijn
The Netherlands
Website: www.kluwerlaw.com

Sold and distributed in North, Central and South America by:
Aspen Publishers, Inc.
7201 McKinney Circle
Frederick, MD 21704
United States of America
Email: customer.service@aspenpublishers.com

Sold and distributed in all other countries by:
Turpin Distribution Services Ltd.
Stratton Business Park
Pegasus Drive, Biggleswade
Bedfordshire SG18 8TQ
United Kingdom
Email: kluwerlaw@turpin-distribution.com

Printed on acid-free paper.

ISBN 978-90-411-3204-8

Printed in Great Britain.

Table of Contents

Acknowledgments

The 2010 edition of *Comparative Income Taxation* builds on the predecessor 1997 and 2004 editions, and the current authors would like to acknowledge the contributions of those who made the initial publication possible. In particular, we would like to thank Albert J. Rädler and J. Mark Ramseyer, Contributing Authors to the prior edition whose work is still reflected in this current edition.

As in prior editions, Carol Hargreaves handled all phases of the preparation of the manuscript for this edition, dealing quickly and efficiently with complex material from many sources, and we gratefully acknowledge her dedicated, cheerful, and competent help. Thanks also to Peter Melz for organizing a preparatory meeting of the authors in Stockholm in May 2003.

Financial support for the project was provided by The Marianne and Marcus Wallenbergs Foundation and the Harvard Fund for Tax Policy Research.

Hugh J. Ault
Brian J. Arnold

Preface

The purpose of this book is to compare different solutions adopted by nine industrialized countries to common problems of income tax design. As in other legal domains, comparative study of income taxation can provide fresh perspectives from which to examine a particular national system. Increasing economic globalization also makes understanding foreign tax systems relevant to a growing set of transnational business transactions.

Comparative study is, however, notoriously difficult. Full understanding of a foreign tax system may require mastery not only of a foreign language, but also of foreign business and legal cultures. It would be the work of a lifetime for a single individual to achieve that level of understanding of the nine income taxes compared in this volume.

Suppose, however, that an international group of tax law professors, each expert in his own national system, were asked to describe how that system resolved specific problems of income tax design with respect to individuals, business organizations, and international transactions. Suppose further that the leader of the group wove the resulting answers into a single continuous exposition, which was then reviewed and critiqued by a wider group of tax teachers. The resulting text would provide a convenient and comprehensive introduction to foreign approaches to income taxation for teachers, students, policy makers, and practitioners.

That is the path followed by Hugh Ault, Brian Arnold, and their collaborators in the development of this fascinating book. Henceforth, a reader interested in how other developed countries resolve such structural issues as the taxation of fringe benefits, the effect of unrealized appreciation at death, the classification of business entities, expatriation to avoid taxes, and so on, can turn to this volume for an initial answer. I am delighted that the Harvard Law School Fund for Tax and Fiscal

Research was able to provide financial support for this important project. The resulting book should greatly facilitate comparative analysis in teaching and writing about taxation in the US and elsewhere.

Prof. Alvin C. Warren, Jr.
Harvard Law School

Table of Abbreviations

PART ONE

Australia

AAT	Administrative Appeals Tribunal
ABN	Australian Business Number
ATO	Australian Taxation Office
FBTAA	Fringe Benefits Tax Assessment Act
GST	Goods and Services Tax
ITAA 1936	Income Tax Assessment Act 1936
ITAA 1997	Income Tax Assessment Act 1997
OPC	Office of Parliamentary Counsel

Canada

CRA	Canada Revenue Agency
GAAR	General Anti-avoidance Rule
GST	Goods and Services Tax
ITA	Income Tax Act
ITCIA	Income Tax Conventions Interpretation Act

France

BOI	Official Tax Bulletin
CA	*Cour d'Appel*
CAA	*Cour Administrative d'Appel*
CE	*Conseil d'État*
CGI	General Tax Code
CRDS	Social Debt Reimbursement Contribution
CSG	Generalized Social Contribution
ECHR	European Convention on Human Rights
ECJ	European Court of Justice

GDP	Gross Domestic Product
IS	Corporate Income Tax
ISF	Net Wealth Tax
IR	Individual Income Tax
LPF	Book of Tax Procedures
TA	*Tribunal Administratif*
TGI	*Tribunal de Grande Instance*
VAT	Value Added Tax

Germany

CITA	Corporate Income Tax Act
FTTA	Investment Tax Law
GFC	General Fiscal Code
GOL	General Order of Levies
IBFD	International Bureau of Fiscal Documentation
IFRS	International Financial Reporting Standards
ITA	Income Tax Act
ITR	Income Tax Regulations
OFD	*Oberfinanzdirektionen*
RTA	Reorganization Tax Act
VAT	Value Added Tax

Japan

CTA	Corporate Tax Act
ITA	Income Tax Act
NTA	National Tax Agency
STMA	Special Taxation Measures Act

The Netherlands

ATR	Advance Tax Rulings
CTA	Company Tax Act 1969
CITA	Company Income Tax Act 1969
DADT	Decree Avoidance Double Taxation 2001
DivTA	Dividend Tax Act
GAT	General Act on Taxation
ITA	Income Tax Act 2001 (Individuals)
VAT	Value Added Tax
WTA	Wages Tax Act 1964

Sweden

BFN	*Bokföringsnämnden*
ITA	Income Tax Act
SFS	*Svensk Forfattningssamling*
SOU	*Statens Offentliga Utredningar*
VAT	Value Added Tax

United Kingdom

CA	Companies Act 2006
CAA	Capital Allowances Act 2001
CGT	Capital Gains Tax
CT	Corporation Tax
CTA	Corporation Tax Act
GAAR	General Anti-avoidance Rule
HMRC	Her Majesty's Revenue and Customs
ICTA	Income and Corporation Taxes Act 1988
IFS	Institute for Fiscal Studies
IHTA	Inheritance Tax Act
ITA	Income Tax Act 2007
ITEPA	Income Tax (Earnings and Pensions) Act 2003
ITTOIA	Income Tax (Trading and Other Income) Act 2005
PAYE	Pay As You Earn
TA	Taxes Act
TCGA	Taxation of Chargeable Gains Act 1992
TLRC	Tax Law Review Committee
VAT	Value Added Tax

United States

AMT	Alternative Minimum Tax
IRC	Internal Revenue Code
IRS	Internal Revenue Service
Treas. Reg.	Treasury Regulation

PART TWO

ACRS	Accelerated Cost Recovery System
CGI	*Code Général des Impôts*
FBT	Fringe Benefits Tax
IFRS	International Financial Reporting Standards
IRC	Internal Revenue Code
ITA	Income Tax Assessment Act
ITAA	Income Tax Assessment Act
OID	Original Issue Discount

PART THREE

CCPC	Canadian-owned 'private' corporations
CGT	Capital Gains Tax
CITA	Corporate Income Tax Act
CTA	Company Tax Act
IRC	Internal Revenue Code
RTA	Reorganization Tax Act

PART FOUR

APA	Advance Pricing Agreements
CFC	Controlled Foreign Corporation
CGI	Code Général des Impôts
CITA	Corporate Income Tax Act
CPM	Comparable Profits Method
CRA	Canada Revenue Agency
CUP	Comparable Uncontrolled Price
DADT	Decree Avoidance Double Taxation
FAPI	Foreign Accrual Property Income
FIC	Foreign Investment Company Legislation
FIE	Foreign Investment Entity
GAT	General Act on Taxation
GFC	General Fiscal Code
IRC	Internal Revenue Code
ITA	Income Tax Act
ITAA	Income Tax Assessment Act
OECD	Organisation for Economic Co-operation and Development
PFIC	Passive Foreign Investment Company
STMA	Special Taxation Measures Act

Introduction

Introduction to the 2010 Edition

The overall structure and organization of the 1997 and 2004 editions appear to have worked well and have been maintained in this 2010 edition. The Introduction to the 1997 edition, set out below, continues to be a guide to this edition. The current material reflects the state of the law through 2009 but, as with the prior editions, is focused principally on structural developments. It should not be used as a source for detailed information. We have made some changes in this edition to facilitate its use as a research tool. Some footnotes have been added, giving legislative and judicial sources as an aid in beginning research on a particular topic. The footnoting has been done sparingly to avoid interrupting the flow of the text, but it should give appropriate starting points for further investigation. In addition, the Bibliography has been omitted and replaced by additional information on basic statutory and interpretative material in the Sources of Law section in each of the Country Chapters in Part One.

Introduction to the 1997 Edition

This work presents a comparative analysis of some of the structural and design issues which are involved in mature income tax systems. It is aimed primarily at professors and students of tax law, both in the United States and abroad, whose central concern lies naturally in working with the concepts and principles of their own domestic systems. For them, the material is intended both to provide information on what other systems actually do, which is interesting in itself, and to suggest other approaches which might represent alternative ways of dealing with corresponding issues in a domestic setting. By introducing a comparative dimension, the materials can be used both to enrich the classroom discussion of domestic problems and to give a starting point for further research and study. For example, who has not wondered, when discussing an interesting question like the child care deduction or the taxation of imputed income, what other countries do in their systems. While the answers are there, they are hard to find and harder to evaluate. This work is at least a beginning in making the approaches of other systems more accessible.

The countries selected for the study, Australia, Canada, France, Germany, Japan, The Netherlands, Sweden, the United Kingdom, and the United States, all have relatively mature and sophisticated tax systems. One would expect a priori that many similar issues and questions would emerge, and this intuition is confirmed by the materials. The responses to the issues, however, vary substantially in many cases though also showing some areas of congruence. Several of the systems belong to the same broad legal 'family'. The approaches of the United Kingdom, Canada and Australia all display some of the expected degree of similarity, given their common historical roots. The Continental systems likewise, though to a lesser extent, have similarities in structure and result. The United States system has developed without much influence from other systems, and the Japanese system has both Continental, especially German, features as well as displaying a strong influence from American ideas in the post-war developments.

Thus while the details differ, there are some recognizable 'family resemblances'. The Commonwealth systems all have, in varying degrees, schedular features. Different classes or categories of income may be taxed in different ways and at different rates, with varying rules for inclusion and deduction. Trust notions of 'income' and 'corpus' have also played an important role in developing tax concepts. Partly as a result of this latter phenomenon, the taxation of capital gains has been the subject of special legislation, often structured as a separate tax regime.

Continental systems, as well, have significant points of resemblance. Financial accounting rules have often been important in the development of tax principles, especially in the computation of business income. In addition, and unlike the Commonwealth tradition, capital gains realized in a business setting have usually been subject to the normal tax rules dealing with business profits. Capital gains of individual investors, however, have at least initially escaped tax, though the traditional approaches have often been modified, extending taxation to certain limited classes of gains.

Beyond these broad features, each of the systems has evolved its own particular set of approaches and principles. These are outlined in some detail in the individual Country Descriptions contained Part One. These individually authored pieces present the overall structure of the systems being considered and try to provide some feel for the 'tax culture' or climate and institutional framework in which the substantive rules operate. They can be read as 'stand alone' descriptions of the systems or referred to subsequently for a better understanding of the later discussion of a particular rule.

It is essential to keep in mind some of the basic features outlined in the Country Descriptions when dealing with the later substantive material. For example, in thinking about the structure of the rules on corporate liquidations, it is crucial to remember that in some countries private capital gains of an individual will not be taxed while business gains will be subject to full taxation. Similarly, in considering items included in the tax base, taxation may depend on into which, if any, of the various taxable categories the item can be fitted. To facilitate the necessary cross-references, some of the more important features of each system are summarized in tabular form at the end of the Part One.

The remaining three Parts deal with Basic Income Taxation, Taxation of Business Organizations, and International Taxation respectively. As will be apparent, the organization is based on an American format and follows in broad outline the issues and questions typically covered in an American law school course on each particular topic.

Within each Part, the various substantive Subparts and Sections begin by outlining some of the structural issues or problems which have arisen in the area under consideration. The responses of the countries to the problems are described together with an attempt to identify common patterns or approaches and to highlight unique or interesting solutions. The descriptions of the substantive rules vary in completeness, and not every issue is discussed in connection with every country. The focus is on structural and design issues, though there is some consideration of extra-fiscal measures.

There is, of course, always a danger in attempting to relate legal rules or concepts in one system to a seemingly similar situation in another system. The institutional and cultural backgrounds may be different and the actual operation of each individual rule depends on the overall structure of both the tax system and the legal system generally. Doing meaningful comparative analysis is especially difficult in the tax area, where political pressure, chance, and historical accident have all had an important influence on the development of the systems. However, with appropriate caveats and cautions, there is much to learn in the tax field from a comparative analysis of common problems. One need not believe in the existence of a Platonic Tax Form to find useful insights in the experience of others.

Part One

General Description

Australia

Prof. Richard Vann

1. HISTORY OF THE INCOME TAX

The federal income tax was introduced in 1915 as a measure to finance the war effort. The first income tax in Australia had been introduced in South Australia in 1884, prior to federation in 1901, and by 1907 all states had an income tax. Interestingly, both at the state and federal level, the income tax was usually introduced in conjunction with a land tax, reflecting the significant influence in Australia of Henry George's work *Progress and Poverty*. Concerns about the operation of the income tax systems led to a Royal Commission in the early 1920s and a new federal income tax statute in 1922. Harmonization of state and federal income taxes was not achieved in this exercise, and a further Royal Commission in the early 1930s produced a new federal tax statute, the *Income Tax Assessment Act 1936*, which is still the current legislation in part and was the model for all state income taxes – that is, harmonization was achieved on this occasion.

The harmonization was short-lived. With the advent of World War II the federal government decided to take over the state income taxes and levy a single federal income tax. A new emphasis on federalism in the 1970s saw the federal legislation amended in a way that permitted states to levy income taxes if they wished, but the necessary precondition for making this a reality – namely, a cut in federal income tax rates to create room for state taxes – did not occur. The more centralist Labour Government of the 1980s and early 1990s repealed the legislation permitting states to levy income taxes.

Although several other commissions of inquiry were instituted from the 1950s to the 1970s, they had little major immediate impact other than giving rise to legislative measures to counter various forms of tax avoidance. There have been two major overhauls of the tax system in general, and the income tax in particular, in more recent times. First, in the mid-1980s the Labour Government introduced a capital gains tax, a fringe benefits tax, a full imputation system in relation to company dividends, and a complete overhaul of the taxation of foreign-source income of residents. These measures generally followed the common 1980s tax reform strategy of base broadening and rate cutting (with maximum individual tax rates falling from 60% to less than 49%).

Second, in 1998 the Liberal National (conservative) Government adopted a comprehensive tax reform agenda with four major elements:

(1) reform of individual and company tax rates, including tax cuts, a tax mix change, and greater integration of the income tax with the social welfare system;
(2) introduction of a value added tax called the Goods and Services Tax, or GST with the revenue going by grants to the states under a major overhaul of fiscal federalism;
(3) overhaul of tax administration, including broader withholding arrangements, integration of several tax collection mechanisms, and binding oral tax rulings for individuals with simple tax affairs; and
(4) substantial changes to the individual and business tax base (50% discount for capital gains made by individuals, uniform capital allowances that abolished accelerated depreciation, introduction of a special regime for small business, anti-avoidance rules on alienation of personal services income and non-commercial losses) and taxation of entities (a simplification of the imputation system, redrawing the debt and equity borderline, rollovers for takeovers and demergers, a comprehensive value shifting regime, new thin capitalization measures, and tax consolidation for 100% common-owned corporate groups).

More than a decade later, one of the elements of the reform in relation to taxation of financial instruments has not been enacted, although it should be during 2009 (indeed, this reform dates back to a 1992 announcement). As time passed, several elements of the 1998 proposed reforms were abandoned, including a complete restructuring of the way in which taxable income is calculated and taxation of partnerships and other joint activities.

Not to be outdone, the new Labour Government, elected in late 2007, announced in 2008 yet another 'root and branch' tax reform. The committee entrusted with this task is due to report at the end of 2009, with decisions and implementation starting to take place in 2010. At this stage it is not clear what shape the reform proposals are likely to take, although one element will concern the ongoing issue of appropriate integration of the tax and social security systems.

2. CONSTITUTIONAL ISSUES

Australia has a federal constitution under which the central government is given power to levy income taxes along with the states. To meet the emergency created by World War II, the federal government effectively excluded the states from the income tax arena. The drastic legislative measures adopted for this purpose, including a forcible seizure of state income tax offices, were upheld in the High Court of Australia, relying in part on the defence power in a major constitutional challenge by the states. Since that time, no state income tax has been levied in Australia and the federal tax is the sole tax. The federal government was able to maintain this dominance in peacetime, mainly through the grants power in the Constitution, which the High Court held permitted the federal government to make grants to the states conditional on the states not levying an income tax.

The federal government also has exclusive constitutional power to levy duties of customs and excise, a provision originally intended to produce a customs union within Australia. The High Court has interpreted this power widely to include the imposition of sales taxes, so that the states are effectively excluded from the major modern tax bases. Australia does not have a history of levying social security taxes, which in any event would almost certainly be at the federal level under constitutional powers conferred on the federal government by referendum in 1946 with respect to the social security area.

3. TAX RATES

The 2008–2009 federal income tax rates for resident individuals are as follows:

$0–6,000	0%
$6,001–30,000	15%
$30,001–80,000	30%
$80,001–180,000	40%
$180,001 and above	45%

There are various tax credits for low-income earners, which raise the zero bracket higher in many cases. In addition, all taxable income of individuals is subject to the 1.5% Medicare levy, which, as its name suggests, is designed to offset a (small) part of the cost of Australia's universal health care system. This levy is collected as part of the income tax, and it is not treated as a social security tax by the Organisation for Economic Co-operation and Development (OECD). There is a phase-in of the levy at lower levels of income so that it is not collected from the very poor, but the phase-in is recaptured by a surcharge so that, above moderate levels of income, it operates as a flat-rate charge. As a result, the maximum individual rate is usually treated as 46.5%; this rate is used, in fact, in the legislation designed to levy tax at top rates on, for example, the undistributed income of trusts. The fringe benefits tax rate is also 46.5%. Recently the picture has become more complicated, with a 1% surcharge for wealthier taxpayers without private health insurance and a tax rebate for those who have private insurance, but 46.5% is still regarded as the effective top tax rate for individuals.

The corporate tax rate is a flat 30%, which applies to public and private companies alike at all income levels. There are a few isolated cases where different corporate tax rates are charged; for example, pooled development funds generally pay tax at 25% (these funds provide venture capital to small and medium-sized enterprises).

4. COMPOSITION OF THE FISCAL SYSTEM

It follows from the constitutional situation discussed above that the states in Australia are denied direct access to the major tax bases. The states are thus forced to rely on a miscellany of taxes (mainly payroll tax, stamp duties on a variety of transactions, and taxes on land and motor vehicles) for about half their revenues, with the remaining half coming in the form of grants from the federal government. With the introduction of the GST on 1 July 2000 and the provision of this revenue by the federal government to the states in lieu of general-purpose grants that had previously been made, some (but not all) of the pressure was taken off the imbalance in the revenue-raising capacities of the respective tiers of government. Including the GST as, in effect, a state tax means that the federal government raises 70% of total taxes and the states 30%. Special-purpose grants are still used to provide federal money to the states (e.g., for the financing of public hospitals).

The major tax in Australia by far is the federal income tax, which raised $189 billion out of total Australia-wide tax revenues of $320 billion in 2005–2006 (the latest OECD data available), or 59% of total taxes. The predominance of the income tax in Australia has existed for many years. Since the OECD first began to collect statistics in 1965, it has been in excess of 50% of total taxation. Even when the federal income tax became the only income tax in Australia in World War II, the income tax represented 42% of total revenues. According to the latest OECD information, taxes totalled 30.6% of Gross Domestic Product (GDP) in 2006, up from around 22% in the 1960s. Total taxes have hovered around 30% of GDP since the 1980s. Thus, Australia can claim to have one of the lowest tax ratios in the OECD, but the comparison is misleading due to the lack of social security taxes and the existence of non-tax mechanisms (compulsory private pension funds) for achieving similar purposes.

5. BASIC STRUCTURE OF THE INCOME TAX

Nominally, Australia has a global income tax system, since the basic inclusion provision covers income according to ordinary concepts (what the courts have held to be income) without reference to categories or sources of income. There are many specific inclusion provisions dealing with particular kinds of income (called *statutory income*), although it is still the case that the vast majority of assessable income in Australia enters through the basic concept of ordinary income. Despite the apparently global nature of income, in fleshing out the concept, the Australian courts have adopted a fairly narrow approach to what is income. This outcome can be attributed to a number of influences.

First, although Australian judges have always recognized that the Australian system is structured quite differently from the explicit schedular nature of the UK system, nonetheless UK case law concepts have often been applied in determining whether specific items are income, and in this way the UK schedules and concept of sources of income have influenced developments in Australia. This explains why, for example, gambling and lottery winnings are not included in the general concept of income.

Second, as in the United Kingdom, which has always had a category of 'other income' in its schedular structure, there are deeper and more ancient sources at work. A major influential concept of income existing in the law when the income tax was introduced in the United Kingdom and Australia was the trust law concept of income. Trust law distinguishes between the capital and the income beneficiaries of the trust, with the former being entitled to any increments in value of the property of the trust that generates its income. The influence of the trust law has been most apparent in the exclusion of capital gains from the basic concept of income in the United Kingdom and Australia.

Third, accounting concepts of profit have had an influence; but since Australia does not use the concept of profit explicitly in the tax legislation in dealing with business income (in contrast to the United Kingdom), the influence has been muted in Australia.

The general valuation rule adopted in the income tax in Australia has also followed that of the United Kingdom, being the amount of money into which a non-monetary item can be converted. Historically, this was a significant limiting factor in the taxation of benefits in kind, although the lack of detailed valuation rules and administrative unwillingness to issue them were also important. Two doctrines that seem to be more peculiarly Australian have been the cause of limitations on the income concept. First, it is clearly established that there is no doctrine under which the reimbursement of an expense that is deductible to a taxpayer will amount to income (although it will be income in certain cases, such as general business receipts). Second, the Australian courts have held that where an amount is received in a lump sum that encompasses income and non-income elements, it is not possible to apportion out the income elements (unless there is clear agreement between the parties to the payment on the breakdown of the amount), and the whole is treated as not being income.

In the tax reform of the 1980s, the introduction of a capital gains tax and a fringe benefits tax added significantly to the tax base and overcame most of these problems, although curiously there still has been no direct and general abolition of the basic valuation and apportionment rules that limit the amount brought into income.

Although the Australian system has thus adopted many of the limiting features of the UK schedular system, the nominal global nature of the system means that many of the features of the UK system are not applied. In particular, generally speaking, special rules are not enacted for the detailed treatment of different categories of income, with the result that all items of income are included on a current year basis and losses on one kind of income generally can be offset against other income (the major exception here being capital losses). Australia has also not been as much influenced by the UK source concept as has, say, Canada, although from time to time there are hints of such a concept. For example, it is still unclear to what extent losses arising from a particular income-earning activity that has come to an end can be deducted.

On the deduction side, Australia has a general deduction provision that covers most deductions incurred to earn income. This provision does not apply to capital items, so it is necessary to find specific provisions dealing with capital expenses. Over the years these specific provisions have been constantly extended on a piecemeal basis to the point where they cover most categories of capital expenses. In 2001 the rules on wasting capital expenses were consolidated and extended in the uniform capital allowances regime, and in 2006 the range of recoverable capital items was further extended, although the coverage is still not complete.

Australia applies essentially the same calculation of taxable income to all taxpayers, including individuals and companies, under the same statutory provisions. Some special rules apply to companies, such as trafficking in company losses, value shifting, intercorporate dividends, the imputation system, and the controlled foreign company regime, and in recent years an increasing number of special rules have been put in place for small business.

6. TAX LEGISLATION

6.1. Legislative Process

The Constitution requires that tax bills originate in the House of Representatives (the popularly elected House of Parliament as opposed to the Senate, which has the same number of senators from each state) and that they deal with only one subject of taxation. The latter requirement has led to some fragmentation of tax legislation, with the result that most tax measures consist of one law spelling out the tax base and another law (or several laws) actually imposing the tax.

Typically, a tax bill takes at least six months to complete passage through Parliament, partly because the Senate prefers to have a committee report on a bill, which means that two sittings of the Senate are necessary for legislation to pass. It is not uncommon for tax bills to take considerably longer to pass if the matter is controversial or if an election intervenes, as all bills lapse when an election is called and need to be reintroduced. Federal elections are held on a three-year cycle in Australia.

All important tax bills originate from the government (the party or parties which control the House of Representatives under the Westminster system of government used in Australia). Although the government of the day in Australia, apart from one recent brief period, has not controlled the Senate for many years and may have to negotiate with minor parties for important or controversial legislation to pass, generally the government (or more accurately the bureaucracy) rather than the legislature is the driving force for tax policy and legislation in Australia.

Tax legislation is so complex that most members of Parliament do not understand it. Apart from major tax reforms, an ongoing tax legislation program arises from various policy announcements from government. In a typical year approximately ten bills dealing with taxation add 500 pages, or often much more, to existing tax legislation.

One highly undesirable feature of the legislative process that is an outgrowth of the tax avoidance problems discussed below is that tax legislation is routinely made retrospective to its announcement date, a practice that does not create any constitutional issues in Australia, unlike some other countries. Initially this was confined to tax avoidance measures but now the same applies even where the legislation concerns systemic issues. The Senate has adopted procedural rules to curb the worst features of this practice – unless the legislation is introduced into Parliament within six months after announcement, the Senate will generally pass the legislation on a prospective basis. The legislation may be subject to major changes in Parliament, and considerable uncertainty among taxpayers results. The new Labour government elected in 2007 is trying to clean up a backlog of about sixty announced but unenacted measures of the previous government, some dating back many years, but with its own tax reform process now underway, it remains to be seen how successful it will be. In 2008 the new government also accepted recommendations from a committee it set up to investigate the tax policy and legislation process, which sets time targets for enacting announcements (six months for retrospective measures and twelve months for prospective measures).

6.2. Statutory Style

From the 1960s, Australian income tax legislation began to be drafted in a peculiarly turgid and convoluted style out of a desire by the drafter to anticipate all possible applications of the specific statutory rules and to prevent their abuse. Partly this approach can be blamed on the literal, nit-picking approach to interpretation of tax legislation formerly used by the judges. However, at least part of the responsibility or blame seems to rest with the unsatisfactory drafting arrangements that existed in Australia, where the Office of Parliamentary Counsel (OPC) had a monopoly on drafting; coordination among this Office, the policy makers in Treasury, and the technical and administrative people in the Australian Taxation Office (ATO) had not worked very well, judging by the results (although Australia is by no means alone in the incomprehensible nature of its tax legislation).

By the early 1990s the Income Tax Assessment Act 1936 could lay claim to the dubious twin titles of being the longest income tax statute in the world and the most unreadable. By that time the basic income tax statute, the Income Tax Assessment Act 1936, was approaching 6,000 pages in length and, together with ancillary legislation such as the Fringe Benefits Tax and the International Tax Agreements Act, occupied four volumes more than 20 centimetres thick printed on wafer-thin pages in closely crowded type. To the original 126 pages of 1936, 500 pages were added in the four decades to 1976, 1,000 pages in the next decade to 1986, and more than double the existing amount of legislation in the decade to 1996 (this explosion in growth being attributable to the extensive tax reform starting in the mid-1980s as well as the ongoing battle with tax avoidance). Australia's income tax, fringe benefit tax (FBT), GST, and related laws consumed almost 13,000 pages and more than 9.5 million words before a clean-out in 2006. The problem is compounded by including virtually all the rules in legislation and leaving little or nothing to regulations (unlike the United States, which with Code and Regulations combined can still claim to being the world champion in terms of verbiage).

Not surprisingly, the bulk and complexity of the legislation has attracted criticism, especially from tax professionals, and there have been several attempts to deal with the problem, none of them successful to date. First, in the period 1994–1998, the government invested substantial resources in the Tax Law Improvement Project, whose brief was to redraft the legislation in a plain-English, user-friendly form without, however, effecting any significant changes in policy or meaning. By 1998 about one-third of the 1936 Act had been rewritten and enacted in tranches into the Income Tax Assessment Act 1997. With the use of diagrams, flow charts, signposts, lists, etc., this redraft was easier to follow and eliminated some of the bulk. The redraft adopted the unusual approach of addressing the taxpayer as 'you', so that the basic charging provision now reads '[Y]ou must pay income tax for each year ending on 30 June'.

When the Liberal National government embarked on its major tax reform program in 1998, it abandoned the Tax Law Improvement Project part-way through. The project had been widely criticized as cosmetic, and there were constant arguments over whether various redrafted provisions had changed the underlying law. The government proposed to address the underlying causes of complexity. An ambitious proposal to redraft the whole legislation in a different structure was, however, abandoned after some years' work, although a significant project to identify and eliminate inoperative provisions in tax legislation proceeded and got rid of a few thousand pages (including, as it turned out, some operative provisions!).

There were also considerable changes in the policy and legislative process within the bureaucracy. A non-statutory but independent advisory body, the Board of Taxation, was created in 2000 and regularly reviews major substantive tax policy issues for the government (such as international taxation and, currently, the taxation of collective investment vehicles). The Board also investigated tax policy and legislation drafting processes, and the government adopted its recommendations. Policy, administrative, and drafting issues were proposed to be approached in an iterative and interactive way rather than in the previously applied linear way (Treasury developed policy, passed the outcome to the ATO to develop drafting instructions, which passed it to OPC to draft). The main concrete consequences so far of the new process are much more consultation on tax measures and the movement of ATO staff to Treasury. The drafting monopoly of OPC remains. The new Labour government was not overly impressed by the results and set up yet another committee to investigate the tax policy and legislation process. In 2008, the government accepted its recommendations, which are designed to produce extensive consultation before initial policy decisions are taken as well as during the development of policy announcements, more attention to the care and maintenance of the tax legislation, and a more transparent policy and legislative process; however, no change of responsibilities within the bureaucracy has occurred. A review of the results has already been promised in advance.

6.3. Statutory Interpretation

Until the early 1980s, the Australian Courts adopted a very strict and literal approach to the interpretation of tax legislation, excluding any reference to extrinsic materials or the purpose of the legislature except insofar as that purpose was ascertainable from the words used. The approach is typified in the following quote:

> It is for the Parliament to specify, and to do so, in my opinion as far as language will permit, with unambiguous clarity, the circumstances which will attract an obligation on the part of the citizen to pay tax. The function of the court is to interpret and apply the language in which the Parliament has specified those circumstances.
>
> The court is to do so by determining the meaning of the words employed by the Parliament which is discoverable from the language used by the Parliament. It is not for the court to mould or to attempt to mould the language of the statute so as to produce some result which it might be thought the Parliament may have intended to achieve, although not expressed in the actual language employed . . .
>
> Parliament having prescribed the circumstances which will attract tax, or provide occasion for its reduction or elimination, the citizen has every right to mould the transaction into which he is about to enter into a form which satisfies the requirements of the statute. It is nothing to the point that he might have attained the same or similar result as that achieved by the transaction into which he in fact entered by some other transaction, which, if he had entered into it, would or might have involved him in a liability to tax, or to more tax than that attracted by the transaction into which he in fact entered. Nor can it matter that his choice of transaction was influenced wholly or in part by its effect upon his obligation to pay tax. The freedom to choose the form of transaction into which he shall enter is basic to the maintenance of a free society.[1]

From this time, three related developments have substantially improved the interpretation process, although it still can hardly be described as ideal. First, the judges began to take a more purposive approach to their interpretation of tax legislation and permit themselves to look at extrinsic material on their own motion.

1. Chief Justice Barwick in *Westraders Pty Ltd* [1980] HCA 24, 144 CLR 55, 60-61. The Barwick court (1965–1981) is widely regarded as having taken literal, indeed taxpayer-biased, interpretations to extremes.

Second, the Acts Interpretation Act 1901, which contains many rules for the interpretation of statutes, was amended to require a purposive approach in interpretation and access to extrinsic material where the statute was ambiguous. This both confirmed and encouraged the change in judicial attitude which was already underway. Third, the approach to drafting the legislation began to change, as already noted, and more detailed, organized, and helpful explanatory memoranda began to be produced (the explanatory memorandum is the official government explanation that is introduced into Parliament at the same time as the legislation). The Tax Law Improvement Project mentioned above was intended to be the culmination of this process, but, as we have seen, it was not and the story is still unfolding. Despite these changes and apart from whether statutory complexity can be eradicated, it remains to be seen whether a coherent and sustainable system of interpretation involving the cooperation of the legislature, the courts, and the administration will emerge.

The following explanation of the interpretive process is representative of the currently stated approach:[2]

> It is now clear, if it ever was in dispute, that the task of construction is not one simply of taking each word used in a statute and applying the dictionary meaning of that word to arrive at a conclusion. The task is not as mechanical as that. While it is clear that the construction of a statute will commence with the words used and that it is a good start to assume that the words mean what they say, that is only a start to the process . . .

However, the English language is seldom so clear and unambiguous that only one construction is open. As a result, judicial decisions in recent times that have discussed the process of construction have attached great importance to 'context'. Perhaps the most famous and often cited passage to this effect is to be found in the judgment of the High Court in *CIC Insurance Ltd v. Bankstown Football Club Limited* where Brennan CJ, Dawson, Toohey and Gummow JJ in a joint judgment wrote:

> It is well settled that at common law, apart from any reliance upon s 15AB of Acts Interpretation Act 1901 (Cth), the court may have regard to reports of law reform bodies to ascertain the mischief which a statute is intended to cure. Moreover, the modern approach to statutory interpretation (a) insists that the context be considered in the first instance, not merely at some later stage when ambiguity might be thought to arise, and (b) uses 'context' in its widest sense to include such things as the existing state of the law and the mischief which, by legitimate means such as those just mentioned, one may discern the statute was intended to remedy. Instances of general words in a statute being so constrained by their context are numerous. In particular, . . . if the apparently plain words of a provision are read in the light of the mischief which the statute was designed to overcome and of the objects of the legislation, they may wear

2. *MLC Limited* [2002] FCA 1491, 126 FCR 37 at paras 31–32 Hill, J.

a very different appearance. Further, inconvenience or improbability of result may assist the court in preferring to the literal meaning an alternative construction which, by the steps identified above, is reasonably open and more closely conforms to the legislative intent.

Judicial interpretation of tax legislation in practice is arrayed along a continuum between literal and purposive, although not so apparently aligned with political and philosophical views of judges as in the United States.

7. COURTS DEALING WITH TAX MATTERS

7.1. Appeal Processes

Australia does not have a specialized tax court, although there is a long history of administrative tribunals with expertise in tax matters. Apart from significant constitutional differences between courts and tribunals, the main practical difference is that tribunals are part of the executive and generally stand in the shoes of the administrator when making decisions; therefore, they can re-exercise discretions that the administrator has. On appeal to a court, the administrative exercise of discretions can be challenged only on grounds recognized in administrative law, such as a decision being *ultra vires*.

When the ATO has made a tax assessment on a taxpayer, the first step in the appeal process is an objection to the assessment. This leads to a reconsideration of the assessment by the ATO. If the assessment stands after reconsideration, the taxpayer can choose to appeal to the Administrative Appeals Tribunal (AAT) or to the Federal Court. In small cases (tax in dispute up to $5,000) there is also a Small Taxation Claims Tribunal (effectively part of the AAT) that deals with matters expeditiously. Hearings before the AAT are in private, can be relatively informal (with the taxpayer often appearing in person), involve smaller appeal fees, and do not lead to orders for costs (i.e., each party effectively bears its own costs of the appeal). The AAT has conference procedures designed to settle matters before they come to a hearing. Court appeals are relatively formal matters, with parties represented by lawyers who make extensive oral and written submissions. Costs follow the event in the usual case (i.e., the loser pays the winner's legal costs). The ATO runs a test case program under which it will fund the taxpayer's legal expenses if it desires to test a matter of important principle in the courts.

In any appeal the onus is on the taxpayer to prove that the assessment is excessive. The onus does not have great practical significance except in cases where the ATO has assessed on the basis of unexplained assets held by taxpayers that do not accord with their income tax returns (i.e., where the ATO considers that the taxpayer is concealing income). Written reasons, often lengthy, are provided for all decisions setting out the facts, the law, and the reasoning by which the decision was reached. Virtually all tax decisions are publicly available in electronic form and are produced by private publishers in hard copy. The commencement of an appeal does not suspend the obligation to pay the tax in dispute, but generally the ATO will suspend recovery proceedings while an appeal is under way (often on condition of payment of a proportion of the tax in dispute).

If the taxpayer chooses to appeal to the AAT, any further appeal to the Federal Court (single judge) can only be on a matter of law. From the Federal Court there is a right of appeal to the Full Federal Court (three judges) on matters of law; from there, appeal to the High Court of Australia (five–seven judges) is not as of right but requires the leave of that Court. In some tax administration situations, cases can be heard in state rather than federal courts. Decisions of higher courts are binding on lower courts and tribunals. At any level of appeal it is usual, but not obligatory, to follow previous decisions at that level on the same legal issue.

The number of income tax decisions in recent years is as follows:

Year	*AAT*	*Federal Court*	*Full Federal Court*	*High Court of Australia*
2000–2002 average	37	33	9	4
2006	59	27	8	1
2007	60	36	18	3
2008	49	30	10	5

Notes

1. Some cases are represented more than once in the sense that the original hearing and any appeals are reported and counted separately, so that a particular case could appear four times.
2. The numbers for the Federal Court and the Full Federal Court also include a small number of cases heard at the same level in the state court hierarchy in those rare cases where state courts still have jurisdiction in federal income tax matters.

It will be evident that there has been some increase in litigation in recent years compared to the period 2000–2002. The main reason is referred to in the discussion of anti-avoidance legislation below. Judgments (reasons for decision) average around 5,000–10,000 words in the AAT, 7,000–15,000 words in the Federal Court, and over 15,000 in the High Court.

7.2. Judicial Expertise

Tax was probably the first area in Australia to have specialist administrative tribunals (originally called Boards of Review). The Boards of Review were constituted by three members – one from the ATO, one accountant, and one lawyer. Because of the influence of the ATO in the appointments, the Boards were often regarded as pro-tax administration. By a quirk of the federal constitution, tax cases went from the Boards directly to the High Court of Australia, the highest court in the land. For a time the system worked well, as the best judges in Australia had a certain expertise in taxation and usually produced sensible decisions.

The High Court managed to dispense with its constitutional jurisdiction in tax matters, first to state courts and then to the newly created Federal Court of Australia from the latter part of the 1970s. When the Boards were replaced by the AAT in the 1980s, a Tax Division was created but the membership of that Division includes many members who do not have previous experience in taxation. One judge on the Federal Court was a tax specialist prior to appointment, and several other judges are regularly involved in tax appeals. No Federal Court judge works full-time on tax matters.

From 1965 to 1981, the High Court under Chief Justice Barwick was generally regarded as strongly pro-taxpayer. Since then, the courts are generally regarded as having moved to a position that favours the tax administration against the taxpayer.

8. TAX ADMINISTRATION

Administration of the income tax (and other federal taxes) in Australia is a huge enterprise, one of the biggest in the country. The ATO has about 23,000 staff, or one staff member per 900 population, and an annual operating budget of about $2.9 billion. The administration of the income tax has been through several major changes and upheavals over the last twenty-five years. The changes started in 1984 and have continued relentlessly since. The Australian experience reflects that of several other countries, which can be attributed to increasing international administrative sharing of experience and cooperation through the OECD and other mechanisms.

One catalyst for change was the Australian Audit Office, which produced a number of highly critical efficiency audits of the ATO in the mid-1980s (and was followed by major reviews by the House of Representatives Standing Committee on Finance and Public Administration in the late 1980s and by the Parliamentary Joint Committee on Public Accounts in the early 1990s). Such audits and parliamentary scrutiny are ongoing, but nowadays the ATO usually accepts and often anticipates the recommendations and works much more cooperatively with its many oversight bodies, which also include the Taxation Ombudsman (effectively a special division of the Ombudsman office) who deals with individual cases and the Inspector General of Taxation who deals with systemic tax administration issues.

Australia has long had a system of universal filing of tax returns by taxpayers. There were 13.5 million returns received in the 2005–2006 year, including 11.5 million individual returns (Australia has a population of about 21 million). Until the mid-1980s all tax returns were manually processed by officers who issued assessments on the basis of the returns with virtually no scrutiny or follow-up audit activity. Where the officer did not agree with the return as filed, an assessment was issued with an adjustment sheet (handwritten with special purple pens) and the taxpayer could then object to the assessment, which initiated the appeal process. While many cases were settled at this stage, there was very little direct contact between tax officials and taxpayers, matters being dealt with by correspondence. Most of the non-assessment resources of the ATO were devoted to withholding, collection, and appeals.

In the mid-1980s the ATO took the first tentative steps toward self-assessment for companies, which was finally completed in the early 1990s, and self-assessment now effectively applies to all taxpayers. Individuals still do not pay tax when filing a return and receive a computer-generated formal notice of assessment advising tax due, whereas companies do the calculations and payments themselves. The most obvious initial effect of this change was to move resources out of assessing into audit, and for the first time many taxpayers actually came face-to-face with tax officers. The large corporate audits in particular generated a lot of heat, and were not assisted from a public relations point of view by well-publicized dawn raids on banks and professionals seeking copies of documents about suspected tax schemes.

In the early 1990s client service became the focus of activities of the ATO, with audit activity being reduced from late-1980s levels (when coverage was still not great) and resources moved into service areas. A non-statutory Taxpayers' Charter was introduced by the ATO in this context. In the late 1990s and early 2000s much of the ATO's resources was devoted to implementing the extensive tax reform announced in 1998, and audit more or less ceased. Tax shelter promoters took advantage of this opportunity so that audit and enforcement once again became an urgent priority when the ATO returned to business as usual. The current ATO approach is a mix of carrots (service) and sticks (audits and penalties) based on a fairly sophisticated risk assessment process and compliance model, as well as so-called 'real time' tax administration, under which the ATO tries to monitor what is happening in the real world of tax on a current basis rather than finding out only when tax returns are lodged some time down the track.

Individual taxpayers responded to the changes in tax administration and the increasing complexity of the tax system after various tax reforms by increasingly seeking the help of professional tax return preparers called tax agents (over 70% now use tax agents). The ATO in turn produced a variety of products designed to assist individuals in preparing their own tax returns during its client-service phase. With the development of the Internet, the ATO is trying to move this population online, which has now stabilized to electronic filing. About half of the individuals who prepare their own tax returns use the Internet to file them. In the process, the ATO is taking the first steps toward simplifying individual tax returns by electronically pre-filling tax information in the possession of the ATO. The current Secretary of the Treasury has expressed a desire to significantly reduce the number of individual tax returns.

With regard to tax administration for business taxpayers, as noted earlier, the 1998 tax reform had significant impacts on tax collection. Withholding on employment income by business has existed for many years in Australia, along with tax instalment systems for business income. In the late 1980s the tax file number used for many years within the ATO was given a formal statutory basis and began to be used for reporting and backup withholding purposes (rather than just for internal tracking of files) in relation to investment income, with some significant improvements in detection and compliance. At the same time the collection and information matching capabilities of the ATO were greatly improved through the use of technology. Annual federal budgets regularly contain quite significant revenue increases arising from administration improvements based around technology, largely affecting business and requiring large tax technology investments by business as well as the ATO.

The introduction of the GST was used as the opportunity of extending the tax collection system. An Australian Business Number (ABN) was introduced and is effectively compulsory for taxpayers registered for GST. Even if they are not registered for GST, taxpayers with business income are well advised to obtain an ABN, since otherwise payments received by them from other businesses are subject to withholding at 46.5% (so-called 'no-ABN withholding'). This system has flushed out many habitual non-filers of income tax returns, including a number of senior lawyers who have subsequently been struck off the rolls of practising barristers. Current GST turnover also began to be used to make instalment payments of tax more current. Effectively, an instalment rate for business income is derived from the last year's income tax return as a percentage of turnover; that rate is then applied to the current monthly or quarterly turnover, depending on whether instalments are due monthly or quarterly.

To implement these changes, a two-page Business Activity Statement was introduced to replace virtually all the various forms that were used previously for withholding and instalment payments of tax. While the idea is appealing in concept, it has been difficult to implement, at least in the transitional phase. The system had to be changed on several occasions, which moved it back closer to the previous system.

Compliance costs in Australia, which a number of 1990s studies suggested were already the highest in the world, are generally thought to have risen following tax reform. The difficulties in the relationship between the ATO and large businesses that emerged with self-assessment have not gone away. The ATO has responded more recently with an independent review of its dealings with corporate taxpayers and various forms of compliance agreements with large businesses.

For tax professionals, there have also been important changes over this period. Self-assessment was accompanied by the introduction of an extensive public and private rulings system that is legally binding on the ATO. An informal private ruling system had been in operation for many years, and non-binding public rulings began to be issued in 1982 as part of the introduction of freedom of information legislation in Australia. In 1992 legislation was passed formalizing this process (as part of the final stages of self-assessment), which has led to significant growth in the numbers of public and private rulings. Public income tax rulings are now issued on matters of general principle as well as for transactions affecting significant numbers of taxpayers (such as capital management activities by large listed companies) or involving widely marketed investment products (especially in the agricultural sector). As a result of the 1998 tax reform, individuals with simple tax affairs can now obtain binding oral rulings for which the ATO has an elaborate recording system. After some scandals with private tax rulings and some technical problems with the original legislation (such as contesting private rulings before the courts) a review of self-assessment in 2004 led to a rewrite of the binding rulings legislation without changing its basic principles. Although nominally available to taxpayers directly, the great bulk of important ruling requests are handled through tax professionals.

With the increasing use of tax agents noted above, questions about their regulation and professional standards have been raised, as well as the responsibilities of tax professionals more broadly. Legislation on the regulation of tax agents, with a view to reforming the rudimentary 1943 system, has been promised for over a decade and drafts have been debated for many years. A bill was finally introduced into Parliament at the end of 2008 but has not yet been enacted. In 2006 civil penalties were introduced for promoters of tax exploitation schemes, which generally are schemes caught by the general anti-avoidance rule discussed below. The definition of 'promoter' is broad and could apply to tax professionals, although 'merely' providing advice about the scheme is excluded.

9. GENERAL PRINCIPLES

9.1. Relationship between Tax and Financial Accounting

The Australian courts generally give the tax legislation primacy over accounting principles. The legislation uses the global system nominally and does not adopt 'profits' as the measure of business income. It is thus easy to interpret the legislation as setting out its own criteria of taxability completely independent of accounting rules. Equally, at many crucial points the legislation does not provide guidance on accounting rules, and the courts could have easily adopted accounting principles as the guide in such cases. As a result, the attitude is very much 'take it or leave it', as suits the particular judge.

So far as any trend can be discerned, the courts seem over time to be moving toward greater consistency with accounting principles. On the other hand, the legislation increasingly specifies tax accounting rules for many areas, partly arising out of bad judicial decisions. Even where these tax rules follow generally accepted accounting concepts, they usually do so through detailed statutory language and so do not have the capacity to change when accounting practice changes.

During the tax reform commencing in 1998, debate arose on whether it would be better to leave the determination of business income to accounting concepts, with differing views on the potential for simplification of the legislation. The Ralph Review of Business Taxation ultimately rejected a European-style approach of explicitly adopting accounting concepts into the tax law. However, it did propose that differences between tax and accounting be systematically identified and removed where there was no clear policy reason for the difference.

The most important recommendation in this area, however, was the proposed new method of calculating taxable income, which had many close parallels with accounting (especially the use of assets and liabilities in the process with definitions very similar to those used in accounting). As noted above, after extensive consultation, the government decided not to proceed with this new method. Hence, the rather haphazard relation of tax and accounting in Australia looks set to continue in the future with one important exception – an option in legislation currently before Parliament to use financial accounting in lieu of the tax rules for taxation of financial instruments.

9.2. Respect for Legal Form

Unless a transaction can be characterized as a sham, in the sense of not having under general law the legal effect that it purports to have, the courts generally respect the form of the transaction adopted for income tax purposes. Thus, the transfer of a right to income that is effective under property law is generally regarded as carrying the income with it for tax purposes (although there is specific legislation directed at this result for shorter-term assignments). Similarly, it has been held that an embezzler was not assessable on interest earned on embezzled funds because the interest was subject to a constructive trust in favour of the company embezzled.[3]

There is, however, no uniform practice on this matter. Courts have been prepared to look at substance in the area of services income (whether payments under restrictive covenants are for genuine restrictions or not), but in the area of deductions, some of the most problematic court decisions in fostering tax avoidance elevated form over substance (e.g., what was really purchase price became deductible if given the form of rent for the use of the property).

In related issues, there has been debate in cases as to whether tax motivations for transactions can affect the tax outcome; the traditional answer, as found in the quote from Barwick, CJ in *Westraders* above, has been no. After acceptance in the lower courts, the High Court of Australia has rejected the UK judicial doctrine of fiscal nullity on the basis that there is a statutory anti-avoidance regime, so that judicial activism is unnecessary. Nonetheless, in some cases, including High Court cases, deductions have been denied on the basis that the expenses were tax-motivated. For example, in a complex annuity scheme that featured large interest deductions early in the period of the annuity and most of the income toward the end, with a power to unwind the transaction before the income arose, the High Court said that where income exceeded deductions, generally there was no need to look at motivation.[4] However, if deductions exceeded income, then motivation was relevant, and if in this case the parties intended to unwind the scheme before the income arose (as was ultimately found to be the case), then the interest deduction was reduced to the amount of income derived in each year. Similarly, a collapsing prepaid interest scheme was found in a lower court not to work, because the

3. *Zobory* [1995] FCA 1226, 64 FCR 86.
4. *Fletcher* [1991] HCA 42, 173 CLR 1.

purpose of paying the interest was to obtain a tax deduction and not to earn income, so that it failed the income-earning test of the statute.[5] Once again, however, it is difficult to find consistency of approach in the courts.

9.3. Tax Avoidance and Anti-avoidance Legislation

The former manual assessment system and the apparent taxpayer bias of the judiciary from the mid-1960s encouraged aggressive tax avoidance activities by taxpayers and their advisers, which still lingers today. There was little chance of getting caught and if you did, then as likely as not, the courts would uphold the scheme. As a result, a large-scale publicly marketed tax-avoidance industry flourished from about the mid-1970s, which to some extent made the payment of tax optional. The government was initially slow to react to these developments, and the early amendments were themselves full of loopholes, which suggested to some observers tacit acceptance of the industry by the government.

By the late 1970s, when lengthy unreadable anti-avoidance legislation seemed to have closed off most of the abuses, advertisements still appeared in the financial press offering to purchase companies for the value of their pre-tax income (less a percentage being the purchaser's fee or commission). There was no shortage of sellers who did not stay to ask what was being done with the companies (the assumption being that they would be put into a tax scheme that wiped out their tax liability). It came to the surface in a royal commission, investigating a notorious labour union heavily involved in criminal activities, that the companies were simply being stripped of their assets by the purchasers, dummy directors with criminal backgrounds appointed, and the records of the companies destroyed (metaphorically consigned to the 'bottom of the harbor' as the scandal came to be called – that is, Sydney Harbour – although the activities were by no means confined to Sydney).

The legislative reaction was severe. It was made a specific criminal offence to render a company unable to pay its tax (although arguably the general criminal law already had this result), and more importantly, retrospective legislation was passed making the vendors of the shares in the companies liable for the company tax that was not paid, even where small listed companies were involved. A new general anti-avoidance rule was enacted to overcome the defects of the previous rule. A significant share of some of the best people resources in the ATO were involved in the exercise well into the 1980s. This included attacking not only the 'bottom of the harbor' cases, but many of the real avoidance schemes. There was considerable success in the courts as the judicial tide turned (one notorious 1974 High Court of Australia case, often considered to be the start of the real 'rot', was ultimately reversed as a precedent in 1989).[6]

One of the root causes of the problem in a policy sense was the combination of a classical corporate tax system with no capital gains tax, so that most share sales

5. *Gwynvill Properties Pty Ltd* [1986] FCA 273, 13 FCR 138.
6. *Curran* [1974] HCA 46, 131 CLR 409, reversed in *John* [1989] HCA 5, 166 CLR 417.

were tax-free. The policy remedy came with the tax reform of 1985, introducing an imputation system of company taxation and a capital gains tax. At the same time, the tax administration was undergoing its own reform, as noted above, partly to ensure that the same debacle could never occur in the future. This development, combined with the not-surprising suspicion of the tax profession among tax administrators arising from the tax avoidance era, has meant that relations between the profession and the tax administration remain somewhat strained despite expressions and intentions of goodwill and cooperation on both sides.

Tax planning went into a less aggressive mode in the 1980s. Rather than seeking to wipe out all tax liability through paper-shuffling circular transactions, tax reduction through exploiting the debt-equity borderline, tax shelters, and timing differences became the main focus of attention, although more aggressive planning on the international scene was also evident. In the mid-1990s, however, the tax avoidance industry began to flourish once again, partly as a result of the diversion of tax administration resources produced by the tax reform beginning in 1998, noted above. Many employees who had bought into the schemes and been refunded virtually all of the tax withheld on their employment income found that no action was forthcoming from the ATO to audit or challenge the schemes because of the ATO preoccupation on other fronts. The schemes consequently mushroomed, particularly among employees in Western Australia, with tens of thousands of ordinary taxpayers participating. Once the ATO began to pursue the taxpayers after the main part of the 1998 reforms affecting administration had commenced, the issue became highly political and the ATO was forced to make generous settlement offers. As work on the schemes proceeded, it became evident that they were prevalent in all segments of the taxpayer population, including among well-paid executives and small businesses, and the efforts to clean them up took several years.

As a result, the ATO began litigating in a significant way the anti-avoidance provision that had been passed in 1981 to deal with the previous round of tax avoidance, with a significant degree of success. Against this background, Australia's anti-avoidance rules can now be considered. Originally the provision was section 260, which read as follows:

> Every contract, agreement, or arrangement made or entered into, orally or in writing, . . . shall so far as it purports to have the purpose or effect of in any way, directly or indirectly:
>
> (a) altering the incidence of any income tax;
> (b) relieving any person from liability to pay any income tax or make any return;
> (c) defeating, evading, or avoiding any duty or liability imposed on any person by this Act; or
> (d) preventing the operation of this Act in any respect, be absolutely void, as against the Commissioner, or in regard to any proceeding under this Act, but without prejudice to such validity as it may have in any other respect or for any other purpose.

Although there were ups and downs in the history, a series of decisions prior to 1980 deprived the provision of virtually any meaning. The major problems were as follows:

(1) With regard to the general inclusion and deduction provisions of the Act, the courts held that they had their own built-in protection if they were interpreted properly (which the courts demonstrably failed to do) and so did not need the assistance of the anti-avoidance provision.
(2) With regard to the specific provisions of the Act, the courts held that where the legislation offered the taxpayer a choice, then the anti-avoidance provision did not apply if the taxpayer exercised such a choice. This was taken to extremes. For example, the Act has different rules for private and public companies, and much elaborate tax planning was directed to avoiding characterization as a private company, which the courts held was the exercise of a choice.
(3) To supply the counterfactual for the application of the provision (what would have happened in the absence of the contract, etc.), the courts tended to look only to what the taxpayer did, so that it seemed necessary for the taxpayer to start down one direction with a transaction and then to change course midway for tax reasons. A well-executed tax plan carried out from the very beginning was thus immune (the false-start principle).
(4) If the section applied, its effect was simply destructive of the contract, etc. It did not allow the Commissioner to construct an alternative that would give rise to tax; the tax liability had to be found in the ruins of the contract, etc.

The legislature enacted the more elaborate Part IVA to take the place of section 260. Under this Part, three elements have to be found: a scheme, a tax benefit, and an objective conclusion (not having regard to the parties' actual intentions) that the primary purpose of the scheme was to obtain the tax benefit. A scheme is defined so broadly as to cover virtually any transaction, although the courts have held that it must be something that can stand and make sense on its own. A tax benefit is obtained when an amount is not included in assessable income of a taxpayer in a year of income where it would have been included, or might reasonably be expected to have been included, if the scheme had not been entered into; there is a specific exclusion for elections under the Act, such as valuing inventory on the basis of cost or market value. A similar tax benefit rule applies in the case of deductions, capital losses, withholding tax, and foreign tax credits. In determining whether the purpose of the scheme was to obtain the tax benefit, eight listed criteria, such as the form and substance of the scheme, the timing of the scheme, the change in financial positions that result from the scheme, and the connection between the parties, are used. The Commissioner is given power when these criteria are satisfied to determine that the Part applies and then reconstruct the transaction to produce the tax outcome that would prevail in the absence of the scheme.

At the time the new rules were introduced, it was stated that they applied to transactions that were 'blatant, artificial or contrived arrangements' as compared to 'normal commercial transactions by which taxpayers legitimately take advantage of opportunities available for the arrangement of their affairs'. They were successful in closing down the round-robin collapsible-paper schemes and for many years acted *in terrorem* against aggressive tax planning in genuine transactions.

As noted above, however, more recently considerable litigation has occurred and is still occurring over the operation of the rules. The High Court established the important point that there was no dichotomy between obtaining a tax benefit and carrying out a commercial objective – that is, the rules go further than was stated at their time of introduction. Further, it is possible to look to the professional advisers in deciding what the dominant purpose of the transaction was (taxpayers cannot claim exemption from the rules because they are ignorant of the complexities of the tax law). Thus, it is possible to apply the provision where the after-tax return on a deposit is higher where funds were artificially moved offshore to take advantage of an international exemption. Similarly, interposing a company between an Australian-resident company and a foreign-resident company to obtain an interest deduction that otherwise would have been quarantined to foreign income was struck down under the provision.[7]

The lower courts, however, initially had some difficulty in working out how much commerciality is enough. It was held that an offshore captive insurance arrangement was not subject to the rules;[8] nor was a sale and leaseback that significantly increased tax depreciation without any offsetting income[9] (these arrangements having been heavily marketed by merchant bankers). When the lower courts held that the rules did not apply to a split loan product marketed by a financial institution, which increased deductibility of interest on an investment property by capitalizing interest on that property and paying off the principal of the part of the loan on the taxpayer's residence (interest on the latter type of loan being non-deductible), the High Court intervened again and held that the rules applied.[10] Since then, the lower courts have generally followed suit for the various schemes that were the subject of the latest round of mass marketing described above. Further, there is an increasing tendency for the courts to hold that, in any event, tax schemes do not comply with the particular provisions they are trying to exploit. The lower courts have struggled in part because the government and legislature have never solved satisfactorily the inherent conflict with anti-avoidance rules arising from tax concessions that encourage certain forms of activity and transactions.

Currently the anti-avoidance rules are a significant deterrent to tax schemes. Some wealthy taxpayers' greed seems, however, to know no bounds, and it is no

7. *Consolidated Press Holdings Ltd* [2001] HCA 32, 207 CLR 235.
8. *WD & HO Wills (Australia) Pty Ltd* [1996] FCA 1284, 65 FCR 298.
9. *Metal Manufactures Ltd* [2001] FCA 365, 108 FCR 150; *Eastern Nitrogen Ltd* [2001] FCA 366, 108 FCR 27.
10. *Hart* [2004] HCA 26, 217 CLR 216.

surprise in view of the history recounted above that some of them have gone underground and resorted to tax evasion schemes offshore. One of the 'advisers' involved was raided in a Melbourne hotel and his computer found to contain a list of clients. A round of prosecutions and extraditions involving some high-profile individuals is under way in a project known as 'Wickenby'. The courts have been busy in recent years with desperate procedural actions by the taxpayers concerned, but the ATO has been largely successful to date in applying criminal and civil sanctions. Even though a fresh round of tax reform is under way, it seems that the ATO has learned the lesson from last time that it cannot sleep where tax avoidance and evasion are concerned.

10. SOURCES ON TAX LAW

Tax is always in the headlines in Australia. It has been the topic or a main topic of many federal elections in the last twenty-five years. As will also be noted from the discussion above, there have been many colourful incidents in the tax system. For the social history of taxation in Australia, there is no better source than the newspapers, many of which are now archived online.

The tax law, cases, and rulings are also readily available through free online sources. As noted above, the income tax is spread over a number of statutes, but the most important parts are in the 1936 and 1997 Income Tax Assessment Acts, which are available at <www.comlaw.gov.au>. Explanatory memoranda are produced for all legislation and are increasingly helpful in the tax area, even to the point that they seem to almost supplant the text of the law. They are available from the same website from 1996 and from <www.ato.gov.au/atolaw/index.htm> going back to 1922 by browsing for extrinsic materials. The ATO now produces an enormous volume of material on the interpretation and application of the law, including rulings and various kinds of guides, which are available on the ATO website, <www.ato.gov.au>. Cases, which are important sources of law both for general rules and for the interpretation of detailed provisions, can be found at <www.austlii.edu.au>, a website that also has a tax-related section, including legislation, cases, treaties, and online tax journals. For tax reform from 1998 on, there are four important websites: Treasury <www.treasury.gov.au>, Review of Business Taxation <www.rbt.treasury.gov.au>, the Board of Taxation www.taxboard.gov.au, and the current tax reform website, <http://www.taxreview.treasury.gov.au>.

Books and journals on taxation matters abound. The pre-eminent text on the general principles of the tax system is Parsons, *Income Taxation in Australia* (1985) which is available free online at <http://www.setis.library.usyd.edu.au/oztexts/parsons.html>. The main commercial publishers in taxation are CCH Australia and Thomson Reuters, which both produce an annual version of tax legislation and several looseleaf and online commentary services. The best account of current tax law in book form can be found in Woellner, Barkoczy, Murphy & Evans, *Australian Taxation Law* (published annually), and there are several student casebooks, such as *Cooper, Krever & Vann's Income Taxation Commentary and*

Materials, (6th edn 2009) and Kobetsky, Krever, O'Connell & Stewart, *Income Tax: Text Materials and Essential Cases*, (7th edn 2008). The main professional organization is the Taxation Institute of Australia, which has three taxation journals, *Taxation in Australia, Tax Specialist*, and *Australian Tax Forum*, as well as many conference papers and series (see <www.taxinstitute.com.au>). Other specialist tax journals include *Australian Tax Review, Australian Journal of Taxation, Revenue Law Journal* and *e-journal of Tax Research*; the final three are available free online (see above). The Australian Tax Research Foundation publishes research studies of Australian taxation and a conference series; see <www.atrf.com.au>.

Canada

Brian J. Arnold

1. HISTORY OF THE INCOME TAX ACT

Canadian federal income tax was first imposed in 1917 as a temporary measure to help finance World War I. Until then, the major sources of federal revenue were customs and excise taxes. Over the period from 1917 to the early 1960s, the income tax became an increasingly important source of government revenue. Rates increased and the tax base expanded on a rather ad hoc basis. Dissatisfaction with the resulting 'system' led to the establishment of a Royal Commission (the Carter Commission) in 1962 to make a comprehensive study of the Canadian tax system. In 1966 the Carter Commission issued its famous report proposing the adoption of a comprehensive tax base. The report led to a major overhaul of the income tax in 1972. The revised system was much more sophisticated and the legislation much more complex. Another less significant tax reform occurred in 1986–1987 in conjunction with, and partly in response to, the worldwide tax reform phenomenon that occurred during that period.

2. CONSTITUTIONAL ISSUES

Under the Canadian constitution, the federal government has unlimited powers of taxation. The provinces have the power to levy 'direct taxation' within the province on income earned in the province and on the worldwide income of persons who are resident in the province. All of the ten provinces and the three territories levy income tax on individuals and corporations. The federal individual tax rates are set taking into account the provincial taxes. The federal corporate income tax contains a 10% abatement to make room for the provincial corporate tax. Pursuant to a long-standing tax collection agreement between the federal and provincial governments, the federal government collects both individual and corporate tax on behalf of most of the provinces. In consideration, the provinces must adopt the federal income tax base, although they apply their own rates and provide a wide range of tax credits. Quebec is the only province that collects its own individual income tax; as of 2009, only Alberta and Quebec collect their own corporate taxes.

3. TAX RATES

The 2009 federal income tax rates for individuals are as follows:

Taxable Income	*Tax Rate*
$40,726 or less	15%
$40,727–81,452	22%
$81,453–123,184	26%
$123,185 and over	29%

Since 2000, brackets have been fully indexed for inflation. Various personal credits are similarly indexed for inflation. There is, however, no comprehensive relief for inflation with respect to amounts included in computing income.

Although the provincial individual income taxes are based on the tax base as defined for federal income tax purposes, the provincial tax rates and brackets vary considerably from province to province. Except for Alberta, which levies a 10% flat-rate tax, the provincial income taxes are levied on a progressive basis with three to five brackets. The rates vary from 5.06% on the lowest bracket in British Columbia to 24% on the highest bracket in Quebec. Three provinces levy substantial surtaxes on individuals. The combined federal and provincial individual rates for the top bracket vary from 39% in Alberta to 48.22% and 48.25% in Quebec and Nova Scotia respectively. Non-resident individuals are subject to a combined federal and provincial rate for the highest bracket of income of 42.92%.

The basic federal tax rate for corporations has been reduced gradually over several years from 28% to 19% effective for the 2009 year. The rate will be further reduced until it reaches 15% effective 1 January 2012. The federal rate is formally ten percentage points higher, but there is a 10% abatement for provincial corporate income taxes. The provincial corporate income taxes are levied on the tax base computed in accordance with the same rules that are used to compute the federal tax base. In 2009 the provincial corporate tax rates varied from 10% in Alberta to 16% in Nova Scotia and Prince Edward Island. The combined federal and provincial corporate rates for 2009 vary from 29% in Alberta to 35% in Nova Scotia and Prince Edward Island. Canadian-controlled private corporations qualify for a special reduced rate of 11% on the first $500,000 of active business income. All of the provinces also provide reduced tax rates for the active business income of Canadian-controlled private corporations.

The federal government and some of the provinces levy capital taxes on corporations. The federal capital tax is imposed only on large financial institutions with capital in excess of $1 billion at a rate of 1.25%.

4. COMPOSITION OF THE FISCAL SYSTEM

For the year ended 31 March 2007, federal income taxes comprised about 64% of total federal government revenues. Of this amount, corporate income taxes accounted for about 17% while personal income taxes make up the remaining 47%. The reliance on personal income taxes has declined over the past five years, from 48.3% for the year ended 31 March 2002 to 40.2% in 2007. Other important sources of federal revenue include employment insurance contributions (6.8%) and indirect taxes – namely, the goods and services tax (a form of value added tax) and customs duties and excise taxes (18.2%). For 2007, personal and corporate income taxes generated approximately $113 billion and $40.6 billion respectively out of total revenues of $242.4 billion. For the same year, income tax revenues constituted 13.3% of GDP. The percentage has declined from 15.1% in 2002.

5. BASIC STRUCTURE OF THE INCOME TAX

In Canada, the basic structure of the rules for calculating income tax payable is the same for both individuals and corporations and is contained in the same statute. Income is calculated on a source basis. Income in the broad economic sense that does not have a source is not income in the legal sense. Amounts that lack a source are not characterized as income and are not taxable unless they are expressly included in income under the Income Tax Act ('the Act'). Perhaps the best example of this fundamental principle is a windfall gain such as a lottery prize, which is not considered to have the quality of income. Capital gains are another example, although since 1972 a portion of such gains (currently 50%) has been expressly required to be included in income. Capital gains are considered to be derived from the disposition of a source of income rather than income from a source; or, to use the well-worn metaphor, a capital gain represents the tree (capital) rather than the fruit (income) from the tree.

The source concept of income finds statutory expression in section 3 of the Income Tax Act, which defines a taxpayer's income as: 'income for the year from a source inside or outside Canada, including . . . the taxpayer's income for the year from each office, employment, business, and property'. Section 4 goes on to provide that a taxpayer's income or loss from any source must be calculated on the assumption that the taxpayer had no income or loss from any other source during the taxation year and that only amounts reasonably applicable to that source of income are deductible. Section 4 also contains a similar provision with respect to the computation of income from sources in a particular place (geographical sources). This provision is relevant for the purpose of determining both a non-resident's income earned in Canada and the credit for foreign taxes on income earned by Canadian residents outside Canada.

It is clear from section 4(1)(a) of the Act that amounts are deductible in computing income from a generic source only if they can reasonably be regarded as applicable to that source. Although it does not necessarily follow that a source of income must exist at the time an expense is incurred in order for the expense to be deductible, the courts have so held. In the absence of an express statutory provision, expenses incurred either before a source of income exists or after it ceases to exist are not deductible because they are not applicable to a source of income.

The source concept of income has its roots in the 'schedular' basis used in early UK income tax statutes.[1] Under this approach, income tax is levied only in respect of amounts included in various schedules. If an amount is not specifically included in one of these schedules, it is not subject to tax. The schedules specify the types of income subject to tax and also the persons subject to tax on such amounts. Generally, income and losses from different schedules cannot be aggregated because each schedule has its own computation rules.

The Canadian income tax system has never followed the UK schedular approach completely. Since 1917, the Canadian Act has required the inclusion of items of income from all sources – a clear attempt to escape the narrow confines of a schedular approach. Generally, however, the courts have limited the definition of income in section 3, referred to above, to income from the specifically enumerated sources: employment, business, and property. In addition, the Canadian system has permitted the aggregation of income and losses from various sources since 1972.

In Canada, as in the United Kingdom, the judicial exclusion of amounts from income on the basis of the source concept has been largely reversed by statute. For example, as mentioned earlier, since 1972 a portion of capital gains has been included in income. Also, subsection 6(3) of the Act ensures that amounts received before employment commences or after it ceases must be included in income if they constitute compensation for services rendered. The increased use of accrual accounting for income tax purposes in recent times has effectively eliminated the problem of including in income amounts received after the cessation of a source of income. The practice has been for the government to overturn by legislation most court cases holding that amounts are not income because they lack a generic source.[2] For example, the Federal Court of Appeal held that a payment received

1. See Part 2 below for a comparison of the schedular and global systems.
2. However, a Supreme Court decision, *The Queen v. Fries* [1990] 2 CTC 439 (SCC) holding without any analysis that strike pay was not taxable, has not been reversed by statute.

by a shareholder for entering into a non-competition covenant on the sale of the shares of a corporation was tax-free.[3] According to the Court, the amount was not income from employment, a business, or property; nor was it a capital gain because the shareholder could not be considered to have disposed of any property. This result will be reversed by proposed amendments to the Act, effective 7 October 2003.[4]

In summary, the Canadian tax base includes most significant items of income whether or not they have a source under the case law. Windfall gains are the most significant items of income that are currently excluded from the tax base because they lack a source.

Although the source concept has been overridden by specific statutory provisions with respect to income items, it has not often been overridden with respect to deductions. When the Act provides for the inclusion in income of amounts that lack a source, the inclusion is generally net of any expenses incurred in connection with the amounts. For example, the amount of a capital gain is the proceeds of disposition less the cost of the property and any selling expenses. Generally, however, expenses are not deductible under the Act unless they relate to income from an existing source. Moreover, there are many instances in which expenses are incurred after a source of income has ceased to exist and there is no ongoing income against which these expenses can be offset. Since 1993, interest can be deducted in certain circumstances after the source of income has ceased to exist.

In summary, there are five major sources of income: office or employment, business, property, capital gains, and miscellaneous. The taxpayer must calculate income and loss from each source separately and allocate reasonable deductions to each respective source. The rules for calculating income from the various sources differ, although for income from business and property, the differences are minor. The major difference between income from employment and income from business or property is that the deductions permitted in computing employment income are severely limited. Once income and losses from the various sources have been computed, they are aggregated to obtain the taxpayer's 'income'.

The next stage is the determination of a taxpayer's taxable income. Taxable income is income less a few specific amounts, such as loss carryovers and dividends, received by a Canadian corporation from other corporations. The relevant tax rate is then applied to the taxable income to determine the tax payable before credits. The allowable tax credits are extensive because all of the personal deductions and exemptions were converted into tax credits in the mid-1980s. In recent years many additional personal tax credits, such as credits for adoption expenses, public transit, children's fitness, home renovations, and first-time home buyers, have been introduced for non-fiscal reasons. Tax credits also include credits for foreign taxes and tax expenditures such as the investment tax credit.

---

3. *Manrell v. The Queen* [2003] 3 CTC 50 (FCA).
4. However, the proposed amendments have been pending for more than six years.

6. TAX LEGISLATION

6.1. Tax Legislative Process

Important tax legislation is usually introduced pursuant to the annual budget of the Minister of Finance. In recent years, however, increasing use has been made of press releases to announce new tax measures. Also, technical tax amendments are often issued in the form of draft legislation for public comment without any announcement in a budget. Like all legislative proposals, tax bills must be passed by both the House of Commons and the Senate and receive Royal Assent from the head of state (the Governor General of Canada acting on behalf of the Queen).

Most tax changes are subject to some public consultations. The Minister of Finance consults widely with other levels of government and interest groups as part of the annual budget process. Draft tax legislation is usually issued to the public for comment before being tabled in Parliament. Department of Finance officials meet regularly with representative groups of tax practitioners.

It can take several years for tax changes to be enacted. Rarely is draft legislation available at the time that a change is announced in a budget or in a press release. The preparation of the draft legislation can take several months. Once the draft legislation is available, it is usually issued for public comment and consultation with tax practitioners. The draft legislation is then revised and introduced into Parliament, although in the case of controversial measures, the revised draft legislation may first be issued for another round of public consultations. The speed of passage of tax legislation through Parliament depends on several factors, such as how important and controversial the legislation is and what other matters occupy the legislative agenda.

The significant delay between the announcement of tax changes and their enactment causes problems in circumstances where the changes take effect on announcement. Such changes are not effective until the legislation is fully enacted but, once enacted, they are effective from the prior date of announcement. This situation puts the tax administration (the Canada Revenue Agency ('the CRA'), formerly Revenue Canada) and taxpayers in a dilemma. Taxpayers can refuse to pay any tax owing pursuant to the pending legislation; however, if the legislation is enacted they will owe the amount with interest. The CRA usually proceeds on the assumption that the changes will be ultimately enacted. As a result, tax returns, forms, and taxpayer information are produced on that assumption. If the changes are not enacted, those items are incorrect and any tax paid pursuant to the proposed changes should be refunded.

6.2. Statutory Style

Prior to tax reform in 1972, the general style of Canadian legislation tended to be broad, generally worded provisions. For example, an income tax was levied on the income of residents of Canada, but there was no definition of a resident of Canada for this purpose. Similarly, the Canadian transfer pricing rules consisted of two simple provisions that required the amount charged in any transactions between a resident and a related non-resident person to be reasonable in the circumstances.

With tax reform in 1972, there was a clear change in the style of statutory drafting. The Act expanded dramatically. The 2008 version of the Act and Regulations consists of more than 2,000 pages. The 1972 Act and virtually all amendments since then have reflected a high degree of technical complexity. Increasingly, the government places reliance on detailed technical rules to resolve tax policy issues. Inevitably, the rules require ongoing revision as the instances in which they operate inappropriately are discovered. Often it seems that these rules are intended to preclude the courts from playing any significant role in the development of tax law. On the one hand, tax professionals complain bitterly about the pace of legislative change and the length and technical complexity of the provisions. On the other hand, they demand that the tax rules be certain, which requires detailed technical statutory rules. Despite these modern developments, there are still some aspects of the Canadian income tax system that are short, simply worded holdovers from the pre-1972 Act.

The style of statutory drafting of tax legislation in Canada is peculiar in several respects. The Income Tax Act is by far the largest Canadian statute. The provisions of the Act are drafted by professionals in the Department of Finance, whereas all other federal legislation is drafted by the Department of Justice. The Income Tax Act was the only federal statute omitted from the periodic consolidation of federal statutes, in which each statute and the amendments to it are consolidated and the provisions are renumbered and reorganized. This exception was justified in part because of the cost to the government and to commercial publishers of republishing forms, brochures, loose-leaf services, etc., to reflect revised section numbers. The statutory drafting convention in Canada is that each provision consists of only one sentence regardless of the length and complexity of the provision. As a result, there are single-sentence provisions that go on for several pages. A recent development in the style of statutory drafting is the frequent use of algebraic formulae for calculations.

Like all Canadian legislation, tax legislation is bilingual; the English- and French-language versions of the Act are equally authoritative. Typically, the Department of Finance develops tax policy and legislation in English; the English version is then translated into French. For purposes of interpretation, both language versions must be taken into account and, if they conflict, the meaning that best accommodates both versions applies (the shared-meaning rule).

6.3. Statutory Interpretation

Until 1984, Canadian courts generally used the strict or literal approach to the interpretation of taxing statutes. This approach was originally adopted from the UK judicial tradition and was deeply ingrained, despite being so obviously inappropriate. Strict interpretation resulted in some shocking judicial decisions.

In 1984 the Supreme Court of Canada, in the *Stubart Investments* case, abandoned strict interpretation in favour of a so-called modern approach:

> Today there is only one principle or approach, namely, the words of an Act are to be read in their entire context in their grammatical and ordinary sense harmoniously with the scheme of the Act, the object of the Act and the intention of Parliament.

The Supreme Court's endorsement of the modern approach was widely accepted by lower courts, the tax authorities, and tax practitioners. However, in a series of cases from 1994 to the present, the Supreme Court made several inconsistent statements about its approach to statutory interpretation. Although the Supreme Court consistently confirmed that the modern approach is the correct approach to statutory interpretation, it nevertheless applied strict interpretation, or what the Court referred to in several cases as a 'plain meaning' approach. In 2005, in the first cases dealing with the general anti-avoidance rule,[5] the Supreme Court referred to the modern approach to statutory interpretation as the 'textual, contextual and purposive approach'. Although the Court emphasized that this approach applies to all statutes, including tax statutes, it went on to indicate that 'because of the degree of precision and detail characteristic of many tax provisions, a greater emphasis has often been placed on textual interpretation where taxation statutes are concerned'. As a result, the Court has reiterated on a number of occasions that if the words of a provision are clear and unambiguous, they must simply be applied; on the other hand, if the words can be reasonably interpreted in more than one way, greater emphasis must be given to the context and purpose of the Act. Even if the words appear clear, however, the Supreme Court admits that context and purpose must be considered to determine if there are latent ambiguities. The Court does not appear to recognize the inherent contradiction in its approach to statutory interpretation: If context and purpose must be considered to reveal latent ambiguities, how is it possible to simply apply clear and unambiguous provisions?

The Supreme Court's approach to statutory interpretation has had important implications for the Court's perception of the role of courts in combating tax avoidance. The Supreme Court has consistently held since 1994 that taxpayers are taxable in accordance with the legal form of their transactions (economic substance or economic realities are irrelevant) and that entering into transactions solely to obtain tax benefits is irrelevant to the determination of the tax consequences. According to the Supreme Court, in the absence of a statutory rule, taxpayers are free to arrange their affairs to avoid tax. Moreover, it is Parliament's

5. *The Queen v. Canada Trustco Mortgage Co.* [2005] 5 CTC 215 (SCC) and *Mathew v. The Queen* [2005] 5 CTC 244 (SCC).

responsibility and not the courts' responsibility to combat tax avoidance. In recent cases, the Supreme Court has stated clearly that, at least in tax cases, judicial innovation is undesirable.

It may seem strange in light of the modern approach to statutory interpretation, but Canadian courts will not admit into evidence the legislative history of a provision for the purpose of interpreting it. There is an exception to this *Hansard* rule if the extrinsic material is used only for the purpose of showing the mischief or problem the legislation was intended to correct. The *Hansard* rule was adopted from the United Kingdom, although it was abandoned by the House of Lords in certain limited circumstances in the early 1990s. It seems likely that Canadian courts will follow the UK courts in expanding access to legislative history. Indeed, in practice, many Canadian judges have been considering legislative history in one way or another for many years.

7. COURTS DEALING WITH TAX MATTERS

Taxpayers who choose to dispute the tax, interest, or penalties levied by the Minister of National Revenue must file a notice of objection to their assessment. This notice triggers an internal appeal process within the CRA. If the assessment is confirmed, the taxpayer may appeal to the courts. Except for certain large corporations, the amount of tax in dispute does not have to be paid until the dispute is finally resolved.

All tax appeals are heard in the first instance by a single judge of the Tax Court of Canada, under either a general procedure or an informal procedure. The informal procedure is available, on an elective basis for taxpayers, for cases involving $12,000 or less of federal tax and penalties or a loss of $24,000 or less. Under the informal procedure there are no formal rules of evidence and taxpayers need not be represented by counsel. There is no appeal as of right from an informal procedure decision, although decisions are subject to judicial review and such review is not uncommon. Decisions in informal procedure cases are not intended to have any precedential value; however, the Tax Court has occasionally followed decisions in informal cases.

The general procedure before the Tax Court is a formal trial with both sides represented by legal counsel. Because tax assessments are presumed by statute to be valid, the initial onus of proof is always on the taxpayer to show that the Minister's assessment is invalid. This initial burden of proof is not important as a practical matter because during the trial the burden shifts back and forth with the presentation of evidence. An adverse judgment of the Tax Court may be appealed to the Federal Court of Appeal by either the government or the taxpayer. A final appeal lies to the Supreme Court of Canada, whose jurisdiction is largely discretionary. Unlike the Tax Court, the Federal Court of Appeal and the Supreme Court hear many cases other than tax cases. An appeal to the Federal Court of Appeal or the Supreme Court is restricted to questions of law or mixed questions of fact and law.

The number of tax cases decided annually by the three levels of courts for the period from 2005 to 2007 is shown in the following table.

Year	*Tax Court of Canada*	*Federal Court of Appeal*	*Supreme Court of Canada*
2005	363	84	4
2006	301	68	1
2007	333	90	2

The total number of tax cases heard by the courts over the past decade has increased significantly.

Case law is an important aspect of Canadian income tax law. It serves to elaborate the meaning of the provisions of the Income Tax Act. Despite the detailed technical nature of the statutory provisions, vagueness and ambiguity are frequent. A considerable amount of case law each year involves the distinction between capital gains and ordinary income, the deduction of business expenses, and the deduction of personal tax credits.

Judicial decisions are binding unless reversed on appeal. The government will sometimes reverse by statute a judicial precedent with which it disagrees. As income tax has become the preserve of specialists, it has become more difficult for generalist courts to handle tax issues properly.

Canadian courts are obligated to provide reasons, usually in writing, for their decisions. Typically, judicial decisions, which are referred to as reasons for judgment, recite the facts of the case, the positions and arguments of the parties, and the decisions of the lower courts before providing the reasons for the court's decision. Dissenting decisions are common with respect to appeals to the Federal Court of Appeal or Supreme Court, where an odd number of judges hear each case (three in the case of the Federal Court of Appeal and five, seven, or nine in the case of the Supreme Court). Judges often cite a wide variety of materials in their decisions, including other cases, books and articles, prior and subsequent versions of the statute, and government reports. Decisions of higher courts are binding on lower courts. A court is not bound to follow its own prior decisions, but usually does so as a practical matter.

8. TAX ADMINISTRATION

The Canadian administration of tax collection is based on a system of 'voluntary compliance' or self-assessment. All taxpayers are legally obligated to file an annual tax return reporting their income and expenses accurately, along with a calculation of the amount of tax owing or the refund due. Slightly over 50% of all individual tax returns are filed electronically. The CRA has established electronic filing of returns as one of its priorities and wants to have 75% of all returns filed electronically within the next few years. Once filed, tax returns are then checked by the CRA to ensure that the required information is correct, the necessary receipts are attached, and the computations are mathematically correct. A notice of assessment showing the amount of tax owing is then sent to the taxpayer. Since less than 1% of all individual tax returns are actually audited by the CRA, the income tax system depends largely on voluntary compliance by taxpayers.

The system is not exclusively voluntary. Payments of salary and wages and other amounts are subject to withholding at source. In addition, the self-assessment system is supported by broad information-reporting requirements.

The rationale for the self-assessment system is cost-effectiveness. Costs to the government include the cost of printing returns, providing information and assistance to taxpayers, processing returns, and auditing a minimal number of returns filed. No other system is nearly as economical.

The CRA is responsible for the administration of the income tax system and other federal taxes such as the Goods and Services Tax. For 2006, the CRA handled just over 23 million individual tax returns and 1.4 million corporate returns. The CRA was created in 1999. Prior to that time, the CRA's responsibilities were carried out by Revenue Canada, an ordinary government department. The shift to agency status was justified on the basis that it would insulate officials from political interference and provide more flexibility in dealing with human resource issues. In substance, the creation of the CRA caused considerable dislocation and expense and produced no significant benefits.

The administrative style of the Canadian tax administration has varied considerably over the past twenty-five years. In the late 1970s and early 1980s the CRA was accused of using 'Gestapo' tactics and being insensitive to taxpayers' legitimate concerns. Indeed, the CRA's performance was an important issue in the 1984 federal election. When the Progressive Conservative Party was elected in that year, it set out to make significant reforms to tax administration. The central thrust of these reforms was to convert the CRA from an enforcement agency to a service agency. This shift in attitude had many consequences, from the silly (taxpayers began to be referred to as 'clients') to the serious (the CRA started to take a rather benign attitude to tax avoidance transactions that complied literally with the words of the Act).

The CRA's preoccupation with service continues today. In the early 1990s a so-called 'fairness package' was adopted, which gave the CRA statutory authority to waive interest and penalties, to accept late-filed elections, and to make refunds for statute-barred years. For 2006–2007, 39,000 out of 75,000 fairness requests to waive interest and penalties were granted. Each CRA office has one or more Fairness Committees to consider fairness requests from taxpayers. It should be noted that the CRA is also responsible for delivering a number of social welfare programs and other spending programs through the income tax system. In these respects, the CRA is a service rather than a tax collection organization. More recently, the CRA has placed increased emphasis on enforcement. In 2005 the CRA initiated a special program to address aggressive international tax planning. The CRA is also part of the Joint International Tax Shelter Information

Center (along with Australia, Japan, the United Kingdom, and the United States), which involves a collaborative effort to deal with international tax avoidance schemes.

The CRA's administrative practices are extremely important in many areas of the tax system. In some areas, the law consists of little more than a generally worded statutory provision and a series of well-known administrative practices. In general, the CRA makes its administrative practices widely known to the public. The CRA publishes its administrative positions, which are available through the Department's online services. The open access to the CRA's administrative positions was effectively forced upon it after the introduction of access-to-information legislation. Commercial publishers used the access-to-information legislation to publish information about administrative positions that were important to tax practitioners. The CRA now publishes its administrative positions itself.

There is very little administrative discretion expressly permitted by the provisions of the Act. Such administrative discretion is viewed with disfavour by both the government and tax practitioners. As a general matter, of course, CRA officials have significant amounts of administrative discretion in administering the Act. However, any exercise of such discretion is subject to judicial review through the normal objection and appeal process. It is also subject to review by a recently appointed ombudsman and by the Auditor General, who scrutinizes all aspects of the CRA's administration of the tax system on a continuing basis. The Auditor General's annual reports on the CRA have attracted considerable public interest and led to important changes in the CRA's practices and in the income tax legislation.

The behaviour of Canadian taxpayers is probably broadly similar to that of American taxpayers. The general public meets its tax obligations grudgingly, and there is probably a good deal of small-scale cheating. Large corporations are sensitive to tax issues, and most do not hesitate to engage in aggressive tax planning.

Corporate and individual tax shelter arrangements have become increasingly problematic despite the adoption of specific anti-avoidance legislation and a general anti-avoidance rule. Tax professionals have become increasingly aggressive over the last twenty-five years.

9. GENERAL PRINCIPLES

9.1. Relationship between Tax and Financial Accounting

Section 9 of the Act provides that a taxpayer's income from a business or property for a year is the 'profit' from the business or property for the year. The term 'profit' is not defined in the Act. The courts have held that profit is the net amount of gross revenue in excess of expenses, computed in accordance with the ordinary principles of commercial accounting and business practice. Although accounting principles and practices are important in the computation of profit, in the

Canderel case[6] in 1998 the Supreme Court reiterated that the computation of profit for tax purposes is a question of law, and accounting practice is not controlling. In many instances the use of accounting principles or practices is expressly overridden by the provisions of the Act. For example, accounting depreciation is not allowed for tax purposes; instead, a separate system of capital cost allowance has been established for income tax purposes. In addition, accounting practise may be displaced by overriding principles of income tax law such as the realization principle. The courts have indicated that there is no requirement of conformity between the treatment of an item for financial accounting purposes and income tax purposes. The taxpayer is free to adopt any method for computing business income as long as it is not inconsistent with the provisions of the Act, case law, or well-established commercial practices. These well-established practices include generally accepted accounting principles, but they are not rules of law; rather, they are interpretive aids. If a taxpayer uses a method for computing income that does not contravene the provisions of the Act, is consistent with the case law principles for measuring income, and gives an accurate picture of the profit of the business for the year, that method is acceptable unless the Minister can establish that another method gives a more accurate picture of the taxpayer's income.

9.2. Respect for Civil or Private Law Form

It is clearly recognized in Canada that the income tax law is generally applied to legal rights and obligations determined under the general law. The Act is replete with terms such as 'employment', 'corporation', 'person', and 'paid-up capital' that derive their meaning from the general law.

There are two difficult aspects regarding this issue. First, because Canada is a federal state, occasionally the legal meaning varies in different provinces. This is particularly the case with respect to the province of Quebec, which follows a civil law system. Ordinarily, the drafters and the courts strive to achieve consistency in the application of the income tax law to taxpayers in various parts of the country. The courts and the CRA generally adhere to the relevant provincial law, although they have sometimes been known to take flexible positions in order to achieve consistency. Special statutory provisions have been adopted with respect to legal concepts used in the province of Quebec, such as usufruct, rights of habitation, and emphyteutic leases. This is part of a broad government initiative called bijuralism to ensure that federal laws apply in the same way in Quebec and the common law provinces. Second, the application of the provisions of the Act to the offshore activities of Canadian taxpayers involves applying the Act to foreign legal rights and obligations. In general, the legal rights and obligations are determined under the foreign law; the Canadian tax law is then applied to those findings, which are, in effect, treated as findings of fact rather than law. For example, whether a foreign entity is characterized as a corporation or partnership for Canadian tax purposes is

6. *Canderel v. The Queen* [1998] 2 CTC 35 (SCC).

based on the legal rights and obligations of the members under foreign law. If those rights and obligations are similar to those of shareholders of Canadian corporations, then the entity will be characterized as a corporation.

9.3. Anti-avoidance Doctrines and Rules

There is considerable confusion in Canada concerning the doctrine of substance over form. Canadian law derives from the House of Lords decision in the *Duke of Westminster* case[7] in 1936. In that case, the House of Lords clearly rejected any doctrine under which the legal form of a transaction could be disregarded in favour of its economic substance. However, the House of Lords did recognize that the legal substance of a transaction prevails over the nomenclature used by the taxpayer to describe the transaction.

The Supreme Court of Canada has reaffirmed on several occasions that the *Duke of Westminster* case is deeply entrenched in Canadian tax law. Nevertheless, on several occasions the Canadian courts, including the Supreme Court, have made references to the doctrine of substance over form or economic realities, which seems to suggest that economic substance will prevail over legal form in certain circumstances. For example, in the *Bronfman Trust* case[8] in 1987, the Supreme Court of Canada stated:

> The recent trend in tax cases [has] been towards attempting to ascertain the true commercial and practical nature of the taxpayer's transactions... Assessment of taxpayers' transactions with an eye to commercial and economic realities, rather than juristic classification of form, may help to avoid the inequity of tax liability being dependent upon the taxpayer's sophistication at manipulating a sequence of events to achieve a patina of compliance with the apparent prerequisites for a tax deduction.

Unfortunately, the Supreme Court did not analyze the connection between this statement and the *Duke of Westminster* case. In another case, the Supreme Court stated, without any elaboration, that substance would apply over form where it was consistent with the wording and purpose of the particular provision.[9]

In the *Shell Canada* case[10] in 1999, the Court rejected its earlier dicta from the *Bronfman Trust* case:

> This Court has repeatedly held that courts must be sensitive to the economic realities of a particular transaction, rather than being bound to what first appears to be its legal form... But there are at least two caveats to this rule.

7. *Duke of Westminster v. CIR* [1936] AC 1, 19 TC 4990, 51 TLR 467 (HL).
8. *The Queen v. Bronfman Trust* [1987] 1 CTC 117 (SCC).
9. *Corporation Notre-Dame de Bon-Secours v. Communauté Urbaine de Québec and City of Québec*, et al. [1995] 1 CTC 241 (SCC).
10. *Shell Canada Ltd. v. The Queen* [1999] 4 CTC 313 (SCC).

> First, this Court has never held that the economic realities of a situation can be used to recharacterize a taxpayer's *bona fide* legal relationships. To the contrary, we have held that, absent a specific provision of the Act to the contrary or a finding that they are a sham, the taxpayer's legal relationships must be respected in tax cases. Recharacterization is only permissible if the label attached by the taxpayer to the particular transaction does not properly reflect its actual legal effect...
>
> Second, it is well established in this Court's tax jurisprudence that a searching inquiry for either the 'economic realities' of a particular transaction or the general object and spirit of the provision at issue can never supplant a court's duty to apply an unambiguous provision of the Act to a taxpayer's transaction. Where the provision at issue is clear and unambiguous, its terms must simply be applied...
>
> [T]his Court has made it clear in more recent decisions that, absent a specific provision to the contrary, it is not the courts' role to prevent taxpayers from relying on the sophisticated structure of their transactions, arranged in such a way that the particular provisions of the Act are met, on the basis that it would be inequitable to those taxpayers who have not chosen to structure their transactions that way... The courts' role is to interpret and apply the Act as it was adopted by Parliament. Obiter statements in earlier cases that might be said to support a broader and less certain interpretive principle have therefore been overtaken by our developing tax jurisprudence. Unless the Act provides otherwise, a taxpayer is entitled to be taxed based on what it actually did, not based on what it could have done, and certainly not based on what a less sophisticated taxpayer might have done.

The main anti-avoidance doctrines referred to by Canadian courts in tax avoidance cases are:

- the sham transaction doctrine. Under this doctrine, a transaction which attempts to give the appearance of legal rights and obligations different from the actual legal rights and obligations created between the parties can be disregarded for tax purposes. The sham doctrine requires an element of deceit and is applied only rarely;
- substance over form. As discussed above, this doctrine is limited to legal substance over legal form. It is similar to the sham doctrine and is rarely applied;
- step transaction doctrine. This doctrine is not well developed in Canadian law, although it has been applied occasionally;
- the business purpose test under which transactions which lack a business purpose, other than the avoidance of tax, may be disregarded. This doctrine was explicitly rejected by the Supreme Court of Canada in the *Stubart* case in 1984.

Although these judicial doctrines are quite limited in scope, the Tax Court and the Federal Court of Appeal have not had difficulty in striking down avoidance schemes by applying the ordinary rules of statutory interpretation or specific anti-avoidance rules. However, in the 1990s the Supreme Court upheld almost every tax avoidance arrangement that came before it, including some blatantly artificial schemes lacking any commercial reality.

In 1987 the government enacted section 245 of the Act as a general anti-avoidance rule ('GAAR'). Under this rule, if a transaction is an 'avoidance transaction', the tax consequences of the transaction may be determined so as to disallow any tax benefit arising from the transaction. An avoidance transaction is defined to be any transaction that results in a tax benefit, which is broadly defined, unless the primary purpose of the transaction is something other than tax avoidance. Even if a transaction is an avoidance transaction, however, there is an exception for transactions that do not involve a misuse of the provisions of the Act or an abuse of the provisions of the Act read as a whole.

In the first two GAAR cases decided by the Supreme Court in 2005 (*Canada Trustco* and *Mathew* referred to above),[11] the Court failed to articulate a principled basis for the interpretation and application of the GAAR. For example, it is difficult to distinguish the results in the two cases (the GAAR was applied in the *Mathew* case but not in *Canada Trustco*) on any principled basis. Throughout the decisions the Court reiterated the necessity for certainty, predictability, and fairness for taxpayers, including taxpayers engaged in aggressive tax avoidance schemes. The Court failed to provide any clear guidance with respect to the crucial issue under the GAAR: how to determine if a transaction is abusive. The Court minimized the role of economic substance, despite an explicit reference to economic substance in the explanatory notes to the GAAR, by holding that economic substance is relevant only if the statutory provision that the taxpayer relies on for the tax benefit refers to or contemplates economic substance; even then, the lack of economic substance is not determinative, but only a factor to be taken into account in deciding whether a transaction is abusive. Finally, the Supreme Court signaled its unwillingness to hear future GAAR cases by characterizing the issue of abuse as a question of fact for the trial court judge and cautioning appeal courts to interfere only in the event of a palpable and overriding error by the Tax Court.

Nevertheless, another GAAR case, *Lipson v. The Queen*[12] was decided by the Supreme Court in early 2009. This case involved a scheme to make mortgage interest on a principal residence deductible. A slim majority of the Supreme Court (4:3) held that the GAAR applied. One of the dissenting justices thought that the GAAR did not apply because the scheme was covered by a specific anti-avoidance rule. Unfortunately, the case does nothing to resolve the uncertainty concerning the interpretation and application of the GAAR.

11. *Supra* n. 5.
12. [2009] 1 CTC 314 (SCC).

10. SOURCES OF TAX LAW

Virtually all federal tax legislation – individual income tax, capital gains, and corporation tax – are contained in the Income Tax Act. That Act also contains some special taxes that are not based on income, such as the capital tax on large financial institutions. Since the early 1980s, all Canadian tax legislation has been accompanied by explanatory notes. These notes sometimes provide useful explanations of the purpose and the operation of the provisions. Sometimes, however, they simply paraphrase the words of the statute. Canadian courts refer to the explanatory notes as an aid to interpretation. The Act is supplemented by Regulations, which are detailed rules adopted by the Cabinet (not passed by Parliament). The Regulations vary enormously, from rules that should probably be in the Act to tables prescribing the amounts for employers to withhold from salaries and wages. Current amendments to the Act and Regulations are available online at <www.fin.gc.ca>. However, most tax professionals use one of the consolidated annotated versions of the legislation produced by the commercial publishers (Thomson/Carswell and CCH).

The CRA issues a wide range of administrative material concerning income taxes. Information circulars, interpretation bulletins, and technical interpretations are particularly useful to determine the CRA's position with respect to the interpretation and application of the provisions of the Act. Most information circulars are intended to provide explanations of areas of the tax system for the general public. Interpretation bulletins and technical interpretations deal with narrower, more technical issues and are intended for tax specialists. The CRA is not legally bound by its administrative positions expressed in these publications, although, as a practical matter, it departs from published positions very infrequently. The CRA also provides binding advance rulings to specific taxpayers on proposed transactions. These advance rulings are used extensively by large accounting and law firms for complex corporate transactions. The CRA charges for its rulings service on a cost-recovery basis. All of the CRA's published material is available on its website <www.cra-arc.gc.ca>.

Relief from tax imposed under the Act may be available under one of Canada's tax treaties. As of late 2008, Canada's tax treaty network consisted of almost ninety treaties, including treaties with most of Canada's major trading partners. The text of Canada's tax treaties and the status of the tax treaty network are available at <www.fin.gc.ca>.

Secondary sources (books, articles, etc.) and government reports are important sources of information on the Canadian income tax system. Courts often refer to this material in their decisions. The leading textbooks on income tax are Vern Krishna, *The Fundamentals of Canadian Income Taxation*, 9th edn (Butterworths, 2006) and Peter Hogg, Joanne Magee, and Jinyan Li, *The Principles of Canadian Income Taxation*, 6th edn (Carswell, 2007). There are two comprehensive looseleaf services (Thomson/Carswell and CCH) and several electronic services. The leading professional organization is the Canadian Tax Foundation, which publishes the *Canadian Tax Journal* (quarterly), an annual conference report, and monographs dealing with tax issues. The Foundation's website is <www.ctf.ca>. The 1966 *Report of the Royal Commission on Taxation* (the Carter Report) is probably the most important government report. The 1997 *Report of the Technical Committee on Business Taxation* (the Mintz Report), which was appointed by the Minister of Finance, provided a detailed analysis of the taxation of business income and made several recommendations to improve the system, only a few of which the government adopted.

France

Prof. Guy Gest

1. HISTORY

The first French income tax system was instituted by three statutes in 1914 and 1917. It was a mixture of the then-English and Prussian systems in that it was characterized by the imposition of seven flat-rate taxes on seven different schedular categories of income (almost the same as today) at the first level and a progressive tax on the total of incomes from all schedular categories accrued to or received by the taxpayer at the second level.

A distinct corporate income tax – of a global type – was created in 1948 (*impôt sur les sociétés*, IS), the base of which was and is still fundamentally determined according to the rules applicable to the industrial and commercial schedular category of income. Previously, the profits of corporations were subject to one of the then-existing flat-rate schedular taxes according to the type of activity carried out (industrial and commercial, agricultural, non-commercial, etc.). Initially 24% (the rate of the former individual income tax on industrial and commercial profits), the normal rate (i.e., the rate of the tax on ordinary income as opposed to capital gains) progressively rose up to 50% in 1958. It remained at that level for almost thirty years.

An integration system was introduced by a 1965 statute. A resident shareholder (or even a non-resident under some tax treaties) was granted a tax credit (*avoir fiscal*) equal to one-half of the dividend received. As a result, the double taxation on regularly distributed profits was partially eliminated.

Beginning in 1986, the corporate tax rate progressively decreased to 33.33% for fiscal years beginning 1 January 1993. From 1989 to 1992, French corporations were subject to a split-rate system: A surtax was assessed when, after having been taxed at the normal rate when earned, the corporate income was distributed; it was designed to bring the standard corporate tax rate on distributed income up to 42%.

With a 33.33% corporate tax rate and a 50% imputation credit (*avoir fiscal*), no double taxation remained on distributed profits. But because of budgetary needs, three surtaxes were successively created, in 1995 and 1997 for all corporations, and in 2000 for large firms only; only the third one is still in force. On the other hand, a process of yearly reduction of the *avoir fiscal* started in 1999, limited to corporate shareholders not enjoying the intercorporate dividends exemption. This process ended in 2005 with the repeal of the imputation credit for all taxpayers. Those corporate shareholders not entitled to the intercorporate dividends exemption no longer enjoy any relief from economic double taxation; for individual shareholders, the *avoir fiscal* has been replaced by a deduction of 50% of the dividend (reduced to 40% in 2006 when the individual income tax schedule was reorganized).

As far as individuals are concerned, apart from an attempt in 1948 to standardize the rates of the seven schedular taxes, which quickly proved unsuccessful, the 1914–1917 system remained fundamentally unchanged until 1960. At that date, the different existing proportional and progressive income taxes levied on individuals were replaced by a progressive individual income tax (*impôt sur le revenu*, IR). But the basis of this tax consisted of the same categories of income as those in the previous system, and important differences in the taxation of these categories, even in the applicable rates, remained. Most of these differences, except those inherent in the nature of these categories, were progressively eliminated in the 1960s and 1970s on the basis of the slogan '*A revenu connu égal, impôt égal*' (equal taxes for equal income once known), while the category of non-business capital gains was added in 1976.

At the same time, the rates rose steadily, with the highest bracket marginal rate in the early 1980s exceeding 70%. Since then a slow process of reduction in stages has occurred so that, since 2006, the top marginal rate has been 40%. But it should be remembered that at the same time new flat-rate individual income taxes have been created.

The new and additional individual income taxes, called the generalized social contribution (*contribution sociale généralisée*, CSG) and the social debt reimbursement contribution (*contribution au remboursement de la dette sociale*, CRDS), were created in 1991 and 1996 respectively to help finance the social security system. In spite of their names and the fact that they partially replaced existing social security contributions, they are not social security contributions, and they apply to all types of income, including capital gains and income on which an additional so-called social levy (*prélèvement social*) has been imposed since 1998. The rate of the CSG has been dramatically raised since its creation and the revenues this tax yields are significantly higher than those from the classical progressive IR.

As far as taxation of income and gains from capital are concerned, the existence of a yearly net wealth tax – presently called *impôt de solidarité sur la fortune* (ISF) – since 1982 (with a three-year interruption from 1986 to 1989) must also be taken into account. Only non-business assets of individuals are taxable; the rate schedule is progressive, with a 0% bracket up to €790,000 and a 1.80% marginal rate over €16,480,000 million in 2009. A savings clause intervenes to cap the total combined amount of income tax and wealth tax due at 85% of a taxpayer's income, such cap being itself capped (!) for the wealthiest. Over the last few years, new exemptions and tax reductions, mainly concerning stock and securities, have been introduced; moreover, the burden of the wealth tax has been otherwise lessened since taxpayers have been able, since 2006, to benefit from the so-called *bouclier fiscal* (tax shield), which prevents them from having to pay more than 50% of their total income (taxable and tax-exempt) in direct taxes (i.e., IR, new flat income taxes, ISF, local taxes on the main home).

2. CONSTITUTIONAL ISSUES

The 1958 Constitution and the texts having the same legal value (i.e., the 1789 Declaration of Rights and the Preamble of the 1946 Constitution) contain some important provisions concerning taxation. It emerges from Articles 34 and 37 of the Constitution as interpreted by the Constitutional Court (*Conseil Constitutionnel*) that rules governing taxation must be laid down by statute, but only those of a 'determining' nature, which means that, in theory at least, some room must be left to government decrees (*décrets*) and, as the case may be, ministerial orders (*arrêtés*) to lay down rules of secondary importance that are necessary for the practical implementation of the statutory rules.

Article 38 authorizes recourse to delegated legislation. Unlike during previous Republics, this possibility has rarely been used in tax matters under the current Fifth Republic.

Moreover, France is a unitary State, and local authorities may collect only those taxes that have been specifically intended for them by Parliament; in certain cases, they may merely choose the rates within predetermined bands. Such taxes are not, however, taxes on income.

Lastly, human rights and fundamental freedoms as enshrined in the 1789 Declaration of Rights and the Preamble to the 1946 Constitution – especially equality of all in matters of taxation – are binding upon those drafting tax statutes.

The conformity of statutes passed by Parliament with constitutional provisions is verified by the Constitutional Court only when certain bodies (President of the Republic, Prime Minister, Presidents of the two Houses of Parliament) or sixty members of one or other of the Houses of Parliament request that this be done. This means that certain tax statutes currently in force may contain provisions that run counter to the Constitution. However, beginning in 2009, it is possible to raise before the courts a defence of infringement of the rights and freedoms guaranteed by the Constitution, in which case the highest court concerned (*Conseil d'Etat* or *Cour de cassation* as the case may be) may refer the matter to the Constitutional Court.

Moreover, in the last few years, on the combined basis of the principle of supremacy of EU law and Article 55 of the Constitution providing that duly ratified international treaties prevail over parliamentary statutes, EU constraints have had major effects on French tax statutes. On pain of being set aside by the court, laws and regulations must not only comply with EC Treaty provisions but must also respect derived Community law – that is, the provisions of regulations and directives adopted by the European bodies in their fields of jurisdiction, whether or not involving taxation. Following decisions handed down by the European Court of Justice or French courts, certain tax provisions have had to be repealed or modified because they run counter to Directives (especially in the field of value added tax, or VAT) or the major freedoms of movement proclaimed by the EC Treaty (e.g., free movement of goods, workers, services, capital, and payments; freedom of establishment) or because of the prohibition laid down in the same Treaty of aids granted by Member States that distort competition.

The European Convention on Human Rights (ECHR) of 1950 and the case law of the European Court of Human Rights have had an impact on French tax law, in particular Article 6 dealing with the right to a fair trial, and have led to a rethinking of the statutory regime of tax penalties. Insofar as the fundamental principles and freedoms contained in the ECHR are largely identical to those contained in the 1789 Declaration of Rights, the verification of the conformity of French statutes with the Convention has in some ways constituted an indirect means of allowing courts to ensure respect for the 1789 Declaration, in particular the principle of equality.

3. TAX RATES

3.1. Progressive Individual Income Tax (IR)

The 2009 IR rate schedule applicable to income received or accrued in the year 2008 contains five brackets (thirteen before 1994):

Taxable Income	*Tax Rate*
€5,852 or less	0%
€5,852–€11,673	5.50%
€11,673–€25,926	14%
€25,926–€69,505	30%
€69,505 and over	40%

This schedule applies to one share of the global annual income of each fiscal household (for a description of the family share system, see below 5.1 and Part 2, Subpart E.1. Typically, one share corresponds to the taxable income of a single person (with no children).

The brackets are indexed for inflation, as are several thresholds concerning tax exemptions, deductions, or reductions.

Flat rates apply to different types of capital income or gains in lieu of the progressive schedule either automatically (e.g., 16% on business long-term capital gains and 18% on non-business gains on the sale of securities), or optionally (e.g., 18% on interest from bonds).

3.2. Flat-Rate Individual Income Taxes

The current rates of the generalized social contribution (CSG) and the social debt reimbursement contribution (CRDS) on wages, business income, pensions, or unemployment benefits are respectively 7.5% (initially 1.1%), 0.5%, and 2%. The CSG is, however, reduced to 6.6% or 6.2% or, in some cases, 3.8%, on most retirement annuities and unemployment benefits. The CSG on capital income and gains is 8.2%, to which must be added the 0.5% CRDS and the 2% social levy and its two additional contributions, amounting to an overall rate of 12.1% since 2008.

When these taxes are added to the IR, the marginal rates of tax on income of individuals are much higher than they appear to be in the IR rate schedule, even allowing for certain differences in their respective bases and to a partial deduction of the CSG from the basis of the IR.

3.3. Corporate Income Tax

As noted above, the normal rate of the corporate income tax (IS) has been 33.33% since 1993. But a 3.3% so-called social surtax is applicable on the IS itself, more precisely on that part of the IS that exceeds €763,000.

Since 1997, small corporations (i.e., those whose turnover does not exceed €7,630,000 and whose equity is at least 75% owned by individuals) have enjoyed a special rate, which is currently 15% on their income plus capital gains not exceeding €38,120.

Moreover, a reduced rate applies to certain passive (rents, interest, dividends) and agricultural income of non-profit-seeking and otherwise exempt entities ('*associations*') – generally 24%, but 10% on most income from securities. More importantly, most net long-term capital gains of corporations (nowadays defined as gains realized on the sale of certain substantial interests occurring within two years after the interests were acquired) have been exempted since 2007. Certain reduced rates, respectively 19% and 15%, apply to long-term gains on stakes in listed corporations whose assets mainly consist of immovable property and to royalties and gains from the sale of patents.

4. BASIC STRUCTURE OF THE FISCAL SYSTEM

One of the traditional basic features of the French tax system was said to be that income taxes represent a small proportion of the tax revenues compared to other developed countries. The main reason for this imbalance was that the individual income tax (IR), although highly progressive, contained many exemptions, allowances, and tax reductions of all kinds, so that its burden was concentrated on the highest income categories, while almost one out of two households was exempt.

While these characteristics of the IR today remain fundamentally unchanged, a clear trend toward a greater part of French tax revenues coming from income tax has become apparent. As a percentage of GDP, income taxes doubled during the last twenty-five years of the twentieth century, with a dramatic increase at the end of the 1990s. Since 2000 they account for about 11% of GDP (according to the latest OECD statistics) – that is, as much as taxes on goods and services, which had for many years been by far the most substantial source of public revenues (excluding social security). This can easily be explained by the creation of the generalized social contribution (CSG), the social debt reimbursement contribution (CRDS), and the other so-called social tax levies to help finance welfare benefits, and by the subsequent marked rise in the rate of the CSG. As a matter of fact, these new-style income taxes, with wide bases and flat rates, have proved productive in terms of revenues – about €92 billion for the CSG and the other flat-rate income taxes, compared to approximately €60 billion, €65 billion, and €180 billion for IR, IS, and VAT respectively, based on 2008 estimates.

At the same time, and for the same reason, social security contributions (not to be mistaken for the above-mentioned social levies, which are income taxes) symmetrically decreased from 18.5% of GDP in the years 1985–1995 to about 16% since 2000. They must be added to income taxes as they are also essentially levied on income, especially on earned income.

Tax revenues as a percentage of GDP have been rather stable, about 44%, since 1996.

5. BASIC STRUCTURE OF THE INCOME TAX

5.1. Income Taxes on Individuals

As noted above, the French tax system comprises no fewer than three different general taxes on the income of individuals (not counting the 2% social levy on capital income and gains and its two additional contributions).

As far as the traditional progressive individual income tax (IR) is concerned, gross taxable income necessarily falls into one of the following eight categories:

- salary and pension income;
- remuneration received by certain company managers;
- industrial and commercial profits;
- agricultural profits;
- real estate income;
- securities income;
- private (i.e., non-business) capital gains;
- personal (non-commercial) services income and other income (catchall category).

From the beginning, the concept of income has been based on the civil law source theory, according to which income encompasses only sums of money that are likely to flow on a periodic basis from a steady source, as opposed to one-off receipts or to those that can be considered as part of the source itself (especially capital gains). This theory still fundamentally inspires the criteria that can be found in the 'other income' category to determine whether income that does not fall within any one of the other existing categories is taxable or not. But in a number of respects, especially as far as capital gains are concerned, the source theory has been reversed by statute.

Business capital gains and losses have systematically been taken into account (except for very small businesses) since the 1930s and taxed within the industrial and commercial, agricultural, and non-commercial schedular categories. In contrast, the principle of the taxation of private – that is, non-business – capital gains was established only in 1976, and there still exist many exemptions and favourable rules governing their taxation.

Each category has its own specific set of rules (and often several different sets of rules) used to calculate the net income or loss. Incomes and deductible charges are normally taken into account at their actual amount. But charges (or certain categories of charges) to income can in some cases optionally be deducted from gross income or turnover on a standardized basis, such as allowances equal to 10% of salary or pension after deduction of social contributions; 71% of turnover of very small businesses (with annual sales below €80,000); 50% of payments for commercial and 34% for non-commercial services rendered by very small businesses (gross income lower than €32,000); and 40% of gross rents (if lower than €15,000).

Except for gains on the sale of securities, fixed securities income, and business long-term capital gains, which are generally, ex officio or optionally, subject to a flat-rate tax (see section 3.3 above), the individual progressive income tax base is, in principle at least, the algebraic sum of net income and losses from all categories realized by the different members of the same fiscal household, from whatever geographical source if the latter are tax residents or from French sources only if they are non-residents. But exceptions to the offsetting of net income and losses have become more and more numerous. Today, some categories of net losses are no longer deductible from positive income of the same year; they can be carried forward only against positive income of the same nature earned during the next five or ten years, as the case may be; these are mainly net losses from renting of real estate and so-called non-professional (non-business) agricultural, industrial, and commercial or non-commercial profits. These losses are said to be ring-fenced (*tunnélisées*).

If the algebraic addition of losses and incomes (subject to the aforesaid restrictions) results in a global net loss, the latter is carried forward for the six following years. Otherwise, there can be deducted from the global income some expenses (mainly alimony) and allowances (for old or disabled low-income people and for fiscal households comprising married children and/or children with family responsibilities, as these children are not taken into account for the application of the family share system). Most deductions from global income have been transformed in the 1980s into *réductions* (i.e., non-refundable credits) or *crédits d'impôt* (i.e., refundable credits) because credits were considered fairer than deductions;

since then, new tax incentives for certain expenses incurred by taxpayers have taken the form of such tax reductions or credits.

The household is the taxable unit. It is composed, as the case may be, of a single person or a married couple or, since 1999, two unmarried partners who have entered into a domestic partnership (*pacte civil de solidarité*), and, subject to certain elections or exceptions, of dependent persons, mainly children.

According to the family share system (*quotient familial*) created in 1945 (see Part 2, Subpart E.1), the household net income is divided by the number of shares approximately corresponding to the number of people in the family, before being subjected to the single progressive tax schedule. The figure so obtained is then multiplied by the relevant number of shares. This gives the gross tax.

Several additional calculations must then be made before arriving at the net tax payable. In particular, tax credits are to be computed. Such credits are equal to a fixed percentage of certain personal expenses, such as gifts to charities, important repairs to the main home and care of young children; some are refundable (the so-called *crédits d'impôt*), and some are not (*réductions d'impôt*). Other credits do not correspond to expenses incurred by the taxpayer, such as the former imputation credit (*avoir fiscal*) or the employment credit to which low-income employees or the self-employed are entitled since 2001.

In short, the system for the computation of French individual income tax is probably one of the most complicated in the world. Fortunately, the computation is not made by the taxpayer.

The computation of the *flat income taxes* (CSG and CRDS) looks relatively simple, but their creation brought in a new factor of complexity in the calculation of the IR, from the basis of which the CSG is partially deductible. Apart from the rate, the CSG and CRDS differ from the IR in many important ways. Their base is wider: It includes the social security contributions, and there are fewer allowances, fewer deductions, and almost no exemptions, and no offsetting exists for losses in one category of income against income belonging to other categories. The taxable unit is not the household and the existence of dependents is not taken into account. Non-residents are not subject to these taxes.

5.2. Corporate Income Tax

The rules applicable to the calculation of the basis of the normal rate (33.33%) of corporate income tax (IS) are fundamentally the same, whatever activity is carried on by the corporation, as those used to evaluate the basis of IR on the industrial and commercial profits of sole proprietorships (other than those whose charges to income are calculated on a standard basis). Both taxes are basically levied on the results of the business for accounting purposes, plus charges not deductible and minus income not includable for tax purposes, and the same accounting principles and rules must be used. As far as non-includable incomes and non-deductible charges are concerned, the general scheme is also the same, even if some are specific to one tax or the other.

One of the differences lies in the scope of long-term capital gains eligible for a reduced rate of taxation: these are gains from the disposal of all sorts of fixed assets by self-employed persons but, since 1997, only gains from the disposal by corporations of certain substantial interests (at least 5%) in other corporations. Corporations can choose the intercorporate dividends exemption rather than including the income from such interests in their tax base.[1]

Corporations are eligible for a three-year carryback of losses, which entitles them to a tax credit, which is not available to sole proprietorships, and which they can choose instead of the unlimited carryforward (five years before 2004, six years for sole proprietorships).

Groups are entitled to opt for the consolidation of a domestic parent and any 95%-or-more domestic subsidiaries (*intégration fiscale*). As an exception to the so-called principle of territoriality, according to which active income is taxable in France only if it is attributable to a French trade or business (mainly a branch or dependent agent), groups may also obtain the consolidation of a domestic corporation and its foreign branches and its 50%-or-more domestic or foreign subsidiaries (*bénéfice mondial et consolidé*). From 2009, small- or medium-sized corporations (with less than 2,000 employees) may opt for the deduction (within limits) of losses of foreign branches or 95%-directly-held foreign subsidiaries. Such losses are recaptured as and when profits are made by such entities, and in any case no later than five years thereafter.

6. LEGISLATION

6.1. Legislative Process

Most tax measures come from Finance Acts, either initial or rectifying. They are normally passed in the same terms by both Houses of Parliament (*Assemblée Nationale* and *Sénat*) under an accelerated legislative process in which the Assemblée Nationale, the only House elected by universal direct suffrage, may, if need be, have the last word. Finance bills are necessarily of government origin, but Members of Parliament may, under strict conditions, table new provisions or amendments as long as they do not result in a reduction of the level of public revenues (Article 40 of the Constitution). Consequently, only those parliamentary amendments agreed to or inspired by the government stand a chance of getting onto the statute book.

Tax provisions may also be found in ordinary statutes, and major tax reforms have been achieved in this manner. They are, however, mostly of governmental origin, and Members' right of amendment is limited for finance bills.

1. Exemption is preferable in most cases; however, there are circumstances (small businesses qualifying for the 15% corporate tax rate or corporations belonging to a consolidated group) in which taxation with a foreign tax credit is preferable.

The legislative process is a rapid one for both ordinary bills and finance bills. Parliament, moreover, has only seventy days in which to vote on finance bills. No formal provision is made for hearings or public consultation, even though interested professional organizations may be informally consulted. It is rare indeed to see tax provisions come from an extra-parliamentary ad hoc committee of experts. The reform improving taxpayers' rights and guarantees in 1986 and 1987 and the one enhancing legal certainty in tax matters in 2009 are striking exceptions to this rule. The major part of debate thus takes place inside Parliament, mainly in the Finance Committees of the two Houses.

The initial Finance Bill for a given year N is passed before the end of December of the preceding year, but the provisions contained as to individual income tax and corporate income tax apply retrospectively, unless expressly otherwise provided for, to income and capital gains realized during the year N-1. Moreover, especially during the 1980s and early 1990s, Parliament passed (at the government's request and often purely for the purpose of reversing by statute case law running contrary to administrative interpretations and practices and with which the tax authorities disagreed) numerous special tax provisions of a retrospective nature. No constitutional provision prohibits tax laws from having retrospective effects. However, the Constitutional Court has laid down limits, in particular by requiring that such special measures be justified by sufficient general interest and by excluding any retrospective increase of tax penalties and any calling into question of court decisions that have become *res judicata*. Such measures have become markedly less numerous over the past few years.

6.2. Statutory Drafting

The French tax code, even considered together with its schedules (government decrees and ministerial orders), is far less voluminous than the US Internal Revenue Code. This is probably because for a long time the French Parliament did not seek to contemplate every particular situation and often preferred, rather than setting out precise, specific, and rigid rules or comprehensive definitions and enumerations, to formulate principles and generally worded, concise provisions adaptable to various and/or new situations through appropriate constructions. Thus, much was left to administrative and judicial interpretation.

This is less and less true. A lot of old-style provisions indeed remain in effect, such as the statutory rules concerning the taxation of corporations in the international field, which date back to 1948 and are condensed into several lines in the tax code. But as in many other legal systems, the style of statutory drafting has greatly changed during the last few decades, in that statutes tend to be much more numerous, detailed, and complex than before. Statutory tax law is also nowadays characterized by frequent changes. Such an evolution reflects the growing complexity of the technical, economic, and social background of the law, as well as the utilization of taxation as a means of leverage in economic and social matters and the growing influence of lobbies on the legislative decision-making process.

6.3. Statutory Interpretation

Case law remains a major source of tax law. This is because many statutes are still worded in general terms and administrative interpretations are not normally binding upon courts (see below). Many tax principles and rules have been set by the tax courts, and judicial interpretations are part of the law.

No interpretation act has ever been enacted; the judgments never explicitly set out the construction principles and methods used; and there are very few academic studies on the subject. It is somewhat difficult to explain how statutes (and decrees) are construed by the courts.

It can, however, be said that, as a matter of principle, the clear wording of the text always prevails over the preparatory works and over tax equity or economic considerations. But it is the judge who decides whether the text is clear, and even if a provision is clear, it may be incomplete, imprecise, or inappropriate to the particular situation in hand. In such cases, as well as when the texts are ambiguous, contradictory, or silent, the judge may use every available method of intrinsic or extrinsic interpretation likely to reveal what the intent of the legislator may have been, although he is rather reluctant to use reasoning by analogy or *a contrario* reasoning, and he rarely explicitly relies on the preparatory works. In practice the judge is very much at liberty to decide what the law is.

This is particularly true for administrative judges, who are in charge of the litigation concerning the main levies (individual and corporate income taxes and VAT). Recent administrative case law, which, because statutory provisions have remained silent, has drawn up a complex method for calculating business capital gains arising from the sale of interests in partnership, offers a good example. Civil courts, which deal with litigation arising from registration, death, gift, and wealth taxes as well as stamp or excise duties, tend to adopt a more literal and strict style of construction.

In the particular case of a domestic tax provision that appears to be incompatible with the EC Treaty, EC Directives, or constitutional rules or principles, the courts attempt whenever possible to interpret the provision in a manner consistent with EC law or such constitutional rules or principles and thus avoid having to strike down the provision. They are no longer reluctant to refer questions of interpretation to the European Court of Justice when the conformity of a national provision with EC law is dependent on the correct interpretation of such law.

7. COURTS DEALING WITH TAX MATTERS

7.1. Structure of the Courts

France does not have any specialized tax courts. One of the traditional peculiarities of the French legal system is, however, to be found in tax matters – namely, the existence of two parallel court systems. Administrative courts that, generally speaking, hear disputes between the administration and the administered (hence their name) most commonly hear taxation cases. However, civil courts, which normally hear cases between private persons or entities, have jurisdiction by statute to deal with litigation arising from registration, death, gift, and wealth taxes as well as stamp or excise duties. This dual court system subsists, notwithstanding frequent criticism, because civil judges are deemed to be more competent than administrative judges to deal with the questions of civil law, which this type of taxation raises. Consequently, the administrative courts hear mainly litigation dealing with major taxes such as income tax, corporation tax, and VAT. Litigation involving the CSG and other flat-rate income taxes can be heard by both types of courts, depending on the type of income concerned.

The taxpayer who contests his taxation on de facto or de jure grounds can never directly refer the matter to a court. He is first required to lodge a complaint with the Service that has determined the taxation and do so before the expiry of a period that, for most taxes, is between two and three years (3,643,134 complaints in 2007 for all taxes, 1,338,562 for State direct taxes). A longer period applies when the tax results from a tax reassessment following a tax audit. This first stage acts as a filter and makes it possible to settle the vast majority of disputes. The lodging of a complaint does not relieve the taxpayer from paying the disputed tax, although he may obtain a further period of grace for such payment by lodging sufficient security with the Treasury.

If the Service involved fails to reply within six months or expressly rejects the complaint, the taxpayer may then, without any time limit in the first case and within two months in the second, refer the matter to an administrative court (*Tribunal Administratif*, or TA) or civil court of first instance (*Tribunal de grande instance*, or TGI). An appeal is possible within two months before the Administrative Court of Appeal (*Cour administrative d'appel*, CAA) or a civil Court of Appeal (*Cour d'appel*, CA), whose decisions may also be appealed to the administrative (*Conseil d'État*, CE) or civil (*Cour de cassation*, Cass.) court of highest jurisdiction. A filter is used at this stage to eliminate patently inadmissible appeals or appeals devoid of serious grounds, but there is no requirement as to the granting of leave. The appeal, called a *pourvoi en cassation*, does not normally prevent a judgment from being executed (is not normally suspensive) and is restricted to questions of law, but this limit is liberally construed.

Number of cases (2007) brought before:	*All taxes*	*State direct taxes (mainly IR & IS)*
Administrative Courts		
TA	25,170	8,444
CAA	3,598	
CE	520	
Civil Courts		
TGI & CA	949	
Cass.	166	

All judgments are delivered by a bench of judges. An attorney is not required before the lower courts (TA and TGI). During the hearing of the case, the taxpayer may always request – and often does so successfully – that the court set aside the provision that is the basis of the disputed tax because it runs contrary to a provision of higher value (statute, tax treaty, EC treaty, EC Directive or Regulation, as the case may be). As from 2009, the taxpayer may raise before the courts the defence of infringement by a legislative provision of the rights and freedoms guaranteed by the Constitution.

The foregoing rules apply when the assessment basis, the amount of the tax, or the manner in which it is assessed is disputed. When the litigation deals with tax collection, a similar system applies, but with certain differences, in particular regarding the time allotted and the apportionment of jurisdiction between civil and administrative courts.

Mention should also be made of the possibility for the taxpayer, independently of any litigation as to the tax itself, to bring proceedings for judicial review on the grounds of an *ultra vires* act before an administrative court to have any illegal governmental decree, ministerial order, or administrative interpretation set aside. When a French provision has been held, during any litigation (tax dispute, proceedings for an *ultra vires* act, EC action for failure to act, or an action for interpretation) not to conform to a higher legal rule by one of the French courts of highest jurisdiction or the European Court of Justice, any taxpayer is entitled to obtain the refund of the taxes paid on the basis of the challenged provision during the three-year period directly preceding the court decision.

7.2. Judicial Style

Judgments are generally short, rarely more than two or three pages long. After a reference to the applicable statutory provisions, and a succinct summary of the proceedings to date and the arguments exchanged by the parties, the grounds are written in a concise and even sometimes over-laconic style. The opinions of the judges – either concurring or dissenting – are not published. However, the opinion given on each case, prior to the deliberation of the court, by one of the members of the court (in the administrative courts, the so-called *Commissaire du Gouvernement*, or *Rapporteur public* as from 2009) constitutes a valuable tool in understanding the decision, even if the latter does not always follow the path traced therein. It is often published in specialized reviews. The doctrine of binding precedent is not applied as such, but once the position of the court of highest jurisdiction (whether administrative or civil) has been clearly established, lower courts tend to follow this example, at least for a certain period.

8. ADMINISTRATION

8.1. Tax Assessment, Collection, and Auditing

French taxes are levied on the basis of tax returns by taxpayers. People are encouraged to make these returns and relevant payments by electronic means, although relatively few natural persons have as yet taken up this possibility (7.4 million in 2008 out of about 35.8 million fiscal (IR) households, 19 million of which are actually IR taxable).

All the income from all schedular categories realized by the different members of each fiscal household must be indicated in the progressive individual income tax (IR) general return. But the tax return forms sent to taxpayers are now partially pre-completed; they contain all relevant information communicated to the tax authorities by third parties about wages and income from securities. Special tax returns concerning the various categories of business profits (industrial or commercial, agricultural, and non-commercial profits) and rents or gains from the sale of immovable property must also be filed and added to the general return.

The amount of individual tax payable is no longer assessed by taxpayers themselves, which is a good thing given the great complexity of the method of calculation.

There is no withholding of tax on wages or pensions. Tax is withheld at source only on some securities income and, in an international context, on certain income of non-residents. But the flat income taxes (CSG, CRDS, and the 2% social levy) are withheld at source for most income. The IR is paid in twice-yearly provisional instalments or, at the option of the taxpayer, in ten monthly instalments equal respectively to one-third and one-tenth of the tax paid in the previous year. When the tax for the year has been calculated by the authorities, a notice of assessment showing the amount of tax owing is sent to the taxpayer, who is then required to pay the outstanding balance or who, in the event of over-payment, is entitled to a refund.

Corporations must also file an annual general tax return to which are attached a bundle of additional returns giving the accounting and tax information and setting out the elements that serve to determine the tax result and the corresponding tax. The tax should in principle be paid when the returns are made, but in fact it is really payment of an outstanding balance, since corporate income tax is also paid by provisional instalments.

Any reassessments following verification of the returns made by individuals and corporations must be notified to the taxpayer before 31 December of the third year after the year for which the tax is due.

The tax files of individual taxpayers now seem to be more systematically reviewed than in the past (office audit). In the business sector, the necessarily limited funds devoted to tax auditing are concentrated on the control of medium-sized and big firms, as the tax result of many small sole proprietorships is still determined on the basis of a standard deduction (see section 5.1 above). In the past few decades the tax audit services have been reorganized, the skill of tax auditors has been improved, and the use of computers has made tax auditing more efficient. But at the same time the tax auditing process has been more and more precisely regulated; many detailed procedural rules that courts generally strictly enforce are now affording the taxpayer complete protection. For the past ten years the number of field audits has remained relatively low (47,851 in 2006 of the more than 3.3 million eligible businesses), as has been the case for in-depth audits of individuals (4,578 in 2006 of 35.8 million households).

For historical reasons, two different administrative agencies have long been in charge of the assessment, calculation, and control of direct taxes on the one hand and the collection of such taxes on the other hand. In 1999 an attempt to unify these agencies, which was clearly desirable for efficiency reasons, failed because the trade unions opposed it. Nevertheless, since 2002 a new special agency called the *Direction des Grandes Entreprises* ('Direction of Major Firms'), whose seat is located near Paris, receives the online returns and payments for almost all direct and indirect taxes due by all corporations whose turnover or gross assets exceed €400 million and their parents and subsidiaries (based on ownership of 50% or more of the shares). Moreover, since 2006, other businesses have had a single local interlocutor for all their State taxes in each newly created *Service des impôts des entreprises* (tax service for businesses). The merger process has also been started for private individual taxpayers – that is, a one-stop scheme for the assessment and payment of taxes that should be completed by 2012.

French taxpayers do not like taxes, and they say they don't. In the 1950s and the 1960s there were some revolts against taxation, especially by small individual businesses. But even if many taxpayers still consider tax evasion as legitimate and the amount of tax evasion remains significant, the relationships between taxpayers and the revenue services seem to have reached a relatively peaceful *modus vivendi* in spite of the increase of tax burdens and the improved efficiency of tax auditing. This is probably because of the new and numerous statutory rights granted to taxpayers, a growing understanding of the link between taxes and State benefits, the growing number of employees compared to small businesses, and an increasing open-mindedness of the tax authorities about economic and international concerns.

In the past, French taxpayers and tax professionals have apparently not shown outstanding skill in tax planning, or at least they have not been engaged in aggressive tax planning, probably partly because of the fear inspired by the anti-abuse of law provision in the Code, which appears to many to be a real sword of Damocles. But under the influence of Anglo-American practice, things have somewhat changed, especially in the international tax field. In response, many loopholes have been closed and the tax services have now been granted many anti-avoidance tools, which they try to use with an ever-increasing efficiency in spite of the obstacles resulting from EC and tax treaty case law.

8.2. Administrative Interpretations

After Parliament has enacted a statute, government decrees (*décrets*) and ministerial orders (*arrêtés*) often outline the meaning and scope of the statutory provisions and their methods of application, but this is not systematic unless Parliament has specifically asked the government to do so.

Published administrative circulars (*circulaires* or *instructions* or *notes*) issued by the Minister of Finance or, under his authority, by the heads of the main tax departments of the Ministry of Finance (mainly the *Direction générale des impôts*) then explain and interpret statutes and decrees as well as outline the practical measures for the application of the same. Before being published, they are more and more often submitted for comments to different organizations (e.g., employers' unions, lawyers and chartered accountants associations). In April 2009, for the first time, a circular was submitted to the general public for comments on the website of the Ministry of Finance.

Circulars cannot lay down new rules, and they are deprived of any force of law in that they are not binding on taxpayers and courts, except when they establish an interpretation of a decree, statute, or tax treaty that is favourable to taxpayers. In the latter situation, no additional assessment is possible against a taxpayer who has complied with such interpretation (a kind of doctrine of estoppel). The tax authorities also make their position known in ministerial replies to questions put by members of Parliament. The circulars tend to be more frequently and more rapidly issued after a statute has been enacted. They also tend to become ever more precise and are increasingly illustrated with ever-longer examples. They are, of course, important and useful to taxpayers. But fields of tax law where decrees and circulars are non-existent or of limited help are not rare, even when the statute is itself generally worded (for instance, in transfer pricing matters).

The French tax authorities do not in principle have any discretionary power and have for long been reluctant to issue advance rulings. There were procedures (*agréments*) – some of which still exist – whereby taxpayers could not benefit from a particular tax regime without the prior consent of the tax services. Things have gradually changed.

In 1987 a new estoppel provision was added to the existing one concerning the interpretation of fiscal texts: The tax services cannot make a tax deficiency assessment on the basis of an estimation of the taxpayer's situation regarding the application of a given tax provision (e.g., the qualification of a business activity for individual tax purposes) different from the one they had previously made, either spontaneously (e.g., on the occasion of a tax audit) or in response to a question by the taxpayer, at least as long as the situation or provision has not been modified.

Parallel to this general guarantee and beginning in the mid-1990s, a dozen specific ruling (*rescrit*) procedures were successively introduced, each of them having a narrow scope (e.g., existence of a permanent establishment, advance pricing agreement (APA), and the like). If the tax services fail to provide an express answer within a certain time (three to six months as the case may be), they are deemed to have assented to the taxpayer's request provided the latter has described his situation in a precise, comprehensive, and good faith manner. Lastly, since July 2009, the taxpayer has, under the same conditions, benefited from the general guarantee concerning any question relating to the application of tax law to particular facts whenever the tax services do not answer within three months. This is a something of a revolution on the French tax scene. It remains to be seen for how long French taxpayers will remain skeptical about procedures of this kind.

9. GENERAL PRINCIPLES

9.1. Relationship between Tax and Financial Accounting

The link between tax and financial accounting is very close. The taxable income of corporations and, in principle, of sole proprietorships carrying on an industrial, commercial, or agricultural activity is fundamentally their book income, to which adjustments are made whenever tax law departs from accounting law. In cases of uncertainty, the courts have shown in the last few years a growing tendency to apply the accounting concepts, rules, and principles unless there are strong reasons to the contrary derived from the purpose of the applicable tax provision. This set of accounting concepts, rules, and principles is set down by the law, and firms must conform to them. By the same token, it is often regretted that tax considerations sometimes 'pollute' the development of accounting rules.

9.2. Respect for Civil or Private Law Form

The doctrine of the autonomy of tax law is nowadays out of favour. Civil, commercial, or corporate law concepts used in tax law normally have the same meaning as under the branch of law to which they belong. This is a major principle of interpretation in civil courts when they deal with tax cases. On the other hand, administrative courts, when judging income tax or VAT cases, may still be more sensitive to the purpose of the particular tax provision involved and consider that it can justify giving a particular term a meaning different from the one it has in other branches of law.

If the parties to a transaction have erroneously characterized the transaction for tax purposes, the tax service is entitled to recharacterize it. In cases when it has been deliberately mischaracterized to avoid or unduly decrease taxation, the tax authorities must invoke the 'abuse of law' doctrine, which constitutes one of the major anti-avoidance weapons.

9.3. Anti-avoidance Doctrines and Rules

Two main doctrines have been traditionally used in French tax law to combat tax avoidance.

The abuse of law (*abus de droit*) doctrine, which has been specifically embodied in a particular section of the tax code, authorizes the revenue service to redefine a specific transaction (e.g., a sale) that in fact disguises (*simulation*) another transaction (e.g., a donation), the tax cost of which is higher and more generally, according to case law, to set aside any scheme that is devoid of any business purpose and has been set up by the taxpayer exclusively for tax purposes (*fraus legis*).

The second anti-avoidance doctrine, which is much more widely used by tax auditors, is the abnormal management decision (*acte anormal de gestion*) doctrine, according to which the consequences of any management decision can be set aside when it unduly deprives a business from receiving income, makes it incur useless expenses or losses, or more generally is not in the interest of the business; such income is taxed as if it had been received, and such loss or expense is not deductible for tax purposes and, in the case of corporations, the corresponding sums are deemed to have been distributed.

These two doctrines are applicable in both domestic and international tax matters. They have inspired several specific anti-avoidance statutory provisions in the international tax field, such as those against transfer pricing, payments to low-tax jurisdictions, 'rent-a-star' companies, and controlled foreign corporations.

10. SOURCES OF TAX LAW

Tax statutes have been codified in a single code since 1950, known as the General Tax Code (*Code général des impôts*, or CGI). Previously, when new statutes were enacted, it was up to the government to insert them in the Code by codifying decrees. Today, however, this is very often no longer necessary since Parliament has adopted the habit of passing provisions that directly vary, complete, or repeal existing articles or introduce new ones. The numbering of articles that results from this permanent re-mix is often very complex, all the more so as it does not contain any system of organized subdivisions.

Since 1992 the vast majority of tax procedure rules (e.g., audits, litigation, collection) have been grouped together in a separate book, known as the Book of Tax Procedures (*Livre des procédures fiscales*, or LPF), which from a legal point of view is part of the General Tax Code. However, when one refers to the General Tax Code, such reference concerns solely those substantive provisions found in the Code.

Government decrees (*décrets*) and ministerial orders (*arrêtés*) are codified in different schedules to the CGI (as narrowly defined above) or in special parts of the LPF.

The new administrative circulars (*circulaires*, *instructions*, or *notes*) are periodically published in the Official Tax Bulletin (*Bulletin officiel des impôts*, or BOI). They used to be periodically integrated, when necessary after redrafting, in a weighty collection of texts that contain the opinions of the tax authorities on all taxes and that are known as the Basic Administrative Documentation (*Documentation administrative de base*), designed for tax agents but also open to the public. Unfortunately, the periodic updating of this collection was considered too expensive and was discontinued in 2002. Circulars currently released, however, attempt to alleviate the consequences of this situation by considering the subject matter modified by the relevant provision in a systematic manner and from every angle; thus, they are increasingly long and precise.

Rulings of general interest are published (in an anonymous way) on the site of the Ministry of Finance (see below).

Selected decisions handed down by the two courts of highest jurisdiction (<www.conseil-etat.fr>; <www.courdecassation.fr>) are published in official collections: *Recueil des décisions du Conseil d'Etat (Rec.*, or *Recueil Lebon*) and *Bulletin des arrêts de la Cour de cassation – Chambres civiles (Bull. Civ.)*. Decisions of the greatest interest, irrespective of the court handing them down, are traditionally to be found in the main tax reviews: *Revue de Jurisprudence Fiscale* (*RJF*), Francis Lefebvre Ed., and *Revue de droit fiscal* (*Dr. fisc.*), LexisNexis Ed. (see below).

The text of the French Constitution (in English, German, Spanish, and Italian) and of the decisions of the Conseil Constitutionnel, some of which are translated into the above-mentioned languages, can be found on the site of the Conseil Constitutionnel (<www.conseil-constitutionnel.fr>).

The most comprehensive, precise, and up-to-date treatise (a new edition every year) is the *Mémento pratique fiscal* (Francis Lefebvre Ed.). The French tax authorities also publish a yearly treatise called *Précis de fiscalité* (see below).

The most exhaustive privately edited tax documentation is probably the one published by *Les Editions Francis Lefebvre* (<www.efl.fr>), which consist of general documentation (*Documentation fiscale* in 12 volumes), a special edition of the CGI and LPF (*Code pratique*), a comprehensive treatise (*Mémento pratique fiscal*), and four reviews: *Feuillets rapides* (weekly), *Bulletin fiscal* (monthly), *Revue de jurisprudence fiscale* (monthly, case law only), and *Bulletin des conclusions fiscales* (monthly, mainly selected opinions of the *Commissaires du Gouvernement/Rapporteurs publics* before the *Conseil d'Etat*). Systematic cross-references between the different elements of this documentation are of great help. Its digital version is called *Navis fiscal.*

LexisNexis (<www.lexisnexis.fr>) also publishes general documentation (*JurisClasseur fiscal* and *Jurisclasseur fiscal international*) with a weekly review attached to it (*Revue de droit fiscal*).

Official websites of major interest:

<www.impots.gouv.fr> (Ministry of Finance)
Tax forms, statistics, rulings, circulars, *Bulletin Officiel des impôts*, *Documentation de base*, Précis de fiscalité, CGI and LPF, Tax treaties.
<www.legifrance.gouv.fr> (Prime Minister)
Constitution; codes (some are in English and Spanish, but not the tax codes); statutes, decrees, ministerial orders, circulars (full text since 1990); case law (constitutional, administrative and civil); links to treaties, ECJ and ECHR case law, official bulletins.
<www.assemblee-nationale.fr> (Assemblée nationale) and <www.senat.fr> (Sénat)
Travaux préparatoires (preparatory works) of statutes (especially Finance Acts), Reports by the Parliamentary Commissions and Committees.

Germany

Prof. Dr Wolfgang Schön

1. HISTORY

Under the constitution of the German Reich founded in 1871, only the German federal states, and not the Reich itself, had the power to impose income taxes. Therefore, the history of modern income taxation in Germany starts with the Prussian Income Tax Act of 1891, which introduced a systematic 'source-based' approach to income taxation. Due to the heavy financial burden of World War I, this legislative power was shifted to the German Reich by the Weimar Constitution of 1919. In 1920, a modern Income Tax Act (strictly following the comprehensive economic concept of income) and the first German Corporate Income Tax Act were enacted. The 1920 act did not survive the hyperinflation of 1922–1923 and was replaced by the pragmatic Income Tax Acts of 1925 and 1934, which provided the basic framework for today's Income Tax Act (ITA). The Corporate Income Tax (CITA) has undergone three major reforms: In 1977 the 'classical' system was replaced by an imputation system, which itself had to give way to a 'shareholder-relief' system in 2000. The Corporate Income Tax Reform in 2007 adapted the 'shareholder-relief system' or 'half-income system' to the final withholding tax system, which has been implemented for all capital income derived from financial assets that are held as private assets ('modified half-income system').

2. CONSTITUTIONAL ISSUES

2.1. Legislative Powers

In fiscal matters, the German Federal Constitution (*Grundgesetz*) of 1949 was designed to strengthen the political power of the states (*Länder*). Therefore, the Federation (*Bund*) is competent to enact tax laws only if the *Bund* is at least partly entitled to the tax revenues (e.g., income tax) or if federal legislation is necessary to ensure equal living conditions or to maintain legal or economic coherence in Germany.[1] If the *Bund* exercises this right, the *Länder* are no longer authorized to legislate in this area. Contrary to the political concept of the *Grundgesetz*, after more than fifty years this has led to an overwhelming importance of federal legislation in tax matters. Nevertheless, under the federal constitution, the *Länder* take part in federal legislation through the instrument of the Council of States (*Bundesrat*). The *Bundesrat* even has the power to veto tax bills if the *Länder* or the local municipalities receive a share in the revenue.[2] Under this system, *Bund* and *Länder* are bound to cooperate in any major tax legislation (e.g., income tax, corporate income tax, value added tax).

2.2. Sharing of Tax Revenue

While tax legislation is mainly a federal matter and tax administration mainly a state matter,[3] the revenue from most of the more important taxes is shared among the *Bund*, the *Länder* and the municipalities (*Gemeinden*).[4] On the other hand, excise taxes go to the *Bund*, while estate duties or real estate transfer tax go to the *Länder*. An important tax on income from trade and business (*Gewerbesteuer*) is raised by the municipalities.

Revenue sharing mandated by the Constitution is one of the major inroads on the constitutional separation of federal and state budgets. In addition, there are horizontal payments between rich and poor states; there are also vertical payments from the Federation to individual states (*horizontaler und vertikaler Finanzausgleich*).[5]

3. IMPACT OF BASIC RIGHTS ON TAXATION

Both the provisions framing the 'fiscal constitution' of Germany with respect to the allocation of powers to different levels of government and the 'basic rights' enshrined in the German Constitution have played an important direct role in

1. Article 105 para. 2 with reference to Basic Law, Art. 72 para. 2.
2. Basic Law, Art. 105 para. 4.
3. Basic Law, Art. 108.
4. Basic Law, Art. 106.
5. Basic Law, Art. 107.

developing German tax law after World War II. Especially in the 1990s, major changes in German tax law have been forced upon the government by the German Constitutional Court, which may be directly approached by taxpayers.

Among the 'Bill of Rights' contained in Articles 1 to 19 of the Federal Constitution, the following have had a special impact on tax matters:

- Article 2, paragraph 1 (Right to Liberty of Person): the Constitutional Court has concluded that the state is not allowed to tax income that is necessary to maintain a minimum living standard.[6] According to a recent judgment, the tax-free amount of income must include not only necessary costs for nutrition, clothing, and accommodation, but also a certain amount of social security contributions for medical services and care.[7]
- Article 3 (Equality): the Constitutional Court has stated that tax legislation must comply with the 'ability-to-pay' principle in income tax matters and avoid inconsistent results (e.g., different valuation principles under the wealth and gift tax acts and different tax treatment for retirement payments have been declared invalid). Most recently, an incoherent provision on commuter expenditures was struck down by the Court.[8] There is an ongoing debate about whether a dual income tax system would be in line with the principle of equality. Furthermore, equality has to be achieved with respect to the practical enforcement of tax liabilities (e.g., taxation of interest income).[9]
- Article 6, paragraph 1 (Marriage and family are under the special protection of the state): the Constitutional Court has decided that the sole fact of a marriage may not increase the total tax burden of the spouses; therefore, the joint assessment of husband and wife was declared null and void; subsequent legislation provided for income splitting.[10] Moreover, the income of minor children must be assessed separately.[11] Finally, tax legislation must grant 'adequate' allowances for child tuition and education.[12]
- Article 14 (Protection of Property): in a controversial judgment dating from 1995, the Court concluded that taxation of income may not exceed (roughly) 50% of income.[13] In 2006, the Court overruled this judgment by denying that an absolute maximum tax rate exists in Article 14.[14]

6. Federal Constitutional Court (*Bundesverfassungsgericht*) judgment of 25 Sep. 1992 2 BvL 5,8,14/91 Reports (BVerfGE) 87, 153.
7. Judgment of 13 Feb. 2008 2 BvL 1/06.
8. Judgment of 9 Dec. 2008 2 BvL 1/07.
9. Judgment of 27 Jun. 1991 2 BvR 1493/89 Reports (BVerfGE) 84, 239; judgment of 9 Mar. 2004 2 BvL 17/02.
10. Judgment of 17 Jan. 1957 1 BvL 4/54 Reports (BVerfGE) 6, 55.
11. Judgment of 30 Jun. 1964 1 BvL 16/62 Reports (BVerfGE) 18, 97.
12. Judgment of 10 Nov. 1998 2 BvR 1057/91 et al. Reports (BVerfGE) 99, 216.
13. Judgment of 22 Jun. 1995 2 BvL 37/91 Reports (BVerfGE) 93, 121.
14. Judgment of 18 Jan. 2006 2 BvR 2194/99.

- Article 20, paragraph 3 (Rule of Law): the Court has concluded that retroactive legislation is admissible only under restricted conditions; retrospective legislation has to pass a proportionality test.[15]

4. TAX RATES

4.1. Individual Income Tax

The German personal income tax rate schedule is based on a formula approach.[16] Effective for 2009, individuals pay taxes according to a progressive rate at between 14% and 45%. Since German income tax law is governed by the nominal-value principle, it does not provide for indexation, with the effect that the average tax rate on real income increases constantly with inflation.

From 2009, the basic personal exemption is €7,834 for a single person and €15,668 for a married couple. The federal income tax rates for individuals are as follows (marginal tax rates for individuals; for married couples the total amounts must be doubled):

€7,834 or less	0%
€7,835–52,551	14.0%–42.0%
€52,552–250,400	42.0%
€250,401 and more	45.0%

Effective as of 1995, a solidarity surcharge of 7.5% (since 1998, 5.5%) of the income and corporate income tax liability (*Solidaritätszuschlag*) was introduced to raise additional revenue to cope with the financial needs caused by German unification.[17]

4.2. Corporate Income Tax

The corporate income tax rate has experienced a dramatic fall over the last twenty-five years. When the imputation system was introduced in 1977, the tax rate for retained profits was aligned with the top marginal income tax rate of that year at 56%. Starting in the late 1980s, the corporate income tax rate was gradually reduced to 40% in 1999. During the same period, the tax rate for distributed profits was reduced from 36% to 30%. When the imputation system was abolished in 2000, the tax rate for retained and distributed profits alike was set at 25%. (For 2003 a rate of 26.5% applied). From 2008, the tax rate is 15%.[18]

15. Judgment of 3 Dec. 1997 2 BvR 882/97 Reports (BVerfGE) 97, 67.
16. Germany, Income Tax Act (ITA), s. 32a.
17. *Solidaritaetszuschlagsgesetz.*
18. Germany, Corporate Income Tax Act (CITA), s. 23 para. 1.

5. COMPOSITION OF THE FISCAL SYSTEM

5.1. Revenue Share of Specific Taxes

Germany is a high-tax country levying a variety of different taxes. Many of these taxes are transaction taxes generating only a small amount of revenue. In 2007, the total tax revenue of the *Bund*, the *Länder*, and the municipalities[19] amounted to €538.2 billion. In relation to the 2007 Gross Domestic Product (GDP) of €2,423.8 billion,[20] the total tax revenue is 22.2%. In relation to the GDP, the share of taxes (not including social security contributions) has varied only between 22% and 25% during the last twenty-five years. For 2007 the most important taxes are listed in the following chart:[21]

Total German Tax Collection 2007 (excluding social security contributions)	*In bn.€*	*% of Tax Revenue*	*% of GDP*
Personal income tax (*Einkommensteuer*), including:			
– Wage withholding tax (*Lohnsteuer*)[22]	131.8	24.5%	5.4%
– Assessed income tax (*veranlagte Einkommensteuer*)[23]	25.0	4.6%	1.0%
– Not assessed taxes on yields (*Kapitalertragsteuer*)	13.8	2.6%	0.6%
– Interest withholding tax (*Zinsabschlagsteuer*)	11.2	2.1%	0.5%
Subtotal	181.8	33.8%	7.5%
Solidarity surcharge (*Solidaritätszuschlag*)	12.3	2.3%	0.5%
Corporate income tax (*Körperschaftsteuer*)	22.9	4.3%	0.9%
Trade tax (*Gewerbesteuer*)	40.1	7.5%	1.7%
Value added tax, including VAT on imports (*Umsatzsteuer*)	169.6	31.5%	7.0%
Real estate transfer tax (*Grunderwerbsteuer*)	0	0%	0%
Insurance tax (*Versicherungssteuer*)	10.3	1.9%	0.4%
Mineral oil tax (*Mineralölsteuer*)	39.0	7.2%	1.6%

19. Under the German federal structure there exists a distinct system of revenue sharing among the different government levels.
20. Source: *Statistical Yearbook 2008 for the Federal Republic of Germany*, <www.destatis.de/jetspeed/portal/cms/Sites/destatis/Internet/DE/Navigation/Publikationen/Querschnitts-veroeffentlichungen/JahrbuchDownlads.psml>.
21. Source: *Statistical Yearbook 2008 for the Federal Republic of Germany*, 572.
22. Before deduction of children's allowance.
23. Before deduction of reimbursements from the Federal Finance Office.

Total German Tax Collection 2007 (excluding social security contributions)	*In bn.€*	*% of Tax Revenue*	*% of GDP*
Electricity tax (*Elektrizitätssteuer*)	6.4	1.2%	0.2%
Tobacco tax (*Tabaksteuer*)	14.3	2.7%	0.6%
Liquor excise tax (*Branntweinsteuer*)	2.0	0.4%	0.1%
Customs (*Zölle*)	4.0	0.7%	0.2%
Car tax (*Kraftfahrzeugsteuer*)	8.9	1.7%	0.4%
Real property tax (*Grundsteuer*)	10.8	2.0%	0.4%
Estate tax (*Erbschaftsteuer*)	4.2	0.8%	0.2%
Total of approx. 20 other taxes	11.6	2.2%	0.5%
Total tax revenue	538.2	100.0%	22.3%

The revenue from assessed income tax, corporation tax, net worth tax, and inheritance tax appears rather low in an international comparison.

Members of Catholic or Protestant churches, as well as some other recognized religious communities, pay an 8% or 9% surcharge on their income tax (church tax, *Kirchensteuer*) which qualifies as an itemized deduction. The total revenue for the Catholic and Protestant churches (as of 2007) amounts to €8.6 billion, which is not included in the chart above.[24]

5.2. Shift from Direct Taxes to Indirect Taxes

Since German reunification took place in 1990, a variety of special tax provisions and subsidies have been introduced to promote investment in East Germany and to restructure the East German economy. Because of the unexpectedly high costs of unification (and a shortfall of tax revenues as of 1993), the German government felt compelled to increase taxes, in particular VAT, mineral oil tax, and other indirect taxes, thereby effecting a shift from direct to indirect taxes.

Between 1995 and 2006 there can be seen a major decrease in the tax rates for personal and corporate income tax (see below) while the tax base has been broadened gradually. On the other hand, VAT rates and special consumption tax rates have been constantly on the rise. In 2006, the general VAT rate has been increased to 19%. 'Ecological Tax Reform' was enacted in 1999 and for the first time an electricity tax (*Stromsteuer*) was introduced. *Stromsteuer* and mineral oil tax have been increased over the last few years to influence energy consumption and to provide extra financing for the social security system.

24. Source: <http://fowid.de/fileadmin/datenarchiv/Kirchensteuereinahmen_im_Vergleich_1968-2007.pdf>.

In relation to the total tax revenue, direct taxes (personal and corporate income tax, trade tax, interest withholding tax, net worth tax, and similar taxes) are as follows:[25]

1970	48.2%	1995	48.6% (estimated)
1975	54.7%	1999	52.4% (estimated)
1980	55.3%	2001	54.9% (estimated)
1985	56.0%	2006	50.5% (estimated)
1990	52.3%	2007	50.6% (estimated)

5.3. Social Security Contributions

German social security contributions currently amount to 40.25%[26] of the wages, salaries, and other compensation paid to employees. The social security contributions are borne by the employer and the employee.

In contrast to taxes, the share of social security contributions as a percentage of GDP has dramatically increased over the last twenty years as a result of an aging population, better and more expensive medical services including dentistry, longer periods for study, and earlier retirement. Several German governments have ineffectively tried to reduce this extra burden on earned income.

6. BASIC STRUCTURE OF THE INCOME TAX

6.1. Individual Income Tax

6.1.1. Principles of the Tax Base

Over the last 100 years, the concept of income under German law has undergone important changes. The Prussian Income Tax Law of 1891 followed a strict 'source' approach, regarding as 'income' only the periodic emoluments of a constant 'source' the gains and losses of which would not be included in taxable income. Under the influence of Georg von Schanz, the German Income Tax Law of 1920 presented an accruals-based income system that did not survive the hyperinflation of the early 1920s. The current system, which was framed mainly in 1925

25. Source: Bundestags-Drucksache 13/2009 of 18 Jul. 1995, Entwicklung des Steueraufkommens und der Steuerstruktur; *Statistical Yearbook 2002 for the Federal Republic of Germany*, 520; Federal Ministry of Finance, Struktur und Verteilung der Steuereinnahmen, Monatsbericht des BMF, August 2007, 55, August 2008, 85.
26. As of the beginning of 2009, the social security tax rates amount to 19.9% for pension insurance contributions (up to an amount of €64,000 income per year), 15.5% for health insurance contributions on average (up to an amount of €44,100 income per year), 2.9% for unemployment insurance (up to an amount of €64,000 income per year), and 1.95% for care insurance contributions (up to an amount of €44,100 income per year).

and 1934, follows a mixed (pragmatic) approach. Income tax is levied on the basis of a 'synthetic income' comprising inputs from different categories.

The particular differences between these different categories have increased over time, so that the possibility of changing from a global to a schedular system has been discussed. The most important aspect is the special treatment granted to capital income. Under the Business Tax Reform enacted in 2000, only 50% of dividends and capital gains on shares are included in the income tax base. Beginning in 2009, income derived from financial assets that are held as private assets is subject to a final witholding tax of 25%.[27] Income derived from shares that are business assets is subject to the regular income tax. The taxpayer can include the income that has been subject to the final withholding tax in his personal income tax declaration if he is subject to an income tax rate lower than 25%. To provide for a 'clean cut' between earned and capital income, the introduction of a 'dual income tax', as in the Nordic countries, was recommended by the Economic Advisory Council to the German government in 2003. In 2006, the Economic Advisory Council published a detailed proposal for reforming corporate and personal income tax, including a draft for a new income tax act.[28]

Another general aspect of German income taxation has been called its 'dualism'. Among the seven sources of income listed in section 2 paragraph 1 ITA there exists one major distinction laid down in section 2 paragraph 2 ITA:

- three categories of 'profit income' (*Gewinneinkünfte*), that is,
  (1) income from agriculture and forestry (sections 13–14a ITA);
  (2) income from trade or business enterprises (sections 15–17 ITA);
  (3) income from professional and certain other independent personal services (section 18 ITA).
- four categories of 'excess income' (*Überschusseinkünfte*), that is,
  (1) income from dependent personal services (wages and salaries, section 19, 19a ITA);
  (2) income from capital investments (e.g., interest and dividends, section 20 ITA);
  (3) rental and royalty income (sections 21, 21a ITA);
  (4) income from certain other sources specifically defined in the ITA, such as from so-called speculative transactions (sections 22, 23 ITA).

For purposes of the first three sources of income, 'income' is defined as 'profit' (*Gewinn*) – that is, as the difference between the net business assets at the end of the tax year and at the end of the preceding tax year, plus withdrawals and less contributions.[29] For the last four sources of income, 'income' is defined as the excess

27. ITA, s. 32d para. 1.
28. *Dual Income Tax, A Proposal for Reforming Corporate and Personal Income Tax in Germany*, ZEW Economic Studies, Vol. 39, 2006.
29. ITA, s. 2 para. 2, no. 1 with reference to s. 4 para. 1.

of receipts over expenditures to acquire, secure, and/or maintain revenue[30] – that is, the cash method applies, supplemented by a deduction for straight-line depreciation.[31]

The main difference between these categories concerns capital gains or losses from the disposition of assets. Under the 'profit income' rule, all gains and losses related to a trade or business (including farming and professional services) are generally fully included in the tax base and taxed at ordinary tax rates upon realization. Under narrow conditions, business capital gains may be subject to rollover relief.

Until 1998, capital gains or losses from the disposition of private assets (company shares, bonds, real estate, works of art) were in principle not subject to income tax. Only if they were derived from the sale of a substantial participation (more than 25%) in the shares of a company[32] or from so-called speculative transactions specifically defined[33] were they included in the tax base. A transaction was assumed to be a speculative transaction if a private asset was sold within two years after the acquisition in the case of real property or within six months in the case of securities and other assets.[34] In 1999 and 2000 the threshold of a 'substantial participation'[35] was reduced to 1%, leaving out only portfolio shareholders in big public companies. Furthermore, the period for 'speculative transactions' was extended to one year in the case of securities and to ten years in the case of real estate.[36] As discussed above, the Business Tax Reform 2007 introduced a final withholding tax of 25% for all profits from private financial assets irrespective of how long the asset is held.[37] An amount of 60% of the capital gain from shares that are held as business assets, or that exceeds the 1% threshold for a substantial participation, is taxed at the individual tax rate.[38] Due to this reform, the general discussion about a fully fledged dual income tax is decreasing in Germany.

In the computation of taxable income from all seven categories, all costs incurred in the pursuit of income are fully deductible[39] (although there is an increasing tendency to restrict the deductibility if there is some connection with the taxpayer's personal lifestyle). Only in the context of 'final withholding tax' on capital income is the deduction of related expenditure prohibited by statute.[40]

30. ITA, s. 2 para. 2 no. 2 with reference to ss 8–9a.
31. ITA, s. 9 para. 1 no. 7 with reference to s. 7.
32. ITA, s.17.
33. ITA, s. 23 para. 1.
34. ITA, s. 22 no. 2 with reference to s. 23. It should be noted that the Federal Tax Court 'invented' the concept of a so-called 'professional real estate trader', thus also applying the 'profit income' method to taxpayers who buy and sell real estate with a turnover of more than three sales within five years.
35. ITA, s. 17 para. 1.
36. ITA, s. 23.
37. ITA, s. 32d para. 1.
38. ITA, s. 3 no. 40, 20 para. 8.
39. ITA, s. 4 para. 4 and 9 para. 1.
40. ITA, s. 20 para. 9 sentence (hereafter sent.) 2.

However, private expenses are not relevant for tax matters, thus separating the accrual of income from the consumption of income – a principle expressly stated in section 12 ITA.

6.1.2. Private Expenses

Only some narrowly defined groups of private expenses – that is, 'special costs' (*Sonderausgaben*) and 'extraordinary costs' (*aussergewöhnliche Belastungen*) as well as certain personal allowances – can reduce the tax base.

Special costs[41] include a wide range of expenses such as certain alimony payments, certain annuities, or church tax paid. The most relevant of these are social security contributions to a public pension scheme, health insurance, or unemployment insurance. Section 10a ITA gives certain taxpayers an additional reduction for private pension contributions. Section 10b ITA allows (up to a limit of 20% of the taxable income) certain donations for scientific, charitable, and specific cultural purposes. Extraordinary costs[42] are private expenses that are recognized if they are unavoidable, based on legal, factual, or moral reasons; they must be higher in comparison to similar expenses of most other taxpayers so that general allowances or tax rate reductions do not cover the situation. A clear concept is missing with respect to the treatment of extraordinary costs.

A major change has occurred in the treatment of expenses of a taxpayer for his own subsistence and family maintenance. In a series of landmark decisions, the German Constitutional Court[43] has forced the government to raise substantially the tax-free threshold for personal minimum expenses (from ca. €2,500 in 1990 to ca. €7,700 in 2009)[44] and for family expenses (including high amounts for the tuition and education of children). In addition, a reduced deduction of child-care costs for single parents has been ruled void.[45]

6.1.3. Non-resident Taxpayers

In the case of non-resident individuals, the same categories and concepts are applied as those described above. Following the 'territoriality' concept of 'limited tax liability',[46] income of non-residents is subject to tax only if it is derived from German sources.[47] On the other hand, foreign residents are denied certain tax advantages and personal allowances.[48] European law has had an increasingly important impact on the treatment of non-resident taxpayers. To avoid a conflict

41. ITA, s. 10.
42. ITA, ss 33 and 33a.
43. Federal Constitutional Court (*Bundesverfassungsgericht*) judgment of 25 Sep. 1992 2 BvL 5,8,14/91 Reports (BVerfGE) 87, 153; judgment of 9 Dec. 2008 2 BvL 1/07.
44. ITA, s. 32a para. 1.
45. Judgment of 17 Oct. 1984 1 BvR 527/08 Reports (BVerfGE) 68, 143.
46. ITA, s. 1 para. 4.
47. ITA, s. 49.
48. ITA, ss 50 and 50a.

with non-discrimination rules under European Community law, the German Parliament has introduced a rule that foreign taxpayers receiving 90% or more of their income from German sources can apply for 'extended unlimited tax liability'.[49] On the other hand, the deductibility of personal tax consulting fees was abolished for all taxpayers when the European Court decided that denying this deduction to non-resident taxpayers in German tax law was an infringement of the right of free movement in the EC Treaty.[50]

6.2. Corporate Income Tax

6.2.1. Taxable Entities

Since 1920, legal persons and other independent entities are subject to corporate income tax under the Corporate Income Tax Act (*Körperschaftsteuergesetz*). The most important entities subject to corporate income tax are corporations (stock companies, limited partnerships with shares, and limited liability companies). Commercial cooperatives, mutual insurance associations, and other juridical persons under private law are, from an overall point of view, less important.[51] Yet it should not go unnoticed that even non-incorporated state-held businesses are subject to CITA, thus avoiding competitive tax advantages for state-owned business.

Partnerships, including a limited partnership with a corporate general partner (*GmbH & Co. KG*) (of which approximately 80,000 exist in Germany), are not subject to corporate income tax. The income of a partnership is assessed on the basis of a single tax return for the whole partnership.[52] It is then allocated for tax purposes to the partners regardless of the actual distribution of profits. The law thus follows a (limited) transparency concept. A rule that would have enabled partnerships to 'opt' for corporate taxation was discussed in the wake of the 2000 business tax reform but did not find enough parliamentary support.

6.2.2. Tax Base

All income earned by corporations is deemed to be income from trade or business.[53] Other entities subject to corporate income tax, particularly associations without legal existence, state-held institutions, certain foundations, and other asset-conglomerations under civil law, are subject to the general income categories listed in the ITA.[54]

49. ITA, s. 1 para. 3 ITA.
50. ECJ, 6 Jul. 2006, C-346/04 (*Conijn*).
51. CITA, s. 1 para. 1.
52. ITA, s. 15, General Fiscal Code (GFC), s. 180 para. 1 no. 2.
53. CITA, s. 8 para. 2.
54. CITA, s. 8 para. 1.

A major feature of the corporate tax base is the treatment of 'hidden distributions' or 'constructive dividends'. Since corporate tax law does not allow the deduction of distributions or constructive dividends to shareholders,[55] it also provides that 'hidden distributions' to shareholders must be added to the corporate tax base. 'Hidden distributions' include any expenditure or waived income of the company that are caused by the relationship between the company and a shareholder (e.g., inadequate consideration for services delivered by a shareholder). The ensuing factual problems concerning the identification of a 'hidden distribution' contribute excessively to the lawsuits between companies and tax authorities and also provide a substantial risk of criminal tax liability.

6.2.3. Tax System

One of the most important factors in German tax policy is the relationship between corporate taxation and income taxation. The corporate tax structure introduced in 1977 contained two fundamental decisions:

(1) The top rate of personal income tax and the top rate of corporate income tax on retained income were equal (at the time 56%). Thus, there was neutrality as to the legal form of an enterprise (corporation, partnership, sole trader).
(2) In the case of distributions, the corporate tax rate was reduced (in 1977 to 36%) and fully credited against the personal income tax of the shareholder. Thus, neutrality as to the allocation of the income (reinvestment or consumption) was achieved. This was also aimed at strengthening the German capital market.

This system worked well for many years but was subject to heavy pressure in the 1990s. On the one hand, there emerged strong tax competition between the Member States of the European Community and beyond. Massive reductions of the tax rate in other industrialized states made it necessary for Germany to reduce its top corporate tax rate gradually to 40% on retained profits in 1999. On the other hand, it seemed – from a revenue perspective – impossible to grant similar tax reductions in the field of income tax. Corporate tax rates and marginal income tax rates drifted further and further apart.

On the other hand, the 'imputation system', which was 'standard' in the 1970s in Europe, displayed discriminatory features that seemed to be no longer sustainable under the fundamental freedoms enshrined in the EC Treaty. The main problem was the fact that the imputation system was not extended to foreign-source dividend income, thus discriminating against investment in companies resident in other Member States. Moreover, foreign residents holding shares in German companies were not granted a tax credit. Finally, domestic permanent establishments of companies from other Member States were effectively taxed

55. CITA, s. 8 para. 3 sent. 2.

at a higher rate than domestic subsidiaries, thus distorting the tax situation between permanent establishments and subsidiaries.

The 2000 Business Tax Reform was designed to modernize the German system. The 'imputation system' was replaced by a 'shareholder-relief' system, which combines a low corporate income tax rate with a substantial tax reduction at the shareholder level. On the one hand, the tax rate that applies to retained and distributed profits alike was set at 25%; on the other hand, only 50% of the dividends paid to an individual shareholder were included in the personal tax base (the 'half-income' method). The combined tax charge of corporate and personal income tax was meant to be approximately the same charge as in the case of other income (e.g., from a trade or business). This reform has managed to provide Germany with an attractive corporate tax rate (although trade tax has to be added) and to remove possible conflicts with EC law, since the half-income method has been extended to dividends from foreign-resident companies. Critics of the new system point out that tax neutrality between different legal forms for business (corporate structures, partnerships) has been sacrificed and neutrality of allocation (reinvestment or consumption) has also been adversely affected.

The 2000 Business Tax Reform also introduced a 'participation exemption'[56] for corporate shareholders, which is the most ardently discussed feature of the new law. Due to the abolition of the imputation system and the introduction of a fixed tax rate for retained and distributed profits alike, the legislature had to find a way to provide relief for inter-company distributions. The 'participation exemption', which has been chosen to provide a single level of taxation on the subsidiary, has in principle been widely acclaimed and is not restricted to domestic shareholdings or to minimum holdings. It has also been extended to capital gains that derive from the retention of (taxed) profits in the subsidiary. The most controversial provision has been to extend the 'participation exemption' even to capital gains in the shares that have not yet been subject to tax at the level of the subsidiary, thus granting to parent companies the option to realize 'hidden reserves' in their subsidiaries tax-free.

Since 2008, the tax rate for distributed and retained profits at the corporate level has been reduced to 15%.[57] All other changes implemented by the 2007 Business Tax Reform came into force on 1 January 2009. A significant part of the 2007 reform concerns capital gains from financial assets. Since the new rules distinguish between shares that are held as business assets and shares that are held as private assets, the new system might also be called a 'dual' tax system. Dividends and capital gains from shares held as private assets are subject to a final withholding tax of 25%.[58] However, the taxpayer can include this income in his personal income tax declaration if his personal tax rate is lower than 25%.[59] There is no deduction for expenses with respect to these profits.[60] If the shares are held as

56. CITA, s. 8b.
57. CITA, s. 23 para. 1.
58. ITA, s. 20 para. 1, para. 2 with reference to s. 32d para. 1.
59. ITA, s. 32d para. 6.
60. ITA, s. 20 para. 9 sent. 2.

business assets, only 60% of the dividends and capital gains are included in the personal income tax base of the individual shareholder.[61] Consequently, only 60% of expenses with respect to these profits are deductible.[62] The increase in the taxable income for the shareholder of up to 60% of the profits is seen as the counterpart to the reduced tax rate of 15% at the corporate level. Dividends and capital gains earned by a corporate shareholder remain tax-free.[63] Only 5% of these profits is deemed to be a non-deductible business expense[64] and that portion of the income in effect remains taxable. Furthermore, the 2007 Business Tax Reform modified the deductibility of interest payments as business expenses. It was mainly the tax planning potential of cross-border financial transactions between a parent and its subsidiary that led the legislature to introduce an 'interest stripping rule'.[65] The rule allows a deduction for interest payments as business expenses only to a limited extent, on the basis of earnings before interest, tax, depreciation, and amortization (EBITDA). It is questionable whether the new rule is consistent with constitutional and EC law. The former thin capitalization rule has been abolished.

Finally, the legislature has restricted the use of losses of a corporation if a single person acquires a significant percentage of the corporate shares (*Mantelkauf*). The new provision[66] limits the use of losses derived if more than 25% of the shares are transferred to one person within a period of five years. If more than half of the shares are acquired within that period, all losses derived at the corporate level that have not been used up to that point are extinguished.

Another feature of German corporate taxation is 'fiscal unity' (*Organschaft*),[67] which has undergone fundamental changes in recent years and is still 'under construction'.

6.3. TRADE TAX

The second major tax to which a German business (whether incorporated or not) is subject is trade tax.[68] For more than 100 years trade tax has been one of the two pillars of tax autonomy at the municipal level (the other is real estate tax). Every trade or business carried on in Germany is subject to this tax, excluding the agricultural and professional sector. Foreign businesses are subject to trade tax if they have a permanent establishment in Germany.[69] According to trade tax statistics,

61. ITA, ss 3 no. 40 and 20 para. 8.
62. ITA, s. 3c para. 2.
63. CITA, s. 8b para. 1.
64. CITA, s. 8b para. 5.
65. CITA, s. 4h, ITA, s. 8a.
66. ITA, s. 8c.
67. ITA, ss 14-19.
68. Trade Tax Act (*Gewerbesteuergesetz*).
69. Trade Tax Act, s. 2.

about 60% of the revenue from trade tax stems from unincorporated businesses and only 40% from corporations.

Trade tax originally comprised the business income, the business net value, and the payroll of its workers. In order to alleviate the tax burden for business, business net value tax and payroll tax have been abolished over time. As a result, trade tax has been transformed into an extra charge on business profits, with extremely volatile results for municipal revenue. Proposals are periodically discussed either to extend trade tax to professional services or even to replace it by a municipal surcharge on general income tax.

The tax base for trade tax is the business profits determined under the income tax rules,[70] subject to various adjustments that are (mostly) aimed to eliminate the effect of financing structures for the enterprise.[71] These add-backs lead to a broadening of the tax base compared with the income tax base.

The rate for trade tax on income is 3.5% (base tax rate)[72] multiplied by a municipal factor (*Hebesatz*), which is determined by each municipality.[73] At present, the average municipal factor is 391%. The trade tax rate varies between 7% and 17.15%, which results in an average tax rate of 12% for trade tax on income.[74]

The 2000 and 2007 German business tax reforms massively changed the character of the trade tax. For corporate taxpayers, trade tax nearly equals the burden of corporate tax, since the corporate tax rate of 15% is complemented by trade tax of roughly 12% of the profits on average. As of the beginning of 2008, the trade tax is not deductible as a business expense for income and corporate taxation.[75] But for unincorporated businesses, trade tax can largely be credited against the income tax (depending on the effect of the adjustments under trade tax described above).[76]

7. TAX LEGISLATION

7.1. Legislative Process

Legislation in income tax matters (both individual and corporate income tax) is essentially framed by the fact that both the Federation and the German States participate in the process. Any change in income taxation requires the consent of the *Bundestag* and the *Bundesrat*, which leads to – sometimes awkward – compromise seeking. Tax legislation regularly starts with a government proposal

70. Trade Tax Act, s. 7.
71. Trade Tax Act, ss 8 and 9.
72. Trade Tax Act, s. 11 para. 2.
73. Trade Tax Act, s. 16.
74. KPMG's Corporate and Indirect Tax Rate Survey 2008, <www.kpmg.de>.
75. ITA, s. 4 para. 5b.
76. ITA, s. 35.

(and simultaneously a proposal by the majority faction in the *Bundestag*), which is discussed in the Finance Committees of both houses. There are public hearings of experts – and indirect influence by political pressure groups. Technical changes are initiated mainly by the tax administration. On average, parliamentary process takes about six to twelve months until the new Act is published in the Federal Gazette (*Bundesgesetzblatt*). Since the political parties rarely have the political power to enact major reforms, some of the most important innovations in German income taxation are due to decisions by the Constitutional Court.

7.2. Statutory Style

There is no single Federal Tax Code in Germany, although there have been several attempts from academic circles to promote such a project. The major tax acts stem from the 1920s and 1930s and still bear their original structure. Nevertheless, an ever-increasing number of changes in the tax acts distort the original logical concept. There is a constant but rather unclear desire for 'simplification' of tax law by politicians, tax professionals, and citizens. Nevertheless, the German tradition of achieving fairness in each case (*Einzelfallgerechtigkeit*) is still strong. The ever-growing number of changes in the tax law is due to several reasons. Politicians use the tax system to further specific economic or other (e.g., environmental) aims by granting tax incentives or disincentives. Moreover, members of the tax administration often demand specific changes to the technical provisions of the tax acts to prevent what they believe to be 'abuses'. It goes without saying that the necessity to find a political compromise during the legislative process at the federal level (e.g., between *Bundestag* and *Bundesrat*) leads to unsatisfactory solutions. Finally – as in most industrialized countries – the complexity of German tax laws is also due to the growing complexity of domestic and international economic relations (e.g., taxation of financial instruments). Several reform proposals presented by academics in recent years have recommended a dramatic reduction in the size and the style of tax legislation.

7.3. Statutory Interpretation

The starting point for the interpretation of German tax acts is the wording of the statute (literal interpretation). Furthermore, the systematic context of the statute, its objective purpose, and the legislative history of a provision must be taken into account. These teleological, systematic, and historical approaches are particularly important where the wording of a statutory provision is ambiguous. The ancient concept that in tax matters there is no 'teleology' beyond the fiscal effect of a tax is no longer valid.

In the 1920s and 1930s a specific 'economic perspective' (*wirtschaftliche Betrachtungsweise*) was promoted by the Tax Courts, which allowed interpretation to extend beyond the limits of the wording of a statute. This concept of a single particular method of interpreting tax statutes is no longer accepted. Nevertheless, leading tax lawyers still support this 'economic perspective' as an application of the general rules of 'teleological interpretation'. Even the Federal Tax Court is split: Some chambers (*Senate*) adhere to a narrow and literal construction of a tax statute, while other judges prefer a broader view. This fundamental difference of attitude reappears in other contexts, such as:

- the question whether tax law interpretation should adhere to the civil law meaning of the text or give way to an 'autonomous' (and more flexible) interpretation of tax law;
- the question whether tax statutes may be extended by way of analogy (or whether the 'rule of law' prevents this extension without express parliamentary consent);
- the question whether the application of 'abuse of law' rules may be employed in order to re-qualify a situation without respect to 'good business reasons' of the taxpayer for the chosen construction.

8. COURTS DEALING WITH TAX MATTERS

8.1. Structure of the Courts

In Germany tax disputes are not adjudicated by the general courts but are referred to a specific pillar of the judicial system.[77] There are two levels of tax courts, the (Lower) Tax Courts established by the *Länder* and, as the final court of appeal in tax matters, the Federal Tax Court. The Lower Tax Courts are responsible both for the investigation of the relevant facts of the underlying case and the proper application and interpretation of the law, while the Federal Tax Court decides only on questions of law.

The lower Tax Courts sit with three professional judges and two laymen, while the Federal Tax Court in Munich sits with eleven chambers (*Senate*), each with five judges. An appeal against a judgment by a lower court may be lodged with the Federal Tax Court only if the taxpayer can show that there exist divergent judgments by lower courts or that the case is of fundamental importance.[78]

A notice of assessment or other formal act of the tax administration is subject to judicial review. The taxpayer must file his appeal with the same tax office that is responsible for the assessment on the administrative level. If the administrative appeal fails, the taxpayer may then appeal to the courts.

In total, about 20% of cases are decided in favour of the taxpayer; this percentage would be higher if one leaves aside the large number of taxpayers' appeals that are rejected for formal reasons. Approximately 60,000 new cases come before the Tax Courts per year.[79] At the end of 2006, there were 67,643 cases pending

77. See Tax Court Act (*Finanzgerichtsordnung*).
78. Tax Court Act, s. 115.
79. Source: <www.bundesfinanzhof.de/www/bfh/03aufbau/aufbau2.html>.

before the Lower Tax Courts and 2,697 cases before the Federal Tax Court.[80] In 2006, 48,606 cases were brought to the Lower Tax Courts and 3,386 cases to the Federal Tax Court. The total number of cases resolved in 2006 was 56,878.[81] It is interesting to note that about 80% of these cases resulted in a judgment of the court. Obviously, the time while the case is pending before the Tax Court is used for negotiations between the taxpayer and the tax administration. The Tax Courts estimate that about one-third of the cases end in favour of the taxpayer.

8.2. Judicial Style

The Federal Constitutional Court has the power to review the compatibility of federal legislation with the German Constitution with *inter omnes* effect. Its decisions are binding for the other governmental bodies of the *Bund* and the *Länder*.

The decisions of the Federal Tax Court (*Bundesfinanzhof*) are binding only for the parties in the specific case. Nevertheless, the decisions of the Federal Tax Court, which in most cases provide ample legal reasoning, carry great persuasive weight. If one chamber (*Senat*) wants to deviate from the *ratio decidendi* of another chamber, it must refer the case to the Great Chamber (*Großer Senat*) to find a solution that is binding for the whole court.

The publication of a particular decision in the Federal Tax Gazette (*Bundessteuerblatt*) or in the administrative tax regulations indicates that the tax authorities have agreed to extend the *ratio decidendi* of a specific decision of the Federal Tax Court to similar cases. Sometimes tax authorities release a decree of non-application regarding a particular decision, which is sometimes to the advantage of taxpayers but often to their disadvantage, since it forces taxpayers to seek recourse to the courts again. In recent years, the official publication of some tax decisions has sometimes been delayed deliberately by the tax authorities for a long time, thus leaving taxpayers and tax officials in a state of uncertainty. In many situations tax authorities have even proposed legislative changes to avoid the consequences of court decisions. These cases regularly lead to a constitutional debate on the retroactive aspects of such legislation and the compatibility with the equality principle under the German constitution.

9. TAX ADMINISTRATION

When the *Grundgesetz* came into existence in 1949, the Western powers insisted that there be no centralized collection of taxes, but that taxes should be collected

80. Source: *Statistical Yearbook 2008 for the Federal Republic of Germany*, 269.
81. *Statistical Yearbook 2008 for the Federal Republic of Germany*, 269.

by the *Länder*. Today, the collection of taxes is decentralized but uniform. Conceptually, federal and state tax administration is exercised by a separate hierarchy of federal and state authorities.[82]

The Federal authorities are, in particular, the Federal Ministry of Finance (*Bundesfinanzministerium*), the Federal Central Tax Office (*Bundeszentralamt für Steuern*), and the main customs offices (*Hauptzollämter*), which are in the field of customs and excise the counterpart to the tax offices. The regional finance offices (*Oberfinanzdirektionen*, or OFD) that still exist in some *Länder* are mixed entities, consisting of federal authorities in the customs field and state authorities in the tax field. The head of each regional finance office is simultaneously a federal and a state government official.

While the constitutional provisions on tax administration may indicate strong differences between the federal states, the reality shows strong uniformity. The general laws on tax procedure and on administrative procedural rules (the current General Fiscal Code, or *Abgabenordnung*, still follows its predecessor from 1919) are identical, as are the career and salary provisions for tax officials. The heads of the special tax divisions of the federal states meet regularly with their federal counterparts.

The Federal Ministry of Finance publishes every two or three years new regulations concerning the most important taxes (i.e., income tax, corporate income tax, turnover tax, trade tax). These regulations are meant to facilitate dealing with these taxes and to ensure a uniform application of the laws throughout Germany.

Over the years the *Bund* has expanded its own tax service in certain areas, particularly in the area of international taxation. The administrative arm of the *Bund* is the Federal Central Tax Office *(Bundeszentralamt für Steuern)*, which administers double taxation treaties, refunds of withholding taxes, refunds of VAT, attribution of ID numbers for EU purposes, etc.

9.1. General

German tax administration works in a quite bureaucratic and formalistic way, governed by strict adherence to the rule of law.

More than 200 million tax assessments are made every year. This estimate includes separate assessments (e.g., for real estate valuation, partnerships, church tax). Some taxpayers may even get more than a dozen assessments for the income tax for a particular year, taking into account subsequent adjustments and corrections, with some of them based on separate assessments for partnerships in which the taxpayer is a member.

82. Basic Tax Law, Art. 108; see also the Tax Administration Act (*Finanzverwaltungesetz*).

9.2. Assessment and Audit

In Germany, all taxpayers are obliged to file an annual income tax return[83] and report their income and expenses accurately. An exception exists only for taxpayers whose income does not exceed the subsistence minimum of €7,664 or who receive relatively low income from employment and no significant further taxable income from other sources. However, such taxpayers will be assessed upon request. Employment income is subject to a withholding system[84] but is included in the annual assessment as well. The same holds true for withholding tax on interest and dividend payments (although the new bill on interest taxation proposes a final withholding tax).

Tax returns are checked by a medium-level tax inspector who scrutinizes the relevant facts and makes sure that the information is sufficient and correct. If any issues arise, more detailed information may be requested. The tax authorities have far-reaching powers to gather evidence.[85] Moreover, if the taxpayer does not fulfil his obligations, he is not entitled to the 'benefit of the doubt' and may be subject to disadvantageous estimates by the tax authorities.[86]

A taxpayer's request for judicial review does not affect the general rule that the amount of tax fixed by the assessment must be paid within the time given (usually one month). Only in rare situations will the execution of the assessment be suspended upon request of the taxpayer either by the tax office or the Tax Court.[87]

This desk audit is concerned mainly with plausibility (i.e., reviewing how the different categories of income of the taxpayer have developed compared with earlier years, as well as with taxpayers in the same trade or profession). Following this preliminary examination, tax authorities are entitled to make their assessment subject to further review. In such cases, desk audits are – depending on the economic importance of the case – succeeded by field audits.[88] Field audits are highly developed in Germany, and most businesses or professional firms of any significant size are typically subject to a field audit. Smaller businesses are audited less frequently; their selection may depend on the existence of certain indicators. The practical execution of field audits is criticized because the audit periods are too long. Quite often field audits deal with transactions that were executed six or more years in the past. Altogether, the German tax administration employs more than 10,000 field auditors.

In order to exert effective control, tax legislation has in recent years significantly raised the level of documentation obligations for taxpayers, regularly stretching back ten years.

---

83. ITA, s. 26 para. 3.
84. ITA, ss 38–42f.
85. GFC, s. 85 et seq.
86. GFC, s. 162.
87. GFC, s. 361, Tax Court Act, s. 69.
88. GFC, s. 193 et seq.

9.3. TAX COMPLIANCE

The ability of the tax authorities to verify whether the declaration of income by a taxpayer is accurate varies significantly among the different types of income.

Due to the field audits in the area of business and professional income tax, compliance levels appear to be high in international comparisons. The same holds true for employment income. Frequent (usually every one or two years) field audits also cover the withholding of wage taxes by employers. Also, smaller enterprises are audited for wage withholding tax on a regular basis. The payment of social security contributions is field-audited separately by agents of the social security organizations.

In the case of income from capital investment, in contrast, tax compliance levels seem to be very low. For many years there was no serious effort to enforce the declaration of interest from bank accounts and bonds. There was no withholding tax on interest, and banks were not required to provide information reporting on interest payments automatically. The tax auditors of banks did not have the authority to copy lists of bank customers who received interest. Consequently, according to estimates accepted by the Federal Constitutional Court in the 1990s, 60%–70% of domestic interest payments received by private investors were not reported. Finally, the Constitutional Court declared the system of interest taxation to be unconstitutional because it violated the principle of equal treatment.[89]

As a consequence, in 1993 a withholding tax of 30% was introduced on interest received by residents (but not by non-residents). At the same time, a basic exemption for capital income was introduced permitting a tax-free amount of €750 per year. Since this withholding tax applied only to banks resident in Germany (and not even to all debtors resident in Germany), there was a substantial outflow of capital, particularly to the subsidiaries of German banks in Luxembourg and Switzerland, in total estimated to be more than DEM 500 billion (ca. US$333.3 billion). As a response to both international and domestic tax evasion, the German government has introduced a final withholding tax of 25% for interest income as part of capital income taxation. The withholding tax applies from 2009 on. The exchange of information within Europe under an EC directive facilitates the taxation of cross-border interest payments.

Compared to other countries, Germany has an extremely high number of criminal tax investigations. It may even be argued that it is the fear of a criminal investigation that keeps the rather complicated tax system running. In recent years, prominent taxpayers, including executives of major companies, have been under investigation. Every year about 30,000 cases of criminal tax investigations are initiated, of which more than 10,000 result in a conviction of tax fraud by a criminal court. The judgment is registered in the criminal record of the taxpayer.

The penalties adjudicated by the criminal courts are usually monetary. So far, imprisonment is rare as far as direct taxes are concerned; prison terms are usually

89. Federal Constitutional Court (*Bundesverfassungsgericht*) judgment of 27 Jun. 1991 2 BvR 1493/89 Reports (BVerfGE) 84, 239; judgment of 9 Mar. 2004 2 BvL 17/02.

suspended. It is not unusual, however, for a suspect to be placed in preliminary detention to prevent him from disrupting the investigation or disappearing to a foreign country. Prominent tax evasion cases in the last few years have resulted in a public debate about stricter penalties in criminal tax law, and reform is on the way.

9.4. ADMINISTRATIVE STYLE

German tax officials are usually well trained and expected to strictly follow the rule of law. Thus, the power of discretion of the individual tax official is relatively small. Moreover, most actions by tax officials are surrounded by a framework of numerous regulations, decrees, and circular letters, which tax officials (but not the courts) are bound to obey. Most internal circular letters are also published to inform taxpayers and their advisers about future treatment by the tax office.

Due to the rule of law, any contracts – and even formal settlements – concerning the amount of the tax and the applicable tax law are not permitted. However, there are some deviations from this principle:

- If the underlying facts of a particular case are difficult to investigate, a mutual agreement on the facts is possible; it is not binding if it leads to an obviously wrong tax treatment.
- The tax administration is also entitled to give rulings on questions of law under statutory provisions.[90] However, the tax office can refrain from giving a ruling when the object of the application would be the achievement of a specific tax advantage such as a tax shelter or a borderline case of tax abuse.

The German tax administration adheres to a high – but not too strict – level of control, especially with respect to its field audits. In recent years two antagonistic developments have been observed. On the one hand, the problematic financial situation both of the *Bund* and the *Länder* leads to increasing pressure on tax offices to apply the rules intransigently (including even the taxation of charities, churches, and state-owned enterprises). On the other hand, the personnel are more and more challenged by the increasing complexity of business transactions and the constant change of the law, both of which lead to a feeling of dissatisfaction within the tax administration. At the federal administrative level, tax policy has become more and more short term, and the increasing application of 'tax abuse' provisions against all sorts of business transactions is interpreted as a sign of nervousness.

Cases of corruption are rare. An important factor in this context is that salaries of tax officials are thought to be competitive with those in the private sector if the more generous retirement plan is included. The decision on a promotion is made according to merit and seniority.

---

90. GFC, ss 204–207.

9.5. Taxpayers' Style

It is rather obvious that due to high German tax rates and the complexity of the German tax base, most taxpayers try to reduce their tax liability. However, the possibilities for different taxpayers to do so vary significantly.

On the one hand, taxpayers earning income exclusively from employment have limited possibilities to reduce their tax burden because most deductions available to them are standardized and income is subject to a withholding system.

On the other hand, most multinational corporations are sensitive to tax issues, and most do not hesitate to engage in reasonably aggressive tax planning. The right of the taxpayer to test the limits of 'tax abuse' is accepted as long as the facts are fully and correctly disclosed to the tax authorities. Mid-sized corporations are also becoming more and more sophisticated in international tax planning.

10. GENERAL PRINCIPLES

10.1. Relationship between Tax and Financial Accounting

German taxation of business income earned by both individual entrepreneurs and corporations is marked by a strong connection between taxable income and accounting income. This 'linkage' (*Maßgeblichkeit*) is based on the principle that the financial accounting treatment controls for tax accounting, provided there are no divergent tax provisions.[91] An interpretation by the Federal Tax Court holds that whenever there is an accounting election, the taxpayer must use in his tax return the option that results in a higher taxable income.

This linkage rule, in combination with the absence of express tax limitations, has the result that reserves and provisions are accepted as tax deductions in Germany more than in other countries. In spite of high nominal tax rates, this timing rule gives fast-growing enterprises a temporary tax advantage compared to foreign enterprises. On the other hand, mature enterprises suffer under the high tax rates, particularly during periods of high inflation.

In recent years, several developments have damaged this traditional 'linkage'. Tax legislation in 1997 and 1999 restricted substantially the opportunities to include tax-free provisions in the tax base[92] and forced enterprises to claw back depreciations of shareholdings or real estate if the market value recovered during the years following the depreciation claim.[93] Moreover, the tax courts have more and more tried to loosen the 'linkage' between tax accounting and commercial accounting because commercial accounting is itself linked to European directives, and tax courts tend to avoid referring matters of domestic taxation to the European Court of Justice.

---

91. ITA, s. 5 para. 1.
92. ITA, s. 5 para. 2a–4b.
93. ITA, s. 6 para. 1 no. 1 sent. 4, no. 3 sent. 3.

The European-wide introduction of International Financial Reporting Standards (IFRS) for publicly traded companies in 2005 has raised the question whether German tax accounting can follow IFRS financial accounting. However, a current reform of national financial accounting rules, which will allow more mark-to-market accounting, does not involve tax accounting. Nevertheless, the pressure on the legislature to further de-link the relationship between financial and tax accounting is currently growing.

10.2. Respect for Legal Form

In Germany, the relationship between civil law and tax law has dramatically changed over the decades. While the 'economic perspective' (*Wirtschaftliche Betrachtungsweise*) prevailed in the 1920s to 1940s, tax courts in the 1950s and 1960s tried to find stability in recourse to civil law concepts. Nowadays, civil law and tax law are largely regarded as separate fields of law, while constitutional law has taken over the role of the 'leading' source of legal concepts. Nevertheless, there are still several connections between tax and civil law. First, it is generally accepted that tax law must be applied to the reality formed by the rights and obligations of taxpayers under civil law (the so-called 'precedence' of civil law). Moreover, the wording of many tax provisions evidently refers to civil law concepts, which must be applied in many circumstances. The civil law meaning serves as a starting point for the interpretation of a statute. It is highly disputed whether interpretation may – under the rule of law – exceed the original civil law meaning of many terms found in tax statutes.

10.3. Anti-avoidance Doctrines and Rules

German tax administration and, to a lesser extent, tax courts have always followed the principle of 'substance over form', with varying intensity. There is a strong tendency in academic writing to apply this substance over form concept generally in the interpretation of tax statutes, thus returning to a predominantly 'economic' approach to tax law. The tax courts have followed this approach openly only in rare cases. Thus, the application of the substance over form concept is primarily based on the general statutory anti-avoidance clause,[94] which provides that tax 'must not be circumvented' by abusive behaviour.

Nevertheless, there is no consensus on the concept of 'abusive behaviour' even within the Federal Tax Court. While it is generally accepted that 'tax abuse' requires that a structure be inadequate (in the sense of 'unusual') to achieve the economic goal strived for, it is controversial whether the Court should (as in the past) look at the 'intent' of the taxpayer seeking to reduce the tax burden and

94. General Order on Levies (GOL) (*Abgabenordnung*), s. 42.

the existence of 'good business reasons'. On the other hand, the Federal Tax Court has declined to apply section 42 if the tax advantage the taxpayer hopes to achieve is in line with the general system of the tax law itself.[95] Therefore, a tax reduction following the distribution of profits by a company is not abusive if this is what the legislature aimed to achieve, even if the profits are subsequently re-contributed to the company. In 2008, section 42 was extended slightly (the original draft proposed a dramatic extension of the anti-avoidance provision).

Over the years, a large amount of specific anti-avoidance legislation has been introduced in the German tax system. Major provisions are controlled foreign corporation (CFC) legislation and an 'interest stripping rule' introduced in the 2007 Business Tax Reform, as well as a disputed new provision on the denial of corporate tax losses in the case of the sale of substantial shareholdings. Although the Federal Tax Court has decided that section 42 should not be applied if there exists some special tax legislation to fight abuses in a specific setting,[96] this judgment has been reversed by an amendment to section 42.

11. SOURCES OF TAX LAW

Income tax cases are covered by the following sources of law, which are formally published in the Official Gazette (*Bundesgesetzblatt*) and/or the Official Tax Gazette (*Bundessteuerblatt*):

- Federal Constitution (*Grundgesetz*), especially the Basic Rights laid down in Articles 1–19 <www.bundestag.de/parlament/funktion/gesetze/gg_pdf.pdf>.
- Income Tax Act (*Einkommensteuergesetz*), which includes the bulk of material law regarding income taxation <www.gesetze-im-internet.de/bundesrecht/estg/gesamt.pdf>.
- Income Tax Regulation (*Einkommensteuer-Durchführungsverordnung*), which covers (mostly) procedural aspects and is released by the Federal Ministry of Finance <www.gesetze-im-internet.de/bundesrecht/estdv_1955/gesamt.pdf>.
- Income Tax Guidelines 2001 (*Einkommensteuer-Richtlinien*), which are binding for the members of the administration but can be ignored by the tax courts; a whole set of circular letters by the Federal and State Ministries of Finance amends the Guidelines <www.einkommensteuerrichtlinien.de>.

Other relevant cases are governed by:

- Corporate Income Tax Act (*Körperschaftsteuergesetz*) <www.gesetze-im-internet.de/bundesrecht/kstg_1977/gesamt.pdf>.

---

95. Federal Tax Court (*Bundesfinanzhof*) judgment of 26 Jun. 2006 I R 97/05 (on a 'self-cancelling' scheme).

96. Federal Tax Court (*Bundesfinanzhof*) judgment of 18 Jul. 2001 I R 48/97; judgment of 20 Mar. 2002 I R 63/99.

- Reorganisation Tax Act (*Umwandlungssteuergesetz*) <www.gesetze-im-internet.de/bundesrecht/umwstg_1995/gesamt.pdf>.
- Trade Tax Act (*Gewerbesteuergesetz*) <www.gesetze-im-internet.de/bundesrecht/gewstg/gesamt.pdf>.

There are also regulations, guidelines, and circular letters discussing these Acts.

In Germany, tax literature is largely found in commentaries and textbooks. The most relevant ones are listed here.

General Textbooks

Dieter Birk, *Steuerrecht*, 11th edn (Heidelberg: C.F. Müller, 2008).
Brigitte Knobbe-Keuk, *Bilanz-und Unternehmenssteuerrecht*, 9th edn (Cologne: Otto Schmidt, 1993).
Klaus Tipke, *Die Steuerrechtsordnung*, 1st edn (3 vol.), 1993 et seq.; 2nd edn (2 vol.) 2000 et seq. (Cologne: Otto Schmidt).
Klaus Tipke & Joachim Lang, *Steuerrecht*, 19th edn (Cologne: Otto Schmidt, 2008).

Commentaries on Individual Income Taxation, Corporate Income Taxation, and Reorganization Taxation

Ewald Dötsch, Werner F. Jost, Alexandra Pung & Georg Witt (eds), *Die Körperschaftsteuer*, looseleaf (Stuttgart: Schaeffer-Poeschel).
Ewald Dötsch, Joachim Patt, Alexandra Pung & Ralf Möhlenbrock (eds), *Umwandlungssteuergesetz*, 6th edn (Stuttgart: Schaeffer-Poeschel, 2007).
Dietmar Gosch (ed.), *Körperschaftsteuergesetz*, 2nd edn (Munich: C.H. Beck, 2009).
Johanna Hey, Ulrich Prinz & Michael Wendt (eds), Herrmann-Heuer-Raupach, *Einkommensteuergesetz und Körperschaftsteuergesetz*, looseleaf (Heidelberg: C.F. Müller).
Paul Kirchhof (ed.), *Kompaktkommentar-Einkommensteuergesetz*, 8th edn (Heidelberg: C.F. Müller, 2008).
Paul Kirchhof, Hartmut Söhn & Rudolf Mellinghoff (eds), *Einkommensteuergesetz–Kommentar*, looseleaf (Heidelberg: C.F. Müller)
Thomas Rödder, Andreas Herlinghaus & Ingo van Lishaut, *Umwandlungssteuergesetz*, 1st edn (Cologne: Otto Schmidt, 2008).
Ludwig Schmidt (ed.), *Einkommensteuergesetz*, 28th edn (Munich: C.H. Beck, 2009).

Commentaries on International Taxation and Double Taxation Treaties

Helmut Debatin & Franz Wassermeyer (eds), *Doppelbesteuerung*, looseleaf (Munich: C.H. Beck).
Hans Flick, Franz Wassermeyer & Hubertus Baumhoff (eds), *Außensteuerrecht*, looseleaf (Cologne: Otto Schmidt).
Florian Haase (ed.), *Außensteuergesetz – Doppelbesteuerungsabkommen* (Heidelberg: C.F. Müller, 2009).

Klaus Vogel & Moris Lehner (eds), *Doppelbesteuerungsabkommen*, 5th edn (Munich: C.H. Beck, 2008).

Foreign-Language Textbooks

German Tax and Business Law (London: Sweet & Maxwell, 2005).
Dossiers Internationaux Francis Lefebvre: Allemagne, CMS Hasche Sigle (Editions Francis Lefebvre, 2007).
International Bureau of Fiscal Documentation (IBFD), *European Tax Handbook 2009*, country chapter Germany.
IBFD, *Global Individual Tax Handbook 2009*, country chapter Germany.
IBFD, *Global Corporate Tax Handbook 2009*, country chapter Germany.

Japan

Prof. Minoru Nakazato, Prof. Mark Ramseyer & Yasutaka Nishikori

1. HISTORY

The Japanese Imperial Constitution was promulgated in February 1889, but the income tax had already been enacted in 1887. Prior to that time, Japanese national revenues had been heavily dependent on the land tax and the liquor tax. As a result, the notion behind the income tax was that the tax burden should be made fairer by assessing tax on those engaged in commerce and industry. At the same time, the introduction of the income tax had important economic implications for the Japanese government. In the Meiji Era, the Japanese government was pursuing the rapid industrialization of the country. It was apparent that the heavy reliance on the land tax and liquor tax, which was suitable to an agricultural economy, had to be modified to accommodate the new industrialized society. The new income tax was a progressive tax with five brackets ranging from 1% to 3% in 0.5% increments. Corporations were not taxed, and capital gains were not included in the tax base of the income tax at that time. Since then, there have been several significant revisions to the income tax. The more prominent are as follows:

(1) In 1899, income was divided into three categories: Type I (corporate income), Type II (interest on bonds), and Type III (individual income). Of these, the first two items were taxed at a low rate, and the third was taxed at progressive rates. Corporate bond interest was taxed independently through withholding provisions; it was not taxed further. Because dividends on stock were not taxed, there was no double tax on corporate

income. At this stage, the income tax was still less important for the Japanese national budget than other kinds of taxes, such as the land tax and liquor tax. As of 1902, the income tax accounted for only 5% of total tax revenues.

(2) In 1920, interest on bank deposits was added to Type II income. Dividends on stock were added to Type III income, but only after a 40% deduction of the amount received.

(3) In 1940, tax burdens were raised to cover the high costs associated with World War II. The income tax was assessed on a wider swath of the population and became central to the national tax structure. At the same time, the Income Tax Act was divided into the Income Tax Act (*Shotokuzeiho*), which principally governed individual income tax, and the Corporate Tax Act (*Hozinzeiho*), which governed exclusively corporate income tax and other corporate taxes.[1]

(4) In 1947, a self-assessment system was introduced on a broad scale. What had been a distinctively Japanese amalgam of a schedular and global system was replaced with a single global system, although the schedular system was maintained with regard to the calculation of income. The scope of taxable income was broadened and capital gains were made taxable. The unit of taxation was changed from the household to the individual.

(5) In 1950, the system was changed yet again to incorporate most of the provisions of a study commission headed by Columbia University economist Carl Shoup. The new system incorporated the latest in tax theory from the United States and used a global progressive tax that took a comprehensive tax base as its ideal. *Inter alia*, capital gains were taxed in full; capital losses were deductible in full; provisions were adopted to integrate the corporate and individual income tax; many special tax measures were abolished; and tax administration was improved.

(6) In 1987, the tax rate structure was flattened; the exemption for deposit interest income was abolished; the tax exemption for capital gains from the sale or exchange of securities was abolished; and the consumption tax was introduced.

(7) In terms of recent movements and future prospects, one can predict a gradual aging of Japanese society by 2025. This necessarily has implications for Japanese tax reform. First, the consumption tax rate must be increased. Second, the corporate income tax rate must be lowered to prevent the outflow of Japanese investment overseas. As of 2009, both of these measures have been implemented, at least in part. The corporate income tax rate was reduced from 37.5% to 30% through the 1998 and 1999 revisions, although this reduction of the corporate income tax rate was coupled with an expansion of the tax base (i.e., elimination of several

1. The terms 'Income Tax Law' and 'Corporate Tax Law', rather than 'Income Tax Act' and 'Corporate Tax Act', are often used for the English translations for *Shotokuzeiho* and *Hojinzeiho*, respectively. We choose the term 'Act' because both are statutes enacted by the Diet.

kinds of special deductions from taxable income). In addition, consolidated returns have been allowed by the 2002 tax revisions. As to consumption tax, the increase in the consumption tax rate from 3% to 5% (including the 1% local consumption tax) was enacted in 1994 (effective as of 1997). It is thought that further increases in the consumption tax rate and relaxation of tax burdens on corporations may be necessary in the future, although the recent recession makes the short-term prospects more ambiguous.

The single event with the most influence on post-war tax policy was the 1949 Shoup Report.[2] Regarding this report, Professor Kaneko has written:

> In 1949, in order to realize the nine principles of economic stabilization, a long-term balanced budget under the Dodge Line was established, and inflation rapidly came under control. Furthermore, in order to accomplish the (long-envisioned) comprehensive reconsideration of the national tax system, SCAP invited from the US a group of experts organized around Columbia Professor Carl Shoup (the 'Shoup mission'). This mission included Shoup and six other specialists in tax theory or tax law. They arrived on May 10, 1949, and investigated and considered the national tax system for about three and a half months. On September 15, they published their large-scale report, the so-called Shoup Report. The mission returned to Japan again in July 1950, and on September 21 published a second report (the *Second Report on Japanese Taxation by the Shoup Mission*). This was a form of 'after care' for the 1949 report. These studies are often referred to together as the 'Shoup Report'.
>
> The Shoup Report recommended on a long-term basis, the way our tax system (both the national and the local systems) ought to be. Its main principles can be summarized by three goals: (a) the establishment of a fair tax system, (b) the reform of tax administration, and (c) the strengthening of local fiscal capacity. In suggesting measures like the revaluation of assets, however, it also considered the need for capital accumulation and economic recovery. As a whole, the Shoup Report urged the establishment of a theoretically coherent fair tax system . . .
>
> The Shoup Report designed a single country's tax system around a coherent theoretical structure. As a result, it was a grand experiment. In content, it systematized the latest in tax theory in the US (from the perspective of tax-system theory, that was the most advanced in the world). For scholarship too, it was a magnificent achievement. Moreover, as one could tell from looking at the members of the mission, it was a heavily reformist group. They understood the vicissitudes of the American tax system, and had high hopes about how that system should be reformed. Precisely because of that, they strove hard to establish a modern idealist tax system that was extremely fair.
>
> In other words, the Shoup Report pointed toward reformist legislation. It contributed greatly toward the modernization of our country's tax system.

2. *Report on Japanese Taxation* by the Shoup Mission (4 vols).

> Moreover, as one can see from the proposals to revalue capital assets, it contained many realistic elements, and contributed to economic stabilization and growth. In part stimulated by the Shoup Report, the study of tax theory and tax law in our country also grew steadily and has now reached a vigorous state. At least indirectly, these scholarly achievements too are a legacy of the Shoup Report.[3]

2. CONSTITUTIONAL ISSUES

Because Japan does not have a federal system, it does not confront constitutional issues regarding the allocation of various taxes among the national government and state or municipal entities, as does, for example, the Sixteenth Amendment of the US Constitution. Rather, the Japanese Constitution provides that Japanese citizens are obliged to pay tax in accordance with law and does not restrict the kinds of tax that may be levied by the national or local governments.

Still, since the enactment of the Japanese Constitution (the 'Constitution') in 1946, various constitutional issues have been argued with regard to the income tax law, especially relating to two principles: (1) tax must be imposed under laws enacted by the Japanese Parliament (tax according to laws), and (2) tax must not be imposed on a discriminatory basis (equality).

The first principle derives from Article 84 of the Constitution, which provides: 'No new taxes shall be imposed or existing ones modified except by law or under such conditions as law may prescribe' [Official translation: the term 'law' here is the Japanese *horitsu*, which might better be translated as 'statute']. This principle leads to the conclusions that (i) no non-legislative regulations, such as cabinet orders and ministerial ordinances, may provide tax requirements without specific delegation by law; (ii) provisions of tax laws and regulations must be specific enough for citizens to understand their meaning; and (iii) no governmental guidelines or circulars can be a source of tax law, no matter how strong an effect they might have on tax practice. This principle also affects the administration of the tax system (see section 8 below).

The first item of this principle is sometimes argued in the course of tax-related suits in which taxpayers challenge the constitutionality of tax laws and regulations on the basis of the overbroad delegation of tax requirements to non-legislative regulations. As to the second item, this does not necessarily mean the prohibition of provisions of tax laws with abstract concepts; in fact, the Japanese income tax law contains conceptual and flexible terms such as 'extremely low' or 'appropriate amount'.[4]

The equality principle derives from Article 14 of the Constitution, which provides, 'All of the people are equal under the law and there shall be no discrimination in political, economic, or social relations because of race, creed, sex, social status, or family origin' [Official translation]. This principle is thought to require (i) taxation

3. Hiroshi Kaneko, *Sozzei ho* [Tax Law], Tokyo: Kobundo, 14th edn (2009), 54–55, 59–60.
4. For example, Income Tax Law s. 59 and Corporate Tax Law s. 34.

according to ability to pay, (ii) equity in taxation, and (iii) neutrality. One of the most important court precedents with regard to this principle was the judgment by the Supreme Court of Japan on the issue of whether the elaborate Japanese withholding tax system applicable to salary income constituted a violation of this principle because of its inapplicability to business income. The Supreme Court held that the withholding tax was constitutional, referring to the necessity of the withholding tax system for the purpose of efficient tax collection.

In addition to these principles, tax laws and regulations are sometimes challenged for violating other principles provided for in the Constitution. For example, the scope of family members who were eligible for income tax exemption was once alleged to violate the Constitution, which declares the government's duty to ensure cultural and healthy life for Japanese citizens; however, the Supreme Court upheld the related provisions in the income tax law.[5] The Japanese human rights legislation has no substantial effect on substantive tax issues, although special tax treatment (e.g., special exclusions and deductions) that is favourable to the socially disadvantaged are sometimes provided for in the income tax law.

As discussed further in detail below, Japanese courts are conservative in the exercise of their judicial powers to determine the constitutionality of tax laws. As a result, tax laws and regulations are rarely concluded to be unconstitutional by courts. Partly because of this conservative attitude, terms and concepts that one might otherwise think unclear are held to be clear enough to be constitutional upon judicial interpretation, despite the existence of Article 84 of the Constitution.

3. TAX RATES

The individual income tax rates imposed at the national level are as follows:

Taxable Income (¥1000)	*Marginal Rates (until 2006)*	*Marginal Rates (2007 and thereafter)*
1,950 or less	10%	5%
over 1,950–3,300	10%	10%
over 3,300–6,950	20%	20%
over 6,950–9,000	20%	23%
over 9,000–18,000	30%	33%
above 18,000	37%	40%

In addition to this national tax, individuals are also subject to the local income tax (*Juminzei*) at a rate of 10%. There are no formal rate bracket adjustments for inflation, but in the 1960s and 1970s the government reduced tax rates frequently, which had somewhat similar effects. In the past decade, the individual income tax

5. *Tsuji v. Izumiotsu zeimu shocho*, 59 Hanrei Jiho 1187 (Sup. Ct., 17 Dec. 1985).

rate structure has been dramatically flattened. Prior to the 1987 revisions, the maximum income tax rate, which was applicable to income exceeding ¥80 million, was 70%; currently, the maximum tax rate is 40%. This reduction reflects the view that a high maximum tax rate interferes with the decision to engage in risky enterprises or businesses in Japan. As specified above, the 2007 revisions have slightly increased the maximum tax rate for the national income tax, except for the 5% reduction for taxable income of ¥1,950,000 or less. However, this change was coupled with a change in the local income tax rate, and the combined national and local income tax rates have not changed. Further, it is worthwhile to note that the effective national income tax rates are lower than those specified above because the income tax law permits various kinds of tax exemptions such as the family member exemption. As a result of such exemptions, as of 2008, an employee with a spouse and two children was totally exempt from the income tax if the amount of gross income was approximately ¥3.2 million or less. The 2007 revisions abolished the 20% special reduction in income tax that had been available since 1999.

The corporate income tax rate for 2008 is 30%. A reduced tax rate (22%) is applicable to the first ¥8 million of taxable income of companies with stated capital of ¥100 million or less. This reduced tax rate is also applicable to non-profit entities. It should be noted that companies are also subject to local income tax and enterprise tax. The effective tax rate including these taxes is approximately 40%. Japanese corporate income tax rates are widely regarded as too high, despite reductions in the rates several years ago. In addition, as is apparent from the statistics below, Japan relies heavily on the corporate income tax compared with other developed countries. The corporate sector consistently insists that further reduction of corporate tax burdens is essential for Japanese companies to survive global competition. However, taking into account the current severe condition of the national budget of Japan, future reduction is expected to be revenue-neutral and to be paired with an increase of other taxes, such as the consumption tax.

4. COMPOSITION OF THE FISCAL SYSTEM

According to the 2008 budgets, the percentage contribution of each kind of tax to national and local revenues (excluding the proceeds of government debts) is:

Type of Tax	*Percentage Contribution*
Individual income tax	30.2%
Corporate income tax, including the enterprise tax	27.7%
Inheritance tax	1.6%
Real estate tax	9.2%
Consumption tax	13.8%
Other taxes	17.5%

Among these, the percentage contribution of each kind of tax to national revenues alone (excluding the proceeds of governmental debts) is:

Type of Tax	*Percentage Contribution*
Individual income tax	29.5%
Corporate income tax	30.3%
Inheritance tax	2.8%
Land tax	Nil
Consumption tax	19.4%
Liquor tax	2.8%
Tobacco tax	1.6%
Other taxes	13.6%

Approximately 30% of Japanese national revenues is supplied by governmental debts. Thus, the aforementioned percentages would be substantially lower if calculated on the basis of total national revenues.

As noted, Japan obtains a relatively large percentage of its revenues from the corporate income tax. The ratio of national to local tax revenues is about 6:4. According to the 2008 budgets, the total of local and national taxes (excluding social security burdens) accounted for 25.1% of national income. After taking the social security burdens into account, this ratio would reach as much as 40%.

5. BASIC STRUCTURE OF THE INCOME TAX

5.1. On Individuals

Japanese individual income tax has two distinct features: The individual income tax heavily relies on the withholding tax, and it maintains a schedular system.

In principle, Japan uses the self-assessment system for individual income tax purposes as well as corporate income tax purposes. In fact, however, withholding rules play a substantial role. Indeed, a substantial portion of individual income tax is collected through the withholding system. For a couple of reasons, this withholding largely obviates the need for self-assessment and filing a tax return. First, wage earners generally make appropriate adjustments to their withholding at the end of the year and this adjustment eliminates the need for wage earners to file a return.[6] Second, much of non-wage income, such as interest on deposits, is also subject to withholding.

Because wage earners usually need not file a tax return, they tend to consider the tax filing obligation bothersome. This was regarded as one of the reasons that

6. ITA, s. 121.

Japanese individuals were reluctant to invest in equity, which used to trigger the tax-filing requirement in general. As of 2003, small- or medium-sized individual equity investors have been excluded from this filing obligation as a result of a new withholding tax system applicable to capital gains on listed equity securities.

Although many individuals are exempted from filing a tax return, if required, each individual, rather than a household, must file a return. A joint return system has not been adopted in Japan.

Individual income tax still maintains a formally schedular system – in the sense that income is divided into ten categories and computed according to distinct rules of calculation. For example, capital gains on equity securities that are not subject to the withholding tax mentioned above are totalled separately from other kinds of income and are taxed according to special tax rates.[7] The theory behind this schedular system is sometimes said to be that the 'ability to pay' varies by category of income. However, this feature of the individual income tax definitely makes tax planning easier by means of changing the character of income from one category to another through sophisticated financial products and other technologies. For example, relatively favourable tax treatment is applicable to Occasional Income, especially compared to Miscellaneous Income. This gives taxpayers incentives to have their income treated as Occasional Income. Other evidence of the schedular character of the Japanese system includes limits on the deductibility of losses in one category against income in other categories. As discussed above, the system has become, in substance, closer to a global regime.

To avoid double taxation on corporate earnings at the individual and corporate levels, Japan has adopted the divided-received credit method. However, because of the limit on the creditable amount, double taxation is not completely eliminated.

5.2. On Corporations

The features of the individual income tax discussed above are not applicable to the corporate income tax in Japan. The tax base of the corporate income tax is, in general, the amount of net profits earned in the whole business engaged in by a corporation and calculated on the basis of the accrual method. No distinct treatments are made according to the nature of income. However, corporations as well as individuals are often subject to withholding tax according to the (Individual) Income Tax Act (ITA), or *Shotokuzeiho*. Of course, corporations are entitled to tax credits of the amount equal to the withholding tax. Yet this feature is sometimes critical for financial institutions because one of the principal sources of their earnings is the time value of money. For this reason, financial institutions are often exempt from the withholding tax, subject to some procedural requirements to enable withholders (i.e., counterparties of transactions with financial institutions) to identify the financial institutions.

---

7. Special Taxation Measures Law, s. 37-10.

Since 2002, corporations have been permitted to file consolidated returns, although a consolidated group subject to such returns may not include non-Japanese entities.

To avoid double taxation, 50% of dividends received from other corporations are excluded from taxable income. This 50% exclusion is increased to 100% exclusion if the distributing corporation is an affiliate of the receiving corporation.

6. TAX LEGISLATION

6.1. Legislative Process for Income Tax Measures

Japanese tax law, including income tax law (i.e., both the individual and corporate income taxes (ITA and CTA)), is amended annually. The effective dates of such amendments are generally set as the first day of the taxable period. As a result, the ITA is usually amended as of 1 January and the Corporate Tax Act (CTA) is usually amended as of 1 April, the taxable period for individuals being the calendar year and the taxable period for corporations being their fiscal year (which, for many Japanese corporations, is from 1 April to 31 March of the following year).

According to current practice, tax amendments are enacted in accordance with the following steps. Although the Constitution provides that the tax must be imposed by laws enacted by the Parliament, most tax legislation is initiated by a government agency rather than Parliament:

First step: The Tax Commission (*Zeiseichosakai*), an advisory committee of the Prime Minister, submits a report to the Minister regarding tax amendments.

Second step: The government party (almost always Liberal Democratic Party) and the Ministry of Finance announces the outline of tax amendments for the next taxable period around December.

Third step: Discussion at Parliament.

Fourth step: Tax amendments pass the Japanese Parliament.

Tax regulations corresponding to the amendments to tax laws are prepared under a similar time schedule by the Ministry of Finance, but are published only after the passage of the related law amendments.

Because the members of the Tax Commission include non-government persons and tax specialists, such as tax law professors, the views of the private sector are indirectly reflected in the first step. In addition, in the first and second steps, informal sounding from the public, and especially from powerful pressure groups, is made. Drafts of tax amendments are rarely subject to substantial modifications during the course of discussion in Parliament.

In Japan, a process of public consultation similar to that applicable to draft IRS regulations is available only in limited circumstances. Because of this, it is difficult for tax amendments to reflect the views of the private sector other than those of strong pressure groups. Even in the case of tax amendments with a technical nature, tax specialists other than the members of the Tax Commission do not have a substantial opportunity to participate in the process of such amendments. Moreover, the process of drafting the provisions for tax amendments in the Ministry of Finance has not been made public. Therefore, the Japanese general public often encounters difficulty in finding any meaningful legislative history of tax amendments.

6.2. Statutory Style

Compared to legislation in other areas of the law, the provisions of Japanese tax laws are quite detailed. This feature may be regarded as a reflection of the 'tax-according-to-laws' principle under Article 84 of the Constitution, as discussed in section 2 above. Note, however, that the statutes – detailed as they may be – still contain flexible terms, such as 'extremely low price' or 'appropriate amount'. In addition, the tax laws delegate the details of tax rules to cabinet orders (*Seirei*) and ministerial ordinances (*Shorei*) issued by the Ministry of Finance. Although Article 84 of the Constitution prohibits absolute delegation of tax requirements to cabinet orders and ministerial ordinances, the volume of such orders and ordinances is much larger than that of tax laws, mainly because of their technical nature.

As a structural matter, there are separate laws for individual income tax (ITA) and corporate income tax (CTA). Further, there is an additional law for 'special tax treatments', which contains provisions that could broadly be considered as tax expenditures. Because of this structure, corporations must refer to all of these laws in order to properly understand the tax effects of transactions. As discussed above, under the ITA, some kinds of withholding taxes are applicable not only to individuals but also to corporations.

6.3. Statutory Interpretation

Courts are sometimes said to pay more attention to the actual text of the statute in tax law matters than in other fields (although this is obviously a difficult claim to measure). This may be because of the existence of Article 84 of the Constitution.

As discussed further below, Japanese courts generally respect the legislative history of laws, including tax laws. Emphasis is placed on (i) answers given by the Tax Commission in response to questions at the time of the promulgation of, or amendment to, the relevant tax law provisions; and (ii) interpretations (whether official or not) given by the staff of the National Tax Agency (*Kokuzei-cho;* the NTA) or the Regional Tax Bureaus (*Kokuzei-kyoku*) within the Ministry of Finance.

The actual legislative drafting is done by young bureaucrats in the Ministry of Finance or the NTA. As a result, it sometimes happens that the most valuable tax legislative materials exist only as internal documents within the Ministry of Finance or the NTA. Sometimes this internal information becomes public when a bureaucrat at the Ministry of Finance or the NTA publishes a book or article in his 'private' capacity.

Judges seldom have deep specialist knowledge of tax law. This might be a reason why Japanese courts frequently defer to the opinions of the tax authorities in tax litigation.

Government interpretations of tax laws and regulations are officially announced by the NTA or other tax authorities in the tax guidelines and circulars (*Tsutatsu*) and in tax rulings. In addition to these official interpretations, and similar to the case of legislative history, interpretations by tax officials are often stated in books or articles written by them. Although these interpretations are unofficial, they are considered to be de facto tax rules in practice, because it can be reasonably expected that the tax authorities will not object to tax planning arrangements that follow such published interpretations.

7. COURTS DEALING WITH TAX MATTERS

7.1. Structure of the Courts

Taxpayers must first bring complaints against decisions by the tax authority (local tax office) regarding tax amounts to the National Tax Tribunal before bringing them to judicial courts. Although the Tribunal is a department of the NTA, the Tribunal may make decisions on complaints independently of the NTA. This system has been adopted to efficiently use sophisticated knowledge of tax laws and regulations held by tax officials. The Tribunal is independent of the NTA in the sense that the NTA may not direct the Tribunal in its decisions on tax disputes. However, the President of the Tribunal, who is the head of the Tribunal and is granted the authority to make final decisions on all tax disputes at the stage of the Tribunal, is appointed by the Commissioner of the NTA. In addition, the members of the Tribunal, who manage tax disputes in practice, are tax officials as well as civil court judges and prosecutors. Although the President makes all final decisions on tax disputes at the Tribunal, such decisions are made based on the opinions submitted by the consultation panel, consisting of three members of the Tribunal.

Appeals against decisions by the Tribunal can be brought to a district court that governs the area where the taxpayer in question resides. In large-scale district courts, such as the Tokyo District Court, the same departments always deal with tax litigation; nevertheless, such departments are still general courts rather than special tax courts. Decisions of district courts can be appealed to the relevant high court and then to the Supreme Court.

In general, Japanese courts do not have specialized tax judges. Japanese judges are under the career system and are frequently transferred to different courts located all over Japan. This system makes it difficult for judges to be specialists in a particular area of law, such as tax law. In addition, many judges are not sophisticated at tax calculations and would encounter difficulty in calculating the amount of tax. These circumstances might promote the tendency of judges to be inclined to accept the government's interpretations of tax laws and regulations and tax circulars issued by the NTA.

The following table illustrates the number of tax disputes heard by the Tribunal and judicial courts. The table also indicates the results of such tax disputes. The number of disputes decided in favour of taxpayers is small.

From April 2006 to March 2007

Level	*Number of Disputes Decided*	*Taxpayers' Win*	*Taxpayers' Partial Win*	*Taxpayers' Loss*	*Others*
Tribunal	2,945	91	270	2,211	373
District Court	228	21	13	150	41
High Court	128	19	5	99	5
Supreme Court	88	11	11	62	4

7.2. Judicial Style

Judicial opinions of Japanese courts, especially those of lower courts, are long and detailed with regard to the interpretation of law and findings of fact. This feature of judicial opinions is called 'minute judgment'. Judicial opinions with respect to interpretation of laws and regulations often refer to their legislative history. Although legislative history is not binding, a traditional approach for the interpretation of law by Japanese courts is that laws should be interpreted according to the intention of legislators. Therefore, especially when courts encounter controversial legal issues, they highly respect the relevant legislative history if it is sufficiently clear.

The aforementioned general analysis is equally applicable to tax cases. In addition to this general nature, with regard to tax cases, it appears that courts tend to respect the government's interpretation of tax laws and regulations as espoused by the NTA or other tax authorities, even if such interpretations are unofficial.

Following the continental influence on the Japanese legal system, judicial opinions are not formally the source of law, at least among equal levels in the judicial hierarchy – although, of course, judicial opinions by the Supreme Court have dominant authority in practice. This analysis does not mean, however, that judicial opinions by district courts, the lowest level of courts in tax litigation, have no authority. Quite the contrary – they have enormous authority for Japanese tax practice. For example, if the tax office loses a case, even if the court is an obscure district court, the tax authority often changes its policies to comport with the court decision. In general, if a court rejects a tax circular, the circular is usually amended.

Japanese courts tend to be conservative in the exercise of their powers to determine the constitutionality of laws and defer broadly to the legislative branch. This tendency is particularly noticeable in fields such as tax law where technical sophistication is at a premium. As the Supreme Court put it:

> Tax today involves more than its basic function of providing for the national fiscal needs. It also redistributes income, appropriately allocates resources, and adjusts economic performance. In deciding each citizen's tax burden, the determination of national fiscal, economic, and social policy on a comprehensive national scale becomes necessary. Because the prerequisites of tax liability must also be decided, however, the process requires specialized technical judgment as well. Accordingly, in the determination of tax law, it is necessary to defer to policy and technical judgment (based on accurate data regarding such issues as the national fiscal situation, the social economy, the national income, and the national living situation) of the legislative branch. At root, the courts have no choice but to respect the discretionary judgment of that branch.[8]

8. TAX ADMINISTRATION

The governmental agency in charge of the income tax administration is the NTA, which is an independent department of the Ministry of Finance. The NTA consists of the head office, eleven Regional Bureaus, and at the lowest level, approximately 500 local tax offices engaged in the day-to-day management of tax affairs. The NTA's head office performs administrative functions and issues tax guidelines and circulars. Tax collection is generally administered by the relevant local tax office or the Regional Bureau. These national tax agencies have a budget of approximately ¥720 billion and employ more than 56,000 officials. For the period between April 2006 and March 2007, the number of audits for income tax was approximately 210,000.

Japanese tax law does not have a special provision for taxpayers' access to tax-related information. Although Japan has a general law regarding the disclosure of government information, in general, disclosure of specific tax-related information is very restricted. Tax officials are subject to a confidentiality obligation with regard to the non-public information they obtain in the course of their work.

In July 2002, a tax rulings system was introduced in Japan. In general, tax rulings are issued by the local tax office in the area where the applicant resides, except that in some cases the Regional Bureau or the NTA issues tax rulings. Tax rulings are to be published within sixty days following the response by the tax authority to the application.

8. *Oshima v. Sakyo zeimu shocho*, 39 Saihan Minshu 2-247 (Sup. Ct., 27 Mar. 1985) (en banc).

The government's administration of the tax system must be carried out in accordance with laws enacted by Parliament. This is a basic constitutional principle in Japan, and the notion is particularly important in tax matters because of Article 84 of the Constitution. Administrative interpretation is provided mostly in the form of guidelines or circulars issued by the NTA. Although guidelines and circulars are not binding interpretations of law, necessarily they are the result of careful consideration by a group of knowledgeable and sophisticated specialists in the NTA. This feature, together with the fact that courts rarely have expertise in tax matters, results in considerable judicial deference to these circulars.

The whole question of Japanese administrative style is a matter of some controversy. The conventional interpretation is that the system is characterized by a strong bureaucracy using informal 'administrative guidance', which is typically followed by the private sector. As applied to the tax area, this would mean that informal interpretations in the form of tax circulars or otherwise would perform the same role as formally issued regulations in a more rule-oriented system. On the other hand, some commentators (including the authors of this description) have taken the position that the Japanese system is not unique in its use of informal regulations. Informal regulations are followed only if and to the extent that the parties believe that the positions taken therein could be transferred into formal rules. By governing informally, both the government and the private sectors save the costs associated with a more formal system.

The relatively small number of judicial cases regarding tax matters in Japan might be viewed as an effect of this administrative style. Many of the decisions by the local tax offices regarding the amount of tax payable are not challenged at judicial proceedings but are accepted by taxpayers, sometimes after some compromise by the local tax office.

At least according to conventional wisdom, Japanese taxpayers do not approach tax planning as aggressively as US taxpayers do. Recently, however, aggressive tax shelters have begun to be marketed. For example, an American bank marketed the following tax-planning scheme as a way of minimizing inheritance gift tax liability: (i) a child became a US resident; (ii) the parent, in Japan, bought US treasury bonds; (iii) the parent gave bonds to the child. The Japanese gift tax applies to the recipient of the gift. If the recipient is a non-resident, the tax applied only to domestic assets, and the US treasury bonds (even if physically located in Japan) are considered to be foreign assets. Accordingly, the Japanese gift tax did not apply to this scheme. On the other hand, the US gift tax applies in principle to the donor but does not cover intangible property. As a result, the gift by a non-resident of treasury bonds was not subject to tax in either jurisdiction. Japanese gift tax law was amended in 2000 to combat this kind of tax shelter. Currently, Japanese nationals are subject to the gift tax in respect of foreign assets as well as domestic assets if they were resident in Japan at any time during the previous five years.

Among taxpayer organizations, there are those that are cooperative with the NTA (e.g., the Blue Return Organization) and those that are uncooperative (e.g., the Democratic Chamber of Commerce). The Democratic Chamber of Commerce has launched many legal challenges against the tax authority. Among the leftist tax adviser (*zeirishi*) groups, there is the Young Tax Advisers Association.

One interesting development in this area is that some court decisions hold tax advisers liable to the taxpayer for any deficiencies resulting from their advice. Suppose that adviser X files taxpayer Y's return. On it, Y claims he owes ¥5 million. If the Tax Bureau audits Y and finds he actually owes ¥8 million, Y pays the ¥3 million deficiency and can then sue X for reimbursement for that ¥3 million. Apparently, these kinds of conclusions have been taken only by lower courts.[9] If widely accepted, however, it would, of course, help explain why tax advisers do not take aggressive positions.

Still, in recent years, financial products developed for the purpose of acquiring tax benefits or other kinds of tax planning schemes have become increasingly common in Japan. The NTA and other agencies are aware of this issue and are making substantial efforts to identify illegal or questionable tax shelters. It appears that the NTA's stance against these tax-oriented products has become more aggressive recently. In any event, the schedular system of the Japanese individual income tax and the high tax rate of the corporate income tax should give taxpayers strong motivation for tax planning. Struggles between the NTA and taxpayers have just started and will likely take a long time to be settled.

9. GENERAL PRINCIPLES

9.1. Relationship Between Tax and Financial Accounting

The taxable income of a corporation is calculated on the basis of the profit-and-loss statement prepared in accordance with the Company Act[10] with adjustments required by the CTA. The accounting provisions dictated by the Company Act, in turn, are based on generally accepted accounting principles.[11] Therefore, for corporations, tax accounting is generally the same as financial accounting, although the tax law has special rules that are different from the Japanese GAAP in certain respects. The reason for this general reliance of the tax law on financial accounting is the need to simplify the tax law; but, at the same time, such reliance raises several problems. For example, suppose that the rules for financial accounting change. If tax accounting should be the same as financial accounting, the tax rules would automatically change as well. Yet that seems to violate the general constitutional requirement of taxation according to law (see section 2 above). One of the issues that has arisen recently is whether the mark-to-market method for evaluation of certain assets, such as financial derivatives transactions, could be adopted without statutory changes for tax purposes, if that method were adopted for

9. *Ryujitsushoji KK v. X* (the name of the defendant is not publicly available), 1654 Hanrei Jiho 54 (Tokyo H. Ct., 13 Mar. 1998).
10. CTA, s. 74.
11. Company Act, s. 431.

financial accounting purposes. Although this issue was actually resolved by changing the tax law according to the changes in financial accounting principles, similar kinds of problems may possibly occur.

For income tax on individuals, taxable income is calculated without regard to the Japanese GAAP. Although the general method for the calculation of individual taxable income is the accrual method, under limited circumstances, the tax law permits individuals to use the cash method.

9.2. Respect for Legal (Civil Law) Form

In general, the Supreme Court's position has been that, where the tax law uses concepts that are commonly used in, or defined under, private law such as the Civil and Commercial Codes, the concepts are interpreted in the same manner as in the Civil and Commercial Codes, unless otherwise defined in the tax law.

According to most observers, courts respect contractual forms and do not impose a tax based on the underlying economic substance, ignoring contractual forms. Because this judicial approach offers opportunities for tax avoidance, the tax authority sometimes asserts a substance-over-form argument. It appears that the tax authority has become aggressive using this kind of argument in recent years, especially in cases involving international transactions.

9.3. Anti-Avoidance Doctrines or Legislation

The Japanese tax law does not have a general provision that authorizes courts to recharacterize tax avoidance schemes. However, some provisions negate tax avoidance schemes under limited circumstances. Perhaps the most important provision is the one that authorizes courts to recharacterize the transactions of family corporations. According to this provision (stripped of a variety of details), if transactions among such corporations unreasonably reduce their tax liability, the courts can recharacterize the transactions and recompute the tax liability.

Although several court precedents have ruled to the contrary, the general scholarly view and some other court precedents have taken the position that the 'tax according to law' principle under Article 84 of the Constitution prohibits courts from recharacterizing legal schemes because of their tax-avoidance nature without a specific provision authorizing such recharacterization. Currently, the tax authorities rarely insist on recharacterization without a specific provision but tend to try to achieve the same goals by narrowly interpreting tax provisions on which taxpayers rely to obtain tax benefits.

In addition to such anti-avoidance provisions for family corporations, a similar provision was adopted for corporations that file consolidated returns at the time of the introduction of the consolidated tax system in 2002.[12] Because this

12. CTA, s. 132-3.

anti-avoidance provision has no history, its detailed interpretation has yet to be tested in the courts. Moreover, a similar kind of anti-avoidance provision has been introduced in relation to corporate mergers or other corporate reorganization transactions.[13]

10. SOURCES OF TAX LAW

10.1. SOURCES OF TAX LAW

Sources of Japanese tax law include (i) the Constitution, (ii) international treaties (or conventions), (iii) laws and statutes, and (iv) government regulations comprised of cabinet orders (*seiriei*) and ministerial ordinances (*shorei,* issued by the Ministry of Finance). Local ordinances (*jorei,* issued by municipalities) may also be sources of local tax law. As discussed above, because Japan is a civil law country, judicial opinions are not formally the source of law, although judicial opinions, especially those issued by the Supreme Court, have practical authority.

In theory, the tax guidelines or circulars (*tsutatsu,* issued by the NTA) are simply internal instructions from bureaucratic superiors to inferiors, and thus neither bind citizens nor constitute the source of tax law. However, in fact, as discussed above, courts almost always defer to these circulars, and taxpayers seldom challenge their validity. These circulars should be understood as playing an important role in making tax administration predictable and thus providing certainty to taxpayers.

Similarly, tax rulings do not constitute a source of law, regardless of their importance in tax practice. Since the introduction of the rulings system in 2002, their number has steadily increased. Further, in 2008 the scope of tax rulings was expanded to include specific transactions as well as tax issues with general applicability. This change may make the tax ruling system more useful.

Japanese tax law does not grant the Ministry of Finance or the NTA general authority to prescribe tax regulations (as discussed in section 2 above, such authorization, if made, would be disregarded because of its unconstitutionality). Therefore, only cabinet orders and ministerial ordinances based on specific delegation by tax law constitute the source of law. The text of the current tax law including cabinet orders and ministerial ordinances can be found at <http://law.e-gov.go.jp/cgi-bin/idxsearch.cgi> (only Japanese versions are available). Moreover, the Japanese text of the tax guidelines and circulars are available at <www.nta.go.jp/shiraberu/zeiho-kaishaku/tsutatsu/menu.htm>.

Although the Japanese government does not provide an official translation of the tax law, the outline of the income tax system applicable to non-residents of Japan is available on its website <www.nta.go.jp/taxanswer/english/gaikoku301.htm>.

13. CTA, s. 132-2.

10.2. Available Materials

The NTA's website <www.nta.go.jp> contains not only the texts of the tax guidelines and circulars, but also many other items, such as a summary of the tax revisions for recent years and copies of tax rulings. With respect to certain items including the annual report of the NTA (National Tax Agency Report), the English translations are also available there.

In addition to the NTA's website, Y. Komi and T. Honjo, *Corporate Tax Law of Japan* (Sozeishiryokan, 2007) offers an English translation of the corporate tax law. The English translations of various other tax laws are also available in looseleaf booklets issued by Eibun-Horei Sha.

H. Kaneko, *Sozei ho* [Tax Law], 13th edn (2008) provides a comprehensive and insightful overview of the entire Japanese tax system. *Sozei ho kenkyu* [Studies in Tax Law], an annual journal, and *Nichi zei ken ronshu* [Essays in Japanese Tax Studies], a collection of essays, include professional and scholarly essays on various topics, including international tax issues. The tax law commentaries issued by Daichi-Hoki-Shuppan and edited by S. Takeda are the most reliable commentaries for Japanese income tax law. These commentaries are authored by current and former NTA officials and accurately reflect the NTA's views.

The Netherlands

Kees van Raad

1. HISTORY OF THE NETHERLANDS INCOME TAX SYSTEM

An 1821 Act provided the first conceptual framework for the taxes existing at that time. Most of these taxes were excise taxes, except for the tax levied under the Patent Right Act of 1819, which was imposed on trades and businesses (operated under a license or 'patent') according to their deemed income as apparent from external characteristics, such as the number of employees. The first true income taxes were introduced in 1892–1893. Income from capital was taxed under the Wealth Tax Act of 1892, under which income from capital was deemed to amount to 4% of the value of the capital. In addition, the Business Tax Act of 1893 subjected to tax income from business and employment activities.

The reason for taxing income under two separate acts was the desire to tax passive (unearned) income more heavily than active (earned) income. This difference in income taxation disappeared when the two acts were replaced by the single Income Tax Act of 1914. In order to continue to subject wealthy individuals to a higher tax burden, however, a wealth tax was introduced in the same year. The 1914 income tax was levied not on the income earned by the taxpayer during the preceding year, but on the income he could be expected to earn during the current year from income sources available to him at the beginning of the taxable year (1 May) and on the basis of the actual amount of income derived from such sources in the preceding year. Disposition of a source of income just before 1 May was therefore a widespread tactic to avoid taxation on income from such sources. Whereas the 1914 Income Tax Act originally covered the income of companies as well, in 1918 a special tax on corporate distributions was introduced (while non-distributed income remained tax-free).

After Germany occupied The Netherlands in 1940, it introduced in The Netherlands in 1941 an individual income tax and in 1942 a company income tax, both based to a large extent on the existing German taxes and both taxing true income rather than deemed income, as was the case under previous acts. Although after the war both acts were substantially amended, not until the 1960s were they replaced by the Income Tax Act of 1964 and the Company Tax Act of 1969. At the time they were enacted, these two statutes, which still reflected many of the notions of the old tax codes introduced by Germany, were models of clear and concise tax legislation; as introduced, each of these acts was less than twenty pages in print. As a consequence, however, of a considerable decrease of tax morality in The Netherlands from the 1970s on and the subsequent international avoidance tactics to which taxpayers resorted, the government was forced to add to the tax code detailed, complex counteracting measures, which often contained elements of overkill. This, in turn, led to further taxpayer reactions and, on the government side, to increases in both the size and detail of the statute and a corresponding reduction of the clarity and conciseness of the tax acts.

In the 1980s The Netherlands joined the worldwide move toward rate reduction and base widening of the income tax. In addition, it paid some lip service to tax simplification. The simplification, however, remained restricted mostly to the replacement of a detailed rate structure of the individual income tax by three tax brackets and an integration of individual income tax rates and general social security contributions. The proposals of a government commission appointed in the early 1990s to come up with suggestions for a true simplification of the individual income tax law received only lukewarm support from the Government. In the late 1990s an ambitious Under Minister of Finance developed blueprints for a partial return to the 1892 roots of the Netherlands income tax system: they provided for three schedules ('boxes') of income (income from 'work and home', 'substantial interest', and 'capital'). The last box provides for taxation of income on a deemed basis (determined to amount to – as in 1892 – 4% of the value of the underlying asset) rather than of real income. Based on these blueprints, on 1 January 2001 the (Individual) Income Tax Act 2001 entered into force.

2. CONSTITUTIONAL ISSUES

2.1. In General

Under Article 104 of the Netherlands Constitution, the State (i.e., the central government) is entitled to levy any taxes provided they are based on a statute. In addition to such State taxes, taxes may also be imposed by local public authorities (provinces, municipalities, and water boards) but under Articles 132(6) and 133(2) of the Constitution, these local authorities are restricted to the taxes enumerated in the pertinent statutes (the Act on Provinces, the Act on Municipalities, and the Act on Water Boards). In contrast, provinces and water boards are generally restricted to user fees. Municipalities may also impose an (annual) tax on the value of real property. The budgetary needs of provinces and municipalities, however, are met mostly through revenue sharing with the central government.

2.2. Impact of Human Rights Conventions and EC Treaty Fundamental Freedom Provisions

As Netherlands statutory law (including tax law) cannot be challenged on the basis of a presumed violation of any Netherlands constitutional provision, individuals and companies cannot invoke the non-discrimination clause laid down in Article 1 of the Constitution. For that reason, the non-discrimination provisions in the human rights conventions to which The Netherlands has acceded are in The Netherlands of greater importance than to litigants in other countries. So far, some of the statutory tax provisions and several administrative positions taken by the Revenue Service have been found by the courts to violate these treaty non-discrimination provisions.

In addition, the fundamental freedom provisions of the European Community Treaty, notably those on the freedom of workers (Article 39) and the freedom of establishment (Article 43), have been decided by the European Court of Justice (ECJ) to forbid differential tax treatment of non-resident taxpayers. For example, in a 1995 decision[1] the ECJ found the Netherlands statutory restriction to resident taxpayers of the right for individuals engaged in business to set up a tax-free old-age reserve violated Article 43 of the EC Treaty. And a June 1996 decision[2] of the ECJ found the former 25% income tax bracket for non-resident individuals in The Netherlands to be in violation of one of the treaty's non-discrimination provisions.

3. INCOME TAX RATES

In the current modified-schedular individual Income Tax Act 2001, different rate structures apply to the three schedules, or boxes. Income from home and work is taxed at the following progressive rates (2009), applicable to both the income tax and the wages tax:

Taxable Income	*Tax Rate*
Under €17,878	2.35%
€17,878–€32,127	10.85%
€32,127–€54,776	42%
Over €54,776	52%

1. Case C-80/94, 11 Aug. 1995 (*Wielockx*).
2. Case C-107/94, 27 Jun. 1996 (*Asscher*).

As of 1990, the individual income tax rates are combined with the contributions for general social security. These contributions are due only on income up to the second bracket (€ 32,127). The combined rates are as follows (reduced social security rates apply to persons over age 64):

Income Tax	*Social Security*	*Combined (> 65)*
2.35%	31.15% (13.35%)	33.50% (15.60%)
10.85%	31.15% (13.35%)	42.00% (24.10%)

Income, comprising ordinary income and capital gains earned by an individual in connection with a 'substantial interest' (i.e., a share interest of at least 5% in a company), is subject to a flat 25% rate. And, as indicated above in section 1, capital income is taxed on a deemed basis: Not the actual return, but an amount equal to 4% of the average value of the assets minus liabilities, is subject to a flat 30% rate, resulting effectively in net wealth taxation of 1.2% of the taxpayer's net wealth.

Dividends are subject to a withholding tax of 15%, which is creditable against the income tax liability of residents and of those non-residents where the dividend is attributable to Dutch-source income for which they are subject to ordinary taxation.

In the company income tax the rate amounts to 25.5%, albeit that the first €40,000 of company income is taxed at 20% and the next €160,000 at 23%.

4. COMPOSITION OF THE FISCAL SYSTEM

	2009 Budget		*2008 Result*	
	*Amount**	%	*Amount**	%
Taxes on consumption (Indirect taxes)	77,818	33.5%	74,317	33.1%
turnover tax (VAT)	45,952	19.8%	43,812	19.5%
purchase tax on cars & motorcycles	3,478	1.5%	3,541	1.6%
excise taxes	11,038	4.7%	10,563	4.7%
tax on legal transactions	6,088	2.6%	6,038	2.7%
use tax on cars & motorcycles	3,350	1.4%	3,001	1.3%
environmental taxes	4,605	2.0%	4,432	2.0%
Other	3,307	1.4%	2,930	1.3%
Taxes on income and wealth	109,502	47.1%	102,946	45.9%
wages tax	90,658	39.0%	84,237	37.5%
income tax (individuals)**	– 6,019	– 2.6%	– 6,029	– 2.7%

	2009 Budget		2008 Result	
	Amount*	%	Amount*	%
dividend tax	3,796	1.6%	4,098	1.8%
company tax	18,435	7.9%	18,269	8.1%
Other	2,632	1.1%	2,371	1.1%
Total taxes and general social security levies	187,320	80.6%	177,263	79.0%
Social security levies employees	45,218	19.4%	47,124	21.0%
Total taxes and social security levies	232,538	100.0%	224,387	100.0%

* × €1 million
** Negative as a result of wages tax and dividend tax credits against income tax liability

5. BASIC STRUCTURE OF THE INCOME TAX

5.1. INDIVIDUALS

The income of individuals is subject to income tax as provided for in the Income Tax Act of 2001 (ITA, *Wet inkomstenbelasting 2001*). With respect to income from current or past employment and to public benefits, recipients are subject, in addition to the income tax, to the wages tax under the rules of the Wages Tax Act of 1964 (WTA, *Wet op de loonbelasting 1964*). Amounts withheld as wages tax are credited against any income tax due. If the resulting amount of income tax does not exceed a given minimal amount, no individual income tax assessment is imposed. As the table in section 4 shows, the income tax currently has a negative net yield, as the amount of income tax refunded by filers who paid wages tax (and/or dividend tax) in excess of the income tax liability is higher than the additional income tax paid by filers with a remaining income tax liability.

Dividends distributed by a Netherlands-resident company are subject to a 15% tax, withheld by the distributing company and creditable against the recipient's individual income tax liability (usually as capital income in box 3). There is no withholding on interest and royalty payments. In terms of interest, however, banks are required to report to the tax administration the amounts of interest they pay on savings accounts and the names of the resident individuals holding such accounts.

Particularly with regard to income taxation of individuals, Netherlands tax law employs a 'source of income' concept. Only income derived from a 'source' is taxable. This term does not refer to the territorial source of the income – that is, the source concept used by most countries to distinguish between domestic-source and foreign-source income. 'Source of income' refers to instances where the taxpayer engages in an economic activity with the intention to derive a benefit therefrom and where such benefit can objectively be expected to materialize. Consequently, activities that are not expected to produce any positive amount of income (hobby farms, 'inventing', etc.) are not considered to constitute a source of income, with the result that expenses incurred cannot be used to offset other income.

Capital gains realized by individuals are generally not subject to taxation. Exceptions apply to business capital gains and gains on the disposition of so-called substantial interest shares (i.e., shares belonging to a 5%-plus interest in a company). Before the Income Tax Act of 2001 came into effect, the absence of capital gains taxation and the relatively high tax rates applicable to ordinary income constituted a strong incentive for taxpayers to try to convert ordinary income into a tax-free capital gain or into a substantial interest gain (that was taxed at 20%). One of the important aims of the 2001 Act was to eliminate such avoidance tactics through the introduction of deemed income taxation of capital income and by subjecting in substantial interest cases both current income and capital gains to the same 25% tax rate.

5.2. Corporations

Companies are taxed on the basis of the Company Tax Act of 1969 (CTA, *Wet op de vennootschapsbelasting 1969*). All income earned by companies is deemed to be business income. For the general rules on the determination of business income and for the taxation of non-resident companies, the CTA refers to the ITA.

In addition, the CTA contains detailed rules on, *inter alia*:

- Corporate reorganizations (*exchange of assets for stock:* Article 14; *exchange of stock for stock:* Article 13i; *legal merger:* Article 13k [in connection with Article 14b ITA], *legal division:* Article 13j [in connection with Article 14a ITA]). To the extent that (cross-border intra-EU) reorganizations are covered by the 1990 Merger Directive (amended in 2005) as implemented in Dutch tax law, the rules on Dutch domestic reorganizations have been made identical to those of such cross-border mergers.
- Participation exemption (Articles 13–13k CTA). Dividends received from a qualifying (resident or non-resident) subsidiary company are exempt from tax in the hands of the parent company. Similarly, capital gains realized on the disposition of shares of such a subsidiary company are exempt.
- Fiscal unity (Articles 15–15aj CTA). Upon the request of all companies concerned, the income of qualifying subsidiaries is taxed to the common parent company.

Further, in the last decade complex rules have been added countering the erosion of the corporate tax base through the deduction of interest payments (particularly to non-resident recipients).

6. TAX LEGISLATION

6.1. Tax Legislative Process

Although Parliament has a constitutional right of legislative initiative, virtually all bills are introduced in Parliament by the government, after the advice of the Council of State has been obtained. The bills are discussed in several rounds in the full Second Chamber of Parliament, which has the right of amendment (through a 'motion' introduced by one or more members of this Chamber). The government, which also may amend a pending bill, has the right to withdraw a bill it has introduced. After a bill has been approved by the Second Chamber, it is introduced in the First Chamber of Parliament that can only approve or reject the bill; this Chamber has no right of amendment.

6.2. Statutory Style

With the exception of the Income Tax Act 2001, the tax acts regarding income taxation (Company Tax Act, Wages Tax Act, and Dividend Tax Act) were drafted in the 1960s. Their overall design at that time was to provide a clear and lean framework of fundamental rules. The predecessor of the current income tax act, the 1964 Income Tax Act, comprising provisions on taxable persons, categories of taxable income, personal deductions, loss compensation, tax rates, and special rules, in most text editions comprised less than twenty pages of print. The other acts were even briefer. Practical details and other specific matters (e.g., amounts that may change frequently, lists) were typically relegated to implementing decrees. By 1996, the 1964 Individual Income Tax Act had grown to more than four times its original size. The 2001 Act, while still clearly structured, is about 40% longer than the last version of its predecessor and reflects the current tendency to counteract undesirable tax planning techniques with detailed statutory provisions.

The 1969 Corporate Tax Act has been expanded over the last decade. Detailed rules have been added with regard to the participation exemption, fiscal unity, and anti-base-erosion measures. These additions have obfuscated the Act's original well-balanced structure. Mostly as a result of the legislature's recurring attempts to counter particular tax avoidance practices, highly detailed rules have been inserted, greatly adding to the size and affecting the accessibility of the statute.

The individual and company income tax acts, and the wages, dividend, and wealth tax acts and implementing decrees currently comprise well over 500 pages of print.

In respect of many income tax provisions, the Minister of Finance has issued interpretative decrees in which he takes particular positions. When such a position is more favourable to the taxpayer than it would be under a strict application of the statute or an implementing decree, the taxpayer is entitled to rely in his tax return on that interpretation. To the extent that a position taken by the Minister of Finance appears stricter than the law, the taxpayer may challenge that interpretation in court.

Newly enacted tax legislation, like all law, is generally not retroactively effective. However, in a 1996 memorandum, the government takes the position that in three situations there may be justification for retroactive effect of newly enacted tax rules: The measure concerns anti-abuse, corrects an obvious legislative error, or announces a new rule that would allow taxpayers to effectuate plans quickly before the new law could render such actions impossible.

6.3. Statutory Interpretation

The Netherlands Constitution provides that taxes may be levied only on the basis of a statute. It also provides that courts may not test the constitutionality of statutes, including tax statutes, but they may test rules enacted by local governments and administrative positions taken by the Revenue Service in interpretative decrees. Equal-treatment provisions laid down in the Netherlands Constitution provide only guiding principles, rather than enforceable rules, when applying statutory provisions. As a result, the non-discrimination provisions of the human rights conventions have had a much greater impact in The Netherlands than in countries where such guarantees are provided in national law.

Because statutory tax provisions may not always be clear and may need interpretation, a substantial body of case law has been developed over the years on the interpretation of statutory law in general and of tax statutes in particular. In general, four methods are applied, without any clear hierarchy among them. The 'grammatical' method emphasizes the literal meaning of statutory terms. The 'historical' method puts the focus on explanatory memoranda published with respect to the draft legislation and on the parliamentary memoranda and debates on the provision concerned. Under the 'systematic' method, particular attention is paid to the structure and cohesion of the statute involved, and finally the 'teleological' method considers the purpose and intent of the statute as decisive factors for its interpretation. However, as courts are free in tax matters to choose the means of interpretation, there is no prevailing order in the use of these four methods.

7. COURTS DEALING WITH TAX MATTERS

If a tax dispute is not solved upon review within the tax administration, the taxpayer may appeal his case to one of five District Courts (*Rechtbanken*). Their decisions can be appealed to one of the five regional Courts of Appeal (*Gerechtshoven*). Further appeal can be made to the Supreme Court (*Hoge Raad*). Each of these courts has one or more special chambers to hear tax cases. In important cases, one of the 'advocates general' (official advisers) to the Supreme Court will issue an advisory opinion ('conclusion') to the Court before it renders its judgment.

Strictly, court decisions are binding only for the case decided. In practice, they are given much greater weight, particularly when the court's phrasing of the decision is more general than the case requires. Nevertheless, in cases where the government strongly disagrees with a position taken by the Supreme Court (*Hoge Raad*), it may submit to the Court a second case on the same issue. If the Court maintains its position, the government will typically consider introducing in Parliament a statutory amendment to change the law.

Netherlands courts do not issue dissenting opinions. Partly as a consequence thereof, the opinions are often quite brief since they are restricted to what the court members (for important cases, three at the District Courts and the Courts of Appeal, and five at the Supreme Court) are able to agree on. Occasionally, the grounds given for a decision are phrased so tersely that the decision reads like a saying by the Delphic oracle, giving ample room for widely divergent interpretations as to its scope.

Since tax proceedings in court are not public, the decisions are anonymous when made public by the court. Curiously, the courts themselves select which cases to publish. While it appears that most cases that are not made public are of no interest except to the litigating parties, in some cases, decisions of wider significance may not be made public. There is a growing sentiment to give an outside authority the power to select for publication the court decisions in tax matters.

One final aspect concerns *prospective overruling*. In the 1990s the Supreme Court issued a few decisions in which it overruled its own earlier case law prospectively only – that is, it protected the taxpayer concerned who had relied on the existing case law and ruled that it would only apply its new viewpoint to the next suitable case.

8. TAX ADMINISTRATION

8.1. In General

Traditionally the Netherlands Revenue Service has been organized in a manner that reflects the categorization of taxes. There were separate departments for direct taxes and indirect taxes. Both departments consisted of divisions, each of which dealt with a distinct tax. As a result, in its contacts with the tax administration a company typically would have to deal with different officials for each of the taxes to which it is subject (company tax, wages tax, turnover tax and, occasionally, dividend tax and tax on legal transactions).

In the 1980s the tax administration underwent a complete overhaul to change it from a government-oriented into a taxpayer-oriented organization. Departments and their divisions merged and to the extent that they did not merge, each (corporate) taxpayer was assigned a coordinating official who generally acts as the single contact for the company. To the extent that questions arise that are outside the area of expertise of this official, he would discuss them with the officials in charge of the tax concerned.

While this reorganization has not changed the fact that taxpayers and Revenue Service have opposite interests, it has certainly improved the efficiency of taxpayers' dealings with the Revenue Service. In addition, it has improved the efficiency of the tax administration's operations, for example, by conducting combined rather than separate audits for company income tax, wages tax, and turnover tax.

A further step toward improving the relationship between the tax administration and taxpayers was the introduction in 2005 of 'horizontal supervision', particularly for business taxpayers. The tax administration aims at concluding covenants with large and medium-size enterprises that provide for replacing audits (conducted after the taxation years reviewed) by monitored agreements on the taxpayer's administrative processes. They further provide for mutual consultations and discussions on changes and developments of the enterprise's business activities. The overall aim is for greater certainty for the taxpayer regarding his current tax position and fewer conflicts regarding the tax consequences of events that already have taken place. The first experiences with this approach, where intrusive after-the-fact control is replaced by transparency and partnership, are encouraging.

8.2. Taxpayer Bill of Rights; Ombudsman

Along with the reorganization of the tax administration, attempts were made to further improve the position of the taxpayer vis-à-vis the Revenue Service. In 1991 the Ministry of Finance promulgated a 'Taxpayer' Bill of Rights', after the example of the United States. In The Netherlands, however, the importance of this Bill is more of a psychological nature than real because the Bill is mainly restricted to restating the taxpayers' statutory rights.

Of more substantive importance to taxpayers has been the extension of the scope of the government's actions in respect of which the 'Ombudsman', an independent authority with whom complaints against the government may be lodged, is entitled to receive complaints from citizens and companies or to undertake investigations on his own initiative. The Ombudsman is not permitted to investigate general government policy and individual cases where the taxpayer had access to regular administrative or judicial remedies. Despite these restrictions, he is called upon by taxpayers in a large number of cases, and in a substantial number of these cases, he has found that the government acted wholly or partly in an inappropriate manner. While the Ombudsman has no legal means to enforce his findings, by publishing his reports, in which he may suggest specific remedial action to the Revenue Service, he is usually successful in having the government comply with his recommendations.

8.3. Release of Government Information to Taxpayers

The 1991 Act on Public Access to Government Information has provided taxpayers and their advisers with an important instrument to obtain insight into tax administration policy in general and individual cases. Over the past decade a body of case law has emerged on the basis of decisions by the Council of State (*Raad van State*). This Council is the highest administrative court that rules on appeals by individuals and companies against refusals of the government to divulge information. The information may range from an audit report on individual taxpayers (under current case law, the entire report must be made available to the taxpayer except for those parts that contain information on sensitive issues such as audit strategies) to internal government studies and private rulings.

8.4. Advance Rulings

These rulings are typically issued on a request submitted by Netherlands- and foreign-controlled internationally operating companies. They have been issued for many decades. Until 2002, they comprised three categories, each category issued by a different tax office. Rulings on the determination of an arm's-length price in individual transactions were issued by the taxpayer's local tax office. If a request for a ruling concerned the taxation of large direct investment projects of (prospective) foreign investors, the Rotterdam Tax Office for New Foreign Investment in The Netherlands was authorized to issue an advance ruling. Finally, when the ruling request concerns the determination of the income of a Netherlands member of an internationally operating company, a Rotterdam-based team of tax inspectors (the 'Ruling Team') is in charge of these rulings. Most of the rulings issued by this team are of one of eight standard types; 'cost plus' rulings and rulings for holding companies, finance companies, and royalty companies are the most common types.

In the spring of 2002, as a result of the enquiries of the EU and OECD into unfair tax practices, the procedures under which the Netherlands Revenue Service issues rulings were revised, with a further revision and update in 2004. First, 'advance pricing agreements' (APAs) were introduced. These are preferably negotiated on a bilateral basis (i.e., involving the revenue authorities of the other country concerned as well) and issued typically for a four- or five-year period. Second, 'advance tax rulings' (ATRs) are made available with regard to the following three determinations: (1) the application of the participation exemption to intermediate and top holding companies where none of the subsidiaries carries on business in The Netherlands; (2) tax treatment of hybrid financial instruments and of hybrid entities; and (3) the issue of whether in given cases a non-resident company has a permanent establishment in The Netherlands. Further, rules have been issued regarding the substance of Netherlands-resident 'financial service companies', transfer pricing (including the institution of Coordination Group

Transfer Pricing), and the principle of good faith that should govern the relationship between treaty partners.

8.5. Assessment, Administrative Appeal, and Appeal to Courts

For income tax (individuals) and company tax (companies), the tax inspector issues a tax assessment after having reviewed the tax return filed by the taxpayer and received that taxpayer's answers to questions that the inspector had asked on the basis of his review. With respect to corporate taxpayers, the questions may pertain to foreign subsidiaries of the taxpayer and to its foreign parent company. Failure to provide adequate answers to such questions may result in the burden of proof shifting from the tax inspector, where it usually rests, to the taxpayer.

For business taxpayers, the tax administration is undertaking efforts to have companies sign up for 'horizontal supervision' covenants (see above, under section 8.1). Under the traditional approach, the inspector will order a field audit every few years before issuing the assessment. The 200 largest companies are subject to a field audit every year. To arrive at an agreement on the facts of the case, the tax inspector may conclude with the taxpayer a contract (*compromis*) in which these facts are determined. If the tax inspector, after he has issued an assessment, learns facts that he did not know (and could not reasonably have known) at the time of issuing the assessment and that increase the taxpayer's tax liability, the tax inspector will issue a supplemental assessment (increased with a penalty if the taxpayer was at fault). Both the original assessment and the supplemental assessment may be appealed by the taxpayer administratively. This appeal is usually decided upon by the same tax inspector who issued the assessment.

The wages tax and value added tax (companies and individuals) and the dividend tax (companies) are self-assessment taxes. If the tax inspector disagrees with the self-assessed amount, he may issue a supplemental assessment (with or without a penalty). This assessment is also subject to administrative appeal by the taxpayer.

The decision made by the tax inspector upon the appeal lodged against an assessment may be appealed to the one of five District Courts (*Rechtbanken*). The taxpayer does not need legal representation for making such an appeal. Cases are heard in this Court by one- or three-member panels of judges. These judges may have a background in administrative law or have typically been recruited from the circles of senior government tax officials, senior tax advisers, and tax academics. In addition, prominent tax advisers and tax professors may serve as part-time deputy judges. A decision by a District Court may be appealed to one of the five Courts of Appeal, which will review both the finding of the facts and the application of the law. Further appeal can be made to the Supreme Court (*Hoge Raad*). In addition to a Civil Chamber and a Criminal Chamber, the Supreme Court has two Tax Chambers (reflecting the prominent role of tax law in The Netherlands judicial process), each consisting of five justices, two or three of whom typically have a tax background. The Supreme Court has no right to refuse to hear a case, but will consider only questions of law. For appeal to the Supreme Court in tax matters, the taxpayer again does not need legal representation. On complex issues presented to the Supreme Court, one of the five independent Advocates General of the Tax Chambers of the Court may issue in advance an Advisory Opinion to the Court. These opinions usually provide excellent analyses of the law at issue. The number of tax appeals, which has been rising over the last two decades, seems to have stabilized now at an annual number of about 13,000 per year for appeals to any of the five Courts of Appeal, and at about 750 per year for further appeals to the Supreme Court.

9. GENERAL PRINCIPLES

9.1. Relationship between Tax and Financial Accounting

In The Netherlands the rules on tax accounting and on commercial (financial) accounting diverge substantially. Whereas the aim of commercial accounting (including the IFRS rules that since 2005 have been compulsory in the EU for quoted companies) is to provide the information necessary to judge the financial policy and operations of a business undertaking, the purpose of tax accounting is to determine the income of a business operation as the basis for paying tax to the government. While the two goals partially overlap, important differences concern the impact of inflation and the degree of discretion in making accounting choices. Tax accounting rules are generally 'nominalist' – that is, require amounts to be taken into account for their nominal value without loss of value as a result of inflation being taken into account, whereas commercial accounting rules are 'substantialist' and take into account the effects of inflation. Further, with regard to valuation of assets and liabilities, tax rules are generally rather strict and conservative. And finally, differences between tax and commercial accounting rules arise where the tax instrument is employed to pursue economic, social, and cultural purposes.

9.2. Respect under Tax Law for the Civil (Private) Law Form of Contracts

Netherlands tax law employs many terms and concepts that are based on civil (private) law. The question may arise as to whether for tax law purposes these terms and concepts necessarily have the same meaning as they have under civil law. Under current doctrine, civil law terms and concepts used in tax law are generally to be understood in their civil law meaning. However, the aim and purpose of a given tax law provision may justify giving to a particular term or expression a meaning that differs from its general civil law meaning.

9.3. ANTI-AVOIDANCE DOCTRINES AND RULES

The application of tax law rules generally involves three steps. First, it must be ascertained whether what is presented as a fact is indeed a fact. Next, it has to be determined whether the (truly existing) facts are to be recognized for tax purposes. Finally, the law must be applied to these ascertained and recognized facts. At either of the last two levels, the issue of substance over form may arise.

For tax law purposes, facts need not be accepted by the tax authorities as they are presented by the taxpayer. Something presented as a fact may not be a fact. For example, if a hobby artist donates a worthless painting to a local museum to obtain a charitable deduction, the 'gift' may be found to be non-existent because what was given had no value (this is called 'simulation' in that non-existent facts are suggested to be true facts). To the extent that facts – or legal situations – truly exist, the next step is to examine whether they should be recognized for tax purposes or whether, on the basis of their substance, they should be re-characterized. For example, illegal income (for instance, income obtained through embezzlement) is subject to tax despite the fact that it does not constitute true income because the recipient may be under the legal obligation to return to the owner the funds obtained (when the funds are returned, a deduction ['negative income'] will be allowed at the time of the payment). Other examples include rental income in cases in which the lessee is related to the lessor and pays an unrealistically low rent and income from a void contract that nevertheless has been implemented.

After the facts have been accepted for tax purposes, the courts may apply the (non-statutory) *fraus legis* doctrine to attach to facts tax consequences different from the consequences that these facts normally entail. While a taxpayer is generally free to organize his affairs in a manner that is most advantageous to him from a tax point of view, there are limits to this freedom. One such limit is reached when the taxpayer (alone, or in collaboration with other taxpayers) is able to lower the amount of his tax liability entirely at his own discretion (e.g., if a parent company pays tax-deductible interest to its subsidiary company on a loan obtained from the subsidiary, and the subsidiary subsequently returns to the parent as a tax-free intercorporate dividend the amount it received from the parent as interest).

To apply the *fraus legis* doctrine, the following requirements must be met: (1) the extraordinary – non-taxable – situation created by the taxpayer is in its non-tax effects identical or similar to the more ordinary – taxable – situation; (2) tax avoidance is the controlling ('primary') motive of the taxpayer; and (3) the tax effects of the situation created by the taxpayer conflict with the purpose and intent of the tax law.

While before 1970 *fraus legis* (and a related statutory substance-over-form rule) were rarely applied, since the 1980s cases involving the application of this doctrine has substantially increased at both the lower court and the Supreme Court levels. Many of these cases involve the erosion of the corporate tax base through interest payments and, with respect to individuals, the taxation of income derived from closely held companies (see section 4.2, above). So far, the courts have restricted the application of this doctrine to national law and have refused to extend it to the application of tax treaties. Consequently, non-resident taxpayers (where individuals, often former Netherlands residents) in particular have been able to shield their transactions from the application of *fraus legis*.

10. SOURCES OF TAX LAW

The official source of statutory tax law is the Official Gazette (*Staatsblad*) where all statutes (and amendments) are published. The amended texts are published commercially by various commercial publishers in both looseleaf and bound editions. Tax decisions by the District Courts, the Courts of Appeal, and the Supreme Court (including the Advisory Opinions of the Supreme Court's advocates general) are made public officially only on the Internet (<www.rechtspraak.nl>) and by commercial publishers in print.

Annotations by scholars to selected tax decisions of the Supreme Court are published in the (prestigious) BNB, and also in a range of weekly and monthly Netherlands tax publications.

Citations of tax statutes, their parliamentary history, and other legislative instruments are traditionally made to the page numbers of the official printed sources. With the reduced use of these sources in practice and their replacement by digital sources, the old system of citations becomes increasingly less functional but has not yet been replaced by a uniform digital source coding system.

10.1. Primary Source Materials (all in Dutch)

- Collection of texts of tax laws: paperbacks (by Kluwer)
- Case law reporters (some decisions annotated):
  - BNB
  - Vakstudie-Nieuws
  - FED Fiscaal Weekblad
  - Nederlands Tijdschrift voor Fiscaal Recht

10.2. Secondary Source Materials: Printed

English

- K. van Raad, Tax Management – Foreign Income Portfolios, 973-4th, *Business Operations in The Netherlands* (Tax Management, 2009) – available both in print form and online
- The following periodicals frequently contain English language articles on Dutch tax law: *Intertax* (Wolters Kluwer), *EC Tax Review* (Wolters Kluwer), *Bulletin for International Taxation* (International Bureau for

Fiscal Documentation), *European Taxation* (International Bureau of Fiscal Documentation), and *Tax Notes International* (Tax Analysts);all are available both in print form and online.

Dutch
Encyclopaedic works covering the entire area of Dutch domestic and international tax law:

- *Fiscale Encyclopedie De Vakstudie*: 13 sets of looseleaf books (Wolters Kluwer) – all available both in print form and online.
- *Cursus Belastingrecht*: set of looseleaf books (Wolters Kluwer) – all available both in print form and on CD-ROM.
- *Nederlandse Documentatie Fiscaal Recht*: 9 sets of looseleaf books (SDU)– all available both in print form and online.

10.3. Digital Materials

Website – Dutch government
<www.overheid.nl>
Contains links to all public services, as well as full-text laws, bills, and other official documents. Some information and links in English: <www.overheid.nl/english/>

Website – Dutch courts
<www.rechtspraak.nl>
Selection of Dutch judgments. Some general information in English: <www.rechtspraak.nl/information+in+english>

Website – Dutch tax authorities
<www.belastingdienst.nl/>
Information for individuals, businesses, and tax consultants regarding tax returns, wage tax and VAT, import and export duties, etc. Some information in English: <www.belastingdienst.nl/english/>

Dutch Ministry of Finance
<www.minfin.nl/>
Information on budget, taxes, financial management, financial markets, international cooperation, state participations, etc. Some information in English: <www.minfin.nl/english>

PricewaterhouseCoopers news in English:
<www.nl.pwc.com/extweb/bn/TaxNews.nsf/indexuk.html?ReadForm>

KPMG Meijburg news in English: <www.meijburg.com/news>

Database

For English-language articles and books on Dutch tax law, the (freely accessible) database of the Library of the Amsterdam-based International Bureau for Fiscal Documentation (<www.ibfd.org>) offers a wealth of information: <http://ibfdlib.ibfd.nl/uhtbin/cgisirsi/ifB8aFP2op/IBFD/185280005/60/502/X>. An advanced search (*country:* Netherland; *language:* English) produced in total 1,642 items – for 2009 (on 15 June 2009) 20 items, for 2008 66 items, and for 2007 89 items.

Sweden

Prof. Peter Melz

1. HISTORY

The income tax originated as a schedular income tax system. The first income tax law was enacted in 1810, influenced by English liberal thought. However, it was repealed in 1812, and instead a schedular system with eight income sources was introduced. During the nineteenth and the beginning of the twentieth century, the development toward a modern income tax went on with important reforms in 1860, 1902, 1910, and 1928. At the same time, the income tax became more important as government revenue from duties and excises decreased.

As a result of successive reforms, schedular differences have decreased. The income concept was broadened by successive inclusions of capital gains. In 1985 the municipal income taxation of corporations was abolished. Since then, corporations pay national income tax only, which has led to simplification because there is no cause for national transfer pricing problems. In 1991 a major reform was enacted. The sources were reduced to three for individuals: income from employment, business income, and income from capital. In principle, however, the Swedish system is still a schedular system, which means that there is no general definition of income. The definitions of income with respect to the different sources, however, are quite broad.

The source principle nonetheless still has some importance: If a specific potential income item cannot be included as income in any of the three sources, it will be excluded from the income tax base. In general, it can be said that taxable income consists of all remuneration for performance of services, yield and gains on capital, and income from a business. After 1991 further important reforms have considered the taxation of proprietorships to equalize such taxation with the taxation of corporations and restructuring of businesses.

2. CONSTITUTIONAL ISSUES

Sweden has a written constitution. There is not one, but four, different basic laws. Constitutional rules of importance for taxation are contained in *Regeringsformen* (the Instrument of Government).

Long before written constitutions, it was accepted as a basic rule that taxes should be levied only with the consent of the people. In the Constitution, it is likewise stated that taxes should be levied in accordance with law and tax rules should be enacted by Parliament (*Riksdagen*).[1] In accordance with this rule, it is not possible for Parliament to delegate legislative power to government or government authorities. Delegated rules may only prescribe how to comply with the statutory rules, and no new rules may be implemented through them. In reality, regulations have great impact in some areas, especially with respect to the procedure to establish assessed values on real estate. This is such a technical field that the complete procedure cannot be prescribed in the statutory rules and must therefore be prescribed in regulations.

Another constitutional rule with importance for taxation is that retroactive legislation is not allowed for penal law and tax law. This prohibition is relevant only for legislation that increases taxation, which is normally the case. Anti-avoidance legislation often takes effect immediately after the intention to pass such legislation becomes public, as the Constitution allows legislation to take effect on the day the government informs Parliament that a bill will be sent to Parliament later.

Constitutional control of legislation is limited. The Constitution states that courts should set statutory rules aside only if they are obviously in contradiction of the Constitution.

Other rules in the Constitution that may act as safeguards for taxpayers are fairly vague. Apart from the prohibition against retroactive legislation, there is a prohibition on expropriation without compensation and a rule that legislation should be applied in a uniform way.

It has become more common for taxpayers to appeal to the European Court of Justice (Strasbourg). So far the tax cases have concerned questions of procedural remedies, etc., and not the substance of tax rules.

3. TAX RATES

The corporate tax rate is simply a flat rate, 26.3% of taxable income. There is a system of double taxation of corporations, and dividends are, with a few exceptions, taxable to individuals, as discussed below.

A number of income taxes and social security contributions can be levied on income of individuals. For income from capital a flat rate of 30% is levied; this is a

1. The Instrument of Government (Ch. 8 s. 2).

national tax only. For earned income (income of employment and business), taxation is progressive. After a basic allowance (see below) local income taxes (county and municipality) are levied on income. The rates are decided by the local governments and are on average 31.52%.[2]

For income above a certain prescribed amount, national income tax will also be levied. For income (after the basic allowance) above 328,800 SEK, the national income tax is 20% and rises to 25% above 495,100 SEK. Rate brackets are adjusted for inflation. In total the tax rate on earned income starts at about 31% and rises to a maximum of about 56%. Further, it has to be taken into consideration that, to a large extent, payments of social security contributions do not result in social benefits.[3] These payments should therefore be considered to be taxes. The combined rate is a bit complicated to calculate, but is about 67% for the top income tax bracket.[4] Social security contributions are paid by employers, 32.42% of income from employment of employees, and 30.71% for self-employed persons. The base for social security contributions is similar to the income tax base for earned income.

Allowances from taxable income are calculated in a complicated way.[5] The basic allowance first increases and then decreases. It starts with an amount equal to the taxable income and then increases to a maximum of 31,600 SEK at incomes between 111,400 and 128,200 SEK. The allowance then decreases to a minimum of 12,100 SEK for incomes above 322,300 SEK.

In 2007 a special in-work tax credit was introduced aimed at stimulating participation in the workforce.[6] It is calculated based on income from employment (salaries, etc., but not pensions). The calculation is very complicated. The maximum credit is 18,340 SEK (for retired persons with salaries, etc., the credit is 30,000 SEK).

4. COMPOSITION OF THE FISCAL SYSTEM

Taxes finance the central government and local governments (municipalities and county councils). In 2007 tax revenues for the general government sector amounted to about 48% of GDP. Around half of the GDP is thus distributed to the government sector. However, nearly half of government expenditures consists of transfers back to individuals and enterprises.

---

2. Rates, etc., are for 2008.
3. It has been estimated that on average about 60% of the contributions could be regarded as taxes. Due to limitations in benefits, this part will, however, be 100% for a high-income earner.
4. For an employee, the marginal rate could be calculated in the following way: An employer pays 100 SEK in salary to an employee and 33 SEK in resulting social security contributions. The employee pays 56 SEK in income taxes with respect to the salary. A total of 89 out of 133 SEK (67%) is paid in taxes and contributions to the government.
5. Income Tax Act (ITA), Ch. 63.
6. ITA, Ch. 65 s. 9a–9d.

In the mid-1990s the government budget had large deficits (e.g., in 1993 net borrowing was 11.9% of GDP). In recent years the budget has either been balanced or had an increasing surplus (in 2008, 2.5% for the consolidated public sectors). Due to the 2008 downturn in the economy, the surplus is decreasing. Parliament has implemented a budget expenditure ceiling that aims to run on average a surplus of 2% of GDP for a business cycle. Government debt was 38% of GDP in 2008.

The Swedish level of taxation is probably the highest in the world. This is partially the result of the design of the Swedish tax system, which in some aspects results in higher gross taxation than in other systems. An example is the fact that Sweden taxes transfers, while in other countries transfers are often not taxed or are even designed as tax deductions rather than open subsidies and grants. Individual social security charges outside the tax system are also common. A government committee (SOU 2002:47) made recalculations for such factors and also made adjustments for deficits and surpluses for a number of countries. The Swedish tax quota for 2000 decreased from 53% to about 44% of GDP, but remained the highest among the countries compared. The comparable figures before and after adjustments for selected countries were: US (29%–37%), UK (37%–37%), Germany (38%–36%), Japan (27%–35%), and Australia (32%–35%).[7]

4.1. Types of Taxes

In the beginning of the twentieth century indirect taxes on trade, consumption, etc., were the most important type of taxes. The trend since then has been the increasing importance of income taxation. However, in recent decades, compelled by the need to increase tax revenues, the relative importance of income taxes has declined, and social security contributions have increased substantially. In the tax reform of 1991, the income tax was further decreased, and the VAT was increased through broadening of the tax base.

Almost every type of tax is used in Sweden: municipal and national income tax on individuals, national income tax on corporations, net wealth tax, inheritance and gift tax, value added tax, taxes on alcohol and tobacco, petrol (and energy in general) tax, sales (stamp) tax on real estate, and real estate tax. In 2006 total tax revenues[8] amounted to 1,422 billion SEK; some of the components were: income taxes 480 billion, social security contributions 336 billion, and VAT 266 billion. The net wealth tax and inheritance taxes have been repealed as of 2006–2007. They raised combined approximately 6 billion.

The national income tax forms a small part of national government revenues, but the combined income tax for national and local governments is still the largest source of tax revenue. Furthermore, social security contributions function to a large extent as an income tax, since they are levied on the same base as the income tax and normally ensure no individually earmarked future benefits.

7. SOU, 2002:47 at 104.
8. All social security contributions included.

Most taxes are levied and constructed only to pursue fiscal goals. However, at least officially, it is considered that the income tax should be used to a certain extent to redistribute income. Certain sales taxes, such as tobacco and alcohol taxes, as well as taxes on energy consumption, are intended to influence consumption behaviour. The new government (conservative-liberal) has made more use of the tax system for non-fiscal goals. In 2007 a tax credit for domestic costs was introduced; the credit is 50% of the costs with a cap of 50,000 SEK per year. Domestic costs include washing, cleaning, gardening, child care at home, etc. In 2008, as a response to the recession, the number of services was enlarged to include construction, maintenance, etc., in owner-occupied houses and flats. The maximum tax credit remains, however, at 50,000 SEK. The credit is a deviation from strict neutrality in the income tax system, but the argument is that market imperfections will be diminished by the credit.

5. BASIC STRUCTURE OF THE TAX SYSTEM

In Sweden, income taxes are paid by individuals to the national government and to two levels of local government (county councils and municipalities). Corporations pay income tax only to the national government. Taxable income for national and municipal purposes is calculated according to the Income Tax Law (*Inkomstskattelagen*, IL).

5.1. Individuals

For individuals income is calculated with respect to three sources: income from employment, business income, and income from capital. The first two sources consist principally of income derived from work, as an employee or as a self-employed person. The source of income from business comprises all forms of independent business (even, for example, agriculture and commercial real estate).

5.1.1. Earned Income

Income from employment and business (earned income) are added together, and the combined income is subject to municipal and national income tax. Municipal tax rates vary according to locality and average around 31%. National income tax is levied only above a prescribed limit (see above section 3).

Employment income is the major source of income. It includes salaries, compensation for various dependent services, pensions, etc. For reasons of simplification, expenses, apart from the most essential categories, are not deductible unless they exceed 5,000 SEK.

The calculation of business income is more complicated. The same rules, with minor exceptions, apply for businesses carried out by individuals and entities. Some of the rules are described below.

If the calculation of income from employment or business results in a loss, as a rule, the loss is not deductible from income from another source. However, such a loss can be carried forward indefinitely and deducted against income from the same source in future years.

5.1.2. Income from Capital

With respect to income from capital, a national income tax is levied at a flat rate of 30% and no municipal tax is imposed. This means that there is often a major difference between the tax rate on capital income on the one hand and the tax rate on employment and business income on the other hand, which makes characterization an important issue. In addition, measures are necessary to prevent taxpayers from converting income from business or services to capital.

The lower tax rate on capital income is intended as a standardized compensation for the inflationary losses incurred in connection with capital income. In the preparatory works for the tax reform, the derivation of the tax rate is shown to be based on a rather simple calculation: a real interest rate of 3% and an inflation rate of 4% were anticipated. Thirty percent tax on a nominal interest rate of 7% means a tax – 2.1% – which is 70% of the real interest rate. This rate is roughly the same – actually some percentage points above – as the rate for a high-income earner on earned income, if social security contribution fees are included.

The inflation rate fell considerably after the tax reform and now conforms to the average European level. The result is that the real tax rate on capital has normally been below what was expected.

Another reason for the choice of the tax rate on capital income was the need to maintain equivalent rates for income from capital, corporations' income, and the municipal tax rate in order to counter tax planning. Because there also is no basic allowance for income from capital and the tax rate is flat, there is no incentive to split income among family members. Further, for most types of assets the full nominal amount of capital gains is taxable at realization, which reduces any incentive to transform capital income into capital gains.

Capital income includes current capital income – interest, dividends, etc. – and capital gains on realization of all types of assets and foreign debt (exchange gains). All types of capital income are taxable in full. As mentioned above, this is motivated by reasons of neutrality and equity and to decrease incentives for tax planning. Some exceptions exist for personal property. Thus, only two-thirds of a capital gain from the sale of personal dwellings is taxable. For personal property, only capital gains above 50,000 SEK per year are taxable. Further taxation of capital gains on personal dwellings can be deferred if a new personal dwelling is bought.

All costs of acquiring capital income are deductible in full. All interest costs are deductible irrespective of the use of the capital. The stated reason is neutrality between persons who are able to invest or consume out of equity capital and persons who need to borrow. Income from capital is taxable at a flat rate of 30%. For losses from capital, 30% of the loss up to 100,000 SEK and 21% of the loss exceeding this amount is credited against national and local income tax due on earned income and real estate tax. The latter reduction of the tax credit was implemented to somewhat deter investments with front-loaded costs and deferred revenues.

The taxation of capital income also has involved a complicated relation to the real estate tax. The real estate tax is levied on most kinds of real estate. In the Swedish income tax system a tax has historically been levied on imputed income from owner-occupied dwellings. It was considered to be a tax on imputed capital income from these investments and could thus be said to form part of the system of capital income taxation. In the tax reform of 1991, the tax on imputed income was taken out of the income tax system and levied as a real estate tax. The tax rate is 1% of an assessed value, which should be 75% of the market value. In 2007 this taxation was dramatically reduced to a municipal real estate fee, which is capped at 6,000 SEK.[9] The rate of the fee remains 1% on assessed values. Despite the considerable reduction of taxation, the deduction for interest cost was not changed. According to general rules deductions are allowed for all personal interest expense incurred in connection with income from capital.

A net wealth tax was previously levied at 1.5% of net wealth above 1.5 million SEK. The tax base contained in principle most types of assets, but wide exemptions have been granted, primarily to capital invested in businesses directly or through close corporations. In 2007 the net wealth tax was abolished. The reasons stated were that the tax had a negative impact on business investment and that it was applied unfairly.

5.2. Corporations

For corporations, all income is derived from one source, namely, income from business. A national income tax at a flat rate of 26.3% is levied on the income. The effective tax rate is lower because up to 25% of the income can be set aside in a tax allocation reserve (*periodiseringsfond*) for six years. The intention is that, apart from that reserve, there should be no more possibilities for special tax reserves, as had been the case under prior law, so that the tax is on the effective income of the corporation.

Income distributed from a corporation as dividends is taxed to individuals as income from capital at a tax rate of 30%. This means a combined tax rate of about $26.3\% + 0.737 \times 30\% = 48.41\%$ on the income earned by a corporation and distributed to its shareholders. In order to place taxation of dividends somewhat on par with taxation of interest, a lower tax rate applies to dividends distributed from corporations whose shares are not quoted on an exchange. The tax rate is 25% and the combined tax on corporate and dividend income, calculated as shown above, is 44.72%.

As stated above, the taxation of income from employment and business for individuals is considerably higher than the taxation of distributed income from corporations. This could create an incentive to transform earned income to capital income (dividends) by decreasing salaries from corporations in order to increase

---

9. Municipal Real Estate Fee Act.

dividends, for example. When the dual system was introduced in the 1991 tax reform, some special provisions were introduced to counter this effect. The aim of these rules[10] is to ensure that income derived by shareholders from their corporations should be taxed at the rate applicable to earned income even if the income is distributed as dividends.

The rules apply to shares in close corporations, which are defined as corporations controlled by four or fewer persons (including close relatives), if owned by a person who is working to a considerable extent in the corporation. When the rules apply, dividends above a certain level (see below) and capital gains will be taxed as employment income for individuals. This results in roughly the same tax burden as for salaries paid by the corporation (if dividends are paid, corporation tax is roughly equivalent to social security contributions payable by corporations that pay salaries). The dividing level is calculated as a normal yield on the shareholders' investment. As a rule, the investment is calculated as the cost price for the shares; the yield rate is calculated as a long-term market interest rate plus nine percentage points. Dividends above this level are taxed as employment income; dividends below this level are considered to be the ordinary return on invested capital and are taxed as capital income, but with a special favourable tax rate of 20%. The overall result of this special regime is normally that most shareholders can avoid taxation of dividends as employment income. The yield rate that establishes the amount of capital income is high. More important for many shareholders is that capital income includes not only income below the yield rate, but also 20% of the salaries in the corporation. This could be a large amount and thus, for many corporations, no dividends are in fact taxed as employment income.

It is an important neutrality aim that differences in the form of business should not result in differences in taxation. The rules for taxation of individuals carrying out business have expressly been shaped to be similar to the rules for the taxation of corporations. However, the taxation of partnerships deviates in several aspects, mainly in order to prevent tax planning; these rules are not covered here. Income from business carried on directly by an individual is subject to social security contributions, municipal income tax, and (if the combined income for the individual is high enough) state income tax. The combined effect could result in a 66% marginal tax rate in the highest income tax bracket (the tax burden on an individual partner's share in a partnership's income is the same). The effective tax rate for distributions from close corporations is almost the same when dividends are taxed as earned income, according to the special rules described in the previous paragraph. Thus, the burden of taxation is almost the same in all three cases.

The level of taxation for income retained in a corporation is 26.3%. Until 1995, income in individual businesses was fully taxed irrespective of whether the income was retained in the business or used for private purposes. The present rules mitigate this hardship by allowing a deduction from income for the part retained in the business. The accumulated amount of such deductions may not exceed the net value (assets minus debts at cost) of the business, which means that retained

10. TIA Chs 56 and 57.

income is supposed to increase the net value of the business. A tax of 26.3% is paid on the deducted amount, which makes the tax equal to the tax on undistributed income in corporations. A decrease in net value of the business is considered to be a distribution of income, which triggers normal income taxation (less tax already paid of 26.3%). The accumulated amount of the deduction is referred to as the expansion reserve (*expansionsfond*).

6. TAX LEGISLATION

6.1. Legislative Process

Tax legislation is normally prepared by work in government committees. A committee can either be parliamentary (members of the committee are MPs) or an expert committee. Minor amendments or urgent legislation – for example, anti-avoidance legislation – can be prepared directly in the Ministry of Finance.

Committee Reports (*Statens Offentliga Utredningar*, SOU) are referred for consideration to central government agencies, special interest groups, courts, universities, or other bodies whose activities may be affected by the proposals. The government then presents a government bill (proposition) to the Parliament (*Riksdagen*). For important proposals, the bill is preceded by a draft that is examined by three Supreme Court judges in the Law Council (*lagrådet*). Amendments in Parliament are rare, probably because the government usually has a controlling majority in Parliament. The bill is scrutinized in Parliament by a Standing Committee for Taxation (*skatteutskottet*).

Government committees usually deal with rather comprehensive questions and could be active for years. The review process normally takes at least half a year and the remaining process in the Ministry and Parliament normally another half to a full year. Not all proposals by committees result in immediate legislation. Some are aborted and some form the basis for further investigations in the Ministry by a new committee.

6.2. Statutory Style

The major changes in the Swedish tax law have been enacted through statutory rules. The statutes have been written in a rather broad way and therefore case law has had the possibility to create law in some important cases. In recent years, especially during the tax reform of 1991, the tendency has been to codify case law into statutory rules.

The Swedish tax codes in the 1930s and the following decades were written in a special way. There was first a rather short and principal statutory rule (paragraph); this rule was then explained more in detail in a regulation (which also was a statutory rule). In the beginning, the regulations were not intended to add any new content, but only to explain, and sometimes even contained arithmetical examples.

In 1999, the old municipal and national income tax laws were replaced with a new comprehensive tax law, the Income Tax Act (*Inkomstskattelagen*). It has a modern structure in line with the standard for laws in Sweden and consists of sixty-six chapters. Each chapter is divided into several sections and sub-sections with headings under which paragraphs are organized.

The statutory rules are rather detailed. However, the aim in recent decades has been to avoid complicated rules – and thereby complicated statutes. This is, however, more a question of the structure of the system (e.g., avoiding different treatment of different kinds of income) than a question of statutory style.

A more general tendency in statutory style in recent decades has been to avoid enumerations and instead to give a more abstract definition. This is intended to give the courts the possibility of dealing with new phenomena (e.g., financial instruments) and placing them in the proper categories. On the other hand, a lot of new mechanical rules have been introduced recently and, because of their mechanical character, the statutory rules regulating them are rather comprehensive. The need for greater clarity in statutes that impose tax has been stressed more in the past decade. This is partly a necessary reaction to a more literal interpretation by the courts and partly a result of increased respect for constitutional and other aspects; increased predictability for taxpayers, however, is a lesser factor in this development. Thus, one can see a tendency for writing statutes more comprehensively and not expecting the courts to remedy shortcomings.

6.3. Statutory Interpretation

There is no uniform system of statutory interpretation in Sweden. In the Supreme Administrative Court, which handles tax cases and other administrative law matters, one method has been in general use, with few exceptions, and that is to give great value to opinions expressed in preparatory works to the legislation, primarily the government bill to Parliament. In some recent cases, however, a new tendency can be seen. There is now more willingness to ignore the preparatory opinions when they are not clearly reflected in the statutes. There is also a tendency to literal interpretation, or at least great respect for the literal meaning of the statutes. Among academics, there are various opinions regarding the degree of authority that should be given to the preparatory works. In cases where the preparatory works and the statutory rule are clearly contradictory, there is a consensus that the statute cannot be set aside. Legislation based on EC directives lacks the traditional preparatory work and thus that source of interpretation is lacking.

7. COURTS DEALING WITH TAX MATTERS

Decisions by the tax authority may be reviewed by the authority itself in order to amend the decision. If the matter is not settled, the taxpayer may appeal to the county administrative court (*länsrätt*) and then again to the administrative court of appeal (*kammarrätten*).

If the case is of importance to the interpretation of the law, the Supreme Administrative Court (*Regeringsrätten*) may grant leave to appeal and try the case.

These courts are not specialized tax courts, but deal with all types of administrative cases (cases where the national or local government is one of the parties). However, until the 1990s tax cases were a clear majority of the cases heard by the courts; now, fewer of the cases are tax cases.

A special board gives advance rulings for important transactions. The board consists of two or three judges (active or former) and five or six laymen (professors, tax officials, tax lawyers, etc.). Taxpayers can apply for a ruling with respect to planned transactions. The government, acting through the Tax Agency, may also apply for a ruling, but only for a pending case. Rulings can be appealed to the Supreme Administrative Court without the need for leave to be granted.

In principle, judgments have the same form in all courts. Facts and reasons forming the basis for the decision are presented. The court is normally presented with a proposal for judgment drafted by one of the judges or a special rapporteur. The tradition is not to write individual decisions, but to adjust the proposal to a joint decision. Of course dissenting opinions may be presented and will be attached to the judgment.

Judgments in the Supreme Administrative Court are more elaborate, due to better resources, access to the analysis in the judgments by the lower courts, and their role as precedents.

Cases decided by the Supreme Administrative Court are deemed to be binding on lower courts. There is no statutory rule to this effect, but precedents are, with rare exceptions, followed. The Supreme Administrative Court seldom changes a precedent, and if it does, the change must be made in a plenary session.

8. TAX ADMINISTRATION

The tax administration consists of the Tax Agency *(Skatteverket)* with regional offices. Formerly there were different regional authorities, but they were merged into one single national tax authority. Tax authorities are responsible for providing information to taxpayers, checking tax returns, etc. The Tax Agency issues Tax Advice *(allmänna råd)*. This advice is not binding. In the advice, the state of law is described based on statutory rules, case law, and preparatory works.

For most taxpayers, the tax return is simplified. Statements of earnings, interest, etc., are supplied by third parties – for example, employers or banks. The Securities Registry Centre provides statements of dividends paid out by the Centre. These amounts are pre-filled in the tax returns. Tax returns are checked annually. In reality, many returns are not actively checked due to lack of resources.

The number of tax field audits has been reduced from more than 18,000 per year in the late 1980s to about 6,500 in 2007. This is partly due to the fact that they increasingly target larger corporations and more difficult cases. The tax claims generated by the field audits were 11 billion SEK in 2007.

The bulk of tax revenues is collected by withholding and prepayments. Taxes on income from business are pre-assessed in twelve instalments per year. Payments are registered in a special tax account for each taxpayer, and it is therefore possible to deviate from the predefined dates for instalments. However, a deficit on the account will result in claims and interest charges.

If the final tax due exceeds the mandatory prepayments, further prepayments can be made to avoid interest charges.

It is a general principle in Sweden that documents submitted to or from government agencies are accessible to the public. Exceptions to this rule are allowed only in accordance with what is stated in the Official Secrets Act. The content of tax returns is secret, but the amount of total taxable income and net wealth are made public. Proceedings and submissions in court cases about taxation are secret, but the judgments are public.

A surcharge is levied if the taxpayer has provided incorrect information in his tax return. The surcharge is normally 40% of the understated tax paid. The surcharge is decreased to 20% in cases where the tax officials could have corrected the fault by information from mandatory statements of earnings, the previous years' tax returns, etc. The surcharge may not be levied in cases where the incorrect information is deemed to be excusable. These rules have for the most part been strictly applied by the courts, and the surcharge may often be considered to be disproportionately harsh. This has led to widespread criticism, and a judgment concerning the Swedish surcharge was issued by the European Court of Justice. The system in general was not considered to be incompatible with the Human Rights Charter but certain rules were criticized and, as a consequence, new rules were enacted effective in 2004. The exemptions from surcharge were widened and a possibility for partial exemption was introduced. The old system presents courts only with the alternatives of full exemption or no exemption, which probably has deterred them from giving exemptions. In 2007 tax surcharges were decided to a total amount of 1.4 billion SEK.

The administrative surcharges are the most important penalties for misconduct. Criminal sanctions can be applied for more serious wrongdoing under the Tax Crime Code. The punishment for tax fraud is imprisonment for up to two years, and for serious tax fraud, up to six years.

9. GENERAL PRINCIPLES

9.1. Relationship between Tax and Financial Accounting

Taxable business income is computed according to generally accepted accounting standards. The accounting profits form the basis for taxation. Corporations must follow the Annual Accounts Act of 1995 and the Book-keeping Act of 1999 in preparing their financial statements. The Annual Accounts Act is based on the EC Fourth, Seventh, and Eleventh Directives. Credit institutions, brokers and dealers in securities, or insurance companies are covered by two special accounting acts. Accounting standards are established primarily by the Swedish Accounting Standards Board *(Bokföringsnämnden)*, which is a government authority, and the Swedish Financial Reporting Board.

In some respects statutory tax rules specify how assets are to be valued. Annual depreciation of machinery and other equipment is allowed at 30% of the residual value or at 20% of the acquisition value. Buildings are depreciated by 2%–5% per year depending on their use.

In the 1991 Tax Reform, the intention was that tax allowances should be as close to commercial depreciation as possible. This is the case concerning buildings, but tax depreciation for machinery may exceed commercial depreciation.

If no statutory tax rule applies, accounting standards are applied. For example, this is the case with respect to the recognition and calculation of most forms of revenue. An important case where accounting standards apply on the cost side is the measurement of inventory; for example, research and development costs normally are deducted immediately instead of being included as part of inventory value.

The connection between tax accounting and accounting standards is thus broadly applicable (almost all revenues and some important costs). An advantage of this approach is a reduction in compliance costs and more neutral taxation when taxable income is closer to real (commercial) income. A disadvantage is the risk that accounting standards will be too conservative to avoid reporting results too early. However, this risk is now reduced since most accounting standards mirror International Accounting Standards (IAS). Another concern may be constitutional issues. Tax law should be enacted by Parliament, but to an important extent, it is now the result of decisions of private accounting boards. However, this could be seen as tax rules mirroring real life, with the possibility for Parliament to change the tax rules if the accounting standards are considered to be inappropriate.

In 2008, a government committee proposed that the connection between tax accounting and accounting standards should be abolished and that, instead, more tax accounting rules should be introduced.

9.2. Respect for Legal Form

In general, words and concepts in tax laws that are similar to those in civil laws are interpreted in accordance with civil law. In many cases the situation is not regulated in detail in civil law and has not been considered in Civil Court because the question of, for example, whether a contract should be deemed a lease or a sale has limited civil law consequences. The tax courts in these instances have to consider what the correct decision is based on civil law.

The form is respected as long as there is some economic substance behind the form. If a transaction is only stated as, for example, a lease in the contract, but is in substance a sale, it will be treated according to its real economic significance. However, the courts are mostly not willing to set the form aside when some substantial consequences of the contract are in accordance with the form. For instance, a sale and leaseback of real estate has been ruled to be treated as a sale, although in reality it was most likely that the transaction in fact functioned as a loan with collateral. Important for the decision was that there existed some, however *ex ante* small, risk that the 'lender' might be stuck with the real estate, with no right to repayment. Special tax aspects may be taken into consideration when interpreting the meaning of complicated transactions because some civil law concepts are vague.

9.3. Anti-avoidance Doctrines and Rules

A special Tax Avoidance Act has been in force for several years. Transactions can be set aside according to the Tax Avoidance Act *(Lagen om skatteflykt)*, if four conditions are fulfilled: (i) the transaction will result in a substantial tax reduction; (ii) the taxpayer has directly or indirectly taken part in the transaction; (iii) the main purpose of the transaction is the tax reduction; and (iv) an assessment based on the form of the transaction contravenes the purpose of the relevant tax rules as interpreted from the relevant rules and the statutory tax rules in general. The law has seldom been used because it is hard to show that these conditions are fulfilled.

The courts have been rather reluctant to use anti-avoidance doctrines other than the Tax Avoidance Act. As mentioned above, courts use only a restrictive form of the substance-over-form doctrine.

The application of the sham transactions doctrine is not controversial in principle, but it is sometimes hard to decide if a transaction is a sham.

10. SOURCES OF TAX LAW

Committee reports are published in the *Swedish Government Official Reports series (Statens offentliga utredningar*, SOU) and *Ministry publications series (Departementsserien, Ds)*.

Opinions expressed by the Law Council *(lagrådet)* are published at their website <www.lagradet.se>.

Government bills are to be found on its website <www.regeringen.se>.

Statutes and amendments to statutes are published in the *Swedish Code of Statutes* (*Svensk Forfattningssamling*, SFS). Current cumulative versions of statutory tax laws are published by the National Tax Board and private publishers. The Swedish Parliament has a website with bills, committee reports, and statutes: <www.riksdagen.se>.

Case law is published in *The Annual Reporter of the Supreme Administrative Court (Regeringsrättens Årsbok)*. The Supreme Administrative Court also publishes recent case law at its website <www.regeringsratten.se>.

Judgments from lower courts are not officially published. However, the Tax Agency publishes summaries of some judgments considered important. Advance rulings are published at the website of the Board for Advance Rulings (*Skatterättsnämnden*) <www.skatterattsnamnden.se>.

The Tax Agency publishes its general advice and information materials at <www.skatteverket.se>.

A large number of academic theses and monographs about tax questions are published. Two major tax journals *(Skattenytt* and *Svensk Skattetidning)* publish ten issues each per year.

Accounting standards are published by the *Bokföringsnämnden*, BFN (The Swedish Accounting Standards Board) at <www.bfn.se> and the Swedish Financial Reporting Board at <www.radetforfinansiellrapportering.se>.

Most of the websites contain pages in English, but with limited content.

The United Kingdom

John Tiley

1. HISTORY: INCOME TAX

History is all-important in the UK tax system. Thus, because the UK tax system has been around since the Middle Ages, the tax year starts, not at some arbitrary date in mid-winter (such as 1 January), but in the spring (6 April). As will be seen in the later sections of this chapter, however, there are indications that some of the old pillars of the system (although not yet the start of the tax year) are under review or even redesign, especially where companies are concerned.

Income tax was introduced in 1798 and has remained in force, except for a gap between 1816 and 1842, ever since. It is, in theory, a temporary tax in that Parliament has to decide each year that there is to be an income tax for that year. This doctrine of the annual tax is a relic from the days when Parliament wanted to make sure that the King would summon a Parliament each year; a perpetual source of income would make calling Parliament less necessary. This doctrine applies also to corporation tax, but not to capital gains tax or inheritance tax.

The income tax was completely overhauled in 1803 by the introduction of the system of the taxation of income as such (as opposed to a person's total income), the abandonment of the general return of income, and the introduction of the schedular system backed up by an extensive system of withholding at source. These principles of deduction at source and a schedular definition of income have been extremely influential. Thanks to the recent Tax Rewrite Programme (see further below sections 5 and 6), income tax is no longer expressed in a series of Schedules, lettered A to F. However, it remains a schedular system in substance. If income does not come within any particular part of the relevant Acts, then it is not chargeable to income tax. Each particular part has its own rules for dealing with, for example, how the specified income should be taxed and defined, what deductions should be allowed, as well as what timing rules should apply. A loss under one Schedule or Part cannot necessarily be set against income under another. Under the new system, one no longer talks of total income but of 'net adjusted income'.

The 1803 system included the taxation of imputed income arising from the occupation of property; this arose under the 1803 Schedule A, a system that remained in place until 1963.

The influence of this overall system is still with us. Thus, even today the income tax consists of various heads of income, each with associated rules. However, today's new legislation finally spells out – in some detail – the different types of income and the different types of taxpayer liable to income tax. It also contains detailed but incomplete rules on how a person's income tax liability is calculated.

Another effect of the 1803 system was to make the introduction of graduation and differentiation a more difficult task; such a system demanded a personal return of total income and was inconsistent with the final character of the scheme of deduction at source. When introduced in 1907, differentiation originally took the form of a lower rate of tax on earned income, but this soon became a relief from income tax; only in 1973 was the tax rate expressed in terms of earned income and a new additional rate applied to investment income; this additional rate was itself repealed in 1984. In 1910 graduation took the form of a new tax – super tax – later remodelled and renamed surtax. Income tax was levied on income, surtax on the total income of an individual. Surtax being additional to income tax, a particular piece of an individual's income might be subject to income tax at 40% and surtax at 20%; it was an excess liability on those better able to pay. Only in 1973 were the two taxes merged, although this is often a matter of form rather than substance, as the continued existence of excess liability shows.

Another historical effect was the astonishing longevity of the preceding-year basis of assessment. Under this system, the income arising for a source in, say, year three is used as the measure of income from that source in year four; it is taxed in year four at the rates relevant to year four, not year three. This was finally repealed in 1996.

Probably the greatest legacy of history is a view of the scope of income and the distinction between income and capital. When income tax was first introduced in 1799, not only were various existing forms of capital already subject to other taxes, but there was also a substantial area of law, that of trusts, where a sharp distinction between income and capital receipts had been drawn. Further, insofar as business was concerned, Adam Smith had already set out the distinction between circulating and fixed capital, between income profits and capital gains. The details of trading income had to be worked out at a time well before the first Companies Act, when the business unit was relatively small and ownership and management were not completely distinct concepts. A tax on income introduced against such a legal and intellectual background would find little room for arguments based on a comprehensive income tax base. Moreover, since the tax was seen as temporary, the taxation of capital gains would have seemed unjust. A separate tax on capital gains (CGT) was eventually introduced in 1965. The distinction between capital and income remains central to the tax system despite a certain amount of convergence, especially with regard to rates of tax, in 1987 for the corporate sector. Convergence of rates in the personal sector was achieved in 1988 but was undone ten years later.

1.1. Corporation Tax

In the United Kingdom, the tax paid by companies on their profits is not 'income tax' but 'corporation tax'; the expression 'profits' covers both income and capital gains. This tax was introduced in 1965, at the same time as CGT. Before 1965 companies paid tax on their profits, but did so through a combination of the income tax (as opposed to surtax or supertax) and special taxes. Dividends were not subject to income tax but were grossed up to give a figure for surtax; this was done whether or not the company paid income tax on its profits.

The fact that a company was subject to income tax, but not surtax, meant that it was advantageous for a high-rate taxpayer to leave income behind the veil of a company, where it would be taxed at lower rates and so multiply more rapidly. Legislation was therefore introduced in 1922 to deal with what were then called one-man companies, in the form of a surtax direction that treated the income of the companies as if it were the income of their owners and therefore liable to surtax. This was the forerunner of the modern close company legislation; the reduction in tax rates over recent years has enabled Parliament to repeal almost all of these attribution-of-income rules. A special tax on profits, the National Defence Contribution, which in due course became profits tax, was introduced in 1937. This was an extra tax on the profits of the company but was not an income tax. This device could be used to levy tax at differential rates on distributed and retained profits; it was in fact used in this way between 1947 and 1958. Since one of the taxes in this two-tax system was income tax, the rate would be altered whenever the government thought it desirable to alter the rate in the personal sector. Profits under the two taxes were computed differently. Not only was profits tax levied on a current, as opposed to a preceding, year, but some items were deductible in computing profits for profits tax that were not deductible for income tax, necessitating two sets of calculations; thus, for example, until 1952 profits tax was deductible for income tax. Further, companies whose profits were less than £2,000 were exempt from profits tax.

This untidy system was replaced in 1965 by a corporation tax based on the classical system. This was in turn replaced in 1973 by a partial imputation system. A number of imputation features were removed between 1997 and 1999; the current corporation tax is a very odd beast, at least in theoretical terms.

The legislation on corporation tax was last consolidated in the Income and Corporation Taxes Act 1988, but, as seen above, certain rules dealing with capital gains are to be found in the Taxation of Chargeable Gains Act 1992. Both Acts are supplemented by (many) provisions in the annual Finance Acts. At the time of writing, the rules on Corporation Tax are being rewritten in two Acts, one of which has now been passed (see further section 6 below). Although the new rewritten legislation contains several rules that are explicable only in terms of a schedular system, there are substantially fewer such rules in Corporation Tax than there are in Income Tax.

2. CONSTITUTIONAL ISSUES

It is notorious that the United Kingdom does not have a written constitution. However, it does have a long constitutional history, and taxation has played a key part in that story. Thus, the Tudor monarchy, in particular, paid for its alliance with the middle classes by allowing Parliament (and especially the House of Commons) an increasing role in government and taxation. Charles I's attempt to govern – and tax – without Parliament led eventually to the English civil war and his own execution. The Bill of Rights of 1688[1] provided that no charge on the subject shall be levied by pretence of prerogative without the consent of Parliament. In the twentieth century, the attempt by the House of Lords to resist major taxation reforms led to the Parliament Act of 1911, which allowed the House of Commons to get certain legislation through despite the opposition of the House of Lords – and also removed any role for the House of Lords in relation to money bills (i.e., most tax laws).

The UK courts acknowledge the sovereignty of Parliament – that is, they recognized that they have no function of judicial review of primary legislation. For this reason, the courts for many years raised no objection to retrospective legislation. As a result, in 1978 an anti-avoidance measure was made to apply to events occurring after March 1976 – a particularly effective form of anti-avoidance measure.

The courts do, however, have a review role in three important aspects. First, they have a full judicial review role in relation to secondary legislation, which includes statutory instruments that are becoming known, increasingly, as regulations. Second, like all other EU Member States, the UK courts acknowledge the twin doctrines of the supremacy and direct effect of EC law. Third, the United Kingdom has been a signatory to the European Convention of Human Rights since 1966 and so the United Kingdom courts give effect to the Convention – but not in an entirely straightforward way.

The human rights dimension needs to be disentangled carefully. The 1966 accession allowed UK complainants to take matters to the European Court of Human Rights (at that time, the Commission and the Court in Strasbourg). The Convention was not implemented in UK domestic law until the Human Rights Act of 1998, which came into force in 2000, and even then did so in a way that preserved the sovereignty of Parliament. The UK courts must interpret legislation so as to give effect to Convention rights but, if this is impossible, they have no power to override the legislation; instead, they may declare it to be incompatible

1. 2 Will. and Mar. (c. 2), Art. 4.

with the Convention. If Parliament decides that it does not want to amend the law, even by the fast-track process prescribed in the Act, there is nothing the litigant can do but follow the familiar path to Strasbourg (equally, there is nothing to stop the Westminster Parliament from repealing the Act itself or withdrawing from the Convention altogether).

Two other Human Rights Act matters should be mentioned. First, section 6 of the Act makes it unlawful for a public authority – an expression covering a court or tribunal and a person whose functions are, even in part, of a public nature (e.g., revenue departments) – to act in a way that is incompatible with Convention rights; judicial remedies are governed by section 8. The court or tribunal must 'have regard to', but is not bound by, the jurisprudence of the 'Strasbourg Organs'. Second, new legislation presented to the House of Commons must carry a certificate from the relevant Minister asserting that the legislation proposed is (or is not) compatible with the Convention rights. Ministers seeking passage for a bill that they state is not compatible are unlikely to succeed.

In addition to these matters, one may note that the Human Rights Convention has been of some influence in the development of other purely UK domestic administrative law rules.

The Convention has been more influential in the development of fundamental principles of EC law, principles said to emerge in part from the common traditions of the Member States. The importance here is that these fundamental principles are capable of direct effect and therefore, thanks to the supremacy of EC law, will override parliamentary sovereignty.

Within the United Kingdom the central government enjoys an almost unparalleled degree of power. There are local authorities in different parts of the country, but they are subject to tight control from the central government in a number of ways. First, a substantial part of their responsibilities is funded centrally rather than by their local taxes. Second, their revenue-raising powers have been made the subject of capping powers. Third, their ability to raise money from businesses has been reduced by the device of the business rate, a rate that applies to businesses but that is fixed centrally and not locally. This leaves the local authorities with little power to raise much money from the local residents; the local tax is called the council tax. The level of the council tax is fixed by the local authority – subject to capping – and that rate is then applied to each house, the house being placed in one of a number of bands of value.

A local income tax has been considered from time to time in the United Kingdom but never implemented. Under the terms of the Scotland Act 1998 the Scottish Parliament may vary the basic rate of income tax by up to 3 pence in the pound, but only for Scottish residents.

Treaties are made by the sovereign under her prerogative power and take effect under the normal rules for public international law. However, treaties (including tax treaties) have effects for individuals only if they are then ratified by the relevant parliamentary procedure. For tax treaties, this procedure is set out in TA 1988, section 788, which states explicitly that the treaty can be given this effect only for the purposes set out therein.

Of all aspects of the UK tax system, the rates of income tax provide the most striking examples of the influence of history – and of politics. The record in this area does not justify the alleged reputation of the British for moderation. Rates of income tax in the last year of the Labour administration (1978–1979) reached 83%; however, if the income was classified as investment income and exceeded a certain figure, a supplementary tax of 15% was due – making a marginal rate of 98%. This was fairly typical of the period after 1945 and showed the great doctrinal belief in equity in the sense of shared misery. It was highlighted by the occasional (twice) surcharge on income, which being expressed as percentage of tax normally due could (and did) mean that the marginal rate of tax could exceed 100%. The ferocity of these rates emphasized the gap between income and capital gain (not generally taxed until 1965), the importance of any gaps in the tax base, and the generally neutral attitude of the courts toward straightforward tax avoidance schemes.

Since the election of the Conservative administration, led by Margaret Thatcher, in 1979, the top rates have been reduced – in 1979 the general rate dropped from 83% to 60%; in 1984 the surcharge on investment income was abolished, and in 1988 the top rate was cut to 40%. In these ways, the doctrinal writings of the 1970s, with their emphasis on neutrality rather than equity, have come to hold sway with the same fervor as those of their predecessors arguing for equity. The New Labour administration, led by Tony Blair and Gordon Brown, which came to power in 1997, did not increase the low nominal rates of tax but did other things to increase revenue. As will be seen in section 3 below, the appalling state of the UK finances means that this promise has been abandoned.

Indexation and inflation adjustments have been part of the UK tax system for many years. Income tax rate brackets are liable to be adjusted for inflation or other causes each year; the same was true of the personal reliefs. In part this was attributable to the fact that the income tax was an annual tax and was therefore subject to annual review. However, all adjustments depended on the needs of the Chancellor of the Exchequer of the day. In recent years, adjustment of these amounts for inflation has been formalized in that they will be changed unless the annual Finance Bill directs otherwise. The annual Finance Bill has directed otherwise more often than not with smaller (or no) adjustments in years when the government needs money and larger adjustments when the government needs votes.

Adjustment for inflation has formed part of the capital gains system since 1982. The current position is that inflation adjustments are made to the base cost of the asset in determining a gain. However, while the adjustment can remove a gain altogether, it cannot create a loss. In 1998 the legislation was changed to substitute a taper relief for indexation. Taper relief did not apply for corporation tax, which remained on the indexation system (see section 5 below). Taper relief was abolished in 2008 in favour of a single rate of capital gains tax (18%).

There are no inflation-based adjustments to the base cost used in determining the amount that may be claimed under the capital allowance system (depreciation).

3. RATE STRUCTURE AND RELIEFS, 2009–2010

The income tax rate structure begins with the rates of tax.

Taxable Income	*Tax Rate*
savings income (but see below) 0–£2,440	10% (starting, savings rate)
non-savings income 0–£37,400 and savings income £2,440–£37,400	20% (basic rate)
over £37,400	40% (higher rate)

Rate brackets and reliefs are index-linked, but the effects of indexing are more often than not overridden by express statutory provision; this overriding has sometimes made the increase smaller (or non-existent) and sometimes larger. The government has announced that it will introduce legislation in the UK Finance Act 2009 for an additional higher rate of income tax of 50% for incomes over £150,000. This will be backed up by restrictions – as from 22 April 2009 – on attempts by taxpayers to forestall these changes by changing pension contributions, for example.

The capital gains tax is no longer charged as if the gain were added to the taxpayer's other income; for virtually all disposals after 5 April 2008, a single flat rate of 18% applies, subject to an annual exemption for individuals, which for 2009–2010 is £10,100. In addition, National Insurance contributions are imposed on both employer and employee; employees currently pay at 11% on their weekly earnings between £110 and £844 and 1% above that figure. The maximum rate for employees is 12.8%. In recent years, these contributions have been raised to help fund the National Health Service. This is an example of the device known as hypothecation, or the earmarking of a tax for a particular purpose; such hypothecation is rare in the United Kingdom. This increase enabled the government to get more money from the public without touching the rate of income tax. The government has also announced that it will legislate for increases of 0.5% in these rates as from April 2011.

Savings income, principally interest, may benefit from the 10% starting rate, as set out in the table above. However, it is available only in limited circumstances; the savings income is treated as the top slice of a taxpayer's income and so will not be available at all if the taxpayer's other – for example, earned – income exceeds the savings rate limit of £2,440. Dividends are taxed at 10%, the dividend ordinary rate, but this rises to 32.5%, the dividend upper rate, once net adjusted income exceeds £37,400. It will be seen that the system requires rules as to which types of income are to be treated as the top slice of income. The reason for the special rates for dividends is to preserve the same overall tax burden enjoyed (or suffered) when the rates were 20% and 40%, but there was an associated credit that was then worth more. A new rate of 42.5% will apply as from 6 April 2010–2011 where dividend income forms part of net adjusted income exceeding £150,000.

The individual tax burden is then adjusted, first by reference to the personal allowance: All residents (and some non-residents) have a personal allowance of £6,475. There is also a special blind persons' relief of £1,890. In an important change of principle, the government has announced that it will legislate that the benefit of the personal allowance of £6,475 should be restricted for those with high incomes. As from 6 April 2010 it will be restricted for those with income over £100,000; the allowance will be reduced by £1 for every £2 of income above £100,000.

In addition to the basic personal allowance, a number of extra reliefs are given by reference to age, marital status, income, and other factors.

The first group of reliefs takes the form of allowances – or deduction from what would otherwise be taxable income. First, the personal allowance of £6,475 is increased for the elderly (but the extra amount is reduced as income rises – by £1 for every £2 of income over £22,900):

Personal allowance (65–74)	£9,490
Personal allowance (75 or over)	£9,640

There is also a special married couples' allowance where the taxpayer was born before 6 April 1965. Like the personal allowance, this is phased out as income rises (by £2 for every £3 of income over £22,900) but has two distinguishing features: (i) this relief is given effect only at 10%, and (ii) there is a minimum value of £2,670 (i.e., £267, assuming sufficient income). Where the elder spouse is 65–74 years of age, the relief is £6,865, and where the elder spouse is 75 or over, £6,965 – with the same minimum of £2,670.

The second group of reliefs are tax credits with their own separate statute, Tax Credits Act 2002. These credits represent a major change, as the tax system is now being used to deliver what had previously been social security goals. The new tax credits took effect from April 2003. The two primary credits are (i) Child Tax Credit, which provides income-related support to the main caregiver and is intended to help all but the richest 10% of families, and (ii) Working Tax Credit, which can apply to a lone parent or to a couple and where at least one is working (this credit includes a significant element for child care). The latter credit is designed to help 1 million single people or couples in low-paid work; the value of this benefit increases if there are children, and there is also an element for child care expenses. The features of this system to note are: (i) that these credits are targeted in that they are reduced in value as incomes rise; (ii) that the relevant income level used in this reduction now turns on the combined income of the parents in the household; and (iii) that the benefit is paid to the primary caregiver (some previous credits were paid through the wage packet, thus placing the burden on the employer – this was abandoned in the new scheme in 2003). In 2009–2010 the maximum value of the child tax credit, using an annual rather than weekly basis, is £2,235 per child with the family as such getting £545 (enhanced for the first year of the child's life). The working tax credit is worth a maximum of £1,890, with a further £1,860 for certain couples and single parents. There is also an element for child care. Credits are reduced as income rises, but the benefits can still be of value to families with an income of £50,000.

Taking these changes since 1997 as a whole, they represent a major shift in resources from families to families with children. The targeting element means that the benefits are withdrawn as incomes rise, resulting in high marginal rates of tax on household incomes.

For corporations, in 2009 the full rate is 28%, with a reduced rate of 21%, which is phased out when income exceeds £300,000; the benefit of this expires at £1.5 million. These figures of £300,000 and £1.5 million are not indexed to inflation and have remained unchanged for many years. For a brief period there was also a starting rate of 0% where profits did not exceed £10,000, but the benefit was withdrawn as profits rose from £10,000 to £50,000. This was abandoned after only a few years.

4. COMPOSITION OF THE FISCAL SYSTEM

The different taxes have different yields. The UK government projections for 2008–2009 put net taxes and social security contributions at £541 billion, or around 38.3% of the UK's GDP. That total breaks down into £160 billion from taxes on personal income (after allowing for tax credits), £52 billion from taxes on corporate income (to which 0.5% should be added for North Sea revenues), £104 billion from social security contribution taxes, and £83 billion from taxes on goods and services (including excise duties); inheritance tax was expected to bring in just £3.2 billion. The effects of the banking crisis and the decline in economic activity mean that these figures are unlikely to be achieved in 2008–2009.

5. BASIC STRUCTURE OF THE INCOME TAX

5.1. On Individuals

The UK system of income tax is a schedular system. Today, as a result of the Tax Law Rewrite Programme, the United Kingdom's legislation on income tax is stretched out over three principal – but not exhaustive – Acts. The Income Tax (Earnings and Pensions) Act 2003 (ITEPA), the Income Tax (Trading and Other Income) Act 2005 (ITTOIA), and the Income Tax Act 2007 (ITA). The purpose of the rewrite is to use modern language to make legislation both more intelligible and more accessible.

One noticeable feature of the project is that it will deal with rules on purely UK situations and with rules on situations with a foreign element (e.g., UK dividends and foreign dividends) in the same part of the legislation. However, the project must ensure that the content of the law itself remains unchanged because it is indeed a rewrite and not a reform. Therefore, placing the rules for UK dividends and foreign dividends together emphasizes how different they are. To make matters worse, as we shall now see, the legislation is not comprehensive.

While the UK income tax is indeed still a schedular system, it is no longer expressed in terms of Schedules A, B, C, etc., but in terms of a list of heads of charge. Unfortunately, the legislation contained in these three acts is not exhaustive of the various heads of charge; moreover, there is no comprehensive list of the heads of charge. These are matters of form. What may be more worrying is the belief implicit in the project that one can rewrite the words – often at great length and usually with a completely different structure – and not change the meaning.

ITA 2007 begins by listing three charges to income tax under ITEPA – all previously under Schedule E:

- Part 2 (income from employment);
- Part 9 (pension income); and
- Part 10 (social security income).

It then lists four heads under ITTOIA:

- Part 2 (trading income), the former Schedule D Cases I and II;
- Part 3 (property income), the former Schedule A;
- Part 4 (savings and investment income), the former Schedule D Case III and Schedule F; and
- Part 5 (miscellaneous income), including the former Schedule D Case VI.

ITA 2007 itself imposes the following charges:

- Part 10 (charitable trusts);
- Part 12 Chapter 2 (accrued income profits); and
- Part 13 (tax avoidance).

ITA 2007 also lists two other heads of charge, but expressly warns that the list is not comprehensive.

With the change in form but not in substance, differences in the fiscal treatment of income from employment (ITEPA Part 2), income from business (ITTOIA Part 2), and income from property (ITTOIA Part 3) persist. The legislation contains many priority rules. ITTOIA section 2 lists many of these rules but then adds, ‘but the rules in those sections need to be read with other rules of law (whether in this Act or otherwise) about the scope of particular provisions or the order of priority to be given to them’.[2] Other major features of the UK income tax, such as the distinction between income and capital, have been mentioned under heading 1 above.

5.1.1. Capital Gains Tax (CGT)

The refusal of the courts and the legislature to widen the scope of income tax to cover capital gains is of great importance in the history of the UK tax system.

2. ITTOIA, s. 2.

Opportunities to convert income into capital were exploited by taxpayers and only occasionally were stopped, and then on a piecemeal basis, by the legislature. Reform eventually came in 1965 with the introduction of the long-term capital gains tax. A short-term gains provision had been introduced in 1962 that was designed to tax gains realized within six months of acquisition and to tax them as income. This was extended in 1965 to gains realized within twelve months and was preserved until 1971, despite the introduction of the long-term CGT in 1965, because of the difference in tax rates – CGT had a flat rate of 30% while income tax could go over 90%. The rates of CGT and income tax were assimilated for companies (i.e., for corporation tax) in 1987. They were assimilated for individuals in 1988 but, as we shall see, this is no longer the case. For disposals on or after 6 April 2008, the rate of tax for CGT on individuals is a flat 18%. With higher incomes due to attract income tax of 50% as from 2010 to 2011, much tax planning activity is expected.

CGT contains its own fundamental doctrines. It is restricted in that there must be a disposal (whether actual or deemed) and the disposal must be of an asset that is relevant to the tax system. Assets relevant to the system include shares and debts on a security, although there is an important exception for qualifying corporate bonds; other debts are not generally relevant assets, although exceptions are made for debts on a security, for certain loans to traders, and for assignees of debts. A liability is not an asset, so that a loss on a loan (e.g., due to the extra cost of paying off a foreign currency loan when sterling has declined against that currency since the original borrowing) cannot give rise to any relief under CGT; conversely, there is no liability on a gain. This gap was the source of much frustration for many taxpayers and led to the introduction of new rules for foreign exchange transactions and risk management instruments in 1995 and a comprehensive new regime for all loan instruments in 1996 – but only for companies subject to corporation tax.

CGT has two other major restrictions. The first, introduced in 1988, is that it does not usually attempt to tax gains that accrued before 31 March 1982. The second restriction is that individuals enjoy a large exemption from tax on the first £9,600 (2008–2009) of capital gains realized each year.

In 1982, the United Kingdom introduced some relief for inflation. For CGT before 1998 – and still for corporation tax – this relief was delivered through the ‘indexation allowance’. By 1998 the indexation relief could not be used to turn a gain into a loss, although this had been so in the past. In 1998, the United Kingdom replaced indexation relief for CGT – but not for corporation tax – with a tapering system. This system distinguished sharply between business assets (where the taper reduces the chargeable gain by 75% after just two years, thus reducing the effective tax rate from 40% to 10%) and non-business assets (where the taper extends over ten years and, at the most, reduces the gain by only 40%, leaving 60% taxable, and so gives an effective rate of 24% for a top-rate taxpayer). Tapering did not reduce a gain to zero. In 2008 tapering relief itself was scrapped as part of a simplification package and replaced by a single rate of CGT of 18% for individuals without indexation relief. The simplification package was found to produce losers as well as winners and so a relief, called 'entrepreneurs' relief', was provided for certain business gains.

Where an asset has a useful life of less than fifty years, it will be classified as a 'wasting asset' and the costs will be written off over the life of the asset to avoid giving relief for the inevitable loss. If the wasting asset is a chattel, it will be exempt from CGT.

The CGT legislation was consolidated in the Capital Gains Tax Act 1979 and again in the Taxation of Chargeable Gains Act 1992. The reason for the change in title is that corporations do not pay CGT on their capital gains but instead pay corporation tax. The 1992 Act consolidates not only the rules for CGT, but also a number of the corporation tax rules that had not been consolidated in the 1988 Act. The Tax Law Rewrite Programme has not yet begun work on the capital gains rules.

Capital losses may be set only against capital gains of the same or any subsequent tax year, a rule that encourages a certain amount of tax planning and results in a certain amount of anti-avoidance legislation.

5.2. On Corporations

Corporation tax is charged on the profits of companies that are resident in the United Kingdom or carry on business through a permanent establishment in the United Kingdom. Profits are determined as the sum of income, as defined under the income tax rules, and chargeable gains under the CGT rules. However, several rules apply only to corporation tax (e.g., those dealing with loan relationships, including foreign exchange matters, and derivatives). Other examples include the research and development tax credit, remediation relief, and the 2002 rules on intellectual property. As already seen, the Rewrite Programme will make the corporation tax legislation quite distinct.

6. TAX LEGISLATION

First, a general comment: Although, as seen above, the tax law rewrite legislation is less than perfect, it does in several respects represent a major improvement on what had gone before. For years immediately before the rewrite, there was an Act known as the Income and Corporation Taxes Act 1988. This was not a complete code of provisions for income tax and corporation tax. Rather, it was the latest in a series of consolidations; these had occurred in 1918, 1952, 1970, and 1988. The 1988 Act could have been amended each year by the annual Finance Act; however, there was no need for the annual Act to do that, and so later Acts instead added their own provisions to the overall patchwork of legislation. One purpose behind the Rewrite Programme is to prevent that situation from arising in the future. It is expected that amendments to the provisions in the three Income Tax Acts will take effect as amendments to those provisions and not be free-standing.

Second, it used to be that the combination of the consolidated or rewritten Acts and the subsequent Finance Acts contained all the relevant tax legislation. This is no longer true; important provisions relating to tax are also to be found in free-standing tax statutes such as the Tax Credits Act 2002 and in more general enactments such as the Criminal Justice and Police Act of 2001.

Because Parliament has to re-enact the income tax each year, there is at least one major piece of tax legislation each tax year; this gives many opportunities for reform, although most of these are put forward by the government. Some will be anti-avoidance measures; others will be more wide-ranging reforms. Because of the nature of the UK political system, the government is almost certain to get its legislation passed – often unscathed. Opposition parties can propose amendments, and sensible (such as technically helpful and zero-cost) ones will often be adopted by the government, but only on the basis that it does the drafting.

Taxation bills originate in the House of Commons, as the powers of the House of Lords are, as we have seen, very limited. Each year a Finance Bill begins in March or April; currently, this is preceded by a pre-Budget report in November of the previous year. Some proposed changes will be announced in November and some in March, but the government can make a statement at any time and announce that legislation will be retrospective to the date of the announcement. Such retroactive legislation is generally regarded as normal and unobjectionable.

In recent years major technical reforms, such as the loan relationship legislation of 1996, have been the subject of an elaborate consultation process, with draft clauses and considerable Revenue explanations to accompany the draft and final legislation – the whole process taking well over a year. However, it has to be said that one effect of this consultation process has been a greater willingness to have detailed legislation backed up by even more detailed subordinate legislation or statutory instruments, sometimes known as regulations. The power to make these statutory instruments sometimes includes the power to change the primary legislation itself; such powers are rare elsewhere in the tax system. They are needed in the technical areas mentioned to enable the tax authorities to adapt the legislation as new instruments or arrangements come along. The Finance Act 2002 rules on intellectual property followed a similar pattern.

6.1. Statutory Style

The traditional UK tax statute was drafted in a precise and detailed way, a way entirely suited to, and perhaps an appropriate response to, the tradition of literal interpretation. Until the last fifteen years or so, there was relatively little resort to delegated legislation (or statutory instruments).

The Rewrite style is very different. The new approach is meant to make tax statutes more intelligible, making the legislation clearer and easier to use but also, inevitably, longer. The new system makes extensive use of 'signpost' provisions. The extensive use of words that do not have any dispositive effect is something of a challenge for those accustomed to traditional legislation. The first great product of this process was the Capital Allowances Act 2001, an Act that applies both to corporation tax and income tax.

Although the courts are now taking a more purposive approach to the interpretation of statues and a 'less blinkered' approach to the facts, it remains the case that the legislation itself is often very detailed. In recent years there has also been a tendency for highly prescriptive rules to be backed up by a purpose-based anti-avoidance rule.

The UK transfer pricing legislation[3] is expressly based on the OECD principles[4] and refers to those in operation when the UK legislation was enacted in 1998 and any later principles adopted by the OECD, but only if approved for this purpose by statutory instrument.

6.2. Statutory Interpretation

The current mantra, which is particularly clearly stated in *Barclays Mercantile Business v. Mawson*[5] in 2005, is that courts approach tax statutes in the same way as any other statutes – by looking at the words to be interpreted in a purposive way, but in their context.

It is too much to expect that any exposition of the principles of statutory interpretation would remove all difficulties in their application because it is in the nature of questions of construction that there are borderline cases about which people will have different views. However, it is possible to achieve some clarity about basic principles. The modern approach to statutory construction, as Lord Steyn explained in *IRC v. McGuckian* in 1997,[6] is to have regard to the purpose of a particular provision and interpret its language, so far as possible, in a way that best gives effect to that purpose. The House traced its change in approach to the interpretation of statutes back from 1997 to the *Ramsay* case in 1981.[7] Before *Ramsay*, the approach of the courts was vitiated by formalism and, in particular, by insisting on treating every transaction that had an individual legal identity (e.g., payment of money, transfer of property, creation of a debt, etc.) as having its own separate tax consequences, whatever might be the terms of the statute. In combination, the literal interpretation of tax statutes and the formalistic insistence on examining steps in a composite scheme separately allowed tax avoidance schemes to flourish. *Ramsay* liberated the construction of revenue statutes from being both literal and blinkered.

The question of the nature of the principle emerging from the *Ramsay* doctrine has been a matter of much discussion. Many saw it as a judicially created anti-avoidance doctrine. A few brave souls saw it more simply – as a much-needed new

3. TA 1988 Sch. 28AA.
4. OECD Transfer Pricing Guidelines (Paris: OECD, 1995).
5. [2004] UKHL 51, [2005] STC 1.
6. *IRC v. McGuckian* [1997] STC 908 at 915, [1997] 1 WLR 991 at 999.
7. *Ramsay (WT) Ltd v. IRC* [1982] STC 174 (HL).

approach to the interpretation and application of tax statutes. In the *Barclays* case the House of Lords decided that the few brave souls had been right.[8]

The extent to which the *Barclays* mantra will produce results different from those obtained by using the older approach is only slowly emerging. The change obviously affects the terms in which cases are argued, but judges have sometimes found that it is often difficult to find a parliamentary purpose that is sufficiently specific to help them decide the particular case before them. The Tax Law Rewrite Programme does not help in this regard because it is not meant to change the law and so is not set out in the form of principles.

A further problem is that when the structure of the Act is looked to, the policy assumptions underlying provisions may change. Thus, the rules about companies buying their own shares clearly assumed that qualifying companies would try to take advantage of the new rules that allowed the transaction to be treated as one involving only capital gains legislation; later changes in the various rates of tax, including corporation tax, CGT, and income tax, made this assumption quite false, and as a result, companies might try to make their transactions fall outside the supposedly beneficial rules.

7. COURTS DEALING WITH TAX MATTERS

7.1. Structure of the Courts

A taxpayer who is dissatisfied with an assessment made by Her Majesty's Revenue and Customs (HMRC) has a right of appeal. Since 1 April 2009 this appeal is made to a completely new system of tribunals. The new rules apply right across the area of administrative tribunals; tax appeals are just one strand of the system.

The new system contains two tiers – a First Tier Tribunal and an Upper Tribunal. Appeal from the Upper Tribunal lies to the Court of Appeal and from there to the House of Lords. As from October 2009, a new Supreme Court will replace the House of Lords Appellate Committee. At the time of writing, many details remain to be settled by statutory instruments (e.g., how business will be allocated between the two tiers).

In the normal course of events an appeal will be taken first to the First Tier Tribunal. There is then a right of appeal to the Upper Tribunal but only on points of law – that is, not facts. If the case started in the Upper Tribunal, the appeal is not confined to questions of law but requires the leave either of the Upper Tribunal or the relevant appellate body.

Among many differences from the old system, two stand out. First, the new Upper Tribunal not only acts as an appellate body from the First Tier but also has the power of judicial review. This should prevent much frustration and expense. Secondly, both the First Tier and the Upper Tribunals have a power to review their own decisions. Naturally this is quite distinct from 'judicial review'. At the time of

8. See further s. 9.3 below.

writing it is unclear whether this power will just be concerned to correct slips or whether it can give rise to a rehearing.

Before April 2009 appeals lay to a body known as 'the Commissioners'. This term is confusing, since the Members of the Board of HMRC are known as the Commissioners of HMRC. The appellate commissioners are either general or special, and their full title is General (or Special) Commissioners for the purposes of the Income Tax; despite the mention of income tax, their jurisdiction extends to other taxes, but not to VAT, which, until April 2009, had its own appeal tribunal.

General Commissioners reflect the English appreciation of the amateur; like magistrates, these are laypeople who sit on panels and are advised on the law by their clerk. The term 'amateur' should not be seen as a condemnation; the tribunal usually comprises people of a wide range of experience who bring considerable expertise to their tax role. It is expected that the General Commissioners will go to the First Tier Tribunal. In contrast, the Special Commissioners are highly trained specialists appointed from the ranks of barristers, solicitors, or accountants, and sometimes from the HMRC itself.

The burden of proof lies on the taxpayer to disprove the assessment. Publication of the decisions of the Special Commissioners began in 1995; previously, these were regarded as confidential to the parties. The Commissioners still sit in private, although the question has been raised whether this is contrary to the Human Rights Act of 1998; they now have the power to award costs in appropriate cases in accordance with the normal rules of litigation in the United Kingdom (i.e., costs follow the cause).

The General Commissioners have had the more exotic areas of tax law removed from their jurisdiction. They sit in private (with the same caveat as to the Human Rights Act); their decisions are not published, and they have no power to award costs. Appeal from their decisions lies by an archaic process, still used in criminal appeals from decisions of magistrates, and known as the case stated. The question of costs under the new 2009 system is still under discussion.

Since appeals lie from Commissioners only on questions of law and not of fact, the issue of the distinction between the two is important. Apart from errors of law in the most obvious sense, the courts have said that they will intervene in three situations that may well amount to the same thing: where there is no evidence to support the determination reached by the Commissioners, where the evidence contradicts that determination, and where the true and only reasonable conclusion contradicts that determination.[9]

7.2. Judicial Review

As just seen, the distinction between appeal and judicial review will become less important – in procedural terms – in 2009. Judicial review is one of the few ways in

9. *Edwards v. Bairstow and Harrison* 36 TC 207 at 229.

which an assessment may be disturbed. In recent years, it has been used to challenge the Commissioners' decision at the hearing of an appeal or at some other procedural step; for example, a hearing was unfair when the taxpayer was not given enough notice. However, judicial review may also be used to challenge decisions by HMRC before, and independent of, any appeal hearing. Consequently, it has been used to question the tax authorities' withdrawal of an informal clearance given by an inspector[10] and HMRC's decisions not to treat a taxpayer as falling within an extra-statutory concession[11] or a statement of practice[12] and not to assess another taxpayer.[13]

Judicial review must be distinguished from an appeal. On appeal, the court may uphold an assessment or vary it; in judicial review the court either upholds the act complained of or quashes it; if it quashes it, it sends the matter back to the original body to exercise its jurisdiction correctly. The court does not substitute its own decision for that of the body reviewed. If the Commissioners have conducted the hearing of an appeal in a way that breaches the rules of natural justice, they will have to hear the appeal again. If an assessment by an inspector is quashed, a new assessment must be made – although it may sometimes be too late for the tax authorities to make a new one. On appeal, the court goes into the merits of the decision; in judicial review, the court looks at the procedures followed and ensures that the public body whose acts are being scrutinized had the power to do what it has done. In judicial review, the court does not interfere with the proper exercise of a power or jurisdiction.

7.3. Judicial Style

UK court judgments tend to be carefully reasoned. The Special Commissioners now tend to give long and detailed judgments. General Commissioners still have to give reasoned decisions and can be asked to 'state a case' for any appeal; this process takes some time and requires them to set out the evidence, the arguments, the facts as they find them to be, and their decision.

Once the case reaches the High Court or its equivalent, normal rules apply. Cases are fully argued (mostly orally) and judgments are fully reasoned. They tend to be long – out of a need to report what has been argued and then what is decided.

7.4. Legislative History

The court may look at the purpose and history of the relevant legislation and, to this end, reference may be made to the state of the law and the material facts and events

10. *R v. IRC ex parte Matrix Securities Ltd.* [1994] STC 272 HL.
11. *R v. IRC ex parte Fulford Dobson* [1987] STC 344.
12. *R v. IRC ex parte Kaye* [1992] STC 581.
13. *IRC v. National Federation of Self Employed and Small Business Ltd.* [1981] STC 260.

with which it is apparent that Parliament was dealing.[14] In *Pepper v. Hart*[15] the House of Lords, reversing centuries of case law, held that the court could consult *Hansard* (as the official record of debates in the UK Parliament is known) in order to interpret the words of the legislation if: '(a) legislation is ambiguous or obscure, or leads to an absurdity; (b) the material relied on consists of one or more statements by a minister or other promoter of the Bill together if necessary with such other Parliamentary material as is necessary to understand such statements and their effects; and (c) the statements relied on are clear'.[16]

7.5. Precedent

As just seen, in some circumstances – for example, on appeal from the First Tier Tribunal to the Upper or from the General Commissioners to the High Court – the higher court can overturn the decision appealed only for errors of law, not for errors of fact. It follows that a court may dismiss an appeal even though the appellate judge might have decided the case differently from the original tribunal; such cases are of little value as precedents. Otherwise judgments of superior courts bind inferior courts, and judgments of the same level of court are usually binding.

8. TAX ADMINISTRATION

Since 2005 direct taxes, previously administered by the Inland Revenue, and indirect taxes, such as VAT, previously administered by Customs and Excise, have been administered by one combined department, HMRC. Both departments work closely with the Treasury but are not subordinate departments of the Treasury, even though they share common Ministers. One positive result of the merger has been a review of the many powers each possessed, leading to harmonization and modernization. With respect to penalties, the new system has three degrees of culpability – 'careless', 'deliberate but not concealed', and 'deliberate and concealed'. The standard penalty is 30% of the lost tax for carelessness, 70% for deliberate but not concealed offences, and 100% for deliberate and concealed offences. The penalties may be reduced if voluntary disclosure is made.

Work on HMRC powers is ongoing. The UK Finance Act 2009 will contain powers requiring senior accounting officers of large companies to take reasonable steps to establish and monitor accounting systems so that they are adequate for accurate tax reporting. Such officers also have to certify annually that the systems are adequate (or explain why). The legislation will also allow HMRC to publish the name of taxpayers, individuals, or companies or businesses, for deliberate defaults leading to a loss of tax of £25,000 or more.

---

14. Lord Macdermott in *IRC v. Rennell* [1964] AC 173, 198.
15. *Pepper v. Hart* [1992] STC 898.
16. *Ibid.*, at 922.

After a long and honourable tradition of assessment to tax by the Revenue, the system changed to one of self-assessment as from 1996, but only for fewer than one half of taxpayers. Self-assessment applies to corporation tax (and so to all companies) and to individuals who have a substantial amount of income outside the system of collection at source.

The corporation tax system requires companies to make a self-assessment and pay the tax due within nine months from the end of the company's accounting period. There is also a system of payment in advance by quarterly instalments beginning six months and thirteen days from the start of the accounting period. This system applies only to large companies, which in broad terms means those with annual profits of £1.5 million or more. However, where a company becomes large for the first time, the system applies only as from the next accounting period unless its profits exceed £10 million. The risk of getting the instalment calculation wrong falls on the company. It is government policy that all corporation tax returns should be made electronically as from April 2011.

Income tax has very different rules. First, only some taxpayers must make a self-assessment. Those taxpayers subject to the self-assessment system who are willing to make their returns electronically must make a return of their income and calculate the tax due no later than 31 January following the end of their tax year (so by 31 January 2011 for the year 6 April 2009–5 April 2010). Taxpayers wanting to make their returns other than electronically must file their return by the end of October 2010. If a taxpayer has not calculated the tax due, the HMRC office will do so on the basis of the figures submitted (and sometimes raise queries on the return). The bonus is that HMRC has to do the calculations and not the taxpayer. Before 2008 this was a considerable advantage because the calculation form issued by HMRC to taxpayers, while brilliant and elegant to tax specialists, was far too complicated for normal human beings. This form has been radically revised and is now much simpler to use. When the tax office calculates the tax due, it is on the basis of the figures submitted by the taxpayer and does not indicate that HMRC accepts them; HMRC may still come back later and make new calculations on some new basis if it is dissatisfied with the return.

Payment of the tax is due when the self-assessment return is made or the due date, whichever is earlier. Some tax will already have been paid by deduction at source of interest payments, under the Pay as You Earn cumulative withholding system from employment income (see below) and the credit that accompanies dividend and most other payments. In addition, there is a system of payment on account in two instalments (31 January and 31 July preceding the date of the return). Continuing with the example of the tax for the year 2009–2010, which is finally due on 31 January 2011, there will have been payments on account on 31 January and July 2010, so that only the balance is due on 31 January 2011 (along with the first payment on account for the next year). The payment on account system is meant to protect HMRC rather than victimize the taxpayer. The amount of the payment on account is related to the amount by which the taxpayer's payments on account fell short of the final bill for the previous year. There is no obligation on the taxpayer to pay more than this even when the income of the current year is greater. Where the payment on account seems to the taxpayer to be excessive, there is a procedure for reducing it – but at the taxpayer's risk with regard to penalties and interest if the reduction proves to be incorrect.

HMRC may give notice when enquiring into a return and has a twelve-month period in which to do this; the subsequent investigation may take longer. The enquiry is ended by a 'closure' notice. Once the enquiry period has passed or the closure notice has been given, HMRC has power to seek unpaid tax if this situation was brought about carelessly or deliberately by the taxpayer and the officer could not have been reasonably expected, on the basis of the information then available, to be aware of the loss of tax.

The ordinary time limit for giving notice is now four years after the 31 January by which the self-assessment return should have been made. This is lengthened to six years if the loss of tax has been due to carelessness and twenty years if it has been deliberate. It is expected that these new periods will be fully in place by April 2010.

Taxpayers outside the self-assessment system have their tax assessed by the HMRC. This has worked quite well because of: (i) the wide band of income taxed at the basic rate of tax and (ii) the scheme for withholding tax at source on many types of investment income, including dividends and interest. In combination with the first feature, this meant that there would be few adjustments made for most taxpayers if tax at the basic rate were withheld at source.

However, perhaps the most important feature of the rules for taxpayers outside the self-assessment system was the introduction during World War II of the rules known as Pay As You Earn (PAYE). This was a system of cumulative withholding at source on all income from employment. The taxpayer would be given a code that would be based on the deductions available to him that year; the deductions would then be allocated on a week-by-week cumulative basis. The rules allowed for an accurate deduction of tax even where the person's income level or employment changed during the year. A drop in income level would bring not simply a reduced tax deduction for the rest of the year but sometimes even a repayment. The purpose of this system was to establish the correct amount of income tax deducted at source by the end of the year so as to avoid additional paperwork. This imposed a substantial extra cost on employers but the system appears to have worked well.

9. GENERAL PRINCIPLES

9.1. Relationship between Tax and Financial Accounting

The traditional stance of UK tax law was to regard tax accounting and business accounting as distinct. The force of this distinction could be exaggerated. Thus, it was clear that in many areas the tax law rules were different from the accounting rules (e.g., in relation to depreciation). Nonetheless, as a practical matter, both tax practitioners and HMRC would start by looking at the business accounts and then making such changes as were needed for tax law.

The recent United Kingdom story has been one of continuous movement, usually gently, toward alignment. The UK tax legislation (TA 1988, sections 18 and 60) charges tax on the full amount of annual profits or gains arising or accruing from a trade, profession, or vocation. By the early 1990s the courts had come to recognize a significant role for business accounting.

A Court of Appeal decision[17] doubted whether any judge-made rule could override a generally accepted rule of commercial accountancy that: (i) applied to the situation in question; (ii) was not one of two or more rules applicable to that situation; and (iii) was not shown to be inconsistent with the true facts or otherwise inapt to determine the true profits or losses of the business. This was carried further by legislation.[18] These provisions require that the profit must be computed in accordance with generally accepted accounting principles 'subject to any adjustments required or authorized by law' in computing profits for those purposes. Depending on the taxpayer, the generally accepted accounting principles are those recognized in the United Kingdom or the International Accounting Standards.

This is still a long way from complete alignment, but there have been substantial legislative changes that have brought the two closer. Thus, the mid-1990s corporation tax rules on loan relationships, financial instruments, and foreign exchange (now merged with the loan relationship rules) all use accounting rules for measuring and timing gains and losses; moreover, they usually override the distinction between capital and revenue. Likewise, the 2002 rules on intellectual property use accounting concepts both in their definition and tax computation rules. One thing these provisions have in common is a willingness to abandon the old doctrines, such as the distinction between income and capital and the realization requirement. In place of the old doctrines is an accrual system of taxation covering both gains and losses and allowing a choice of accounting systems.

In 2002, the government consulted on a more radical extension of these changes to the rest of the corporate tax system by proposing the adoption of business accounting principles for depreciation, for annual revaluation of capital assets, and for scrapping the schedular system in favour of a global definition of income. These proposals eventually faded away.

Some business people still want tax law to follow accounting treatment – usually believing that they can get more reliefs than are available at present and hoping to save on accountants' bills for making tax returns. However, some accounting specialists want to be free to develop their accounting ideas, which are based on how to report profits to shareholders and other interested parties without fear that that their proposals will be rejected because of adverse tax implications. Some tax specialists want nothing to do with it, believing that some of the answers produced by the accounting theorists are not only bad tax, but also bad accounting.

This dispute reminds one of the words of Lord Hoffmann, who once wrote, 'Like many rival tribes accountants and lawyers have opinions of each other which

---

17. *Gallagher v. Jones* [1993] STC 537, especially 555-6, per Sir Thomas Bingham M.R.
18. FA 1998, s. 42 for corporation tax and ITTOIA, s. 25 for income tax.

are largely based on ignorance. . . . In fact both professions are deeply engaged in the intolerable wrestle with words and meanings, which give rise to philosophical problems having much in common with each other.'[19]

9.2. Respect for Legal Form

The distinction between private law and public law has had little impact on UK substantive law – as opposed to procedural law – and it has been quite unnecessary to decide whether tax law is part of public law. The English genius for not categorizing things unless one must, combined with its instinctive wish to proceed on a purely pragmatic basis, is well illustrated by this issue, which is of such concern to lawyers brought up in the civil law tradition.

In answering the question of how far the UK tax law has respect for legal form, we must divide the question into different issues. We start by recognizing that the rights and duties created by people in their personal or business dealings are part of the facts to which the tax law must apply its concepts; thus, the rights created by legal form are as much fact as the state of the weather or a person's age. As section 9.3, which follows, shows, the UK courts have wrestled hard with the question of how far they can go in re-characterizing the facts where tax avoidance schemes are concerned. As the speech of Lord Hoffmman in *MacNiven*, cited below in section 9.3, makes clear, there will be many contexts in which the courts give a strict legal meaning to a particular expression in the tax legislation. It would not occur to these judges that they are having 'respect' for the legal form; they are simply interpreting the relevant (tax) legislation. Apart from the avoidance context, there will be many occasions on which the tax legislation uses concepts which have familiar legal meanings. Thus, the question whether a person's income comes from employment or business turns on whether the relevant contract is one of service or for services, a distinction familiar to tort and labour lawyers. The question whether a business is being carried on by a company or by a partnership will have to be answered with the Partnership Act definition of a partnership very much in mind. Likewise, questions of status such as whether a person is married, or whether Y is the child of X, will normally be answered by reference to family law rules. To take another example, the technicalities of property law will also be relevant in analyzing issues such as whether a person still has an 'interest' in property.

In response, the tax legislature may deliberately avoid the use of a word with existing technical overtones. This may be further encouraged by the fact that the tax legislation has to apply to Scotland as well as to England, and therefore the language should be able to accommodate two sets of concepts; this may be done by referring explicitly to English terms and then to Scottish terms – for example, the definition of 'settlement' for Inheritance Tax purposes[20] or by adopting broader

19. Foreword to Freedman and Power (eds), *Law and Accountancy: Conflict and Cooperation in the 1990s* (1992).
20. IHTA s. 43.

terminology not confined to one system or the other. The UK tax system pays considerable respect to the legal form of the transaction. The issue, in all cases, is how far the legal form of the transaction determines the tax consequences, but this is a matter for the process of interpreting tax statutes.

9.3. ANTI-AVOIDANCE DOCTRINES AND RULES

The periodic shifts in the UK tax environment can also be seen in the willingness or unwillingness of the courts to control tax avoidance by judicial doctrine. As seen above in section 6.2, the effect of the *Barclays* case is that the courts now try to look for the purpose behind the statute and to take a less blinkered approach to the facts. While *Barclays* does much to settle the intellectual basis for interpretation, it does little for certainty in the application of the rules. Despite the new judicial approach, tax legislation is still drafted in the traditional way with highly prescriptive rules, sometimes backed up by a purpose-based anti-avoidance rule. Some of these rules have proved difficult to interpret.

The UK tax system has a large number of anti-avoidance provisions, some broad, some narrow. The courts have shown a willingness to interpret in a broad way anti-avoidance provisions that are phrased in general language that deliberately eschews legal terms of art. The story is long and drawn-out and erratic, as the following quotation from nearly forty years ago shows:

> We seem to have travelled a long way from the general and salutary rule that the subject is not to be taxed except by plain words. But I must recognize that plain words are seldom adequate to anticipate and forestall the multiplicity of ingenious schemes which are constantly being devised to evade (*sic*) taxation. Parliament is very properly determined to prevent this kind of tax evasion (*sic*) and, if the courts find it impossible to give very wide meanings to general phrases, the only alternative may be for Parliament to do as some other countries have done, and introduce legislation of a more sweeping character which will put the ordinary well-intentioned person at much greater risk than is now created by a wide interpretation of such provisions as those which we are now considering.[21]

The House of Lords has shown itself capable, on the one hand, of depriving a provision of any effect, and, on the other, of imposing double taxation.

Apart from the question of the strictness or otherwise with which statutes are construed, there is the closely related issue of the characterization of the facts, particularly where avoidance schemes are concerned. There has been no shortage of leading cases on the judicial approach to problems of tax avoidance, but one still begins with *IRC v. Duke of Westminster*.[22] This case lays down that, in applying the tax legislation to the facts, the courts must have respect for the legal rights the

21. Lord Reid in *Greenberg v. IRC* [1972] A.C. 173 (HL) at 198.
22. *IRC v. Duke of Westminster* [1936] AC 1; 19 TC 490.

parties have created, even if those rights were created for tax avoidance purposes. In this form, the decision is still good law, but it does not tell us what those legal rights are, and it is here that the new approach has made its impact.

As a result of some occasional odd drafting and an aggressive tax-avoidance industry, a number of avoidance schemes were peddled in the 1970s. These schemes frequently involved circular and ultimately self-cancelling transactions carried through according to some timetable. A typical example was *Ramsay v. IRC,*[23] where the House determined that it would be consistent with the *Westminster* doctrine to treat such circular and self-cancelling transactions as one single transaction for tax purposes. Although the scheme in *Ramsay* failed not only at this abstract level but also on a narrow point of tax law, the decision was important. If the scheme had succeeded, the tax (CGT) would have become voluntary – one would have paid either HMRC or the tax adviser. In assessing this apparently complacent attitude on the part of the judges, it should not be forgotten that Parliament passes a Finance Bill every year and that loopholes could be filled by appropriate provisions. Moreover, the traditions of party discipline and of allowing clauses drafted by good professional draftsmen meant that the government would usually get its way, and do so in a workable form.

In *Furniss v. Dawson,*[24] the *Ramsay* decision was extended to a linear transaction in a preordained series having no purpose (as opposed to effect) other than the avoidance of tax. This was the high-water mark of what became known as the New Approach or the *Ramsay* doctrine. The case itself involved the use of a share-for-share exchange to achieve a deferral of capital gains tax on a corporate reorganization. The effect of that decision, exacerbated by some wide statements by some members of the court, was to reduce much tax advice to a valueless exercise in guessing what the courts might do next. This period of uncertainty ended in 1988 when the court, in considering what was meant by a preordained series of transactions, concluded that such a series of transactions existed only when it was 'practically certain' at the time of the first step that the second would follow.[25] This case also restricted the New Approach, so that the United Kingdom was left with a narrow step transaction doctrine that applied where there is no business purpose other than the avoidance of tax. However, the New Approach may well have had other effects, particularly in encouraging the courts to look more broadly at the facts even where there is no tax-avoidance motive. Meanwhile, the courts have stressed the need for tax to live in the 'real world'.[26]

The nature of the common law is such that the process of judicial development of doctrine is anything but smooth; much depends on the nature of the case before the court and the particular judges. Two further judicial decisions make this point. The first was *McGuckian v. IRC* 1997 in which, as we have seen, the House of Lords enunciated the purposive approach to the interpretation of tax statutes, and

23. *Ramsay v. IRC* [1981] STC 174, [1982] AC 300.
24. *Furniss v. Dawson* [1984] STC 153, [1984] AC 474.
25. *Craven v. White; Bayliss v. Gregory* and *IRC v. Bowater* [1988] STC 476.
26. For example, *Ensign Tankers* (Leasing) *Ltd v. Stokes* [1992] STC 226.

two of the five members of the House of Lords sitting in that case were prepared to take a broad approach to an avoidance case without going through the step transaction doctrine at all. The other, and more dramatic, decision was the unanimous decision of the House of Lords in 2001 *MacNiven v. Westmoreland Investments Ltd*,[27] in which the leading and most complete speech was given by Lord Hoffmann. This case held that the step transaction doctrine did not have any role where the term in issue was 'juristic' as opposed to commercial. The commercial/juristic distinction proved difficult to apply, and in the *Barclays* case it was downgraded to being a useful insight. However, what mattered was that the House held in *MacNiven* that the question whether to apply the new approach was itself a question of construction. The courts have no power to strike down avoidance schemes; Parliament has not given them such power, and while they can develop purposive interpretations or a step transaction doctrine, the matter remains one of judicial attitude.

In the late 1990s HMRC consulted on the possibility of introducing a statutory general anti-avoidance rule (GAAR). The result of the consultation was that the proposal was withdrawn – however, that was before the decisions in *MacNiven* and *Barclays.* Tax planners seem to have become ever more aggressive in recent years. The legislative response so far has been to increase the number of anti-avoidance rules in new legislation, with the result of ever-longer annual statutes.

Meanwhile, the European Court of Justice has developed its own approach to these issues. It has refused to give effect to transactions which 'abuse' EU rules; this is closely related to a refusal to give effect to transactions which are wholly artificial. The court applies this approach both to VAT and direct taxes. We wait to see how long the UK courts take to adapt them to purely domestic direct tax situations.

10. SOURCES OF TAX LAW

10.1. Legislation and Materials and Cases

A statute's legislative history can be traced not only in the legislation passed year-by-year together with the accompanying debates, but also in the annual reports made to Parliament by HMRC. These are accompanied by many statistics. There is also useful information of a background variety in another government publication called *Social Trends*. Explanatory notes prepared by HMRC for Ministers when presenting the bill to Parliament are now publicly available – and can be traced through the HMRC website <www.hmrc.gov.uk> – a long-overdue change. Legislation produced under the Tax Law Rewrite Programme can be traced through the various exposure drafts as well as the extensive explanatory notes that accompany the final legislation. These are available electronically via the HMRC website.

27. [2001] UKHL 6, [2001] STC 237.

The texts of the statutes are available through the normal commercial websites (e.g., LexisNexis and Westlaw). There are no official hard copy versions of the complete tax statutes – everyone relies for hard copy on the annual versions produced by Tolley LexisNexis and CCH.

The House of Common Parliamentary Papers dating back to the eighteenth century are now available on the website <http//parlipapers.chadwyck.co.uk>. This covers, for example, bills, statutes, Parliamentary Committee Reports, and the Annual Reports of HMRC. The debates, reported in *Hansard,* are now available online for the House of Commons dating back to 1988 and for the House of Lords dating back to 1996; this work is continuing; see <www.publications.parliament.uk/pa/pahansard>.

UK judicial decisions are available online through websites such as Westlaw. The cases are also published weekly through series such as Simons Tax Cases and its CCH counterpart. There is also a series called 'Tax Cases'. These are published by HMRC. They are produced only when the case is finally settled but have the advantage that the reader can find the decision of the original tax tribunal and all successive stages of appeal together in one place.

10.2. Official Practice and Rulings

HMRC (formerly Inland Revenue) for many years published extra-statutory concessions and statements of practice. The latter became more systematic in 1978. The scope of the legal basis for making these concessions has been the matter of much debate; recent legislation enables the Treasury to give legal effect to existing concessions by order. Since 1978, HMRC has published Revenue Interpretations and Decisions in their own magazine called *Tax Bulletin.*

Other sources include the publication of HMRC's own manuals for the guidance of inspectors; some of these are particularly useful (e.g., those dealing with specialized matters such as banking and international transactions). Publication of the manuals is not complete – various passages, such as those on avoidance schemes, are omitted.

Pre-transaction rulings have been a feature of some parts of the tax code but are not generalized. Informal advance clearances have long been available provided full disclosure is made. The development of pre-transaction rulings is part of a recent HMRC process of improving its working relation with large businesses. The process is intended to develop an 'enhanced relationship' between the taxpaying company and HMRC, with better and quicker service and each company having its own Customer Relationship Manager at HMRC. This is all part of HMRC's goal to make best use of its resources and to use a risk-based analysis for its compliance activities. HMRC also hope that this relationship may lead to less aggressive tax planning.

The question whether one can use concessions for tax-avoidance purposes was considered in *R v. IRC ex parte Fulford-Dobson.*[28] The court held that since the

28. *R v. IRC ex parte Fulford-Dobson* [1987] STC 344, 60 TC 168.

official booklet published by the Inland Revenue and setting out these concessions stated that the Revenue would not allow them to be used for avoidance purposes, the taxpayer could not reverse that refusal by judicial review. This is of considerable interest as there is, of course, no general anti-avoidance provision in the tax legislation itself.

Where an application for judicial review is made on the basis of a ruling, in the case of an informal clearance, HMRC will be bound only if the taxpayer gave full details of the specific transaction on which he sought the ruling, made it plain that a fully-considered ruling was sought, indicated the use he intended to make of any ruling given, and if the ruling or statement made was clear, unambiguous, and devoid of qualification. A breach of a representation by HMRC will not amount to an abuse of power if the taxpayer knows that clearance at the local level is not to be treated as binding on HMRC or if the taxpayer has not fully disclosed all relevant material to the inspectors. There is not necessarily full disclosure merely because sufficient information has been disclosed to enable inferences to be drawn.

10.3. TREATIES

The United Kingdom has an extensive network of double tax treaties.

10.4. SECONDARY SOURCES

There are two leading practitioners' works. *Simons Direct Tax Service*, recently completely revised and reissued, is available both electronically and in hard copy (10 volumes); it is published by Butterworths LexisNexis. CCH publishes a similar service. The best accounts for lawyers are to be found in the series of volumes published by Sweet and Maxwell and some stemming from the work of G.S.A. Wheatcroft in the 1960s; this is known collectively known as the *British Tax Library*. *Wheatcroft and Whiteman on Income Tax,* 3rd edn, was published in 1988 and is kept up to date by annual cumulative supplements.

The last Royal Commission on income tax reported in 1955. There have been various government documents or reports of committees on particular issues since then (e.g., the Keith Committee Report on the Powers of the Revenue Departments in 1983). As seen above, the House of Commons Parliamentary Papers dating back to the eighteenth century are now available on the website <http://www.parlipapers.chadwyck.co.uk>.

There is much other writing on tax. Some of the most important is produced by the fiercely independent Institute for Fiscal Studies (<www.ifs.org.uk>) and, of special interest to lawyers, its influential Tax Law Review Committee (TLRC). Publications from the IFS also include occasional commentaries, their famous green budgets, which are surveys of options for future government action and incisive comments on past choices, and the journal *Fiscal Studies*. Textbooks include *Tiley's Revenue Law*, 6th edn (Hart Publishing, 2008, with electronic supplements from the publisher), *Revenue Law Principles and Practice*, 26th edn (Tottel Publishing, 2008), and *Tiley and Collison's UK Tax Guide* 2008–2009 edn (LexisNexis: Tolley); the latter two are annual publications and cover more taxes than does Tiley.

The leading journal is the *British Tax Review*, founded in 1956. There are also some articles of interest in *The Tax Journal* and *Taxation* (both published by LexisNexis and the *Tax Adviser*, which is published by the Chartered Institute of Taxation (<www.ciot.org.uk>).

Some relevant websites have been mentioned already but are repeated here. The Revenue and Customs website is <http//:www.hmrc.gov.uk>, but those interested in policy matters and current legislation should also refer to the Treasury website at <www.hm-treasury.gov.uk>. The IFS website <http//:www.ifs.org.uk> has links to many other tax-related sites.

The famous *Structure and Reform of Direct Taxation,* also known as the 'Meade Report', was published by the Institute for Fiscal Studies in 1978. A successor volume, *Tax by Design: Reforming the Tax System for the 21st Century*, the Mirrlees Review, is to be published in 2009. A volume of commissioned papers is already available online. It will be published as *Dimensions of Tax Design, 2009.*

The United States

James R. Repetti

1. HISTORY OF FEDERAL INCOME TAX

The United States first adopted a tax on the income of individuals in 1864 to finance the Civil War. A taxpayer's income included his share of undistributed corporate income. The tax, which was repealed in 1872, affected only 1% of potential taxpayers because of a generous exemption.

Over twenty years passed before Congress adopted a new act in 1895 that imposed a tax on the income of both individuals and corporations. The US Supreme Court declared this act unconstitutional because Congress lacked authority to adopt an individual income tax without apportioning the tax among the states based on their relative populations. The final enactment of an individual income tax required the adoption of the 16th Amendment to the Constitution, which was ratified by the states in 1913.

The original 1913 income tax and subsequent changes through 1938 were enacted as self-contained Revenue Acts. Each new Revenue Act would supersede the prior Revenue Act and would contain all the income tax provisions. As a result, the process of referencing and amending the statutes was very complex and cumbersome. To remedy this problem, Congress codified all the revenue provisions in effect in 1939 into the Internal Revenue Code of 1939. The change to a Code allowed subsequent statutory enactments to occur as amendments to the Code, rather than as a re-enactment of the entire Revenue Act.

Congress replaced the 1939 Code with the Internal Revenue Code of 1954. The 1954 Code revised the income tax treatment of partnerships, trusts and estates, annuities, and corporate distributions. It also introduced several new deductions and provided more accelerated depreciation rates. The most significant changes in the 1954 Code occurred in the 1980s. In 1981 Congress substantially reduced individual rates and adopted significant new tax incentives for savings and investments, including greatly accelerated depreciation rates. In 1986, Congress adopted additional significant changes in the income tax structure. The Tax Reform Act of 1986 broadened the tax base, substantially eliminating many tax incentive provisions and reducing individual rates still further. The deduction for personal interest was eliminated (except for home mortgage interest), as was the preference for capital gains. To mark the significance of the changes, Congress renamed the Code as the Internal Revenue Code of 1986.

The period 1986 through 2000 witnessed several amendments to the Code that tended to increase the maximum statutory rates for individuals. Concerns about budget deficits dominated legislation during that period, with little attention paid to the impact of the changes on the overall structure of the Code. Frequently, Congress hastily adopted amendments to the Code, with the result that still more 'technical' amendments were necessary to correct the earlier changes. The focus on revenues, however, helped eliminate a budget deficit and, with the help of strong economic growth through 2000, created a surplus.

From 2001 through 2006, a Republican President and a Republican majority in both houses of Congress existed for the first time in almost half a century. The result was a series of tax cuts. In 2001, Congress enacted a major tax cut intended to decrease revenues by $1.35 trillion dollars for the period 2001 through 2010. The tax decreases generally took the form of reduced rates for individuals. In addition, the estate tax was repealed effective in 2010. Interestingly, the decreased tax rates will end on 31 December 2010, and the pre-existing higher rates, as well as the estate tax, will be restored in 2011, unless Congress votes to make the reduced rates and elimination of the estate tax permanent or to modify them. In 2003, Congress reduced the maximum tax rate for individuals on capital gain and dividend income to 15%. In late 2004, bowing to pressure from the EU, Congress finally repealed the FSC/ETI regime and replaced it with provisions that allow special deductions for domestic 'manufacturers' (a term defined broadly to include, among others, film producers and software creators). Despite the fact that Republicans lost control of the House of Representatives in 2007, concerns about economic conditions prompted more generous depreciation and expensing provisions in 2008.

2. CONSTITUTIONAL ISSUES

The Sixteenth Amendment to the US Constitution grants Congress broad powers to assess an income tax. Earlier cases that seemed to impose some restrictions on the Sixteenth Amendment on the ability of Congress to use tax statutes to accomplish objectives not related to raising revenue are now commonly disregarded. For example, it is now clear that Congress may use taxes to discourage certain activities without any consideration of whether the tax will in fact raise revenues.[1]

1. See, e.g., *Sunshine Anthracite Coal Co. v. Adkins*, 310 US 381 (1947).

Moreover, Congress may favour some groups with tax preferences without favouring all groups so long as the distinction among groups is not based on a suspect classification such as race. For example, in *Regan v. Taxation With Representation of Washington,*[2] the Supreme Court ruled that the fact that Congress allows veterans' organizations to use tax-deductible contributions to engage in political lobbying did not mean that Congress has to extend the same tax subsidy to other organizations. The Court explained that Congress has 'broad latitude in creating classifications and distinctions in tax statutes'.

Consistent with this 'broad latitude' is the Supreme Court's treatment of tax statutes that apply retroactively. The Court has stated that the enactment or amendment of a tax statute that applies retroactively will be held unconstitutional under the due process clause of the Fifth Amendment only where 'the nature of the tax and the circumstances in which it is laid [are] so harsh and oppressive as to transgress the constitutional limitation'.[3] Under this standard, the Supreme Court has permitted tax rates to increase for the calendar year in which the legislation was adopted, although adopted late in the year.[4] Similarly, in *United States v. Carlton,*[5] the Court held that an amendment in 1987 that applied retroactively to 1986 was not unconstitutional where Congress had acted promptly to correct a mistake in the statute adopted in 1986.

Another area illustrating the US courts' view of the expansive nature of Congressional taxing power is the courts' application of Article 1, section 7, clause 1 of the US Constitution. That provision states, 'All Bills for raising Revenue shall originate in the House of Representatives; but the Senate may propose or concur with amendments as on other bills.' In 1982 the House of Representatives adopted a tax bill consisting of three pages, which it then sent to the Senate. The Senate removed the provisions which the House had adopted and substituted over 500 pages of new amendments to the Code. Both the House and the Senate then adopted the 'revised' bill, and it was signed by the President. All the US Courts of Appeals, which have addressed the validity of this process, have held that the Senate's 'revision' did not violate the above-quoted Article 1, section 7, clause 1.

3. TAX RATES

The rates of the US income tax have fluctuated widely depending upon revenue needs and economic objectives of Congress. Initially, in 1913, the maximum statutory tax rate was 6% for individuals and 1% for corporations. In subsequent years the rate for individuals peaked at 91% and for corporations at 52% (excluding the excess profits tax, which during World War II subjected corporations to an overall maximum rate of 80%).

---

2. 461 US 540 (1983).
3. *Welch v. Henry*, 305 US 134, 147 (1948).
4. See, e.g., *United States v. Darusmont*, 449 US 292, 297 (1981); *United States v. Hudson*, 299 US 495, 500-01 (1937).
5. 512 US 26 (1994).

The Internal Revenue Code of 1986 significantly reduced both the level and progressivity of the rates, establishing the maximum statutory rate for individuals at 28% and the corporate rate at 34%. Since then, rates have varied depending on the political and fiscal climate. In 1993, Congress increased rates to 39.6% for individuals and 35% for corporations. In 2001, Congress adopted legislation that would decrease rates for individuals during the five-year period through 2006. In 2003, Congress accelerated the decrease, with the result that the maximum individual rate is 35% for 2009.

Different rate schedules are provided for different categories of individuals. The brackets for the lower rates are broader for married individuals filing joint returns and for heads of households as compared to the brackets for unmarried individuals. The brackets for rates that apply to all individuals are adjusted annually to reflect inflation. The rates for the 2009 taxable year are as follows:

Unmarried Taxpayer

Taxable Income	*Rate*
$0–$8,350	10%
$8,351–$33,950	15%
$33,951–$82,250	25%
$82,251–$171,550	28%
$171,551–$372,950	33%
$372,950 or more	35%

Married Taxpayers Filing Jointly

Taxable Income	*Rate*
$0–$16,700	10%
$16,701–$67,900	15%
$67,901–$137,050	25%
$137,051–$208,850	28%
$208,851–$372,950	33%
$372,951 or more	35%

Taxpayer Who is Head of Household

Taxable Income	*Rate*
$0–$11,950	10%
$11,951–$45,500	15%
$45,501–$117,450	25%
$117,451–$190,200	28%
$190,201–$372,950	33%
$372,951 or more	35%

The tax rates for corporations are not adjusted annually to reflect inflation. The corporate tax rates for 2009 are as follows:

Corporations

Taxable Income	*Rate*
$0–$50,000	15%
$50,001–$75,000	25%
$75,001–100,000	34%
$100,001–335,000	39%
$335,001–$10,000,000	34%
$10,000,001–$15,000,000	35%
$15,000,001–$18,333,333	38%
$18,333,334 or more	35%

The corporate rate of 38%, which is applied to taxable income between $15,000,001 and $18,333,333, exists in order to reduce the benefit of the lower rates that were applied to lesser bracket amounts.

4. COMPOSITION OF THE FISCAL SYSTEM

In addition to the income tax, the US federal government also imposes a wealth transfer tax, social security taxes, and various excise taxes. There is no federal sales or value added tax. Each state in the federal system is also allowed to impose taxes. The states in general impose some combination of income, property, wealth, sales, and excise taxes.

Social security taxes in the United States represent a significant tax that is imposed on net income from self-employment or on wages from employment. For 2009, self-employed individuals pay social security taxes of 15.3% on net earnings of $106,800 or less. Income from self-employment in excess of $106,800 is taxed at 2.9%. Employees pay social security taxes of 7.65% on their wages of $106,800 or less and their employers also pay taxes of 7.65% on each employee's wages up to $106,800. The employee and employer each pay a tax of 1.45% on the employee's wages in excess of $106,800.

Federal receipts, as a percentage of gross domestic product ('GDP'), have been fairly steady since 1960. During the period 1978 through 2007, federal receipts ranged from a low of 16.4% of GDP for the year 2004 to a high of 20.9% for the year 2000.[6] Revenues in 2007, constituting 18.8% of GDP, were down from the high of 20.9% in 2000 as a result of the tax decreases adopted in 2001 and an economic recession. The largest source of receipts for the US government is the individual income tax. In 2007, 45.3% of federal receipts were from

6. *Budget of the United States Government, Fiscal Year 2009*, Historic Tables, Table 2.3 (2008).

the individual income tax.[7] The next-largest category of receipts by the IRS is social security taxes, which accounted for 33.9% of IRS receipts in 2007.[8] Taxes from corporations accounted for only 14.4% of receipts in 2007.[9] Receipts from the estate and gift tax represented 1% of federal receipts in 2007.[10]

It is interesting to note that the relative contributions of the corporate income tax and social security taxes have reversed over the past sixty years. In 1944, social security taxes accounted for 7.9% of federal receipts, while the corporate income tax accounted for 33.9% of receipts.[11] In contrast, in 2007, corporate income taxes accounted for only 14.4% of receipts while social security taxes accounted for 33.9%.[12]

5. BASIC STRUCTURE OF THE INCOME TAX

5.1. Individuals

The US income tax is global. It taxes the income of US citizens and US residents regardless of the geographic source or character of the income. The starting point for calculating the tax is gross income. The term 'gross income' is defined broadly to include all accessions to wealth, with a few well-defined exclusions. Some significant exclusions are gifts, bequests, and proceeds from life insurance policies. Scholarships paid to degree-seeking students are also excludable from income if the scholarship is for tuition or book expenses and the student is not required to perform services. A broad range of fringe benefits is excluded from income, the most important ones being employer-provided health insurance and employer contributions to pension plans.

Income from the cancellation of debt is excluded from income only in certain narrow situations, such as when the taxpayer is insolvent or in a bankruptcy proceeding. Windfalls and gambling wins are clearly includable in income.

Although no statutory provision addresses the issue, imputed income is not taxed in the United States. For example, taxpayers do not recognize income for the imputed rental value of their homes. Similarly, a taxpayer is not taxed with respect to the care provided by a spouse, parent, or child.

Gross income is recognized upon the occurrence of a realization event. The scope of transactions that result in a realization event is fairly broad. For example, an exchange of one item of property for another qualifies as a realization event where the properties differ 'materially in kind or in extent'. Under this

---

7. *Ibid.*, at Table 2.2.
8. *Ibid.*
9. *Ibid.*
10. Estate and gift tax receipts were $26 billion in 2002 out of a total of $2.568 trillion in total receipts. *Budget of the United States Government, supra* n. 6, at Tables 2.1 and 2.5.
11. *Ibid.*
12. *Ibid.*

approach, the change in the yield of a debt instrument by more than 25 basis points will generally be treated as an exchange of an old debt instrument for a new instrument. In the corporate context, the distribution of appreciated property is now normally a realization event to the distributing corporation, although it took Congress a surprisingly long time to reach this result.

The United States does not treat death as a realization event. Indeed, the appreciation inherent in property held by a taxpayer at death permanently escapes income taxation because the tax basis of the property is stepped up to its fair market value at the time of death (or its fair market value at the time six months after death if the alternative valuation date is selected). Property owned by the taxpayer at death is subject, however, to the US estate tax, which is a wealth transfer tax.

An old Supreme Court decision, *Eisner v. Macomber,*[13] initially created some doubt about whether Congress had the authority to treat the mere appreciation of an asset as a realization event. However, the Court's statement in a subsequent decision,[14] which described the realization requirement as 'founded on administrative convenience', has largely eliminated any doubt about the authority of Congress to define a realization event in any way it wishes. Congress has elected to take a 'mark-to-market' approach in narrow circumstances. For example, taxpayers in general are required to recognize any appreciation or diminution in value that has occurred during the tax year only with respect to certain futures contracts and options.

After calculating gross income, individual taxpayers may deduct expenditures that the statutes expressly provide are deductible. Taxpayers are permitted to deduct expenses that they have incurred in producing income in a trade or business. Difficult judgments occur, however, where expenses that are incurred in the conduct of a trade or business also involve aspects of personal consumption. The US tax system's treatment of such expenditures has been somewhat arbitrary. Some expenditures that involve mixed aspects of income production and personal consumption are always non-deductible in full regardless of whether the income-producing aspect dominates. For example, child care expenses and the costs of commuting from a taxpayer's residence to her principal place of business are not deductible.[15] Other expenses, such as business-related meals and entertainment, are partially deductible pursuant to a statute that arbitrarily allows a deduction for 50% of such expenditures.

The trade or business expenses that may be deducted currently are limited to expenses that do not have a significant benefit extending beyond the current taxable year. In general, expenses that have a benefit extending beyond the current year must be capitalized, although there has been substantial disagreement as to exactly how the test should be formulated. These capitalized expenses may be amortized or depreciated under various Code provisions. In general, the period

13. 252 US 189 (1920).
14. *Helvering v. Horst*, 311 US 112, 115 (1940).
15. A special credit is allowed, however, for a portion of the expenses incurred in caring for children under age 14.

for depreciation or amortization is determined by statute. Currently, the periods for real property correspond roughly to their economic useful life. In the past seven years Congress has increasingly allowed capital expenditures involving tangible personal property to be expensed in order to encourage investment.

Trade or business expenses are generally deductible from gross income to obtain the statutorily defined amount of 'adjusted gross income'. Most other deductions (the 'itemized deductions') are then taken from adjusted gross income to determine taxable income. The calculation of adjusted gross income is significant because many of the itemized deductions are limited by reference to adjusted gross income. For example, the deduction for charitable contributions of appreciated property is in general limited to 30% of adjusted gross income. Medical expenses are deductible only to the extent that they exceed 10% of adjusted gross income.

Most itemized deductions represent 'tax expenditures'. These deductions include medical expenses, casualty losses, and interest on loans secured by residences. In addition to the tax expenditure deductions, expenses incurred in profit-seeking activities that do not rise to the level of a trade or business and that are not related to rent- or royalty-producing property are also deductible only from adjusted gross income in calculating taxable income.

Most of the expenses deductible from adjusted gross income in calculating taxable income are decreased by up to 80% for high-income taxpayers. The decrease takes the form of a 'phase-out' of the deductions as income increases. Congress indicated that the purpose of the phase-out was to more closely match tax burdens with ability to pay.[16] Excluded from this phasing-out are medical expenses, casualty losses, and interest expenses incurred in connection with the production of investment income.

Moreover, some itemized deductions (the so-called 'miscellaneous' itemized deductions), such as expenses incurred in a profit-seeking activity and expenses of an employee that have not been reimbursed by the employer, are deductible only to the extent that they exceed in the aggregate 2% of adjusted gross income. Congress stated that the purpose for the 2% floor was to reduce the burden of record keeping and to account for the fact that the expenses subject to the 2% floor often contained some element of voluntary personal expenditure.[17]

In lieu of itemized deductions, individual taxpayers may deduct a so-called standard deduction. Usually, taxpayers will deduct the standard deduction if it exceeds the total amount of their allowable itemized deductions. The standard deduction is not subject to the 2% floor rule or to the phase-out that applies to many itemized deductions. The main purpose of the standard deduction is to reduce the need for record keeping for expenses; it also functions to exempt from tax a certain amount of income for those taxpayers, particularly in low brackets, who do not have such expenses. The standard deduction is adjusted annually to reflect

16. H.R. Rep. No. 881, 101st Cong., 2nd Sess. 361 (1990).
17. Staff of the Joint Committee on Taxation, *General Explanation of the Tax Reform Act of 1986*, 78 (1987).

inflation. For the 2009 taxable year, the standard deduction is $5,700 for unmarried individuals, $8,350 for heads of households, $5,700 for married individuals filing separately, and $11,400 for spouses filing jointly.

All individual taxpayers may also deduct a 'personal exemption' amount, which is adjusted annually to reflect inflation. For the 2009 taxable year, the personal exemption amount is $3,650. Taxpayers are also allowed additional exemptions for dependents. The exemptions are phased out for higher-income taxpayers. The phase-out of these deductions and the itemized personal deductions for high-income taxpayers generates a complex pattern of marginal rates.

After the various deductions, a tentative tax using the progressive tax rate is then calculated. Allowable tax credits, such as the child care credit and earned income tax credit, are subtracted to determine tax liability. Most credits are not refundable. However, the earned income credit is a refundable credit, which causes it to function as an income supplement system for low-income workers.

In calculating the tentative tax liability and actual tax liability, preferential tax rates apply to dividends and capital gains. The maximum rate for both types of income is 15%. In general, qualifying capital gains are gains attributable to capital assets that have been held for more than one year. A capital asset is generally defined in the Code as property that the taxpayer did not hold for sale to customers in the ordinary course of business and that was not depreciable property used in a trade or business. Special rules extend the preferential tax rate to gain from depreciable property used in a trade or business that is not held for sale to customers in the ordinary course of business. The portion of gain from depreciable property that is attributable to depreciation is recaptured as ordinary income. The portion of gain from depreciable real property that is attributable to depreciation is taxed at a rate of 25%. Any excess gain from depreciable property (real or personal) is taxed at a rate not greater than 15%. Special rules also apply to gain from the sale of 'collectibles' (e.g., stamp collections, rare coins and the like) held for more than a year. Gain from such items is taxed at a maximum rate of 28%.

In recent years, the US tax system for individuals has tended toward a schedular system. Several categories of expenses are limited in their deductibility to similar categories of income. For example, losses from 'passive activities' may be deducted only from income generated by passive activities. In general, a passive activity is a profit-seeking activity to which the taxpayer does not devote a significant amount of time. Similarly, investment interest expenses are deductible only from investment income. Where a personal residence is partly used for profit-seeking activities, expenses attributable to the personal residence (other than mortgage interest expenses) may in general be deducted only from income generated by the residence. Lastly, the treatment of capital gains is schedular. Taxpayers may fully deduct capital losses from capital gains but can deduct only $3,000 of capital losses from ordinary income annually.

Another aspect of the individual income tax is the alternative minimum tax (AMT). The AMT is, in effect, a 'shadow' tax system that accompanies the regular US tax system. Congress adopted the AMT 'to ensure that no taxpayer with substantial economic income can avoid significant tax liability by using exclusions, deductions and credits'.[18] The AMT functions as an alternative calculation of a taxpayer's taxable income by limiting or eliminating many tax expenditure deductions and exclusions. Where the taxpayer's AMT liability exceeds her regular income tax liability, the taxpayer must pay the AMT liability. Recently, the AMT has become quite controversial. Although Congress sought to apply the AMT to a taxpayer's 'economic income', the AMT frequently overestimates economic income because it denies a deduction for expenses incurred in a profit-seeking activity. Moreover, exemptions from the AMT have not been fully adjusted to reflect inflation. Consequently, in a result not anticipated when the AMT was first enacted, many middle-class taxpayers living in areas with high local taxes, which are not deductible for AMT purposes, have found themselves subject to the AMT.

5.2. Corporations

The United States has a modified classical corporate tax system that taxes income at the corporate level and again taxes distributions at the shareholder level, although at a reduced rate.

The income of a corporation is calculated in a manner similar to that with respect to individuals, but with several important variations. There is no adjusted gross income for a corporation, since expenses and losses incurred by a corporation are generally assumed to be connected to a trade or business. Instead, deductions are subtracted directly from gross income to calculate taxable income.

Capital gains are not taxed at a preferential rate, as they are for individuals. However, corporations are restricted to deducting their capital losses against capital gains. Unused capital losses may be carried back three years and forward five years.

Since the corporation is treated as a separate taxable entity, special rules are necessary to prevent the recognition of income upon the formation of the corporation. In general, shareholders will not recognize income when they transfer appreciated property to the corporation in exchange for stock if they will own 80% of the corporation's stock after the transfer. The corporation itself never recognizes gain upon the transfer of its own stock to a shareholder in exchange for property.

Because corporate income is taxable to the corporation when recognized and is taxable again when distributed to shareholders, special rules are necessary to prevent the 'cascading' of corporate-level tax with respect to intercorporate distributions that qualify as dividends.[19] These rules allow a deduction for a percentage of the dividend a corporate shareholder receives. The amount of the deduction depends on the level of shareholding. The entire dividend can be deducted if the corporate shareholder owns 80% of the stock of the distributing corporation.

18. Staff of the Joint Committee on Taxation, *General Explanation of the Tax Reform Act of 1986*, 432 (1987).
19. Dividends are distributions to stockholders of the corporation's 'earnings and profits' – that is, the corporation's taxable income with several adjustments.

Special rules apply to curtail the potential for tax arbitrage. For example, a provision prevents corporations from purchasing portfolio stock with borrowed proceeds in order to obtain the tax benefits of the interest deduction with respect to the borrowed proceeds and the dividends-received deduction with respect to amounts paid on the debt-financed portfolio stock. Similarly, Congress has sought to prevent corporations from obtaining capital loss deductions that are attributable to declines in the value of stock as the result of dividends paid to the corporations that were not taxed at all or only partially taxed.

Corporations are also allowed to acquire other corporations without triggering a corporate- or shareholder-level tax in certain transactions called 'reorganizations'. To qualify as a reorganization, several requirements must be satisfied. A business purpose for the transaction must exist, and a significant portion of the shareholders in the acquired corporation must receive stock in the acquiring corporation. Also, the acquiring corporation must continue to conduct at least one of the target's historic businesses or to use a significant amount of the target's assets. Finally, the structure of the transaction must correspond to one of the forms set forth in the statutes. There appears to be no substantive purpose for the transactional forms set forth in the statute, and their intricacies are the product of historical accident. The rationale supporting non-recognition – that the shareholders have not significantly changed their relationship to the target's business – appears to be better addressed by the continuity of interest and business requirements.

Historically, dividend distributions to shareholders who are individuals were taxed at higher rates than the rates applicable to gains on the sale of stock. The result was a substantial body of the corporate tax rules aimed at preventing shareholders from 'bailing out' corporate earnings at capital gains tax rates. For example, special rules were formulated to determine whether a sale of stock to a corporation or a related corporation would be treated as a disguised dividend or as a sale. In general, the form of the transaction as a sale would be respected where there had been a significant reduction in the shareholder's stock ownership of the company. Similarly, special rules were adopted to prevent shareholders from recognizing capital gains with respect to preferred stock that was distributed to them by the issuing corporation to the extent that the corporation had earnings and profits at the time the stock was issued. The importance of these rules has diminished as a result of the 2003 legislation, which causes dividends and capital gains both to be taxed at a maximum rate of 15%. Individual taxpayers will still have an incentive to 'bail out' corporate earnings as capital gains, however, if they have a high basis in their stock.

As in the case with the individual income tax, the corporate income tax also has an AMT. The AMT rate for corporations is 20% after allowance for a $40,000 exemption, which is phased out. The corporate AMT was adopted to ensure that corporations will pay a minimal income tax. It also attempts to measure the economic income of the corporation more accurately than the regular corporate income tax. Because of the complexity of the computations and the lack of guidance for some key aspects of the corporate AMT, it is not clear that the benefits arising from the corporate AMT outweigh the significant burdens imposed on corporate taxpayers.

6. TAX LEGISLATION

6.1. Legislative Process

The US Constitution requires that all tax bills originate in the House of Representatives. The House Committee on Ways and Means commences the process by conducting a public hearing on proposed bills.

The proposer of the new legislation is normally the first witness to appear at the hearing. If the President is the proposer, which is usually the case, the first witness to appear will be the Assistant Secretary of the Treasury for Tax Policy, followed by other members of the executive branch, such as the Chair of the Council of Economic Advisors. Members of the public, including various special interest groups, then testify.

After the hearing, the House Ways and Means Committee members meet to consider the general outlines of the bill and the policies to be implemented. The Committee members do not draft the statutory language. Rather, attorneys at the Office of House Legislative Counsel compose statutory language that implements the policy objectives adopted by the Committee. The Office of House Legislative Council also drafts a report to accompany the bill. The Committee then reviews the statutory language and report. Following approval of the language and report by the Committee, the entire House considers the bill.

The Senate normally starts to consider the bill at the same time as the House and follows the same process. (The requirement that tax legislation originate in the House is satisfied by a sleight of hand: The number of the original House bill is assigned to the bill ultimately adopted by the House and Senate.) The Senate Finance Committee conducts hearings. It then adopts statutory language and a committee report, which it submits to the entire Senate for its approval.

Differences between the House bill and Senate bill almost always exist. The differences are resolved at the Committee of Conference of the House and Senate (the 'Conference Committee'), which consists of members of the House Ways and Means Committee and the Senate Finance Committee. The Conference Committee issues to the House and Senate a Conference Report that sets forth the revised bill with a brief explanation. The Senate and House cannot amend the Conference Report, but must either approve or reject it. If approved, the bill is sent to the President, who can either sign the bill or veto it.

6.2. Statutory Style

The Internal Revenue Code is immense. What initially started as sixteen pages in section II of the Tariff Act of 1913 has blossomed into a tome of approximately 6,000 pages.

There are many reasons for the current complexity of the Code. The use of tax expenditures, however, accounts for much of the complexity. The presence of tax expenditures requires additional provisions to prevent taxpayer abuse of the tax rules. For example, a preferential rate for capital gains necessitates many additional provisions to prevent taxpayers from converting ordinary income into capital gain. Tax expenditures also require courts to engage in difficult factual inquiries about whether the taxpayer has satisfied the applicable statutory requirements. Moreover, the ability of taxpayers to use tax expenditures to eliminate or significantly reduce their tax liabilities has caused Congress to adopt the AMT, which is supposed to ensure that all taxpayers pay a minimal income tax when tax expenditures would otherwise eliminate or reduce tax liability.

Another source of complexity has been the willingness of Congress to disguise tax increases for political reasons. In 1990, for example, rather than increasing revenue simply by raising the maximum statutory rate, Congress adopted provisions that decrease many of the itemized deductions for high-income individuals. Moreover, Congress had earlier adopted another provision that allows deductions for 'miscellaneous itemized deductions' only to the extent that the total of such deductions exceeds 2% of the taxpayer's adjusted gross income. Both of these provisions require classification of deductions that are subject to the limitations. Based on no overriding principles, they reduce or eliminate the 'transparency' of the system for the ordinary taxpayers to whom they apply.

Complexity is also produced by the tendency of the Code to assign different meanings to the same word in different parts of the Code. For example, the term 'property' often has a different definition for different Code sections. In addition, the use of different rates for different types of capital gains reduces transparency.

Lastly, in recent years, Congress has tried to anticipate many of the ways that taxpayers will attempt to abuse tax provisions and address them in the statute. This practice is in contrast to earlier years when Congress would rely on the courts to police the boundaries of compliance. It is not clear that this approach is productive. The failure of Congress to address all abuse situations may create an inference that Congress intended to permit the abuses not addressed in the statute.

6.3. Statutory Interpretation

In the United States, as in all systems, there is a tension between a strict, literal approach to statutory interpretation and an approach that attempts to achieve the intent of the legislature. The Supreme Court has stated:

> There is, of course, no more persuasive evidence of a statute than the words by which the legislature undertook to give expression to its wishes. Often these words are sufficient in and of themselves to determine the purpose of the legislation. In such cases we have followed their plain meaning. When that meaning has led to absurd or futile results, however, this court has looked beyond the words to the purpose of the act. Frequently, however, even when the plain meaning did not produce absurd results but merely an unreasonable

> one 'plainly at variance with the policy of the legislation as a whole' this Court has followed the purpose, rather than the literal words.[20]

As the foregoing statement clearly illustrates, the US courts have traditionally sought to determine the legislative purpose for a specific statute in order to determine whether the statute's plain meaning is unreasonable. In seeking to identify the legislative purpose for a particular Code section, the courts will normally examine reports from the House Ways and Means Committee, the Senate Finance Committee, and the Conference Committee. They may also examine an explanation of the statute drafted by the staff of the Joint Committee on Taxation, records of hearings, and analyses by commentators, although they will normally accord less weight to these sources.

Currently, however, a vocal minority of the Supreme Court, including its Chief Justice, has been urging that legislative material, such as Committee reports, not be used in statutory interpretation. For example, the majority opinion in *Gitlitz v. Commissioner*[21] interpreted a tax statute without referring to the statute's legislative history, although a House Committee report suggested that Congress had intended an interpretation for the statute that was different from that adopted by the majority. Such a textualist approach, if continued, could have a significant effect in the tax field. For example, some have suggested that increased use of the textualist approach may contribute to the proliferation of tax shelters.[22] Tax shelters often involve transactions that comply with the literal language, but not the legislative intent, of the statute. A textualist approach may make it more difficult for a court to determine that the legislature did not intend the statute to be applied in the manner exploited by the tax shelter because the court cannot consult the statute's legislative history.

Although the inclusion of the word 'Code' in the name 'Internal Revenue Code' implies a self-contained, systematic statutory treatment of the tax laws, the courts have developed many common law principles that aid their efforts to apply tax provisions. In general, the courts narrowly interpret exclusions from gross income. That is, an item (other than imputed income) is generally excluded from gross income only where an express statute authorizes such exclusion. Similarly, the courts view deductions as a matter of legislative grace. They disallow a deduction unless it is permitted by statute and interpret the statute narrowly.

The courts have also created several requirements that are not in the statute. In order for a transaction to qualify for favourable tax treatment, the courts generally require that it be entered into for non-tax purposes. For example, the Supreme Court denied favourable tax treatment to a transaction that satisfied all the literal requirements of the governing statute because the transaction lacked a

20. *United States v. American Trucking Ass'n*, 310 US 534, 543 [1945].
21. 531 US 206 (2001).
22. Noel B. Cunningham & James R. Repetti, 'Textualism and Tax Shelters', *Va. Tax Rev.* 24 (2004) 1.

business purpose.[23] Similarly, the courts ignore an entity's existence if it was not formed for a business purpose and has no business activity.[24]

In applying tax statutes to a transaction, the courts seek to identify the substance of the transaction rather than blindly follow the form cast by the taxpayer. For example, although the taxpayer may have drafted a financial instrument in the legal form of debt, the courts treat it as equity if the taxpayer fails to respect the formalities of debt, such as prompt payment of interest and principal. Similarly, rather than accept a transaction as a sale or a lease because the taxpayer had structured it in that legal form, the courts analyze whether the burdens and benefits of ownership have shifted in order to identify the nature of the transaction for tax purposes. Lastly, the courts may combine several steps into a single transaction where it appears that the taxpayer intended a single transaction. Under the 'step transaction' approach, for example, if a taxpayer sells stock shortly after having acquired it in a tax-free corporate acquisition to the acquiring corporation, the court may treat the taxpayer as receiving cash in the transaction rather than stock.

7. JUDICIAL STRUCTURE AND STYLE

The United States has no specialized system of courts that hears only tax cases. One court of first instance, the Tax Court, hears only tax matters and has jurisdiction if the taxpayer resists the payment of a tax asserted by the Internal Revenue Service. Alternatively, the taxpayer can pay the tax asserted and sue for a refund, either in the United States District Court, a court of general jurisdiction, or in the United States Court of Federal Claims, a special court that handles claims against the government. The taxpayer may request that a jury be the finder of facts in the United States District Court, but is limited to a judge as the fact finder in the Tax Court or United States Court of Federal Claims. Decisions from the United States District Court and Tax Courts may be appealed to the Court of Appeals for the circuit in which the taxpayer resides. Decisions from the United States Court of Federal Claims may be appealed to the Court of Appeals for the Federal Circuit. Thus, the taxpayer has a number of judicial options in contesting her tax liability, and this structure creates a certain amount of 'forum shopping'.

All decisions may then be reviewed by the Supreme Court, although there is no right to review unless a constitutional issue is involved. In the event that the Courts of Appeals reach differing results on the same issue, the Supreme Court will usually agree to hear a case that will resolve the issue.

Judicial decisions are issued in the form of full opinions that set forth the relevant facts and apply the law to those facts. Because courts rely on cases as precedents in deciding future cases, the judges are usually careful to set forth their reasoning in full.

23. *Gregory v. Helvering*, 293 US 465 (1935).
24. See, e.g., *Moline Properties Inc. v. Commissioner*, 319 US 436, 438–439 (1943).

Despite the extensive statutory material in the US system, the courts have been responsible for a significant part of the doctrinal development in the tax area. In some instances, principles based in case law have subsequently been taken over in the statute. In others, the case law remains the primary source of law. For example, the determination of the taxpayer to whom income should be attributed is almost entirely based on case law. In addition, the case law principles of statutory interpretation discussed above have had an important influence on the development of the law.

8. ADMINISTRATIVE, TAXPAYER, AND JUDICIAL STYLE

8.1. Administrative Style

The US tax system is a self-assessing system that is backed up with extensive informational reporting and withholding. For example, most employers who pay wages must file with the IRS the amounts paid to each of their employees and are also required to withhold income taxes on those amounts. The bulk of individual income taxes collected by the United States are through employer withholding. In 2007, for example, approximately 67.9% of individual income taxes were collected from withholding.[25] There are also reporting requirements for persons who employ independent contractors in the course of their business, for persons receiving $10,000 or more of cash, and for most forms of capital income, including gains on sale of investment assets.

The audit rate for taxpayers had been declining until recently. In 2007, the United States audited 1.0% of individual income tax returns,[26] compared to only .57% in 2002 and 1.67% returns in 1995.[27] For individuals with income over $100,000, the audit rate was 1.77% in 2007,[28] compared to a rate of only 0.86% in 2002,[29] and 2.79% in 1995.[30]

In 2007, the United States audited 1.7% of all corporate tax returns,[31] compared to 0.97% in 2002[32] and 2.05% of all such returns in 1995.[33] The audit rate

25. See Internal Revenue Service, *2007 Data Book*, Table 1 (2008) (noting that in 2007 $1.366 trillion was collected from the individual income tax and that $928 billion of such receipts had been withheld by employers).
26. *Ibid.*, at Table 9; GAO, *Tax Administration: IRS should continue to expand reporting on its enforcement efforts* (January 2003), Table 6.
27. Internal Revenue Service, *2007 Data Book*, Table 1; GAO, *Tax Administration: Audit Rates and Results for Individual Taxpayers* (26 Apr. 1996), Table 1.1.
28. IRS, *Fiscal Year 2007 IRS Enforcement and Service Statistics* (2008).
29. GAO, *Tax Administration: IRS should continue to expand reporting on its enforcement efforts* (January 2003), Table 7.
30. GAO, *Tax Administration: Audit Rates and Results for Individual Taxpayers* (26 Apr. 1996), Table 1.4.
31. IRS, *2007 Data Book*, Table 1 (2008).
32. IRS, *2002 Data Book* (2003), Table 10.
33. IRS, *1995 Data Book* (1996), Table 11.

for corporations in 2007 with assets between $10 million and $50 million was 15% in 2007,[34] compared to only 7.80% in 2002.[35] For corporations with assets of $250 million or more, the audit rate in 2007 was 100%[36] compared to only 34.37% in 2002.[37]

To discourage taxpayers from playing the 'audit lottery', the IRS charges interest on tax deficiencies at a rate equal to the federal short-term rate plus 3% and assesses penalties equal to 20% of the tax deficiency unless there was a reasonable cause for the deficiency. In addition, increasingly sophisticated use of computer checking of information returns reduces the audit lottery odds.

Perhaps because of the self-assessing nature of the US income tax, the Internal Revenue Service has tended in recent years to provide detailed regulations. In addition, the Service publishes 'public revenue rulings' similar to memoranda of law that address various issues not resolved in the regulations. Taxpayers seeking additional advice may request the Service to issue a private ruling to the taxpayer stating how the law will be applied in a situation the taxpayer has presented to the Service. These private rulings are published in a redacted form to prevent discovery of the identity of the taxpayer.

The IRS is not permitted to disclose tax returns to the public.[38] However, it may disclose the returns to other federal agencies, state tax officials, and foreign officials (pursuant to tax treaties). In addition, the IRS is permitted to aggregate data from several returns, so that information cannot be traced to a particular taxpayer, and to publish that aggregate data.

8.2. Taxpayer Style

Taxpayers in the United States, both corporate and individual, tend to be aggressive in interpreting the law to their advantage. During the period 2001 through 2003, there was a significant decline in revenue from corporations, which many attributed to the extensive use of corporate tax shelters during that period. Investment banks and accounting firms had been aggressively marketing tax shelters to corporations and wealthy individuals that involved transactions that complied literally with the statute but not with the statute's legislative purpose. Frequently, the fees for such tax shelters were a percentage of the tax savings. Tax shelter promoters also often provided opinions of legal counsel with respect to the shelters that advised that it was more likely than not that favourable tax treatment would be sustained by the courts. The opinions were highly suspect, however, because they often did not address the applicability of the business purpose and substance-over-form doctrines to the tax shelter. They merely stated that the determination of

34. IRS, *2007 Data Book* (2008), Table 9.
35. IRS, *2002 Data Book* (2003), Table 11.
36. IRS, *2007 Data Book* (2008), Table 9.
37. IRS, *2002 Data Book* (2003), Table 11.
38. Internal Revenue Code (IRC), s. 6103.

business purpose and substance-over-form is highly factual and then assumed compliance with those doctrines.[39]

Corporations were willing to invest in such investments because of the low audit rates. Even if the corporations were audited, the transactions were often buried in so much paperwork that it was unlikely that the auditor would identify their true nature. As discussed above, audit rates have increased since 2003. The increased number of audits of corporations, coupled with more rigorous standards governing the issuance of legal opinions about tax shelters, may account for the rebound in corporate revenues since 2003.[40]

9. GENERAL PRINCIPLES

9.1. Relationship Between Tax and Financial Accounting

In general, tax accounting is totally distinct from financial accounting. The principle of conservatism in financial accounting creates a bias in favour of a rapid recognition of expenses and a delayed recognition of income.[41] In contrast, tax accounting seeks, broadly speaking, exactly the opposite. That is, tax accounting seeks generally to recognize income as soon as it is reasonable to expect the taxpayer to pay tax but to recognize expenses only to the extent that they can be matched to the recognized income.

For example, tax accounting generally requires taxpayers who receive a cash payment before they have earned it by performing services or delivering property to include the payment in income regardless of whether they use the cash or accrual method of accounting. Moreover, even if an accrual-method taxpayer has a fixed liability that would normally justify a current deduction, the taxpayer may frequently not recognize the expense for tax purposes until it is actually paid. Similarly, while financial accounting principles require the establishment of reserves for estimated expenses that relate to current income, tax accounting does not generally permit such reserves.

Like financial accounting, tax accounting employs an annual accounting period that has been interpreted fairly strictly by the courts. Events that occur after the close of the year will not, in general, affect the tax treatment in the year. Nonetheless, taxpayers are allowed a deduction for items that they have included in income and are subsequently required to return. Moreover, in certain situations, the taxpayer may, in lieu of a deduction, be able to reduce current tax liability by the amount of taxes paid in the prior year attributable to the inclusion of the item in

39. For a detailed discussion of the abuses, see Cunningham & Repetti, *supra* n. 22.
40. Revenues from the corporate income tax as a percentage of GDP more than doubled from 2003 to 2007, increasing from 1.2% in 2003 to 2.7% in 2007. *Budget of the United States Government, Fiscal Year 2009,* Historic Tables, Table 2.3 (2008).
41. Unfortunately, recent scandals in some US companies indicate that some accountants have not been applying the conservatism principle properly.

income. In the converse situation, taxpayers who have deducted an expenditure that is subsequently refunded must recognize income to the extent that the earlier deduction resulted in a tax saving. Expenses incurred in a trade or business that exceed business income may be carried back two years and forward twenty years.

9.2. Respect for Legal Form

As discussed earlier in section 6.3, US courts will look behind the form of a transaction to determine its substance. For example, a lease may be treated as a sale for federal income tax purposes, even though the governing instrument is a lease for state law purposes, if the lease effectively conveys all the burdens and benefits of ownership to the lessee.

In addition, the courts will refuse favourable tax treatment for a transaction if the only reason for the transaction was to save federal income taxes.[42] Where the generation of a profit is the asserted business purpose, some courts will weigh the profit potential against the tax benefits from the shelter.[43] In contrast, other courts have concluded that the existence of any profit motive is sufficient to have a transaction respected.[44]

9.3. Anti-avoidance

As discussed earlier in section 6.3 on statutory interpretation, the courts have created several common law doctrines to curtail taxpayer avoidance activities. Although there has been significant debate about whether a general anti-avoidance statute would be useful, Congress has not adopted such a provision.

In narrow contexts, Congress has either adopted anti-avoidance legislation or expressly authorized the IRS to adopt anti-avoidance regulations that address specific abuses. In section 269, Congress sought to prevent a corporation that had acquired another corporation from deducting expenses or claiming credits with respect to the acquired corporation where 'the principal purpose for which such acquisition is made is evasion or avoidance of Federal income tax by securing the benefit of a deduction, credit or other allowance'. In 1993, Congress also adopted section 7701(1), which authorizes the Secretary to 'prescribe regulations recharacterizing any multiple-party financing transaction as a transaction directly among any two or more of such parties when the Secretary determines that such recharacterization is appropriate to present avoidance of any tax by this title'. Pursuant to this statute, the IRS has promulgated regulations that allow it to treat an entity as a conduit if a principal purpose for using the entity in the transaction was to avoid the

42. *Gregory v. Helvering*, 293 US 465 (1935).
43. See, e.g., *ACM Partnership v. Commissioner*, 157 F.3d 231, 257–258 (3rd Cir. 1998).
44. *IES Industries, Inc. v. Alliant Energy Corp.*, 253 F.3d 350 (8th Cir. 2001).

US income tax on income of foreign corporations that is not effectively connected with a US trade or business.[45]

As discussed earlier, the courts recharacterize a business transaction if it lacks a business purpose. Where the business purpose is generating a profit from the transaction, some courts compare the magnitude of the profit to the tax savings. In the context of partnership taxation, the IRS has sought through regulations to require that the magnitude of the partnership's business purposes for entering into a transaction be substantial in comparison to the transaction's tax savings.[46] In addition, the IRS has sought to require that courts interpreting partnership tax provisions expressly consider the legislative purpose for the tax provisions. Commentators disagree about whether the IRS has the authority to impose such requirements without a directive from Congress.

10. SOURCES OF TAX LAW

The primary source of tax law is the Internal Revenue Code. Traditionally, in interpreting particular Code sections, the courts examine reports from the House Ways and Means Committee, the Senate Finance Committee, and the Conference Committee. They may also examine an explanation of the statute drafted by the staff of the Joint Committee on Taxation, records of hearings, and analyses by commentators, although they will normally accord less weight to these sources. However, as discussed earlier, a minority of courts do not employ any legislative materials, such as Committee reports or records of hearings, in interpreting the statute.

The Treasury Department issues regulations that interpret the Code. The regulations are given significant deference by the courts if they address issues not spoken to in the statute and they are reasonable interpretations. In general, courts will invalidate only regulations that adopt positions that conflict with the statute's legislative purpose.

In addition to regulations, the Treasury Department, acting through the IRS, which is a division of the Treasury Department, issues several other forms of guidance. One form of administrative guidance, the Revenue Ruling, is similar to a memorandum of law. It states the issues to be addressed, the facts pertaining to the issues, and a legal analysis of the issues. Revenue Rulings may be relied upon by all taxpayers unless the law upon which the Ruling is based has changed. The IRS has stated that its 'general practice [is] . . . to make . . . revocation or modification prospective only'.[47] Another form of guidance that may be relied upon by all taxpayers is the Revenue Procedure, which is usually an explanation of a procedural issue. The IRS also issues private letter rulings to taxpayers who request guidance from the National Office of the IRS; only the taxpayer to whom the private letter ruling is addressed may rely upon it. Technical advice memoranda and field service advice

45. See Treas. Regs. s. 1.881-3(b)(1).
46. Treas. Regs. s. 1.704-2.
47. Rev. Proc. 89-14, 1989-1 C.B. 814.

are similar to private letter rulings, except that the District Director of the IRS, not a taxpayer, requests that the National Office render advice pertaining to an issue that has arisen in the audit of a taxpayer. The taxpayer being audited is permitted to file a brief and request a hearing before the National Office renders a ruling. Although private letter rulings, technical advice memoranda, and field service advice have no precedential value for any taxpayers not directly involved, tax advisers study the rulings carefully to glean the IRS's perspective on the issues addressed. The rulings are published in redacted form to prevent disclosure of the identity of the taxpayer.

Lastly, all the courts described in section 7 above render written opinions that are available to the public. The impact of the opinion depends upon which court issued it. Supreme Court opinions are binding on all lower courts. Opinions of the Courts of Appeals for the various circuits, in contrast, bind only the lower courts whose decisions are appealed to that particular Court of Appeals. The Tax Court and United States District Courts are bound by the decisions of the Court of Appeals for the circuit in which the taxpayer resides. The Claims Court is bound by decisions of the Court of Appeals for the Federal Circuit.

Set forth below are the web sites for obtaining important court decisions and IRS rulings.

US Supreme Court <www.supremecourtus.gov>
Courts of Appeals

- 1st circuit <www.ca1.uscourts.gov>
- 2nd circuit <www.ca2.uscourts.gov>
- 3rd circuit <www.ca3.uscourts.gov>
- 4th circuit <www.ca4.uscourts.gov>
- 5th circuit <www.ca5.uscourts.gov>
- 6th circuit <www.ca6.uscourts.gov>
- 7th circuit <www.ca7.uscourts.gov>
- 8th circuit <www.ca8.uscourts.gov>
- 9th circuit <www.ca9.uscourts.gov>
- 10th circuit <www.ca10.uscourts.gov>
- 11th circuit <www.ca11.uscourts.gov>
- Federal circuit <www.fedcir.gov>

US Court of Federal Claims <www.uscfc.uscourts.gov>
US Tax Court <www.ustaxcourt.gov>

IRS Administrative Rulings

Revenue Rulings, Revenue Procedures, Announcements, and Notices issued since January 1996 can be obtained on the IRS.gov web site <www.irs.gov/irb>.

Private Letter Rulings and Technical Advice memoranda may be obtained at <www.irs.ustreas.gov/foia/article/0,,id=110353,00.html> under the heading, 'Non-precedential Rulings & Advice'.

Part Two

Basic Income Taxation

Subpart A. Global Versus Schedular Design of Income Tax

From a theoretical perspective, income tax is often said to be structured on either a global or a schedular basis. A global income tax involves tax applied to a person's total income, and income consists of all types of income. All amounts, whatever their nature or source, are included in income, and deductions are permitted without regard to the type of income in connection with which they were incurred. In short, income and deductions are combined to produce an overall taxable income amount to which the tax rate is applied.

In contrast, a schedular income tax involves separate taxes on different types or sources of income. For each category of income, amounts included in income and deductions allowed are determined separately. If an amount is not included in any schedule, it is not taxable, although there is usually a schedule that includes residual amounts (i.e., amounts not covered in other schedules). For certain income categories, such as investment income, the deduction of expenses may be limited or even prohibited. An overall loss in one category can generally not be offset against income in other categories. The rate of tax applied to the income in the various categories often differs. Similarly, the assessment and collection measures often differ. The tax on some types of income may be collected by withholding, the tax on others by filing returns.

A schedular income tax system presents difficulties that do not arise under a global system. First, to the extent that the tax rates of the various schedules differ, taxpayers will attempt to manipulate the character of amounts to minimize tax. The classification of different types of income can be quite difficult and take up considerable administrative resources. Second, a schedular income tax system makes it difficult to implement progressive taxation of individuals in accordance with the ability-to-pay principle. Tax is imposed separately on the income of each schedule rather than on the taxpayer's total income. As a result, for example, a taxpayer may be subject to significant taxation if the taxpayer has income in one schedule, even where the taxpayer has no overall income because of an offsetting loss in another schedule. In addition, personal exemptions, rebates, and other types of relief are difficult to implement under a schedular system.

The theoretical global and schedular systems described briefly above represent the ends of a spectrum. In between these extremes are income tax systems in which elements of both global and schedular systems are combined, although one type of system may be predominant. All of the countries studied in this book have income tax systems that combine global and schedular elements to various degrees. Countries such as Australia, Canada, and the United States, which take a global approach generally, have numerous provisions that reflect a schedular approach. For example, the deductibility of expenses or losses with respect to certain types of activities may be restricted to the gross revenue from those activities. In addition, some types of investment income (dividends and interest) are often subject to withholding tax, and capital gains are often subject to a lower rate of tax than other types of income. Similarly, the European countries and Japan, which generally have schedular income tax systems, often have provisions that modify the effects of the schedular approach and introduce global elements. For example, some countries allow losses from one category to offset income from other categories.

Applying a global or schedular label to a country's income tax system does not adequately reflect the combined global and schedular elements in its system. However, an awareness of the basic structural principles on which the system is built is important to understand a country's general approach. The effect of a country's general approach is pervasive. It affects the way in which the country determines which amounts are included in income, which expenses are deductible, how losses are treated, which rules for computing income apply, etc. Understanding whether a country's general approach to income tax is global or schedular can assist in explaining why particular aspects of its income tax system are as they are.

Subpart B. Inclusions in the Tax Base

The determination of the items to be included in the tax base is a central question in all income tax systems. As the information in Part One has shown, the countries here under consideration vary substantially in their formal definitions of income. In general, each country's approach to the determination of amounts included in income is affected fundamentally by whether its income tax system reflects a global or schedular approach, as discussed above.

The *United States* has the most extensive statutory definition of income, essentially a tautological statement that income is income 'from whatever source' and then a non-exclusive list containing the most commonly occurring items.[1] Specific items that would otherwise fall within the broad definition are expressly excluded. The *Australian* system, as well, has a global income approach, but, influenced by trust concepts, the judicially developed concept was not extended to capital gains, which required additional legislation. In the 1997 re-enactment of the legislation, income was separated into two categories, ordinary income (what the judges have decided is income) and statutory income (what is made income by specific statutory provision), but the basic concept remains global.[2] The judges, in deciding what is ordinary income, have drawn from UK case law, which is to some degree an oddity given the different nature of the UK system.

In contrast, the *United Kingdom* definition is based on a number of categories of income.[3] As seen above in Part One, until the Tax Law Rewrite Project, this definition was expressed in Schedules (sometimes subdivided into Cases); to be

1. United States, Internal Revenue Code (IRC), s. 61.
2. Australia, Income Tax Assessment Act (ITAA) 1997, s. 6-5, 6-10.
3. United Kingdom, Income Tax Act 2007, s. 3 referring, *inter alia*, to the Income Tax (Earnings and Pensions) Act 2003, here called ITEPA, and the Income Tax (Trading and Other Income Act) 2005, here called ITTOIA. As noted in Part One, there is no definitive list of all the categories of income.

taxable, a particular item had to fall within one of the Schedules. The Schedules evolved historically and reflected the relative importance of the different sources of income that existed at the time of the original legislation in 1802; as seen in the description in Part One, the rewritten legislation adopts a different order. Some Schedules have broad coverage – for example, profits of a trade – and others are narrow, such as income from foreign securities. The modern list of sources reflects all too well the absence of a general theory of income; the United Kingdom simply finds that a receipt is subject to income tax if it fits into a part of the scheme and is not excluded by some other rule (e.g., for being capital). Where income falls into a particular Part (formerly Schedule), the rules of that category must be applied; this affects both the method of computation and the ability to offset losses in one category against income in another category.

The existence of the Schedules has also influenced other aspects of the system. Conceptually, each Schedule or Part is viewed as listing separate categories or 'sources' of income; thus, trading income is distinct from employment income, and each trade is a separate source. If a receipt has no taxable source, it cannot be included in income. The receipt of what would otherwise be income in a year in which the source no longer exists does not, in principle, give rise to tax, but this principle has been much eroded by specific legislation. In addition, the realization of a gain on the disposition of a 'source' is not itself treated as an item of income, thus leading to the necessity of special rules to capture such receipts as capital gains.

The *Canadian* system, influenced historically by the United Kingdom and the United States, has a global definition of income based on the source concept. Only amounts that have a source constitute income subject to tax. The principal sources of income – business, property, and employment – are specifically mentioned in the statutory definition of income.[4] As in the United Kingdom and Australia, special legislation was required to extend taxation to capital gains, but unlike the situation in the United Kingdom, losses from various sources can, in general, offset income from other sources. In addition, the statute has been amended to include in income most amounts that lack a source. Consequently, the source basis of taxation is of relatively minor significance.

The *Swedish* system, although growing out of a different tradition, also distinguishes between income from employment, business, and capital. The *Dutch* system likewise separates employment, business, and investment categories, with an additional category for periodic income.

The *Dutch* system, as was explained in the country section in Part One on The Netherlands, has employed since 2001 a schedular ('box') system under which (1) income from (employed and self-employed) work and the rental value of an owner-occupied residence, (2) income and gains from substantial interest participations, and (3) income from capital are taxed separately.

The *German* system provides in the statutory structure for seven income categories, with two basic methods of income calculation applicable to the various

4. Canada, Income Tax Act (ITA), s. 3.

categories.[5] As a result of a recent Business Tax Reform, capital gains in shares and other securities realized outside a business are now subject to a final withholding tax of 25%.[6] The former tax exemption for these gains has been abolished. The alienation of real estate is still tax-free for owner-occupied houses and rental houses held for more than ten years.[7] The *French* system has similar statutorily delimited categories, although the extent of capital gains taxation is broader.

In *Japan*, the approach to income definition is an intermediate one and reflects both the pre-war European schedular tradition and the post-war American global view. While income is divided into several categories in accordance with a schedular approach, capital gains on non-business assets are subject to tax and a broad category of 'Miscellaneous' income gives the system a global character.[8]

Despite these differences in starting point, however, there is more similarity in results than the formal definitions would suggest. The following material analyzes the treatment of a number of specific items in the determination of the tax base in each country. Subpart C will consider deduction issues.

1. EMPLOYEE FRINGE BENEFITS

1.1. General

The issue of the appropriate treatment of employee fringe benefits arises in a similar fashion in both schedular and global systems. The inclusion of fringe benefits in the tax base is necessary both in terms of horizontal equity and in order to prevent the erosion of the cash compensation base. A number of structural issues, however, are involved in the taxation of fringe benefits. In the first place, there is the question of whether an employee can be said to have obtained a personal or consumption benefit from the item in question or whether it is simply part of the 'working conditions' of his employment. Even where some non-work-related personal benefit is clearly present, there is an important issue of valuation. Often the employee does not have a choice as to whether to accept the benefit, and including the full market value in income may be an inappropriate measure. From an administrative point of view, ensuring that the item is in fact included in the employee's tax base can be difficult, particularly in the case of small amounts or benefits that are shared among many employees. Similarly, where wage income is subject to withholding at source, the inclusion of fringe benefits provided in kind can be a problem. Finally, some categories of fringe benefit, such as child care, may be expressly excluded from the tax base for social policy reasons.

The systems under consideration here show a wide range of responses to the taxation of fringe benefits. They include the outright exclusion of some significant

5. Germany, Income Tax Act (ITA), s. 2 paras 1–2.
6. Germany, ITA, s. 20 para. 2.
7. Germany, ITA, ss 22 no. 2 and 23 para. 1 no. 1.
8. Japan, Income Tax Act (ITA), ss 21-35.

benefits, some arbitrary 'standard' values used for employee inclusion of specific benefits, valuations that clearly undervalue the benefits, the denial or limitation of the employer's deduction for benefits that are not included by the employee, and finally, a separate employer-level fringe benefits tax (FBT), which in effect includes the value of the benefit in the employer's tax base in lieu of taxing the employee. To a certain extent, some exclusions apparently reflect differing societal views on what is appropriately viewed as a non-taxable working condition – for example, a free glass of beer in Germany and Australia[9] (provided the employer is a brewer and the beer is consumed on the employer's premises) and free coffee in Sweden. Several countries exclude certain benefits, such as gifts on special occasions, that are provided to employees in their personal rather than employee capacities. More generally, the countries' practices differ significantly in the extent to which a real attempt is made to tax the economic benefit accruing to employees. Several countries use unrealistic standardized amounts for certain types of commonly recurring fringe benefits such as automobiles.

In the *United States* system, detailed statutory provisions deal with fringe benefits. The principal rules enacted in 1984 supplanted administrative practice, which was increasingly unable to deal with the proliferation of fringe benefit programs.[10] The statutory pattern establishes a general rule that fringe benefits are taxable but then creates a number of exceptions. Under the 'working condition fringe' exception, an employer-provided benefit is not taxable if the expense would have been deductible if incurred directly by the employee. In addition, *de minimis* amounts of fringe benefits are excluded. In a concession to the transportation industry, services provided to employees at 'no additional cost' to the employer are not taxed, thus allowing that form of compensation to be given to transportation employees on a tax-free basis. Employer discounts are also excluded, subject to some limitations. Exclusion is also available, usually subject to dollar limitations, for certain employer-provided transportation, reimbursed moving expenses, day care programs, educational assistance, group life insurance, and meals and lodging in certain situations. From an economic point of view, one of the most important non-taxable fringe benefits is employer-funded medical care. Medical benefits provided directly or under insurance-financed plans are not taxable. The ability to obtain medical care on a before-tax basis has been identified as one of the factors affecting the escalation of medical care costs.

Where fringe benefits are taxable, they are in principle taxed at fair market value. The employee's 'subjective perception' of the value of the benefit is not relevant. Detailed regulations establish the values of employer-provided automobiles and aircraft. A statutory provision requires the taxation of employer-provided parking to the extent that the value of the parking exceeds $190 per month.

In *Germany*, the employment income category in principle includes all 'benefits' received by the employee to the extent that they can be determined to have a

9. Australia, Fringe Benefits Tax Assessment Act (FBTAA), s. 41.
10. United States, IRC, s. 132.

cash value.[11] The theoretical justification for the inclusion is based on the notion that the benefit results in an increased 'ability to pay' because the employee has been saved an expense which he would otherwise have incurred. The fact that the benefit cannot be converted to cash is not relevant. A *de minimis* rule excludes from income up to €44 per month of otherwise taxable benefits.[12] Special employer discounts are taxable only if their net value exceeds €1,080.[13]

There is a long statutory catalogue of items that are not taxable for what are perceived to be social policy reasons, including employer-provided day care, employer-provided passes for public transportation between home and workplace,[14] and extra pay for overtime work on Sundays, holidays, or at night.[15] The private use of technical equipment in the workplace is tax-free because these benefits are hard to evaluate.[16]

In addition, several exceptions based in case law focus on the benefit to the employer of a happy workforce (firm outings, 'occasional' gifts, free beer) but seem to ignore the parallel benefit to the employee. Recent cases[17] have tended to reduce the scope of the case law exceptions and treat the statutory exemptions as exclusive.

Benefits are, in principle, valued at retail market value.[18] There are, however, standard value tables for meals and lodging, and other benefits that apply unless there are unusual circumstances – for example, a luxury apartment provided to an executive; these tables generally undervalue the benefits. In the case of employer-provided cars, the employee may choose between a standard value method or an 'exact' method.[19] The standard value method is based on the list price of the car and requires a percentage of that value to be included in income. Alternatively, the employee can use the 'exact' method based on actual costs and a driving record establishing private and business-related driving.

Special 'lump sum' rules apply at the employer level with respect to certain fringe benefits.[20] In effect, these rules make the employer-level tax the final tax on the benefit; it is not included in the employee's assessable income. The rules also provide a lower rate of tax on certain benefits for policy reasons.

In *Sweden*, in principle, all benefits that fall into the category of income from employment are taxable. However, no attempt is made to tax employee benefits such as free coffee, sport training facilities, and the like. The justification relates principally to ease of administration. Where benefits are taxable, in principle, valuation should be done on the basis of fair market value. Standard values are

11. Germany, ITA, ss 19 para. 1 no. 1 and 8 para. 1.
12. Germany, ITA, s. 8 para. 2, sentence (hereafter 'sent.') 9.
13. Germany, ITA, s. 8 para. 3.
14. Germany, ITA, s. 3 no. 32.
15. Germany, ITA, s. 3b.
16. Germany, ITA, s. 3 no. 45.
17. Federal Tax Court (*Bundesfinanzhof*), judgment of 22 Jun. 2006 VI R 21/05.
18. Germany, ITA, s. 8 para. sent. 1.
19. Germany, ITA, s. 8 para. 2 sent. 2.
20. Germany, ITA, s. 40.

used for meals and cars, the two most commonly provided fringe benefits. For meals, average restaurant prices for 'normal' meals are calculated periodically, and that valuation is generally controlling. For employer-provided cars, a standardized amount is calculated based on the price of the car. The rule has been criticized from an environmental point of view in that it, in effect, establishes a zero marginal cost for additional personal driving.

Another item with special treatment is employer-provided health care. Sweden has an extensive public health care system that involves long waits for certain kinds of services. If the employer pays the costs of private care, the amount is not deductible to the employer and is not taxed to the employee. The tax rate of the (corporate) employer is usually lower than the employee rate (and the employer does not bear the burden of social security contributions), and thus an incentive is provided for this kind of benefit. A partial justification is the advantage to the employer of getting the employee back to work sooner.

In *The Netherlands*, most fringe benefits are included in income. Valuation is based on resale value or, if it is not possible or usual to sell the benefit received, the amount the employee is assumed to have saved because of the employer benefit. In the case of employer-provided housing, a fair market rental must be used as the standard for valuation. Special – and generally realistic – valuation rules apply to, *inter alia*, meals, low-interest loans, stock options, and transportation provided by the employer. Cars provided by the employer and also used privately are taxed to the employee at 14%, 20%, or 25% of the car's list price (depending on its CO_2 emissions).

The *French* system, in principle, includes benefits at retail value, but there are several substantial exceptions and special rules that result in undervaluation, especially in connection with meals and lodging.[21] Since 2005, the level of employees' income is irrelevant to the valuation, and food and lodging are valued on a lump sum basis (€4.30 per meal in 2009). The value used for a separately imposed 'housing tax' is optionally applicable for lodging and is not in fact generally related to fair market value. As to employer-provided cars and electronic equipment (computers, mobile phones, etc.), the real costs attributable to private use or, at the employer's option, a given percentage of the purchase price or of the total annual costs (rents, maintenance, insurance) or subscription rate, as the case may be, are included in the employee's taxable income.

Canada has a broad statutory provision that taxes 'benefits of any kind' received by an employee,[22] but some benefits are excluded by statute (e.g., health benefits, group term life insurance) or by administrative decision (e.g., merchandise discounts, subsidized meals where the employee pays cost, and recreational facilities).[23] Courts have held that reimbursement of moving expenses, of the loss on the sale of a house, and even of increased mortgage expenses arising in connection with a move, are not required to be included in income; however, the latter

21. France, *Code général des impôts* (General Tax Code, hereafter CGI), s. 82.
22. Canada, ITA, s. 6(1)(a).
23. Canada Revenue Agency, Interpretation Bulletin, IT-470R, 1999.

two results have been changed by statutory amendments.[24] Free parking spaces are generally considered to be a taxable benefit unless the employee does not have exclusive use of the space or is required to travel frequently in the course of employment. Complex rules attempt to value employer-provided automobiles. In general, it is difficult to find any consistent criteria in either the administrative practice or the jurisprudence on which to distinguish between taxable and non-taxable fringe benefits.

In *Japan*, although all benefits are in principle taxable, administratively sanctioned exemptions include gifts related to years of service or the anniversary of the company, discount sales of employer goods and services, and meals and housing provided at below-market rates to employees.

The *United Kingdom* initially had difficulty in taxing fringe benefits because of a court-developed principle that benefits could be taxed only to the extent that they could be converted to cash.[25] This led to a widespread use of fringe benefits that could not be resold or where real or nominal restrictions reduced or eliminated the resale value. In response, a special statutory regime was introduced for directors and employees with incomes over a certain level (£8,500).[26] The income level was originally set to cover only higher-paid employees but has not been increased for inflation, thus expanding the coverage of the statutory rules. The rules apply to a wide range of benefits. However, the benefits are generally valued at the marginal cost to the employer, which allows substantial value to be derived free from tax by the employee. One particular aspect of these statutory rules has become important and requires mention. The benefit is caught if it was provided 'by reason of the employment'. This condition is satisfied automatically if the benefit is provided by the employer and the employer is a company; it may be rebutted in limited circumstances if the employer is not a company.[27] Thus, a payment by such an employer to an employee who is the victim of a terrorist attack is taxable income.

A standard value approach is used for company cars and other commonly recurring situations. Free parking is expressly excluded from taxation. The court-developed principles remain applicable outside the statutory regime and continue to limit inclusion of such benefits to their cash conversion value (i.e., the resale price for employer-provided goods).

While the contours of the rules differ, most of the systems described above allow substantial amounts of employment income in the form of fringe benefits to escape tax because of the administrative and valuation problems involved in taxing such benefits. *Australia* has taken a different approach to the treatment of fringe benefits. In general terms, rather than attempting to value the benefit and collect the tax at the employee level, in 1986 Australia introduced a separate employer-level tax on fringe benefits while excluding such benefits from the employee's tax base.

---

24. Canada, ITA, s. 6(19)–(23).
25. *Tennant v. Smith* [1892] 3 TC 158, now ITEPA, s. 62.
26. The rules are gathered in United Kingdom, ITEPA, Part 3.
27. United Kingdom, ITEPA, s. 201.

Apart from the technical aspects referred to below, the decision to impose an FBT was very much a political one. The tax was introduced by a Labour (centrist-socialist) government whose constituency was to a large extent based in the trade union movement. Because of defects in the system for taxing fringe benefits at the employee level, untaxed or low-taxed fringe benefits had become widespread among all classes of employees and had been, at least in part, capitalized into wage rates. If the income tax on fringe benefits had been imposed on employees, there would have been an immediate reduction in after-tax wages, whereas the levy of the tax on the employer meant that, in most cases, the initial incidence of the tax fell on the employer. This resulted largely from the fact that wage rates in Australia were then set out in officially approved awards and could be changed only by elaborate procedures. After enactment, the burden of the tax has gradually been shifted to employees through the bargaining process.

From a technical viewpoint, the FBT was introduced primarily because of the perceived administrative difficulties of assessing and collecting tax on fringe benefits at the employee level. In addition, in principle, imposing the tax at the employer level allowed the tax to be collected without the allocation of the value of the total benefit to individual employees, which was one of the major administrative difficulties in the case of shared benefits.[28] The basic issue of the valuation of the total amount of the benefit, of course, remains, although the level of the inquiry is shifted to the employer. The FBT legislation sets up a variety of valuation rules that roughly parallel the types of rules used in the income tax systems in other countries. However, since the FBT was completely new, more attention was given to details and the logical structure of the rules than is usually the case for gradually evolving rules for taxing fringe benefits to employees. On the other hand, commonly recurring items such as employer-provided parking have continued to be a problem in the FBT system, and complicated and arbitrary valuation rules have been required.

The use of a separate tax to deal with fringe benefits, while it has administrative advantages, raises its own problems. Several issues arise in the interaction between the FBT and the income tax. If the FBT is non-deductible under the income tax and the employer is tax-exempt or the employer's tax rate is less than the FBT rate, the FBT is not a perfect substitute for taxing employees on fringe benefits. This is because that part of the tax collected through the income tax (via non-deductibility of the FBT) varies as between employers taxed at the same income tax rate as the FBT rate, employers taxed at a different income tax rate to the FBT rate, and tax-exempt (zero tax rate) employers. To equalize the treatment of the three categories of employers, it is necessary to make the FBT deductible in relation to the income tax on the employer and to gross up either the value of the fringe benefit (as Australia now does) or the FBT rate (as New

28. In fact, the Australian system requires the allocation of benefits to employees in many situations – for example, in order to apply a fixed exemption level that is allowed for each employee. However, the possibility in principle of avoiding an allocation of benefits is present in the fringe benefit tax approach.

Zealand does) by a factor of t/(1 – t) where t is the FBT tax rate. For example, if the FBT rate is 25%, the gross-up factor is 0.33. The original version of the Australian gross-up did not apply to all tax-exempt employers and thus left a significant number of tax-exempt bodies in an FBT-favoured position. More recently, the government has capped the amount of benefit per employee of employers that still receive favoured treatment at $17,000 for hospital employees and $30,000 for other favoured bodies.[29]

In addition, if the rate of the fringe benefit tax (as appropriately adjusted) is set at a rate below the maximum individual rate, there will be an advantage for fringe benefits to highly compensated employees who would have been taxed at a higher rate under the income tax. On the other hand, using the maximum individual rate indirectly overtaxes other employees. The problem of overtaxation of employees who are not subject to the maximum individual tax rate can be overcome by having employees 'buy' the benefit from the employer, since this reduces the FBT base and, with it, the tax rate to the employee's actual rate (because the benefit is bought with after-tax dollars).

Another problem involves the treatment of fringe benefits that would be deductible by the employee if paid for directly by the employee. Since the FBT taxation takes place at the employer level, there is no way to 'wash' the employee inclusion and deduction, as would normally be the case with employee-level taxation. A notional deduction in the FBT, the 'otherwise deductible' rule, was created to reduce the taxable value of fringe benefits that would have been deductible if paid for directly by the employee (e.g., in relation to payments of employee expenses by the employer).[30] In other cases, the issue is handled by the way the benefit is valued. Thus, in the case of, for example, a company car used for both business and personal travel, the FBT valuation rules isolate the personal use, and for this purpose, the business use can be established by a travel log or through statutory formula that applies a percentage to the cost of the car depending on the number of kilometres driven.[31] While the 'otherwise deductible' approach solved the 'wash' problem, it re-introduced the question of allocation of benefits: To determine if the amount would be 'otherwise deductible', it must be allocated to a particular employee (or class of employees) to determine whether an employee-level deduction would have been available.

There are other difficulties with having two parallel systems for dealing with normal employee compensation in the income tax and fringe benefits in a separate tax. Borderline classification issues between normal compensation taxable to the employee and fringe benefits taxed at the employer level have complicated the administration of the system. Eliminating the fringe benefit from employee taxation creates problems with means-tested benefits and other programs based on taxable income. In Australia's recent tax reform, this problem was addressed by requiring that the value of fringe benefits (with some minor exceptions) be

29. Australia, FBTAA, s. 5B(1E) Steps 2 and 3.
30. Australia, FBTAA, s. 24.
31. Australia, FBTAA, ss 9 and 10.

included in the employee's annual income statement received from the employer and basing other income-related benefits on the combined salary and fringe benefits figure.[32] As a result, allocation of virtually all benefits to employees is now required. Further, it is not a simple matter to adapt separate fringe benefit taxation on the employer to international tax and treaty relationships. On the whole, the introduction of the FBT in Australia has improved the tax treatment of such benefits. Nonetheless, some feel that if as much legislative and administrative effort had been put into improving the income tax treatment of fringe benefits as went into the construction of the new tax, the overall results would have been even better. In the 2009 tax reform exercise, the possibility of shifting the tax on fringe benefits to employees is again under review.

1.2. Employer-provided Pension Benefits

Employer-sponsored pension or retirement plans are fringe benefits that frequently receive special tax treatment. The importance of privately based pension plans is directly related to the extent to which public or quasi-public retirement arrangements exist. While the details of the provisions vary, they typically allow a current deduction to the employer for amounts set aside for employee retirement payments to be made in the future with no current tax to the employee. In some cases, the amounts must be transferred to a separate fund or trust, while in others they simply represent a liability of the employer. Where the contributions are set aside in a special trust, the earnings accumulated in the trust prior to distribution are often not taxed.

In the *United States*, an extensive system of employer-provided pension plans covers nearly half of full-time workers and supplements the somewhat limited public social security benefits.[33] Extensive and complex rules govern the 'qualification' of the plan, including requirements dealing with funding, non-discriminatory coverage, limitations on contributions and benefits, and the 'vesting' of employee rights. From a structural point of view, the plan utilizes a trust to which both employer and employee contributions are made. The plans take basically two forms, a 'defined benefit' plan and a 'defined contribution' plan. Under a defined benefit plan, the employee is entitled to specific benefits on retirement, typically tied to the period of service and level of compensation. The employer makes whatever contributions are actuarially required to fund the anticipated payments. In a defined contribution plan, a specified percentage of the employee's salary is contributed to the plan and the benefit is whatever the accumulated fund generates.

From a tax point of view, employer contributions are currently deductible but are not currently included in the employee's income. Similarly, employee contributions, when present, are currently deductible. Both employer and employee contributions are subject to a fixed monetary limitation and a limitation based

32. Australia, FBTAA, Part XI B.
33. United States, IRC, s. 401.

on a percentage of the employee's income from employment. Employees can also make non-deductible after-tax contributions to the plan. The earnings of the qualified plan are not subject to tax in the hands of the trust and the distributions, when made, are fully taxable to the employee. A special rule imposes an additional 10% tax if withdrawals are made before reaching the age of 59½ unless the withdrawal is made by a person at least 55 years old who is unemployed. This rule attempts to ensure that the tax-preferred savings are really being used for retirement. Similarly, benefits have to begin at age 70½. Rollover provisions are broadly available on a change of employment.

Other tax-favoured mechanisms are related to employees' retirement income. So-called 'cash' or 'deferred' plans allow employees to make their own contributions in lieu of current cash salary to plans subject to generally the same rules and restrictions as qualified plans.[34] Payouts from such plans can be accelerated only in the case of the employee's disability, death, termination of employment, or the occurrence of an emergency that causes severe financial hardship. In addition, certain specially favoured qualified plans ('Employee Stock Ownership Plans') are allowed to make investments in the stock of the employer corporation and give the employees the right to receive the stock on retirement.

The overall economic impact of qualified plans in the United States is substantial, accounting for over $121.4 billion in lost revenues in 2008.

Employee pension plans are the most important source of retirement income in *Canada*. The government-provided pensions – Canada (or Quebec) Pension Plan, to which all employees must contribute, and Old Age Security – are relatively modest.

To qualify for tax benefits, employee pension plans must be registered with the tax authorities, and registration is permitted only if various conditions are met. In addition, pension plans must meet several conditions imposed by provincial law. Legally, the plans are trusts. Registered plans must be either money purchase plans or defined benefit plans. Limits on the contributions by both employers and employees are related to the maximum pension benefit that an individual can receive. In addition, the limits are integrated with the limits on contributions to private retirement savings plans.

Both employer and employee contributions to registered pension plans are tax-deductible within limits. In addition, income earned by the plan is not taxable. The investments that can be made by registered pension plans are restricted. For example, no investments can be made in the employer or persons related to the employer. Amounts are taxable when withdrawn from the plan, except for certain rollovers to other registered plans.

The situation in *Japan* is somewhat different. Although initially employer pensions were uncommon, beginning in the late 1950s it became more usual for employers to provide for employees' pensions, typically by paying premiums to a bank or insurance company that agreed to pay the retirement income. The premiums are currently deductible by the employer and, if the plan qualifies,

34. United States, IRC, s. 401(k).

are not currently taxed to the employee, who is taxed only on the pension when paid. However, the pension reserves are subject to a special corporate tax in the hands of the company[35] providing the benefit to compensate for the fact that the premium is currently deductible by the employer and not included currently by the employee. Before 2002, all the employer-sponsored pension plans that qualified for this special tax treatment were 'defined benefit' plans. Since 2002, 'defined contribution' pension plans have also become available as plans qualifying for similar tax treatment.[36]

In *Sweden*, employers can claim deductions for pension costs either through a deductible reserve against profits, a transfer to a qualified pension fund, or the purchase of pension insurance. The amount deductible is the same as the cost recorded in the financial accounts, but normally with a limit equal to the lower of 35% of the employee's salary or an indexed amount, which in 2009 was about SEK 428,000.[37] The amounts are not taxed currently to employees.

In *The Netherlands*, an employer may deduct as a business expense pension premiums paid to an insurance company or to a pension fund that operates for an entire industry or branch of business activities. Alternatively, the employer may create, but not control, a special pension fund for employees that meets certain statutory requirements. Contributions to the fund are deductible currently. With respect to pensions for persons who are both shareholders and employees, the company may deduct an addition to a self-managed pension reserve where the legal right to the pension has not yet vested in the employee, although the employer has expressed an intention of granting a pension on retirement.

The employee's right to future benefits is treated as postponed wage income and is not taxed until actually received. Most pension funds are exempt from tax, with the result that the accumulated earnings of these funds typically go untaxed. There have been proposals to tax the capital surplus of such funds, but no legislation has yet been enacted.

Dutch pension benefits are typically quite generous, albeit recently with a slight downward trend. Many employees were typically entitled to a pension that, when combined with the relatively substantial governmental social security old age benefit, was equal to 70% of their last year's earnings, with the amount often indexed for inflation or even for changes in general wage levels. In light of the demographic situation and the potentially increasing number of retired persons, there has been a move to 70% of the weighted average lifetime salary.

In *Germany*, the use of employer-provided pension plans is fairly widespread, with nearly one-third of all companies providing a plan. Close to one-half of the working population is covered by an employer plan. Under labour law, the employee can demand an occupational pension plan if he is willing to finance the contributions by deductions from his wages (*Entgeltumwandlung*). Since the

35. This special corporate tax is temporarily suspended until the end of March 2011 (Special Taxation Measures Act (STMA), s. 68-4).
36. Japan, Corporate Tax Act (CTA), s. 84.
37. Sweden, Income Tax Act (ITA), Ch. 28.

retirement benefits from the state-run social security system were reduced in 2001, employer-provided pension plans have become more important in Germany and enjoy some tax advantages.

Plans can be structured by a direct commitment by the employer to pay the pension or through a third party as pension insurance, as a pension fund, as direct insurance, or as a 'benevolent' fund. Large and medium-sized companies typically use the direct method, while smaller enterprises fund the pension obligation by purchasing insurance. Direct pension commitments are funded through the creation of deductible pension reserves.[38] For tax purposes, the reserve can first be established when the employee reaches the age of 27 and is based on the actuarial calculations of the future pension obligation using a 6% discount rate. Subsequent adjustments to the reserve can be made. There is no restriction on the employer's use of the funds in the reserve. However, employers are legally required to participate in a special guarantee fund. Although the employee has a legal right to the future pension at the time the reserve is formed, there is no taxation at the employee level until payments are received.

In contrast, if the employer finances retirement benefits through direct insurance, the payment of the premium is currently deductible by the employer.[39] For the employee, the premium is generally taxable income.[40] However, up to €2,544 per year is tax-exempt.[41] When the retirement payments are made by the insurer, they are fully taxed to the extent that the payments are based on the tax-exempt pension premiums. The part of the retirement payment that results from non-deductible and non-exempt contributions is taxed partially.[42] If pension benefits are funded through a pension fund or pension insurance, the pattern of taxation is the same as for direct insurance; the employer has a current deduction for the contributions,[43] and the employee has current income[44] that is partially tax-exempt.[45] The fund itself is generally tax-exempt and is subject to substantial governmental oversight and regulation.[46] A final method for funding involves so-called benevolent or relief funds. Benevolent funds are subject to less government supervision than formal pension funds, and correspondingly, there are substantial restrictions on the employer's deduction.[47] The contributions of the employer are not income for the employee because he does not have a legal right to the future pension payment. The pension payments are taxed as wages.[48]

38. Germany, ITA, s. 6a.
39. Germany, ITA, s. 4b.
40. Germany, ITA, s. 19 para. 1 no. 3.
41. Germany, ITA, s. 3 no. 63.
42. Germany, ITA, s. 22 no. 5.
43. Germany, ITA, s. 4c.
44. Germany, ITA, s. 19 para. 1 no. 3.
45. Germany, ITA, s. 22 no. 5.
46. Germany, Corporate Income Tax Act (CITA), s. 5 no. 3.
47. Germany, ITA, s. 4d.
48. Germany, ITA, s. 19 para. 1 no. 2.

In the *United Kingdom*, legislation dealing with pensions has been radically liberalized and simplified, with the new rules taking effect in 2006.[49] The new rules apply both to employer-provided schemes and to personal arrangements. Before 2006 it was not necessary for employees to join their employers' schemes.

The United Kingdom permits various types of entitlements, including terminal salary schemes (defined benefit plans) and money purchase schemes. These now have a maximum value, called the lifetime allowance; in 2009–2010 the allowance is £1.75 million. The individual may make a contribution at any time. The annual allowance (i.e., the maximum that may be contributed) is set for 2009–2010 at £245,000 of relevant earnings (whether from employment or business, but not usually from a property business). A person may also contribute up to £3,600 a year from any source in certain circumstances. As noted above in Part One, the United Kingdom charges higher rates of tax on certain incomes. As from 6 April 2011, individuals with incomes over £150,000 will be given relief only at the basic rate of income tax (currently 20%) and not at the marginal rate; the legislation will include rules to prevent abnormal contributions in the two intervening years (beginning on 22 April 2009).[50] On retirement, these workers may take a pension or commute a part of that pension into a fixed sum; the effect of this sum is to reduce the remaining pension.[51] The maximum tax-free lump sum is 25% of the member's pension rights or 25% of the lifetime allowance, whichever is less. Benefits must be taken by age 75 at the latest, and this will usually be by way of pension scheme or lifetime annuity. Income withdrawal is allowed instead for a money purchase scheme. Benefits may not usually be taken before age 50. Breaches of the rules, such as straying beyond the lifetime or annual allowances, entail substantial penalties.[52]

Employer-provided pensions require that a fund be established under a trust, complete with an administrator who is responsible for dealing with the tax authorities. Employer contributions are deductible currently, and income and capital gains from the funds held by the pension scheme are normally exempt from tax.[53] However, the imputation tax credit accompanying a dividend is not repayable.

In recent years great differences have emerged between these final salary schemes and defined contribution schemes or money purchase schemes; the last two may not be tied to terminal salaries. The 2000 downturn in stock market values and accounting rules requiring companies to be much more cautious in assessing their pension liabilities led to quite a disgraceful pension panic. Many companies switched their employee pension schemes from defined benefit to money purchase plans by closing their defined benefit schemes to new employees and even by making existing employees make the change for future years of service. Some of these companies took advantage of the stock market boom to make no

49. United Kingdom, Finance Act 2004, Part 4.
50. United Kingdom, legislation forthcoming.
51. United Kingdom, Finance Act 2004, Part 4 Ch. 3.
52. United Kingdom, Finance Act 2004, Part 4 Ch. 5.
53. United Kingdom, Finance Act 2004, Part 4 Ch. 4.

contributions at all during the years of plenty, and now their employees are reaping the consequences. Those employed in the public sector may have their pensions paid for by the state. The question whether the costs of these pensions have been are properly calculated is matter of current political concern.

Australia's arrangements for private retirement income, which is generally referred to as superannuation, have deviated significantly from those of other countries and are worth examining in more detail. In contrast to some other countries here considered, there is no public social security scheme funded by a special tax in Australia; the universal old age pension funded out of government general revenues is basically a flat-rate payment equal to 25% of average weekly earnings (currently under review) that is strictly means tested. Thus, employer-provided or self-provided benefits are extremely important.

Prior to 1983, employer contributions to superannuation funds (in the legal form of trusts) were deductible within generous limits; superannuation funds were tax-exempt; and lump sum payments on retirement were effectively tax-free, while pensions were taxable. Less than half the labour force was covered by private superannuation and coverage was heavily skewed in favour of upper income groups. In 1983, taxation on lump-sum payouts was introduced, and in 1988 (mainly to fund a reduction in the company tax rate and to overcome arbitrage activities involving superannuation funds), a 15% tax on employer contributions and on fund income was introduced along with a 15% tax rebate for pensions paid from superannuation funds. That is, the intention was to accelerate revenue rather than significantly affect the tax expenditure involved in the superannuation area. In 2009, the tax expenditure in respect of the superannuation system is estimated at $29.4 billion, far and away the largest item in total tax expenditures of $56.9 billion.

In 1992 a superannuation guarantee charge was introduced to make superannuation contributions compulsory in respect of all employees, with the required rate of employer contribution being phased in over a number of years and reaching a maximum of 9% of salary in 2002. The proceeds of this charge, which applies only when employers do not provide 'voluntarily' the required level of private superannuation coverage, are paid into a special fund for the benefit of the relevant employee, who may direct payment into a superannuation fund. To prevent the system from being burdened by small amounts that are eaten up by administration charges, employers do not need to contribute for employees with salaries of less than $450 per month (i.e., low-paid part-time employees).

Employee contributions to a superannuation fund are generally made out of after-tax income and are not subject to the contributions tax or to tax on payout from the fund. There is thus a bias against employee contributions in the system. Employer contributions are without limit, but limits are indirectly applied by imposing excess contributions taxes on superannuation funds (the amount permitted being $50,000 per annum, per employee, indexed for inflation). Deductible employer contributions are not included in the income of the employee but, as mentioned, are subject to the 15% contributions tax in the hands of the superannuation fund.

The income of a complying superannuation fund (one that has been approved by the Australian Prudential Regulation Authority as meeting certain criteria for vesting, age limits, portability, etc. or is otherwise qualified) is taxed at a rate of 15%, in contrast to the 45% top individual rate. Superannuation funds are entitled to the benefit of corporate imputation credits to reduce the contributions tax and the tax on investment income. A fund may not invest more than 10% of its assets in the sponsoring employer or its associates but otherwise is relatively unrestricted in investment policy, although the trustee must formulate and implement an investment strategy.

In general, superannuation pensions prior to 1 July 2007 were taxable in the ordinary way as other income (apart from the employee's non-deductible contributions), but subject to a flat tax rebate of 15% in recognition of the tax paid on deducted contributions and fund income. Because of concerns about the aging of the population, the government instituted a major reform in 2007, the centrepiece of which was the abolition of tax on superannuation benefits paid to persons aged 60 or over. The purpose of this and other detailed changes was to create an incentive for persons considering retirement to remain partly or fully engaged in the workforce while at the same time being able to access their superannuation benefits.

An elaborate system for rolling over amounts paid from superannuation funds on change of employment, etc., is designed to ensure that they remain within the special tax regime until specified age limits are reached (generally not earlier than age 60). Contributions and income can be made and accumulated within the system until age 75. Schemes can take defined contribution and defined benefit forms, and there are many special rules in relation to unfunded schemes for public sector employees.

As noted above, although the superannuation system is private rather than a public system, it is compulsory for all employees, with contributions required of employers and enforced by the superannuation guarantee charge. The government has made the superannuation system the centrepiece of achieving the twin objectives of increasing the private savings rate in Australia and insuring against effective bankruptcy of the public sector as the population ages. To that end, and in addition to the system described above for employees, a similar arrangement applies to the self-employed; indeed, there is no requirement that a person be employed or self-employed to participate in the superannuation system. A person can obtain an 18% tax credit for contributions up to $3,000 per year to a complying fund in respect of a low-income spouse, and low-income employees are entitled to a government co-contribution ($1.50 for every $1.00 contribution by the employee, with a maximum co-contribution of $1,500).

For the vast majority of *French* employees, retirement benefits come exclusively from the compulsory social security system, so that employer pension plans are uncommon and private pension funds do not exist as such. Before 2004, employers could freely create internal or external plans from which all or certain categories (e.g., managers) of employees could benefit. Contributions to such plans were deductible. But the conditions for the non-inclusion of such contributions in the employee's taxable income and the deductibility of employer contributions were in practice rarely met, and the corresponding pension benefits were taxable. Things changed slightly starting in 2004: a Pension Reform Act enacted in July 2003 provides for a new type of optional pension plan to which more generous tax benefits are attached. Pursuant to defined contribution pension plans negotiated with the employee representatives and established by a firm, a group of firms, or a branch, contributions to mutual funds (tax-exempt) are deductible from profits within strict and complex limits. The employee's contribution is deductible and the employer's contribution is not included in the employee's taxable income, subject to a combination of absolute and percentage limitations applicable to the total amount. The corresponding pension is taxable when actually received.[54]

2. IMPUTED INCOME FROM OWNER-OCCUPIED HOUSING

The in-kind return from the ownership of personal assets and self-provided services has long been recognized as an economic benefit, but only in the case of owner-occupied housing has there been a serious effort to include the benefit in the income tax base. The treatment of imputed income from owner-occupied housing is an important part of the overall treatment of housing for tax purposes. Failure to tax imputed income, when coupled, as it often is, with a deduction for interest costs incurred in purchasing a personal residence and preferential treatment of gain on sale, may lead to a serious under-taxation of housing expenditures and a corresponding overinvestment in this sector as compared to rental housing. This has clearly been the case in the *United States*. Failure to tax imputed income from owner-occupied housing also creates equity problems in the relative treatment of renters and homeowners. On the other hand, real property taxes may to some extent operate as a surrogate for the taxation of imputed rental income. Thus, in *France*, for example, the taxation of owner-occupied housing was abandoned in 1966, but local taxes apply both to the owner of the property and to the occupant.

In the systems considered here, the results with respect to the taxation of owner-occupied housing are varied. In *Canada* and the United States, although the matter has been discussed from time to time, no legislative proposals to tax income from owner-occupied housing have been seriously considered. In other countries, the taxation of imputed housing income was attempted but then dropped because of difficulties in applying the tax on a realistic basis. For example, prior to 1987, *Germany* included in the category of rental income the income from owner-occupied housing. The rental value was based on either the assessed value of the real estate, which was seldom an accurate measure of the market value, or on comparable rentals, which also presented some valuation problems. Since interest costs (as well as maintenance costs in the case of the comparable rentals approach) were deductible, the result was often a loss that could be used against other income.

54. France, CGI, s. 163 *quatervicies*; see also s. 163 *bis* B and 237 *ter*.

After a transition period beginning in 1987, taxation of imputed income was eliminated. However, a recent reform of the tax rules for private pension contributions has re-introduced, to a certain extent, an imputed income rule for owner-occupied housing.[55] A person whose private pension contributions qualify for certain tax advantages can use these contributions to finance a house or condominium for his own living purposes; when he retires and occupies the home, there is a deferred taxation of a fictitious pension income associated with the housing.

For similar reasons, abolition of tax on imputed rent occurred earlier in *Australia* (1922) and *France*. France, however, continues to tax the imputed rental income of moors, meadows, forests, and bodies of water used for private hunting or fishing, as well as non-resident ownership of real estate in some cases.[56] In the *United Kingdom*, the tax was abandoned because of the perceived difficulty of obtaining accurate valuation of property for purposes of the tax at a time when rental controls meant there was no open market for real property.

In *The Netherlands*, imputed housing income is, in principle, subject to tax. From a policy point of view, the taxation of imputed income from home ownership is intended to help equalize the after-tax living costs of owners and renters but has also been an important means to stimulate home ownership in a country where people historically have been renters rather than homeowners. The latter goal is accomplished by using a (modest) deemed semi-net rental amount from which any (mortgage) interest paid can be deducted, resulting for many taxpayers in a loss that offsets other income (within box 1: income from employment and business). The imputed income is based on a formula intended to reach results approximating the market rental value of similar occupied properties. The numbers used in the formula are reviewed periodically to take into account changes in actual rentals, and in recent years the required inclusion has been set at about 1.3% of the fair market value of the property. Gain on the sale of the residence is not taxed, consistent with the general pattern of non-taxation of capital gains.

Similarly, imputed income from owner-occupied housing has historically been subject to income tax in *Sweden*. Originally, the fair market rental value was included as revenue in the tax base. The same rule was applied (and still is applied) to the use by the owner of property held in a business (e.g., personal use of an apartment in an apartment building). Valuation problems made the application of the system difficult in the case of owner-occupied private housing and was replaced with a system using standardized amounts. The imputed return was taken to be the interest rate on long-term government bonds, with no deductions for any expenses except interest expense. Thus, in effect, the return on the taxpayer's equity invested in the house was taxed.

In the tax reform of 1991, the basic principle of taxing imputed income was retained for equity reasons, but the structure of the tax was changed. A separate real estate tax was imposed at a rate of 1.5% (later decreased to 1%) of the assessed value of the property, which should, in principle, be equal to 75% of the

55. Germany, ITA, ss 92a and 92b.
56. France, CGI, ss 14 and 30.

market value. The rate was set with reference to the historical real yield on government securities. The combination of the tax rate and the calculation of the base was intended to tax the return at a rate equivalent to the rate for income from capital, after inflation adjustments are taken into account. A deduction is allowed for interest expense when income from capital is computed (tax rate 30%). An important part of the system is that the assessed values have been kept fairly accurately in line with market values, with assessments every third year. In areas with a rapid increase in market values (which was an unbroken trend from the mid-1990s until 2008) the effect was a considerable increase in tax payments. Many homeowners found they were unable to fund further tax increases. Some specialized reforms were carried out in order to mitigate these effects for persons with low incomes. The opposition (non-socialist) parties did promise to abolish the tax and, upon forming the government, they introduced a bold reform in 2007. The tax (renamed the municipal fee) is now capped at 6,000 SEK.[57] The rest of the system remains in place: a 1% fee on assessed value (with the cap) and unlimited interest deductions. Sweden may thus be moving from one extreme of taxing imputed income from owner-occupied housing to another extreme.

For cooperative apartment houses, a common legal arrangement in Sweden, the taxation model is the same as for owner-occupied houses. Overall taxation (fees) is lower for cooperative apartments than for owner-occupied houses, before and after the reform.

Japan does not, in principle, tax the imputed value of privately held assets. However, there is a mechanism that effectively may allow for the taxation of some imputed income if a personal asset is later sold. In general, a deduction for depreciation is not allowed with respect to personal assets. Nonetheless, the taxpayer must adjust the basis of the personal asset as if depreciation had been taken. If the personal asset is later sold at a gain, the gain must be calculated from the adjusted basis.[58]

3. GIFTS

The proper taxation of gifts in a family context has been a matter of some discussion from a theoretical point of view in systems with a global approach to income definition. Because the person who receives the gift (the donee) has the power to consume or save the proceeds, there is some logic in including the gift in income. On the other hand, because the donor has typically paid tax on the funds used to make the gift initially, taxing the donee represents a second tax on what is the same economic income. One response to this problem would be to give a deduction to the donor for the gift, but in systems with a progressive rate structure that approach would encourage income shifting to reduce taxes. The final possibility, which is the rule generally adopted, is not to tax the donee but also to give no deduction to the

57. Sweden, Municipal Real Estate Fee Act.
58. Japan, ITA, s. 38 para. 2.

donor, thus ensuring that the initial income stream from which the gift is made is taxed only once (although, from one point of view, to the wrong person).

In schedular systems, the issue arises somewhat differently. In the case of private gifts, the issue of income inclusion generally does not come up, since typically the receipt does not fall within any taxable schedule. In some systems, the 'other' category of income includes receipts from whatever source if they arise on a periodic basis (e.g., a series of gifts over a period of time, reflecting an underlying notion of periodicity as an important characteristic of income). In all of these situations, the existence of transfer taxes also may have an impact on the view taken of gifts from an income tax perspective.

A related problem involves gifts or bequests of appreciated or depreciated property. Some systems treat the gift or bequest as a realization event. Others postpone current taxation and preserve the potential taxation of the appreciation at the time of the gift by providing a carryover tax cost[59] in the property to the donee.

Some countries, in particular the United States and the United Kingdom, allow a fair market value tax cost in the hands of the transferee for transfers at death without treating the transfer as a realization event. These aspects are dealt with briefly here and discussed in more detail in the subsequent section dealing with realization generally.

Additional issues are raised by gifts in a business context, typically when the donor deducts the payment, and are considered after the treatment of non-business gifts.

3.1. Gifts Outside a Business Setting ('Personal' Gifts)

The *United States* is an example of the treatment of personal gifts in a global income setting. Gifts in a private context are not taxable to the donee and are not deductible by the donor.[60] In the case of appreciated property, the gift is not treated as a realization event, and the donee's tax cost is the tax cost of the donor, thus preserving the possibility of tax on the appreciation in the hands of the donee.[61] A special rule prevents the shifting of loss in the case of depreciated property. Bequests are treated similarly with respect to deduction and inclusion, but the property receives a tax cost equal to fair market value in the hands of the transferee, thus allowing pre-death appreciation in the property to escape tax altogether.[62]

In *Germany*, gifts of private assets between private persons are neither taxable to the donee nor deductible by the donor. The tax cost of appreciated assets

59. The various systems use different terminology to express the notion of the taxpayer's capital investment in an asset for tax purposes. The US term is 'basis' or 'tax basis'. Other systems refer to 'cost', 'tax cost', 'acquisition cost', 'tax book cost', or some equivalent term. These materials will generally use the term 'tax cost' to refer to this basic concept.
60. United States, IRC, s. 102.
61. United States, IRC, s. 1015.
62. United States, IRC, s. 1014.

carries over.[63] In *France*, the same pattern of taxation applies, but the transferee takes a fair market value tax cost for both gifts and transfers at death.

For the deduction and inclusion of gifts, similar principles are applied in the *United Kingdom, Canadian*, and *Australian* systems. Personal gifts are non-taxable, since they are not derived from a taxable 'source' and similarly are not deductible by the donor. The Commonwealth systems differ, however, in their treatment of gifts and bequests of appreciated property. In Canada, both *inter vivos* transfers and transfers at death are treated as realization events for the transferor, with the transferor being deemed to receive proceeds equal to the fair market value of the property and the transferee taking a fair market value tax cost.[64] In Australia, *inter vivos* transfers are similarly realization events, whereas transfers at death result in a carryover of tax cost, thus postponing the possible taxation of pre-death appreciation.[65] The United Kingdom treats an *inter vivos* gift as a realization event.[66] As in the United States, however, in the case of a transfer at death, there is no realization and the transferee takes a fair market value tax cost. Unlike Australia and Canada, the United Kingdom still has an estate tax on death; on death, the single rate of 40% applies once the transfers exceed £325,000 (for 2009–2010).[67]

Japan and *Sweden* reach the same results as to deduction and income inclusion and generally provide for a carryover of tax cost if a gain on the sale of the asset would be taxable.[68] The same is true for *The Netherlands*, except that where the gift concerns a substantial participation (5% or more of the shares) in the shares of a company (the only type of personal asset in respect of which capital gains are taxable), the gift is treated as a (deemed) disposal, giving rise to taxation of the donor and a step-up in basis for the donee.

3.2. Gifts in a Business or Employment Context

Gifts in a business or employment context raise somewhat different issues. The donor who has made the gift for business reasons will typically deduct the amount of the gift as a cost of doing business, so if, as in the case of personal gifts, the gift continues to be exempt in the hands of the donee, the entire amount would escape tax. The response to this problem is either to deny the deduction to the donor or to require the gift to be taxable to the donee. Both approaches have been taken in the systems under consideration.

In the *United States*, most gifts over a *de minimis* amount from an employer to an employee are taxable to the employee and deductible as a business expense by

63. Germany, ITR (Income Tax Regulation), s. 11d.
64. Canada, ITA, ss 69(1), 70(5) and (6).
65. Australia, ITAA 1997, ss 116-30(1), 128-10, 128-15.
66. United Kingdom, Taxation of Chargeable Gains Act 1992 (TCGA), s. 17.
67. United Kingdom, Inheritance Tax Act 1984, on threshold, see Sch. 1.
68. Japan, ITA, ss 9 and 60.

the employer.[69] Special rules apply to exclude tangible property awarded for length of service and other similar achievements (the 'golden watch' exception). In the case of gifts in the business context to non-employees, in principle, the donee may be able to exclude the gift as an expression of disinterested generosity by the donor (i.e., a true gift), but in that case the deduction is denied to the donor, thus ensuring that the gift is not excluded from the tax base entirely.[70]

In the *Commonwealth* countries, business gifts are typically taxable to the recipient (or subject to the FBT in Australia in the case of employees) as arising from an employment or other business relationship. The gift can be excluded if the taxpayer shows that it arose out of personal regard, but the fact that the payer has deducted the payment may raise a presumption that it is taxable in some countries. In the *United Kingdom*, the special rules that apply when employment earnings exceed £8,500 are relevant here. If the person providing the gift is the employer, it is deemed to arise by reason of employment and so is taxable; this presumption cannot be rebutted where the employer is a company and otherwise only in limited circumstances. Certain long-service awards (£50 per year but only if total years exceed 20) are exempt, as are certain gifts from third parties (£250 a year). These statutory rules have no application to the business context, a vivid example of the schedular or Part system. In *Canada*, by administrative concession, certain gifts to employees (e.g., Christmas gifts) if limited to two per year and to a *de minimis* amount (currently $500) are not required to be included in income but are deductible by the employer.

In *Germany*, in general, gifts over a *de minimis* amount (€35) are not deductible by the donor as a business or income-related expense even if they have a clear business purpose,[71] but such gifts may be excluded by the donee only if they are true gifts. If the purported 'gift' is sufficiently related to a clearly identifiable service, then the cost of the transfer is deductible by the payer and must be included in the recipient's income.

Gifts of business property made for non-business reasons are subject to a complex set of rules emerging from general principles dealing with the withdrawal and contribution of business assets.[72] The donation of an asset for non-business reasons is treated as the withdrawal of an asset by the donor. The 'fair value' of the asset has to be included in the calculation of that year's profit, so that all 'hidden reserves' are taxed.[73] There is no deduction for the transfer under the general rule denying deduction for gifts. The donee receives the gift free of income tax in his personal capacity. If the donor gives the gift to the donee, who uses the asset for business purposes, it must be included in the balance sheet as a 'contribution' at fair market value at the time of transfer, but that amount is not included in income.[74]

69. United States, IRC, s. 102(c).
70. United States, IRC, s. 274(b).
71. Germany, ITA, s. 4 para. 5 no. 1.
72. Germany, ITA, s. 4 para. 1 s. 1.
73. Germany, ITA, s. 6 para. 1 no. 4 sent. 1.
74. Germany, ITA, ss 4 para. 1 sent. 1 and 6 para. 1 no. 5 sent. 1.

The *Swedish* rules are similar, except that the transfer for business reasons results in realization and a corresponding fair market value deduction for the transferor.

Gifts made by corporations or commercial law partnerships in *Japan* are, in principle, subject to income tax in the hands of the recipient and deductible by the payer. If the gift is not related to any particular category of income of the recipient, it is taxed as Occasional Income, which is subject to a preferential rate and special deductions. Otherwise, the gift falls into the appropriate income category, sometimes subject to a special rate.[75]

In *The Netherlands*, gifts that occur in a business or employment context are treated as deductible by the payer and are generally taxable to the recipient, although exceptions are made for gifts received by an employee on special occasions. In the case of appreciated property, the transfer is a realization event.

In *France*, business gifts to clients, employees, etc., are generally not taxable if they are not directly related to services performed. This condition is strictly construed as far as employees are concerned but has received an express statutory exception in the case of gifts of fully depreciated computer hardware or software.[76] They are, however, deductible if they are made in the interests of the business and the amounts are not too large.[77] The gift of a capital asset would be considered a realization event for capital gains taxation purposes.

4. PRIZES AND AWARDS

As in the case of gifts, the income definitional issues for prizes and awards arise somewhat differently in global and schedular systems. In a global system, the logic of the system clearly points toward taxation of the recipient unless extra-fiscal considerations are thought to justify exclusion. In schedular systems, the question is whether the prize 'fits' in a taxable category. In both systems, special rules sometimes apply to prizes or awards in the employment context.

In the *United States*, prizes and awards are in general fully taxable, regardless of the nature of the activity or accomplishment being recognized.[78] Thus, for example, the Nobel Prize is taxable, as are athletic awards. Special rules exempt certain prizes and awards in the form of tangible property for employee service or achievement and, since the amounts remain deductible by the employer, the entire amount escapes tax.

In *Germany*, prizes and awards are taxable if they can be related in a loose way to one of the income categories.[79] In addition, they may be taxed as 'other' income if they are awarded for a specific accomplishment. Awards to employees for

75. Japan, ITA, s. 34.
76. France, CGI, ss 81 and 31 *bis*.
77. France, CGI, ss 39.5 and 54 *quater* (clients), s. 82 (employees).
78. United States, IRC, s. 74.
79. Federal Tax Court (*Bundesfinanzhof*), judgment of 23 Apr. 2009 VI R 39/08.

suggestions, improvements, etc., are taxable. On the other hand, prizes in recognition of a life's work (the Nobel Prize, Goethe Prize, etc.) are not taxable. Lottery prizes are exempt, even if the lottery takes place in a business setting, as long as the chances of winning are low and all employees are entitled to participate. But a prize awarded to a candidate in the context of a TV show can be taxable, since it represents consideration for 'occasional' services.[80]

Similarly, in *The Netherlands*, prizes and awards are taxable if they relate to the recipient's professional or business activities (e.g., a prize to a professional author if the recipient could reasonably expect to receive the award). Prizes for 'hobby' activities (e.g., at an amateur dog show) would not be taxable, because there is no taxable source; however, if too much effort is involved, a business or profession may be present.

In *Japan*, prizes and awards received from corporations or commercial partnerships as part of advertising and publicity campaigns are taxable as Occasional Income. Scholarly and scientific prizes are not taxable.[81]

Under the *Swedish* schedular system, prizes and awards that cannot be characterized as 'remuneration' for a 'performance' are not taxable. Thus, lottery prizes where the winner is chosen by chance are not taxable. However, they may be subject to a special lottery tax paid by the organizer.

On the other hand, a case held that a prize for entering an advertising slogan in a contest was taxable. The court rejected the taxpayer's argument that there were so many entries that the jury could not have read all of them and that therefore the prize was in fact based on chance. It was not relevant that the amount of the prize had no relation to the value of the performance. Prizes won on TV shows are taxable even if based on chance; the element of performance is supplied by the act of appearing on the program. In addition, lottery prizes won in a draw that is limited to employees are taxable as fringe benefits arising out of the employment relation.

In Sweden, the Nobel Prize has been held (not surprisingly) to be non-taxable, in part on the theory that the accomplishments on which the prize was based were not undertaken in order to obtain the prize (the case was decided before *The Double Helix* was written).

The *Australian* and *Canadian* rules reveal similar principles, with prizes arising in a field of endeavour regularly carried on by the taxpayer or paid on a periodic basis being taxable as income resulting from a taxable 'source'. The position in the *United Kingdom* is similar but may not be identical. In the United Kingdom, a prize awarded to an author voluntarily (and not solicited by the author) was treated by the tax authorities as a windfall and therefore was not taxable. Some countries have an exemption for general public prizes such as the Nobel Prize; the United Kingdom does not. The treatment of prizes was recently litigated in *Australia*, with the High Court holding that prizes, grants, bonuses, and sponsorships received by

80. Federal Tax Court (*Bundesfinanzhof*), judgment of 28 Nov. 2007 IX R 39/06.
81. Japan, ITA, s. 9.

an Olympic-standard athlete were all taxable.[82] In Canada, Olympic medals are considered taxable.

In *France*, statutory law excludes the Nobel Prize and a specific list of other equivalent international literary, scientific, or artistic prizes.[83] Other prizes, especially domestic ones, awarded by an independent jury can be exempted according to administrative regulations.[84] State grants awarded to Olympic medal holders are also traditionally excluded from taxable income by a specific parliamentary decision.

5. SCHOLARSHIPS AND GRANTS

The tax treatment of scholarships is related both to the global or schedular structure of the tax system and to the overall system for the provision of educational services in the country. In countries that provide extensive no-fee or low-fee public education, scholarships involving tuition are generally not an issue and scholarship payments are usually in the form of support for living expenses. In a schedular system, one of the typical schedules of taxable income is periodic payments for living expenses; scholarships easily fit into this taxable category. Similarly, in a global system that focuses on consumption as an important component of the tax base, payments for living expenses would be a clear candidate for taxation.

In addition, where tuition is generally privately financed, the issue of scholarships covering tuition must be faced, with potentially different outcomes in global and schedular systems. Non-fiscal arguments concerning the importance of supporting education also play a role. Finally, even where, in principle, some scholarships are exempt, they may be taxable if they are sufficiently closely related to employment or some other taxable category of income. The systems under consideration here combine these principles in various forms.

In the *United States*, scholarships that cover tuition and related educational expenses are excluded from income.[85] Payments for other expenses, such as lodging or meals, do not qualify for the exclusion. The recipient must be a candidate for a degree at a recognized educational institution. The exclusion is not available to the extent that the student is required to perform teaching, research, or other services as a condition of the grant. In that situation, the amount equal to the fair market value of the services performed is taxable and the remainder, if any, can be excluded as a scholarship. The reduction or remission of tuition fees for the children of employees of an educational institution is excluded from income as a qualified scholarship, as long as such reduction is available on a non-discriminatory basis (i.e., not limited to professors).

---

82. *Stone* [2005] HCA 21, 222 CLR 289.
83. France, CGI, s. 92 A.
84. France, Administrative Documentation 5 G-2222, paras 9–11.
85. United States, IRC s. 117.

In *Sweden*, despite the extensive low-cost public education system, a special statutory provision exempts scholarships. There were discussions in the context of the 1991 tax reform to repeal the exemption, but it survived based on arguments about the necessity of supporting research. Payments in support of education that can be characterized as remuneration for services are taxable. For example, a 'scholarship' paid by a publishing house to an author whose works were published by the publisher was held to be taxable. In some cases, a series of payments in support of research may be taxable based on the historical notion that periodicity is an essential characteristic of income. Periodic payments by domestic tax-exempt organizations have been made exempt by statute; however, a series of payments over three years by a foreign foundation to a Swedish researcher was held to be taxable.

In *Germany*, most scholarships are tax-exempt under a statute.[86] To qualify, the payments must be made by governmental or charitable organizations and must not require any specific performance of services on the part of the recipient. The purpose of the payments must be to further research or education. The Federal Tax Court has recently extended this tax exemption to scholarships covering cost of living even for senior scholars.[87] Scholarships that do not meet these requirements are taxable income.

In contrast, in *The Netherlands*, while public 'study grants' are exempt from tax, private scholarships and grants are taxable if they take the form of periodic payments. This reflects the early role of periodicity in income definition. On the other hand, lump-sum payments are not taxed.

In *Canada*, which also has extensive public education, scholarships, fellowships, and bursaries are excluded from income to the extent that they are received in connection with the recipient's enrolment in an elementary, secondary, or post-secondary school program.[88] Other scholarships, fellowships, bursaries, and prizes are included in income to the extent that they exceed $500. Research grants must also be included in income, but only to the extent that the amount received exceeds the research expenses incurred.[89] Personal and living expenses other than research-related travel expenses may not be claimed as deductions against a research grant. In contrast, in *Australia*, although scholarships would normally be taxable as periodic payments covering living expenses, a specific statutory exclusion applies for full-time study at a school, college, or university unless the purported amount is conditional on providing services currently or in the future.[90] The *United Kingdom* similarly exempts scholarships, although amounts in support of study provided to children of employees by an employer are taxable to the employee under the fringe benefits legislation. The latter rule does not apply if the scholarships are provided

86. Germany, ITA, s. 3 no. 11, no. 44.
87. Federal Tax Court (*Bundesfinanzhof*), judgment of 20 Mar. 2003 IV R 15/01.
88. Canada, ITA, ss 56(1)(n) and 56(3).
89. Canada, ITA, s. 60(o).
90. Australia, ITAA 1997, ss 51-10 and 51-35.

under a trust scheme in which at least 75% of the relevant payments to beneficiaries are to those who are not relatives of employees.[91]

In *France*, state-provided educational assistance, which is awarded on the basis of social criteria, is not subject to tax but is treated as social assistance. Otherwise, scholarships and grants are taxable whenever there is some kind of consideration on the part of the payee or some legal or contractual obligation on the part of the party funding such scholarships or grants.

In *Japan*, financial assistance for educational expenses is excluded from taxable income. Educational expenses must be directly related to educational activities and, therefore, financial assistance for meals is not excluded, while that for tuition is excluded from taxable income. In addition, this exclusion does not apply to financial assistance that can be considered to be consideration or compensation for services rendered. In this regard, employer-sponsored scholarships available to the children of employees are not generally excluded from the income of the employees.[92]

6. CANCELLATION OF INDEBTEDNESS

Where funds are borrowed, income is typically not realized under any of the systems dealt with here. The traditional explanation is that the increase in assets caused by the loan is offset by the corresponding liability to repay the loan, so in balance sheet terms there is no increase in net worth at the time of the loan. Under this approach, all systems must deal with the situation where, contrary to expectations, the loan is not fully repaid. In principle, the failure to repay the loan in full results in additional taxable income to the borrower, because the loan proceeds were originally received on a tax-free basis on the expectation that they would be repaid in full. In many cases, however, where the debt is being forgiven in whole or in part, it is because the taxpayer is in financial difficulty, raising the practical issues of the desirability and feasibility of assessing and collecting a tax at this time.

The countries examined here have taken a wide variety of approaches to the problem. Most recognize in principle the taxability of forgiveness of indebtedness, although in the context of a schedular system, the debt must be related to a taxable category of income. However, all of the systems make some concessions for financially troubled taxpayers. In some cases, no income is required to be recognized unless the taxpayer is made financially solvent after the forgiveness. However, some systems require the reduction of other tax attributes – for example, the tax cost of property or the availability of accrued operating losses – that have been, in effect, financed out of the loan proceeds.

The evolution of the rules in the *United States* shows some of the interplay among these principles. Income from cancellation of indebtedness is in principle

91. United Kingdom, exemption in ITTOIA, s. 377; further rules in ITEPA, s. 211 et seq.
92. Japan, ITA, s. 9.

included in income, although there are a number of exceptions.[93] In the private context, the cancellation may qualify for exclusion as a gift. Special rules in effect from 2007 through 2012 also allow taxpayers to exclude income from the cancellation of debt that was used to purchase or renovate their principal residences. In a business setting, specific statutory rules exclude cancellation of indebtedness from income if the taxpayer is in a bankruptcy proceeding or is insolvent both before and after the forgiveness. Otherwise, cancellation in a business setting results in taxable income. Where exclusion is available, the taxpayer is generally required to reduce certain tax attributes as a condition for the exclusion. The reduction is made first in any net operating losses, which are in effect treated as if funded by the forgiven loan. If those losses are not sufficient to absorb the forgiveness, the taxpayer must reduce the tax cost of other assets, thus increasing potential income in the future by reducing deductions or losses or increasing the amount of gain on the disposition of the assets.

Under an earlier statutory regime, all business taxpayers could elect to exclude cancellation income if tax attributes were correspondingly reduced. This rule was found to be too generous and was eliminated, thus limiting the exclusion to insolvency and bankruptcy situations.

In *Germany*, in principle, cancellation of indebtedness is taxable if the debt arises in connection with a source of taxable income. If the debt has been incurred for private reasons, no income results from its cancellation. The conceptual basis for the inclusion of business-related cancellation lies in the increase in net worth of the business that the forgiveness causes. A statutory exemption for a cancellation of debt in connection with the reorganization of a failing business was repealed some years ago. On the other hand, the forgiveness of a debt by an associated person due to a personal relationship with the debtor is seen as a private asset of the debtor and treated as a tax-free contribution to his business.[94]

In *Sweden*, cancellation of indebtedness is taxable if it takes place in a business context, unless the debtor is insolvent. Where the cancellation does not result in income, the right to deduct a loss is limited by the same amount. In effect, the cancellation income must be offset by the otherwise available loss carryovers that could be used to reduce income in later years. It has been suggested that if there are no such loss carryovers, the tax cost of assets acquired with the loan should be reduced. Outside the business context, cancellation of indebtedness does not result in income.

Similarly, in *The Netherlands*, cancellation occurring in a business context is taxable unless it can be established that the debt could not have been repaid. Insolvency or bankruptcy is a factor in that determination but is not controlling. If the cancellation of a debt is not taxable, the amount of the forgiven debt must be

---

93. United States, IRC, s. 108(a).
94. Federal Tax Court (*Bundesfinanzhof*), judgment of 9 Jun. 1997 GrS 1/94 Federal Tax Gazette (*Bundessteuerblatt*) 1998, part 2, 307; judgment of 31 May 2005 I R 35/04; it should be noted that only the market value of the forgiven debt is regarded as a tax-neutral contribution, while the difference between the nominal value and the market value is ordinary taxable profit.

used to offset any current losses or available loss carryforwards. In *Japan*, in principle, cancellation of indebtedness results in income to the debtor. However, in administrative practice if the debt is cancelled in circumstances in which it is extremely unlikely that the debt will be repaid, no income results.

The treatment of forgiveness of indebtedness income in *Canada, Australia*, and the *United Kingdom* has been influenced by the capital gain – ordinary income distinction. Cancellation of debts arising in the business context, such as trade payables, have always been included as business income in Canada. When the taxation of capital gains was introduced, the possibility of treating the forgiveness of other types of liabilities as a taxable capital gain was considered but rejected. Instead, loss carryovers and the basis of depreciable property were required to be reduced to the extent possible by the amount of the forgiveness. If the amount forgiven exceeded the available tax attributes, there were no tax consequences to the excess of the debt forgiven. Effective in 1994, the debt forgiveness rules were revised extensively.[95] The amount of the forgiveness is still applied to reduce loss carryovers and the tax cost of various assets; however, one-half of any remaining balance must be included in income unless it is transferred to a related taxpayer.

In *Australia*, there is no general legislative rule that cancellation of indebtedness results in income. If a company involved in a finance business buys back its long-term debt obligations at below face value, the corresponding profit is taxed as part of business income. However, if a commercial company does the same transaction, no income results because the capital gains tax, which would seemingly be applicable to gains in this type of situation, deals explicitly with assets and not liabilities. Rules requiring the reduction of losses or tax cost similar to those in Canada were introduced in 1996.[96] A 1999 tax reform report suggestion that Australia move to a system more akin to the US system was not adopted.

The *United Kingdom* continues to have restrictive rules on cancellation of indebtedness income. In general, income arises only if the loan was employment-related, made to a shareholder of a closely held corporation, or involved a liability that had previously been deducted (e.g., in the business income context).[97]

In *France*, the cancellation of a debt in a private context has no tax effects. In a business setting, the cancellation results in income even if the debtor is in bankruptcy.[98] In some circumstances, the cancellation by a parent corporation of an advance to a subsidiary may be excluded from income and treated as an increase in stated capital.[99]

95. Canada, ITA, s. 80.
96. Australia, ITAA 1936, Sch. 2C.
97. For example, for employment issues see ITEPA, s. 188; for close companies see ITTOIA, s. 415 (income tax) and TA 1988, s. 419 (CT); on repayment of released debt see ITTOIA, s. 97 (income tax) and CTA 2009, s. 94, replacing and TA 1988, s. 94 (CT).
98. France, CGI, s. 38-2.
99. France, CGI, s. 216 A.

7. GAMBLING

The inclusion of gambling income is strongly influenced by the schedular or global nature of the system. In the global system in the *United States*, gambling winnings are, in principle, subject to tax whether they arise from occasional transactions or are received by a professional gambler. However, even in the case of a professional gambler, gambling losses for the year can be deducted only to the extent of gambling income.[100] This essentially schedular approach to gambling income may be influenced to some extent by the concern with artificial gambling 'losses'. As well, the gambling losses may be viewed as consumption. The restrictions in *Japan* are even stricter. Gambling income is taxable as Occasional Income and losses incurred in gambling are not deductible against other types of income. Moreover, because each gambling occasion is a separate event, gambling losses arising on one occasion cannot be deducted against gambling winnings derived on another occasion. These restrictions presumably reflect both the administrative difficulties of verifying losses and the possible characterization of the gambling losses as consumption.[101]

In many schedular systems, gambling income is taxable only if the gambler can be found to be in the business of gambling. For example, in *Germany*, case law holds that gambling income of a professional card player is taxable as business income.[102] Gambling winnings in TV shows are taxable 'other' income to the extent that they are the result of a certain accomplishment.[103] Similarly, in *The Netherlands*, an entrepreneur who gambles with his business proceeds and incurs gambling losses will not be able to deduct such losses from his business income, as no reasonable businessman will engage in gambling with business money.

As discussed above, *Sweden* taxes gambling if the income can be considered to arise from the performance of a service, but not if it results purely by chance. Winnings in the Swedish lottery are expressly exempt. The tax exemption for lottery prizes has recently been expanded not only to cover Swedish lotteries, but also lotteries arranged within the European Union. In a case decided by the European Court of Justice (ECJ), the previous Swedish rules, restricted to Swedish lotteries, were considered to be a restriction on freedom of establishment.

In *Australia, Canada*, and the *United Kingdom*, income derived from gambling or lottery-type prizes is not taxable unless the activity amounts to a business. Otherwise, there is no taxable 'source', and accordingly gains are not taxable and losses not deductible. *France* reaches the same results as far as its progressive income tax is concerned,[104] but such amounts are specifically subject to the new flat-rate income taxes.

---

100. United States, IRC, s. 105(d).
101. Japan, ITA, s. 34.
102. Federal Tax Court (*Bundesfinanzhof*), judgment of 26 Aug. 1993 V R 20/91, *Deutsches Steuerrecht* 1994, 56.
103. Federal Tax Court (*Bundesfinanzhof*), judgment of 28 Nov. 2007 IX R 39/06.
104. France, Conseil d'État, 21 Mar. 1980, no. 11235.

8. ILLEGAL INCOME

In all of the systems considered here, in general, the fact that income is derived from illegal activities does not prevent its taxation *(pecunia non olet)*. The common principle is that the taxpayer cannot use the illegal nature of his activities as a defence against taxation.[105] In a schedular system, the income must, of course, fall into a taxable category. Thus, for example, in *Germany*, illegal income often falls into the category of income from trade or business or even miscellaneous income from the occasional performance of services (e.g., espionage).

Since illegal income typically involves a civil law obligation to repay the amounts taken, the taxpayer has no legally recognized right to keep the income, and this has influenced the income inclusion issue in some situations. For example, an *Australian* case held that earnings on embezzled funds were not taxable to an embezzler who was caught and had to return the funds with interest.[106] Some early *United States* cases reached a similar result on the ground that the taxpayer (an embezzler) had no 'claim of right' to the income, although the result was later reversed.[107] A *Canadian* case held the proceeds of embezzlement to be taxable and rejected the claim of right argument on the ground that the taxpayer had no intention of repaying the funds.[108] Sometimes a line must be drawn between embezzlement and an informal loan (typically with an intention to repay). The latter characterization requires the real or assumed acquiescence of the 'lender'. A related issue involves the deduction for the repayment of illegally obtained funds that are included in income.

In *Sweden*, there is in principle full taxation of illegal income that arises in a business. However, in most cases, illegal income is forfeitable and as such, deductible, so there is no net income. Illegal income that does not arise in a business is not taxable. It is also considered that the illegal activity could not alone establish a business.

In *France*, according to the principle known as 'tax law realism', income from illegal activities is taxed like lawful income in whatever income category is appropriate. For example, income from procuring is commercial profit, while the income of a prostitute is either wages or non-commercial profit,[109] depending on the circumstances. Similarly, in *The Netherlands*, income from illegal activities has always been recognized as taxable. Recent examples from case law include income from theft, trade in narcotics, bank fraud, and bribery. In the *United Kingdom*, case law holds that the profits of prostitution are taxable as business income – but whether as a trade or as a profession has not been decided.[110] Prostitution is not

105. Germany, GOL (General Order of Levies), s. 40.
106. *Zobory* [1995] FCA 1226, 64 FCR 86.
107. *James v. United States*, 366 U.S. 213 (1961).
108. *The Queen v. Poynton* [1972] CTC 411 (Ont. CA).
109. France, Conseil d'État, 5 Nov. 1980, no. 13222.
110. *IRC v. Aken* [1990] STC 497.

an illegal activity in the United Kingdom, whereas living off such earnings of another person is.

The treatment of expenses such as bribes and fines and other penalties that often arise in connection with illegal income is discussed below in Subpart C.

9. WINDFALLS

The logic of a global system extends to the taxation of windfall gains such as found property, and this approach is followed in the *United States*. *Japan* treats windfalls as taxable Occasional Income. In *Germany*, the treatment of windfalls depends on the situation. Normally, found property is not taxable. Another example is the sale of a patent developed by a research student without the intention to earn income. However, if it arises in a business setting, it is included as part of the business profits. Therefore, money found by a businessman on his premises is taxable. Likewise, in *The Netherlands*, windfalls are in general not taxable unless they fall within a taxable category (typically, business income). Personal injury damages are not taxable if the injury has permanently reduced the victim's capacity to earn, but are taxable if the payment compensates for temporary loss of income. The same applies to awards for immaterial injury. In *Sweden*, windfalls have historically not been taxable, since they are not the result of efforts to earn income and are not periodic. In the *Commonwealth* countries, a windfall is not derived from a taxable 'source' of income and is not included in the income tax base.[111] The subsequent extension of taxation to capital gains typically did not affect this result.

Damages represent a special category of windfall gains. In general, in schedular systems damages are taxable to the extent that they relate to assets or activities that are taxable. Awards for damage to property are typically treated as reducing the tax cost of the asset, with gain resulting if the total amount recovered exceeds the cost. In some cases, the gain can be deferred through the use of a reserve or rollover if the property is to be repaired or replaced. Damages for personal injuries are typically not taxable even if calculated with reference to lost earnings or earning capacity. In the *Commonwealth* systems, the introduction of a capital gains tax expanded the taxation of damage awards, which previously had sometimes escaped tax, although the exclusion for damages to person or profession (e.g., defamation) was typically retained.

In *France*, personal injury damages are normally excluded from the tax base to the extent that they do not set off a loss of income. In some exceptional occurrences, damages can, however, be taxed when paid in the form of an annuity.[112]

Germany taxes damages if they are paid as compensation for a lost opportunity to earn income.[113] Damages that occur in the personal sphere are not taxable income.

111. *Graham v. Green* [1925] 2 KB 37.
112. Especially when not exempted by CGI, s. 819 *bis*.
113. Germany, ITA, s. 24 para. 1 lit.a.

Personal injury damages are excluded from income in the *United States* only if the injury is physical in nature. Emotional distress does not qualify as a physical injury for this purpose.

10. SUBSIDIES

The treatment of governmental subsidies raises a number of structural issues. In the simplest case, when the payment is a form of payment for services (e.g., payments to private carriers for mail transport), it is typically taxable as business income. At the other extreme, some subsidies are so indirect or diffuse that even with a global income definition, they would not be included in the tax base. In still other cases, the payment is not includable directly in income but the tax cost of assets acquired or other tax attributes must be reduced accordingly, so that the payment is indirectly included over the life of the asset. Public welfare payments are typically not taxed unless they are in the form of wage supplements such as unemployment compensation. In the *United States*, the rules follow this pattern in general.

Similarly, in *Germany*, for business-related subsidies, capital contributions may be treated either as current income or as a reduction in the tax cost of assets produced or acquired with the funds, at the taxpayer's election. In the latter case, an income effect will result from the reduction of the depreciation base or from a higher profit on a disposal of the asset. If the subsidies are not used to finance an asset, they are fully taxable. However, if they relate to conduct to be performed over a period of years (e.g., not producing milk for five years), the payments may in effect be included over the period of the performance of the service as an accounting matter. Public welfare subsidies for individual taxpayers are not taxable, but in some cases must be taken into account in determining the applicable tax rate on other income ('exemption with progression').

In the same way, in *Sweden*, governmental subsidies are currently taxable if they are intended to subsidize current costs in a business. If they are in the nature of capital contributions, the basis of the appropriate assets is reduced correspondingly. It is not clear whether these statutory rules would apply to subsidies provided by private organizations such as research foundations. Such subsidies probably would not be taxable; instead, the tax authorities may attempt to deny the deduction of expenses financed by the tax-exempt subsidies. The result is the same as if the subsidy had been included in income and the deduction of the expenses allowed.

In *The Netherlands*, subsidies granted in respect of the acquisition of assets are not currently taxable but result in a basis reduction. Subsidies received in respect of current expenses reduce the amount of any deduction for such expenses. The same approach applies in *Japan*, although corporations may elect for the subsidies to be added to their current income.[114]

Under case law principles, in the *United Kingdom*, subsidies for current operations are included in income, but payments to recoup a capital investment are

114. Japan, CTA, s. 42.

exempt as non-taxable capital receipts.[115] This line is not easy to draw. Subsidies are taken into account in calculating the tax cost of property under the capital gains or capital allowance legislation.[116] *Australia* follows the same pattern, although recent interpretation of a long-existing statutory provision, the introduction of the capital gains tax, and recent case law on general principles of income may have narrowed the scope of the exclusion for capital receipts.[117] There is an increasing tendency to deal expressly in the tax legislation with the tax status of newly introduced subsidies. In *Canada*, government subsidies (broadly referred to as inducements or assistance in any form) are expressly included in income to the extent that they have not otherwise reduced the cost of property or the amount of any deductible expenses incurred by the taxpayer.[118] Where the subsidy relates to depreciable, non-depreciable, or intangible property, the taxpayer has an election to include the amount currently in income or reduce the tax cost of the property.

In *France*, public subsidies are generally exempt from tax unless they are a substitute for taxable income, as in the case of unemployment compensation. In a business context, subsidies for current costs are fully taxable. Payments for capital costs may be spread over ten years (non-depreciable assets) or taken into account at the same time and rated as depreciation.[119] In some situations, the basis of the asset purchased may be increased for depreciation purposes by a portion of the subsidy.[120]

11. REALIZATION AND RECOGNITION OF GAIN

In all of the systems examined here, in general, income and capital gains must be 'realized' before being taken into account for tax purposes. This realization principle is quite obvious with respect to the taxation of capital gains and losses. A capital gain or loss is realized, in general, only if the property is sold, exchanged, or otherwise disposed of. Until such time, any change in value of the property resulting in an accrued gain or loss in respect of the property is not relevant. The realization principle also operates with respect to business income, although it functions there somewhat differently. Income from a business is usually computed on an 'accruals' rather than a 'cash receipts and disbursements' basis. In this setting, realization is not synonymous with a cash method of accounting. For example, under a system based on realization, business income from the performance of services is usually realized when the services are performed and billed, although the collection of the fees may only take place at a later time. Thus, in the

115. *Seaham Harbour Dock Co.* [1930] 16 TC.
116. For example, see United Kingdom, TCGA, s. 50 and Capital Allowances Act 2001, s. 209 et seq.
117. Australia, ITAA 1997, s. 15-10, as interpreted in *First Provincial Building Society Ltd* [1995] FCA 1101, 56 FCR 320; *GP International Pipecoaters Pty Ltd* [1990] HCA 25, 170 CLR 124.
118. Canada, ITA, s. 12(1)(x).
119. France, CGI, s. 42 *septies*.
120. France, CGI, s. 39 *quinquies* FA.

business context, the realization principle means that income arises only when a transaction, such as the performance of services, occurs. Therefore, in some settings, the realization requirement might be referred to as the transactional basis underlying the income tax. In other cases, a change in tax status – for example, ceasing to be a resident – is treated as a 'deemed' realization with respect to certain assets held by the taxpayer.

The definition of realization events or the identification of transactions that give rise to income or gain is critical to all realization- or transaction-based income tax systems. In all of the countries examined here, some transactions, such as sales of property, are clearly realization events. However, some of the countries go much further and treat certain transactions as realization events even where no consideration is received by the transferor. Thus, for example, gifts, transfers on death, and the withdrawal of property from a business for personal use are considered to be taxable dispositions in several countries.

While the concept of realization is firmly anchored in all of the systems, it seems that the realization requirement is increasingly being abandoned in certain areas. For example, several countries have adopted some sort of accrual or 'mark-to-market' method of taxation for financial instruments. This development began with the treatment of the implicit interest element in bonds issued at original discount and has been extended to other types of instruments. These matters are discussed in more detail in Subpart D, as the approach has historically been tied to accounting rules. In addition, the realization principle has frequently been abandoned in the taxation of foreign investment companies. There a mark-to-market approach is often used, as well as the technique of imputing a specified rate of return on such investments for tax purposes where the mark-to-market method proves difficult to apply. These matters are discussed in Part Four.

All systems also contain rules that allow for the deferral ('rollover') of realized gain in some circumstances. These provisions typically involve property-for-property exchanges, reinvested realization proceeds (especially if the realization event was involuntary), and other similar situations. The rules vary substantially, both in their requirements and in the techniques used to establish deferral. Various corporate exchanges that involve rollovers, usually in the context of corporate reorganizations, are discussed in Part Three.

In the *United States* system, there is substantial case law on the doctrine of realization. Originally thought to be constitutionally required, the realization requirement is now recognized as essentially a question of administrative convenience.[121] Any exchange of properties in which there is a 'material difference' between the properties exchanged will result in realization.[122] The gratuitous transfer of property *inter vivos* or at death, however, is not treated as a realization event. In the case of gifts, a carryover of tax cost preserves the possibility of taxing accrued gains in the hands of the donee, but for transfers at

121. *Commissioner v. Glenshaw Glass*, 348 U.S. 426 (1955).
122. *Cottage Savings Assoc. v. Commissioner*, 499 U.S. 554 (1991).

death, the heir or legatee receives a fair market value tax cost, and appreciation to the date of death escapes tax altogether.

The placing of a mortgage on property, even if the mortgage is non-recourse and involves no personal liability for the repayment of the funds, is not treated as a realization event. As a corollary of this rule, the transfer (or abandonment) of property subject to a mortgage is treated as involving an amount realized equal to the face amount of the mortgage.

A special statutory rule requires securities dealers to report gains and losses on securities on a mark-to-market basis as if the property had been sold on the last day of the taxable year.[123] In addition, taxpayers holding futures contracts that are traded on an exchange are also generally required to mark the contracts to market.

Realization of gain is also required where the nominal owner of stock, certain types of debt, or a partnership interest enters into a short sale, offsetting notional contract or forward sale of such asset.

'Rollover' provisions allow realized gain to be deferred in certain situations. These include the exchange of like-kind depreciable property and real estate held for investment or used in a trade or business, and the reinvestment of proceeds from damage or condemnation of property involved in an 'involuntary conversion'.[124] A provision that allowed taxpayers to roll over their gain from the sale of their principal residences has been replaced with an exemption. The exemption allows a taxpayer to exclude $250,000 ($500,000 for married individuals filing a joint return) of such gain from income.[125]

In *Germany*, gains on dispositions of property are taxable and losses correspondingly are deductible if they occur in the context of a business or similar income category.[126] The taxation of the gain is subject to the 'accrual method' of income determination; the overall profit of the business includes both operating profit and capital gains insofar as the value of the consideration received for an asset exceeds its book value. The mere increase in value does not lead to taxation as long as there is no disposal of the asset.[127] If, however, the increase 'recaptures' former impairment losses, it must be taken into account for tax accounting purposes.[128]

Several rules provide for the taxation of 'hidden reserves' if an asset is withdrawn from the business without consideration. This withdrawal of an asset from a corporation, a sole proprietorship, or a partnership is added to the taxable profit according to the 'fair value' of the asset.[129] The transfer of assets to a foreign permanent establishment and all other cross-border transfers of assets, where the subsequent gain would not fall under the German taxing jurisdiction, is also treated

123. United States, IRC, s. 475.
124. United States, IRC, ss 1031 and 1033.
125. United States, IRC, s. 121.
126. Germany, ITA, s. 2 para. 2.
127. Germany, ITA, s. 5 para. 1 with reference to German Commercial Code, s. 252 para. 1 no. 4.
128. Germany, ITA, ss 6 para. 1 no. 1 and 4, no. 2 sent. 3.
129. Germany, ITA, ss 4 para. 1 sent. 1 and 6 para. 1 no. 4.

as a withdrawal and therefore taxed as an immediate realization event.[130] If the asset is transferred to an EU Member State, the taxpayer is allowed to take the gain into account over a period of five years unless there is an actual disposition of the asset by the foreign branch at an earlier stage.[131] It is highly doubtful whether and how far these rules comply with the EC provisions on the Internal Market.

Several provisions in the German system allow the deferral or rollover of a realized gain. In the case of real estate held in a business context, current recognition can be avoided if the sales proceeds are reinvested in real estate.[132] Otherwise, the taxpayer can avoid current recognition of gain by establishing a tax-deductible investment reserve which reduces current income. The reserve may be maintained for four to six years depending on the type of asset. If the reserve is dissolved because no reinvestment is undertaken in the prescribed period, an annual interest charge of 6% is imposed on the amount of the reserve. Moreover, in the course of reorganizations of business entities, the transfer of assets to a partnership or a corporation can lead to rollover if the transfer does not involve any cash consideration and the taxpayer becomes a partner or shareholder in the firm.[133]

The Netherlands has the same basic pattern of rules, although the technical details differ somewhat. For example, reinvestment must be in similar property and the reserve may not be maintained for more than three years.

In *Sweden*, in general, all property gains are taxed only on realization. One significant exception is gains on claims and debts denominated in foreign currency arising in a business, which are taxed on a mark-to-market basis, following accounting principles. Gain realized on an involuntary conversion of property can be deferred if the proceeds from insurance, damages, etc., are reinvested. Gain on the sale of a personal residence can likewise be deferred if the sales proceeds are reinvested.[134]

In *Japan*, a sale or exchange of an asset is also necessary for gain realization. This includes the contribution to capital by a shareholder, which is a realization event. Gain on business assets may be deferred in a like-kind exchange. Under prior law (influenced by the Shoup Commission and Stanley Surrey), a gift of appreciated property was treated as a realization event, but the system was very unpopular and was replaced with a carryover basis mechanism (which extends to transfers at death).[135] Since 2000, the corporate income tax has used the mark-to-market method for financial derivative products and securities held for the purpose of trading.[136]

---

130. Germany, ITA, s. 4 para. 1 sent. 3.
131. Germany, ITA, s. 4g.
132. Germany, ITA, s. 6b.
133. Germany, ITA, ss 6 para. 5 and 16 para. 3 sent. 2; RTA (Reorganization Tax Act), ss 20 and 24.
134. Sweden, ITA, Ch. 47.
135. Japan, ITA, s. 60.
136. Japan, CTA, ss 61-3 and 61-5.

France requires realization, although in the business context, foreign currency gains on claims are taxed on a mark-to-market basis[137] and unrealized losses on non-depreciable capital assets can be taken into account through the use of reserves.[138] Transfer of business property by gift or death is a realization event, as is the withdrawal of assets from a proprietorship or the cessation of the taxpayer's business.[139] There are relatively few rollover provisions outside the context of corporate reorganizations.

All of the *Commonwealth* systems are based on the realization principle. The realization requirement was originally developed by the courts in the context of trading profits. With the subsequent introduction of capital gains taxation, broad statutory realization rules were enacted that in general treat any disposal or disposition (as compared to the 'sale or exchange' language used in the United States) of an asset as a realization event. Thus, in *Canada*, for example, realization occurs if the taxpayer disposes of most of the important incidents of ownership in the asset. In some cases, changes in the terms of debt or stock can, in the view of the fiscal authorities, be treated as a realization. In addition, as previously discussed, disposition of property by gift or a death is generally treated as a realization event (although rollovers are available for interspousal and certain other transfers). In general, rollover relief is limited to capital gains and losses. However, recapture of capital cost allowance (depreciation) in respect of depreciable property may be deferred where the property is disposed of involuntarily and a replacement property is acquired.[140] Similarly, deferral is permitted with respect to dispositions of eligible capital property, including goodwill, and real property used in a business where the taxpayer acquires a replacement property.[141]

Special rules in Canada require financial institutions to account for gains and losses on certain debt and equity securities on a mark-to-market basis.[142] There are several other narrow exceptions to the realization requirement. For example, if property used in a business is converted to personal use or vice versa, the property is considered to be disposed of for its fair market value. Similarly, certain 'transfers' of inventory, intangible property, and depreciable property by a Canadian resident to a foreign branch or vice versa are considered to take place at fair market value. Decreases in the value of inventory are recognized pursuant to the lower of cost or market accounting convention prior to the sale of the inventory.

The *Australian* approach is similar, with statutory rules (principally in the capital gains tax) dealing with what are called 'CGT events'. The Australian system contains special provisions dealing with the taxation of assets that could be viewed as 'created' at the same time they are disposed of – for example, the entering into of a covenant not to compete. A broad rule treats as a CGT event any

137. France, CGI, s. 38-4.
138. France, CGI, Regulatory Sch. III, s. 38 *sexies*.
139. France, CGI, ss 201 and 221.
140. Canada, ITA, s. 13(4).
141. Canada, ITA, s. 14(6).
142. Canada, ITA, s. 142.5.

payment received with respect to an asset.[143] In 2009, Australia is introducing a comprehensive accrual system for the treatment of financial assets. It will use a mixture of internal-rate-of-return and mark-to-market principles for calculating income and expense on a broad range of financial instruments; this new system is discussed in more detail in Subpart D.

Australia has a number of rollover provisions covering a wide range of circumstances, including involuntary dispositions, death, and certain property exchanges. For historical reasons, the technical details differ depending on whether the property involved is inventory, depreciable business property, or capital property.

The *United Kingdom* system similarly focuses on 'disposal' as the principal test of realization for its capital gains tax; several of the various income schedules have their own concepts of realization, using either a receipts basis or an earnings (accrual) basis. The term 'disposal' is not defined for CGT but has been held to cover any transfer of beneficial ownership. If the disposal is other than at arm's length, it is deemed to be at fair market value. There are a number of 'deemed' realization situations, including, for example, value shifting by changing rights attached to shares in a company.[144]

A case law principle treats the withdrawal of an inventory asset from business to personal use as, in effect, a deemed sale at fair market value resulting in realization of income. This has now been turned into a statutory principle. Special legislative rules govern the interaction of this case law principle with the capital gains tax regime.[145]

Rollover of realized capital gain is permitted in a variety of situations, including the replacement of business assets within three years of disposal. Express rollover provisions are not needed for reinvestment of sums realized from assets subject to capital allowances or giving rise to ordinary income.

Since 1996 the United Kingdom has introduced a number of statutory rules dealing with loan relationships, foreign exchange, and derivative contracts. These are based on accounting principles and disregard the distinction between income and capital. They apply only to corporation tax.[146]

12. CAPITAL GAINS AND LOSSES

Although the term 'capital gain' or its linguistic equivalent is frequently used in the tax systems under consideration here, the precise contours of the concept vary

143. Australia, ITAA 1997, ss 104-35 and 104-155.

144. United Kingdom, Capital Gains TCGA, ss 2 (general rule), 17 (gift), 21 (disposal), 29 et seq. (value shifting). On bases for employment income, see ITEPA, s. 16 et seq., and for trading income see ITTOIA, ss 25–27 (income tax) and CTA 2009, ss 46–48.

145. The case law principle is *Sharkey v. Wernher* [1956] AC 36, TC 275 made statutory as ITTOIA, s. 172A et seq. and CTA 2009, Part 3 Ch. 10. On the interaction with CGT, see TCGA, s. 161.

146. See now United Kingdom, CTA 2009, Part 5-9 ss 292–931.

considerably from country to country. In addition, the concept plays a different role in different systems. In general terms, the notion is of a non-recurring gain that is not part of the normal stream of income from a business or investment. The distinction may rest on agricultural notions distinguishing between land and the yield from land, or the tree and its fruit. In Anglo-Saxon systems, it has its origin to some extent in trust concepts, which distinguish between current income and gains allocated to corpus for trust accounting purposes. Gains attributed to corpus are generally not available for distribution to income beneficiaries.

Regardless of how a capital gain is defined, several basic patterns of capital gain taxation emerge. In some countries, typically Continental, all income that arises in a business is taxed in the same fashion. There is no distinction between income and capital gains. Thus, for example, gain on the disposition of an asset used in the business is treated the same as a gain from the sale of inventory. On the other hand, gain on an asset that is not connected with a business or other taxable category of income often will not be taxed at all, although sometimes there is an exception for short-term gains. Thus, gains realized by individuals on investment assets often are not taxed or are taxed only in special circumstances.

In systems influenced by the United Kingdom, the distinction between ordinary income and capital gain is applied both to business enterprises and to private persons. Initially, capital gains were not subject to tax because such gains were not income from a source, but rather gains from the disposal of the source itself. Subsequent legislation, typically in the form of a separate capital gains tax regime, ultimately brought capital gains into the tax base, often employing a preferential rate of tax.

Finally, in countries with a global approach, capital gains were always included in the tax base, although here too taxation at a preferential rate was common. In most systems, capital losses are subject to limitations, reflecting either the special treatment of the gain or the fact that timing of the realization of the gains and losses is usually within the control of the taxpayer, especially in the case of investment assets.

These differing approaches can generate different structural issues in the various systems. In many Continental systems, since all income arising in corporations is business income, there is no need to classify assets as capital or ordinary in that context. On the other hand, for assets held by individuals, the issue is whether the assets are held as business assets or privately, leading either to full taxation or to exemption. In a global system like that of the United States, the corresponding issue at the individual level is whether the assets qualify for preferential treatment or are subject to normal taxation. In systems that give a preferential rate for business-related capital gains on depreciable assets, some mechanism is necessary to 'recapture' excess depreciation on the sale of an asset as ordinary income; in systems that tax all business income in the same fashion, this issue does not arise.

In all systems, the existence of a different treatment for a certain class of gains has led to statutory and jurisprudential complexity in attempting to delimit the classification. This problem is heightened by the lack of any consensus as to why gains from the disposition of certain types of assets should be given special treatment.

The taxation of capital gains in the *United States* has had a long and complicated history. Gain on the disposition of assets has traditionally been included in the tax base, whether or not arising in a business context. However, for both individuals (since 1922) and for corporations (since 1942) certain gains have usually qualified for preferential treatment. Deduction for capital losses has in general been available only to the extent of the amount of capital gains, although individual taxpayers may claim a limited amount of capital losses against ordinary income if no capital gains are present. Unused capital losses can be carried forward.

At the present time, capital gains are taxed at a lower rate for individual taxpayers who would otherwise be taxed at higher progressive rates, whereas corporate gains are taxed in full.[147] Both the treatment of capital gains and the definition of the class of gains entitled to such treatment have varied substantially over time. The result is a hodgepodge of technical rules that is impossible to rationalize.

In general terms, capital gain entitled to preferential treatment is gain realized on the sale or exchange of a capital asset that has been held for over one year. Substantial statutory and case law material defines 'capital asset', the central concept in preferential gain treatment. The definitional process is complicated by the fact that all gain is initially included in the capital gain category, with a number of exceptions then applying to treat the gain as ordinary income. Capital asset status is thus denied for inventory and other property held for sale to customers in the ordinary course of a business. The scope of this rule, especially in the context of real estate, has generated an enormous amount of litigation.[148]

Under complex provisions, gains on real estate and depreciable personal property used in a business are treated as capital gains if the disposition of all such property in the taxable period results in a net gain, but, inconsistently, a net loss can be deducted against ordinary income.[149] To the extent that the gain on depreciable assets is attributable to depreciation deductions that reduce the tax cost of the property, all or a portion of the gain is taxed at less-favourable preferential rates or as ordinary income, depending on the nature of the property.[150] Copyrights and other literary or artistic property cannot generally qualify as capital assets in the hands of the person who created the property.[151] An exception adopted in 2007, however, treats copyrights held by musical composers as capital assets. Patents held by inventors can also qualify as capital assets, even in some circumstances where they would appear to be inventory.[152] Special rules also apply to gain from

147. United States, IRC, s. 1(h).
148. United States, IRC, s. 1221.
149. United States, IRC, s. 1231.
150. United States, IRC, ss 1245 and 1250.
151. United States, IRC, s. 1221(a)(3).
152. United States, IRC, s. 1235.

the sale of 'collectibles' (e.g., stamp collections, rare coins) held for more than a year. Gain from such items is taxed at a maximum rate of 28%.

Gain from the disposition of personal assets is taxed, but a deduction for losses is not allowed. Individuals may exclude $250,000 ($500,000 for married individuals filing a joint return) of the gain from the sale of a residence that was the seller's principal residence for at least two of the five years preceding the sale.

Germany was typical of the schedular approach to capital gains taxation on the Continent, but has changed its tax system substantially in recent years. The general rule remains that private capital gains are not subject to tax and all gains realized in business are included in taxable business profit.[153] Gains from the disposal of real estate are taxable if the real estate is held for less than ten years,[154] and the disposal of other assets is taxable if held for less than one year.[155] A reduced rate applies to the sale of a sole proprietorship, all of the shares of a wholly owned company, or a partnership interest. Correspondingly, private losses are in general not deductible, while losses realized in the course of a business are deductible in full.

Until 31 December 2008, gains resulting from the sale of corporate shares held for more than one year by private persons were taxable only if the participation exceeded a certain threshold.[156] Over the years, the threshold has been reduced from 25% to 10% to 1% of the company capital. Today, capital gains from stock that is held as a business asset or that exceeds the threshold of 1% is taxed at the individual tax rate, but only to the extent of 60% of the gain. Capital gain from shares held by a corporate shareholder is tax-free.

From 2009 on, all remaining capital gains (e.g., from the sale of portfolio stock or other securities that are held as private assets) are taxable.[157] They are subject to a final withholding tax of 25%.[158] The taxpayer can include the capital gain in his personal income statement if he is subject to a lower tax rate.[159] Capital losses can be set off only against capital gains of the same kind.[160]

Basically the same pattern applies in *The Netherlands*,[161] except that the minimum level of shareholding for a taxable substantial participation is 5%. Capital gains and other income from a substantial participation are taxed as box 2 income at a 25% rate. Losses from a substantial participation can be carried over against gains from substantial participations; or, if the taxpayer no longer has a substantial participation, losses can generate a tax credit of 25%, which can be used against the tax liability arising from income from business or employment (i.e., box 1 income) in the year in which the loss is incurred, and can be carried

153. Germany, ITA, s. 2 para. 2.
154. Germany, ITA, ss 22 no. 2 and 23 para. 1 no. 1.
155. Germany, ITA, ss 22 no. 1 and 23 para. 1 no. 2.
156. Germany, ITA, s. 17.
157. Germany, ITA, s. 20 para. 2.
158. Germany, ITA, s. 32d para. 1 sent. 43.
159. Germany, ITA, s. 32d para. 4.
160. Germany, ITA, s. 20 para. 6.
161. Netherlands, ITA, Art. 4.2.

forward if there is no current tax liability. Also, there is no special tax on short-term gains, but such gains are taxed if they are the result of more-than-normal investment activities (e.g., restoring a building) or are based on special insider knowledge so that a sale at a gain could be reasonably foreseen.

In *Sweden*, capital gains realized by individuals outside a business context were initially taxed only if they were speculative and short-term. However, through successive reforms, taxation of capital gains has been extended; now all such gains are taxable as income from capital. The tax rate, 30%, is lower than the rate for business or employment income, partly reflecting the impact of inflation. The principle set down in the tax reform of 1991 was that capital gains should be fully taxable. From the beginning, however, there were exceptions to this rule. The exceptions from the basic rules have proliferated since then, and capital gains for owner-occupied houses and flats in cooperative apartment houses are taxable at a 22%/30% rate. The justification for this rule is in part based on a desire to reduce the lock-in effect (although a rollover is available for reinvested gains).

The basic principle for capital losses is that they are deductible, but only to a limited amount. The main rule is a limitation to 70% of the total loss. This limitation is intended to counter to some extent the taxpayer's ability to realize losses currently while deferring gains. Here, too, the exceptions have proliferated, and there is no limitation for capital losses on bonds that are publicly traded. Losses on publicly traded stock can be deducted in full against corresponding gains realized in the same year. On the other hand, a loss on a personal residence is limited to 50% of the loss, paralleling the preferential treatment of the gain.

If there is an overall loss in the capital income category, it can be used against income in other categories after appropriate adjustment is made to reflect the fact that capital income is taxed at a preferential 30% rate. The allowable loss is converted into a 21% credit (70% loss × 30%), which reduces the tax on income in other categories.

Like some Continental systems, *Japan*, in general, has no special rules dealing with capital gains realized by a corporation. However, there is a complex set of rules for capital gains of individuals. In general, gains on assets held for less than five years are fully taxable. Only one-half of the gain is included in income for assets held for more than five years.[162] Prior to 1989, gains on securities were not taxed. Presently, while capital gains on debt securities are not taxed in general, net gains on equity securities are taxed at a special 20% rate (excluding local tax), except that listed equity securities are entitled to a preferential tax rate.[163] A separate set of rules applies to gains from real estate. In general terms, in some circumstances, these rules apply higher-than-normal rates to real estate gains (e.g., in the case of short-term gains). They also provide for the classification of real estate gains as business income, capital gain, or Occasional Income, with differing consequences both as to the calculation of the gain and the rate of tax. These rules

162. Japan, ITA, s. 22.
163. Japan, STMA, s. 37-10.

reflect the special role that real estate gains have played in the Japanese domestic economy.

In *France*, net gains by sole proprietorships on fixed assets held for more than two years are taxed at a preferential rate (16% instead of progressive income tax, plus 12.1% total flat-rate income taxes);[164] long-term gains on real property used in the course of business benefit from an annual 10% deduction beginning in the sixth year of holding and are thus exempt after fifteen years.[165] Moreover, small businesses are generally not taxed on short- and long-term gains.[166] A gain is always treated as ordinary income to the extent of depreciation taken. Since 1997, corporate assets eligible for long-term capital gain treatment have been restricted to substantial interests (5% or more) in other corporations and are now exempt.[167] Private capital gains historically were not subject to tax but since 1976 have been covered by a special tax regime characterized by preferential rates (18% for gains on stocks and securities and 16% for gains on real property instead of progressive income tax, plus 12.1% total flat-rate income taxes), frequent exemptions (e.g., personal assets and residences), and annual standard deductions leading to exemption after a given number of years of holding (eight years for stock and securities, fifteen years for real property).[168]

The development of capital gains taxation in the *United Kingdom, Canada*, and *Australia* has, in general, taken a somewhat different course. As indicated above, initially, gains on the disposition of assets outside the business context generally were not taxed. Within the business context, a distinction was drawn between inventory and current assets as compared to fixed and long-term assets. Only gains on assets in the former category were subject to the income tax. In both the private and business settings, gains from the disposition of 'capital assets' were not included in the tax base because of the 'trust' concept of income. (The income beneficiaries of a trust were not entitled to any appreciation in the value of the trust assets.) Also, under the source concept of income, a capital gain could be considered to be derived from the disposition of the 'source' itself rather than as income from a source. Subsequently, all three systems (United Kingdom [1965], Canada [1972], and Australia [1985]) adopted separate systems for the taxation of capital gains, which cover both private gains and gains on the disposition of capital assets used in business. In addition, in the case of the United Kingdom and Australia, and to a lesser degree, Canada, the capital gains tax legislation was used to mitigate certain defects and problems that had emerged in the operation of the traditional income tax system. Thus, the capital gains tax system is, to some degree, a parallel taxing system that does substantially more than simply include the gain from a certain class of assets in the tax base. With their somewhat parallel histories, the Commonwealth systems thus have a number of features in common.

---

164. France, CGI, ss 39 *duodecies* and 39 *quindecies*.
165. France, CGI, s. 151 *septies* B.
166. France, CGI, ss 151 *septies* and 238 *quindecies*.
167. France, CGI, s. 219 I-a.
168. France, CGI, ss 150-0 A sq. (stock and securities) and 150 U sq. (real property).

The *United Kingdom* adopted a short-term capital gains tax as part of the income tax in 1962 and then enacted a separate tax on capital gains in 1965. The system has been modified several times since then; the short-term tax was repealed in 1971. In formal structure, the capital gains tax is a separate tax for individuals but part of the corporation tax for capital gains realized by corporations. The outcomes are often, but not always, the same.[169] The basic structure of the tax is to impose a charge on gains from all dispositions of assets and then to exempt a number of types of gains from the tax. These include gains that are otherwise subject to the income tax – for example, profit on the sale of inventory, gain from certain private assets (cars and personal residences), gain on certain government securities, and a number of other miscellaneous exceptions, including gain on the disposal of a decoration for valour acquired otherwise than for money or money's worth. A *de minimis* rule excludes gains and losses on personal assets that are disposed of for less than £6,000. Relief for the effects of inflation was introduced in 1982;[170] this took the form of an adjustment to the tax cost of the asset. In its present form, the indexation system does not apply to create a loss on the disposition of a capital asset, although previously such treatment was possible. This indexation basis still applies for the corporate income tax, but in 1998 it ceased to apply to those subject to capital gains tax, principally individuals and trusts; from 1998 to 2008, these had a 'taper relief' instead. Taper relief was introduced in 1998 and applies only for years since then – so that an asset held since 1990 and disposed of in 2007 would have its early years dealt with under the indexation system and its later years under taper relief.[171] The taper relief is applied to the gain. The relief distinguished between business assets and non-business assets, with business assets attracting a more generous taper. Business assets attract a 75% reduction after just a two-year holding period, so that a gain otherwise taxable at 40% is taxed only at 10%; non-business assets get a maximum reduction of 40%, and only after ten years, so that a gain taxed at 40% is taxed at 24%. The relief never results in a 0% rate. In 2008, taper relief was abolished for those trusts and individuals subject to capital gains tax – as part of the simplification of the new 18% rate. Also as part of the simplification the indexation relief that had been frozen since 1998 was abolished (i.e., for all disposals after 5 April 2008).[172]

The rate of tax on capital gains has varied, with a preferential rate applicable for certain periods. There is no preference for corporations at the present time. As noted above, individuals are different; they have a single rate of 18% and an annual exemption of £10,100 in 2009–2010.[173] This rate applies to all disposals on or after 6 April 2008. A special 'entrepreneur's relief' in effect applies a 10% rate

169. United Kingdom, TCGA, s. 1; CTA 2009, ss 2 and 4.
170. United Kingdom, TCGA, s. 52A et seq.
171. For (repealed) taper relief see United Kingdom, TCGA, s. 2A and Sch. 7.
172. United Kingdom, TCGA, s. 4 as amended by Finance Act 2008, s. 8.
173. United Kingdom, TCGA, s. 3.

on business gains up to £1 million (per lifetime).[174] Trustees pay tax on trust gains realized during administration at the trust rate, currently 40%; this may actually be higher than if the receipt had been treated as income. An annual exemption is available for trusts at a maximum of £5,050 and a minimum of £1,010, depending on the number of settlements the settler has made. If the trust is for a 'vulnerable beneficiary', the trust is ignored and the gains are charged as if they had accrued to the beneficiary.[175]

Capital losses are, in general, deductible only against capital gains, although losses on securities in unlisted trading companies can be deducted in full. Individuals and trusts can sometimes apply trading losses against capital gains. There is a broader offset for trading losses against capital gains receipts in the corporate income tax.[176]

In *Canada*, initially one-half of net capital gains was included in income; the includable portion was later increased to three-quarters and then reduced again to one-half in 2000.[177] A substantial lifetime exemption for individuals was provided in 1988, but was controversial and has been eliminated except for family farms and shares of small business corporations. Capital losses are in general deductible only against capital gains, although full deduction is allowed for certain losses incurred in investments in small business corporations (referred to as 'allowable business investment losses'). Losses can be carried back three years and forward indefinitely.

Special rules apply to 'personal use' property. If the proceeds of disposition or adjusted cost base of the property are less than $1,000, the proceeds or cost are deemed to be $1,000. This provision is a type of *de minimis* rule that is intended to eliminate the need to keep records with respect to relatively small properties. In addition, losses are deductible only with respect to personal use assets that have a potential investment character (e.g., coins, rare books, art works) and can be used only against gains on the same type of property. Thus, deduction for losses due to the decline in value of consumer durables is not allowed. In addition, gain on the disposition of a principal residence is exempt.

In an attempt to reduce the amount of litigation concerning the distinction between ordinary income and capital gains, certain taxpayers are permitted to make a one-time irrevocable election to treat all gains in respect of all subsequent dispositions of 'Canadian securities' to be on capital account. This election prevents taxpayers from claiming capital gains treatment in respect of gains and ordinary loss treatment in respect of losses from dispositions of Canadian securities. This election is not available to traders in securities, financial institutions, or non-residents.

---

174. United Kingdom, Finance Act 2008, s. 9 inserting TCGA, s. 169H et seq.
175. On trusts generally see United Kingdom, TCGA, Part 3 Ch. 2.
176. United Kingdom, TCGA, s. 2; on set-off of trading loss see TCGA, s. 261B and Income Tax Act, s. 261C. On trading losses for CT, see TA, 1988 s. 393.
177. The capital gains rules are found mostly in ss 38–55 of Canada, ITA.

The *Australian* system taxed capital gains at ordinary rates, with indexation of gains but not losses, until 1999.[178] Indexation applied only if the asset was held for more than twelve months. It was based on a broad consumer price index and effectively compared the index in the calendar quarter of acquisition and the calendar quarter of disposal. Thus, for example, for an asset acquired in the third quarter of 1985 and disposed of in the fourth quarter of 1995, the cost indexation factor would be 1.582, reflecting a 58% inflation over that period. Indexation related only to the asset and not to associated liabilities, so that the interest on a loan used to purchase an income-producing asset remains deductible on a nominal basis. To limit the tax shelter possibilities this system offered, interest deductions related to real estate investments were at one time limited to the income the property produced. These restrictions were repealed after only a short period of operation. In 1999, indexation was frozen and thereafter individuals are given the choice of indexation up to 1999, or a 50% discount on the gain after offset of losses if the asset is held for twelve months. Companies are not entitled to the discount but can still have indexation up to the end of September 1999. The result is that for assets acquired after that time, there is no indexation, and for assets acquired before that time, indexation will become less and less valuable as time passes.

Capital losses are deductible against capital gains, but not other income. Excess capital losses may be carried forward indefinitely to offset capital gains. Rules similar to those in Canada apply to gains and losses on personal assets and exempt gains on the disposition of a principal residence.

When *Canada* and the *United Kingdom* introduced the taxation of capital gains, assets were valued at the time of enactment for purposes of calculating gain or loss, so that only capital gains or losses occurring after that time were taken into account. The United Kingdom rule was subsequently changed to a later valuation date in connection with the introduction of indexation.[179] *Australia* applied its capital gains tax only to assets acquired after a certain date, thus necessitating complex rules preserving the 'pre' and 'post' character of gains (e.g., in the case of rollovers).

The following **Table II-1** summarizes some of the inclusion rules discussed in Subpart B. To deal with the issues that arise in connection with schedular systems, the headings indicate the type of situation being considered. For example, in connection with Windfalls, the assumption is that the windfall does not occur in a business setting or in connection with profit-seeking activities. Similarly, with respect to Illegal Income, the assumption is that the income would otherwise fall into a taxable category if the factor of illegality were not involved.

---

178. The capital gains general rules are found in Australia, ITAA 1997, Part 3-1.
179. For the original rule, see United Kingdom, Finance Act 1965; for 1982 rebasing, see TCGA, s. 35.

Some Aspects of the Tax Base: Inclusions

	Imputed Rental Income from Residence	*Personal Gifts*	*Business Gifts*	*Windfalls (non-business/profit-seeking)*	*Illegal Income (otherwise taxable)*	*Public Subsidies (business context)*	*Debt Cancellation (business context)*
Australia	Excluded	Excluded	Included	Excluded	Included	Generally included	Reduce tax cost or losses if capital; taxable if ordinary
Canada	Excluded	Excluded	Included	Excluded	Included	Included or tax cost reduction	Reduce tax cost or losses if capital; taxable if ordinary
France	Excluded	Excluded	Excluded generally	Excluded	Included	Generally included	Included
Germany	Mainly excluded	Excluded	Included under certain conditions	Excluded	Included	Included or tax cost reduction	Included
Japan	Excluded	Excluded	Included	Included	Included	Included or tax cost reduction	Included
The Netherlands	Included	Excluded	Included generally	Excluded	Included	Generally not included	Generally excluded (exception regarding prior losses)
Sweden	Excluded	Excluded	Included generally	Excluded	Included	Included or tax cost reduction	Included if solvent; if not, excluded but loss

							reduction
United Kingdom	Excluded	Excluded	Excluded (if not for business purposes)	Excluded	Included	Included (unless specific)	Generally excluded (unless business tax benefit from prior deduction)
United States	Excluded	Excluded	Generally included (employee always includes)	Included	Included	Included or tax cost reduction	Included or tax cost/loss reduction

Subpart C. Deductions

The basic notion that an income tax is, in general, imposed on gross income reduced by deductions and not on some broader category of receipts, is a fundamental premise of all of the systems considered here. Although the implementation of this principle takes numerous forms, there are some common features. All systems recognize that, in general, expenditures deductible in computing income must have some connection to taxable activities and that expenditures for personal consumption should, at least in most cases, not be deductible. The systems also distinguish between expenses that reduce income of the current period and capital expenditures that are taken into account through some sort of capital cost recovery system. In some systems, all income-related expenses are in principle deductible unless otherwise limited. In others, deduction is restricted to a more specific catalogue of expenditures. In addition to a deduction for expenses necessary to properly determine net income, some systems allow deductions for certain personal expenses.

Beyond the definition of deductible expenses, all of the systems have important schedular aspects in connection with deductions. Even where income is defined in a global fashion, various classes of deductions are often limited to certain categories of income.

Many systems have special rules dealing with deductions by employees. Some systems allow a standardized deduction from employment income but disallow specific employee deductions. In other situations, only a limited class of employee deductions is allowed, and then often only to the extent that the expenses exceed a certain floor. Limitations of this sort are based on the administrative difficulty of policing such deductions and the concern that, without limitations, substantial amounts of personal, living, and consumption costs would be deducted. These limitations are usually not applicable to an individual's business or professional income, although arguably the same problems exist there. Where employee deductions are restricted and not offset by some sort of lump sum or standard deduction, but professional and business deductions are allowed without limitation, the general effect is to favour higher-income taxpayers.

Another recurring feature in the treatment of employees is an inconsistency between those costs that can be deducted if incurred directly and those that are excluded if reimbursed by an employer. The exclusion rules are usually more generous than the deduction rules. This may be explained in part by the assumption that the income-earning connection is more likely to be predominant if the employer is willing to bear the cost, at least in those cases where it is clear that the expense does not simply represent additional compensation. The exclusion thus serves as a netting of income and deduction for costs that are assumed to be income-earning because they are reimbursed.

Other limitations typically restrict losses arising from interest and capital recovery deductions. These limitations frequently arise in response to perceived problems with 'tax shelter' investments. The various limitations on deductions are discussed after consideration of the substantive deduction rules.

1. MIXED BUSINESS AND PERSONAL EXPENSES

All of the systems must deal with the basic problem of expenditures that have both an income-producing and a consumption dimension. The responses to the problem are somewhat different, both in the general approach and the specific rules. After a description of the countries' general approaches to the problem, there is a discussion of selected expenses that usually have both personal and income-earning components.

At one extreme, *Germany* has a general statutory provision that disallows the deduction of any expense of 'mixed' character[180] unless there is a specific statutory rule allowing a deduction (e.g., business meals). The 'prohibition of division and deduction' appears to be based on the idea that, for reasons of tax equity, consumption should be included in the tax base, even if the consumption necessarily takes place in a business context. Only in limited circumstances where the personal element is *de minimis* or the business and personal elements can be clearly separated will any deduction be allowed.

The *United Kingdom* reaches the same result using a somewhat different analysis, but attention must be paid to the particular source of income. In relation to a trade or profession, deductions are allowed if they are incurred 'wholly and exclusively' in connection with trade or professional activities. For business income, the test is based on the purpose behind the expenditure. However, the apparent breadth of this rule is offset by an absolute prohibition on the deduction of a 'dual-purpose' expenditure and by the refusal of the courts to apply the purpose test simply on the basis of what taxpayers say their purpose was.[181] By contrast,

180. Germany, ITA, s. 12 no. 1.
181. *Mallalieu v. Drummond* [1983] STC 665.

where the deduction relates to employment income, the general test requires that the expense be incurred wholly, exclusively, and necessarily in the performance of the duties of the office or employment. This language has been interpreted to mean that expenses of getting into a position to earn income, as opposed to the actual performance of the activities that generate the income, are not deductible. This interpretation has influenced the treatment of expenses involving commuting, moving, child care, and the like.[182] The divergence between business and employment income deduction rules should not be exaggerated. In many of these instances, the expenditure will not be deductible for business income either, usually on the ground that it was incurred for mixed personal and business purposes.

In *Canada*, the treatment of mixed business/personal expenses is a hodgepodge of statutory rules and administrative practice. In general, expenses must be categorized as either personal or business. They are either deductible in full or not at all, with the exception of business meals and entertainment, one-half of which is deductible. Where, however, an expense can be apportioned on some objective, verifiable basis, such as automobile expenses, the tax authorities will allow the appropriate portion of the cost to be deductible. Nothing in the statute prohibits the apportionment of mixed business and personal expenses.

Even in countries like *Australia*, where apportionment of expenses as deductions is explicitly recognized,[183] the occasion and nature of the apportionment is still debated. For example, if a person flies to a foreign country for one week of business activities and one week of holiday, it is necessary to apportion the costs of accommodation, but it is not clear if the airfare would be subject to apportionment or subject to an all-or-nothing test.

In *Sweden*, the general approach is to attempt to identify the portion of the cost related to the business aspect of the expense. For example, costs for books and other reading material cannot be deducted, even if used in a business, if the material is such that it could reasonably be assumed that it would have been purchased for non-business reasons. On the other hand, an instrumentalist in an orchestra was allowed to deduct dental costs that were necessary for him to continue performing and that he would not otherwise have incurred.

The *French* approach is somewhat similar. No general principle prohibits the deduction of mixed expenses, and apportionment is made on a case-by-case basis.

In *The Netherlands*, as of 2001, employees are not entitled to deduct any expenses apart from commuting expenses (which are deductible at fixed amounts). For businesses, some categories of mixed expenses are always (i.e., irrespective of whether incurred by the employer or the employee) non-deductible, and any allowances paid to employees for such expenses incurred by employees are taxable to the employees. Other types of mixed expenses are not deductible only when incurred by the employer.

Whatever the general rules typically developed in case law, commonly recurring costs such as commuting, business entertainment, and moving often are dealt

182. United Kingdom, ITTOIA, s. 34, CTA 2009, s. 54; ITEPA, s. 336.
183. Australia, ITAA 1997, s. 8-1.

with in special statutory provisions setting forth the conditions for and limits on deduction. The rules are not always consistent with any general theory. One common approach is the allowance of a specified percentage of costs that typically have a significant consumption content, such as meals and entertainment. Strict substantiation requirements are also usually associated with such expenses.

The following material examines some selected deductions that involve mixed business and personal aspects.

1.1. Commuting

Commuting expenses have a clear business connection in that they are necessary to place the taxpayer in a position to begin income-producing activity. On the other hand, the level of commuting expense is tied up with the personal decision as to where to live in relation to the workplace and the means of transportation used. While several systems deny commuting deductions altogether, some give a limited deduction.

Thus, in the *United States*, the costs of commuting, defined as travelling from the taxpayer's personal residence to the principal place of work, are in general non-deductible. However, once the taxpayer is in 'work status', travelling expenses between work sites are deductible. A complex set of case law and administrative rules deals with the myriad issues that arise in applying this distinction. For example, the costs of occasional travel directly from the personal residence to a secondary work site are deductible; the taxpayer is not required to go first to his principal work site.

The commuting expenses of employees that qualify for deduction, like most other employee expenses, are subject to a limit. Such employee expenses are deductible only to the extent that they, together with other miscellaneous deductions, exceed 2% of income.

Similarly, commuting expenses are not deductible in *Canada*, following earlier UK cases that had reached the same result. Costs incurred to put the taxpayer in the position to earn income are not incurred in the course of work and are viewed as essentially personal. The costs are also related to the personal choice of where to live. As in the United States, the expenses of travelling in the course of business are generally deductible. In some Canadian cases, taxpayers attempted to circumvent the rule by establishing home offices and claiming the home/business trip was in the course of business. Substantial restrictions on the deductibility of home office expenses eliminated this tactic.

In the *United Kingdom*, the deduction of commuting expenses was denied in the case of a barrister who worked at home. The barrister's office was his principal place of work, and the cost of travel home in the evening was held to be personal even though he also worked there. The cost of travel was not 'wholly and exclusively' business related.[184] On the other hand, travel between two (exclusive) work

184. *Sargent v. Barnes* [1978] STC 322.

sites is allowed as a deduction. The legislation on employment income (rewritten in 2003) allows a deduction first for travel expenses necessarily incurred in the performance of the duties of the office, words that usually mean the taxpayer's claim to deduct the costs of travel from home to work fails. A further rule allowing the costs of travel for 'necessary attendance' contains an express exclusion for 'ordinary commuting'.[185]

Australian case law has followed the same pattern, also basing its analysis on UK cases. A recent decision in the High Court of Australia disturbed the common understanding that work-related travel was deductible when two separate income-earning activities were involved (in the particular case, one source was employment and the other was a business).[186] The Government has legislated to preserve the common understanding.[187]

In *Germany*, the deductibility of commuting expenses has been the subject of much political debate, legislative action, and a recent judgment of the Constitutional Court. In 2007, the legislature abolished the rule that gave a deduction for a fixed amount (€0.30 per kilometre for the shortest route between the taxpayer's home and workplace regardless of the method of transportation). From 2007 on, the fixed amount is allowed only for commuting between home and workplace in excess of the first twenty kilometres.[188] The Constitutional Court held that this distinction violates the principle of equality, since it was based on purely fiscal factors.[189] The Ministry of Finance has announced that it will re-introduce the deductibility of €0.30 per kilometre for the full distance between home and work.

In *Sweden*, although commuting expenses are viewed in principle as personal, a special statutory provision allows the deduction of commuting expenses to the extent that they exceed SEK 7,000 per year. Only 'reasonable' expenses are allowed, which in practice means the cost of public transportation. The taxpayer can deduct the costs of travelling by car only if it can be established that use of the car saves at least two hours per day in commuting time. The deduction is limited to a per-kilometre amount intended to cover the marginal costs of the car. The trip must be between the taxpayer's 'residence' and workplace, which has excluded costs of travelling from a summer house to work (a common occurrence in Sweden).

In *The Netherlands*, commuting costs were originally considered to be personal and non-deductible. Later, as housing shortages caused more people to live at a substantial distance from their work, case law began allowing deductions in some situations. Beginning in 1964, legislation has allowed employees a limited fixed deduction for commuting expenses.

185. United Kingdom, ITEPA, s. 337 et seq.
186. *Payne* [2001] HCA 3, 202 CLR 93.
187. Australia, ITAA 1997, ss 25–100.
188. Germany, ITA, s. 9 para. 2.
189. Federal Constitutional Court (*Bundesverfassungsgericht*), judgment of 9 Dec. 2008 2 BvL 1/07 et seq.

Since 2001, the deduction has been restricted to expenses for commuting by public transportation (with a maximum of eighty kilometres of travel, one-way). However, if the employer provides to the employee an allowance for commuting by private car, the allowance is not taxed to the employee to the extent that it does not exceed certain limits based on a maximum distance of twenty kilometres.[190] These rules are intended to reflect both environmental and traffic considerations as well as the mixed nature of the expenses.

The treatment of commuting expenses in *Japan* has been revised several times. Commuting costs are usually paid by the employer, and these payments are tax-free up to a certain level. Initially, deductions were not permitted for specific costs, including commuting expenses in excess of the tax-free amounts, if incurred by employees in connection with income that fell into the employment category. Instead, income in that category was subject to a large 'standard' deduction, whose relative size varied with income but amounted to 30% to 40% of compensation. While the deduction performed several functions, its main role was to avoid the administrative burden of dealing with itemized deductions for employee expenses.[191] This technique proved controversial and constitutional objections were raised that it discriminated against wage-earners in relation to other taxpayers, in particular the self-employed who enjoyed such deductions. Although the constitutionality of the approach was ultimately upheld, the statutory rules were changed to allow a limited number of employee deductions, including commuting expenses, to be taken if the total of such deductions exceeded the standard deduction. Thus, 'ordinary and necessary' commuting expenses can be deducted by individuals in some circumstances.[192] While important as a matter of principle, in practice, a very small number of taxpayers actually itemize employee deductions.

In *France*, the general principle is that commuting expenses can be deducted, either in their actual amount or based on a per-kilometre rate,[193] provided that distance between home and work is not 'abnormal'. This means a maximum of forty kilometres unless the taxpayer can justify the extra distance on social or business grounds.[194] Most employees (95%) do not take itemized deductions for expenses such as commuting, but elect a standard deduction of 10% of their compensation.[195]

---

190. Netherlands, ITA, Art. 3.87.
191. In addition to this administrative burden, it has been suggested that the large standard deduction was related to the fact that more wage income was likely to be reported than income in other categories, that taxes were paid more promptly due to withholding, and more broadly, that it functioned as a surrogate for a deduction for 'human capital'.
192. Japan, ITA, s. 57-2.
193. France, Administrative Documentation 5 G-2354, no. 9–43.
194. France, Circulars 4 C-4-04, no. 21 and 5 G-5-04, no. 5 (self-employed), and CGI, s. 83 3 para. 7 (employees).
195. France, CGI, s. 83(3) paras 2–4.

1.2. Moving Expenses

Like commuting, moving expenses have both business and personal elements. Some moves may be entirely personally motivated and others required by the employer. Again, the countries' approaches vary. However, in many cases employer-reimbursed expenses are not included in income, although directly incurred expenses in the same situation are not deductible. This approach, in effect, uses the fact of employer reimbursement as a proxy for the establishment of a necessary income-earning connection for the move.

In the *United States*, case law originally held moving expenses to be non-deductible in the same manner as commuting expenses. However, administrative practice allowed the exclusion of certain employer-reimbursed expenses, creating a disparity both between directly incurred expenses and those reimbursed, and between different categories of reimbursed expenses. The final statutory resolution was to allow a deduction for a limited category of moving expenses or, alternatively, to allow a taxpayer to exclude from gross income a reimbursement received for such expenses from the employer.[196] To be deductible or excludable, the move must be in connection with the commencement of work at a new place of business and meet certain distance requirements. Unlike commuting expenses, moving expenses are not subject to a percentage-of-income limitation.

In *Germany*, there are no special statutory rules dealing with moving costs. They are deductible in some circumstances under case law principles interpreting the general deduction for income-producing expenses. The move must be exclusively or nearly exclusively for a business reason. The most frequent justification is the change of job location (which is itself assumed to be business related). Without a change of job, a move can be business related if it results in a saving of travel time to the job of at least one hour per day. If the move is found to be business related, a deduction is allowed for moving expenses incurred up to the amount that would have been paid as reimbursed expenses to a civil servant for a similar move, without proof of actual cost. Higher costs can be deducted, but the taxpayer must establish the business connection of all of the costs. A reimbursement of moving costs paid by a public employer to an employee is tax exempt.[197]

In the *Commonwealth* systems, as a matter of general principle, moving costs are considered to be personal in the same way as commuting expenses. However, a special statutory rule now allows moving expenses in limited circumstances in *Canada*.[198] Moving expenses are deductible if they arise in connection with the commencement of employment or business in a new location. The move must result in the new residence being at least forty kilometres closer to the new work-place than the old residence.

Originally, this distance requirement was interpreted by the tax authorities and the courts as measured in a straight line. As a result, a taxpayer was denied a

196. United States, IRC, ss 217 and 132(a)(6).
197. Germany, ITA, s. 3 no. 13.
198. Canada, ITA, s. 62.

deduction when he moved from the Quebec side of the Ottawa River to the Ottawa side, even though the distance limitation was satisfied if measured in terms of normal driving distance.[199] This strict interpretation was reversed by the Court of Appeal in favour of a more flexible interpretation that takes into account the normal means of transportation available.[200] The Canadian tax authorities do not give up easily. In a 2007 case, they argued that the distance requirement should be determined by using the shortest distance between two locations generated by a computer software program, despite the fact that in this case the route involved 17 right turns, 18 left turns, and went through several heavily populated areas. The Tax Court rejected this approach as the triumph of mechanical irrationality over common sense.[201]

The statutory deduction was added in part to remove discrimination between employees who received reimbursement of their moving expenses from their employers and those employees who had to bear the costs of moving themselves. The court cases consistently held that such reimbursements were not included in income.

In the *United Kingdom*, moving expenses are not deductible. However, a special statutory provision exempts employer reimbursements of certain costs up to £8,000 per move; the £8,000 figure has not been reviewed for many years.[202] *Australia* reaches a similar result by not allowing an employee deduction for directly incurred expenses but exempting employer reimbursements from the otherwise applicable FBT at the employer level.[203]

In *Sweden*, in principle, moving expenses are not deductible, partly on the basis that they are personal costs and partly on the ground that they represent non-deductible capital costs incurred in acquiring a new source of income. A case law exception allows a deduction where the move was required by the employer.

Sweden has a statutory exclusion for employer-reimbursed moving expenses of certain kinds, even when those expenses would not be deductible if incurred directly. The somewhat unsatisfactory justification of the exclusion of employer-borne costs is to encourage labour mobility in a geographically large country. Size of country, however, does not seem to be a consistent factor in the treatment of moving expenses, given the restrictive rules in Australia and the United Kingdom and the more liberal provisions in Canada.

In *Japan*, moving expenses incurred because of a move at the request of the employer may be deducted in the same way as commuting expenses if the total of all itemized expenses exceeds the standard deduction.[204] As indicated above, *The Netherlands* does not permit the deduction of any expenses incurred by an employee in connection with employment. However, within certain limits, the

199. *Cameron v. The Queen* [1993] 1 CTC 2745 (TCC).
200. *Giannakopoulos v. The Queen* [1995] 2 CTC 316 (FCA).
201. *Nagy v. The Queen* [2007] 5 CTC 2642 (TCC).
202. United Kingdom, ITEPA, s. 271 et seq.
203. Australia, FBTAA, ss 58AA–58F.
204. Japan, ITA, s. 57-2.

reimbursement of moving expenses by the employer is not taxable to the employee.[205]

In *France*, while moving expenses are in principle deductible if the move is made in connection with a change in job, most employees choose the 10% standard deduction.

1.3. Clothing

Clothing is a classic example of a mixed business and personal expense, and the results in all of the systems are similar, involving an objective test as to the suitability of clothing for wear outside work, regardless of the lifestyle of the particular individual.

The approach in the *United States* is to allow a deduction for clothing that is not adaptable to personal use, is not so worn, and is required as a condition of employment. Thus, costs of military uniforms that can be worn when off duty are not deductible, whereas the cost of required clothing such as fatigues, whose off-duty use is restricted, qualifies for deduction.

In *Germany*, under the basic principle of no apportionment of mixed costs, clothing expenses are either fully deductible or non-deductible. 'Typical' professional clothing, such as uniforms for police, fire, military, and airline employees, that is necessary because of the nature of the business, are deductible even if they can be worn privately. Special protective clothing, shoes, and the like are also deductible. The cost of 'civilian' clothes that are not associated with a particular profession and that can be worn in normal public settings are not normally deductible, even if as a practical matter they are necessary for the profession (e.g., dark suits for lawyers). However, cases have allowed the deduction of the cost of formal attire of a mortician, a waiter's tuxedo or trousers (criticized in the literature), and the black suit of (Protestant) clergy.

The *French* rules are broadly similar, but most employees take the standard deduction.

In *Canada*, clothing represents in general a personal expense and is not deductible. Special employment-related clothing expenses are not deductible by employees in Canada, since that is not one of the enumerated employee deductions. However, employer-provided special clothing and uniforms are not includable. Self-employed persons can deduct special clothing and uniform costs.

In the *United Kingdom*, administrative practice that has been put into statutory form provides special fixed allowances, varying from job to job, for tools and special clothing purchased by an employee.[206] For self-employed persons, in a leading UK case, a female barrister was not entitled to deduct the cost of cleaning ordinary clothing worn under court robes that she had purchased specifically to wear in court; the costs of cleaning the wig and gown and other court robes,

205. Netherlands, ITA, Art. 3.17.
206. United Kingdom, ITEPA, s. 367.

however, were deductible.[207] The *Australian* rules are similar, although they have one special feature. In order to prevent employers from providing 'uniforms' that are not noticeably different from ordinary clothing, on a tax-free basis, such clothing has to be registered in a Register of Approved Occupational Clothing, which sets the standards for 'borderline' clothing, specifying requirements (e.g., logos of a certain size) that must be met.[208]

In *The Netherlands*, the costs of 'work clothing' incurred by employees are not deductible, in keeping with the general prohibition on the deduction of expenses by employees. However, reimbursement of clothing expenses by the employer is not taxable to the employee.[209] 'Work clothing' is defined as clothing that must be worn during work activity and that is exclusively or almost exclusively suited for such use. Uniforms, overalls, and professorial gowns are examples.

Sweden is more restrictive and approaches the issue from a somewhat different angle. No deduction is allowed for clothing costs even if the clothes are special, such as uniforms, etc. The theoretical justification is that the expenses for business clothing are not in excess of the alternative 'avoided' expenses for private clothing that would have been incurred in any event. Thus, there is no incremental cost attributable to the business connection. This reasoning is not applicable to outer clothing, such as overalls, that is required in addition to normal clothing, and the cost of such items can be deducted. Free clothing provided by the employer that is not suitable for private wear is excluded from income (although self-incurred costs for the same clothes would not be deductible).

1.4. Business Travel

Deductions for costs incurred in business travel involve two separate issues. In those systems in which commuting expenses are either not deductible or are deductible only within limits, one issue involves distinguishing between the cost of business travel and commuting expenses. The other issue is the treatment of meals and lodging that are typically involved in business travel. The systems differ in the extent to which they attempt to capture the potential consumption element in the latter expenses.

In the *United States*, travel expenses, including meals and lodging, incurred while 'away from home' on business are in principle deductible.[210] In order to prevent the deduction of commuting expenses, 'home' in this context has been interpreted administratively (although not by all courts) to mean the taxpayer's principal place of business. Similarly, to prevent the deduction of 'normal' expenses for meals during the business day, 'away' has been interpreted to mean a situation in which a stop for sleep or rest is necessary. Thus, generally speaking,

207. *Mallalieu v. Drummond, supra* n. 181.
208. Australia, ITAA 1997, Division 34.
209. Netherlands, ITA, Art. 3.16.
210. United States, IRC, s. 162(a)(2).

the costs of overnight business travel are deductible. However, the principles have been applied to myriad factual situations, with results that are not easily reconcilable. If the taxpayer is away from home for more than one year, his 'home' in the sense of principal place of business is, in effect, deemed to have been established in the new work location; thus, lodging and meal expenses are no longer deductible because he is no longer 'away' from home.

For domestic travel, the transportation costs are fully deductible if the 'primary' purpose of the travel is business related. Meal and lodging expenses must be allocated between business and personal activities. More restrictive rules apply to foreign travel. The taxpayer may choose between substantiating actual expenses or claiming a geographically based per diem amount. Meal expenses that would otherwise be deductible under these tests are limited to 50% of the costs incurred, as discussed in more detail below in connection with entertainment expenses.

In *Sweden*, travel expenses are, in principle, deductible to the extent that they exceed the personal costs that would have been incurred in any event. This means that travel and lodging are fully deductible. Meals are deductible only if the trip involves a stay overnight. In that case, a standard amount is allowed as a deduction to offset the increase in expense over the meals at home (a larger standardized amount can be excluded if the employer reimburses the meal expenses). The employee can get a larger deduction by showing that the increase in costs is, in fact, higher. For travel abroad there are special amounts for each country.

In *Canada*, travel expenses incurred while 'away from home' are, in general, deductible. The deduction extends to employees as well, although subject to some restrictions. Only 50% of the cost of business meals is deductible. If a conference fee includes meals and beverages, $50 per day of the fee is considered allocated to meals and subject to the limitation, although no allocation is required for meals on airlines or trains.

Australia reaches roughly the same results through a combination of employee deductions and fringe benefits taxation in the case of reimbursed costs. In the former situation, there are detailed record-keeping requirements if the amounts claimed exceed the travel allowances given to public officials. If the expense is incurred by the employer, the same rules effectively apply through the operation of the FBT.

The rules in the *United Kingdom* are more restrictive. Travel expenses must be incurred 'wholly and exclusively' for the purposes of business. In a leading case, a lawyer was denied the deduction for attending conferences where he admitted that there were social and holiday purposes associated with the trip. In another case, however, an accountant successfully argued that the social aspects of a similar trip were simply incidental to his business purpose, and so was allowed a deduction. Thus, for example, doctors visiting patients in the South of France during the winter are able to deduct the travel costs if their sole purpose in incurring the expense is to look after their patients – and the pleasure of being there is simply an effect of the expenditure. In practice, apparently, some portion of the costs of 'mixed' travel is sometimes allowed.

In *Germany*, transportation expenses can be deducted on the basis of receipts for actual expenses incurred or a per-kilometre allowance can be used. Lodging expenses are deductible in full based on actual costs (although the portion of the amount attributable to breakfast must be treated as a meal expense). For foreign travel, the taxpayer can use either actual costs or a per-diem amount. For food costs, deduction is limited to a fixed per-diem amount depending on how long the taxpayer is away from the work site. For periods of twenty-four hours or more, a deductible per diem of €24 is allowed. Special amounts are laid down for foreign travel. If the taxpayer stays for more than three months in one place, he is no longer considered to be in travel status; as a result, the meals and lodging costs are no longer deductible and transportation costs are limited to commuting expenses.[211]

The *French* rules on business travel are fairly relaxed, requiring only that the expenses be normal and incurred in the course of the business. Deductions for meal expenses of employees must be reduced by the deemed cost of a meal at home, the standard value of which is the same as that of an employer-provided meal (i.e., €4.30 in 2009).

In *The Netherlands*, travel expenses incurred by employees are, like all expenses incurred in connection with employment, not deductible. However, employer reimbursements of travel costs are not taxable to the employee (and are deductible by the employer). Itemized deductions are not available to employees with respect to travel expenses, unlike commuting expenses. This does not mean, however, that business travel expenses are not deductible, but simply reflects common business practice under which travel expenses are borne by employers. For self-employed persons and corporations, travel expenses are deductible to the extent that they are incurred in the course of business.

1.5. Business Entertainment

While the business connection may influence the value of the entertainment somewhat compared to freely chosen personal expenditures, the consumption element of entertainment activities is clear. Entertainment provided in a business context is particularly susceptible to abuse and, not unexpectedly, subject to special limitations in all the countries. These limitations typically take the form of an overlay of additional requirements, especially substantiation, for any deduction at all, and a percentage limit on qualifying expenses. In view of the administrative difficulties, none of the systems attempts to tax the recipient of the entertainment directly. The denial or limitation on the deduction ensures that some amount is included in the tax base, although it is not taxed to the person enjoying the consumption.

In the *United States*, entertainment expenses must meet the normal tests of deductibility and, in addition, be either 'directly related to' or 'associated with' the taxpayer's trade or business. The rules are relaxed for meals and other recreational

211. Germany, ITA, s. 4 para. 5 no. 5.

facilities provided on the business premises or to employees, for meals in restaurants serving the general public, etc. Deductions for club dues are disallowed entirely. Special substantiation requirements apply. Only 50% of otherwise-qualified expenditures may be deducted.[212]

In *Germany*, the deduction of entertainment expenses is generally restricted in accordance with the 'reasonableness' of the cost incurred.[213] Several items are not deductible at all (e.g., costs incurred for the maintenance of establishments for hunting, fishing, or yachting). In the case of meals provided to business partners, 70% of the 'reasonable' amounts paid for food and beverages are deductible. In order to assess the 'reasonableness' of expenses, there must be an analysis of the situation from the point of view of a 'conscientious business manager' (a construct often used in German tax law), the relation of the expenditure to particular business transactions, the size and profitability of the business, and the amounts spent by comparable businesses in this field. The taxpayer must provide proof of the place, the date, the participants, and the reason for business meals.

The pattern in *Sweden* is similar. In addition to meeting the normal deduction tests involving the relation of the expense to a business activity, entertainment expenses must, under special statutory provisions, have a 'direct connection' with the business. The expense must be incurred 'solely' to establish or maintain a business relationship. This restriction would prevent, for example, the deduction of expenses of a yacht that was used to entertain customers, but also used personally. Assuming that the 'direct connection' is present, the deduction is limited to a 'reasonable' amount. In the case of business meals, a standard amount is based on restaurant prices for lunch (currently SEK 90, excluding VAT, per person).[214]

This reasonable amount has been successively decreased, partially because reduction of this deduction has been considered a simple way to finance reforms of business taxation (all government committees are under instruction not to propose amendments that could decrease tax revenues without suggesting alternative increases of tax revenues).

When the amount that can be deducted is limited, the recipient is not required to include the value of the meal in income. Thus, if an employee participates in a business lunch with a client that is paid for by the employer, neither the employee nor the client is required to include any amount in respect of the meal in income. Though the employer's deduction may be less than the actual cost of the meal, the denial of the deduction for the excess still results in a lower total tax than if the meal had been fully deductible and includable in the income of the employee (e.g., as a taxable fringe benefit), given the difference in corporate and individual rates.

In general, no deduction is allowed in the *United Kingdom* for entertainment expenses incurred by employees. If amounts are reimbursed, there is no employee inclusion, but the employer is denied the deduction. Otherwise, expenses must meet the 'wholly and exclusively' test and then are still subject to substantial

212. United States, IRC, s. 274.
213. Germany, ITA, s. 4 para. 5 no. 2.
214. Sweden, ITA, Ch. 16 s. 2.

additional statutory limitations that bar any deduction except for the entertainment of staff. This rule also prohibits a deduction for the costs of providing many sorts of gifts, although a deduction for those costing less than £50 is allowed if they contain a conspicuous advertisement for the trader.[215] *Australia* also has a special statutory rule that in general denies a deduction for entertainment expenses, subject to a number of exceptions, such as restaurant meals of restaurant reviewers consumed as part of their jobs, business trips, and the like. In addition, there is an exception for in-house dining facilities for employees. The latter exception has made it common practice for large legal and accounting firms to have quite lavish private dining facilities. Club fees and the like paid by employers are generally not deductible.[216]

The overlay of the FBT in Australia makes the situation quite complex, since entertainment of employees and their associates is subject to the FBT while entertainment of non-employees is subject to the denial-of-deduction rule. To alleviate the potentially onerous record-keeping burden, two alternative elective methods for dealing with entertainment expenses apply, a straight fifty-fifty split and a split based on a typical twelve-week period.[217]

In *Canada*, 50% of directly connected entertainment expenses involved in business activities is deductible. No deduction is allowed for entertainment expenses incurred by employees, except salespersons in limited circumstances. Reimbursement of entertainment expenses by the employer does not result in an income inclusion for the employee. The Canadian rules expressly disallow any deduction for club dues and the expenses for the use of yachts, camps, lodges, and golf courses. *The Netherlands* allows businesses to deduct entertainment expenses only to the extent that they exceed €4,200 (2009).[218] For employees, no deduction for entertainment expenses is allowed. If the expenses are reimbursed by the employer, the reimbursement is tax-free and the employer can deduct any amount in excess of the threshold.

The *French* rules are much more liberal. There is no particular standard of reasonableness and no percentage limitations apply. However, a special statutory provision disallows a deduction for costs incurred in connection with hunting, fishing, yachting, country houses, and real estate used for entertaining.[219]

In *Japan*, employees are not allowed any deduction for entertainment expenses. For self-employed persons, the expenses may be deducted only if the greater part of the expenses is business related and the business portion of the expense can clearly be identified. Special rules substantially restrict the deduction of entertainment expenses by corporations.

The common technique of limiting the deduction for entertainment expenses as a substitute or surrogate for attempting to tax the beneficiary of the expenditure

---

215. United Kingdom, ITEPA, s. 356 et seq., ITTOIA, s. 45 et seq., CTA 2009, s. 1298 et seq.
216. Australia, ITAA 1997, ss 26–45 Division 32.
217. Australia, FBTAA, ss 37B–37CF.
218. Netherlands, ITA, Art. 3.15.
219. France, CGI, s. 39-4.

itself raises some problems. For example, it has no impact on tax-exempt organizations. This aspect led Australia to include under its FBT a special rule to impose the tax on entertainment expenses of tax-exempts.[220] As a more general matter, as the Swedish situation shows, where there is a difference in tax bracket between the payer and the recipient, denial of the deduction can have quite different effects from the inclusion of the payment, although it ensures that at least some amount is included in the tax base at some point.

1.6. Child Care

The treatment of child-care expenses has been controversial in many systems. Historically, the courts have treated the expenses as personal and non-deductible. However, as single-parent and two outside-worker families became more common, pressure to allow some tax relief for child-care expenses increased. The impact of non-deductible child-care expenses on labor supply generally, and especially with regard to secondary workers, was an important factor in the policy debate. The response was typically to continue to treat the expenses as personal from an income definition point of view but to provide some limited personal deduction or credit for the expenses. No country allows full deduction of child-care expenses as a business expense. However, a number of systems, while disallowing a deduction for directly incurred child-care expenses, allow an exclusion for employer-provided care.

The approach to child-care costs in the *United States* has varied considerably over the years. Although treated by the courts as personal expenses, early statutory provisions allowed a limited deduction for single parents and couples with low incomes. Subsequent legislation expanded the scope of the deduction but continued the dollar limitations. Currently, the expenses are not deductible, but a limited credit is provided for employment-related child-care expenses.[221] In addition, some forms of employer-paid child care can be provided as a non-taxable fringe benefit.

Canadian and *United Kingdom* courts have traditionally held child-care expenses to be personal and non-deductible. The United Kingdom continues to follow this approach, although there is a limited exclusion for employer-provided child care. The still relatively new tax credit scheme contains a substantial element for child care, but only for expenses incurred with registered establishments; this preference for care outside the home is controversial.[222] The provision of more publicly provided pre-school child care is a matter of great political interest. In Canada, a special statutory provision allows a limited deduction for expenses incurred for a variety of child-care services, including day nurseries, and boarding

220. Australia, FBTAA, s. 39.
221. United States, IRC, s. 24.
222. On the child-care exemption, see United Kingdom, ITEPA, s. 318 et seq.; on credits, see Tax Credits Act 2002, s. 12.

schools or camps. The payments must be made to unrelated parties, and the taxpayer must provide the social security number of the recipient. The effect of the deduction has had some positive effect on secondary workers entering the workforce, but the effect is limited by the fact that the deductible amount does not approximate actual child-care costs. There is a limited amount of governmental subsidies for child-care facilities. Proposals for universal child care surface from time to time but have not been adopted for budgetary reasons.

In 1994, the Canadian Supreme Court considered an important case involving child care expenses.[223] The taxpayer, a partner in a large law firm, whose spouse also worked, tried to deduct the costs of a full-time nanny as ordinary business expenses, quite apart from the limited statutory deduction. She claimed that the limited deduction violated the Canadian Charter of Rights and Freedoms (Constitution) because it discriminated against women. In a seven-to-two decision, a majority of the court (all males) disallowed the deduction, holding that the statutory deduction for child-care expenses excluded the possibility of deducting the expenses as ordinary business expenses; the provision was not discriminatory, since there was no showing that child-care expenses were paid disproportionately by women. Two dissenters (both women) would have allowed the deduction. They argued that there was no conflict between the deduction of child-care expenses by business taxpayers and the limited statutory deduction (even though it applied explicitly to business taxpayers). The dissenting female justices also concluded that the statutory deduction for child-care expenses was discriminatory against women. The majority opinion intimated that, in the absence of the special statutory deduction, 'the changing composition of the business class and changing social structure' might require the reclassification of child-care expenses as business expenses.

Case law in *Australia*, influenced by the United Kingdom, has also denied the deduction for child-care expenses as business expenses, viewing them as not being incurred 'in the course of' employment. There are some limited exceptions from the FBT for employer-provided child care. There is no generally provided governmental child care. A tax credit for child care was available between 2004 and 2007 and was then replaced by a direct payment. There are some studies showing a negative effect of the lack of recognition in the tax and social welfare systems for child care on secondary workers. Recent government initiatives in the area have been criticized on the basis that the funds found their way into the pockets of child-care providers through increased fees; one particular private provider came to dominate the child-care market before its bankruptcy in the 2008 global financial crisis. This situation has caused the government to rethink its policy.

In *Sweden*, child-care costs are not deductible. However since 2007, a taxpayer can apply for a tax credit for domestic costs, including child care. The credit is 50% of the costs with a cap of SEK 50,000 per year.[224] This is a deviation from the principle that the income tax system should be neutral and not used for

223. *Symes v. The Queen* [1994] 1 CTC 40 (SCC).
224. See the chapter on Sweden in Part One for more details.

non-fiscal purposes. In this case, the tax credit is justified on the basis that it is necessary to rectify market imperfections. The personal choice to incur private expenses instead of using the available public facilities heightens the consumption element of the expenditure.

Germany has changed the treatment of child-care expenses substantially over the years. After the Constitutional Court ruled in 1977 that child-care expenses are deemed to have a private character and are not business-related, there was no possibility to deduct such expenses at all.[225] Nevertheless, in 1984 the Constitutional Court stated that single and disabled parents should be entitled to deduct a certain lump sum amount in order to cope with child-care expenses – not as a 'business-related-deduction', but as a special allowance for their personal hardship.[226] Later, tax legislation introduced a general deduction for household services, which also included expenses for a nanny. In 1998, the Constitutional Court changed the whole picture and held that, while there should be a reasonable tax-free threshold for child care, its applicability should not depend on whether the parents themselves take care of the children or employ another person.[227] This decision has been criticized strongly in the literature (because this would lead to the deduction of 'opportunity costs'), and the legislature has not followed the advice of the Court. Currently, there is a two-pronged approach: child care can be deductible either as a personal expense or as a business expense depending on the relevant circumstances. A general child-care deduction of €1,080 is recognized without having regard to actual expenses, and a further deduction for two-thirds of the actual costs incurred up to €4,000 per child annually is applicable.[228] Moreover, there are additional deductions for the maintenance of children in general.

In *Japan*, child-care expenses are considered purely personal and are not deductible, although municipalities often provide some monetary assistance to parents that is usually excluded from taxable income. Employer-provided child care is not taxed to the employee as a fringe benefit.

In *The Netherlands*, as of 2005 child-care expenses have been 'de-fiscalized': they are no longer deductible but the Government provides a (tax-free) subsidy for child care.

France considers child care as a non-deductible personal cost but provides an annual credit of 50% of the costs of child care outside the home with a maximum of €1,150 per child under the age of seven.[229] There is also a credit for 50% of the salary paid for au pair and housecleaning services (maximum credit €6,000, if one child, €7,500 if two children or more). This latter provision was intended to

225. Federal Constitutional Court (*Bundesverfassungsgericht*), judgment of 11 Oct. 1977 1 BvR 343/73 et al., Reports (BVerfGE) 47, 1.
226. Federal Constitutional Court (*Bundesverfassungsgericht*), judgment of 17 Oct. 1984 1 BvR 527/80 et al., Reports (BVerfGE) 68, 143.
227. Federal Constitutional Court (*Bundesverfassungsgericht*), judgment of 10 Nov. 1998 2 BvR 1057/91 et al., Reports (BVerfGE) 99, 216.
228. Germany, ITA, ss 4f and 10 para. 1 no. 8.
229. France, CGI, s. 200 *quater* B.

stimulate employment and does not require that both parents work to qualify for the credit, but the credit is refundable only if both parents work.[230]

2. 'HOBBY LOSSES' AND THE CRITERIA FOR DETERMINING BUSINESS VERSUS PERSONAL ACTIVITIES

Activities that are ostensibly aimed at making a profit but involve the potential for substantial personal consumption raise some of the same issues as mixed business and personal expenses and are frequently dealt with by special rules. The questions come up somewhat differently in schedular systems and in systems that operate with a more global income concept. In a schedular system, for either the profit to be taxable or losses deductible, the activity in question must fit within one of the taxable categories. Thus, for an occasional activity (e.g., stamp collecting) that does not fall in any taxable category, neither income nor expenses typically would be taken into account for tax purposes. In a global system, the profit is taxable; the real issue involves the deduction of the costs that arise in the activity (and that will usually be larger than the income).

The *United States* has had a series of statutory provisions dealing with the hobby loss problem. Under the current version, if an activity carried on by an individual is found to be 'not engaged in for profit', the deductions generated by the activity may be used only against the income from the activity.[231] However, deductions that would be available even in the absence of profit-seeking activity have to be 'stacked' first against the income. The effect of the provision is thus typically to deny a portion of the deduction for maintenance and depreciation expenses of the hobby activity against other income. The factors considered by the courts in determining if a profit-seeking activity is present include the nature of the activity as potentially recreation (e.g., horse raising, car racing), an assessment whether the activities are carried on in a 'businesslike' manner, the use of expert advisers, and the history of profits and losses from the activity and its potential for profit. The provision may be overly generous to taxpayers as, to some extent, it allows what are consumption expenses to be offset against the otherwise-taxable income the activity generates.

While originally aimed at limiting the deduction for the consumption element in what were essentially personal activities, the provision has been applied to tax-motivated transactions that were not likely to generate a profit apart from the tax benefits.

In *Canada*, the distinction between business and personal activities is closely related to the source concept of income discussed earlier. If an activity is clearly commercial in nature and there is no personal element, the activity is a source of income. If there is a personal element, the taxpayer must establish by reference to

230. France, CGI, s. 199 *sexdecies*.
231. United States, IRC, s. 183.

objective 'indicia of commerciality' or 'badges of trade' that the predominant intention is to make a profit from the activity. In a 2002 case, the Supreme Court rejected any requirement for an activity to be carried on with a reasonable expectation of profit.[232] The Court even went so far as to indicate that the intention of eventually realizing a capital gain may support a finding that an activity is commercial in nature. Under the Supreme Court's approach, if a taxpayer's activities constitute a business, the revenues derived from the activities will be included in computing income, and the expenses incurred in connection with the activities will be deductible. In contrast, if there is no business, any revenue derived from the activities is not taxable, and any expenses are not deductible. Taxpayers argue that they have a business source of income if they have a net loss from their activities, or only a hobby (no source of income) if they have net profits. In late 2003, the government introduced proposals to reverse the Supreme Court case and re-introduce a reasonable expectation of profit test; however, those proposals were flawed and remain unenacted.

A special rule applies to hobby farmers, a common phenomenon in Canada. Even if the activity is a business, where the hobby farmer's chief source of income is not farming or a combination of farming and some other source, there is a dollar limit on the amount of the loss that can be deducted against other income. Non-deductible farm losses can be carried forward and deducted against farm income in later years.

The *United Kingdom* approach has evolved somewhat differently. Under the basic case law tests, it was fairly easy to establish a 'trading' activity which would, in principle, allow the deduction of costs. However, this rule is supplemented by a special provision that requires that the trade must be carried on a commercial basis and with a view to a realization of profit. A further special rule applies to farming, which disallows losses after five consecutive years of loss unless it can be established that there would be a reasonable expectation of profit if the business were carried on by a competent person.[233] As seen elsewhere (see section 6.3), the United Kingdom now has some restrictions on the right of a person to set a trading loss against income from other sources for that year ('sideways' relief) if the person is not actively involved in running the business. Under the UK system, a loss cannot arise from employment.

In *Germany*, extensive case law deals with the issue of whether the taxpayer's activities constitute a 'business', self-employment, rental, etc., or are private and hence not taxable. The basic test is framed in terms of an intention to make a profit. While formally a subjective test, the cases have consistently based their decisions on the objective facts that indicate such intent. The cases deal both with 'classical' hobby loss situations and also with tax shelters. The statutory provision expressly states that a reduction in taxes is not considered a profit. It is evident that activities with a 'consumption element' (e.g., writing, art, sports) receive particular scrutiny by the tax authorities.

232. *Stewart v. The Queen*, [2002] SCC 46 (SCC).
233. United Kingdom, ITA s. 66 et seq.

For income to be taxable and losses deductible, there must be proof of the intention to generate income, based on objective evidence of the probability of a 'total' profit – that is, that the activity will generate a net profit at some point in a 'reasonable' time after the activities have been started. It is not sufficient that profits be made in later years after early years of losses; the income must be sufficient to cover all costs of the operation and result in an overall profit. In determining if a profit is probable, it is appropriate to take into account possible increases in the value of the assets involved as well as operating income, as long as the gains on those assets would be taxable. Thus, in the case of rental activities that do not constitute a business, the gain on sale of the property would not be taxed and thus cannot be taken into account in determining if a total profit will result. Although the case law allows an initial starting period of losses, a longer period of losses is seen as an indication of private activity unless the taxpayer restructures his activity. On the other hand, it is acceptable for a taxpayer to start a loss-making activity that is meant to support another profitable activity (e.g., an art gallery combined with a restaurant) as long as overall profitability is envisaged.

Prior to the tax reform of 1991, the *Swedish* system made a distinction between hobby and business activities based on the intention to make a profit. If the requisite profit motive was not present, neither the income nor the expenses were taken into account for tax purposes. In the tax reform of 1991, changes were made in the definitions of taxable sources of income. Income from the performance of services is now taxable without regard to the existence of a profit motive. As a result, income from a hobby involving the performance of services is taxed in the 'services' category. In principle, deductions should not be allowed but are permitted up to the amount of the income. Any excess loss cannot be deducted against other income, on the theory that the costs are personal.

In *The Netherlands*, there is substantial case law dealing with the definition of a 'business' (enterprise) that draws a distinction between taxable business and non-taxable personal activities. For a business to be present, there must be (1) a permanent organization of labour and capital, (2) participation in an economic interchange, and (3) a profit-making goal and reasonable expectation of success. These requirements, in effect, place most hobby activities on the personal side of the line, with the result that no receipts are taxed and no expenses are deductible. In some cases, a hobby activity may be viewed as involving 'income from other activities', but in practice, if there is a history of losses, it is unlikely that the deductions would be allowed.

Australia has no objective criterion of the likelihood of profit as the test for determining if the taxpayer is engaged in a business, and as a result there has been considerable litigation over the business/hobby borderline. There have been some unsuccessful attempts to limit the deductibility of farming losses against other income. To deal with the problem, Australia introduced non-commercial loss rules in 2000.[234] Under these rules, losses on hobby-type businesses are not deductible currently but can be carried forward to future years for offset against income from

234. Australia, ITAA 1997, Division 35.

the same type of activities. The rules do not apply if the revenue from the business is $20,000 or more in the year, the business has made a profit in three of the last five years (including the current year), or the business utilizes real property worth $500,000 or more or other property (excluding cars) worth $100,000 or more. There is discretion to relax the operation of the rules in hardship cases (such as fire or flood in the case of farms).

Hobby loss issues have not been extensively litigated or debated in *Japan*. There is, however, some administrative guidance with regard to owners of race horses. If certain requirements as to the number of horses, the manner in which the operations are conducted, etc., are met, then the income will constitute business income and any net loss can be used against other income in other taxable categories. If the tests are not met, the income is included in the Miscellaneous Income category and, while the expenses could be used to offset the racing income, any excess loss cannot be used against other income.

In *France*, a general trend in the case law is to restrict the situations in which amounts are excluded from income. In accordance with this general trend, income and losses from hobbies are usually taken into account in computing taxable income. An amount is excluded only if it is a windfall and not part of any determined profit-making scheme. This would apply, for instance, when a race horse owner who is not a breeder merely entrusts the horse to a trainer; however, whenever the taxpayer undertakes some kind of activity in order to tip the scales in his favour (e.g., choice of horse races, control over trainer), any income (even non-periodical income provided it is likely to recur) is taxable in the 'Other Income' category.[235] The corresponding losses cannot, however, be set against income arising in other taxable income categories; they may be carried forward only to the six following years and offset against income of the same nature (i.e., non-professional).[236] The same rule applies to losses that arise in an agricultural activity when income from other sources exceeds a certain level (€104,239 for 2008 income, with an annual increase); in these circumstances, the taxpayer is presumed to be a hobby farmer.[237]

3. CAPITAL COSTS AND RECOVERY METHODS

3.1. Determining Capital Costs

All of the systems recognize the distinction between currently deductible costs and capital costs. Capital costs are generally recovered under some sort of capital cost recovery system or on the disposal of the asset. While the details of the rules and the formulation of the distinction differ, in general, costs that create a benefit in future years must be capitalized if they represent a relatively large and non-recurring

235. France, CGI, s. 92.
236. France, CGI, s. 156 I 2.
237. France, CGI, s. 156 I 1.

expenditure. In some systems, the treatment of capital gains for accounting purposes is an important element in determining the tax treatment of such costs. There is an unavoidable arbitrariness in the classifications in all of the systems, although a surprising amount of similarity occurs in the results.

Taking the *United States* as an example, the formulation of the current/capital distinction in the case law has varied over time. At one point, the test was whether the expenditure could be said to have created a separate and distinct asset. More recently, however, the focus has returned to the issue of the existence of a significant benefit from the expenditure that extends beyond the taxable year.[238] Even here, however, the test is not applied consistently. For example, advertising expenses can generally be deducted currently despite, in many situations, the clear benefit in later periods.[239]

In the *German* system, a specific statutory provision requires capitalization of any expenditure that has created an 'asset', defined as a transferable object subject to separate valuation, the useful life of which will last for more than one tax period (one year).[240] However, in practice, the courts and the fiscal authorities have allowed a current deduction for major outlays that have a recurring nature in the particular business involved. Similarly, current maintenance expenses are deductible but modifications that substantially alter the condition or character of the asset must be treated as capital costs. Expenses such as painting, which would normally be maintenance, must be capitalized if incurred in connection with the original construction or a major renovation of the asset. Assets whose costs do not exceed ca. €150 must be deducted currently.[241] As discussed in more detail below, under the basic German approach to the relation between tax and financial accounting rules, the same treatment must be used for financial accounting purposes.

In the *Commonwealth* systems, the basic distinction has historically been between currently deductible expenditures incurred in connection with the income-earning process and capital outlays. The latter are not deductible except as expressly provided by statute. Various court-developed tests have been applied in the United Kingdom, Canada, and Australia and parallel, to a large extent, the pattern in the United States. The formulations have included whether the expenditure creates an enduring benefit for the business, whether it is a once-and-for-all expenditure, and whether it relates to a specific and identifiable asset of a capital nature.[242] In the case of expenses giving rise to intangible benefits, the courts were relatively generous in allowing current deductions, as otherwise the result would often be that no recovery of the cost occurred at all due to the narrowness of the capital cost recovery systems.

238. *INDOPCO, Inc v. Commissioner*, 503 U.S. 79 (1992).
239. United States, Reg., s. 1.162-20(a)(20).
240. Germany, ITA, ss 4 para. 1 sent. 1 and 5 para. 1 sent. 1 with reference to Commercial Code, ss 246 et seq.
241. Germany, ITA, s. 6 para. 2.
242. E.g., *Tucker v. Granada Motorway Services* [1979] STC 393.

In *Sweden*, a current deduction is allowed in calculating business income for the cost of assets whose useful life does not exceed three years and for *de minimis* costs of ca. SEK 20,000. Otherwise, costs must be capitalized.

When calculating employment income in Sweden, the deduction of capital costs is based on the cash receipts method of accounting. However, case law requires that the cost of assets that can be used for an extended period must be capitalized. In some cases the rejection of a current deduction for capital costs is well founded, as with assets of mixed personal and employment use. It may not be clear enough in advance to determine to what extent such an asset will be used in the employment to justify the current deduction of the full cost. In other cases, the reasons not to allow current deduction are not so clear.

In the *French* system, historically the focus for capitalization has been on the creation or acquisition of a distinct and legally identifiable asset (with the statutory exception of materials, equipment, or software with a cost not exceeding €500) or a substantial modification in the condition, character, or useful life of an existing asset. With respect to intangibles, however, case law has taken the position that all costs that create a steady and durable source of income must be capitalized. In the case of payments for a licence to exploit a patent or a trademark, however, the asset so created must be assignable.[243] But the scope of this 'patrimonial' approach to capital assets, under which only things owned by a firm and assignable by it can constitute capital assets, seems to be limited to those particular assets; it has been held not to apply to other intangibles such as an undertaking not to compete.[244] In addition, such limitation has been confirmed by the new accounting regulations, applicable for tax purposes since 2005, which, under the new international standards, no longer require ownership of assets but focus on control.[245] In *Japan*, subject to some exceptions for *de minimis* amounts, a general rule in the income tax law requires capitalization of any expenditure whose benefits continue for more than one year. A detailed list of the items that must be capitalized in accordance with this rule is set out in the guidelines issued by the tax authorities, and Japanese practice generally follows those guidelines.

In *The Netherlands*, historically a distinction is made between currently deductible expenses and capital assets. This distinction has given rise to a sizeable body of case law dealing with, *inter alia*, research and development expenses, payments for goodwill, and advertising expenses. It is also necessary to distinguish between capital costs and capitalized expenses to determine whether certain tax incentives for capital investment apply, although this distinction has not resulted in much litigation.

243. France, Conseil d'État, 21 Aug. 1996, no. 154488.
244. France, Conseil d'État, 3 Nov. 2003, no. 232393.
245. France, Regulation CRC 2004-06, 23 Nov. 2004.

3.2. Capital Cost Recovery Systems

While there is a great deal of variation in the systems of capital cost recovery, all systems seem to have three types of rules. First, there are attempts, however rough, to allow a deduction for the capital costs over something like the actual useful life of wasting assets to properly reflect the taxpayer's income. Second, completely arbitrary rules are used in some situations as a matter of administrative convenience. Third, certain types of capital costs are allowed to be written off immediately or over a short period to encourage investments in particular types of assets or to achieve other non-fiscal goals.

In the *United States*, depreciation rules have been modified repeatedly, and the development of the rules reflects both changes intended to simplify the administration of the system and changes in the attitude toward using accelerated depreciation allowances as an incentive for particular forms of investment. Historically depreciation was mandatory and was based on the useful lives of assets to reflect actual experience with particular types of assets. The system was initially based on the experience of the particular taxpayer, but then relaxed to provide for generally applicable classes of assets that allowed the taxpayer to vary the applicable lives somewhat. Straight-line methods were generally used, although more recently accelerated methods were permitted to reflect the fact that certain assets declined more in value in early years and to provide investment incentives.

The system was changed substantially in 1981. Under the Accelerated Cost Recovery System (ACRS), class lives were established for all assets that generally had no relation to the actual useful life of the asset, either in general or in the hands of the particular taxpayer.[246] For example, real estate was assigned a class life of fifteen years. Accelerated depreciation methods were applied to the class lives, which substantially increased the availability of early deductions. The high-water mark of non-economic depreciation policies came in 1981. Since that time, while the class-life system has been retained, most class lives are now more realistic (although not entirely so) and straight-line depreciation is required for some assets. For example, the useful life of commercial real estate has been extended to thirty-nine years and straight-line depreciation is required. Congress has continued to adjust depreciation rates, however, in light of changing economic conditions. In 2002, Congress adopted a 'temporary' provision that allowed an additional depreciation deduction equal to 30% of the tax cost of an asset in the first year that qualifying property (generally, tangible personal property and leasehold improvements) was placed in service. In 2003, Congress increased the amount of the first year's deduction to 50% of the qualifying property's tax cost. This 50% deduction is still available in 2009.

With respect to intangibles, traditionally, all assets that had a determinable useful life could be amortized over that life. Other assets, such as goodwill, were not amortizable. These rules put substantial pressure on the allocation of costs between arguably short-lived intangibles such as customer lists, favourable

246. United States, IRC, s. 168.

contracts, and covenants not to compete and non-depreciable goodwill. In response to a large amount of litigation over these issues, a statutory amendment in 1993 allowed all non-financial intangibles, including goodwill, obtained in the acquisition of all or part of a business, to be amortized over a fifteen-year period on a straight-line basis.[247] This simplifying rule allows a deduction for goodwill amortization but also requires that assets with actual useful lives of less than fifteen years be amortized over the uniform fifteen-year period.

A number of special rules continue to apply for certain types of assets and expenditures. Research and experimentation costs can be deducted currently or amortized over a five-year period at the election of the taxpayer. Pollution control facilities are subject to special rules, as are some costs in natural resource exploitation. Subject to some limitations, up to $250,000 of costs for tangible property and computer software used in a trade or business can be deducted currently. Special rules limit the deductions with respect to cars, computers, and other assets that would typically be used for both business and personal purposes.

Canada has a comprehensive system of capital cost recovery for all tangible and intangible capital assets.[248] Tangible assets and certain intangibles that have a limited useful life, such as patents and trademarks, are classified into different 'classes' (currently, there are 40 classes), and rates of depreciation are prescribed for each class based on rough estimates of their useful lives. Cost-recovery deductions are determined on a declining balance basis for all of the assets in a class or pool. The cost of purchases of property of a particular class is added to the pool. In the case of a disposition, the lesser of the cost of the asset or the proceeds of disposition is subtracted from the pool. If the result in the pool at the end of a year is negative, that amount is included in income as recaptured depreciation. In contrast, if there is a positive balance in the pool at the end of the year and there are no assets left in the class, the unrecovered balance is currently deductible. Although the maximum amount of depreciation is determined for each pool or class on the basis of the prescribed rate of depreciation, the taxpayer can choose on a year-to-year basis to deduct a smaller amount. Thus, a taxpayer without sufficient income to absorb the available depreciation deductions may postpone the depreciation deduction until later years rather than taking the deduction and creating an operating loss.

Land does not qualify for depreciation. Similarly, any asset that is not acquired for the purpose of earning income cannot qualify for depreciation. Certain types of property, such as pollution control equipment and certain manufacturing and processing assets, qualify for accelerated depreciation.

Prior to 1972, the cost of goodwill and other intangible capital property with no limited useful life could not be deducted and was not covered by the capital cost recovery system. Legislation, later amended, now provides for the deduction of 75% of the costs of intangible capital property on a declining basis at 7%.[249] On the sale of such property, 75% of the proceeds are taken into account.

247. United States, IRC, s. 197.
248. Canada, ITA s. 20(1)(a), Regulation 1100, and Sch. B.
249. Canada, ITA ss 14 and 20(1)(b).

The expenses and proceeds are accounted for on a pooled basis using the same techniques as those for the capital cost recovery system.

The *Australian* system, like the Canadian, begins with a general prohibition on the current deductibility of capital costs. Various depreciation regimes were then provided for plant and equipment, buildings, mines, a host of specific expenditures on tangible assets, and a limited class of intangibles such as patents. In general, there is no amortization for goodwill or other similar intangibles. However, one-half of the capital gain is exempt from tax on the sale of a business (including goodwill) with a net worth of less than $6,000,000 or turnover less than $2,000,000. This exemption is in addition to the general 50% discount in the case of individuals, so that 25% of the total gain may be all that is taxed. In addition, in some situations, capital costs that do not fit within the statutory or case law pattern are effectively not taken into account for tax purposes at all. This phenomenon of so-called 'nothings' underlines the lack of a comprehensive system for depreciation. In 2001, the capital cost recovery provisions were rewritten to bring them all within a single framework rather than the patchwork that had previously prevailed and to broaden the costs that could be recovered.[250] The coverage is still not comprehensive, especially in the area of intangibles. The government subsequently expanded the expenses entitled to cost recovery in 2005 but purchased goodwill is still generally excluded until the time of sale.

Where depreciation is available, it is based on estimated useful lives and a choice of the straight line ('prime cost') or declining balance ('diminishing value') method. Prior to 1999, there were significant elements of acceleration in the system, but these were abolished for assets acquired in later years. This change required revision of the tables of useful lives published by the fiscal authorities. These had not been reviewed for many years because they were only indirectly relevant to the rate of depreciation during the 1980s and 1990s. Hence, some of the pain of the 1999 change was delayed for assets with lives in the tables that were shorter than their actual useful lives. As the revision proceeded, it became evident that there could be devastating effects in some industries, and so since 2002 the government has 'capped' the lives of assets in the affected areas (mainly airlines, energy production, and primary production). A further element of acceleration came back into the system in 2006 when the loading for the declining balance method was increased from 150% to 200%. The tables of useful lives are not binding on taxpayers, who may determine shorter or longer economic lives. Taxpayers may recalculate the useful life over time and must do so if expenditure amounting to 10% more of cost is incurred on the asset in an income year. Expensing was allowed for assets with a life of less than three years and for *de minimis* amounts until 2002. Now a simplified elective pooling system applies for assets costing less than $1,000 that operates on an assumed life of four years. If this system is elected, all assets under that amount must be included. Some provisions allow expensing, and even deductions in excess of amounts actually expended for incentive purposes with regard to certain activities (e.g., research and development). Depreciation for

250. Australia, ITAA 1997, Division 40.

buildings is allowed under a separate regime on a straight-line basis at 2.5% or 4% depending on the nature of the asset. Oddly, the deduction is recaptured on sale even though the purchaser must use the cost of the original person who incurred the expenditure in calculating depreciation deductions (i.e., the purchaser does not get a step-up in the cost of the property). The effect is that, in tax terms, a taxpayer is better off holding a building until it falls down or is replaced than selling it. Even though intellectual property is included under the unified capital allowances regime, it is also given a fixed statutory life and is written off on a straight-line basis.

In the *United Kingdom*, the class of assets subject to depreciation is more limited than in other systems.[251] Depreciation is only rarely allowed, for example, for office buildings or retail stores. The principal current depreciable asset is machinery and equipment; the allowances for industrial buildings and agricultural buildings are being phased out by 2011. The rate of depreciation has varied greatly, and neither the period of depreciation nor the rate has had any connection to the actual useful life of the asset. In the 1970s, an immediate write-off was allowed for machinery and equipment, and 50% of the cost of an industrial building could be deducted immediately, with the remainder recoverable over twenty-five years on a straight-line basis. Later changes reduced the rates of recovery to straight-line depreciation over twenty-five years for buildings and a pooled basis for machinery with a 25% rate. In 2008, the 25% rate was reduced to 20%, but there is also now an annual investment allowance of £50,000. In 2009, as one of the measures to assist with cash flow in the economy, the 20% rate is to be increased to 40%. Taxpayers can elect not to claim the deduction in whole or in part in a particular year, thus deferring the deduction to a later period. The present government has introduced new and more generous reliefs for expenditure on certain assets; the list currently includes energy saving and other environmentally friendly assets, business premise renovations, and the conversion of certain types of buildings into flats (but not high-value flats).[252]

In *Germany*, as a general rule, tax accounting follows commercial accounting. With respect to depreciation, tax law contains several specific provisions that in turn influence commercial statements. First, depreciation for wasting assets is based on useful lives as determined in depreciation tables published by the Ministry. The tables are not binding on either the tax authorities or taxpayers, but are followed in the vast majority of cases, and deviations must be specifically justified. Until 2007, the taxpayer could choose between the straight-line method and a declining balance method for wasting assets. The justification for the declining balance method was that the decline in market value in the early years of use is high and maintenance expenses low, while in later years the reverse is true. In 2008, the declining balance method was abolished to generate tax revenue to offset reductions in the corporate tax rate. Currently, although there is discussion to re-introduce it as a means for promoting economic growth, the taxpayer can only

251. United Kingdom, Capital Allowances Act 2001 (CAA).
252. United Kingdom, CAA, s. 39 et seq.

use the straight-line method based on the estimated useful life of the asset. Special rates of depreciation exist for buildings. Since 1986, business goodwill can be depreciated on a fifteen-year straight-line basis (different principles based on case law apply to professional goodwill). Depreciation can also be based on the production from the asset, comparing the performance in the year with the total anticipated production.

Several provisions allow accelerated depreciation to encourage investment in particular assets (e.g., environmental protection, hospitals, ships, small businesses). With respect to investments in former East Germany, an immediate deduction of 50% of certain acquisition and construction costs was initially allowed but has been phased out. Special provisions also existed for investments in Berlin. These rules apply only if the taxpayer includes the deductions in the financial statements.

While extraordinary depreciation can be taken for technical or economic obsolescence or heavy use, no general deduction for impairment losses is available for all sources of income. However, in the calculation of business profits, a special statutory rule allows all assets (including land and stock interests) to be written down to 'going concern value'. The basic notion is that the business assets should be valued as if the entire business had to be disposed of to one potential buyer and the appropriate part of the purchase price had been allocated to the asset in question. The going concern value cannot be less than the price the asset would have obtained if it had been sold separately, or more than the replacement cost. The taxpayer has the burden of proof as to going concern value, and the impairment must also be included in the financial statements. Although the going-concern principle introduces substantial uncertainty in the calculation of income, it is an accepted part of German rules on income determination. Such write-down has to be recaptured in later years following a recovery of the original value.[253]

In *Japan*, the taxpayer can elect between either straight-line or declining balance methods based on useful life tables that are determined by the tax authorities, subject to some exceptions (e.g., only the straight-line method is available for buildings).[254] The tables are extremely detailed and are sometimes revised. Although it is hard to generalize, the tables seem to reflect realistic estimates of actual lives. However, there are some attempts to use artificial useful lives to encourage particular investments, and accelerated depreciation is available as an incentive to encourage certain investments. Assets that are not used for business purposes cannot be depreciated.

In *France*, the same rules normally apply for accounting and tax purposes. In principle, depreciation or amortization is allowed for all assets the benefits of which are likely to be exhausted over a determinable period. Subject to this condition, according to case law, amortization of acquired goodwill (clientele) is now possible provided that such asset is clearly identifiable and, because of its characteristics, distinguishable from the other elements of the goodwill.

253. Germany, ITA, ss 6 para. 1 no. 1 sent. 4 and no. 3 sent. 3.
254. Japan, ITA, s. 49 and CTA, s. 31.

Since 2005, however, when commercial accounting rules relating to fixed assets were changed to adapt them to new international accounting standards,[255] depreciation rules for tax purposes have been more often at variance with rules for accounting purposes, either for the sake of simplification (e.g., no dividing of an asset into its components in certain circumstances) or to keep previous rules applicable (e.g., no deduction from cost of the probable market value of the asset at the end of its useful life; departure from true useful lives for assets other than components, in which case useful life is determined by reference to generally accepted business practices). Both straight-line and declining balance methods are generally used, and special incentive provisions encourage certain investments (e.g., acquired software). These incentives typically allow depreciation over periods shorter than normal useful lives, generally twelve months.[256] If the taxpayer is operating at a loss, in certain circumstances, all or a portion of the otherwise available depreciation can be deferred and carried over to later years without limitation.[257]

In *The Netherlands*, the rules regarding depreciation are quite flexible. All depreciation methods are allowed as long as they are used consistently and meet the standard of 'good business practice'. This standard requires that depreciation be based on historical cost and not replacement value. In 2001, a general rule was introduced regarding minimum useful life and, since 2007, buildings generally cannot be depreciated below certain percentages of their (realistic) real property tax value.[258] Previously, accelerated depreciation methods were used to encourage certain types of investments but were replaced with a direct grant program, which was in turn allowed to effectively expire. Currently, there are accelerated deductions for small-scale investments and investments in energy efficiency and the environment, and several provisions allow arbitrary depreciation. Such depreciation methods are available for certain assets, such as assets specifically designated for environmental protection, employee-friendly tools and equipment, and assets used in the promotion of the Dutch movie industry.

Sweden allows depreciation deductions over standardized lives that are shorter than the actual useful lives for machinery and equipment. Depreciation rates are 20% straight-line or 30% declining balance, at the taxpayer's choice. For buildings, the depreciation is straight-line over a period depending on the type of building (e.g., residential houses are depreciated over a period of fifty years and normal factory buildings over a twenty-five year period). The rules on the deduction of maintenance costs are quite liberal and the combined deductions for real estate are quite generous. Research and development costs are currently deductible in accordance with generally accepted accounting principles. Costs involved in inventory production are capitalized and deducted when the product is sold, in accordance with financial accounting rules.

255. France, Regulation CRC 2004-06, 23 Nov. 2004.
256. France, Circular 4, A-13-05.
257. France, CGI, s. 39 B.
258. Netherlands, ITA, Art. 3.30a.

4. EDUCATIONAL COSTS

Education costs can involve personal consumption, business-related current expenses, or investment in 'human capital' depending on the circumstances in which they arise. All of the systems take generally the same approach, disallowing the expenses of basic education but allowing deductions where the taxpayer is improving or maintaining existing skills. Thus, in the *United States*, expenses that maintain or improve the taxpayer's skills in an existing trade or business are generally deductible. However, if the expenses in fact qualify the taxpayer for a new trade or business or are necessary to meet the minimum educational requirements of a trade or business, no deduction is allowed.[259] The test is an objective one; even if the taxpayer never intends to and never does enter the new profession, the expenses are not deductible. Thus, an accountant who attends law school cannot deduct the expenses even if he undertakes the expenses only to further his accountancy career, since he is in fact qualified for a new trade or business. For non-deductible expenses, there is no provision for the amortization of the investment in 'human capital'.

In *Sweden*, in general, the same approach is taken. Educational expenses are usually not deductible. This is especially the case where they result in qualification for a new position. On the other hand, educational expenses to maintain an existing competence are deductible. Similarly, in *Japan*, educational expenses are usually not deductible, although employees can deduct such expenses if the education or training is required by the employer.

In *Canada*, education expenses are not deductible. The expenses are viewed as personal, capital, or a mixture of both. Continuing education or training expenses of a taxpayer already established in a business are deductible as ordinary business expenses. Education or training expenses incurred by employees are not deductible. A tax credit is available for certain postsecondary school and occupational training costs.

The *Australian* system is along the same lines, with only educational costs involved in an existing trade or profession being deductible, although for historical reasons they must be in excess of a fixed threshold amount.

The *United Kingdom* followed these principles until 1991 when a deduction for qualifying vocational training payments was introduced. The deduction had to be abandoned in 2001 owing to fraud. There are various exclusions from tax for training or retraining courses provided by employers so that the employee incurs no tax liability in respect of these costs incurred by the employer.[260] Business-related expenses, such as the cost of attending conferences, are usually deductible under general principles; there are no special rules for conference expenditures.

In *Germany*, there was a distinction between 'basic' and 'continuing' education, with only expenses for the latter being deductible. Nevertheless, in recent case

259. United States, Treasury Regulations (Treas. Regs.), 1.162-5.
260. United Kingdom, ITEPA, s. 250 et seq.

law the deductibility of education costs has been extended significantly. Under this case law, even the cost of a first academic qualification incurred to improve the career prospects of the taxpayer in his current profession is deductible.[261] This jurisprudence has led to an amendment of the Income Tax Act. Basic education costs are classified as personal expenditures and are deductible only to a limited extent under the provision for 'special' personal costs (from 2009 on, €5,000).[262]

In *The Netherlands*, education expenses incurred by an employee to maintain his current skills are treated as employment expenses and are not deductible. Costs incurred in training for a higher-level job or other occupation are personal expenses that are nonetheless deductible, but only to the extent that they exceed €500, but not €15,000.

The *French* system allows a deduction for educational costs to maintain or improve skills and, in the case of employees, to qualify for a new position. In addition, students (up to twenty-five years old) may either be included in the fiscal household of the parents or taxed separately. In the first case, the result is a decrease in the parents' income tax because of a special tax credit combined with the increase in the number of (family) shares generally (see Subpart E, section 1, below) or with the grant of a standard deduction in the case of children who are married or members of a civil partnership or/and have family dependants.[263] And, where separate taxation is the case, payments made by the parents to the student can be deducted within limits as far as adult children are concerned.[264]

In *Japan*, theoretically, educational expenses are deductible if they are necessary for business. However, in practice, no educational expenses can be deducted from taxable income except for (i) those specifically provided in the law as tax-deductible (such as expenses for obtaining a driver's license)[265] or (ii) those with an apparent relationship with business, such as tuition for certain business seminars.

5. DEDUCTION OF PERSONAL COSTS

As discussed in the Country Descriptions in Part One, personal costs are in general reflected in a personal exemption or personal allowance, which in effect frees from tax a certain minimum level of income. In addition, some systems allow a deduction for specific personal costs, such as medical costs or personal losses.

261. Federal Tax Court (*Bundesfinanzhof*), judgment of 20 Jul. 2006 VI R 26/05.
262. Germany, ITA, s. 10 para. 1 no. 7.
263. France, CGI, ss 6-3 and 196 B.
264. France, CGI, s. 156 II 2.
265. Japan, ITA, s. 57-2, para. 2.

5.1. Interest

All of the systems allow a deduction in general for interest expenses incurred in connection with income-earning activities, and all countries other than the United Kingdom allow a deduction for such expenses in connection with personal investment activities. The deduction is sometimes limited to the amount of current investment income to prevent a current deduction for interest when the income is deferred. In addition, some systems require the capitalization of certain interest expense, typically interest incurred in connection with the production of long-lived assets such as buildings. The most striking difference in the systems here considered is in the treatment of interest expense that does not have a connection with income-producing activities. From a theoretical point of view, whether personal interest – that is, interest related to personal consumption – should be deductible has been the subject of considerable debate. There is general agreement that consumption should be included in the tax base. However, personal interest can be viewed, not as additional consumption, but simply as the cost of a preference for current as opposed to deferred consumption. By borrowing to consume now, the cost of the consumption is increased by the amount of the interest expense but the absolute amount of the consumption, which is the appropriate measure of the tax base, has not changed. The person who borrows to finance current consumption should be treated no differently from a tax point of view than the person who finances the consumption by 'dissaving' and selling income-producing assets. If this analysis is accepted, a deduction for personal interest expense would be appropriate.

On the other hand, if the starting point of the analysis is that business-related expenses are the only type of expenses that should be deducted, personal interest would be disallowed. In addition, allowing a deduction for personal interest is often thought to encourage consumption rather than savings, which may not be desirable from an economic point of view. From a structural point of view, if a distinction is made between deductible and non-deductible interest, some mechanism must be provided for distinguishing between the two classes of interest expense. These varying considerations have played out differently in the systems examined here.

In the *United States*, prior to 1986, all interest expense was allowed as a deduction without any limitations on the deduction of personal interest. Limits on the deduction of personal interest were imposed in 1986 to restrict the deduction for personal interest to interest on loans used to acquire a personal residence (within some dollar limitations). In addition, interest may be deducted on up to $100,000 of loans secured by a residence, no matter to what use the proceeds are put.[266] Complex tracing rules are applied to assign the interest expense to the appropriate category, based on the flow of funds, with some simplifying assumptions.

266. United States, IRC, s. 163(h).

In *Germany*, personal interest is, in principle, not deductible. Prior to 1974 such interest was fully deductible as a 'special expense'. Until 1994, a limited amount of interest on personal residence mortgages was deductible.

New statutory rules for the allocation of interest expense include a fairly complex tracing approach. Interest on business-related debt is not deductible insofar as there have been 'excessive withdrawals' from the business funds. An 'excessive withdrawal' is deemed to occur if the amount of the withdrawal exceeds both the business profit and the contributions made by the taxpayer to the business in the same period.

The rules in *Canada* are similar. Interest is deductible only if the borrowed funds are used for the purposes of earning income, and personal interest is thus not deductible. A proposal to allow the deduction of home mortgage interest is periodically raised (usually around election time) but rejected as unfair and involving too much revenue loss. Non-deductible personal interest involved in the purchase of a personal asset is also not capitalized despite the fact that the capital gain on the sale of the asset is taxable, although at a preferential rate; the expense may be viewed as relating to the untaxed imputed return on the asset. A tracing-of-funds approach is the primary method used to establish the nature of the interest expense, although other methods, such as an ordering rule and apportionment, are occasionally used if tracing is impossible. It is an accepted standard practice for taxpayers to use their savings or equity to finance consumption and to borrow for income-producing purposes. A recent Supreme Court case held that commingling of borrowed funds and savings did not preclude the taxpayer from deducting interest.[267] Although the taxpayer could not trace the borrowed funds to an income-earning use, it was sufficient for the taxpayer to show that an amount equal to the borrowed funds was being used for an income-earning purpose.

Australia and *Japan* follow the same basic approach. The issue has recently attracted a great deal of interest in Australia. The High Court applied the general anti-avoidance rules to a so-called 'split' loan, which is a product offered by financial institutions under which borrowings finance the purchase of a family home and an investment property. All repayments go to pay down the loan on the home while the interest on the investment property is capitalized, so that the part of the loan relating to that property grows in proportion of the amount borrowed.[268] Further, in two controversial decisions, the courts have denied deductions on loans classified as capital for banking regulatory purposes, although one of these cases is currently being appealed.[269] Conversely, the courts decided in favour of a taxpayer in relation to a capital-protected loan (i.e., the financier accepted recourse only to the asset in exchange for a higher interest rate), but legislation was passed to deny a

267. *The Queen v. Singleton* [2002] 1 CTC 121 (SCC).
268. *Hart* [2004] HCA 26, 217 CLR 216.
269. *Macquarie Finance Ltd* [2005] FCA FC 205, 146 FCR 77 and *St George Bank Ltd* [2008] FCA 453, 69 ATR 634 (currently under appeal).

deduction for that element of the interest payment that related to capital protection.[270]

In the *United Kingdom*, deduction for personal interest was originally allowed without restriction. However, since 1969 the deduction has been subject to substantial limitations.[271] If the interest is not connected to a taxable source of income, such as a trade or rental real estate, it must be related to a 'qualifying purpose' to be deductible. The statutory list of accepted purposes is quite limited and includes investment in a closely held company or employee-controlled company, machinery and equipment used in employment or in a partnership (e.g., a car), and certain types of life annuity. At one time the most important qualifying purpose was the purchase of a personal residence. The deduction was restricted in that it applied only to interest on a loan up to £30,000. Further legislation has reduced the value of this deduction by not allowing it to be set against the top rate otherwise payable and by limiting it first to the basic rate of 25%, then to the lower rate of 20%, then to a notional rate of 15%, and then 10%. It was finally abolished in 2000; the exercise represents an interesting example of how to phase out a relief measure by progressively eroding its value.

In *France*, personal interest is not deductible and more generally, no deduction is allowed for investment-related expenses even when the acquired asset is income-producing (e.g., interest on loans used to acquire investment securities). Interest incurred in connection with rental real estate, however, is deductible.[272] While the acquisition by employees or corporate executives of shares of corporations for which they work has for a long time been considered as a purely personal expense, interest incurred in connection with such acquisitions is now deductible from wages and remuneration earned, provided that such a purchase is useful for their activity and the amount of such interest is not disproportionate.[273] On the other hand, interest expense incurred in connection with certain personal expenses, such as the purchase or building of a personal residence, carries entitlement to special tax credits.[274] In contrast, in *Sweden*, there are in principle no restrictions on the deductibility of interest. Interest connected with a business is deducted from the income in that category. All other interest, including personal interest, is deducted in computing income from capital. In general, a tracing rule is used to determine the treatment of the interest expense. Since business income is taxed at a higher rate than income from capital, a special rule prevents taxpayers from allocating excessive private interest expense from capital income to business income. If the amount of debt allocated to the business results in 'negative' equity when compared to the tax cost of the business assets, interest is calculated on the 'negative' equity using the government borrowing rate plus 1% point. The interest amount is treated as additional income in the business category and as additional expense in the capital

270. *Firth* [2002] FCAFC 95, 120 FCR 450, overridden by Australia, ITAA 1997, Division 247.
271. See United Kingdom, ITA s. 383 et seq.
272. France, CGI, s. 31 I 1-d.
273. France, CGI, s. 83(3) last paragraph.
274. France, CGI, s. 200 *quaterdecies*.

income category, thus in effect reallocating a portion of the excess interest expense to the more lightly taxed capital income.

In 2008, restrictions on interest deductions claimed by corporations were introduced in reaction to a potentially widespread tax planning scheme. A simple description of the scheme is as follows. Parent P sells subsidiary A – with a profitable business – to another subsidiary B. The purchase is financed by a loan from P to B. The loan receivable is transferred as a capital contribution from P to a third subsidiary, C, in a country with low or no taxation of interest income. B starts paying interest on the debt to C. In order for B to receive income covering the interest deduction, A – now a subsidiary of company B – gives a deductible group contribution[275] to B. The combined result is reduction of taxable income in A and resulting increase of income in C (no or low tax). According to the main rule in the new legislation,[276] interest on debt created as described in the first step above is deductible only if the tax rate on interest in the creditor country is 10% or more.

In *The Netherlands*, prior to the 2001 tax reform, personal interest was fully deductible without limitation. After 2001, however, personal interest is not deductible.

5.2. Personal Losses

While losses incurred in connection with personal assets are generally not deductible, in some situations a deduction is allowed if the loss occurs in particular circumstances. Thus, in the *United States*, a loss due to damage to personal assets can be deducted if the damage is attributable to a 'casualty', which has been interpreted to mean a sudden and unexpected event.[277] There is a substantial amount of interpretive material around the issue of what constitutes a casualty, including an administrative rule that termite damage is not sufficiently sudden to qualify for a casualty loss. When available, the amount of the loss is limited to the tax cost of the asset and then is deductible only if the total of all losses exceeds a percentage of the taxpayer's income.

In *Germany*, gains and losses on the disposition of private assets are generally not taken into account. The extension of taxability of private capital gains to real estate sold within ten years after acquisition and other assets sold within one year after acquisition has led to the recognition of private losses either within the same period or under carryback and carryforward rules.[278] These losses can be set off only against gains from the same source. The same holds true for losses on privately held shares and other securities under the new rules on the 'final withholding tax'.[279] Under this new regime, losses arising from the alienation of privately held portfolio securities can be set off only against capital gains arising from

275. Group contributions are deductible if the prerequisites in ITA, Ch. 35 are met.
276. Sweden, ITA, Ch. 24, s. 10 a–e.
277. United States, IRC, s. 163(h).
278. Germany, ITA, s. 23 para. 3 sent. 7–9.
279. Germany, ITA, s. 20 para. 6.

the alienation of privately held portfolio securities. This rule extends to casualty losses. Even if the casualty loss has some business connection, no deduction is allowed (e.g., loss of jewellery on a business trip or a firm outing). However, as discussed in Part One, the German tax system recognizes a general deduction for 'extraordinary expenditures'. The expenditures must be unusually high when compared with similarly situated taxpayers and must be unavoidable. Casualty losses are covered by this provision. It is highly disputed whether the deduction applies only to uninsurable losses.

In *Canada* and *Australia*, casualty losses involving personal property are in general not deductible. However, with respect to 'listed personal property' (referred to in Australia as 'collectables') – that is, stamps, coins, jewellery, art works, etc. – losses are deductible but only against the gains from such property. The loss is limited to the tax cost of the property. The *United Kingdom* restricts the loss on personal-use items that are tangible movable property by excluding any gain or loss where the assets are disposed of (including worthlessness) for less than £6,000 and by excluding any gain or loss where the asset is tangible movable property with a useful life of less than fifty years.[280] Australia uses a similar rule to eliminate small gains on non-listed personal assets, but based on cost, so that records do not need to be kept if the cost is below the limit ($10,000). These results all follow from the structure of the capital gains legislation in these jurisdictions.

In *France, Japan, The Netherlands*, and *Sweden*, gains and losses on private assets are not generally taken into account regardless of how those gains or losses come about. Thus, for example, in The Netherlands, neither the loss on an uninsured personal residence destroyed by fire nor the gain from insurance proceeds in excess of basis is relevant for tax purposes. In contrast, in Sweden, personal losses on personal dwellings are taken into account because capital gains on such dwellings are taxable. In Japan, insurance premiums for certain kinds of earthquake insurance are tax-deductible to a limited extent.[281]

5.3. Medical Expenses

Medical expenses may be deducted or claimed as a tax credit in several of the systems, although they are viewed as personal expenses. In the *United States*, where there is no comprehensive public health-care system, a deduction is available for medical expenses that exceed a percentage of income.[282] What constitutes 'medical' treatment has been interpreted quite broadly, although there is a statutory prohibition against the deduction of the costs of cosmetic surgery. Premiums for private health insurance are deductible but, because of the percentage-of-income threshold, persons who are insured typically do not benefit from the deduction.

280. United Kingdom, TCGA, ss 45 and 262.
281. Japan, ITA, s. 77.
282. United States, IRC, s. 213.

As discussed with respect to fringe benefits in section 1, employer-provided health care is not taxable.

Canada has a publicly funded health-care system, although not all costs are covered. A credit is available for 15% (the lowest rate of federal tax) of the medical costs over a threshold amount of the lesser of $1,500 (indexed to inflation) or 3% of income. The credit is available for a lengthy list of medical costs. If a clearly legitimate cost is not listed, no credit is available. There is usually some time lag between the development of new medical technology and its addition to the list of qualifying costs in the medical expense credit. Canada also provides a similar credit for persons with severe and prolonged disabilities to recognize the non-itemizable expenses that such persons incur. The *Australian* system provides a similar credit of 20% for medical costs in excess of $1,500 and also of 30% of the cost of private health insurance (even though Australia has universal public health-care).[283] Health expenses in connection with work-related injuries may be deducted under the general deduction provisions where such injuries are a clear occupational hazard.

Business-related medical expenses may also be deducted in the *United Kingdom*. There is no general deduction for medical costs, but a limited deduction was at one time available for medical insurance by persons over sixty; this was repealed by the Labour government in 1997. Where medical expenses arise outside the United Kingdom, and are thus not covered by the National Health Service system, special legislation allows an employee to avoid the income inclusion that would otherwise arise if the employer bears the cost of providing medical insurance or treatment.[284]

In *The Netherlands*, medical costs were deductible until 2009 to the extent that they exceeded absolute and percentage-of-income limitations. The deduction has been replaced by a subsidy that is available only for chronically ill and handicapped persons. In *Japan*, medical costs exceeding ¥100,000 per household are deductible.[285]

In *Germany*, there is no specific deduction for private medical expenses. A business deduction is allowed for medical costs that arise from a sickness incurred in the course of business (e.g., radiation sickness in the case of a radiologist, tuberculosis in the case of a pulmonary doctor). No deduction, however, was allowed in the case of a heart attack suffered by a lawyer.

For medical expenses with no business connection, the general deduction for 'extraordinary expenses' above a certain minimum is available for some types of medical expenses.[286] The expenses must be 'direct' medical costs (e.g., doctor's costs, hospital costs, drugs). 'Indirect' costs are not deductible and there is considerable litigation over the 'direct-indirect' distinction. An example of a non-deductible indirect expense is the cost of a move to improve breathing for

283. Australia, ITAA 1936, s. 159P, ITAA 1997, Subdivision 61-G.
284. United Kingdom, ITEPA, s. 325.
285. Japan, ITA, s. 73.
286. Germany, ITA, s. 33.

bronchitis. No deduction is allowed for preventive medical costs. Medical insurance premiums can be deducted subject to limitations as 'special' expenses. Recently, the Constitutional Court has ruled that German legislation must extend the deductibility of insurance cost to a large extent.[287]

Sweden has an extensive public health-care system that provides free or low-cost service. As a result, personal medical costs are not deductible. Employers are not allowed a deduction for the medical expenses of employees, and the benefits are not included in the employees' income.

In *France*, mandatory contributions to French public health-care systems are deductible.[288] Non-reimbursed health costs are considered to be personal, unless they are vital for carrying on an income-producing activity (e.g., dentures for someone who is in charge of public relations).

5.4. Charitable Donations

Most of the systems allow a deduction or credit for contributions to organizations, private or public, that perform charitable, religious, cultural, or educational services. There are typically limits on the deductible amounts based on a percentage of the taxpayer's income. Thus, in the *United States*, gifts to qualifying organizations can, in general, be deducted up to 50% of the taxpayer's income.[289] More restrictive limitations apply for gifts to 'private' foundations – that is, organizations that are not supported by the general public but by one or several large donors. Excess donations can be carried over and deducted in subsequent years to the extent that current deductions do not exceed the limitations. In the case of certain gifts of property, the fair market value of the property is deductible, thus giving a deduction for the appreciation in value of the property that has not been included in the tax base. No deduction is allowed for the contribution of services, although out-of-pocket costs in rendering services to charities may be deducted. If the donor receives some benefit as a result of the contribution, the deductible amount is reduced to the extent of the value of the benefit. There are significant substantiation requirements.

In *Canada*, individuals are entitled to a tax credit of 15% (the lowest rate of federal tax) for the first $200 of contributions to registered charities and 29% (the highest rate of federal tax) for donations in excess of that amount. Gifts must be evidenced by a written receipt, which must be filed with the tax return or maintained if the tax return is filed electronically. Donations are limited to 75% of the taxpayer's income for a year with a five-year carryforward. However, gifts of cultural property and ecologically sensitive land are not subject to this limitation. In the case of a donation of appreciated property, the taxpayer may elect to treat any

287. Federal Constitutional Court (*Bundesverfassungsgericht*), judgment of 13 Feb. 2008 2 BvL 1/06.
288. France, CGI, ss 154 *bis* and 154 *bis*-0 A (self employed) and 831 (employees).
289. United States, IRC, s. 170.

amount between the cost basis of the property and its fair market value as the contribution. The amount elected is also treated as the amount realized on the disposition of the property for purposes of realizing gain.

The *Australian* system has few limitations on charitable deductions, although previously it had similar limits on gifts of appreciated property as Canada. In recent years tax benefits for charitable gifts have been increased in a number of ways. Normally, a gift is a realization event at market value, but the gain is now exempt in some cases of charitable giving and a deduction is allowed for the fair market value of the property. Charitable deductions cannot give rise to a tax loss for a year, but the donor can elect to spread the deduction over five years in the percentages the donor elects. There are elaborate administrative procedures for qualifying an institution as charitable before deductions are allowed, and the administration of these procedures has been tightened in recent years partly because of the more generous concessions now available.[290]

In the *United Kingdom*, a deduction is generally allowed for payments of money to charity. There are also special rules for gifts of land, shares, and securities. Under the UK capital gains tax rules, the transfer of an asset to a qualifying charity gives rise to no chargeable gain to the donor. The receipt of various benefits from the charity may lead to the loss of the deduction.[291]

In the *Japanese* system, charitable contributions are deductible to the extent that they exceed an absolute floor of ¥5,000 and do not exceed 40% of the taxpayer's income. The contribution must be made to a government agency or a limited number of government-approved public-interest organizations. The deduction for gifts of appreciated property is limited to the tax cost of the property.[292]

Charitable contributions are deductible in *The Netherlands* to the extent that their total amount exceeds both 1% of income and €60. The deductible amount may not exceed 10% of income.[293] No restrictions apply if the donor is obliged to make annual gifts for at least five years.

In *Germany*, charitable contributions are deductible as 'special' personal expenses.[294] Contributions must be made to governmental agencies or government-approved organizations. The deduction is generally limited to 20% of a taxpayer's income for the year. In the case of businesses, an alternative limitation of 0.004% of the payroll and turnover may be used. Donations to publicly approved foundations can be deducted up to €1 million over ten years. If an individual gift subject to the 20% limitation exceeds that limit, the deduction can be carried forward to the extent that there is 'excess' limitation in future years.

Normally, for contributions of property the fair market value of the property is deductible. Since private capital gains are not generally taxed, the problem of

290. Australia, ITAA 1997, Division 30, s. 118-60.
291. United Kingdom, ITA ss 413-446 and 518-564; for corporation tax see TA 1988, s. 505 et seq.
292. Japan, ITA, s. 78.
293. Netherlands, ITA, Art. 6.32.
294. Germany, ITA, s. 10b.

appreciated property contributions does not arise. If assets are withdrawn from a business and given to a charity, the withdrawal is not a realization event.[295]

The charitable contribution is denied if the donor receives consideration in return; the transfer is no longer considered to be a 'contribution'. The nature and amount of the contribution must be documented. In 2009 the ECJ ruled that German tax law must extend the deductibility to charities located in other Member States of the European Union.[296]

In *France*, charitable contributions to a wide variety of organizations are entitled to a credit that has progressively replaced previous deductions from income and has become more and more generous over the years. Presently, the credit is generally equal to 66% of the total amount of the contributions, up to a limit of 20% of the taxpayer's taxable income or 60% up to 5/1,000 of the gross receipts of businesses; self-employed taxpayers can elect one or the other of these two limits. Contributions in excess of these limits may be carried forward for the five following years.[297]

Only in *Sweden* are charitable contributions not deductible to any extent and are viewed as a personal expense. Since gifts outside a business context are not treated as realization events, however, any appreciation in respect of the gifted property escapes tax. A Government Committee was appointed in 2008 to make a proposal to allow deductions for charitable contributions.

6. LIMITATIONS ON DEDUCTIONS AND LOSSES

6.1. Illegal Payments, Fines, Penalties

Where expenses are incurred that under normal principles would be deductible but are illegal, a number of the systems limit the deduction. This is sometimes the result of a specific statutory provision – for example, disallowing a deduction for bribes – and sometimes follows from a general principle of denial of deductions that offend '*ordre public*' or public policy. Similarly, the deduction of business-related fines or penalties may also be limited.

In the *United States*, case law established the principle that illegal payments and fines were not deductible if the deduction would 'frustrate sharply defined national or state policies'.[298] Using this 'public policy' principle, the cases disallowed deductions where the payment itself, such as a bribe, was illegal, or where the deductibility of a fine or penalty would reduce its effectiveness. Subsequent legislation narrowed the limitation of deductions on 'public policy' grounds to several statutorily defined situations.[299] A special provision disallows all

295. Germany, ITA, s. 6 para. 1 no. 4.
296. ECJ, 27 Jan. 2009 C-318/07 (*Persche*).
297. France, CGI, ss 200 and 238 *bis*.
298. *Com'r v. Tellier*, 383 US 687 (1966).
299. United States, IRC, s. 162(c).

deductions for expenses (other than for cost of goods sold) incurred in connection with the illegal sale of drugs. Another provision deals with the circumstances in which payments to foreign governmental officials can be deducted.

In *Canada*, until 1990, illegal payments were deductible subject to the ordinary restrictions on deductibility of expenses. This rule parallels the rule with respect to the inclusion in income of illegal amounts. In 1990, a statutory amendment denied the deductibility of bribes and similar payments.[300]

Until 2000, judicial or statutory fines and penalties were not generally deductible because any deduction would lessen the deterrent or regulatory impact of the fine. However, case law and administrative practice permitted a deduction for fines or penalties where the breach of law was relatively minor, the fine could be considered a normal risk of the business, and the breach did not endanger public safety and was not deliberate or the result of negligence. For example, it was held that fines for overloaded trucks are deductible.[301] In 2000, the Supreme Court held that fines levied on an egg farmer for deliberately exceeding his quota were deductible because they were incurred for the purpose of earning income.[302] According to the Court, public policy considerations are irrelevant to the question of the deductibility of fines and penalties. This result was overturned by statute in 2004.[303]

As a result of entering an international convention, in 1999 *Sweden* introduced statutory rules prohibiting the deduction of bribes. The case law before this was not clear but according to the general opinion – not shared by the Swedish contributor to this book – the cost of bribes was considered to be a deductible business cost, at least in practice. Fines are not deductible.

Similarly, in *Japan*, there are no public policy limitations on the deduction of illegal payments as long as the payments can be established as 'necessary' for the business, although the courts may scrutinize the alleged necessity carefully. By a specific statutory provision, fines are not deductible,[304] although fines paid abroad can be deducted if the other requirements for deductibility can be met.

In *France*, all expenses related to business activities are, in principle, deductible regardless of their nature provided they are incurred in the interest of the business. Case law tends, however, to adopt a more restrictive approach in the category of income from non-commercial services (e.g., lawyers, public accountants) for which the Code specifies that, to be deductible, expenses must be 'necessary for the carrying on of the professional activity'.[305] Statutory exceptions to deductibility have recently increased. Since 2007 a general principle prohibits the deduction from commercial and industrial business income of all types of penalties incurred for non-compliance with legal obligations, including those

300. Canada, ITA, s. 67.5.
301. *Day and Ross v. The Queen* [1976] CTC 707 (FCTD).
302. *65302 British Columbia Ltd. v. The Queen* [2000] 1 CTC 57 (SCC).
303. Canada, ITA, s. 67.6.
304. Japan, ITA, s. 45.
305. France, CGI, s. 93 1.

related to the assessment and collection of taxes and to tax evasion.[306] Bribes to foreign public officials are also non-deductible.[307]

In *The Netherlands*, fines and penalties imposed by a Dutch court are not deductible (and reimbursement by the employer of such amounts incurred by an employee is taxable to the employee).[308] Equivalent foreign fines, however, are deductible as are penalties imposed by professional bodies. Like any other business expense, bribes are deductible if they are made for business purposes. The tax authorities generally assume a business purpose to exist if it is demonstrated by the taxpayer that in view of the nature of the business, the amount paid does not deviate from what is commonly paid in similar circumstances. However, it may be difficult in practice to prove that a bribe has actually been paid.

In *Australia*, a specific statutory provision disallows a deduction for fines and penalties, a result that had been reached in case law as well.[309] Illegal payments, however, seem to be allowed in principle under the general deduction rules. It was recently held by the Full Federal Court that a drug dealer was entitled to a deduction when the proceeds of his drug dealing were stolen. Due to the public outrage caused by the decision, the government amended the law to prevent deductions in future to the extent that amounts are incurred directly in relation to an indictable criminal offence for which the taxpayer has been convicted.[310] In line with an OECD recommendation, Australia has also amended its law to deny tax deductions for bribes to foreign public officials.[311]

In the *United Kingdom* particular rules forbid the deduction of any expenditure incurred in making a payment that constitutes the commission of a criminal offence (e.g., bribery) or, if made outside the United Kingdom, would have been a crime if it had taken place in the United Kingdom. A similar rule applies to payments made under a threat of blackmail or, in Scotland, extortion; this does not apply if the crime of blackmail or extortion is committed outside the United Kingdom. Under general principles based on public policy considerations, the payment of a fine is not deductible in computing business profits.[312]

Statutory provisions in *Germany* deal with the deduction of both fines and penalties and illegal payments. Fines and penalties are generally not deductible if imposed by a German, European Union, or foreign court.[313] In the latter case, however, they may be deductible if the penalty is based on considerations in the foreign jurisdiction that are inconsistent with the basic principles of the German legal system. Non-judicially imposed penalties that result from legal infractions are also not deductible, unless the purpose of the penalty is simply to make restitution.

306. France, CGI, s. 39 2.
307. France, CGI, s. 39 2 *bis*.
308. Netherlands, ITA, Art. 3.13-1.c.
309. Australia, ITAA 1997, s. 26-5.
310. Australia, ITAA 1997, s. 26-54, overriding *La Rosa* [2003] FCAFC 125, 129 FCR 494.
311. Australia, ITAA 1997, ss 26-52 and 26-53.
312. *McKnight v. Sheppard* [1999]; STC 669 ITTOIA s. 55 CTA 2009 s. 1304.
313. Germany, ITA, ss 4 para. 5 no. 8, 9 para. 5 and 12 no. 4.

Bribes and similar payments are not deductible if they are of such a nature as to be punishable under the German penal code. In some cases, payments to foreign recipients can be deducted if the recipient is named. From 1999 on, the deduction of payments to foreign recipients has been substantially restricted.[314]

6.2. Expenses Associated with Tax-exempt Income

The question of relating expenses to tax-exempt income in a global system arises when certain categories of income are expressly exempted from tax, such as interest from state and local obligations in the US context. For schedular systems, a similar problem arises in dealing with expenses related to items of income that are not formally exempt but simply do not fall into any taxable category.

In the *United States*, an express statutory rule in general denies a deduction for expenses incurred in connection with tax-exempt income.[315] If an expense is directly related to an item of tax-exempt income, the deduction is denied completely. If expenses are related to several categories of income, an allocation is made based on the amounts of income, or in some cases, the value or cost of the assets generating the income. A special rule applies to interest expense incurred in connection with exempt interest income on state and municipal obligations. In this situation, the interest deduction is denied if the purpose of the borrowing is to purchase or 'carry' tax-exempt securities. Thus, interest expense can be denied if the borrowing allowed the taxpayer to continue to hold tax-exempt securities. In the case of financial institutions, interest expense must be allocated between tax-exempt interest income and other taxable income based on the tax cost of the assets involved.

The deduction of expenses associated with tax-exempt income is also specifically prohibited in *Canada*.[316] However, deduction is allowed for expenses incurred in connection with dividends, even though certain dividends are tax-free, because dividends are expressly excluded from the definition of exempt income. A similar approach applies in *The Netherlands*. In general, in Canada whether an expense is associated with exempt or taxable income is determined under a tracing method. Although capital gains are partially taxable, expenses incurred to generate such gains are not deductible (or capitalized). If the asset generates income (or is acquired for the purpose of generating such income) apart from the potential capital gain, the expenses are fully deductible. The *Australian* system reaches similar results since the general deduction rule requires that the deduction relate to assessable income. Deductions for some expenses related to exempt foreign income are designed to avoid international double taxation, especially for interest expense under new thin capitalization rules introduced in 2001. As in Canada, there is no deduction for the costs incurred in connection with capital gains, although the

314. Germany, ITA, s. 4 para. 5 no. 10.
315. United States, IRC, s. 265.
316. Canada, ITA, s. 18(1)(c).

costs, including carrying costs, generally can be included in the cost basis of the assets in most cases.

In the *United Kingdom*, the schedular system is usually enough to protect the tax base; there is no general principle barring a deduction of expenses related to exempt income – it is all a matter of statutory interpretation for each category of income. The loan relationship rules introduced in 1996 specifically deny a deduction for interest incurred for a trade that is carried on outside the scope of the UK corporation tax; this model has been used frequently since.[317] The United Kingdom insists on distinguishing trading companies from companies with investment businesses, but the same results are reached in this area.[318]

In *Sweden*, in general, expenses are only deductible if associated with a taxable income source. In some cases where income that would otherwise fall in a taxable source is explicitly exempt, the exemption has been interpreted to apply to the gross income and not the net income. Accordingly, the associated expenses were allowed as a deduction against other income in the source. Interest is deductible even if the debt to which it relates does not produce taxable income.

Japan has no explicit rule dealing with deductions relating to tax-exempt income. The limitation flows from the basic rule that to be deductible, expenses must be related to a taxable category of income. The same approach is taken in *France*. When no direct allocation can be made, expenses related to taxed and tax-exempt income in the same income category can be allocated on a gross-income basis.

Germany has a specific statutory rule disallowing the deduction of expenses that have a 'direct economic connection' with exempt income.[319] The most important application of this rule in practice used to occur with respect to foreign or domestic intercompany dividends that were typically exempt under tax treaties, as discussed in Part Four. A limited deduction (60%) is granted for expenditures in connection with dividend income that itself is only taxed up to 60% (if the shares are held by an individual or a partnership in a business context).[320]

6.3. 'Quarantining' and Other Limits or Restrictions on Certain Categories of Expenses

In an otherwise global system, sometimes activities or expenses are treated specially, and expenses and losses in those categories cannot be used to offset other items of income. In effect, there is a schedular overlay on the global system. In explicitly schedular systems, a similar result is achieved if an overall loss in a particular category cannot be used to offset or 'compensate' income in other categories. Limitations have typically been applied in response to deductions

317. United Kingdom, CTA 2009 s. 327 (imported losses).
318. United Kingdom, CTA 2009 Part 16.
319. Germany, ITA, s. 3 para. 1.
320. Germany, ITA, s. 3 para. 2.

generated in tax shelter transactions or in activities in which personal consumption is likely.

The *United States* has an extensive system of limitations on deductibility of losses, the most important of which are the so-called 'passive activity loss' rules. Adopted in response to the widespread use of tax shelters in the 1970s and 1980s, the passive activity loss rules restrict the deductibility of losses that arise in any activity in which the taxpayer does not 'materially participate'.[321] This requirement has been administratively interpreted to require in general that the taxpayer spend at least 500 hours per year in the activity, although there are a number of other situations in which a material participation requirement will be satisfied. Special rules apply to real estate activities.

Losses incurred in passive activities can be used only to offset income from passive activities. In this context, 'portfolio' income, typically investment income, is not passive activity income and cannot be reduced by passive activity losses. Unused losses are suspended and can be used in later years against passive activity income. When the passive activity is completely disposed of in a taxable transaction, suspended losses may be used against other income. While originally aimed at the 'artificial' losses arising in tax shelter activities, the rules can apply to real economic losses where the taxpayer does not meet the material participation test.

The application of the rules on an activity-by-activity basis and the special treatment of portfolio income are extremely complex. In effect, the taxpayer is required to categorize each of his activities into 'normal' business activity, passive activity, and portfolio investments, making an allocation of income and deductions to each category. In addition, to determine if an activity has been disposed of so that suspended losses may be used, the exact scope of each separate activity must be determined. The rules in effect turn the otherwise global system of income definition into a schedular system in which each activity is potentially a separate income category.

There are some other, less extensive, limitations on the deductibility of certain expenses. The deduction of investment interest expense not incurred in a trade or business is limited to the amount of investment income, including realized capital gains in some cases.[322] Expenses incurred in connection with the business use of a residence – for example, an office in the home or the rental of a summer house – are limited to the income the activity generates.[323] As discussed previously, capital losses can generally be deducted only against capital gains, although a limited deduction against ordinary income is allowed.

In the case of unreimbursed expenses of employees or expenses involved in income-producing activities that do not amount to a trade or business, the expenses can be deducted only to the extent that they exceed 2% of income. The effect of this limitation is to reduce substantially the availability of deductions for a large

321. United States, IRC, s. 469.
322. United States, IRC, s. 163(d).
323. United States, IRC, s. 280A.

number of taxpayers. Unlike other countries, no specific lump-sum deduction is granted to employees as a substitute for the deduction of these expenses.

In *Sweden*, losses in the category of business income cannot be used to reduce income in other taxable categories. The loss can be carried forward without limitation against business income in future years. The same rule applies to income from employment. There are, however, some exceptions. Losses from business as an artist can be offset against employment income. Business losses during the initial five years of the business are deductible against employment income (up to SEK 100,000 per year). A loss on the termination of a business can be deducted against income from capital.

A different technique is used for losses in the category of income from capital. The loss is converted into a credit at a 30% rate (the basic rate on income from capital) for up to SEK 100,000 and at a 21% rate for the excess. The credit can then be used to offset tax on income in the other categories. The restriction on excess losses is intended to limit the ability to use current losses (principally from interest deductions in highly leveraged investments) where the gain on the investment is deferred.

In *Japan*, losses are restricted as a result of the schedular system. Losses in the dividend, occasional, and miscellaneous categories cannot be used against other types of income. Timber and retirement income are calculated separately. The taxpayer can elect to have dividend income and interest income calculated separately.

A similar system applies in the *United Kingdom*. The UK distinguishes between relief carried forward to be set against income from the same source and 'sideways' relief where the loss is applied against other types of income. It is usually possible to carry losses forward indefinitely to be set against later income from the same source. It is sometimes possible to carry a loss backwards.[324]

Thus, where income arises under ITTOIA Part 3 (Land) whether in the United Kingdom or abroad and the taxpayer is subject to income tax, losses may only be carried forward and set against other income from the property business (which is taken to include all the various pieces of property in one trade). Sideways relief is also available – for the loss-making year and the next year – in calculating net income. It follows that the loss cannot be set against capital gains. A less restrictive rule applies to losses from property businesses for corporation tax. Here the loss can be set off against any sort of (income) profits.

Losses arising in a business can be used sideways and set against income in other categories for the same and, this time, the preceding year. Any unused loss can be carried forward and set off against income profits indefinitely but only if they are income profits *of the same trade*.[325] Because sideways relief was abused, there is now a £25,000 cap on sideways relief for trading losses if the taxpayer is not actively involved in the business. There is also a complete ban on tax-generated

324. United Kingdom, ITA, Part 4.
325. United Kingdom, ITA, s. 83 et seq.

losses.[326] More generous loss offset rules in the early years of a trade allow the loss to be carried back and set off against general income of earlier years.[327] There are also more generous rules for terminal losses. In the case of wholly foreign trades, the loss must be set against foreign profits.

For those subject to capital gains tax, capital losses can be used only against capital gains, with an indefinite carryforward, but (generally) no carryback, of excess capital losses.[328] Trading losses can sometimes be set against capital gains, but capital losses cannot be set against ordinary income. If a trading loss is set off against capital gains, the £25,000 cap for losses where the taxpayer is not active in the business applies here also. More relaxed rules apply for corporation tax, but there is still a bar on the use of capital losses against income. Sometimes, for example, in the case of income from securities or dividends from shares accruing to those subject to income tax, no deductions are allowed and so no loss can arise in the first place.

Under the *Canadian* system, as a general rule, the net results from the various income sources are consolidated in computing total taxable income. However, some special rules operate to limit certain types of losses. Capital cost recovery allowances with respect to rented depreciable property cannot be deducted in excess of the income the particular property generates. In general, capital losses are deductible only against capital gains, and capital losses on certain personal use assets such as coins, stamps, and the like can be deducted only against gains on such assets. In addition, the lifetime exemption for capital gains in respect of farm property and shares of small business corporations is reduced by the taxpayer's cumulative net loss from investments, thus in effect restricting the deductibility of such losses. To the extent that business losses cannot be deducted in the current year, they can be carried back for three years and forward for twenty years. Capital losses can be carried back for three years and forward indefinitely, but are deductible only against capital gains.

Australia has a similar treatment for capital losses. For a brief period in the 1980s, there were rules restricting interest deductions on real property investments to the income the property generated.

In *The Netherlands*, since the introduction in 2001 of the three boxes of income for individuals, a loss in income boxes 1 and 2 (i.e., not box 3 losses regarding capital income) can be carried back three years and forward nine years to offset income of the same box (and, with a small exception, not income of another box). Personal deductions, however, reduce income in boxes 1, 3, and 2, in that order, with any excess being carried forward to future years and applied to income in the boxes in the same order.

Germany as a rule allows losses in particular income categories to be used against income in other categories. In recent years, however, tax legislation has severely restricted these deductions. Losses incurred by individuals with respect to privately held capital property (depending on the length of the holding

326. United Kingdom, ITA, ss 74A–74D.
327. United Kingdom, ITA, ss 72–74.
328. United Kingdom, TCGA, s. 2; note also s. 16A on restriction of relief for capital losses where avoidance is involved.

period – ten years for real estate and one year for other assets such as portfolio securities) can be set off only against gains from the same source.[329] For business or professional taxpayers, all losses from industrial and breeding activities, as well as from particular financial derivatives and certain shareholder loans, can be deducted only against profits from the same source of income.[330] A provision that allowed set-off for losses with respect to domestic shareholdings but restricted set-off for foreign shareholdings[331] was declared invalid by the ECJ.[332]

All other losses can be offset against other profits in the relevant tax period. If the losses exceed the profits of any tax period, they can be carried back to the last tax period up to an amount of €511,500.[333] All remaining losses can be carried forward to future tax periods.[334] But again there are limitations: While an amount of €1 million annually can be deducted without constraint, only 60% of the excess income can be set off by former losses. Non-used losses can be carried forward to the next period.

No deduction is granted with respect to capital losses where the corresponding gain would not be taxable (i.e., where the holding period requirement would not be met) and hobby losses. Moreover, no loss is attributable a partner in a limited partnership insofar as the loss exceeds his capital contribution.[335] Special rules in connection with foreign losses are discussed in Part Four.

In *France*, in principle, the positive and negative results of the various income categories are consolidated, but there are a number of anti-avoidance rules that limit the offset possibilities. Typically, where those rules apply, losses can be taken only against income in the same category in the same year or in the following six or ten years, depending on the type of income. These anti-avoidance rules apply to losses from rental real estate in excess of €10,700 (not considering interest, the excess of which is automatically carried forward), losses from activities in which the taxpayer does not participate on a personal and permanent basis, portfolio investment losses, and losses from hobby farming.[336] Long-term capital losses in business can only be deducted against long-term capital gains, with excess losses qualifying for a ten-year carryforward.[337] Real property personal investment losses are not taken into account at all.[338]

The following **Table II-2** summarizes some of the deduction rules discussed in Subpart C. The notation 'limited deduction' indicates that either the class of costs deductible is restricted in some fashion or that there is a limit on the amount deductible – for example, a non-deductible floor or a ceiling on deductible amounts. In addition, the generality of the table does not capture many of the refinements, such as the distinction frequently made between domestic and foreign illegal payments.

329. Germany, ITA, ss 20 para. 6 and 23 para. 3 sent. 7–9.
330. Germany, ITA, s. 15 para. 4.
331. Germany, ITA, s. 2a para. 1 no. 3.
332. ECJ, 29 Mar. 2007 C-347/04 (*Rewe Zentralfinanz*).
333. Germany, ITA, s. 10d para. 1.
334. Germany, ITA, s. 10d para. 2.
335. Germany, ITA, s. 15a.
336. France, CGI, ss 156 I and 150-0 D 11.
337. France, CGI, s. 39 *quindecies* I-2.
338. France, CGI, s. 150 VD.

Some Aspects of the Tax Base: Deductions

	Commuting Costs	*Entertainment Expenses*	*Illegal Payments*	*Child-Care Costs*	*Personal Interest*	*Medical Expenses (non-business-related)*	*Charitable Contributions*
Australia	No deduction	No deduction	Deductions limited	No deduction	No deduction	Limited credit	Deduction with generous limit
Canada	No deduction	Percentage limitation (no deduction for most employees)	No general limitation (bribes and fines non-deductible)	Limited deduction	No deduction	Limited credit	Limited credit
France	Limited deduction	Full deduction if related to business	No general limitation	No deduction; limited credit	No deduction	No deduction	Limited credit
Germany	Deduction (reinstated by Constitutional Court)	Limited deduction	No deduction	Standard deductible allowance; actual expenses in excess deductible	No deduction	Limited deduction	Limited deduction
Japan	No deduction	Full deduction for individual; limited for corporation	No general limitation	No deduction	No deduction	Limited deduction	Limited deduction

Some Aspects of the Tax Base: Deductions Contd

	Commuting Costs	*Entertainment Expenses*	*Illegal Payments*	*Child-Care Costs*	*Personal Interest*	*Medical Expenses (non-business-related)*	*Charitable Contributions*
The Netherlands	Limited deduction	Limited deduction	No general limitation	Limited deduction	No deduction	Limited deduction	Limited deduction
Sweden	Limited deduction	Limited deduction; standard values	No deduction	No deduction	Fully deductible	No deduction	No deduction
United Kingdom	No deduction	No deduction unless own staff	No deduction	No deduction but tax credit system	Limited deduction (e.g., interest in business)	No deduction (insurance premiums for over 59 deductible)	Limited deduction
United States	No deduction	Percentage limitation	Deductions limited	No deduction; limited credit	Limited deduction (personal residence)	Limited deduction	Limited deduction

Subpart D. Accounting

All systems must contain rules governing the assignment of the various items involved in the computation of taxable income to taxable periods. Since the same task must be performed for financial accounting purposes, a basic question in all systems is the extent to which the timing rules used in determining financial income also control questions of timing for tax purposes. While all the systems considered here use commercial accounting principles and concepts to some extent, they also generally recognize the need for special tax rules in many situations. The most obvious case where tax rules are needed is where the taxpayer, typically an individual employee or investor, does not normally keep commercial books and records. Thus, all systems recognize a simplified 'cash' method of accounting for some taxpayers. In addition, and more fundamentally, in some cases, the goals and purposes of financial accounting are deemed to be so different from the requirements of the tax system that the results produced by the financial accounting rules are viewed as inappropriate for tax purposes. Here, there is a wide variation among the countries concerning the degree to which financial accounting principles are followed in the tax system. The differences rest in part on the extent to which legally binding accounting rules are incorporated into the tax system, in contrast to accounting principles that are developed on the basis of professional standards. In the latter case, the flexibility allowed by the accounting principles is often not accepted for tax purposes.

The following materials examine the basic tax accounting methods used and their relation to commercial accounting principles and then consider some specific situations in which special tax rules have been developed.

1. BASIC ACCOUNTING METHODS

In the *German* system, the method of accounting is determined by the category of income involved.[339] Thus, for example, a taxpayer may use one method for computing business income and another for computing income from employment. The 'excess income' method, which is essentially a cash method of accounting,[340] is used to determine income from employment, capital, rents and royalties, miscellaneous income, and the income of small proprietorships and partnerships. Income is recognized when the taxpayer receives money or other assets at his disposition. Checks are treated as cash and taxable on receipt as long as the check clears in the normal course. Expenses are recognized at the time the taxpayer pays the amount or disposes of the funds. A special statutory rule applies to items of income or expense that regularly occur and are paid 'shortly before or shortly after' the period to which they relate, such as rent for December received in January. Such amounts are taken into account for tax purposes in the period to which they economically relate. Expenditures for depreciable assets are not deducted immediately but must be capitalized and recovered through depreciation deductions.[341]

One of the basic elements of this 'excess income' approach is that the sale of assets in the course of the taxable activity does not constitute a taxable event. Thus, the sale of real estate that was employed to generate rental income, or the sale of a car that was used in the course of employment, has no tax effect. The general rule that private capital gains are not taxed (if the statutory holding period is met) also prevails but does not cover capital gains from securities and other financial instruments after the 2007 Business Tax Reform.

For most taxpayers engaged in business, the use of an accrual method of income computation is required. In general terms, income or loss for the period is determined by comparing the assets and liabilities at the end of the tax period with the assets and liabilities at the end of the preceding period.[342] Thus, when performance of a contract is completed and income has been earned, an asset in the form of an account receivable is entered in the balance sheet and will be reflected as income as a result of the balance sheet comparison at year end. Similarly, a liability that is recognized for commercial accounting, and hence tax purposes, functions as the accrual of a deduction item. A modified version of the accrual method (which contains some elements of the 'excess income' method but does include capital gains) may be used by taxpayers having income from independent personal services or agriculture.[343]

339. Germany, ITA, s. 2 para. 2.
340. Germany, ITA, ss 9–11.
341. Germany, ITA, s. 9 para. 1 no. 7 with reference to s. 7.
342. Germany, ITA, ss 4–7k.
343. Germany, ITA, s. 4 para. 3.

The obligation to use the accrual method is tied to the commercial and corporate law requirements to maintain certain books and records.[344] Correspondingly, there is a close connection between the financial balance sheet and the tax balance sheet used in the net worth comparison. Under the traditional principle of 'linkage' *(Maßgeblichkeit)*, the tax balance sheet must be based on the commercial balance sheet and, unless a special tax rule provides otherwise, the recognition and valuation of assets and liabilities shown on the commercial balance sheet are relevant for tax purposes. This linkage has far-reaching implications for income determination because it incorporates in the tax system the basic 'prudence principle' that is the basis for many German generally accepted accounting principles. Unrealized losses, which are recognized under the rules for financial accounting, are also effective for tax purposes. Similarly, provisions or reserves required for financial accounting reduce taxable income. Starting in 1997 German tax legislation gradually reduced the application of the 'prudence principle' for tax purposes (i.e., by abolition of provisions for future losses or by the introduction of a discount on liabilities and provisions),[345] thus eroding the original strong linkage between commercial and tax accounting under German tax law. Apart from the mitigation of the prudence principle, the statute contains a number of special tax rules for the valuation of assets and liabilities.[346] For example, the principle of valuation according to 'going concern value', discussed above in connection with depreciation, is expressly sanctioned.

On the other hand, a principle of 'reverse' linkage *(umgekehrte Maßgeblichkeit)* also applies.[347] If tax law provides advantageous treatment for an item and that treatment is elected for tax purposes, that treatment must be followed in the commercial statements to be effective. This can mean, for example, that the decision to accelerate deductions for tax purposes will reduce financial statement income and the ability of a corporation to pay dividends. Pending legislation might abolish this reverse linkage altogether.

The mandatory introduction of International Financial Reporting Standards (IFRS) for the consolidated accounts of corporate groups listed in the stock market in 2002 has led to a debate on the future of the linkage between financial and tax accounting. So far, individual company accounts that are relevant for tax accounting are still prepared under traditional 'conservative' commercial accounting rules. While the legislation for individual company accounts moves more and more in the direction of IFRS, German legislation might in the interim require an autonomous set of rules for tax accounting.

The *French* system is governed by roughly the same principles as the German one. The cash method is used to account for income from employment, renting of real estate or securities, profits of small businesses (which can choose that method), and non-commercial personal services (unless the professional has opted for the

344. Germany, ITA, s. 5 para. 1 sent. 1.
345. Germany, ITA, ss 5 paras 2a–4b and 6 para. 1 no. 3, 3a.
346. Germany, ITA, s. 6 para. 1.
347. Germany, ITA, s. 5 para. 1 sent. 2.

accrual method).[348] Income is taxable when received or available for collection,[349] but there is no rule similar to the German one concerning income or expenses paid 'shortly before or shortly after' year end.

As in Germany, a balance sheet comparison method is used for computing the tax results of most taxpayers engaged in business – more precisely, corporations – and, in principle, sole proprietorships carrying on an industrial, commercial, or agricultural activity.[350] The linkage between book and taxable income is particularly close. General accounting principles and concepts apply for tax purposes unless tax law explicitly or implicitly derogates from them.[351] In particular, both for book and tax purposes, income must be recognized and an account receivable entered in the balance sheet when property is delivered or the performance of the service is completed. The taxable net income is determined by making adjustments to book income whenever tax law departs from accounting law (e.g., expenses deductible for book but not for tax purposes, exempt dividends from subsidiaries, long-term capital gains taxable at reduced rates); such adjustments have become more numerous subsequent to modifications in accounting rules in the mid-2000s to conform to new international standards, but the tax authorities refused to modify the tax treatment accordingly. Also, as in Germany, the accounting principle of prudence explains why the deduction of reserves and provisions is liberally accepted for tax purposes. Under the same principles, on the deduction side, expenses are taken into account as liabilities as soon as they are incurred. Conversely, in the minds of some, accounting law has often been 'tax polluted', for instance, as far as depreciation rules are concerned.

In *Sweden*, like Germany, the method of accounting is determined by the category of income. Income from capital and income from employment are accounted for on a cash basis. The principle of 'constructive receipt' taxes income prior to actual receipt if it is possible for the taxpayer to obtain payment earlier. Capital gains are subject to a special rule that in effect puts them on the accrual basis. The rule was introduced in 1991 to discourage deferred payment sales of property.

Business taxpayers, including all corporations, must account for tax purposes on the accrual method. Generally accepted accounting principles are controlling wherever there are no special tax rules. As a general matter, income items are usually determined under financial accounting rules, while there are some special tax rules for deductions. Under normal accounting rules, only the present value of potential future expenditures is deductible. Special tax rules limit the deduction for anticipated guarantee expenses. Because of the importance of accounting rules for tax purposes, tax considerations have often influenced the development of the financial accounting rules. This situation has been criticized as resulting in a distortion of the clear presentation of income for financial accounting purposes.

348. France, CGI, s. 93 A.
349. France, CGI, s. 12.
350. France, CGI, ss 38-2 and 209 I.
351. France, CGI, Regulatory Sch. III, s. 38 *quater*.

The relation between tax accounting and financial accounting is much different in the *United States* system. While the taxpayer must in general report income for tax purposes on the same method of accounting as that used for his commercial books, special tax rules substantially modify the accounting principles. For example, under the accrual method, the use of reserves for estimated future expenses is much more limited for tax purposes than the normally applicable rules for financial accounting. The courts have specifically recognized the 'difference in objectives' between tax accounting and financial accounting in developing special tax rules.[352] In addition, the fiscal authorities can require modifications in accounting methods to 'clearly reflect income' and under this standard a number of accounting practices have been rejected for tax purposes.[353]

The taxpayer can elect a method of accounting, and the statute specifically recognizes the cash method and the accrual method as well as 'other methods' that meet the above standards.[354] For taxpayers on the cash method, typically individuals and small businesses, income is taxable on receipt or in situations in which the taxpayer has 'constructive receipt' of the income because of his access to the income. A check is treated as cash if it clears in due course. IRS regulations state that the receipt of a note in exchange for services is income to a cash-basis taxpayer to the extent of the note's fair market value, but several court decisions appear to create numerous inconsistent exceptions to this rule. Although the receipt of a note in exchange for property is also income, a statutory provision generally permits a taxpayer to avoid recognizing income until payment on the note is received.

On the deduction side, deductions are taken into account when an expenditure has actually occurred, usually when an amount is paid. The taxpayer's use of his own note does not constitute payment. Prepaid expenses are generally treated as capital expenditures. Special rules allow farmers on the cash basis, in effect, to deduct prepaid expenses, but those rules are in turn limited to 'real' farmers to prevent the use of prepayments in tax-shelter transactions.

The accrual method is used by most business taxpayers. If the business involves production, inventories must be used, and purchases and sales are required to be accounted for on the accrual method. On the income side, income must be recognized when the right to receive the income has been established and the amount can be determined. In general, any consistent method of accounting is accepted even if the right to the income has not technically accrued. The treatment of advance payments to taxpayers on the accrual basis is discussed below.

On the deduction side, deduction was historically allowed when 'all events' had occurred that established the liability to make the payment. Although contingent or uncertain liabilities were not deductible, this rule allowed taxpayers to accrue fixed liabilities currently at their nominal amount even when the payment would not actually be made until some time in the future. This approach overstates the true cost of the deduction since it does not take into account the time value of

352. United States, *Thor Power Tool Co. v. Commissioner*, 439 U.S, 522 (1979).
353. United States, IRC, s. 446(b).
354. United States, IRC, s. 446(a).

money between the period in which the deduction accrued and the time it is in fact paid. In extreme situations, the taxpayer could actually be better off with the current accrual of the liability than if he had not incurred the liability at all. In response to this situation, the statute was amended to require that there be 'economic performance' of the obligation before the 'all events' test could be met.[355] This rule basically defers the deduction until payment is actually made or property or services are delivered or performed (e.g., in mining reclamation). For 'recurring' items – that is, normally occurring business expenses – deduction is allowed currently if the amount is paid within eight and one-half months after the end of the tax year, the time requirement for filing a tax return. This economic performance approach makes the accrual of deductions for tax purposes much more restrictive in the United States than in the other jurisdictions.

Japan requires the use of accrual accounting as a general rule. However, small businesses have the option of using cash method principles under strict conditions (selecting the special 'blue return' system).[356] Where the accrual method is used, it usually follows financial accounting principles that are generally accepted to be 'fair and reasonable'.[357] There are also more detailed tax accounting rules. Under the accrual system, liabilities are taken into account at face value, and special provisions allow reserves for mining restoration, oil spill cleanups, and similar occurrences. Paralleling the adoption in financial accounting of the mark-to-market method with respect to some financial instruments, including derivative transactions, the Japanese corporate income tax law was amended to apply the mark-to-market method to such financial instruments.

Under the *Canadian* system, income from employment, farming, and fishing is calculated on a cash basis. Income from business and property, however, must be accounted for generally on the accrual basis. While the tax accounting rules are based on financial accounting principles, they have developed into an independent body of law.[358] Special tax rules specifically displace financial accounting rules. In addition, courts have sometimes rejected financial accounting rules as inconsistent with more basic tax law principles. For example, LIFO accounting for inventory costs has been held unacceptable for tax purposes despite its recognition in financial accounting. Liabilities are generally taken into account at face value in the year incurred as long as they are not contingent with respect to liability or amount.[359] In some cases, however, present value accrual is at least acceptable and might be required.

In the *United Kingdom*, the appropriate accounting regime is determined by the particular part of the Act (e.g., Schedule) applicable to the income. In some cases, the receipts or cash method is used but for trading profits, the most important income category, an 'earnings' basis is generally required. According to a statutory

355. United States, IRC, s. 461(h).
356. Japan, ITA, s. 67.
357. Japan, CTA, s. 22.
358. *Canderel v. The Queen* [1998] 2 CTC 35 (SCC).
359. Canada, ITA, s. 18(1)(e).

amendment in 1998, the profits of a trade, profession, or vocation must be computed in accordance with generally accepted accounting practice subject to any adjustment required or authorized by tax law in computing those profits.[360] Even before 1998 there were signs that the courts were moving closer to a financial accounting base in those cases where there was no specifically developed tax rule.

The mention in the 1998 rule of adjustments required or authorized by law is of great importance. Specific statutory rules deal with specific issues – for example, preventing a current deduction of interest where there is no corresponding income inclusion. Other rules displace depreciation in accordance with financial accounting; instead, the recovery of capital costs is governed by the elaborate rules in the capital allowance legislation.

In the early 2000s the United Kingdom considered a yet more radical move to adopting a financial accounting base for corporation tax. This would have meant following the financial accounting treatment for all things and so, for example, giving effect to depreciation of capital costs. The proposals would also have included moving the taxation of capital gains from a realization basis to an accrual basis, requiring the annual valuation of assets. The proposals even suggested the abolition of the schedular system by allowing losses of any type to be set off against profits of any type. The idea eventually fell away, but it still surfaces in non-governmental tax reform proposals from time to time.

The situation in *Australia* is quite different. Tax accounting rules (at least until recently) have been developed through the interpretation of the statutory terms 'derived' in relation to income and 'incurred' in relation to deductions. While courts have sometimes looked to accounting principles, the tax rules have developed to a large extent independently. For example, whether an expense has been 'incurred' depends in some sense on legal liabilities rather than the commercial outcome and thus parallels the US experience. In general, a cash method has been accepted for employees and small businesses and an accrual method for larger businesses. Under the accrual method, income is included when it is 'earned', and case law establishes the contours of that concept. A special statutory regime is provided for inventory, which in general follows financial accounting principles, although it has some important deviations. For example, the use of the lower of cost or market is optional and not mandatory.[361]

In contrast to the other Continental systems, in the *Dutch* system tax accounting rules have developed relatively independently from financial accounting. Income from employment and a substantial participation in a company are accounted for on a cash basis. Amounts are included in income when received or available for collection even if they are not actually collected. Income from business activities is determined in accordance with 'sound commercial practice' *(goed koopmansgebruik)* applied in a consistent manner. There is substantial case law developing this concept. The principles are different in many important aspects from financial accounting rules, and there is no necessary connection between

360. United Kingdom, ITTOIA, s. 25, CTA 2009, s. 46.
361. Australia, ITAA 1997, Division 70.

financial treatment and tax treatment. However, in the interests of 'prudence', the rules do allow the deduction of unrealized losses if there is a good chance the loss will be incurred and it can be quantified. This tax rule is nonetheless stricter than the corresponding commercial accounting rule. The tax rules emphasize the 'realistic' possibility of a loss.

2. INCLUSION OF ADVANCE PAYMENTS

The treatment of advance payments is a classic example of the possible conflict between financial accounting principles and tax accounting. Where amounts are prepaid prior to delivery of goods or the performance of services, from a financial accounting point of view, income would in general not be taken into account since the unconditional right to the income has not yet been established. Current inclusion of the income would prevent it from being accounted for in the period in which it was earned. On the other hand, from the perspective of the tax system, the fact that the taxpayer has received the cash and is in a position to pay the tax suggests the appropriateness of current inclusion of the income. In addition, the taxation of the advance payment to the seller can be seen as a surrogate for the failure to tax the implicit interest involved in the transaction to the purchaser. The systems have resolved this conflict in a variety of ways.

In the *United States*, the treatment of prepaid income has generated a substantial amount of litigation, including three cases in the Supreme Court. In general, the courts have upheld the tax authorities' assertion that the inclusion of prepayments in income currently is necessary to 'clearly reflect income'.[362] The decisions rest primarily on the discretion of the tax authorities to determine what practices clearly reflect income. While litigation establishes that prepaid income must in principle be included currently, the rule has been relaxed somewhat in administrative practice. In the case of services, income recognition can be postponed until the taxable year after the year of receipt. For sales income, advance payments for inventory can be deferred to the next year. In addition, specific statutory provisions allow the deferral of advance payments. For example, deferral is allowed in the case of dues prepaid to an automobile club for road service, one of the situations in which the courts had required current inclusion.

Canada deals with the problem in a specific statutory provision. Prepaid income must be included in taxable income in the year in which the payment is received, even where the amount is not properly accruable.[363] However, the taxpayer is allowed to deduct a reserve in the same amount, thus neutralizing the initial inclusion.[364] The reserve in turn must be included in income in the following year but if the amount has still not yet been earned by the end of the year, another reserve may be claimed. The period of the reserve is thus, in effect, unlimited,

362. United States, *Schlude v. Commissioner*, 372 U.S 128 (1963).
363. Canada, ITA, s. 12(1)(a).
364. Canada, ITA, s. 20(1)(m).

except in the case of articles of food and drink and unredeemed transportation tickets, where a special rule limits the period to one year.

Despite the general absence of financial accounting principles in the *Australian* tax system, case law doctrine has adopted the financial accounting rule for prepayments. Such amounts are includable only when earned.[365] In the *United Kingdom*, there is also case law support for the position that prepayments may be deferred until the income has been earned, but only if the taxpayer can establish that this is indeed the appropriate financial accounting treatment.[366]

Similarly, in *The Netherlands*, case law interpreting 'sound commercial practice' has allowed the deferral of prepaid income until the period in which it is earned. It is essential that consistent practice be followed. *Sweden* likewise follows general accounting principles that allow the deferral of the recognition of prepayments until the amounts are earned.

Using the balance sheet comparison approach to income determination, *Germany* treats advance payments as neutral from both a financial accounting and tax point of view. The transaction is treated as 'pending' and its effects are thus suspended until completion.[367] The increase in assets on the balance sheet caused by the payment is offset by the reverse liability to deliver goods or the performance of services. Therefore, an advance payment generally has no tax results. *France* and *Japan* reach the same results, although the techniques are somewhat different.

3. INCOME TREATMENT OF DEFERRED PAYMENTS

Where property is sold with the financing in effect being provided by the seller in the form of some sort of purchase money security, accounting rules would usually require the immediate recognition of the income from the transaction. This would be the normal result under accrual methods of accounting and could also be applicable under the cash method, depending on the nature of the buyer's obligation. The systems have reacted in different ways to deferred payments. In some cases, a special rule allows the deferral of the recognition of the income until the payments are in fact received under the note. In other situations, the cash basis taxpayer, who would normally be able to defer the recognition of gain until receipt, is in effect put on the accrual basis and required to take the gain into account when the property is delivered.

The *United States* is an example of the first approach. Under the so-called 'instalment sales' provisions, the taxpayer reports the gain on the disposition of non-inventory assets in the years in which the payments are received.[368] The payment is treated partly as a tax-free return of tax cost and partly as gain, depending on the overall ratio of gain to total purchase price. The instalment obligation

365. *Arthur Murray (NSW) Pty Ltd* [1965] HCA 58, 114 CLR 314.
366. *Symons v. Weeks* [1983] STC 195.
367. Germany, ITA, s. 5 para. 1 sent. 1 with reference to Commercial Code, s. 252 para. 1.
368. United States, IRC, s. 453.

must bear a market rate of interest. There are a number of restrictions on the use of the instalment method. It does not apply if the property sold or received is publicly traded. In addition, instalment treatment is not available for any gain on the property that represents previously taken depreciation deductions. Even where deferral is allowed, if the amount of the outstanding indebtedness held by the taxpayer exceeds $5 million, an interest charge is imposed on the deferred tax. The disposition of an instalment obligation causes the recognition of all deferred gain, even in a transaction in which nothing is received in return.

Japan has a specific provision to allow deferral of recognition of earnings on instalment sales until their due dates. In general, this treatment applies to instalment sales with an instalment period of two years or more.[369]

Under the *Dutch* system, the courts have allowed the deferral of income recognition in certain cases of deferred payment as an aspect of sound commercial practice.

Sweden has taken a quite different approach to deferred payment sales. Whether the taxpayer is on the cash basis or accrual basis, gain on the disposition of capital gain property must be included in the year the sale takes place. The purpose of the rule is to limit deferral of taxation of capital gains. The *Australian* system, in general, also requires profit on the sale of inventory and capital property to be taken into account in the year of sale. The same result is obtained in *Japan* by the fact that almost all transactions have to be accounted for on the accrual basis. In general, the time when a taxpayer must take into account the amount realized from the sale or exchange of a capital asset is not affected by the time of the receipt of the consideration.

Similarly, using the balance sheet comparison method of income determination, in *Germany* the existence of the claim for the payment results in an increase in assets and hence in net worth. The claim is usually valued at its nominal amount, although it may be discounted if some sort of hidden interest is involved in the transaction. A judge-made modification applies in the case of the sale of a whole business if the consideration is paid in instalments; the taxpayer can elect to have the proceeds taxable at the time of sale (and receive beneficial capital gains treatment) or to spread the proceeds over the period during which the instalments are paid.[370]

In *France*, under the accrual method, gains from credit sales are always taxable in the year when the delivery takes place, regardless of the time of the payment and even in the case of a clause permitting termination of the contract in the case of non-performance. The taxpayer can deduct a reserve if, according to the circumstances, the debt will probably not be paid. Under the cash method, payment is generally decisive, with few exceptions. For instance, gain on the sale of a building or of stock or securities by an individual (not acting in a business context) is taxable when the sale occurs regardless of the payment date.

---

369. Japan, CTA, s. 63.
370. Germany, Income Tax Regulations (*Einkommensteuer-Richtlinien*), s. 16 para. 11.

The *Canadian* system takes an intermediate position. When business property is sold with deferred payments, the taxpayer is entitled to set up a reserve for the portion of the profit from the sale that is not due until after the end of the taxable year. However, the maximum period for which the reserve may be claimed is three years.[371] In the case of capital gain property, the same approach is taken. The maximum period for the reserve is five years and at least one-fifth of the amount of the capital gain must be included each year.[372]

The *United Kingdom* also makes a distinction between capital gain property and trading property. In the former situation, gain must be recognized currently based on the value of the consideration received, with no discount for the fact that the payments will take place over time. The actual payment of the tax, however, can be deferred if the consideration is payable for a period of over eighteen months. The situation with respect to business income is more complex. On the deduction side, statutory rules allow a write-off of debts that are bad, estimated to be bad, or are released as part of a statutory insolvency arrangement; the corporation tax rules reflect accounting language and talk of debts that are 'impaired'.[373]

4. ORIGINAL ISSUE DISCOUNT OBLIGATIONS AND OTHER COMPLEX FINANCIAL INSTRUMENTS

Where obligations are issued at a discount from the stated amount payable at maturity, questions of both timing and character of income and expense arise for the borrower and the lender. From an economic point of view, the difference between the issue price and the amount due on redemption clearly represents an interest expense for the borrower and interest income for the lender. However, it has taken some time for tax systems to translate this economic reality into legal rules. In some of the systems dealt with here, there is still no satisfactory resolution of the problem of original issue discount (OID), with the legal form of the transaction controlling its tax treatment in many situations.

Similarly, the emergence of complex financial 'products', typically with hybrid or derivative characteristics, has also raised difficult timing and characterization issues. In general, there is an increasing tendency to abandon traditional realization and tax accounting approaches in this area and to tax such instruments on an internal rate of return or mark-to-market basis. The exact scope of such rules, however, is still uncertain, and many of the systems are currently evolving new approaches to these issues.

In the *United States*, prior to the enactment of explicit statutory provisions, the treatment of OID in the case law was uncertain, with some cases following the legal form of the transaction and treating the discount element as capital. Though the Supreme Court eventually determined that the discount element was properly

371. Canada, ITA, s. 20(1)(n).
372. Canada, ITA, s. 40(1)(a)(iii).
373. United Kingdom, ITTOIA, s. CTA 2009 s. 55; on loan relationships see s. 476.

characterized as ordinary income, Congress had, in the meantime, intervened with a specific statutory provision denying capital gain treatment to the discount realized at maturity. The next legislative response to OID was to require holders of OID bonds to include the original discount amount in income ratably over the life of the bond regardless of the normal accounting method. Subsequent provisions modified the method of inclusion to require the discount element to be treated on an 'economic' or 'constant interest' accrual basis (i.e., with less interest in early years and more in later years), reflecting the implicit reinvestment of the interest element.

Finally, in 1984, rules were introduced dealing with the calculation of OID when bonds are issued for property.[374] Except in the case of traded property, where bonds are issued for property, the value of the property is uncertain and hence the issue price of the bond and the resulting discount cannot be directly ascertained. To deal with this problem, the legislation in general terms provided for the determination of the issue price by discounting the payments to be made under the bond by a stipulated discount rate and treating that amount as the current value of the property, and hence the issue price of the bond. If the amounts to be received under the instrument exceed the hypothetical issue price, the excess is OID and is included and deducted currently under the usually applicable OID principles.

Several special and complex rules deal with obligations providing for contingent payments or a variable interest rate. Proposals have been made (although subsequently withdrawn) to apply OID rules to 'hybrid' obligations, such as convertible bonds, under a 'bifurcation' approach, which would treat separately the option embedded in the convertible bond and the actual loan, applying OID principles to the loan portion of the transaction. Currently, the OID rules are applied to the entire convertible debt instrument. However, when a debt instrument is issued with a separate option that is not embedded, bifurcation is required.

A different set of rules applies to so-called 'market discount' – that is, discount arising from a purchase of bonds in the market that have declined in value because of interest rate changes. No current accrual of the discount is required, but the gain is not entitled to capital gain treatment on disposition.[375] The realization rules are relaxed with respect to the disposition of market discount bonds, so that a gift of the bond would constitute a realization event. In addition, there are limitations on the deduction of interest expense incurred in connection with market discount bonds. The taxpayer may elect to accrue market discount currently, in which case the interest expense is fully deductible.

Beyond the treatment of discount bonds, the rules dealing with more complex financial instruments are still evolving. A mark-to-market approach is taken with respect to many types of commodities futures, foreign currency, and options contracts. In addition, dealers in securities and derivatives are required to use a mark-to-market method for certain forward and option contracts and notional principal

374. United States, IRC, ss 1271–74.
375. United States, IRC, ss 1276–78.

contracts not covered by the general rule.[376] A broader accrual approach has been discussed in the academic literature.

The development in *Sweden* has been similar, although it took place somewhat later. Prior to extensive statutory revisions in 1991, it was unclear whether OID was to be treated as taxable (and deductible) interest or as potentially non-taxable capital gain. Case law principles treated the income on obligations held to maturity as interest, but the treatment of income on a sale during the period the bond was outstanding was never satisfactorily resolved.

Under statutory provisions enacted in 1991, OID on obligations held by private persons is treated as interest but is not taxed until actually received, either on sale or on the maturity of the bond. For corporations and individuals holding bonds as business assets, the general application of financial accounting principles for tax purposes requires the accrual of OID currently as interest income. Business issuers of OID obligations similarly can accrue the interest expense currently.

Japan did not have general tax rules dealing with OID until 1998, although there was a movement to adopt a mark-to-market approach with respect to certain kinds of financial instruments such as derivative financial instruments. In 1996, the mark-to-market method was first applied to banks and securities companies with respect to derivative financial instruments and marketable securities. This treatment has been generalized since 2000, and all companies in Japan are currently required to apply the mark-to-market method to their derivative instruments and marketable securities, except for some hedging transactions.[377] With respect to zero coupon bonds or similar kinds of bonds that do not fall within the category of marketable securities, the amount of OID attributable to a certain fiscal year must be included in the taxable income of holders. Such amount must be calculated on a straight-line basis rather than on an implicit interest basis.

Contrary to the tax treatment for corporate entities, for individuals, OID is not taxable until the maturity of the relevant obligations or their transfer. The tax deferral effect of this approach is somewhat reduced by a special 18% withholding tax on the OID elements, which is imposed at the time of the issue of the relevant obligations. This withholding tax is applicable to zero coupon bonds, subject to limited exceptions.

In *France*, OID has been subject to special rules since 1985. For individuals who do not hold the obligations in a business, the difference between the issue price and the amount ultimately received (excluding annual interest actually paid) is treated as interest income in the year received. The same rule applies in a business context for small discounts but if the discount exceeds 10% of the acquisition price, the interest must be computed on a yield-to-maturity basis and included in income annually.[378] With respect to futures contracts, options, and derivative instruments, statutory provisions require mark-to-market treatment if

376. United States, IRC, s. 475.
377. Japan, CTA, ss 61-3 and 61-5.
378. France, CGI, s. 238 *septies* A sq.

the instruments are traded on an organized market or have a value determined with respect to such a market.

The *German* rules have a similar pattern. If both the issuer and the holder of an obligation are required to use the accrual method of accounting generally – that is, they are business taxpayers – the OID is accounted for currently as interest expense and interest income, calculated on a yield-to-maturity basis. In addition, subsequent changes in interest rates that increase the value of the liability in the hands of the issuer are also taken into account currently, although the corresponding gain to the holder continues to be deferred. From 1999, the calculation of a discount is not dependent on the actual agreement between the creditor and debtor or the content of the obligation (i.e., any liability or provision the maturity of which exceeds one year must be discounted in the balance sheet).[379] As explained above, an exception to this rule exists for obligations that are based on advance payments.[380] The OID is taxed only at redemption or on sale and is treated as interest income and not as tax-free capital gain.

The current rules for 'private' cash basis holders were introduced in 1994 in response to the increased issuance of various forms of bonds with disguised discount, which arguably qualified as tax-free capital gain under the prior system. This topic has largely lost its importance due to the introduction of a general capital gains tax on privately held securities.

There seems to be some movement in the direction of an overall mark-to-market treatment of derivative financial instruments. After years of the basic conservative approach of accounting rules, Germany is now reforming its financial accounting rules for derivative financial instruments held by financial institutions that are 'available for sale', allowing a limited mark-to-market rule. However, this reform does not affect the valuation of financial instruments in tax accounting because the original acquisition costs serve as a valuation cap for tax accounting matters.

The Netherlands has attempted to avoid timing and recognition issues involving bonds and complex financial instruments by adopting rules for taxing capital income on a deemed return basis in 2001. For business taxpayers, under case law (interpreting 'good commercial practice') the annual amount of interest accrued on discount bonds, etc., is taken into account for tax purposes currently.

With regard to the taxation of financial derivatives, tax inspectors generally apply the rules of 'good commercial practice' (a deduction can be taken if there is a more than negligible risk that a loss will be suffered; income not yet earned need not be reported) and taxpayers apparently have accepted this treatment.

The *Canadian* Income Tax Act does not contain comprehensive rules dealing with OID or sophisticated financial products, including derivatives. As a result, the tax consequences of these products must be determined by applying the basic provisions dealing with the character, source, and timing of income and deductions. Not surprisingly, financial products have been used by taxpayers to

379. Germany, ITA, s. 6 para. 1 no. 3.
380. Germany, ITA, s. 6 para. 1 no. 3.

manipulate tax consequences. In certain cases, the government has responded with specific legislation on an ad hoc basis.

As a result of a misreading of old English cases, Canadian courts have traditionally considered interest to be a non-deductible capital expense. Accordingly, there is a special statutory deduction for interest expense incurred in respect of borrowed money, or the unpaid purchase price of property if the money or the property is used for the purpose of earning income.[381] The statutory requirement for borrowed money is an important limitation on the deduction. For example, interest in respect of unpaid (compound) interest would not be deductible in the absence of a special provision, since the unpaid interest is not borrowed money.[382] A special provision permits a deduction for compound interest only when it is actually paid.[383]

According to the express wording of the Act, interest is deductible if it is paid in the year or becomes payable in respect of the year. Nevertheless, by administrative practice, interest other than compound interest is deductible on an accrual basis. Interest is not defined in the Act, but the case law has established that interest is restricted to amounts that represent compensation for the use of money, that are computed in reference to a principal sum, and that accrue on a daily basis.

An OID, premium, or bonus is considered to be interest only if a loan does not provide for interest or provides for interest at less than a reasonable rate. If OID is not interest, it is deductible only when paid. In the case of a 'shallow' discount (the issue price is not less than 97% of the principal and its annual yield is not greater than 4/3 of the stipulated interest rate), the full amount of the discount is deductible.[384] For other 'deep' discounts, only one-half of the amount of the discount is deductible when paid. The disallowance of 50% of the OID as a deduction reflects the fact that generally only 50% of the discount would be included in the income of the holder; in other words, the discount is treated as capital gain to the holder.

Taxpayers could avoid the treatment of OID as capital by issuing zero coupon bonds. Because these bonds have no stated rate of interest, the discount is treated as interest for tax purposes. However, the Canada Revenue Agency takes the position that the interest must be bifurcated into simple interest and compound interest. The simple interest is deductible on an accrual basis, but the compound interest is deductible only when paid on the maturity of the obligation, as discussed earlier. This treatment effectively precluded Canadian corporations from using zero coupon bonds and OID as an effective means of borrowing.

In 1990, the government introduced detailed provisions with respect to certain long-term prepaid debt obligations.[385] These rules were intended to require the prepayment of interest to be treated as a reduction of the principal amount of the

381. Canada, ITA, s. 20(1)(c).
382. Canada, ITA, s. 20(3).
383. Canada, ITA, s. 20(1)(d).
384. Canada, ITA, s. 20(1)(f).
385. Canada, ITA, s. 18(9.2)–(9.8).

obligation. Inadvertently, the rules work in such a way that corporate borrowers can achieve exactly the same result as with a zero coupon bond simply by prepaying interest. In other words, under these rules the amount of the prepayment is deductible on an actuarial basis over the term of the obligation. This result was clearly unintended.

The Canadian tax system does not contain comprehensive accrual rules dealing with financial products. Accordingly, the tax consequences of various products have been established largely by administrative practice and case law. Gains and losses in respect of futures and forward contracts are considered to be on income account if the transactions are connected with the taxpayer's business. Otherwise, a taxpayer may report such gains and losses as ordinary income or loss or as capital gains or losses, but must do so consistently. Originally, the tax authorities applied a linkage approach to the treatment of foreign exchange gains and losses and swap transactions. In other words, the treatment of the gains and losses from the foreign currency fluctuations or the swap was dependent on the treatment of the underlying transaction. This type of approach leads to a mismatch where a capital asset or liability is hedged. Accordingly, the Canada Revenue Agency has taken the position that all interest rate swaps should be treated on income account. However, the Supreme Court decided in a 1999 case that a gain realized on a hedge of a long-term borrowing in a foreign currency was a capital gain.[386]

Financial institutions and investment dealers are required by legislation to use mark-to-market reporting for certain debt and equity securities. For other taxpayers, gains and losses are recognized only when realized. However, if the property constitutes inventory of a business, the lower of cost or market rule of inventory valuation will require the losses to be accrued.

Currently the *Australian* system is a mixture of partial regimes dealing with various aspects of the issues considered in this section. While comprehensive legislation will operate from 2010, with respect to existing law, doubts still persist whether OID is treated as capital gain or ordinary income in a business context, although the practice is to treat it as ordinary income. Under case law both deferred interest and OID are deductible over the term of the instrument for an accrual basis taxpayer.[387] To deal with the problem of mismatches where an accrual basis taxpayer 'borrows' using OID or deferred interest from a cash basis taxpayer (the average individual investor) and problems of capital indexed securities, stripped securities, etc., an accruals regime was introduced in 1984 for a wide range of debt securities issued at a discount or otherwise providing at issue for returns in forms other than periodic interest. This regime uses the internal rate of return method on both the income and deduction side, but does not apply to all debt securities.[388] For example, market discounts where the value of a security has fallen because of a rise in interest rates are not subject to the accruals regime. However, a statutory

386. *Shell Canada Ltd. v. The Queen* [1999] 4 CTC 313 (SCC).

387. *Australian Guarantee Corporation Ltd* [1984] FCA 240, 2 FCR 483; *Coles Myer Finance Ltd* [1993] HCA 29, 176 CLR 640.

388. Australia, ITAA 1936, Part III Division 16E.

amendment in 1989 required that such amounts be treated as ordinary income to prevent capital gains indexation being available.[389] Similarly, foreign exchange gains and losses are subject to a special realization-based statutory regime. An earlier version of this regime, which the courts interpreted very narrowly (by requiring the actual conversion of currency), was replaced in 2003 with much more detailed rules[390] as the first step toward the comprehensive regime; these rules are due to be replaced again for large taxpayers when the new regime commences in 2010.

The new comprehensive regime[391] is a mixture of internal rate of return and realization systems based on whether the return on the arrangement is 'sufficiently certain'. This determination has two elements: The gain or loss must be 'effectively non-contingent', and the amount of the gain or loss must be 'fixed or determinable with reasonable accuracy'. There are important elective elements for using financial accounts, marking to market, matching the timing and character for hedges, and foreign currency translation. Further, the regime will apply on a mandatory basis only to large taxpayers. Other taxpayers generally remain subject to the current rules unless they elect into the new regime. The definition of 'financial arrangement' starts from the idea of a 'cash settlable legal or equitable right' to receive a financial benefit, or a 'cash settlable legal or equitable obligation' to provide a financial benefit. No financial arrangement will arise if either party has a right to receive, or an obligation to provide, something other than a financial benefit or something cash settlable, and the value of that other item is not insignificant (i.e., cash flows on both sides of the transaction are generally required). Most debt, hybrid, equity, derivative, and foreign currency transactions potentially will be within the scope of the rules. However, the rules will have limited impact in certain situations (e.g., equity interests will be largely unaffected unless a taxpayer makes certain elections). A special regime already applies for tax-exempt leasing of plant and equipment.[392] Leasing is not generally covered by the definition of financial arrangement because it does not involve cash flows on both sides.

The *United Kingdom*, like the United States, began with a struggle to fit low-interest and zero coupon bonds into the tax framework. The taxability of a profit arising from a discount has been part of the UK tax system since 1802, when such profits were listed as falling within Schedule D Case III. However, in practice, while the holder was taxable on the discount, the income inclusion occurred only on redemption. This meant that the holder was not taxed on the profit made on a realization before redemption; conversely, however, at redemption the holder was taxed on the whole of the profit arising from the discount, a rule that meant anyone who held such a bond would sell it to a tax-exempt body such as a charity or a pension fund, so that no tax was collected at all. A court decision in 1983 made it more likely that the holder of a bond would be taxed on an intermediate profit but

389. Australia, ITAA 1936, s. 26BB.
390. Australia, ITAA 1997, Division 775.
391. Australia, ITAA 1997, Division 230.
392. Australia, ITAA 1997, Division 250.

the introduction of the 1984 rules, discussed below, meant that this result has not been explored further. Under administrative practice, the discount was not deductible by the issuing company until redemption, when it was deductible in full. Thus, the regime was at least symmetrical.

Statutory provisions dealing with the situation were introduced in 1984. For deep discount bonds, an income element was treated as arising, strictly in line with an algebraic formula, during the life of the bond; a discount was deep if it was greater than 15% or ½% per annum. The issuing company deducted the income element under the formula on a year-by-year basis. The holder, however, paid tax only on an actual (or deemed) disposal; there was no deemed disposal simply because a year had ended. When the holder disposed of the bond, the income element that had accrued up to that day was included in income; if the actual price difference was greater or less than that given by the formula, the balance was treated as capital gain or loss, or income gain or loss, under ordinary income/capital gains tax rules. If the discount was not deep, or for some other reason the bonds fell outside the 1984 rules, the original administrative practice still applied.

The deep discount rules apply only where the gain could be calculated at the start (e.g., where the redemption price was fixed). Some other instruments fell within subsequent rules created in 1989 for 'deep gain' securities where the formulary approach was not possible, but with extensive exemptions (e.g., for convertible securities, qualifying indexed securities and certain government bonds).

In 1996, the United Kingdom introduced new rules for the tax treatment of any 'loan relationship' entered into by a company, thus covering discount bonds but having a much wider scope.[393] A loan relationship arises where the company is a debtor or creditor in respect of a money debt that arises from a contract for the lending of money; it follows that a simple trade debt does not give rise to a loan relationship. The 1996 rules apply for both income inclusion and deduction of expense. After further rule changes, the legislation now authorizes any generally accepted accounting practice. Sometimes special rules apply – for example, where related parties are involved. The foreign exchange rules were merged into the loan relationship rules in 2002; the rules for derivatives were also rewritten at that time.[394]

These loan relationship rules apply only to corporate holders and issuers. For other taxpayers, a revised version of the 1984 and 1989 rules or, in exceptional circumstances, the original administrative practices, continue to apply. The revised version of 1994 merges the two sets of rules and adopts the simple approach of repealing the algebraic formula and subjecting the holder to income tax only on the realized gain, but with equivalent relief for any loss. This 1994 legislation has been rewritten as part of ITTOIA 2005.[395]

393. United Kingdom, CTA, 2009 Parts 5 and 6.
394. United Kingdom, CTA, 2009 Part 7.
395. United Kingdom, ITTOIA, Part 4 Ch. 8.

Subpart E. Attribution of Income

A final element in the structure of an income tax is the attribution of the various elements of the tax base to the taxable person. Several different questions are involved. The most fundamental is the choice of taxable unit. Who is 'the taxpayer' for purposes of applying the various substantive rules of the tax system? Once that question has been answered, a second related issue involves taxpayer attempts to shift income among taxable units to reduce the overall tax burden of taxpayers who are, broadly speaking, related but who constitute separate taxable persons. To what extent and under what conditions will those income transfers be respected? While the issue arises primarily in the context of progressive rate structures, where splitting the income among several taxpayers can reduce the total tax burden, it can also involve taking advantage of various special deductions or allowances.

A related problem concerns the treatment of payments arising out of divorce and separation. Where a married couple is, at least for some purposes, treated as a taxable unit, a question arises as to how payments that result from the dissolution of that relationship should be handled. And even in systems in which the individual is the taxable unit, there may be special rules for payments between divorced or separated spouses and payments for the support of children.

The following material first examines the basic question of the taxable unit and then explores the related issues.

1. DEFINITION OF TAXABLE UNIT

The choice of the appropriate taxable unit involves complex issues of social and economic policy and has been the subject of much discussion in many of the countries here under consideration. Any decision regarding the taxable unit involves emphasizing some policy goals and social values at the expense of others. For example, a decision to treat the individual as the taxable unit may mean that couples with the same amount of income and otherwise similarly situated may pay a different amount of tax depending on how much income is earned by each partner. On the other hand, a decision to treat a couple as the taxable unit may mean that such couples are treated differently from other couples whose economic and social arrangements are functionally similar. In addition, depending on the structure of the rate schedule, a decision to treat married couples as the taxable unit may result in a change in overall tax burden as a result of marriage (or divorce).

The resolution of these conflicting policy goals has taken several forms in the systems here considered. In some cases, each individual is treated as a taxable unit, and there is no aggregation of income of family members. A variation on this approach is to treat the individual as the taxable unit for the purpose of taxing earned income but to have special rules dealing with unearned income. The taxation of each individual separately on earned income allows the decision about entry into the workforce to be independent of the income earned by the other spouse. On the other hand, some type of aggregation of unearned income prevents the shifting of such income within the economic unit to reduce tax burdens.

Other systems either require or allow the married couple (or certain other forms of cohabitation) to be treated as a taxable unit. This approach is sometimes accompanied by a rate structure that 'splits' the income between the two partners equally – which means that, in the case of progressive rates, marriage does not increase the total tax burden on the couple. On the other hand, a differentiated rate for married couples raises the issue of the proper relationship in the rate schedules between the rates for married couples and single persons.

Whatever approach is taken to the taxation of adults, the treatment of the income of dependent children raises a separate issue. Should they be treated as separate taxpayers or taxed together with the adults who have the responsibility for their care?

The development of the rules on taxable unit in the *United States* illustrates the interaction of these various considerations. Prior to 1948, the individual was the only taxable unit. As a result, the tax burden on married couples varied depending on whether the income was earned by one spouse, both spouses equally, or something in between these two extremes. In addition, the Supreme Court had held that, in states that had adopted the civil law community property system, each spouse was taxable on one-half of the income, regardless of who earned the income. As a result, under the progressive rate structure, married couples in community property states could pay less tax on the same amount of combined income than couples in common-law jurisdictions. In 1948, in response to this problem, couples were permitted to elect to file 'joint' returns and to aggregate their income and compute their tax under a rate structure that had brackets twice as wide as the corresponding brackets used by unmarried persons. The election was available only to couples who were married for civil law purposes. While the couple could still file separate returns if they desired, it was almost always advantageous to take advantage of the splitting of income the joint return entailed.

The introduction of joint returns meant that a couple paid significantly less tax than an individual with the same amount of income filing separately.

The perception that individuals were overtaxed in relation to couples under the rate structure introduced in connection with joint returns led in 1969 to the introduction of a new system of rate schedules. The new system retained the separate schedule for married couples but changed the relation among the brackets to reduce the difference between married and single brackets. Under the new system, the bracket differences no longer represented a 'splitting' of income between the spouses. The old rate schedules were retained for married couples who elected to file separately to prevent them from taking advantage of the new lower individual rates.

However, moving away from a system of splitting introduced a new problem. If two single persons with roughly equal income married, their tax burden would be increased, since the aggregation of their income in the married rate structure would increase the impact of the progressive rates. This 'marriage penalty' was partially addressed in 1981 with the introduction of a deduction for two-earner couples. The deduction was eliminated in 1986 when a substantial reduction in the progressivity of tax rates made the marriage penalty much less significant. However, as marginal tax rates have increased since that time, concern about the impact of marriage on tax burdens has reappeared.

There seems to be a growing recognition in the United States that in a system of progressive rates it is impossible to have an equal treatment of married couples, a differential between the taxation of individuals and married couples that does not reflect income splitting, and no significant change in tax burdens as a result of marriage. Choices and compromises must be made, and the relative importance accorded these policy objectives has varied over time. Currently, attention is focused on the 'marriage penalty' under existing law and the impact of aggregate taxation on entry into the workforce by secondary workers. In 2001 and 2003, Congress increased the size of the 15% tax bracket for married taxpayers to eliminate the marriage penalty for income taxed at that rate.

Dependent children in the United States are in general treated as separate taxpayers. However, the unearned income of children under 19 years old (24 years old for full-time students), although technically still treated as separate income and not aggregated with the parents' income, is taxed at the parents' highest marginal rate. In certain situations the income is aggregated in what could be viewed as a first step toward a wider definition of the taxable unit.[396]

The *German* system also provides an election for joint taxation of married couples living together (although not for other couples in marriage-like relationships). For electing couples, the total income of each partner is assessed and the sum of both amounts aggregated and divided by two in determining the statutory tax rate.[397] For private expenditure, husband and wife are treated as one taxpayer, but tax-free thresholds or maximum amounts for deductions are doubled. Recurrently, the impact of splitting on the tax burden of high-income families is subject to political discussion due to diverging views of the role of traditional marriage in society. Children are treated as separate taxpayers for most purposes. In recent

396. United States, IRC, s. 1(g).

397. Germany, ITA, s. 26 para. 1.

years, there has been an ongoing debate as to whether splitting for married couples should be replaced by splitting for families with children, irrespective of the legal status of the couple. There has been no political consensus so far to introduce the 'splitting procedure' for 'married' same-sex couples.

The *Canadian* system takes a different approach. The individual has always been the taxable unit, although there has been periodic discussion to establish spouses or the family as the taxable unit. However, the income of both spouses (formally married or common-law partner, which is defined to include same-sex partners) is aggregated for purposes of determining the entitlement to certain personal tax allowances. The *Australian* system is quite similar. The individual is treated as the taxable unit. As in Canada, the spousal tax credit[398] is reduced as the income of the other spouse increases, so in the case of a couple where only one partner has income there is some limited reduction of tax for the family unit. The amount of the credit and the income level at which it cuts out are relatively low. 'Spouse' for these and other tax purposes is defined as a person of the opposite sex living as husband or wife, although recently federal law has largely eliminated discrimination against same-sex couples without treating the couples as spouses. Over the last decade an increasing number of refundable tax credits, or their functional equivalent, have been introduced. These credits significantly affect the amount of tax paid by low- and middle-income taxpayers; they generally use family income as the basis of measuring qualification for the benefits. In both the Canadian and Australian systems, there are rules to prevent the shifting of income, as discussed below.

Historically, the *United Kingdom* in effect treated the married couple as a taxable unit by attributing all of the wife's income to the husband. Because the husband was the technical taxpayer, he was primarily responsible for the payment of the tax and for all dealings with the tax authorities. This approach was gradually liberalized, with the wife first given the authority to deal directly with the tax authorities, and subsequently, the couple could elect to have the wife's earned income taxed separately. Given the rate structure and other secondary consequences of the election, it was most advantageous to higher-income taxpayers. In 1990, a system of separate taxation was introduced covering both earned and unearned income. In the case of income from property, if the property is owned jointly, the income is divided evenly unless the parties can establish a different underlying ownership and elect to be taxed on that basis.[399] The reasoning behind the change included a need to recognize the changing role – and greater independence – of women in society and to provide them with privacy with regard to their income. Separate taxation applies for purposes of the capital gains tax as well, with a separate annual exemption for both spouses. Children are also treated as separate taxpayers for both income and capital gains tax purposes. There are

398. Australia, ITAA 1936, s.159J.
399. United Kingdom, ITA, ss 836–837.

rules to prevent the artificial splitting of income, but they do not apply where there is an outright gift between the spouses.[400]

Since 1997 the United Kingdom has introduced a series of tax credits to assist families.[401] Since these credits are based to a large extent on the income of households rather than individuals, the effect is to reduce significantly the number of households in which separate taxation is the rule. It will be noticed that the tax credit system looks to the income position of the household, regardless of whether the parties are married or not.

The UK has a concept of civil partnership for those of the same gender. The spouse rules apply to civil partners just as they do to spouses.

The *Japanese* system also adopts the individual as the taxable unit. At one time, there were rules that attempted to assess investment income of family members to the principal wage earner, but they were dropped because of administrative problems. A spousal allowance is provided if the income of one spouse is less than a certain limited amount. The allowance is phased out as the lower-earning spouse's income increases, so that if both spouses earn more than the base amount no allowance is available. The effect of this provision has been criticized as discouraging women from entering the workforce on a full-time basis and was partly abolished in 2003.

The *Dutch* approach is based on individual taxation with some modifications. 'Couples' are taxed separately on business and employment income, income from substantial participations, and capital income. The term 'couples' refers to taxpayers who are married or are registered partners, or have a common household with another person or persons, including parents or siblings, for more than six months and are registered at the same address.

All other income and personal deductions are divided among the individuals concerned at their discretion (with the exception that mortgage interest can be taken into account only by the person to whom the rental value of the residence is taxed). Minor children are taxed on their own business and employment income but all other income is taxed to the parents (and allocated between them at their discretion).

Sweden currently also has a system of individual taxation. In the past, the system was based on a form of aggregate taxation of couples, defined for tax purposes as those formally married or living together and having (or having had) a child together, or having been formerly married. The rules were modified in 1987 to provide for individual taxation on earned income, with unearned income taxed to the partner with the highest earned income and 'stacked' on top of the earned income. A principal reason for the change was to encourage secondary workers, primarily women, to enter the workforce by ensuring that the marginal tax rate on such persons was not affected by the income level of the other partner. This system was subsequently modified again to provide for individual taxation on unearned income. Since the rate on capital income currently is essentially proportional,

400. United Kingdom, ITTOIA, s. 626; for interpretation, *see Jones v. Garnett* [2007] STC 1536.
401. See United Kingdom, Tax Credits Act 2002.

there is no significant problem with income shifting and no need for the attribution of income to the higher-earning spouse.

The *French* system has taken a completely different approach.[402] The taxable unit is the *foyer fiscal* ('fiscal household'), which is composed of husband and wife (or unmarried partners of the same or different sex bound by a *pacte civil de solidarité*, a civil partnership akin to marriage), dependent children, and any qualified disabled person regardless of family relationship who lives with the family. The incomes of all members of the household are first aggregated. The total income is then taxed according to the *quotient familial* or 'family share' system. The taxpayer and spouse or partner are each attributed one 'share'; an additional one-half share is given for up to two additional household members. An additional full share is given for further members. Thus, a family of husband, wife, and two children would constitute three shares; a family with three children would constitute four shares, etc.

The same system applies to single persons (unmarried, widowed, or divorced persons) but, in order to decrease the tax burden on single persons, especially women with dependent children, they are granted an additional one-half share if they actually support, solely or principally, at least one child. Conversely, whenever two single persons (e.g., divorced) share the cost of the upkeep of a child, each parent can benefit only from one-half of a half-share (i.e., one-quarter) or one-half of a full share (i.e., one-half), as the case may be. Unmarried couples (except those joined by a *pacte civil de solidarité*) always constitute two distinct fiscal households. Married persons may, in exceptional circumstances, file separate tax returns provided they live separately.

The total income of the family is divided into the relevant number of shares for the purpose of determining the tax applicable to one share of income in accordance with the individual income tax progressive schedule (seven brackets, from 0% to 40%). The total tax payable by the fiscal household (before any tax credit) is then determined by multiplying the tax on one share by the number of shares.

The basic theory behind this system, which was instituted just after the Second World War, is to take into account the consumption capacity of each member of the family and to tax the family accordingly. A family is composed of a certain number of consumption units who share a given amount of income; globally, it should not pay an amount of income tax different from the sum of the separate income taxes that the family members would have paid if they had been single persons among whom an amount equal to the family global income had been equally split. Initially, each dependent child or person was considered a one-half consumption unit and so was granted a one-half share. But, considering a given total income, the greater the number of children, the smaller the tax reduction from each additional child. For this reason, in the 1980s a full share (instead of one-half) was granted to each child beginning with the third one. As the reduction in income tax resulting from the combination of the family share system and the progressive rate schedule proved to be higher for high-income households than for low-income households,

402. France, CGI, ss 6 and 7, 156, 193–199.

such reduction was at the same time limited to a set amount (€2,292 for 2008) for each one-half share in addition to the full shares accorded each spouse or the single head of household, as the case may be.

The concept of a dependent child is also complex. A child who is eighteen years or older is normally taxed as a single person, but he or she may elect to be attached to his parents' fiscal household provided he or she is less than twenty-one years of age or less than twenty-five if still in school or university, and of whatever age if disabled or performing military service. Even married (or partners in a *pacte civil de solidarité*) children may, up to the above limits, elect to be part of the parents' household, but this does not result in an increase in the number of shares, the only effect being the deduction of a set amount for each attached person, child, spouse, and grandchild (€5,729 for 2008).

This complex system concerns solely the traditional progressive individual income tax. It was not retained by Parliament in the 1990s when the new flat-rate income taxes were created. Under the new taxes, the taxable unit is the individual; the family structure is not relevant.

2. ALIMONY AND CHILD SUPPORT

The treatment of payments that arise out of the dissolution of a marriage also raise attribution of income issues. Suppose, for example, that as the result of a divorce, a husband is required to make monthly payments to his former wife. There are several ways in which such payments could be viewed. One approach would be to treat the payment as a kind of 'splitting' of the income between the two former spouses. Under this view, the alimony would in effect be deductible by the husband but taxed to the wife. On the other hand, the payment could be viewed as a personal expense to the husband and non-deductible. As for the wife, the payment could be taxable, on the view that it has increased her separate net worth and power to consume or, alternatively, treated in the same manner as interfamilial gifts, which generally do not result in taxation to the recipient. The same issues arise with respect to payments of child support to the custodial parent by the non-custodial parent. The systems examined here have taken a variety of approaches to these questions.

The *United States* system makes a basic distinction between alimony and child support. Historically, both alimony and child support were treated as personal expenses, non-deductible and not includable. Successive statutory enactments beginning in 1942 allowed a deduction and required a corresponding inclusion for alimony payments while continuing the non-deductible-excludable treatment for child support payments. The distinction between the two types of payments, often turning on intricacies of state family law, led to substantial litigation. The law was simplified in 1984 by providing a federal definition of alimony that gives the parties substantial leeway in determining which payments will be treated as alimony.[403] To qualify, the payments must be made in connection with a divorce

403. United States, IRC, ss 71 and 215.

decree or written agreement of separation, must be in cash, and the parties must be living apart. The payments must end after the death of the payee and cannot be linked to events that indicate they are in the nature of child support payments (e.g., changes made when a child reaches a certain age). Special complex and largely ineffective rules also are provided to prevent 'front loading' of payments in what is essentially a property settlement rather than periodic alimony.

Even when the statutory requirements for alimony treatment are present, the parties can avoid these tax results by providing in the agreement that the statutory taxing pattern is not intended to apply. This provision gives the parties maximum flexibility in allocating the tax burden of the payments.

Payments for child support and property settlements, which are essentially all payments that do not meet the statutory definition of alimony, are non-deductible and not includable. Property settlements in connection with a divorce continue to be covered by the rollover treatment usually applicable to transfers between spouses.

The *Swedish* system is essentially the same as that in the United States. Periodic payments of alimony are deductible by the payer and taxable to the recipient. Alimony is viewed as an independent source of income for the recipient and is treated as income from services. Other periodic support payments, including those to children, are not deductible and not taxable.

Canada and *Australia* offer interesting contrasts. Under the Canadian system, until 1995, periodic payments of both alimony and child support were deductible by the payer spouse and taxable to the recipient spouse. Lump-sum payments and property settlements, in contrast, were neither deductible nor taxable. It was common practice in the determination of the level of alimony, child support, and property payments to take into account the relative tax brackets of the parties and to utilize the form of payment that maximized the overall tax benefit. In a 1994 case, the Supreme Court of Canada rejected a constitutional challenge to the inclusion of child support payments in the income of the recipient.[404] It was argued that the rule violated the equality provision of the Charter of Rights and Freedoms, as only separated custodial parents were taxed on child support. Despite its victory in court, the government introduced sweeping changes to the treatment of child support payments, including the elimination of the deduction for such payments and the taxation of the payments to the recipient. Alimony and spousal maintenance payments, however, remain subject to the deduction-inclusion system. Transfers of property between divorced or separated spouses qualify for rollover treatment.

The *Australian* system makes no distinction between alimony and child support payments. Both are in effect taxed to the payer, since they are not deductible, and are exempt to the recipient.[405] Administratively, child support payments are collected with the support of the tax administration. Where property has been set aside in trust to fund maintenance payments, the payments are taxable

404. *Thibaudeau v. The Queen* [1995] 1 CTC 382 (SCC).

405. Australia, ITAA 1997, ss 51–50.

to the recipient and are in effect deductible by the payer, since the income is excluded from his return. As for property settlements, there is an automatic rollover on property division between divorced or separated spouses.[406]

The *United Kingdom* similarly does not make any distinction between alimony and child support. Prior to 1988, both types of payments were deductible by the payer and taxable to the respective recipients. In 1988, a new system was introduced that eliminated the general deduction for such payments and also made them tax-free in the hands of the recipient. Initially, a limited deduction was allowed based on the married couple's allowance, which had survived the switch to separate taxation. That deduction was subsequently converted to a credit; it is now relevant only where one of the parties was born before 6 April 1935.[407]

The elimination of the deduction for support payments in 1988 took place at a time when there was a substantial reduction in tax rates, and it is unclear if the change was simply part of a general base broadening or reflected a 'family values' policy that was intended to make it more expensive to support separated families.

In *Germany*, alimony is historically treated as a personal expense and is therefore not deductible. This concept is based on the idea that alimony payments concern the consumption of income, not the accrual of the income itself. Correspondingly, such payments are not taxable in the hands of the recipient. However, under a special statutory provision, up to €13,805 of alimony payments may be deducted and correspondingly included in the income of the recipient if both parties so agree.[408] In addition, in some circumstances, alimony payments which do not qualify for this special treatment can be considered as an 'extraordinary burden' and may be deducted subject to a limitation of €7,680 on such expenses per year.[409]

Traditionally, payments for child support (within or outside marriage) were also regarded as non-deductible consumption expenses. Over the years, the German Constitutional Court has relentlessly argued that funds required for child support are not 'at the disposition' of the taxpayer and therefore – according to the ability-to-pay principle – must be deductible for tax purposes. Currently, a tax-free threshold for child support of €1,824 per parent (€3,648 per couple) is laid down in the statute to which the 'child care threshold' (€1,080/€2,160) must be added (see the discussion of child care expenses above).[410] In practice, these tax expenditures are regularly 'set off' against the payment of child subsidies by the government. Thus, only insofar as the tax advantage resulting from the tax-free threshold exceeds the child subsidies are they recognized in the tax assessment (dual system).

In the *Dutch* system, periodic alimony payments, whether paid to a former spouse or a spouse from whom the taxpayer lives separately, are deductible as a

406. Australia, ITAA 1997, Subdivision 126-A.
407. United Kingdom, ITA, s. 454(3).
408. Germany, ITA, ss 10 para. 1 no. 1 and 22 no. 1b.
409. Germany, ITA, s. 33a para. 1.
410. Germany, ITA, s. 32 para. 6.

qualified personal expense and includable by the recipient. In addition, a lump-sum payment in lieu of periodic payments is deductible when made to a former spouse. A deduction for child support payments is allowed based on a fixed statutory amount related to the age of the child. The payments are not included in income.

In *France*, amounts paid in compliance with the obligation imposed on family members by the Civil Code to support their children or parents are tax-deductible provided they are reasonable in relation to the wealth of the payer and the needs of the payee. The deduction of support for children is possible if they are not attached to the payer's fiscal household but, in the case of adult children, it is limited to a set amount (€5,729 for 2008 income or double this amount if the child is married). Alimony and most other court-ordered payments to an ex-spouse are also deductible provided the parties are separated. Alimony and child support are taxable to the payees if deductible by the payer.[411]

In *Japan*, payment of periodic alimony is not common, and there are no special tax rules. Divorce settlements typically involve a lump-sum payment that is neither deductible nor taxable. Such payments are treated by analogy to tort damages for personal injury. Periodic child support payments are also non-deductible and non-taxable.

3. LIMITATIONS ON ASSIGNMENT OF INCOME

In a system with progressive rates, taxpayers have an incentive to attempt to shift income to related taxpayers who are not treated as part of the same taxable unit but who are part of the same economic family unit. The pressure for income shifting is a function of the definition of the taxable unit and is greatest where husband and wife are treated as separate taxpayers. Techniques to shift earned income typically involve contractual arrangements that create rights to income in related parties. With respect to income from property, the transaction often involves a transfer of the right to the income while the transferor retains the underlying property. In both situations, a basic question is the extent to which the tax system will respect the underlying civil or commercial aspects of the transaction. The systems have reached a variety of results in these situations.

In the *United States*, case law early on established the proposition that earned income was taxable to the earner, and the tax burden could not be shifted by contractual arrangements, even if those arrangements were not tax motivated and were effective for civil law purposes.[412] With respect to income from property, the principles are more complex. Where the entire property is transferred, the tax on both the gain on the disposition of the property and the current income from the property will be shifted to the donee. Where the right to the income is given away but the underlying property is retained, the transfer generally will not be respected

411. France, CGI, s. 156 II 2.
412. United States, *Lucas v. Earl*, 281 U.S. 111 (1930).

for tax purposes.[413] Where the only right the transferor has is the right to an income stream (e.g., a series of royalty payments), and the entire right is transferred, the transfer may be effective if the income stream is of long enough duration. On the other hand, the transfer of the right to one year's income while retaining the remaining stream would not be effective. Special rules deal with the transfer of property to trusts.[414] In general, the transferor must give up nearly all rights to the property (a *de minimis* reversionary interest is allowed) to shift the tax burden to the trust or the trust beneficiaries. Under prior rules, if a ten-year income interest was transferred, the transfer was effective for tax purposes. This rule led to significant amounts of income shifting through trusts and was replaced by the present requirement of a complete transfer.

In business relations between related parties, in general, arm's length principles must be followed. A special statutory rule recognizes partnerships with family members as partners but requires that partners performing services must be reasonably compensated, thus preventing the indirect shifting of income to the partners (typically minors).[415]

In the case of interest-free or low-interest loans, either an arm's length interest rate is imputed or the income generated by the loan is taxed directly to the lender, depending on the circumstances of the loan.[416]

As might be expected, *Canada*, which has the most extensive system of individual taxation, also has the most restrictive rules on assignment of income. Where the taxpayer transfers property to a spouse or minor child, any income from the property, or any property substituted for it, is attributed to the transferor. A similar rule applies to capital gains, but only to property disposed of to a spouse. The attribution rules also apply to interest-free or low-interest loans. Certain dividends and certain income derived through a trust or partnership by a minor are subject to a special 'kiddie tax' at the top marginal rate.[417] Beyond the spouse or child situation, where the taxpayer assigns the right to income to a third party in a non-arm's length transaction, the income remains the income of the transferor. This rule prevents the assignment of salary income as well as income from property where the transferor retains the underlying property. A special statutory rule attributes the income generated on an interest-free or low-interest loan to a person related to the lender. Commencing in 2007, spouses are entitled to elect to split pension income received by one spouse.[418]

The rules in the *United Kingdom* are more liberal. An outright gift of property is effective to shift the burden of tax on the income to the transferee. If property is transferred in trust, the settlor remains taxable if he has retained any interest in the property. Special rules apply to trusts for the benefit of spouses, with the income of

413. United States, *Helvering v. Horst*, 311 U.S. 112 (1940).
414. United States, IRC, s. 674-77.
415. United States, IRC, s. 704(e).
416. United States, IRC, s. 7872.
417. Canada, ITA, s. 120.4.
418. Canada, ITA, s. 60.03.

the trust remaining taxable to the grantor in most cases, even if the grantor does not retain any interest in the trust. The term 'trust' is widely defined for these purposes and includes any transfer or arrangement. There are even wider rules treating income of unmarried minor children of the settlor as income of the settlor, but these rules do not apply to income that is accumulated and not distributed.[419] At one time, the UK capital gains tax had its own rules under which gains accruing under a trust in which the settlor retained an interest were treated as gains of the settlor. With the 2008 changes in the rates of capital gains tax, it would have been advantageous for taxpayers to bring themselves within this anti-avoidance rule; the rule was therefore repealed.

In *Australia*, outright transfers of property between spouses are also effective to shift the incidence of the tax. In addition, various income-splitting schemes involving a division of professional income through the leasing of assets and the provision of services by a related trust have had varying degrees of success. Splitting of income with children has been prevented by a special statutory rule that taxes the unearned income of children (with limited exceptions, including the income from property received by will or transferred under a divorce settlement) at the highest marginal tax rate, regardless of the rates of the parents.[420] In addition, a special provision prevents short-term (less than seven years) transfers of income rights.[421] In the 1998 tax reform, the government indicated that it would not be seeking to close down the income-splitting opportunities in current law, especially involving trusts. The former Prime Minister was a supporter of the family unit of taxation, and income splitting goes some way to achieving this end.

Sweden has no special statutory rules on assignment of income. In the case of earned income, case law principles have required that income be taxed to the person who earned the income. The income source is performance of services, and therefore the income belongs to the person performing the services. Thus, income earned by an employee that, under contractual arrangements, is received directly by the employee's spouse, is taxed to the employee. The rules are more liberal in the case of income from property. Dividend income can be transferred effectively for tax purposes while the transferor retains the underlying shares. In the case of an outright gift of property, the carryover basis results in the tax on the gain being shifted to the donee. No interest is imputed on interest-free loans, allowing the transfer of the income to the borrower.

The *German* rules on assignment of income are not set out in explicit statutory provisions but are judge-made to a large extent. Because there is no general assignment provision in the Income Tax Act, it is accepted that the issues are resolved by the definitions laid down in the provisions governing the particular source of income. The taxpayer is the person who 'derives' income.[422] Therefore, income from a trade or business is assigned to the person who carries on that specific

419. United Kingdom, ITTOIA, ss 619 et seq.
420. Australia, ITAA 1936, Part III Division 6AA.
421. Australia, ITAA 1936, Part III Division 6A.
422. Germany, ITA, s. 2 para. 1.

business or trade. Income from rent or royalty payments is attributed to the persons who are parties to the relevant contracts under civil law. Capital income is attributed to the person who is the (beneficial) owner of the underlying capital.

In practice, these general rules lead to highly disputed questions of law. In the case of *Treuhand/fiducia* (which is similar to the 'trust' concept of the common law), the prevailing opinion accepts the attribution of income to the 'settlor' or the 'beneficiary' only if that person controls the 'trustee'; otherwise, the income is attributed to the trustee. With respect to partnerships and companies, there is an ongoing discussion as to whether the assignment of a profit strictly follows the civil law treatment or whether there has to be some 'adequate' relationship between the original contribution of a partner/shareholder and his stake in the profits. In the case of married couples, in most cases, the 'shift' of income to a spouse is not relevant because the couple is entitled to be taxed according to the 'splitting' system, as described earlier. There is abundant case law and literature on the tax treatment of children participating in their parents' business. They may be recognized as limited or silent partners if actual legal and economic rights are transferred and exercised.

Much of the case law in the assignment of income area involves the treatment of usufruct (*Niessbrauch*), a civil law institution roughly equivalent to an income interest or term of years in the common-law tradition. A usufruct can be created in personal or real property but is most commonly a real property right; it can be either gratuitous or for consideration. In general terms, in the case of a gratuitous usufruct, the income is taxed to the transferee-usufructuary. However, where the asset is a wasting one, no depreciation is allowed, since the usufructuary does not bear the tax cost. Correspondingly, the transferor-owner is denied any depreciation deductions because he is not in receipt of any taxable income. The denial of the deductions makes the transaction unattractive from a tax point of view if the purpose is to shift income. In case of a usufruct on a business, the transferee must manage the business to qualify as the relevant subject of the income thereof.

With respect to income from capital, if only the bare right to income (e.g., a dividend on stock or interest on a bond), is transferred, the income remains taxable to the holder of the underlying asset.[423] In more complex situations, the question is whether the rights transferred amount to an opportunity to influence the economic course of events through voting or management rights, which may be sufficient to shift the income stream but may also be found to be a transfer of the asset.

Japan has no special rules on assignment of income. Contractual arrangements to shift earned income would be treated as taxable to the earner with a subsequent gift of the income, possibly subject to the gift tax. Attempts to shift property income have not been an issue since, under civil law concepts, it is not possible to effectively divide the right to the income from the underlying property.

In *France*, because of the aggregate household system of taxation, there are no special anti-assignment of income provisions. Mention should be made, however, of the limit placed on the deductibility of the wages paid by one spouse carrying on

423. Germany, ITA s. 20 para. 5.

a commercial or industrial business to the other spouse as an employee, because wages are still in some ways more favourably treated than industrial and commercial profits.[424]

In *The Netherlands*, particular income elements and deductions can be assigned between couples at their discretion, as discussed above.

424. France, CGI, s. 154.

Part Three

Taxation of Business Organizations

The taxation of business organizations generally falls into two basic patterns. 'Corporate' taxation typically imposes a tax on the income of certain types of commercial organizations, usually formed under special enabling legislation, and also taxes the profits distributed to the holders of ownership interests, usually adjusting the taxation in the hands of the owners to reflect the fact that the income has been taxed to the organization. The other model, 'partnership' or 'flow-through' taxation, taxes the income derived by the organization directly to the owners, whether or not distributed, and makes appropriate adjustments to reflect this fact when the income is in fact distributed. The following Subpart A deals with corporate taxation, while Subpart B treats partnership taxation.

Of course, these two models do not exhaust the possible patterns of the taxation of business organizations. In Australia, for example, substantial amounts of closely held commercial activity are carried on in the form of 'trading trusts', and foundations or other types of organization are important in other jurisdictions. Nonetheless, most of the issues in the taxation of business organizations revolve around corporate and partnership patterns.

Subpart A. Corporate-Shareholder Taxation

The corporate tax systems in the countries here under consideration have at various times ranged from traditional 'classical' systems of full corporate- and individual-level taxation of distributed profits (United States, The Netherlands, Sweden) to complete integration of corporate and individual tax on distributed profits (Germany, France, Australia). Currently, a wide variety of taxing patterns exists, with imputation systems falling out of favour (except in Australia) and being replaced with direct shareholder-level relief.

This Subpart begins with a brief overview of the structure of the rules governing corporate taxation in each of the countries. The material then examines a number of technical problems common to all systems. Following this, a more detailed discussion of the relation between corporate- and shareholder-level taxation explores the extent to which the various systems deal with the 'double taxation of dividends' and the related topic of capital gains on the disposition of shares in companies.

The function a particular rule performs is affected by the system in which it is operating, which in turn may partially explain the contours of the rule. For example, a distribution of profits may bring with it a shareholder credit in an imputation system but be subject to unrelieved shareholder-level taxation in a classical system. Thus, the role the rule plays within the particular system must be kept in mind when considering matters on a comparative basis. Hence, there is some intermingling of the common issues and the relief of double taxation, but as far as possible, the discussion is kept separate in what follows.

1. OVERVIEW OF CORPORATE TAX SYSTEMS

In the last fifty years, the two predominant corporate tax systems have been the classical system, which taxes the company on its income and then taxes the shareholder separately on distributions received from the company, and the imputation system, which gives the shareholder a credit for corporate tax paid, thus eliminating in whole or part the double taxation of dividends. More recently, many countries have changed the basic structure of their corporate tax systems away from the classical and imputation systems to systems that give approximate or 'rough and ready' relief from double taxation. Because of this state of flux of corporate tax systems, the descriptions that follow often include an indication of changes that have occurred in the last decade or so. Much of the change has been driven by international considerations. These are dealt with in Part Four.

Currently, one classical system survives among the countries covered, and even it is different from the traditional classical system in that special rates apply to the taxation of income from capital generally, including dividend income. Thus, *Sweden* has a classical system, although for a brief period in 1994 dividends were exempt from individual taxation. The basic corporate tax rate is 28%, down from 52% prior to 1991. For individuals, dividend income is usually taxed as income from capital at a flat 30% rate (compared to a top individual rate for other non-capital income of 55%). Capital gains are also subject to 30% tax as income from capital.

The corporate tax system in *The Netherlands* was a pure classical system until changes were made in 1997 and 2001. Since then the system is difficult to classify in traditional terms, although it may be regarded as a variant of the classical system. The Netherlands has a corporate rate of 25.5% (with rates of 20% and 23% for corporate income below €200,000, in order to encourage small business).[1]

In The Netherlands before 2001, individual progressive rates ranging from 37.7% to 60% applied to dividends received by individuals. In addition, before 1997 capital gains on stock were not taxed to individuals unless the level of shareholding amounted to a 'substantial interest', defined as at least a 33.3% interest held by the taxpayer, his spouse, or close relatives (and at least 7% held directly by the taxpayer or his spouse) at any time within five years of the disposition. Gains on the disposition of a substantial interest were taxed at 20%. This system led to individuals investing in growth funds, which in turn invested in companies and reinvested the dividends received. The result was that individuals were not taxed on the reinvested dividends and were exempt on the capital gain.

Beginning in 2001, shares held by individuals that are not part of a substantial shareholding are taxed as part of their net wealth on a deemed yield of 4% of the value of the shares at a rate of 30%, regardless of the actual dividends or capital gains received. On sale, the capital gain is not taxed but is taken into account in determining the base for the tax on the deemed yield. The base uses the average of the beginning and year-end value of the shares, or the beginning value and sale price if the shares are sold during the year. This change was part of a larger change to the taxation of income from capital, which is described in the Netherlands Country Description in Part One. From 1997, for substantial shareholdings of individuals, dividends and capital gains are now subject to tax of 25%.

1. Netherlands, Company Tax Act 1969 (CTA), Art. 22.

At the same time, the threshold for substantial shareholdings was lowered to 5% to be consistent with the substantial participation exemption for corporations holding shares. In this way, individuals with substantial shareholdings are generally taxed at similar rates to individuals who operate businesses in non-corporate form, while portfolio investments in shares are covered by the 'deemed yield' regime.

The *United States* has abandoned its classical system in recent times. Corporate profits are generally taxed at 35%, although there are lower rates for some brackets of income. These lower rates are phased out at various higher income levels, giving an odd pattern of marginal rates.[2] Since 2003, distributed profits are taxed to individual shareholders at preferential rates that do not exceed 15%. For individuals, the maximum tax rate on capital gains is also limited to 15%.[3] Previously, dividends were taxed at 'normal' individual marginal tax rates. Compared to the previous system, the preferential rates benefit upper-bracket taxpayers whose dividend income and capital gains would otherwise be included in higher marginal brackets. On the other hand, the change reduces the element of double taxation of dividends and capital gains on shares. Capital losses can be used only to offset capital gains, although for individuals, $3,000 of capital losses annually can be used against normal income.

The *Japanese* system has a similar degree of integration of corporate and shareholder tax. The corporate tax rate is 30% national tax and approximately 41% combined (including municipal and local taxes) falling from about 50% in 1997. For individual taxpayers with income below ¥10 million, there is a credit for 10% of the amount of the dividend distribution, which can reduce the individual tax on the dividend and the tax on income falling in other schedules. Where the income exceeds the threshold, the credit is limited to 5% of the dividend in excess of that amount and 10% on the remaining amount of the dividend. From 2004, taxpayers may elect not to report dividends received from publicly traded corporations in their tax returns. In this case, only the 20% (10% until the end of 2011) withholding tax is imposed on such dividends (compared to the top individual tax rate of 50% less the credit); all tax rates include municipal and local income tax. Dividends received by corporations are excluded from tax for holdings of 25% or more; otherwise, half of the dividends received are taxed. Capital gains on listed shares realized by individuals were previously taxed at 1.05% of the sale price of the shares; otherwise, at 26% (including 6% municipal and local income tax) of the gain. From 2004, listed shares are taxed at 20% (10% until the end of 2011), including municipal and local income tax. Capital gains on shares realized by corporations are generally taxable at ordinary rates.

In contrast to these systems, the *German* system for many years combined a split rate on distributed profits with an imputation credit to eliminate fully the impact of the corporate tax on profits distributed to resident individuals. In 2000 the system was radically changed. The imputation and split-rate system was abolished and replaced with a 'shareholder-relief' system. This system is intended

2. United States, Internal Revenue Code (IRC), s. 11.
3. United States, IRC, s. 1(h).

to achieve integration in a 'semi-classical' setting by relying on partial integration in the form of relief at the shareholder level, combined with an overall reduction in the corporate tax rate. The starting point in the changes was a substantial reduction in the flat corporate income tax rate from 40% (retained profits) and 30% (distributed profits) to a 25% rate irrespective of whether profits are retained or not. In 2008, the corporate tax rate was reduced to 15%.[4] To provide some 'rough and ready' relief for the payment of tax at the corporate level, until 2008, only 50% of the cash dividends were taxed in the hands of the individual shareholder. From 2009, dividends from shares held as private assets are subject to a final withholding tax of 25%.[5] The tax is applied on a gross basis and no deductions are available. If the stock is held as a business asset, only 60% of the dividends is taxable in the hands of the shareholder at the individual tax rate.[6] To avoid discrimination against foreign investment, this 'part-income method' is also extended to dividends from foreign-based companies. The prior system did not take foreign corporate-level taxes into account. Intercompany dividends are totally free of tax, (even in the international setting).[7] But there is a kind of 'shadow tax' on 5% of the dividend, which amount is deemed to represent the portion of expenses allocable to the otherwise non-taxable dividend.[8]

Unlike the former imputation system, the new corporate tax system also tries to align the treatment of dividends and capital gains. Capital gain from stock that is held as a private asset is taxed with a 25% withholding tax.[9] The bank managing the custody account withholds the tax. If an individual owns at least 1% of the capital stock, or if the shares are held as business assets, 60% of the capital gain is taxed at the individual tax rate.[10] Ninety-five percent of the gain on the sale of shares held by a corporate shareholder is free of tax to parallel the treatment of intercompany dividends.[11]

The *United Kingdom* repealed its advance corporation tax system in 1999 and now has a system where dividends from resident corporations to resident individuals carry a fixed credit and are taxed at reduced rates. The basic rate of corporation tax is 28%. A lower 21% rate is applicable to profits below £300,000 and is phased out as profits exceed that amount, reaching the 28% rate at £1.5 million.[12]

Dividend distributions by resident corporations to resident individuals carry a fixed tax credit of one-ninth of the dividend. As the credit is included in taxable income, the credit equals 10% of the dividend plus the tax credit (the grossed-up

4. Germany, Corporate Income Tax Act (CITA), s. 23 para. 1.
5. Germany, CITA, s. 32d para. 1 sentence (hereafter sent.) 1.
6. Germany, Income Tax Act (ITA), ss 3 no. 40 and 20 para. 8.
7. Germany, CITA, s. 8b para. 1.
8. Germany, CITA, s. 8b para. 5.
9. Germany, ITA, s. 20 para. 2.
10. Germany, ITA, ss 3 no. 40, 17 para. 1 and 20 para. 8.
11. Germany, CITA, s. 8b para. 2.
12. The rates of tax are set by the annual Finance Act. The provision for the lower rate is United Kingdom, Income and Corporation Taxes Act 1988, s. 13.

amount).[13] In addition, individuals are taxed at reduced progressive rates on receipt of dividends. The 20% personal tax rate is reduced to 10% and the 40% tax rate to 32.5% (the 45% rate proposed for 2011 will be reduced to 37.5%).[14] The relation between the taxation of capital income earned directly and distributed corporate profits depends on the rate applicable at the corporate level. In the case of a corporation paying tax at 28%, approximately one quarter of the 28% corporation tax remains unrelieved, but where the corporation is taxed at a rate of 21%, virtually all of the corporation tax is relieved. The United Kingdom used this relatively complicated credit method to replace its imputation system in order to address various international tax issues, which are discussed in Part Four.

For individuals, since 2008, capital gains are taxed at a flat rate of 18%. This reform targeted perceived abuses of the prior taper relief system, including by the controllers of private equity funds. The reform was accompanied by retention of the effective 10% rate for certain gains realized by entrepreneurs. The substantial annual exemption for net capital gains of nearly £10,000 continues.[15]

Intercorporate dividends received from resident corporations are exempt.[16] Capital gains on the disposal of shares by corporations are, however, fully taxable with indexation relief. A substantial shareholder exemption was introduced in 2002 but is available only where the subsidiary is a trading company.[17]

France was one of the first European countries to adopt an imputation system after the Second World War, and the degree of integration has varied. Initially, a credit (*avoir fiscal*) of one-half of the dividend distributed was available to resident shareholders. Where dividends carrying the credit were paid from income that had not borne full corporate level tax, a compensatory tax (*précompte mobilier*) was imposed. From 1993, when the corporate tax rate (initially 50%) was reduced to 33.33%, the imputation credit provided full relief for distributed profits. Corporate shareholders holding a 5% or more interest were entitled to elect either to exclude dividends received from income or to include them with the imputation credit. Since 1999, however, the rate of the credit granted to corporate shareholders not entitled to intercorporate dividend relief has been progressively reduced.

Finally, the cost to the Treasury of the system was significant (particularly since non-residents were entitled by many tax treaties to a payment equivalent to the imputation credit). In addition, questions concerning the conformity of the *avoir fiscal* to the EU freedom of establishment and free movement of capital principles had been raised.[18] In response to these factors, the 2004 Finance Act repealed the *avoir fiscal* in 2005 and replaced it with a deduction (first 50%, then 40% since the reorganization of the progressive rate schedule in 2006) at the individual shareholder level for dividends received. The deduction applies to

13. United Kingdom, Income Tax (Trading and Other Income) Act 2005, ss 397 and 398.
14. United Kingdom, Income Tax Act 2007, s. 8.
15. United Kingdom, Taxation of Chargeable Gains Act 1992, ss 3, 4 and 169H–169S.
16. United Kingdom, Corporation Tax Act 2009, s. 1285.
17. United Kingdom, Taxation of Chargeable Gains Act 1992, Sch. 7AC.
18. See ECJ, 7 Sep. 2004, C-519/02 (*Manninen*) dealing with incoming dividends and EFTA Court, 23 Nov. 2004, E-1/04 (*Fokus Bank ASA*) dealing with outgoing dividends.

dividends from French companies and, in addition – because of EC law and non-discrimination clauses – to dividends from corporations having their seat in the EU or in countries having concluded with France a tax treaty that includes an exchange of information clause. Such dividends after the deduction (i.e., 60% of the dividend) are then subject to the progressive individual income tax rate schedule, which ranges up to 40% (plus 12.1% additional flat-rate levies) but, since 2008, the taxpayer has been able to opt for a flat 18% tax (plus 12.1%) on the whole dividend. Gains from the disposal of shares are taxed as private capital gains – that is, subject to an 18% flat rate (plus 12.1%) when realized by individual shareholders not holding the shares in a business. Gains that are treated as business capital gains are taxed as ordinary income if they are short-term (i.e., held for less than two years), or at a 16% flat rate if long-term, plus 12.1% in both cases.

No relief from economic double taxation is available for corporate shareholders that are not entitled to the intercorporate dividend exemption. Gains realized by such shareholders on the disposal of their shares are also taxed at the normal corporate tax rate. Those that are entitled to the intercorporate regime (holding 5% or more interest in the distributing company) benefit from a full exemption on dividends received[19] and, since 2007, on gains on the disposal of their holdings.[20]

The *Canadian* imputation system allows full imputation of the corporate tax in the case of Canadian-controlled privately held corporations and, until 2007, allowed partial imputation for publicly traded companies and other private corporations, with the degree of integration depending on the nature of the corporate activity.

In 2007, significant changes were made to the integration system in response to the elimination of the benefit of so-called income trusts. In the decade before 2007, many corporations, including large public corporations, were converting into income trust structures to eliminate the double taxation of income earned by Canadian corporations. In effect, the shareholders became unitholders in a trust, and the trust's income was reduced or eliminated through interest deductions. After allowing these income trust structures to flourish, and even promising that they would not be eliminated, the government was forced to counteract the loss of tax revenue. The legislative response was a tax on distributions by income trusts and a reduction in the tax on dividends paid by corporations so that there would no longer be any benefit for corporations to convert into income trusts. After 2011, when the changes are fully phased in, the result will approximate full integration for dividends (called eligible dividends) received by Canadian-resident individuals from Canadian corporations (other than those paid by a Canadian-controlled private corporations out of active business income, which qualify for a reduced tax rate).

One of the most striking features of the Canadian system is that it provides the dividend credit regardless of whether the corporation distributing the dividend has actually paid the corporate-level tax. Thus, it goes beyond simply eliminating the

19. France, France, *Code général des impôts* (General Tax Code, hereafter CGI), ss 145 and 246.
20. France, CGI, s. 219 I-a.

double tax on corporate profits and amounts to an incentive to Canadian-resident individuals to invest in Canadian corporations. Intercorporate dividends are entitled to a full dividend received deduction. Capital gains on shares are subject to the usual 50% capital gains exclusion for both individual and corporate shareholders.

Australia has the only remaining full imputation system among the countries covered. It gives full relief from corporate-level tax on distributions, but the technique is somewhat different. The basic corporate rate is 30% currently, reduced from 49% since 1988. When fully taxed corporate profits are distributed, domestic individual shareholders receive a refundable credit for the full amount of the corporate tax.[21] The corporation distributing the dividend attaches or 'franks' the dividend with a specified amount of corporate tax based on its estimates of the tax it has paid and dividends it has received on which tax has been paid. If over the course of the year a company attaches more corporate tax than it has paid to dividends, a compensatory tax is levied, which can be offset against future company tax liabilities but with penalties if over-franking exceeds 10%. The corporation must inform the shareholder of the amount of credit attached to each dividend payment. 'Anti-streaming' rules prevent dividends being paid from franked accounts to shareholders entitled to the credit and other non-franked dividends to other shareholders.[22] Capital gains on shares acquired after the effective date of the capital gains legislation are taxed at ordinary rates, with individuals entitled to a 50% discount on the amount of capital gain brought to tax if the shares have been held for more than a year.[23]

Table III at the end of Subpart A summarizes these and other features of each of the systems.

2. DEFINING ENTITIES SUBJECT TO TAX

A basic structural decision in the design of a corporate tax is the determination of which entities or organizations should be subject to the tax. Depending on the state's commercial or business organization law, there may be a number of forms of business organization that would be possible subjects for the corporate tax. In some systems, the determination is made on the basis of a statutory list or enumeration of organizations, which is exclusive. More typically, a non-exclusive list and some more general description of characteristics will cause an organization to fall under the corporate taxing scheme. For organizations that are not subject to the corporate tax, some pattern of single-level 'pass-through' taxation is typically applicable and is discussed in Subpart B.

In the *United States* system, all entities formed under the general domestic corporate laws of the states are treated as corporations for federal tax purposes.[24]

---

21. Australia, Income Tax Assessment Act 1997 (ITAA 1997), Divs 67, 207.
22. Australia, ITAA 1977, Divs 201–205.
23. Australia, ITAA 1977, Div 115.
24. United States, Treasury Regulations (Treas. Regs.), ss 301.7701-2(b)(1)–(7).

Thus, the tax applies in principle to both a one-person corporation and a publicly traded corporation with thousands of shareholders. Other forms of business organization in the United States, that is, partnerships and limited liability companies with more than one member, which are not publicly traded, are taxable as flow-through entities unless they 'check the box', that is, elect to be taxable as corporations.[25] Publicly-traded entities are always taxable as corporations regardless of their form of organization.[26] Limited liability companies with only one member are disregarded ('tax nothings') unless they elect to be taxable as corporations.[27] The 'check-the-box' rules replace earlier regulations that were a technical morass and created differences in classification based on relatively insignificant factors.

Some of the other systems here under consideration have taken an approach to classification for tax purposes that follows more closely the commercial law classifications. Thus, in *Canada*, entities formed under the corporation law are subject to the corporate income tax, while those formed under partnership provisions are treated under pass-through rules. There is no attempt to classify civil law partnerships as corporations.

Swedish rules follow the same pattern. There are no tax rules classifying entities for tax purposes, and classification is based on private law characterizations. In general, all entities (except partnerships) that have to be registered are treated as corporations for tax purposes.

In the *German* system, the Corporation Tax Law lists specific organizational forms that are subject to the tax.[28] In general, these forms correspond to the forms of organization under the civil or commercial law and other organizations that are treated for civil law purposes as 'legal persons'. A special catchall provision includes associations, institutions, foundations, and other 'conglomerations of assets' to the extent that the participants are not subject to tax directly. The list is exclusive, and only the enumerated forms are subject to corporate tax. General and limited commercial partnerships, as well as civil law partnerships, are not subject to the corporate tax. This has led to the construction of limited partnerships with a corporate general partner, typically with low capitalization (*GmbH & Co. KG*). Despite their economic resemblance to corporations, these entities are not subject to corporate tax. As the European Court of Justice (ECJ) has recently forced Germany to recognize the legal personality of foreign companies that have their 'real seat' in Germany but their registered office in another EU Member State, and as the 'Societas Europaea' has been introduced as a new supranational company form, Germany changed its tax legislation to include foreign and supranational corporate forms explicitly. When the corporate income tax rate was lowered to 15%, an 'election' for partnerships to be taxed under corporate income taxation

25. United States, Treas. Regs., ss 301.7701-3(b).
26. United States, IRC, s. 7704.
27. United States, Treas. Regs., ss 301.7701-3(b).
28. Germany, CITA, s. 1 para. 1.

was considered but gave way to a reduced tax rate on reinvested partnerships profits within the framework of the income tax.[29]

The *Dutch* rules are similar. The entities subject to corporate tax are defined in the Corporate Income Tax Act both in a 'specific' manner – that is, through enumeration (where Dutch entities are concerned, such as the NV and the BV) – and in a 'generic' manner – that is, through listing of generic criteria (e.g., entities created under Dutch or foreign law whose capital is divided into shares).[30] As a result, all entities whose interests are freely transferable and whose income does not accrue directly to the participants, but requires a decision as to distribution, are subject to corporate tax. Certain other entities are also subject to the corporate tax to the extent that they carry on a business.[31]

In *France*, in general, the form of civil organization is determinative for tax classification. The tax code enumerates different types of business organizations, specifically those whose equity interests are evidenced by shares, which are subject to the corporate income tax regardless of their activity. All of these organizations provide limited liability to their participants. The code also contains a catch-all provision under which all entities (other than partnerships) that have a juridical personality under civil law are subject to the corporation tax if they carry on profit-seeking activities.[32]

There are some interesting special rules. The share of profits attributable to limited partners is subject to corporate tax. Thus, the corporate tax is the price for limited liability. General partnerships are given an election to be treated as corporations for tax purposes.[33] Conversely, since 2008 small newly created corporations whose shareholders are mainly individuals have had the opportunity to opt out and be taxed as partnerships for up to five years.[34]

The situation in *Japan* is somewhat different. All organizations that constitute 'juridical entities' under civil law concepts are, with some explicit statutory exceptions, subject to the corporate tax. Both general and limited partnerships formed under the Company Law are juridical entities and are thus subject to the corporate tax. In contrast, unincorporated associations that are not juridical entities are not subject to the tax. This includes, for example, 'undisclosed associations' that are structurally similar to 'silent' or undisclosed partnerships under Continental civil law concepts. In this situation, the business is operated by the disclosed 'partner' in his own name and for his own account, and there is a contractual arrangement to share the profits (and, if provided in the agreement, the losses) with the silent partner. Although the arrangement is functionally similar in some respects to a limited partnership, the fact that it is not formally a partnership under the

29. Germany, ITA, s. 34a.
30. Netherlands, CTA, Art. 2.
31. Netherlands, CTA, Art. 2.1.e.
32. France, CGI, s. 206-1.
33. France, CGI, s. 206-4.
34. France, CGI, s. 239 *bis* AB; see also, CGI, s. 239 *bis* AA.

Company Law – and thus not a juridical entity for tax purposes – means that it is not subject to the corporate tax.[35]

In *Australia*, the statutory definition of 'company' for tax purposes is quite broad, including all 'bodies or associations corporate or unincorporate' with a specific exclusion for partnerships and unincorporated joint ventures.[36] A variety of special rules for associations, clubs, and the like would formally fall under the definition but are not the usual subjects of corporate-shareholder taxation.[37]

The *United Kingdom* similarly taxes all incorporated bodies and unincorporated associations other than partnerships.[38]

3. ISSUES IN CORPORATE FORMATION

If a corporation is formed by the transfer of cash to the corporation in exchange for the issuance of its shares, the taxpayer will typically have a tax cost or basis in the shares equal to that amount. From a corporate law point of view, the amount received will usually be accounted for as paid-in capital or capital surplus. In some systems, the corporate law treatment of the capital contribution and its possible subsequent repayment will affect the tax rules applicable to the shareholder and to the corporation. In other jurisdictions, the corporate law treatment is irrelevant for tax purposes.

If appreciated or depreciated property is transferred in exchange for shares on formation, the transfer would in principle be an exchange causing gain or loss realization by the shareholder. Several systems take this approach and require current taxation as the general rule in these circumstances. However, a number of systems allow a tax-deferred incorporation if certain conditions are met. The clearest situation is where a sole proprietorship is continued in corporate form, the former owner receiving all the shares on incorporation. Arguably, the transferor has changed only the legal form of his investment, which is now represented by shares rather than direct ownership; to require gain recognition in those circumstances would be inappropriate. There are a number of possible variations, however. Suppose that the assets transferred do not constitute a business, or that the transfer is to an existing corporation and the transferor receives back only a small share interest or receives shares and other consideration. The systems examined here have given quite different answers in these circumstances. In some cases, special rules deal with corporate formations. In others, more general

35. Japan, Income Tax Act (ITA), s. 5 and Japan, Corporate Tax Act (CTA), s. 4.
36. Australia, ITAA 1997, s. 995-1(1) definition of company.
37. Australia, ITAA 1997, s. 50-45 (exemption in relation to sports, culture, arts, and film). Australia inherited the doctrine of mutuality from the United Kingdom, under which persons cannot make a taxable profit out of themselves. This doctrine is applied to members' clubs (*The Bohemians Club* (1918) 24 CLR 334).
38. United Kingdom, Income and Corporation Taxes Act 1988, s. 832(1) ('company') and Income Tax Act 2007, s. 992.

non-recognition principles, which also apply to corporate reorganizations and restructuring, give the possibility of tax-deferred corporate formation.

In the *United States* system, in general, neither gain nor loss will be taken into account, regardless of the nature of property transferred, as long as persons transferring property in the formation transaction collectively have an 80% or greater stock interest in the corporation following the transaction.[39] The theoretical justification for this rule is that the incorporation merely represents a continuing investment by the shareholder in the underlying assets transferred and is not an appropriate time to require taxation of the gain or allow a deduction for the loss. In addition, if the transaction were taxable, it might discourage taxpayers from changing their form of investment through incorporation. However, in effect, such treatment allows several taxpayers to engage in partial exchanges of their assets on a basis that does not require a current payment of tax on the gain. This result is accepted to prevent tax impediments to a combining of assets that would be desirable for business reasons. To prevent abuse, there are restrictions on the ability of taxpayers to pool passive investment assets on a tax-free basis.

As is generally the case with respect to exchanges where no gain or loss is recognized currently, the transferor takes as his tax cost or basis in the shares he receives the historical tax cost of the assets transferred.[40] This 'substituted' basis thus potentially preserves the taxation of the deferred gain at the shareholder level on the sale of the stock. In addition, in the United States system, the corporate transferee takes as its tax cost for the assets the historical cost of the assets in the hands of the shareholder.[41] Thus, after corporate formation, there is the possibility of two gains or losses for tax purposes for what is economically the same gain (or loss) that would have been taxed (or deducted) only once if it had been realized by the shareholder.

If the transferor receives property other than shares of the transferee corporation – for example, cash or a debt obligation – the appreciation in the transferred assets is taxed to that extent and the transferor is entitled to increase his tax cost in the shares by that amount.[42] Losses, on the other hand, cannot be recognized regardless of the consideration received.[43]

The above rules apply not only to the formation of a new corporation but also to transfers of assets by shareholders to an existing corporation where the 80% stock ownership requirements are met.

In other systems, the treatment of the shareholder on formation varies considerably and in general offers more explicit selectivity than does the United States system. Thus, in the *Canadian* system, in principle, the transfer of property in exchange for shares is a taxable disposition. However, the transferor and the

39. United States, IRC, s. 351(a).
40. United States, IRC, s. 358.
41. United States, IRC, s. 362(a).
42. United States, IRC, s. 351(b).
43. United States, IRC, s. 351(b).

corporation can elect the amount treated as received for the property.[44] By electing to treat an amount equal to the tax cost of the property as the value of the shares received, the taxpayer can defer gain. As a consequence, however, both the shareholder and the corporation keep the historical basis of the property for the assets they hold, thus creating the possibility of two gains in the future. There are some limitations on the elective treatment. The amount elected cannot be more than the fair market value of the transferred property, thus preventing the creation of a potential double loss. Similarly, the elected amount cannot, in general terms, be less than the tax cost of the property, thus preventing the creation of a current artificial loss.

The transferor may receive other property in addition to shares in the transferee corporation, and the elected amount is allocated first to that property to the extent of its fair market value. The remaining elected amount is allocated to the shares received. In this way, tax on appreciation in the transferred property is deferred through a reduced tax cost in the shares.

There is no requirement that the transferor control the corporation or receive any minimum percentage of shares. However, there are some special anti-avoidance rules. If the transfer is to a corporation controlled by the transferor or related parties, no loss is recognized. A similar rule prevents the shifting of value to related-party shareholders. There are also restrictions on the type of property that can be transferred. Real property held as inventory and capital property owned by a non-resident, for example, are excluded.

The *Swedish* rules are somewhat more restrictive but have a similar pattern. The basic statutory rule is that a withdrawal of assets from a business is a realization event and is treated as if the assets had been sold for fair market value. However, case law had created exceptions that did not require realization in many situations. No statutory rules exist on formation, liquidation, and reorganization that expressly permit taxation to be deferred in certain defined situations. In practice, incorporation of a business in Sweden is done by selling the assets to an existing corporation at a price equal to their book value. The excess market value of the assets over book value is, in principle, taxable as a withdrawal, but the tax can be deferred under the rules mentioned above. This result is functionally similar to the Canadian result, since the appreciation in the assets remains to be taxed to both the shareholder and the corporation and the setting of the (non-arm's length) sales price amounts to an election by the taxpayer of the amount (if any) that will be subject to tax on the transfer.

In *The Netherlands*, the transfer of a business carried on as a sole proprietorship or in partnership would normally be a taxable event. Under a set of administrative conditions, however, the transfer can be effected without current tax if the entire business (or share of the business in the case of a partnership) is transferred to a newly formed corporation in exchange for stock.[45] More technically, the tax-free transfer is conditional on a number of requirements including: (a) at least 95% of

44. Canada, Income Tax Act (ITA), s. 85(1).
45. Netherlands, Income Tax Act 2001 (ITA 2001), Art. 3.65.

the consideration must be shares of the transferee corporation (provided that the cash paid as 'boot' does not exceed €25,000); and (b) the shares must be held for at least three years by the transferor. If these (and other) conditions are met, the transferor is not taxed, but takes as the tax cost for the shares received the net amount of the book values of the assets and liabilities transferred, reduced by any boot received (prior to 2001, the transferor took fair market value as his tax cost, but this rule was changed to follow the pattern used in most other countries). Because the transferee corporation retains the historical cost basis of the assets, the preformation appreciation will be subject to tax later in the hands of both the transferring individual and the transferee corporation.[46]

In *Germany*, the transfer of business assets in exchange for shares would in principle be a realization event, with the transferor realizing gain or loss and taking as the tax cost in the shares the fair market value of the transferred assets.[47] The transfer of private assets would not result in income recognition, as the disposition of such assets is generally not subject to tax. Despite the general rule of income recognition where business assets are concerned, the special rules dealing with tax-deferred corporate reorganizations may apply to the incorporation of a business. This is subject to a specific act, the Reorganization Tax Act (*Umwandlungssteuergesetz*). Basically, the tax treatment of the transfer of an existing business or independent division of a business in exchange for the newly issued shares of a corporation depends on the way the transaction is treated by the transferee. The transferee has the right to enter the assets in its books at any figure between the old book value of the assets and their 'going concern' value, and this amount is deemed to be the price paid for the assets transferred. Thus, to the extent that the assets are written up in the books of the transferee, the transferor must recognize gain; if the assets are entered at book value, the transaction is tax-free. The corresponding figure is the acquisition cost of the shares in the hands of the transferor. This treatment is available only for a business or division, and the transfer of individual business assets would be a taxable event.

The *Australian* rules on formation distinguish between types of property transferred and are not comprehensive. The capital gains rules require that the transferor hold 100% of the issued shares of the transferee company after the transfer. In addition, the provisions do not apply to transfers by several persons unless they first form a partnership, which is the formal transferor. However, the formation of a partnership will have capital gains consequences, which means that this does not offer a route to overcome the narrowness of the rule. When the rules apply, they provide for a carryover of the tax cost of the transferred assets and a corresponding tax cost for the shares received. Liabilities may be assumed in the transfer. Anti-avoidance rules seek to prevent value shifting in the rollover transactions.[48]

46. Details (the 'standard conditions') are laid down in a Decree of 12 Jul. 2001 (amended 11 Aug. 2004).
47. Germany, ITA, s. 6 para. 6 sent. 1.
48. Australia, ITAA 1997, Div 122.

In the *United Kingdom*, a deferral of the otherwise applicable capital gains tax is available if there is a transfer of an entire business by an individual in exchange for shares.[49] The business must be transferred as a going concern, and all non-cash assets transferred. Consideration other than shares may be received, but the roll-over relief applies only to the extent of the transfer for shares. If the transferor has unrelieved losses incurred in the business, these may be used against income in the form of dividends, interest, or employment income subsequently received from the corporation.[50] The tax cost of the transferor's shares will be the same as that of the assets transferred, while the corporation will take market value as the tax cost of the assets transferred (a step-up in tax cost).[51] Often an incorporator will not seek this rollover relief, as stamp duty will be payable on the transfer of some types of assets such as land. In this case, only some of the business assets may be transferred and a different form of rollover relief used. This relief is available for assets gifted to the corporation but will not result in a step-up in cost for the corporation.[52] An incorporator may not desire rollover in any case because the 18% capital gains tax rate and the annual exemption (nearly £10,000) may mean that an incorporator's capital gains tax liability is not great. A somewhat different set of rules applies to the transfer of a business from one corporation to another.[53]

In *Japan*, in general, the transfer of an asset to a corporation as consideration for the issuance of new capital stock constitutes a taxable event, whether or not such transfer is made in the course of its incorporation. A limited exception to this general rule was modified in 2001. Before 2001, the related gain recognition was deferred only in the case of the formation of a subsidiary by a parent corporation. In addition, such parent had to obtain at least 95% of the subsidiary's stock. The 2001 income tax revisions, which were intended to establish a consistent taxation system applicable to all kinds of corporate restructuring transactions, have changed the scope of the exception. Under the new legislation, if a transfer of an asset for the new stock of the transferee corporation falls within any of the following descriptions, the transfer is deemed to be made on the basis of the book value of the relevant assets for income tax purposes. No taxable income is deemed to be recognized by the transferor, with the transferee taking the transferor's tax basis, in the following three cases:

(a) a transfer of an asset between companies with a 100% equity relationship (i.e., cases where (i) the transferee or the transferor is a wholly owned subsidiary of the transferor or the transferee, as the case may be, or (ii) both the transferee and the transferor are the wholly owned subsidiaries of a common parent);

(b) a transfer of a business (not a specific asset) between companies with more than a 50% equity relationship meeting several criteria that ensure the continuity

49. United Kingdom, Taxation of Chargeable Gains Act 1992, s. 162.
50. United Kingdom, Income Tax Act 2007, s. 86.
51. United Kingdom, Taxation of Chargeable Gains Act 1992, s. 17.
52. United Kingdom, Taxation of Chargeable Gains Act 1992, s. 165.
53. United Kingdom, Taxation of Chargeable Gains Act 1992, s. 171 and United Kingdom, Income and Corporation Taxes Act 1988, s. 343.

of the business (e.g., approximately 80% or more of the employees who were engaged in the transferred business in the transferor company must be assumed by the transferee); and

(c) a transfer of business (not a specific asset) establishing a joint venture with a non-related entity that meets several other criteria.

This rule is compulsory; therefore, any transfer of assets or business meeting these criteria must always follow this rule. The special rules apply only to corporate transferors; all transfers by natural persons remain fully taxable.[54]

In *France*, as well, the transfer of assets to a corporation on formation is generally a taxable event. There are two exceptions, however. First, in the case of the transfer of a sole proprietorship for the stock of the transferee corporation, the transferor can elect to defer taxation of the gain on non-depreciable fixed assets until the stock received is disposed of or the corporation disposes of the assets. With respect to appreciated depreciable assets, the transferor may be taxed currently or the appreciation may be taxed over a five-year period (fifteen years for buildings) to the transferee, thus roughly correlating income recognition and depreciation. If the assets are disposed of during the period, taxation is accelerated. Inventory may be transferred on a tax-deferred basis as long as the book value is continued by the transferee.[55]

Second, a corporation can transfer all of the assets constituting a complete business for the stock of a newly formed corporation on a tax-favoured basis if it agrees to hold the stock for three years. The shares continue the tax cost of the transferred assets. When gains are realized on the assets transferred, they are deferred according to the same rules as apply in a merger reorganization (see section 7.2 below).[56]

4. ISSUES INVOLVING CAPITAL STRUCTURE

Commercial and corporate law principles have traditionally recognized a sharp distinction between ownership interests in a corporation in the form of shares and creditor interests in the form of bonds or other debt obligations. For corporate tax purposes, whatever the pattern of corporate taxation, important tax distinctions have also historically turned on the classification of an investment as 'equity' or 'debt'. In 'classical' systems, payments of interest on debt obligations are typically deductible by the corporation, unlike dividend distributions, which bear full corporate-level tax. The importance of the distinction is reduced somewhat in systems that have some degree of corporate-shareholder integration. Even in such systems, however, the distinction between an interest payment on a debt obligation and a dividend payment on equity can be of significance in some circumstances and is always an issue when the shareholder is not entitled to the imputation credit.

54. Japan, CTA, ss 2, paras 12–14 and s. 62–4.
55. France, CGI, s. 151 *octies*.
56. France, CGI, s. 210 B.

Thus, all systems must deal with this classification for tax purposes. In addition, whatever the domestic rules, a number of countries have special debt-equity restrictions where the shareholders are non-residents. These aspects of the problem are discussed in Part Four.

In the *United States*, the debt-equity distinction was initially developed in the case law. In general, courts have not felt themselves bound by the civil or commercial law characterization of the investment.[57] Instead, the case law has examined a variety of factors, including the legal rights created by the instrument, the economic source of the funds for the payments required, the relation between creditor and shareholder interests, the ability of the corporation to obtain similar financing from third parties, and the relation between the amount of equity and debt financing – that is, whether the corporation is 'thinly' capitalized.[58] The results of the case law are difficult to reconcile in any principled manner and are very fact-specific.

Dissatisfaction with the case law approach led to an attempt to provide clearer administrative rules. Those rules focused more directly on the economic characteristics of the instrument in question and the relative importance of 'debt' or 'equity' features. The rules were ultimately rejected on the ground that they were too complex. As a result, the case law-based system of classification is still generally applicable.

Some special statutory rules have been enacted with respect to certain types of obligations. These rules often 'bifurcate' an instrument with both debt and equity characteristics and treat each part of the obligation separately. The 'normal' amount of interest is allowed as a deduction and the remainder is disallowed or deferred.[59] Thus, for example, where a bond issued at a discount bears excessive interest, the excessive amount is not deductible as interest.[60] Special rules on 'earnings stripping' are principally important in the international context and are discussed in Part Four.

Most of the systems here under consideration have traditionally given more weight than the United States to the civil or commercial law classification of the instrument in determining its tax classification. Thus, in *Canada*, there are no general statutory rules, and the case law usually makes the distinction based on the legal form of the obligation. Special rules apply in some circumstances with respect to certain preferred stock.[61] In general terms, the rules are intended to prevent corporations that are unable to use interest deductions from, in effect, transferring the advantage of the interest deduction to corporate investors who receive tax-free intercorporate dividends. While not formally debt-equity rules, they do impose limits on the ability to utilize the interest deduction. When the rules limiting 'after-tax financing' apply, they impose a tax on the distributing

57. See, e.g., *Slappey Drive Industrial Park v. United States*, 561 F.2d 572 (5th Cir. 1977).
58. *Ibid.*
59. United States, IRC, ss 385, 163(e)(5), 279, 163(j), and 163(l).
60. United States, IRC, s. 163(j).
61. Canada, ITA, Parts IV.1 and VI.1.

corporation, which can then be offset against the corporation's mainstream income tax liability. This ensures that, where the distribution is tax-free in the hands of the recipient, a single level of current tax will have been paid by the distributing corporation on the income out of which the distribution was made.

Like Canada, *Australia* prior to 2001 had no specific rules to distinguish debt and equity, and the tax classification generally followed the legal form. In 2002 comprehensive debt-equity rules were introduced as part of the substantial business tax reform that commenced in 1999. Under these rules, four types of interests used to finance a company are classified as 'equity' unless they meet the 'debt test', namely: shares, interests whose return is at the discretion of the company or its associates, interests whose return is contingent on the company making profits, and interests convertible into one of the three preceding types of interests. A security satisfies the 'debt test', and is thus not equity, if the company has a non-contingent obligation to ultimately return to the investor an amount that is substantially more likely than not to equal or exceed the amount received by the company from the investor. In measuring the values of the amount received and the amount returned, nominal values are used if the security has a life of ten years or less, and present values if the security has a life of more than ten years.[62]

Returns on debt interests are treated generally like interest (deductible and not included in the imputation system) while returns on equity interests are treated generally like dividends (non-deductible but potentially carrying a tax credit). As a result of the new rules, redeemable preference shares are now usually classified as debt interests, while returns on converting preference shares (shares that automatically convert into ordinary shares) are equity interests. The new rules do not apply for all purposes where shareholding is relevant; for example, the disallowance of losses where there is a 50% change in ownership still depends only on share ownership in the traditional company law sense, not on equity interests in the new tax sense. In addition to the debt-equity rules, in international situations deductions for interest paid on debt interests can be limited under thin capitalization provisions, which apply in addition to the debt and equity rules but do not lead to recharacterization as equity.

The *United Kingdom*, too, has followed commercial form in general in distinguishing debt and equity (e.g., treating a perpetual debt instrument as debt). However, a number of complex statutory provisions deal with special situations. For example, if interest paid on a debt security is above a normal commercial rate, the excess is treated as a distribution. In addition, interest may be treated as a distribution where it is received in respect of convertible notes, certain securities linked to shares, or debentures where the return is dependent on the results of the company's business. Due to perceived abuses, these latter rules do not apply to interest paid between two resident corporations or to a UK permanent establishment of a non-resident corporation.[63] For individuals, the reclassification by statute in the United Kingdom is in one direction, from interest to distribution.

62. Australia, ITAA 1997, Div 974.
63. United Kingdom, Income and Corporation Taxes Act 1988, s. 212.

For example, there is no attempt to reclassify dividends paid on redeemable preference shares as interest. In 2005, new rules were enacted for corporate shareholders that can treat shares as debt (and so deny the intercorporate dividend exemption).[64] The types of shares covered are those that resemble interest-bearing debt, potentially including redeemable shares. The effective reclassification is only for the recipient; for the paying corporation, the dividend remains non-deductible, producing a form of economic double taxation. The overall impact of the UK system is a series of discrete rules targeted at particular problems, with the result that the effective nature of an instrument as debt or equity for tax purposes may change depending on who holds it.

In *Sweden*, no general statutory rules deal with the debt-equity distinction, although there are specific provisions on participating loans for closely held corporations.[65] If the interest rate is determined by dividends paid or the profits realized by the corporation, the interest deduction is denied. The payment remains interest in the hands of the recipient. Apart from this rule, the civil law characterization is in general controlling. The court will examine whether the instrument was in fact a debt under civil law, and if so, it will be treated as such for tax purposes. Thus, where an instrument that was in form a debt had a provision for conditional repayment, the court found the obligation was not a debt for civil law purposes and denied the interest deduction. The tax authorities have on occasion tried to use transfer pricing principles to recharacterize debt as equity but have not been successful.

In *The Netherlands*, the civil law form of the instrument generally controls its treatment for tax purposes. There are important statutory exceptions with regard to interest on loans granted under conditions that effectively make the creditor a participant in the business ('participating loans')[66] and interest payments that are considered to erode the Netherlands tax base (interest paid by a parent to its loss-making subsidiary, interest paid in certain cases to a foreign related company, and interest on convertible and/or profit-sharing bonds).[67] In addition, courts have recharacterized purported debt if the parties' real intention was not to make a loan, or, in the case of corporate shareholders, if the circumstances indicated that there was no expectation that the loan would be repaid ('bottomless pit loan').[68]

A 2003 decision by the ECJ (*Bosal*)[69] held that the statutory denial of an interest deduction for amounts a parent pays on loans concluded with a foreign subsidiary organized in the EU violates EC law where similar payments to a domestic subsidiary would be deductible. In reaction to this case, the statute now makes all such interest payments deductible and, in order to counter the use of excessive loans, includes thin capitalization rules.

---

64. United Kingdom, Corporation Tax Act 2009, Part 6 Ch. 7 (ss 522–535).
65. Sweden, Income Tax Act (ITA), Ch. 24 ss 5–10.
66. Netherlands, CTA, Art. 10.1.d.
67. Netherlands, CTA, Art. 10a.1.
68. Supreme Court (Netherlands), decision of 11 Jan. 1988, BNB 1988/217.
69. ECJ, 18 Sep. 2003, C-168-01 (*Bosal Holding*).

There is little developed law in *Japan* on the debt-equity distinction in the domestic context. It is anticipated, however, with the increasing internationalization of capital markets and the emergence of more complex 'hybrid' forms of debt financing, that the issue will receive more consideration. There are already some special rules limiting the deductibility of interest in the case of loans by controlling foreign shareholders, which are considered in Part Four.

France, in contrast, has specific rules that, although they do not recharacterize debt as equity, limit the deductibility of interest.[70] From January 2007, these rules were modified to comply with EC case law[71] and to make them more efficient. In general, interest paid on a loan by a shareholder can be deducted only to the extent that it does not exceed the average bank lending rate. Excess interest remains taxable in the hands of the lender as a constructive dividend. In addition, there is a special limitation on interest paid to corporations belonging to the same group in the case of thin capitalization – that is, when the following conditions are met: the loans made by related corporations exceed one-and-one-half times the stockholders' equity, and interest paid on related-party loans exceeds both interest received on such loans and 25% of current income before tax (plus such interest and depreciation). Unless the corporation can show that its debt-equity ratio is not higher than that of the group, interest exceeding the highest of the above-mentioned limits is not deductible. However, it is not taxable as a constructive dividend; it is carried forward (within the above-mentioned limits) subject to a yearly 5% deduction.

The situation in *Germany* provides two interesting examples of the evolution of debt-equity rules. Historically, court decisions in Germany followed the civil and commercial law characterization of obligations as debt or equity for tax purposes. Only company stock could generate corporate profits and dividends. This has – beginning in the 1920s – resulted in the development of 'hybrid' participations, which did not grant a 'share' in the company under civil law but provided for an obligatory entitlement to a share in the profit of the company and a share in the assets distributed in the event of liquidation. As early as 1934 the Imperial Tax Court held that annual payments for these 'jouissance rights' must be included in the taxable profit of the company, as there was no 'economic' justification for distinguishing between profits distributed to shareholders and profits distributed to holders of 'hybrid' participations. This jurisprudence was subsequently incorporated in the statute. On the other hand, payments to 'silent partners' who also receive a share in the profit of the company's business are regarded as ordinary expenses – just like interest payments to common creditors.

The second example concerns 'thin capitalization'. As the case law adhered to the tradition that interest payments are expenses even if the debt-equity ratio is 'excessive' from a business perspective, the German Parliament responded in 1993 with a statutory provision setting out detailed tax rules dealing with 'excessive' debt capitalization. In the domestic situation, taxation of dividends and interest in

70. France, CGI, s. 212.
71. ECJ, 12 Dec. 2002, C-324/00 (*Lankhorst-Hohorst GmbH*).

the hands of the shareholder or creditor did not lead to major differences; thus, the rules applied only to foreign shareholders and domestic tax-exempt organizations. In 2002 the ECJ ruled that this provision was in conflict with the fundamental freedoms of the EC Treaty.[72] Germany initially chose to extend its complex 'thin capitalization' rules to domestic situations to comply with the requirement of non-discrimination but now has replaced the thin capitalization regime with an interest-stripping rule that limits the deductibility of interest payments at the level of the corporation.[73]

5. TAXATION OF CORPORATE DISTRIBUTIONS

5.1. Basic Structure of Distribution Rules

All systems must have rules that characterize for tax purposes payments to shareholders with respect to their stock and determine the consequences of that characterization. The payments can potentially be treated as a distribution of corporate profits, a distribution of the corporation's stated capital or capital surplus, or a return of the capital of the shareholder invested in the stock, all with differing tax results.

In the *United States* system, the tax treatment of distributions to shareholders depends on whether the source of the distribution is from 'earnings and profits'.[74] Earnings and profits are corporate taxable income, with several important modifications.[75] For example, tax preferences or deductions that have reduced corporate taxable income may nonetheless be included in earnings and profits. The composition of earnings and profits and its attendant complexities are historically rooted and have no particular current policy justification.

Distributions of earnings and profits are classified as 'dividends' for tax purposes.[76] The corporate law characterization of the distribution as a formal dividend, a capital reduction, or even an illegal distribution that impairs capital is not relevant for tax purposes. Similarly, the treatment of the distribution on the books of the corporation has no effect on the tax characterization. Although dividends paid to individual shareholders were historically subject to normal income tax rates, such dividends currently are taxed at the same preferential rates as capital gains. Dividends paid to corporate shareholders are taxed as normal income, but the dividends-received deduction, which provides various degrees of intercompany dividend relief based on the percentage of stock owned in the distributing corporation, usually reduces the attendant tax liability.

---

72. *Ibid.*
73. Germany, ITA, s. 4h.
74. United States, IRC, s. 316.
75. United States, Treas. Regs., ss 1.312-6–1.312-15.
76. United States, IRC, s. 316.

To the extent that a distribution exceeds earnings and profits, it is treated as a tax-free return of the shareholder's tax cost in the shares.[77] If the distribution exceeds the stock investment, it is treated as gain on the disposition of the stock.[78] Since dividends and capital gains are taxed at the same preferential rates for individuals, the significant difference for individuals as to the source of the distribution is the opportunity to receive a tax-free return of their tax cost in their shares when the distribution exceeds the corporation's earnings and profits.

The patterns in other systems are generally quite different, in some ways more restrictive and in others more inclusive. Often corporate law and accounting treatment play more of a role in tax characterization. Timing rules tend to relate the distributions to earnings of a particular year. On the other hand, the limitation of taxable dividends to distributions of corporate earnings is frequently not present. In *Canada*, for example, under case law principles, any distribution made by a corporation that is not in liquidation or pursuant to an authorized reduction of capital is taxed as a dividend regardless of the existence of profits at the corporate level.[79] In the *United Kingdom*, the concept of a 'distribution' is central for determining the treatment of both the distributing corporation (non-deductible) and the shareholder (carrying a dividend tax credit). To the extent that a 'distribution' includes a dividend, the concept follows corporate law as to what is a dividend and what is a return of capital, the latter being expressly excluded from the definition of distribution.[80] To the extent that 'distribution' includes items other than corporate-law dividends, it is irrelevant whether the corporation in question has profits (although in some cases, the distribution must be out of the assets of the corporation).

Similarly, in *Sweden*, there is no connection between the earnings or income of the corporation and the taxation of the corporate distribution. (Special rules may recharacterize a favourably taxed dividend as employment income in some situations.) In the *Netherlands*, any economic benefit received by the shareholder as such is taxable without regard to the financial results of the corporation. Thus, where a corporation with no earnings makes a lawful distribution from capital surplus in anticipation of profits in the future, the amount is taxed as a dividend despite the lack of corporate earnings.

The *Japanese* rules were substantially changed in 2006, corresponding to the overhaul of corporate law in the form of the introduction of the new Company Law. Although the Company Law still maintains restrictions on the payment of dividends (creditors can require improperly paid dividends to be repaid to the corporation by the shareholders), the Company Law now allows dividends to be paid out of capital surplus as well as retained earnings. As to dividends attributable to

77. United States, IRC, s. 301(c).
78. United States, IRC, s. 301(c).
79. *Northern Securities Co. v. The King* [1935] 1 DTC 282 (Ex. Ct).
80. United Kingdom, Income and Corporation Taxes Act 1988, s. 209.

retained earnings, the amount is taxed as a dividend at the shareholder level. As to dividends attributable to capital surplus, only a portion of such dividends is taxed as dividends, while the rest may be taxable as capital gains.[81]

In *Australia*, significant changes were made to corporate law rules on maintenance of capital in 1998, which had tax consequences as well. As a result of these changes, combined with the introduction of new debt-equity rules discussed above, the taxation of distributions has become much more complex. A dividend for tax purposes must be 'out of profits', which was traditionally determined with reference to company accounts or financial statements,[82] although a recent public ruling, with some support from an even more recent case, now suggests that anything not debited to share capital is out of profits. In addition, the High Court of Australia recently held (in the view of many, incorrectly) that distributions that do not fit within the definition of dividend and the out-of-profits requirement can in any event be income under ordinary concepts apart from the definition of dividend – which means they are assessable in full without any imputation credit. The case concerned a right that a company issued to its shareholders to sell back 10% of their shares to the company at a premium to the market price.[83] In addition, even amounts debited to share capital can be taxed as unfranked dividends instead of as a return of capital, as explained below. Dividends on shares classified as debt interests under the new debt-equity rules are nonetheless still taxable as dividends in the hands of the recipient, even though they are deductible at the corporate level and do not carry the imputation credit.[84] Distributions on an equity interest that is not legally a share under the corporate law are taxable without regard to profits (because the company will be expensing these items in its accounts and not treating them as distributions of profits), but they are non-deductible at the corporate level. An indirect 'out-of-profits' requirement applies before such distributions can be franked under the imputation system. In the case of corporations that do not maintain adequate records, the tax authorities can reconstruct the accounts to establish the requisite profits.[85]

The situation in *France* is also rather complex. The definition of taxable corporate distributions encompasses much more than dividends in cash or property properly distributed to the shareholders in proportion to their capital interests. A taxable distribution is deemed to occur whenever a corporate decision results in a 'disinvestment' – that is, a decrease in the value of the corporation's net assets to the benefit of a shareholder, even if the corporation does not have available earnings. Where non-shareholders receive benefits, they can also be treated as a taxable distribution if corporate profits are available. Capital distributions as such

81. Japan, ITA, ss 24 and 25, and Japan, CTA, ss 23 and 24.
82. Australia, Income Tax Assessment Act 1936 (ITAA 1936), s. 6(1) definition of dividend, 44(1); *Sun Alliance Investments* (2005) 225 CLR 488.
83. Australia, Ruling TR 2003/8, *McNeil* (2007) 229 CLR 656.
84. Australia, ITAA 1936, s. 44(1), ITAA 1997, ss 25-85 and 202-45(d).
85. Australia, ITAA 1936, s. 44(1), ITAA 1997, s. 26-26, Div 215.

are prohibited by corporate law. Special rules apply to capital distributed in redemptions or liquidations and are discussed in those sections.[86]

5.2. Relating Distributions to Corporate Earnings

Where a distinction exists for tax purposes between types of distributions, ordering rules are necessary to determine the characterization of the distribution. Thus, in the *United States* system, because of the earnings-and-profits requirement, complex rules are provided that connect distributions and profits. In general terms, profits are deemed to be distributed first, regardless of the formal corporate characterization of the distribution. If the corporation has earnings for the year and an accumulated deficit, a distribution during the year is nonetheless taxable. Distributions are taxable to the shareholder receiving them even if they relate to earnings that were accumulated in years prior to the investment by the shareholder and thus, in an economic sense, represent a return of his original investment in the shares.

For countries that generally tax distributions without regard to the existence of earnings at the corporate level, this type of rule is not necessary. Therefore, under the new corporate tax rules applicable in *Germany*, specific 'baskets', which categorized income according to the tax burden it had borne and which were used under the imputation system, are no longer necessary. Only a distribution from paid-in capital reserve is tax-free.[87]

France as well had complex rules for determining when a distribution is deemed to be from preferentially taxed earnings and was thus subject to the compensatory tax (*précompte mobilier*). The repeal of the imputation system in 2005 made such rules superfluous.

Similarly, for countries that allow the tax-free distribution of share premium or stated capital, rules are necessary to identify such distributions. Often the characterization for corporate law purposes is controlling. In the *Canadian* system, distributions of paid-up capital, which is determined under the applicable corporate law subject to certain adjustments required under income tax law, are deemed to be made before profits distributions, with only the excess over the paid-up capital reduction taxable as a dividend. However, the recovery of capital before corporate profits is available only for certain transactions, such as liquidations, redemptions of shares, and authorized reductions of capital.[88]

The *Japanese* rules after 2008 also generally follow the characterization under the Company Law between dividends attributable to retained earnings and those attributable to capital surplus. Distributing companies are required to inform their shareholders of the amount of dividends attributable to their capital surplus.

The changes to *Australian* company law in 1998 abolished the use of par value for shares and with it the need for a share premium account. Distributions that are

---

86. France, CGI, ss 108–117.
87. Germany, ITA, s. 20 para. 1 no. 2 sent.1.
88. Canada, ITA, s. 84.

treated for corporate law purposes as repayments of share capital are generally tax-free and reduce the tax cost of the stock, with any excess being taxable as a capital gain. If the distribution of share capital is part of a scheme involving the contribution of share capital by one shareholder and its distribution to another, an anti-avoidance rule may treat the distribution as a dividend. Those who benefit more from such distributions compared to dividends, mainly non-resident shareholders and shareholders with pre-CGT shares who are not subject to the CGT, are now subject to three different rules to prevent the streaming of capital.[89]

5.3. Constructive Dividends

All systems have either statutory or case law principles that tax as distributions benefits received by shareholders without the formal declaration of a dividend or profit distribution. In some situations the payment is treated as a dividend for all purposes, although often, to discourage such payments, they will not carry the imputation credit or qualify for intercorporate dividend relief.

The *United States* system has rules based on case law that treat shareholder benefits as dividends. Under a special provision, unreasonable compensation may be disallowed as a deduction at the corporate level even when the payment is not formally recharacterized as a dividend to the shareholder, although the rule is normally applied only in the case of payments to shareholders.[90] Loans to shareholders may be treated as dividends.[91] Even when a loan is not recharacterized, if the loan does not bear a stipulated interest rate, under a special statutory rule a dividend in the amount of the foregone interest is imputed to the shareholder, followed by a deemed transfer of that amount of interest to the corporation.[92] The deemed interest payment may be deductible by the shareholder subject to the normal limitations and is included in the income of the corporation.

In *France*, there are specific statutory provisions dealing with loans to shareholders, excessive remuneration, interest on loans by shareholders that is higher than the average bank lending rate, and expenditures deemed to be extravagant.[93] In addition, case law has developed a principle that treats as constructive dividends any distributions that have been made in situations in which the corporation did not receive an appropriate benefit for the payment. Such an 'abnormal management decision' will result in a taxable distribution. Typical situations involve bargain sales or rentals of corporate assets, payment of personal expenses, and the like. Abnormal benefits granted to third parties who are not shareholders may be treated

89. Australia, ITAA 1936, s. 6(1) definition of dividend paras (d), 6(4), 44(1B), 45, 45A, 45B; ITAA 1997, ss 104–135.
90. United States, IRC, s. 162(a)(1); Treas. Regs., 1.162-7(b)(1).
91. See, e.g., *Crowley v. Commissioner*, 962 F.2d 1077 (1st Cir., 1992).
92. United States, IRC, s. 7872.
93. France, e.g., CGI, ss 111a, d, and e, and 112-4.

as constructive dividends insofar as, after such benefits have been (re)included in its taxable income, the corporation realizes a taxable profit.[94]

In *Canada*, any benefit conferred on the shareholder must be included in taxable income.[95] Typical situations are bargain purchases and sales, rent-free use of property, and payment of personal expenses. A special rule, with some exceptions (such as loans to shareholders who are also employees for the purpose of acquiring a home, automobile, or shares of the corporation), treats as income loans by a corporation to an individual shareholder or related person if the loan is not repaid within one year.[96] These various shareholder benefits must be included in the shareholders' income but are not treated as dividends. As a result, they do not qualify for either the imputation credit or the intercorporate dividend deduction.

In *Australia*, specific legislation treats certain benefits provided to shareholders in closely held companies as non-deductible dividends – in particular, bargain sales of property, interest-free loans, forgiveness of shareholder debts, and excessive compensation or retirement benefits to shareholder-employees or associates.[97] Rent-free use of property probably was not covered, but amendments announced in 2009 will eliminate this loophole. Payment of personal expenses would typically be covered by the fringe benefits tax. As in Canada, the constructive dividend does not bring with it the imputation credit, except in hardship cases at the discretion of the tax administration.[98]

The *United Kingdom* also has special rules dealing with shareholder loans in the closely held context and broadens the concept of 'distribution' to cover benefits in kind provided by a closely held corporation to its shareholders.[99] In addition, a rule applicable to all corporations (but which is most frequently applied here) may treat a transfer of assets or liabilities to shareholders, or vice versa, not in exchange for equal value as a distribution.[100] This applies where value passes from the corporation to the shareholder. By contrast, where in such a transaction value passes from the shareholder to the corporation, there is no reclassification as a contribution to capital.

Dutch case law also deals with constructive dividends. Benefits to the shareholder in his capacity as a shareholder are generally taxable as dividends where both the corporation and the shareholder were aware (or should have been aware) of the advantage to the shareholder.[101] In *Sweden*, prior to the 1990s, special statutory provisions dealt with constructive dividends in the case of closely held corporations, sometimes resulting in heavier taxation than would have applied to actual dividends. These rules were abandoned to improve tax conditions for small businesses and because tax consequences applicable to constructive dividends

94. See France, CGI, s. 109 as construed by the Conseil d'État.
95. Canada, ITA, s. 15(1).
96. Canada, ITA, s. 15(2).
97. Australia, ITAA 1936, ss 109B–109F.
98. Australia, ITAA 1936, s. 109RB, ITAA 1997, s. 202–45(g).
99. United Kingdom, Income and Corporation Taxes Act 1988, ss 218 and 219.
100. United Kingdom, Income and Corporation Taxes Act 1988, s. 209(4).
101. Netherlands, Supreme Court, 2 Dec. 1953, no. 11.414, BNB 1954/22.

under basic tax rules were considered sufficient. A special rule is still applicable to all types of corporate loans made to shareholders that are improper under company law. Such transactions are taxed in full as dividend distributions even if the loans are at arm's length. The rule was introduced as owners of closely held corporations refrained from taking dividends or salary from the corporation and instead used loans to receive necessary funds from the corporation. Constructive dividends are most common in the case of closely held corporations. In the case of publicly held corporations, constructive dividends have been found in some cases, but minor benefits, such as rebates to shareholders for purchases in the corporation's stores, have not been taxed as they have been found to be offered primarily for commercial reasons.

Germany has a statutory basis[102] and highly developed case law for the treatment of constructive dividends. Any transaction between shareholder and corporation that is not undertaken at arm's length is a potential constructive dividend. To avoid constructive dividend treatment, agreements between shareholder and corporation must meet the 'prudent manager' test and must be shown to be in the interests of the corporation and not simply undertaken to benefit the shareholder. Agreements between the corporation and its controlling shareholder must be legally binding, in clear terms, and concluded in advance. If the agreement deviates from the 'standard', there is a danger that the courts will hold the whole transfer of assets (not just the 'excessive' part) to be a constructive dividend. Moreover, even arm's length contracts may lead to constructive dividends if the courts find that they are aimed at 'siphoning off' substantial parts of the company's profit. For large companies, dealings between subsidiaries and group-wide transactions are a constant source of contention between taxpayers and the tax administration. For small and medium-sized companies, the 'adequacy' of salaries for executives who are also shareholders, including 'reasonable' bonus payments and pension reserves, is the major point of disagreement. Before 2008, due to separate assessment procedures, a constructive dividend could be found at the shareholder level regardless of the treatment at the corporate level, and vice versa. This effect has been eliminated in recent legislation. The shareholder relief provisions for the taxation of dividends now depend on a corresponding adjustment for the constructive dividend at the corporate level.[103]

5.4. Intercorporate Dividends and Capital Gains

All of the systems have special rules dealing with distributions by domestic corporations to domestic corporate shareholders. (Special considerations that apply if the corporations are foreign are discussed in Part Four). Although the basic purpose of the various provisions is to prevent the 'cascading' of levels of corporate tax on distributions that move up a corporate chain to the ultimate individual shareholder,

102. Germany, CITA, s. 8 para. 3 sent. 2.
103. Germany, ITA, s. 3 no. 40 lit.d sent. 2 and 3; CITA, s. 8 para. 3 sent. 5.

the structures of the provisions have significant differences, both in terms of the degree of relief granted and the techniques used. Because of the possibility of substituting intercorporate capital gains for dividends and vice versa (by paying out dividends or retaining earnings and selling the shares), many countries have special rules in these areas. Further, a number of countries seek to achieve consistency in the taxation of intercorporate dividends and corporate capital gains on shareholdings.

In the *United States*, the mechanism for relief is a deduction for a certain percentage of the dividend received. The amount of the deduction varies with the degree of share ownership. In the case of 100% share ownership, the full amount of the dividend is deductible, while for portfolio investment (below 20%) the amount is 70% of the dividend.[104] Corporate capital gains are taxed at normal rates.

A series of special provisions restricts the ability of the corporate shareholder to combine the dividends-received deduction with other deductions. Where a portfolio investment is financed with debt, the dividends-received deduction is reduced to that extent, thus preventing a tax arbitrage between the fully deductible interest and the partially taxable intercorporate dividend.[105] Similar rules restrict the ability to claim a dividends-received deduction for a dividend and then claim a tax loss attributable to the stock's decline in value immediately after the dividend payment (sometimes referred to as 'dividend stripping'). The rules generally require that the stock on which the dividend was received be held for a period of time before the loss on sale will be allowed.[106] In some situations, the amount paid for the stock must be allocated between the dividend to be received and the stock itself, thus limiting the amount deductible as a loss when the stock is sold.[107]

Since intercorporate dividends are taxed at a reduced rate while capital gain on the sale of stock is fully taxable, a corporate shareholder may attempt to withdraw dividends from the corporation prior to the sale in order to reduce the taxable capital gain. Case law principles have limited the use of this technique for 'capital gain stripping', especially if the funds used to pay the dividend come indirectly from the buyer.[108] The purported dividend payment is treated as additional sale proceeds.

Canada also allows a deduction for intercorporate dividends but, unlike the situation in the *United States*, the relief is complete.[109] One hundred percent of the dividends are deducted without regard to the degree of share ownership. To prevent closely held corporations from being used as 'incorporated pocketbooks' to hold portfolio investments of individuals, dividends received by these corporations are subject to a special refundable tax intended to replicate the tax that would have

104. United States, IRC, s. 243.
105. United States, IRC, s. 246A.
106. United States, IRC, s. 246(c).
107. United States, IRC, s. 1059.
108. See, e.g., *Waterman Steamship Corp. v. United States*, 430 F.2d 1185 (5th Cir., 1970).
109. Canada, ITA, s. 112(1).

been due if the dividend had been received by an individual shareholder.[110] Other limitations apply to prevent the conversion of taxable capital gains into tax-free dividends. Under these rules, dividends received in some circumstances are deemed to be proceeds of sale of the shares and as such are taxable. The rules are in effect limited to gain which is not attributable to previously taxed corporate earnings.[111] In addition, no loss is allowed on the sale of stock preceded by a dividend distribution that is entitled to intercorporate dividend relief.[112]

The situation was similar in *Australia* but has recently changed. Intercorporate dividend relief is now given by means of the imputation system. A dividend received by a company is taxable and relief is given only to the extent that imputation credits are attached to the dividend.[113] Hence, if a company receives a dividend that is franked only as to half, it pays tax at 30% on the other half of the dividend. This change, combined with the introduction of consolidation of corporate groups, has also led to an alteration in the stacking rules for deductions. Companies now have the option not to claim deductions if they would offset tax-free dividends and the deductions would then be turned into a loss carryforward.[114]

Even with these changes, 'dividend stripping' schemes are still an issue. The schemes typically involved the sale of stock by individuals of closely held corporations that had substantial accumulated earnings. The sale transaction converted the potential dividend income into preferentially taxed (or tax-free) capital gain. The purchasing corporation (the 'stripper') could extract the earnings from the purchased corporation on a tax-free basis and then dispose of the stock at a (deductible) loss. Several statutory provisions continue to deal with this technique. First, in some cases, under general anti-avoidance principles, the seller of the shares may be deemed to have received a taxable dividend rather than tax-preferred proceeds of sale.[115] In addition, more specific statutory rules deny the imputation credit to the purchaser.[116] Former problems of 'capital gain stripping' transactions are now comprehensively dealt with by taxing the unfranked part of dividends and treating certain distributions of capital as unfranked dividends under several anti-avoidance rules.[117]

In the *United Kingdom*, distributions by a resident corporation to another corporation are exempt from corporation tax. In principle, this exemption is available irrespective of whether the profits from which the distribution is made have been subject to UK tax or not. Capital gains on shares held by corporations are generally taxable with indexation relief. If the corporation selling the shares holds 10% or more of the shares in another corporation and both are trading companies,

110. Canada, ITA, Part IV.
111. Canada, ITA, s. 55(2)-(5).
112. Canada, ITA, s. 112(3)-(7).
113. Australia, ITAA 1997, Divs 67, 207.
114. Australia, ITAA 1997, Div 36.
115. Australia, ITAA 1936, s. 177E.
116. Australia, ITAA 1997, ss 207-145(1)(d), 207-150(1)(e), and 207-155.
117. Australia, ITAA 1936, ss 45, 45A, and 45B.

the capital gain is exempt.[118] If a corporation borrows to acquire shares in a resident corporation, the interest expense is deductible, although there are special restrictions on deductibility if the loan is not for the purposes of a trade of the corporation.[119] As in other countries, the United Kingdom has dividend stripping rules that grant broad discretion to the tax administration and other rules that counteract the reduction in the value of shares through excessive intercorporate distributions ('depreciatory transactions' and value shifting).[120] The participation exemption for capital gains is also subject to anti-avoidance rules.

The situation in *Japan* is similar to that in the United States. Intercorporate dividends may be excluded entirely if the share ownership is 25% or more, and 50% excludable in the case of ownership below 25%. There are special limitations on the deductibility of interest expense incurred with respect to stock-paying tax-exempt dividends.[121] Corporate tax applies to capital gains on shares held by companies at ordinary rates.

France allows 100% exclusion if the stock interest is over 5% and the parent corporation has held it or undertaken to hold it for more than two years. As a corollary of the exemption, related expenses are non-deductible. They are deemed to amount to 5% of the dividends (plus foreign tax credit, if any) but cannot exceed the total of expenses of all kinds incurred by the corporation during the tax year concerned.[122] The exclusion is elective, but in practically all cases this treatment is more favourable than including the dividend in the tax base. Unless the assets of the subsidiary consist mainly of immovable property, capital gains realized on the disposal of the stock interest enjoy a similar 100% exclusion (with up to 5% non-deductibility) when the selling corporation is entitled to the 100% exclusion for dividends received or is otherwise treated as having a substantial participation.[123]

In the *German* system, the special rules for intercorporate dividends that were introduced by the corporate tax reform in 2000 remain applicable after the 2007 business tax reform. As there is no imputation of corporate tax at the shareholder level, the legislation provides that all intercompany dividends are in principle tax-free.[124] To avoid discrimination, this rule is extended to dividends received by corporate shareholders from foreign companies. Following recent judgments by the ECJ,[125] the European Commission currently urges Germany also to abolish withholding tax on dividends paid to corporate portfolio shareholders resident in

118. United Kingdom, Taxation of Chargeable Gains Act 1992, Sch. 7AC.
119. This is by reason of the loan-relationship rules that appear in United Kingdom, Corporation Tax Act 2009, Part 5 and, in particular, s. 297.
120. United Kingdom, Income Tax Act 2007, s. 682-703 and Taxation of Chargeable Gains Act 1992, ss 29–34 and 176–177.
121. Japan, CTA, s. 23.
122. France, CGI, ss 145 and 216.
123. Mainly in France, CGI, s. 219 I-a.
124. Germany, CITA, s. 8b para. 1.
125. ECJ, 12 Dec. 2006, C-446/04 (*Test Claimants in the FII Group Litigation*) and 23 Apr. 2008, C-20105 (*Test Claimants in the CFC and Dividend Group Litigation*).

other EU Member States. Against this background, the German government is considering the re-introduction of full taxability for dividends paid to corporate portfolio shareholders resident in Germany to avoid discrimination while maintaining revenue from withholding tax.

To deal with gain reflecting undistributed profits that would have been tax-free on distribution, the German legislation also provides for a 'participation exemption' under which all gains on sales of shares by German companies are tax-free.[126] This rule applies to the entire gain and includes gain that has no relation to retained profits. The rule also applies regardless of whether the subsidiary is domestic or foreign. There is no minimum shareholding requirement. Expenses (stewardship and finance expenses) that are related to tax-free dividends or capital gains may be deducted. On the other hand, 5% of the dividends are deemed to be non-deductible expenses. This deeming provision applies even when there are no costs relating to the participation. In effect, therefore, only 95% of a dividend is exempt.[127]

In *The Netherlands*, there is an exclusion for dividends received on 'participations', defined generally as a 5% or greater stock interest in the distributing company. The exemption for participations also extends to the gain on the sale of the stock.

Sweden likewise has an exclusion for intercorporate dividends.[128] Dividends from non-listed corporations are in general exempt, with exceptions for special tax avoidance situations. Other dividends may also be exempt if the recipient corporation has a 10% or greater voting interest in the distributing corporation or there is a business relation between the two corporations. For other 'portfolio' investments, the dividend is taxable in full. Where shares are sold at a loss as the result of a tax-free dividend distribution, the deduction of the loss is disallowed. In addition, in 2003 Sweden introduced a participation exemption for capital gains and losses. If the conditions described above for dividends are met, an exemption applies for both capital gains and losses. The rules were intended to eliminate a 'third' layer of corporate tax. Moreover, by making capital losses non-deductible, the taxpayer was prevented from manipulating exempt foreign capital gains and deductible domestic capital losses.

5.5. Distributions of Appreciated or Depreciated Property

When appreciated or depreciated property is distributed, if the gain or loss is not recognized at the corporate level at the time of distribution, it will no longer be subject to the corporate taxing regime. While the logic of treating the distribution as a taxable event seems clear, the *United States* historically did not take this approach; neither gain nor loss was recognized on distribution. The rule was

126. Germany, CITA, s. 8b para. 2.
127. Germany, CITA, s. 8b para. 5.
128. Sweden, ITA, Ch. 24.

changed, however, in 1986 and now, in principle, the distribution is a recognition event, with some exceptions. The rules apply whether the shareholder is an individual or a corporation.

In the case of ongoing dividend distributions, gain is recognized on the distribution of appreciated property, but loss is not recognized.[129] The limitation with respect to property with an accrued loss reflects the fact that the timing of the distribution is in the control of the taxpayer. As a result of the rule, however, the possibility of deducting the loss on the property is totally eliminated because the shareholder takes the fair market value as his tax cost. Where property is distributed in complete liquidation of the corporation, both gains and losses are recognized as the possibility of shareholder manipulation is not present.[130] However, there are restrictions on the deductibility of losses on property that has been recently contributed to the corporation. Distributions on the liquidation of an 80%-owned corporate subsidiary are not taxed; the parent corporation takes the historical cost of the assets as its tax cost.[131]

The other systems here under consideration typically require the recognition of gain or loss on property distributions. In *Canada*, the corporation is considered to have disposed of the property at its fair market value, while the shareholder includes the fair market value in income as a dividend and is considered to have acquired the property at a cost equal to that fair market value.[132] These rules are intended to ensure that the consequences of a dividend in kind are the same as those for a sale of the corporate assets followed by the distribution of the proceeds. In *Germany*, any distribution of an appreciated asset is a realization event, regardless of whether the distribution is treated as a dividend to the shareholder or is a return of capital. Similarly, in *The Netherlands* the distribution is a taxable event, although there is the possibility of deferring the tax on the gain by the use of a replacement reserve if the property is going to be replaced.[133] In *Sweden*, the distribution is treated as removal of the assets from the business, which is in principle a recognition event. *Australia*, as well, treats the distribution of an asset as subject to capital gains tax at the corporate level. Where the transferor is a 100% subsidiary of the transferee, either a rollover is available on the transfer if the companies concerned cannot consolidate (e.g., if a non-resident company is involved) or the transaction is ignored in consolidation.[134] Special rules restrict the ability to use such property distributions to shift value among shares. These rules were considerably strengthened in 2002. The *United Kingdom* rules are similar to those in Australia, although the threshold for rollover on transfer between group corporations is 75%.[135]

129. United States, IRC, s. 311.
130. United States, IRC, s. 336.
131. United States, IRC, ss 332 and 334(b).
132. Canada, ITA, s. 52(2).
133. Netherlands, ITA 2001, Art. 3.54.
134. Australia, ITAA 1997, Div 126-B, s. 701-1.
135. United Kingdom, Taxation of Chargeable Gains Act 1992, s. 171.

The situation in *Japan* is somewhat more complex, especially in the event of liquidation of a corporation. The 2006 tax revisions lifted the prohibition on dividends in kind, and recipients are subject to income tax based on the fair value of the distributed property. In turn, a distributing corporation must recognize gain or loss based on the value of the property and its tax cost. However, if the distribution is in liquidation, the gain or loss is calculated as the difference between the fair market value of the property distributed and the sum of the legal capital and capital and profit reserves for tax purposes. A special 'liquidation' tax at the rate of 27.1% is applicable to this amount.[136]

Prior to 2001, this liquidation tax was also applied to merged corporations (i.e., disappearing corporations) in merger transactions; the liquidation tax at that moment was calculated based on the difference between the par value of the stock (together with the fair market value of any non-stock property) received by the shareholders of the merged corporation and the amount of the legal capital and the statutory reserves. After the 2001 revisions of the income tax law, the liquidation tax is no longer applicable to mergers (although it remains applicable to actual liquidations). Instead, the excess of the fair market value of the net assets of merged corporations over their book value is taxed under the general corporate income tax system, subject to some exceptions in which the related appreciation or depreciation is deferred until the disposition of the assets.

In *France*, there is no developed law on the distribution of appreciated or depreciated property as a normal dividend, although for accounting purposes it would be treated as a recognition of gain, and this treatment is considered applicable for corporate tax purposes as well. In the case of liquidations, the rules are quite fully developed. The distributing corporation must realize all gains and losses on distributed assets, which are taxed as capital gain or ordinary income, as the case may be. In addition, any income items that have previously escaped tax as deferred income or tax-free provisions must also be included in the tax base.[137]

5.6. Distributions Involving Changes in Corporate Capital Structure

5.6.1. General

Apart from formal or constructive dividends, many changes in corporate capital structure may involve distributions to shareholders. Typical examples would be distributions in connection with a reduction in capital or a redemption of outstanding shares, or the capitalization of earnings through an increase in stated capital followed by a stock dividend. In all these situations, the distribution must be characterized for tax purposes, and a recurring issue is the extent to which the

136. Japan, CTA, s. 92–100.
137. France, CGI, ss 221-2, 201-1 and 3.

corporate or commercial law characterization of the transaction will be controlling for tax purposes. Here the systems show wide variation.

In the *United States*, as a general matter, the corporate law aspects of a change in the capitalization of a corporation are not relevant for tax purposes. Thus, if a corporation formally reduces its capital and repays that amount to the shareholders, the distribution will be taxed as a dividend as long as the corporation has earnings for tax purposes; the fact that from a corporate law point of view the payment is a return of invested capital is of no significance.[138] Similarly, if a corporation increases its stated capital by transferring undistributed earnings to the capital account, the corporate transfer has no effect on the 'pool' of earnings for tax purposes that determines the taxability of later distributions.[139]

In the systems of most other countries, corporate law concepts play a more important role in determining the treatment of such distributions. In *Canada*, for example, amounts received by the shareholder from a reduction in the paid-in capital of a corporation, other than a public corporation, can be received tax-free.[140] However, if the amount received exceeds the portion of stated capital allocated to the shares, the excess is taxed as a dividend, regardless of the absence of accumulated profits. Similarly, if a reserve against earnings is transferred to capital, the transfer will, subject to some exceptions, constitute a dividend because, after the earnings have been transferred to the capital account, they could be repaid free of tax.[141] In some circumstances, distributions of capital by publicly traded companies are fully taxable as dividends.

Australia has extensive rules to deal with problems of this kind, one of which – the streaming of capital distributions – has already been covered. In addition, if profits are converted to capital, the share capital account of the company becomes 'tainted', with significant consequences. There is an immediate loss of an amount of available imputation credits, and all distributions out of share capital are thereafter treated as unfrankable dividends (so that they are taxed in full without imputation credits). The company can 'untaint' the share capital account by utilizing a process operated through the imputation system, which effectively leads to a tax of 47.5% on the transferred profits.[142]

In the *United Kingdom*, payments effecting a reduction in capital are not treated as distributions. This rule extends to repayments of loan capital even where the interest payment itself is treated as a distribution. The exception is that the repayment of capital on stock dividend shares (within certain periods of time either before or after the issue of the shares) is treated as a distribution.[143]

138. United States, IRC, ss 316(a) and 312.
139. United States, IRC, ss 316(a) and 312.
140. Canada, ITA, s. 84(4) and (4.1).
141. Canada, ITA, s. 84(1).
142. Australia, ITAA 1997, Div. 197.
143. United Kingdom, Income and Corporation Taxes Act 1988, ss 209, 210, and 211.

France also allows the tax-free distribution of amounts resulting from a capital reduction, but only to the extent that the reimbursement to the shareholders of the paid-up share capital exceeds all profits reserves and undistributed profits.[144]

Germany also allows the repayment of stated capital or capital reserves on a tax-free basis.[145] In the case of capital reserves, they may be distributed only after all profits and profit reserves have been distributed. If the shareholder holds the stock as a business asset or has more than 1% of the stock, the distribution of the stated capital or capital reserves is deemed to be a disposal.[146] Following the recent business tax reform, a capital gain that includes the repayment of stated capital is taxable even if the shares are held as private assets.[147] The distribution reduces the acquisition costs of the stock and can result in a taxable gain if it exceeds that amount. *Sweden*, in contrast, treats distributions of the amount of the reduction in the nominal value of stock as dividends without regard to the existence of corporate profits.

5.6.2. Stock Dividends

The distribution of dividends in the form of stock or 'bonus' shares to existing shareholders typically involves a transfer for corporate law purposes of retained earnings into stated capital. It can been viewed as a deemed distribution of a cash dividend to the shareholders followed by a corresponding contribution to capital or solely as an event at the corporate level that has no effect on shareholders, whose economic interest in the corporation is unchanged by the receipt of additional shares. The systems have taken varied approaches to the stock dividend problem. The treatment is in part a function of the rules dealing with distributions of stated capital.

The *United States* rules on the taxation of stock dividends are quite detailed. The basic rule is fairly straightforward: Pro rata distributions of common stock of the same class as the stock on which the distribution is being made are not taxable.[148] The principal justification behind the rule is that the shareholder has not had a significant change of position as a result of the distribution. He simply has more pieces of paper representing an unchanged underlying investment, and thus the receipt of the stock dividend is not an appropriate time to treat the underlying corporate profits as having been distributed. This rule is possible in part because the United States system ignores the effects of the capitalization of earnings for corporate purposes that typically accompanies a stock dividend. As soon as one moves beyond the simple pro rata stock distribution, however, the situation becomes more complex. If the shareholder has the right to choose between a cash dividend and a stock dividend, the stock dividend will be taxable, even if all

144. France, CGI, s. 112-1.
145. Germany, ITA, s. 20 para. 1 no. 2.
146. Germany, ITA, s. 17 para. 4.
147. Germany, ITA, s. 20 para. 2 sent. 2.
148. United States, IRC, s. 305(a).

shareholders elect to receive stock and the distribution is thus pro rata.[149] The shareholder is in effect deemed to have received the equivalent of the cash dividend he might have received.

Where the distribution is not pro rata and thus results in an increase in the proportionate interest of the shareholders receiving the stock dividend, the distribution is generally taxable.[150] Technically, the distribution will be taxable if it results in the increase in the proportionate interest of some shareholders and the receipt of a property distribution by others. Thus, for example, if a corporation has two classes of stock, one of which pays stock dividends and the other of which pays cash dividends, the stock dividends would be taxable. The increase in proportionate interest of shareholders who do not have their stock redeemed when others are redeemed can result in a 'constructive' taxable stock dividend.[151]

The rules in other jurisdictions are simpler, and the results are varied. In *Sweden*, stock dividends are in principle not subject to tax, being viewed as the equivalent of a split in the old stock. Tax cost of the old shares is allocated between the old shares and the new shares of the same type. If the stock is of a different class or type, it has a tax cost of zero. In *Japan*, the commercial law prior to 1990 allowed stock dividends, and they were treated for tax purposes as if the corporation had distributed a taxable cash dividend that had been reinvested. After 1990, stock dividends are no longer possible as a matter of corporate law. However, stock splits are still possible. Until 2001, although the stock split itself was not a taxable event, if it was accompanied by a transfer of amounts from a profit reserve to stated capital (as is usually the case), the shareholder was deemed to have dividend income in that amount. The 2001 revisions have abolished the deemed-dividend tax in such circumstances.[152]

In *The Netherlands*, stock dividends received by individuals are taxed as box 3 income – that is, they are not taxed as such but, as with all capital income, the underlying investment is taxed on the basis of a deemed yield (4%) of the value of the shares.[153] Where the stock dividend is received by a holder of a 'substantial participation', it is tax-free. Stock dividends are, however, subject to dividend withholding tax on their nominal value, but the tax withheld will be credited or refunded to resident shareholders. Stock dividends paid to corporate shareholders are not taxable in any event, even if the holding (if less than 5%) does not qualify for the participation exemption.

In *Canada*, in general, a stock dividend is treated as a taxable dividend to the extent that the stated capital of the corporation is increased as a result of the payment of the stock dividend.[154] Because the capitalized earnings can be

149. United States, IRC, s. 305(b)(1).
150. United States, IRC, s. 305(b)(2).
151. United States, IRC, s. 305(c).
152. Japan, ITA, s. 25, and Japan, CTA, s. 24.
153. Netherlands, ITA 2001, Art. 5.1.
154. Canada, ITA, s. 248(1). 'Dividend' is defined to include a stock dividend and 'amount' is defined to prescribe the amount of a stock dividend.

distributed tax-free in certain circumstances, it is necessary to tax the earnings at the time they are capitalized.

Australia also taxes certain stock dividends that capitalize profits, and the dividends carry with them the imputation credit, with the tax cost of the total shareholding increased by the amount of the dividend. This allows corporations that wish to retain after-tax income for commercial purposes to capitalize the income through the stock dividend, resulting in effect in full integration of corporate and individual tax on undistributed earnings. However, as a result of the tainting of share capital rules referred to above, this treatment is effectively available only for dividend reinvestment plans, under which a shareholder elects to receive shares in lieu of dividends.[155] Australia also permits stock splits, bonus issues that do not alter share capital or profit reserves (functionally equivalent to stock splits), and stock consolidations that do not result in any transfer of profit reserves to stated capital on a tax-free basis. The tax cost of the original shares is spread over the new or consolidated shares.[156] Australia also permits so-called 'bonus plans' for listed companies, under which shareholders can elect to get bonus shares in lieu of dividends, but the shares are not treated as dividends and tax cost spreading applies.[157] The mechanism is different from dividend reinvestment plans, although the two are economically equivalent. Such plans are attractive to shareholders who are not subject to the capital gains tax but they can entail risk of the application of the capital streaming rules mentioned above.

As a general rule, the *United Kingdom* does not tax the issue of stock dividends (so-called 'bonus shares'), and the cost of the original shares is spread over those shares and the bonus shares.[158] There are exceptions to this treatment. The amount paid up as share capital on the issue of bonus shares may be treated as a distribution where the issue is made within ten years of a share capital reduction. Similarly, share capital repaid within ten years after a bonus issue may be treated as a distribution.[159] The other exception is where the taxpayer has the choice whether to receive dividends or bonus shares. In this case, an election in favour of shares gives rise to a distribution, usually in the amount of the cash dividend foregone, and a cost in the shares of an equal amount.[160] While the tax treatment of such a distribution is formally different from other qualifying distributions (there is no gross-up for stock dividends), since the removal of advance corporation tax in 1999, they are treated in a similar way.

French law distinguishes between stock dividends as such and bonus shares resulting in the capitalization of reserves or earnings. In the former case, the shareholder, as a matter of corporate law, has a choice between the receipt of cash or a stock dividend. If a stock dividend is chosen, it is taxable in the same way as a

155. Australia, ITAA 1936, s. 6BA.
156. Australia, ITAA 1936, ITAA 1997, ss 112-25, 124-240, and 130-20.
157. Australia, ITAA 1936, s. 6BA(6), ITAA 1997, s. 130-20.
158. United Kingdom, Taxation of Chargeable Gains Act 1992, s. 127.
159. United Kingdom, Income and Corporation Taxes Act 1988, ss 210 and 211.
160. United Kingdom, Income and Corporation Taxes Act 1988, s. 249.

cash dividend. In the case of bonus stock, the stock is not taxable currently because it is not viewed as increasing the assets of the shareholder.[161] However, the capitalized earnings, unlike capital attributable to original contributions, cannot normally be distributed on a tax-free basis.[162]

Germany represents another variation. Generally, stock dividends are emoluments from the capital and treated as taxable income.[163] However, the allocation of new stock in the course of a formal capital increase created from reserves is not subject to tax. Subsequent repayment of capital increases resulting from stock dividends, however, leads to taxable dividends.

5.6.3. Redemptions

Redemptions – that is, the purchase by the corporation of its own stock from its existing shareholders – are in form the purchase of shares. If that characterization is followed, the shareholder would have a gain or loss on the shares determined by the difference between the tax cost of the shares and the amount received. This gain or loss would be treated under the normal rules dealing with property dispositions. Thus, the gain might be fully taxable, taxed at a preferential rate, or exempt from tax depending on the structure of the capital gains regime. On the other hand, a redemption differs from a sale to a third party in that property is leaving the corporation and remaining in the hands of the shareholder, which is similar in some respects to a dividend distribution and also to a repayment of stated capital. The systems considered here treat redemption transactions in widely varying ways.

In the *United States*, specific statutory rules deal with redemptions.[164] A redemption will not be treated as a profits distribution if it is 'not essentially equivalent to a dividend'. Substantial case law deals with this standard, which focuses on whether the taxpayer has had a 'meaningful reduction' in his ownership interest in the distributing corporation. In addition to this general standard, there are several 'safe haven' rules. If the distribution is 'substantially disproportionate', exchange treatment is applicable. To meet this test, the shareholder must have a more than 20% reduction in his ownership interest in the corporation and must own less than 50% of the corporation after the redemption. Thus, a redemption that reduces a shareholder's interest from 50% to 39% would qualify for sale treatment. A redemption that terminates a shareholder's interest is also treated as an exchange.

In applying these tests, stock owned by related persons and entities is attributed to the shareholder whose stock is being redeemed. Thus, in the above example, if the remaining stock in the corporation were owned by the taxpayer's wife or son, the redemption would not qualify. The ownership rules based on

161. France, CGI, s. 112-7.
162. France, CGI, s. 112-1.
163. Germany, ITA, s. 20 para. 1 no. 1.
164. United States, IRC, s. 302.

family relationship are waived in some cases, such as where the shareholder being redeemed sells all of the shares he actually owns.

Any redemption that does not qualify as an exchange under the general test or the various safe havens is taxable as a dividend to an individual shareholder to the extent that it represents a distribution of earnings and profits.[165] For a corporate shareholder, a redemption not treated as an exchange would qualify for intercompany dividend relief. The tax cost of the redeemed shares is attributed to the remaining shares.

In the other systems, redemptions tend to take place less frequently, often because the reduction in stated capital with which a redemption is often accompanied is a complex procedure as a matter of corporate law. In addition, the corporate law accounting for the redemption has an important influence on the tax treatment.

In *Japan*, the 2001 revisions of the corporate income tax law significantly changed the tax treatment of redemptions. Some technical changes were also made in 2006 corresponding to the changes in corporate law. Under the current system, the capital account of a corporation is divided for the purpose of the income tax into the profit reserve and capital (which consists of stated capital and capital surplus). The amount of the profit reserve and capital is calculated separately from similar concepts under the Company Law, although the profit reserve is, in many cases, equivalent to the accumulated earnings, and the capital is, in many cases, similar to the sum of the stated capital and the capital surplus under the Company Law. In the case of redemptions, the amount distributed to shareholders that is attributable to the profit reserve is taxed as a dividend. Such amount is calculated on a proportional basis. The difference between the remaining amount of the distribution and the book value of the shares would be taxed as a capital gain.[166]

In *Canada*, concepts are similar but the system is somewhat differently structured. In the case of redemptions, the shareholder is deemed to receive the paid-up capital of the redeemed shares first on a tax-free basis, regardless of whether the redemption changes the shareholder's proportionate interest in the corporation.[167] If the amount received on the redemption exceeds the paid-up capital of the shares redeemed, the excess is taxed as a dividend. The redemption transaction is also treated as a disposition for capital gains purposes. However, for this purpose the proceeds of disposition are reduced by any amount deemed to be a dividend.[168] Accordingly, if the acquisition cost of the shares is more than their paid-up capital, a capital loss will result; on the other hand, if the acquisition cost is less than the paid-up capital, a capital gain will result. As an exception to these rules, gains on shares acquired by a corporation in open-market transactions are taxed to the seller entirely as capital gains.[169]

165. United States, IRC, s. 301.
166. Japan, ITA, s. 25, and Japan, CTA, s. 24.
167. Canada, ITA, s. 84(2).
168. Canada, ITA, s. 53(2)(a)(iv).
169. Canada, ITA, s. 84(6).

Australia also treats buybacks involving traded stock as capital gains transactions (taxability being determined by whether the stock is an asset subject to the capital gains regime) provided the transaction occurs in the ordinary course of trading on the stock exchange. In other situations, the purchase price is treated as a dividend to the extent that it exceeds the amount charged to share capital in the buyback.[170] The dividend portion carries the imputation credit. Where the redemption involves traded stock and receives capital gains treatment in the hands of the shareholder, the transaction is still treated as a dividend for imputation purposes from the company point of view to the extent that it exceeds the amount charged to share capital, with the result that imputation credits are lost to the company and the shareholder.[171] There are limits on creating capital losses for company shareholders, and these are currently being extended to other types of shareholders. Other changes were announced in 2009 to make off-market share buybacks by listed companies easier to achieve, as this method has become an increasingly important capital management tool for listed companies in the last decade. It is also possible to achieve redemptions by a reduction of capital that extinguishes the share. In this event, the entire amount received is treated as out of share capital unless any of the anti-avoidance rules referred to above are applied (such as those for capital streaming).[172]

The *French* corporate law allows redemptions only in limited circumstances. Recent statutory provisions have to some extent clarified the tax status of gains on redemptions, which now depends on the type of redemption involved. In the case of a stock redemption that reduces stated capital (other than because of losses), any amount received in excess of the greater of two amounts – the shareholder's share of paid-in capital or the acquisition cost of the shares – is taxed as a dividend, which would qualify for intercompany dividend relief. Moreover, a gain or loss may be recognized based on the difference between the redemption price and the acquisition cost (after adjustment for the portion of the redemption amount taxed as a dividend). The gain or loss is treated as a business capital or ordinary gain or loss, as the case may be, if the shareholder is a business entity; otherwise, the preferential regime of non-business gains from sales of securities is applicable.[173]

In the case of stock redemptions made in view of a distribution to employees (stock option plans, employees' profit sharing) or of a stock redemption plan by a listed company, the redemption price is treated as a capital gain or loss to the extent that it exceeds or is exceeded by the tax cost of the shares.

In *Germany*, redemptions have become more frequent in recent years after several company law restrictions were abolished. There was serious discussion as to whether the redemption should be regarded as a 'partial liquidation' of the company, which would have led to dividend-like taxation. In the end, the tax administration decided to treat the redemption like any other share transaction.

170. Australia, ITAA 1936, Part III Div. 16K.
171. Australia, ITAA 1997, s. 205-30(1) Table Item 9.
172. Australia, ITAA 1936, s. 6(1) definition of dividend para. (d), ITAA 1997, s. 104-135.
173. France, CGI, ss 109, 112-6, 120-3°, 150 0A II-6, and 161.

As a consequence, the capital gain resulting from the redemption is taxable in the hands of the taxpayer at his individual income tax rate if his participation amounts to at least 1% of the share capital (this is hardly ever the case in the portfolio situation) or is held in a business context. Capital gains from a redemption of shares that are held as private assets are subject to the withholding tax of 25%.

In *The Netherlands*, to the extent that the distribution in redemption exceeds the allocated share of average paid-in capital, it is considered to be income of the shareholder. However, as box 3 income, it is not taxed as such but rather, as with all capital income, the underlying investment is taxed on the basis of a deemed yield (4%) of the value of the shares.[174] In cases where the shareholder owns a 'substantial participation' in the company that redeems the shares, the gain or loss realized by the shareholder upon such redemption is treated like any capital gain or loss made in respect of shares that are part of the 'substantial participation'.

Share redemptions in the *Swedish* system are treated as a sale. In the *United Kingdom*, if the redeeming corporation is engaged in a trade and its shares are not quoted on an exchange, the redemption is treated as a capital transaction, with capital gains consequences.[175] Capital gain treatment is available, however, only if the company can establish a business purpose for the redemption and meet other anti-avoidance tests. If the conditions for capital gain treatment are not met, the excess of the amount distributed over the amount paid up on the shares is treated as a distribution.[176] In the normal manner, such distributions are exempt in the hands of a corporate shareholder, but this does not extend to any corporation tax on capital gains.[177] Shareholders that have their shares bought back on the market receive capital gains treatment.

6. LIQUIDATIONS

The liquidation of the corporation is the last opportunity to tax at the shareholder level any undistributed corporate profits that have not yet borne shareholder tax. It is also an occasion to tax the shareholder on the appreciation in value of his stock investment. The systems vary considerably in the extent to which they emphasize one or the other of these two aspects of liquidation. In the *United States*, a liquidating distribution is treated entirely as an exchange transaction. The corporation has a gain or loss to the extent that appreciated or depreciated assets are involved, and the individual shareholder has a capital gain or loss determined by the difference between the tax cost of the share and the fair market value of the distribution.[178] The property received on liquidation takes the fair market value

174. Netherlands, ITA 2001, Art. 5.1.
175. United Kingdom, Income and Corporation Taxes Act 1988, ss 219–229.
176. United Kingdom, Income and Corporation Taxes Act 1988, s. 209(2)(b).
177. *Strand Futures and Options Ltd v. Vojak (Insp of Taxes)* [2003] EWCA Civ 1457 (CA).
178. United States, IRC, ss 331 and 336.

as its tax cost.[179] No attempt is made to tax the undistributed corporate profits as a dividend; the assets they represent are simply included in the calculation of capital gain or loss.

Where the liquidating corporation is a subsidiary (at least 80%-owned) of a corporate shareholder, a special rule applies. The liquidation is tax-free to both the distributing corporation and the corporate shareholder.[180] The assets transferred to the corporate parent retain their tax cost in the hands of the subsidiary; the parent's tax cost in the stock simply disappears.[181]

This pattern of rules makes the form and timing of the liquidation important. If, for example, the corporation first makes a dividend distribution and then a liquidating distribution to an individual shareholder, the dividend will be taxed in full, while the (reduced) amount received on liquidation will be treated as a tax-free return of the shareholder's cost and as a capital gain to the extent that it exceeds such cost. If the entire amount had been distributed in liquidation, only the tax-free return of the shareholder's cost and capital gain treatment would have applied. On the other hand, a dividend paid to a corporate shareholder would qualify for the dividends-received deduction, while a distribution on liquidation would be taxed in full as capital gain to the extent the liquidating distribution exceeds the corporate shareholder's cost in the shares.

Many of the other systems use the occasion of the liquidation to tax the accumulated corporate profits as a dividend and to allow the repayment of the paid-up capital on a tax-free basis. In *Canada*, where a corporation makes a liquidating distribution, the rules are essentially the same as for a redemption of stock.[182] The taxpayer's share of paid-up capital can in general be received on a tax-free basis. Any additional amount received by the shareholder is taxed as a dividend. Further, a capital gain will result to the extent that the acquisition cost of the shares is less than the paid-up capital. Special rules allow the tax-free liquidation of 90%-owned domestic corporate subsidiaries.[183]

The pattern in *Japan* is very similar. The amount of liquidation proceeds that is attributable to the profit reserve is taxed as a dividend. The difference between the remaining amount of the proceeds and the book value of the shares would be taxed as a capital gain. The special 'liquidation' tax discussed in section 5.5 would be applicable at the corporate level.

France also makes a distinction between paid-in capital, acquisition cost, and taxable dividends, and the tax treatment is substantially the same as in the case of stock redemptions in view of capital reductions (see section 5.6.3. above).[184]

The *Australian* system treats liquidating distributions to the extent of after-tax taxable income (as opposed to after-tax profits, which are usually larger) as

179. United States, IRC, s. 334(a).
180. United States, IRC, ss 332 and 337.
181. United States, IRC, s. 334(b).
182. Canada, ITA, s. 84(3).
183. Canada, ITA, s. 88(1).
184. France, CGI, s. 112-3°.

dividends,[185] which carry with them the imputation credit. As in Canada, for capital gains tax purposes, the total amount of the liquidating distribution is treated as consideration for the disposal of the stock, but the amount of the gain is reduced by the amount taxed as a dividend.[186] No loss is allowed unless the total amount received (whether characterized as a dividend or not) is less than the cost base of the shares. It is possible in Australia to overcome this problem by making interim distributions during liquidation that are treated as dividends because the tax cost reduction mechanism is not operative for such distributions and a loss can emerge on cancellation of the shares. With respect to the liquidation of a 100% subsidiary, in certain cases there is a rollover of the tax cost of the subsidiary's assets outside the consolidation regime, although the transaction is still treated as a disposition of the parent company's shares, with the tax consequences outlined above.[187] No fixed ordering rules distinguish between distributions of share capital and retained earnings; in practice, the liquidator has considerable flexibility in obtaining the most favourable tax results on the liquidating distribution,[188] subject to the dividend and capital streaming and other anti-avoidance rules that have been previously discussed.

In the *German* system, where a corporation is wound up and liquidated, it is generally taxed on the difference between the book value of the assets at the beginning of the winding-up period and the value of the assets distributed to the shareholder at the end of the period.[189] If appreciated assets are distributed in kind, the appreciation is subject to tax. In the hands of the shareholder, there is a two-step approach. First, the distribution is treated like a dividend to the extent that it exceeds the capital contribution attributed to the shareholder. This means that the payment to a corporate shareholder is largely tax-free for the latter, whereas the tax treatment of dividends to an individual shareholder depends on the nature of the holding. Dividends from shares held as private assets are subject to a 25% withholding tax. If the shares have been held as business assets or amount to at least 1% of the capital of the corporation, 60% of the dividend is taxed at the shareholder level. Second, with regard to the repayment of capital, the shareholder may realize a capital gain or capital loss if his historical acquisition cost is lower or higher than his share in the company capital. This will be the case if the shareholder has acquired his shares after the formation of the company at a price not identical with the nominal share value. If the shares are held as a business asset or amount to a participation of at least 1%, a gain would be taxable and a loss deductible. If the shares are held privately and do not reach the 1% limit, the gain or loss is subject to the withholding tax of 25%. Special rules apply if the business is not wound up but rather transferred to a partnership composed of the shareholders or continued as a sole proprietorship. If the taxpayer wants the transaction to be tax-free, the book

185. Australia, ITAA 1936, s. 47.
186. Australia, ITAA 1997, s. 118-20.
187. Australia, ITAA 1997, s. 126-85.
188. *Archer Brothers Pty Ltd* (1953) 90 CLR 140.
189. Germany, CITA, s. 11.

values of the transferred assets are continued. If the tax cost of the shares is lower than the book value of the assets, gain is recognized to that extent by the transferee.

In *The Netherlands*, for individual shareholders not holding their shares in a business, a liquidation distribution up to the amount of the average paid-in capital can be received on a tax-free basis. Any excess is treated as a dividend. The shareholder's acquisition cost in the shares is not relevant (as private capital gains are not taxed). A special rule treats a sale in certain circumstances as a liquidation if the corporation is liquidated shortly after the sale and the purchaser (e.g., a non-resident) would not be subject to income tax on the amount in excess of paid-in capital. If the shareholder is a corporation whose holding does not amount to a participation or an individual holding the shares in his business, the difference between the tax cost of the shares and the liquidation payment will be subject to tax as a gain on sale. If the corporate shareholder qualifies for the participation exemption, the gain is not taxed; however, as a result, losses are not deductible.

Sweden treats a liquidation entirely as a capital transaction. This means that if a loss results, it is subject to the 70% deduction limitation discussed above in Part Two, Subpart B, section 12. This result obtains despite the fact that the realization of the loss is typically not a voluntary act by the shareholder and the 70% rule is generally aimed at intentionally realizing losses while deferring gains. If a subsidiary is in effect liquidated into its parent corporation in a merger, the transaction is tax-free to both parties with a carryover basis in the subsidiary's assets. As in the US situation, the tax cost in the shares of the subsidiary disappears in the transaction.

The *United Kingdom* also treats liquidating payments as capital distributions, resulting in capital gains treatment to both the corporation and the shareholder.[190] There is no attempt to treat a portion of the payment as a dividend distribution.

7. CORPORATE REORGANIZATIONS AND RESTRUCTURING

7.1. General

Most of the systems here under consideration have special rules dealing with the tax treatment of corporate reorganizations.[191] Transactions covered include corporate mergers and acquisitions, divisions, changes in capital structure, and other similar rearrangements of corporate affairs. Several structural issues of corporate taxation are typically involved in such transactions. First, the exchanges and

190. United Kingdom, Income and Corporation Taxes Act 1988, s. 209(1).

191. For France, Germany, The Netherlands, Sweden, and the United Kingdom, the EU Merger Directive requires domestic legislation to allow mergers, share exchanges, and certain transfers of assets to take place on a tax-deferred basis when the participating companies and shareholders are organized or reside in different EU states. In modifying their legislation to the requirements of the directive, several of the countries also modified the rules applicable to purely domestic transactions.

rearrangements of interests that take place in reorganization transactions are usually events that would cause a recognition of gain or loss under normal tax principles. Each system must determine the conditions and circumstances under which those rules will be supplanted by special provisions permitting tax-preferred treatment. The factors taken into account might include the business or commercial reasons for the transaction; the corporate and commercial law aspects of the transaction; and the character of the assets involved and their role in the existing and emerging enterprises. In addition, the change in the extent and character of the ownership interests in the corporation is often an important factor in deciding if the normal recognition rules should be displaced. While the form of the investment may change, that change may not be deemed to be a sufficient modification of the 'continuity of ownership interest' to require a recognition of gain or allow a recognition of loss.

Where the judgment is made that the transaction should be only partially tax-free and some income must be recognized, rules must be provided to characterize that gain. To the extent that an exchange is involved, capital gain or loss treatment may be appropriate. On the other hand, if property is coming out of the corporation, it may be similar to a dividend distribution in connection with the otherwise tax-free reorganization. The effect of exchange treatment or dividend treatment will differ in some situations depending on the nature of the shareholder and the extent to which integration relief is available. Finally, rules must be provided for the continuance or carryover of various corporate tax attributes (e.g., tax cost, carry-overs) of the corporations involved.

Sometimes these issues are dealt with in detailed statutory rules, sometimes under broad general principles such as continuity of business or ownership interest, and sometimes with a combination of both approaches. The basic pattern of reorganization transactions and their effects is considered here. The next section deals with the carryover of corporate tax attributes in these situations and the limitations to which carryovers may be subject.

7.2. MERGER TRANSACTIONS

In a typical merger transaction, an existing corporation disappears and its assets and liabilities are taken over by another corporation that continues the business activities of the disappearing corporation. The shareholders of the disappearing corporation may continue as shareholders of the continuing corporation or may receive cash, property, or creditor interests in the continuing corporation for all or a part of their shares. As a formal matter, the merger may take place under special corporate law provisions or may be a 'practical' merger, with an actual transfer of assets in exchange for stock or other property by the corporation ceasing business.

In the *United States*, the rules dealing with mergers have been developed both in case law and in detailed statutory provisions that apply to all qualifying reorganizations, including mergers. Under the statutory structure, a series of corporate rearrangements, including mergers, are defined as 'reorganizations';[192] other rules then determine the consequences of the various transfers and exchanges involved in the reorganization.[193]

Beyond the statutory definition of reorganization, however, there are a number of judicially developed doctrines that have been adopted in modified form in regulations and that limit the scope of reorganization treatment even when the formal statutory requirements are met.[194] First, the reorganization must have a business or commercial purpose. While this requirement is usually easily satisfied, it stands as a barrier to reorganization transactions that are focused exclusively on the tax benefits of reorganization treatment. In addition, the business of the acquired corporation must to some extent be continued, although substantial variation and changes are allowed. Most importantly, the shareholders in the disappearing corporation must have a significant continuing ownership interest in the acquiring corporation. This requirement of 'continuity of ownership interest' is based on the idea that tax deferral is appropriate only when the shareholder has not changed the basic nature of his investment. However, as the doctrine has developed, in fact it allows substantial variation in the economic characteristics of the investment as long as it continues in the form of an ownership interest. Thus, for example, a merger transaction in which a target corporation wholly owned by a single shareholder merges into a publicly traded corporation in which the former shareholder receives only a small percentage of the stock of the acquiring corporation would still qualify under the continuity-of-interest test. This would be true even if the stock interest had substantially different characteristics (e.g., limited voting rights).

While the exact degree of required continuing ownership is not clearly defined in the case law, something less than 50% would be acceptable. That is, if the shareholders of the disappearing corporation, taken together, received at least, say, 45% of the consideration for their shares in the form of stock in the acquiring corporation, the requirement would be met. Exactly where the lower limit is, however, is not clear. Regulations also require that the shareholders participating in the reorganization transaction not sell their shares to the acquiring corporation or a related person for a period of time after the transaction. Thus, a sale immediately after the reorganization to the acquiring corporation will defeat the required 'post-reorganization' continuity if it involves a sufficiently large number of shares.

Assuming that the merger transaction meets the various requirements, the statute provides special rules to determine the tax treatment of the participants.[195] If only stock in the acquiring corporation is used in the merger, neither the acquired corporation that transfers its assets in the merger nor the shareholder who exchanges his shares for shares in the acquired corporation will recognize gain or loss. The tax cost of the assets carries over to the acquiring corporation, and the

192. United States, IRC, s. 368.
193. United States, IRC, ss 354–362.
194. United States, Treas. Regs., s. 1.368-1.
195. United States, IRC, ss 354–362.

shareholder takes as his tax cost in the new shares his historical cost in his old shares. If other property, such as cash or a creditor interest in the acquiring corporation, is received, then gain, but not loss, will be recognized. If this receipt of the non-stock property is functionally equivalent to a dividend distribution made in connection with the merger, dividend treatment will result. Otherwise, gain will be recognized on the disposition of the shares, which would ordinarily be capital gain. The shareholder is allowed to increase his tax cost in the new shares by the amount of the recognized gain (or dividend), and the acquiring corporation is given a similar increase in the tax basis of the assets.

Some special provisions allow reorganization treatment when the stock consideration used is the stock of the parent corporation controlling the actual acquiring corporation. The extremely technical rules for these 'triangular' forms of merger reorganizations have developed in a haphazard fashion and represent no consistent policies beyond the general notions of continuity of ownership interest and continuation of the business enterprise.

The *Canadian* treatment of the functional equivalent of a merger transaction is determined in part by the nature of the transaction for corporate law purposes. Federal and provincial laws allow two or more corporations to 'amalgamate' and continue as a single corporation. The amalgamating corporations do not cease to exist for corporate law purposes; rather, they continue in the form of the amalgamated corporation. As a result of this approach, there has formally been no transfer of assets or discontinuation of business; in an analogy often used in the case law (and appropriate for Canada), it is as if two streams had flowed together to form a river.

The tax law accepts this characterization to some extent, and thus the transfers involved in the amalgamation transaction are not treated as dispositions for purposes of gain or loss recognition. As a result, no rollover is necessary on an amalgamation for the assets of the predecessor corporations. On the other hand, some special tax rules do not follow the corporate concept. Thus, for some purposes, the resulting entity is treated as a new corporation, and the statute provides detailed rules for the carryover of various corporate tax attributes from the predecessor corporations to the new corporation pursuant to the amalgamation.[196]

At the shareholder level, where the shareholders of the 'old' corporation receive only shares of the new corporation, the exchange is tax-free and the shareholders continue the tax cost of their old shares. There is no requirement that the shares received be held for any particular period of time. If there is a difference in the values of the shares given up and the shares received and that benefit in effect accrues to a person related to the shareholder, gain is recognized to that extent. As a prophylactic measure, no increase in basis of the shares is allowed for the gain recognized. If the shareholders receive non-share consideration in the amalgamation, the rollover does not apply and the shareholders are considered to have disposed of their shares in the amalgamating corporations for proceeds equal to the fair market value of the shares in the amalgamated corporation.

196. Canada, ITA, s. 87.

Apart from amalgamations under corporate law, the rules discussed in connection with corporate formation may apply to a transfer of property for shares that is, at the corporate level, similar to a merger. However, the distribution of the shares to the shareholders would be a taxable event under normal principles.

Under *Dutch* law, mergers can take place on a tax-deferred basis provided that the statutory conditions are met. In that case, the tax attributes of the disappearing company are transferred to the surviving company, and the shareholders of the resulting company transfer their tax cost of the old shares to the new shares.[197] Any consideration the taxpayer receives in cash (except for a small amount of 'boot') is taxable up to the amount of the gain. The statutory conditions require, *inter alia*, that the merging companies be subject to the same tax regime.

Germany has a special statute that deals with reorganizations both of corporate and non-incorporated businesses, with differing requirements for the tax-free status of various types of reorganizations.[198] In the case of corporate mergers, a transaction may take the form of downstream or upstream mergers or the combination of two corporations into a newly established third corporation. The shareholders of a dissolved corporation receive shares in the surviving corporation. If the merger does not include cash payments to the shareholders of the dissolved corporation and the book values of the assets are transferred to the surviving or newly established corporation in circumstances in which the potential gain will remain subject to tax in Germany, no gain or loss is recognized by the transferring corporation.[199] However, it is up to the transferring corporation to decide whether the transfer will be entered at book value, fair market value, or a freely chosen intermediate value. The receiving corporation must enter the assets on its books at any value chosen by the transferring corporation between the book value and the fair market value. Insofar as the chosen value exceeds the book value, the transferring corporation must realize a gain. If the receiving corporation exchanges its shares for the assets of the transferring corporation at fair market value, there is no taxable gain at the level of the receiving corporation.[200] However, in case of an upstream merger, 5% of the gain for the receiving corporation is treated as non-deductible expenses.

As for the shareholders, the tax cost of the old shares can be rolled over to the new shares received in the course of the merger if the later taxation of the hidden reserves in the shares is not excluded or limited.[201] Otherwise, the shares of the transferring corporation are deemed to be disposed at fair market value, which leads to a realized gain for the shareholder. The fair market value of the old shares then serves as the tax cost for the new shares. If, as result of the merger, a former portfolio interest becomes a participation that would be subject to tax, the shares take a fair-market-value tax cost. In the converse situation, if a substantial

197. Netherlands, CTA, Art. 14b.
198. Germany, Reorganization Tax Act (RTA) (*Umwandlungssteuergesetz*).
199. Germany, RTA, s. 11.
200. Germany, RTA, s. 12 para. 2.
201. Germany, RTA, s. 13.

participation is changed into a portfolio interest, the tax cost of the shares is carried over and a subsequent disposition of the shares would remain taxable. Cash payments may be received in some circumstances, although gains are taxable to that extent.

In *France*, as well, reorganizations can take place on a tax-deferred basis under conditions and circumstances precisely stated in the statutory provisions. For corporate and tax law purposes, the merger may take the same forms as in Germany. According to the new accounting standards, if both corporations belong to the same group, the transferred assets normally keep the book value they had in the dissolved corporation. In other situations, the assets normally receive a stepped-up basis (market value) and the taxation of the gains is deferred. A distinction is made between depreciable and non-depreciable assets. As to depreciable assets, the gains are then subject to normal corporate tax in the hands of the transferee corporation ratably over a five-year period (fifteen years in the case of buildings), and their depreciation and the gain stemming from their disposal by the transferee corporation are calculated on the basis of their stepped-up value. As to non-depreciable assets, the gains from the sale by the transferee corporation are calculated on the basis of the value they had in the accounts of the transferring corporation. The unrealized profits on the current assets transferred can either be immediately taxed or taxed later as they are sold.[202] At the shareholder level, the taxpayer may elect to defer gain until the disposition of the shares received on the exchange.[203] Cash up to 10% of the nominal value of the shares can be received and is currently taxable.

United Kingdom corporate law does not provide for mergers proper, but similar results can be achieved for commercial law purposes through the transfer of a business owned by the target corporation and issue of shares by the bidding corporation to the shareholders of the target. If the target is wound up as part of the arrangement (under the arrangement provisions of the corporate law),[204] there should be no distribution for tax purposes by the target to its shareholders (e.g., of the shares in the bidding corporation). Rather, the target shareholders will be treated as having received a capital distribution in respect of their shares in the target, which may result in a capital gain.[205] However, if the transactions qualify as a reorganization for tax purposes, no disposition is deemed to take place and the new holding is treated as a continuation of the old. One of the statutorily defined forms of reorganization is a reconstruction of a company or the amalgamation of two or more companies. To qualify, the reorganization must have a bona fide commercial purpose, and the exchange must not be part of a scheme for tax avoidance.[206]

202. France, CGI, ss 210-0 A and 210 A.
203. France, CGI, ss 38-7 *bis*, 150-0 B, and 150-0 D-9.
204. United Kingdom, Companies Act 2006, Parts 26 and 27.
205. United Kingdom, Taxation of Chargeable Gains Act 1992, s. 122.
206. United Kingdom, Taxation of Chargeable Gains Act 1992, Part IV Ch. II (ss 126-140).

The *Japanese* rules on reorganizations were quite restrictive and far from consistent before the 2001 tax revisions. Before 2001, in general, the corporation that disappeared in the merger was subject to the 'liquidation' tax discussed in connection with property distributions. Thus, it had to recognize gain on its appreciated property and include in income any deferred profits or reserves. This gain was calculated as the difference between the paid-in capital, surplus, and legal reserves of the disappearing corporation, and the par value of the stock received, together with the fair market value of any non-stock property received in the merger. This approach allowed the fair market value of the stock received in excess of its par value to escape tax; the only concern was the increase in stated capital for the acquiring corporation. However, if the acquiring corporation entered the assets on its books for more than the par value of the stock given and the non-stock consideration, it was required to realize income to the extent that this value exceeded the book value of the asset in the hands of the merged corporation. Thus, in effect, any increases in paid-in capital resulting from the merger were taxed to the merged corporation, and any write-up in asset value beyond the par value of the shares transferred was taxed to the surviving corporation. Shareholders who received shares in the acquiring corporation were taxed to the extent that the par value of the shares received exceeded the par value of the old shares. If the market value of the shares was higher than the par value, that potential gain was deferred until the shares were disposed of in a taxable transaction.[207]

The 2001 tax revisions apply identical rules to all kinds of reorganization transactions. The general position is that any corporate reorganization transaction should be regarded as a taxable event triggering all unrealized gains accumulated in the companies subject to reorganization. Therefore, in the event of a merger, the corporation that disappears in the merger transaction would be subject to the corporate income tax on such unrealized gains as well as on its annual profit. In addition, the excess of the fair market value of the shares or other assets delivered to the shareholders of the disappearing corporation over the amount of the capital, etc., of such corporation should be taxed as a dividend, and the remaining amount of the delivered shares and assets may be taxed as a capital gain. The new law also provides unified rules regarding the category of restructuring transactions that are not treated as taxable events. These non-taxable merger transactions are: (a) a merger between companies with a 100% equity relationship (i.e., cases where (i) one company is a wholly owned subsidiary of the other or (ii) both companies are the wholly owned subsidiaries of a common parent); (b) a merger between companies with more than a 50% equity relationship that meets several criteria to ensure the continuity of the business (for example, approximately 80% or more of the employees who were employed by the disappearing company must be assumed by the other corporation); or (c) a merger for the purpose of establishing a joint venture between non-related entities that meets several other criteria. Non-taxable mergers must be pure stock-for-stock transactions, and no other consideration should be paid to the shareholders of the disappearing corporation. In the case

207. Japan, CTA, ss 2, para. 12-8, and 62-2.

of a non-taxable merger, the tax otherwise imposed on the shareholders of the disappearing company is deferred until the moment of disposition of the shares of the surviving corporation.

Sweden has special tax rules dealing with merger transactions based on the EU merger directive. These rules apply to transactions where a corporation is dissolved without liquidation. In Sweden this applies only to mergers controlled by rules in corporate legislation. Corporations with different owners could be merged without taxation by combining several steps. For example, if a shareholder transfers shares to a corporation for newly issued shares, the exchange is tax-free. A cash payment is taxed as gain on the exchange. Thereafter, under the general merger provision, the acquired corporation can be merged into the acquiring corporation, thus providing the functional equivalent of a merger of the two companies, with the shareholders of the old company becoming shareholders of the acquiring company.

In *Australia*, corporate law does not generally provide specific procedures for mergers by transfer of assets, except with respect to the banking industry or by a complex procedure involving court approval. Accordingly, most mergers are effected by acquisition of shares, either for cash or in share-for-share exchanges. Generally, mergers involving asset transfers give rise to taxation consequences in the normal way, although one school of thought holds that mergers in the banking sector achieved through universal succession are tax-free on the basis of general tax principles. In addition, effectively tax-free 'contractual' mergers (referred to as dual-listed companies) have been used in international settings (all with the United Kingdom), under which two listed companies agree to operate in concert in future through common management and boards of directors, with dividend and other distributions by the companies being made at the same time and equal in amount. Mechanisms for equalization payments between the companies are provided to deal with situations where one company cannot meet its payment to its shareholders.

7.3. Share Exchanges

A second typical form of reorganization involves an exchange of shares entirely at the shareholder level. Unlike the merger transaction, no transfers of assets are involved and the acquired corporation is unaffected at the corporate level. Normally, a share exchange would be a taxable event in the systems here under consideration, but special provisions allow such an exchange to be treated on a rollover basis if certain conditions are met.

In the *United States*, one form of statutorily recognized reorganization is the acquisition by one corporation of 80% ('control') of the stock of another corporation *solely* in exchange for the voting stock of the acquiring corporation.[208]

208. United States, IRC, s. 368(a)(1)(B).

The courts have strictly interpreted the voting stock requirement, and even a *de minimis* amount of non-qualifying consideration can prevent non-recognition.[209]

The 80% control need not be acquired in one transaction as long as the final acquisition results in the 80% test being met. However, if some of the prior acquisitions have been made for consideration other than voting stock and are considered as part of an integrated acquisition transaction, the entire exchange would be taxable.[210] If the prior acquisitions were for voting stock, the subsequent acquisition of control could be done on a tax-free basis. Where the transaction qualifies as a reorganization, the shareholder retains the tax cost of his old shares for the new shares.

The *Canadian* rules are quite different. Shares can be exchanged for shares in the acquiring corporation in any amount on a tax-free basis as long as the selling shareholders and any non-arm's length persons do not have, after the exchange, shares in the acquiring corporation representing more than 50% of the value of all the shares or have control of the acquiring corporation.[211] In addition, the acquiring corporation and the selling shareholders must deal with each other at arm's length. Shares can also be acquired for other consideration in the same transaction as long as the vendor can clearly identify which shares were exchanged for cash and which were exchanged for shares. Similarly, the rollover applies to a fraction of the shares exchanged for other shares as long as the purchaser's offer indicates that the shares are exchanged for a specified fraction of the acquired shareholder's shares and cash or other consideration for the remaining fraction. The tax-free rollover treatment applies only to the shares or fraction of shares that are disposed of for shares. The shareholder keeps his tax cost in the old shares as his tax cost for the new shares, and the acquiring corporation takes as its cost the lesser of fair market value or the paid-up capital allocated to the shares. The tax-free exchange applies only to exchanges of shares in Canadian corporations.

Australia introduced similar rules for 'scrip-for-scrip' mergers in 1999.[212] The shareholders of the company that is being acquired in the merger can get rollover treatment for shares they dispose of in the merger in exchange for shares, provided the acquiring company obtains 80% of the voting shares in the acquired company. To the extent that the shareholders receive cash, they calculate gain or loss in the ordinary way for the relevant proportion of shares. If the shareholders have shares that were acquired before the introduction of the capital gains tax, that status is not maintained after the merger. Instead, such shareholders get a market value tax cost for the new shares so that the gain on the previous shares held up to that time is protected from tax. This was considered necessary to ensure that mergers were not used to keep shares out of the capital gains net forever. It is necessary that all shareholders can participate in the offer on substantially the same terms. The rules allow a subsidiary of the acquiring company to acquire the shares

209. See, e.g., *Helvering v. Southwest Consolidated Corp.*, 315 U.S. 194 (1942).
210. See, e.g., *Chapman v. Commissioner*, 618 F.2d 856 (1st Cir. 1980).
211. Canada, ITA, s. 85.1.
212. Australia, ITAA 1997, Div. 124-M.

in exchange for shares of the acquiring company. Generally, the acquiring company has a cost base in the acquired shares based on the market value of the shares it uses in the acquisition. If, however, there is a significant degree of continuity of control from the acquired company to the acquiring company, then the original tax cost of the acquired interest is transferred to the acquiring company. This treatment applies when a person (including associates) holds 30% of the acquired company before and 30% of the acquiring company after the merger, or a person holds 80% or more of both companies before and after the merger. These rules are designed to prevent the rollover being used to increase the tax cost of shares in anticipation of a sale of the shares to a third party. Recently, a further restriction was introduced to prevent the market value tax cost given to the shares acquired from being combined with the allocation of cost rules in the consolidation regime (considered below) in order to obtain a considerable increase in the depreciation deductions available. The market value cost for the shares acquired is no longer available if a company without significant assets of its own acquires another company (so-called 'top hat' restructures) in a scrip-for-scrip (that is, stock-for-stock) transaction.[213]

The *Dutch* rules allow a tax-deferred exchange of shares if the acquiring corporation obtains over 50% of the voting stock (reduced from 90% in compliance with the EU merger directive and made applicable to domestic as well as EU-related transactions) of the acquired corporation.[214] Pre-existing ownership of shares may be counted for purposes of the 50% test. Cash payments of up to 10% of the nominal amount of the stock are allowed, although it is not clear if these payments must be pro rata or could be made on a disproportionate basis to buy out a shareholder. Special rules ensure that the later disposition of the shares by a holder of a substantial participation remains taxable if, after the exchange, his share interest no longer qualifies as a substantial participation.

The *German* rules were changed in 1994 to comply with the EU merger directive. This led to an alignment of domestic and EU transactions. In 2007, a new set of statutory rules for the exchange of shares was put in place as part of the reform of the rules for business organizations.[215] An exchange of shares by which the acquiring corporation A contributes shares of company B in the course of a capital increase of a third corporation C and obtains a majority of the voting rights in the acquired corporation C leads to a tax-free rollover in the accounts of corporation A. As in the case of formal mergers, the acquiring corporation has the option of entering the shares acquired at their book value, the fair market value, or any value in between those amounts on condition that there is a 'qualified exchange' of shares (meaning the acquiring corporation acquires a majority of voting rights). If an amount in excess of book value is chosen, the exchanging

213. Australia, ITAA 1997, ss 124-784A–124-784C.
214. If shareholder is a company: Netherlands, Art. 13i.1 CITA (shareholding company entitled to participation exemption) and Art.13i.2 CTA (not entitled to participation exemption). If shareholder is an individual: Art. 3.55 ITA.
215. Germany, RTA, s. 21.

shareholder will recognize a gain to that extent, the tax treatment of which depends on the status of the shareholder.[216] Germany required this 'doubling' of hidden reserves at the level of the shareholder and at the level of the corporation with respect to cross-border reorganizations, thus requiring the foreign acquirer to enter the German book value into its foreign accounts. The ECJ held this requirement to be incompatible with the EC Merger Directive in 2008.[217]

Apart from the case where shares are used as a 'contribution in kind' in the course of an acquisition, case law prior to 1999 allowed a tax-deferred exchange of shares if the shares received were identical in value, type, and function to the transferred shares. This option has been explicitly repealed.[218] In the corporate context, a similar result can be achieved by using the 'participation exemption' for share sales by corporate shareholders.

In general, in *France* an exchange of shares is a taxable event. However, gains from exchanges made in the context of a public exchange bid are deferred until the shares are disposed of.[219] Rollover treatment is also available when 50% of the capital of a company (or, under certain circumstances, contributions of shares conferring at least 30% of the voting rights in a company) is exchanged for newly issued shares of the acquiring company if the shares received are held for at least three years.[220] However, this provision has lost most of its relevance because, from 2007, long-term capital gains from the disposal of 5% or more holdings are tax-exempt. In both cases, cash consideration cannot exceed 10% of the nominal value of the shares.

In the *United Kingdom*, certain share exchanges are treated as reorganizations not resulting in a disposition for capital gains purposes. There are several qualifying transactions.[221] If the acquiring company already owns 25% of the stock of the acquired corporation or, as a result of the exchange, obtains voting control, the exchange may be made on a tax-deferred basis. Tax-deferred treatment is also available if the exchange is part of a general offer to obtain control. Finally, the exchange is tax-deferred if it in fact results in the acquisition of control of the acquired company. The reorganization must have a bona fide commercial purpose and the exchange must not be part of a scheme for tax avoidance. In the hands of the acquiring corporation, the shares in the target will have a cost equal to the value of the shares given by the acquiring corporation (step-up in cost).

As mentioned above in connection with merger transactions, in *Sweden* shares may be transferred on a tax-free basis for newly issued shares of the transferee corporation. *Japan* does not have a rule enabling tax-free share acquisitions, except that Japanese income tax law allows compulsory share swaps for creating a wholly

216. Germany, RTA, s. 21 para. 2.
217. ECJ, 11 Dec. 2008, C-285/07 (*A.T. v. FA Stuttgart-Koerper-Shaften*).
218. Germany, ITA, s. 6 para. 6 sent. 1.
219. France, CGI, s. 38-7.
220. France, CGI, s. 210 B-1.
221. United Kingdom, Taxation of Chargeable Gains Act 1992, s. 135.

owned subsidiary to be tax-free if such share swaps meet certain criteria that are similar to those for non-taxable mergers.[222]

7.4. Non-merger Asset Reorganizations

Some systems have special reorganization provisions dealing with asset transfers or 'enterprise' mergers that involve the transfer of assets in a transaction that does not formally constitute a merger for corporate law purposes. In the *United States*, this type of 'practical' merger is possible if certain statutory requirements are met.[223] The corporation whose assets are being acquired must transfer 'substantially all' of its assets to the acquiring corporation. At least 80% of the consideration received for the assets must be voting stock of the acquiring corporation (or a parent corporation in control of the acquiring corporation). In addition, liabilities of the acquired corporation can be assumed subject to some special limitations. The corporation whose assets were acquired must be liquidated and distribute the consideration received to its shareholders. If these requirements are met, the acquired corporation recognizes no gain or loss on the transferred assets, and the acquiring corporation takes over the tax cost of the assets. At the shareholder level, the shares of the acquiring corporation can be received on a tax-free basis, with the tax cost of the old shares attaching to the new shares. If non-stock consideration within the permissible limits is involved, that amount is taxable, either as gain on the share disposition or as a dividend, depending on the circumstances. The income inclusion increases the tax cost for the new shares. In addition, the acquiring corporation is allowed to increase its tax cost in the assets received by the amount of the income recognized at the shareholder level.

Japan has no rules identical to the US 'practical' merger rule, as described above in connection with corporate formation, but tax-free business transfers are available with regard to transfers in exchange for stock, subject to certain criteria. In addition, a transfer of assets or business from a corporation to its wholly owned subsidiary that meets certain requirements can be a tax-free transaction, if made within two years after the incorporation of the relevant subsidiary.[224]

Although other systems include provisions that allow a tax-deferred transfer of assets to an existing corporation in exchange for shares, there is typically no mechanism to permit the shares received in exchange for the assets to be distributed tax-free to the shareholders unless the transaction meets the requirements of a tax-deferred division, discussed in the next section.

Thus, in the *Canadian* system, there is no equivalent of the US 'practical' merger described above. The special rollover rules described above in connection with corporate formation allow the transfer of assets in exchange for stock to take place on a tax-deferred basis. However, there is no provision allowing the

222. Japan, CTA, ss 2, paras 2-16 and 2-17, and 62-9.
223. United States, IRC, s. 368(a)(1)(C).
224. Japan, CTA, ss 2, para. 2-15, and 62-5.

tax-deferred distribution of the stock of the acquiring corporation to the shareholders of the acquired corporation. The *United Kingdom* has no rollover rules under which one corporation transfers a business to another unrelated corporation in return for shares in the unrelated corporation. Further, the distribution by the transferor corporation to its individual shareholders of shares in the unrelated corporation would be a taxable distribution unless made in a winding-up. However, if the shares in the unrelated corporation are issued directly to the transferor corporation's shareholders, rollover relief is available, as described above in section 7.2.[225] In this case, the only form of consideration that the transferor corporation may receive is the transfer of its liabilities to the unrelated corporation.

Sweden has comprehensive legislation dealing with tax-free reorganizations. Some of these rules have already been mentioned above. The classical method for tax-free reorganization is a sale of business assets at a price equal to the cost basis. However, gain could nevertheless in principle be taxed, because the statutory rules require all sales of business assets to be treated as if sold for fair market value.[226] To prevent gain from being recognized in these circumstances, the reorganization rules provide that a sale below market value will be accepted, and there will be no deemed constructive dividend as a result of the transaction if certain conditions are met.[227] For example, the transferee corporation cannot have losses from activity prior to the transfer, a gain cannot be transferred from a corporation qualifying under a special tax regime to a 'normal' corporation outside the special regime, and any transferred gain must remain subject to Swedish tax. This method of tax-free transfer means that the purchaser will have the same tax base as the seller, and thus the gains will eventually be realized and subject to tax.

Another set of rules makes it possible to exchange assets for shares in the transferee corporation free of tax. A prerequisite is that all assets and liabilities of one or more branches of its business activity must be transferred. The cost basis of the assets is transferred to the shares. These rules are in accordance with the EC merger directive.

In *Australia*, the 'scrip-for-scrip' rollover and new consolidation regime for corporate groups can be used to similar effect. However, a recent amendment to the scrip-for-scrip rules, discussed above, prevents a tax cost increase through the insertion of a new holding company that is more or less entirely held by the same shareholders (in other words, in the absence of a real acquisition or merger involving two companies with their own businesses and different shareholders).

Both *Germany* and *The Netherlands* similarly allow the transfer of, broadly speaking, an independent business unit in exchange for shares on a tax-deferred basis. In Germany, a business unit transferred to a corporation for shares enters at book values if (1) the business unit is part of the corporate tax base of the acquiring corporation, (2) the liabilities of the business unit do not exceed its assets, and (3) the taxation of the hidden reserves at the level of the acquiring corporation is not

225. United Kingdom, Taxation of Chargeable Gains Act 1992, ss 136 and 139.
226. Sweden, ITA, Ch. 22 ss 3 and 7.
227. Sweden, ITA, Ch. 23.

eliminated or limited.[228] However, tax legislation attempts to prevent companies from shifting business units to subsidiaries on a tax-deferred basis to sell the subsidiary tax-free under the rules of the newly established 'participation exemption'. Under the pre-2007 legislation, the participation exemption applied only to the sale of shares in a subsidiary if a tax-free transfer of a business unit was not undertaken within seven years before the shares are sold. This could lead to over- or under-taxation because the current value of the shares has no logical connection to the previous value of the contribution. Under the new rules introduced in 2007, a sale of shares in the subsidiary will lead to a retroactive realization of capital gains in the originally transferred business division. The potential capital gain subject to retroactive taxation will be reduced by one-seventh for each year following the reorganization.[229]

In Germany, the treatment of the transaction, as in the merger and share exchange situations described above, depends on the extent to which the transferee corporation elects to write up the assets in excess of their book value. To that extent, the transferor will recognize gain and have a corresponding increase in the tax cost of the shares.

In the Dutch system, the transferor corporation takes as its tax cost in the shares received the fair market value of the shares, thus eliminating the theoretical (in that the transferring company will almost always be entitled to the participation exemption with regard to the shares received) corporate-level tax on the appreciation in the transferred assets. The transferee corporation acquires the assets at their historical tax cost and thus bears the burden of the tax on disposition.[230] There is a requirement, however, that the stock be held for at least three years to prevent what is essentially a cash sale from being converted into a tax-deferred exchange.

In *France*, it is possible to transfer an independent business activity for shares on a tax-deferred basis (see section 7.3 above). The transferring corporation can distribute the shares to its shareholders if prior approval is obtained to waive the normally applicable three-year holding period.

7.5. CORPORATE DIVISIONS: 'DEMERGERS'

The division of the assets of an existing corporation can take a variety of forms, but all have in common the splitting of ownership at the shareholder level. In a typical 'demerger' situation, shareholders of the original corporation emerge from the transaction with stock interests in two or more corporations.[231] The splitting of

228. Germany, RTA, s. 20 para. 1.
229. Germany, RTA, s. 22 para. 1.
230. Netherlands, CITA, Art. 14.
231. In the terminology often used in connection with corporate divisions, the pro rata distribution of the stock of a subsidiary to the existing shareholders is referred to as a 'spin-off'. If the distribution is in exchange for the stock of the distributing corporation, the transaction is termed a 'split-off'. A split-off is often done on a non-pro rata basis and results in a change

ownership at the shareholder level raises several tax issues. In the first place, since property has left the original corporation, gain might be recognized by the distributing corporation under normally applicable rules. In addition, since the shareholder has received a property distribution, the usual rules for dividends or redemptions (if shares in the original corporation are exchanged for the distributed shares) are implicated at the shareholder level. Finally, since the shareholder now has two interests in place of his original single interest, it is possible to sell a part of his investment while retaining the remainder, thus involving the usual rules, including preferential or tax-free treatment on the sale shares. From a policy point of view, the issue is whether and to what extent the results of the normally applicable rules should be modified when the transaction constitutes a corporate division.

The systems examined here have reacted quite differently to the tax issues that arise in corporate divisions. In some countries, special rules allow tax-free treatment and are crafted to limit the perceived tax avoidance possibilities in the transaction. In others, no attempt has been made to change the normally applicable rules to allow tax-free treatment. In contrast, in the United States, detailed rules allow for a tax-deferred division of, broadly speaking, active businesses, but have substantial restrictions intended to prevent the 'bailing out' of corporate profits in a divisive transaction.[232] In Canada, there are no special rules on demergers, but normally applicable principles may allow divisive transactions in some circumstances, although typically not without administrative approval.

Even among those jurisdictions that allow some form of tax-deferred division, there are substantial differences in the requirements that must be met. Almost all jurisdictions, however, recognize that some sort of 'business' or commercial purpose must be established for the division and have rules preventing the division of business and investment assets.

The rules on corporate division are most developed in the *United States* and involve both case law principles, which have been codified in the regulations, and statutory provisions. The rules apply both to the distribution of an existing subsidiary and the transfer of assets to a newly formed subsidiary followed by the distribution of the stock to the shareholders. As a basic requirement, the division must have a demonstrable business purpose to justify the transaction from a commercial point of view.[233] The purpose must be, in general, a 'corporate' purpose, as opposed to a 'shareholder' purpose, and must justify the division of ownership at the shareholder level. Thus, for example, a desire to insulate risky activities in a separate corporation is not a sufficient business purpose for the distribution of the stock of the corporation to shareholders. On the other hand, where shareholder disagreement is affecting operations at the corporate level, a corporate division may be commercially justified.

---

in the ownership of the distributing corporation. Finally, in a 'split-up', the distributing corporation transfers assets to new or existing subsidiaries and then liquidates.

232. United States, IRC, s. 355.
233. United States, Treas. Regs., s. 1.355-2(b).

Assuming that the division has a business purpose, several statutory requirements are intended to prevent the division from being used to distribute corporate profits to shareholders.[234] First, both the corporation making the distribution and the distributed corporation must be engaged in the active conduct of a trade or business and have been engaged in such business for at least five years prior to the division. This requirement prevents the concentrating of passive or investment-type assets in one corporation that could then be disposed of at preferential capital gain rates after the division. In addition, the statute requires that the stock of a distributed subsidiary must not have been acquired in a taxable acquisition in the past five years. This prevents the distributing corporation from using its earnings and profits to purchase a corporation with an active business and then make a tax-free distribution of that corporation shortly thereafter. The statute further mandates that the division cannot be 'used principally as a device for the distribution of [earnings]'. Although the 'device' and 'active business' requirements overlap to some extent, the former focuses particularly on the possibility of a post-division sale of one of the businesses and takes this as an important indicator of a distribution 'device'.

If the above requirements are met, then at the corporate level, both the transfer of the assets to a subsidiary corporation (if an existing subsidiary is not involved) and the distribution of the stock do not result in the recognition of gain or loss. The receipt of the stock by the shareholders is similarly tax-free, and the tax cost of the shares with respect to which the distribution is made is allocated to the shares of the distributed and distributing companies.

In contrast, *Canada* has no special provisions dealing with divisive transactions, but a complex transactional form – the 'butterfly' reorganization – allows what is in effect a demerger transaction.[235] The most important structural requirement is that each transferee corporation must receive the same proportionate share of property of the corporation being divided, *viz.* business property, investment property, and cash. Thus, the transaction cannot be used to 'bail out' cash or liquid investment assets.

Since 1980, the *United Kingdom* has had extensive statutory rules dealing with demergers. Basically, three situations are covered: (1) the distribution by the parent company of the shares of an existing subsidiary; (2) the transfer of a subsidiary by the parent company to another company in exchange for the other company's shares and a distribution of those shares by the transferor company; and (3) the transfer of a business of the parent company to a subsidiary in exchange for its shares and the distribution of those shares by the parent company.[236] The most important conditions are that the company is a trading company or a member of a trading group and that the demerger is of some benefit to the trading activities. This latter test requires more than merely showing some commercial purpose to the transaction. An advance ruling or clearance for the transaction can be obtained

234. United States, IRC, s. 355 (a)-(e).
235. Canada, ITA, s. 55(2)-(5).
236. United Kingdom, Income and Corporation Taxes Act 1988, s. 213.

from the fiscal authorities. If the various requirements are met, the distribution of the shares will not be treated as a distribution for tax purposes and will be tax-free in the hands of the recipient; the cost of the original shares will be spread over those shares and the new shares. In general, the company faces no capital gains consequences in distributing shares or transferring assets or shares.[237]

The situation is similar in *Australia*. Prior to 2002, there were no special rules dealing with demergers, but a transactional form of demerger was possible in the context of a corporate group. The subsidiary to be distributed could issue stock rights to the shareholders of the parent company without the distribution being treated as a dividend or otherwise taxable.[238] The exercise of the right was not taxable and resulted in the shareholders owning stock directly in the subsidiary. The tax cost of the stock was the exercise price of the option, and thus any transfer of value was taxed to the shareholders when the stock was sold. There were no restrictions on this form of transaction based on the business or commercial purpose of the transaction, although a special statutory provision was applicable to certain spin-offs taking this form where the distributed entity was a unit trust subject to single-level taxation.

In 2002, as part of Australia's ongoing business tax reform, special and very generous demerger relief provisions were introduced in addition to the rules outlined above.[239] The new rules allow the 'head company' of a demerger group to distribute shares of a company in the group to shareholders in the head company tax-free, from both capital gains and dividend treatment, for both the demerger group and the shareholders. Several conditions must be satisfied. The head company must hold at least 20% of the demerged entity and must distribute at least 80% of its shares in that entity. The value of the shareholders' new and continuing interests must be the same proportion of the value of the demerger group after the merger as before it, and no cash or other benefit can be distributed to the shareholders in the transaction. Shareholders must be treated equally in the demerger. The shareholders' original tax cost and capital gains tax (CGT) status (shares acquired before the introduction of CGT are excluded from the tax) are allocated between the shareholders' continuing and new shares. Anti-abuse rules deal with value shifting at the corporate level in the demerger and remove the dividend exclusion if the capital and profit elements of the demerger do not reflect the circumstances of the demerger.

In *Sweden*, under special statutory rules for publicly traded corporations (occasioned by the restructuring of Allmänna Svenska Elektriska Aktiebolaget (ASEA) into ASEA Brown Boveri (ABB) in 1991), a pro rata distribution of all shares of a previously owned subsidiary corporation is possible on a tax-free basis. This requirement indirectly prevents investment asset bailouts. The tax cost of the

237. United Kingdom, Taxation of Chargeable Gains Act 1992, ss 136, 139, and 192.
238. This was the generally accepted position at the time, but it was thrown into doubt by a subsequent court decision (*McNeil* (2007) 229 CLR 656), referred to in relation to taxation of distributions above.
239. Australia, ITAA 1936, s. 44(3)-(6), ITAA 1997, Div. 125.

shares of the distributing corporation is allocated between the distributing and distributed corporation based on fair market values. There is generally no tax at the level of the distributing corporation as long as the shares are investment assets and not current assets.

In accordance with the EU Merger Directive, rules for partial demergers were introduced in 2007.[240] Recent changes in corporate law have also made it possible to effect a complete demerger in accordance with the rules for tax-free reorganizations.[241] In practice, a demerger could, however, be accomplished tax-free at both the level of the distributing corporation and the recipient shareholder by using statutory rules for sales below market value (see above, section 7.4).

Germany introduced the tax-deferred demerger in 1994 when it changed its domestic laws to comply with the EU Merger Directive.[242] Under the German system, two forms of demerger are recognized: a division and a split-off. In a division, two or more potentially independent businesses are transferred to new or existing subsidiary corporations. The shareholders of the distributing corporation acquire shares of the receiving corporations and the distributing corporation is dissolved. In a split-off, one or more businesses are transferred to subsidiary corporation(s) with the distributing corporation continuing to operate at least one business. The transfer can be made without recognition of gain to the distributing corporation if the parties elect to retain the book values of the assets involved and the 'hidden reserves' or appreciation of the assets are taxable at the level of the receiving corporation. The shares of the receiving corporations given to the shareholder of the contributing corporation enter at book value if the capital gain realized at disposal would be fully taxable in Germany. In the division, any existing loss carryforward and the pools of net equity are allocated between the surviving corporations based on fair market values.

In *France*, both the transfer of assets preliminary to a demerger and the distribution of the stock would be, in principle, taxable events. However, a division can be made on a tax-deferred basis if prior governmental approval is obtained. In addition, under legislation passed in 1995, prior approval is no longer necessary for tax-deferred treatment when a corporation operating at least two independent businesses transfers those businesses to two (or more) corporations whose shares are distributed to shareholders on a pro rata basis and the shareholders hold the stock for at least three years.[243]

The *Japanese* system was substantially changed in 2001. Prior to 2001, while assets could be contributed on a tax-deferred basis to a newly formed subsidiary, no special rules permitted the tax-deferred distribution of the shares of a corporation; the distribution was treated as a taxable dividend or redemption. Under the 2001 legislation, corporate demergers are generally regarded as taxable events for both the dividing corporations and their shareholders. However, the Japanese income

240. Sweden, ITA, Ch. 38a.
241. Sweden, ITA, Ch. 37.
242. Germany, RTA, s. 15.
243. France, CGI, ss 210-0 A and 210 B.

tax is deferred at both the corporation and shareholder levels for (a) a corporate demerger between companies with a 100% equity relationship (i.e., cases where (i) the transferee company or the transferor company is a wholly owned subsidiary of the transferor company or the transferee company, as the case may be, or (ii) both companies are the wholly owned subsidiaries of a common parent); (b) a corporate demerger between companies with more than a 50% equity relationship that meets several criteria to ensure the continuity of the business (for example, the principal portion of a certain kind of business must be transferred to the transferee company); and (c) a corporate demerger for the purpose of establishing a joint venture between the transferor and the transferee that meets several other criteria. To prevent tax-motivated transactions, the 2001 tax revisions introduced an anti-avoidance provision that is generally applicable to any kind of corporate reorganization transaction.[244]

In *The Netherlands*, under a qualifying tax-deferred demerger, the new companies take the tax cost that the acquired assets and liabilities had in the hands of the demerging company.

8. TRANSFER AND LIMITATIONS ON TRANSFER OF CORPORATE TAX ATTRIBUTES

In many systems, when a corporation goes out of existence in connection with a merger or similar transaction, its tax attributes are transferred to the successor corporation. The tax attributes transferred typically include the tax cost of assets, various reserves and provisions, and most importantly, loss carryforwards. In connection with loss carryforwards, there are often restrictions on the ability of the successor corporation to use the losses against subsequently arising income. These limitations are intended to prevent the 'selling' of loss carryforwards by the corporation that incurred the losses to third parties. They are typically triggered by changes in the ownership of the loss corporation and/or changes in its business activities.

The *United States* has highly developed rules concerning both the carryover of attributes and limitations on those carryovers.[245] Basically, in situations that qualify as reorganizations under the various statutory definitions, the corporate attributes of the disappearing corporation are inherited by the surviving corporation. In situations involving divisions where there is more than one surviving corporation, some of the existing corporate tax attributes are divided among the surviving corporations. In addition, in the liquidation of a corporate subsidiary, the subsidiary's attributes are inherited by the parent.

There are substantial limits on the carryover of losses, credits, and other tax benefits in those situations in which attributes are inherited.[246] The limitations

244. Japan, CTA, s. 2, para. 12-11, and ss 62-2 and 62-3.
245. United States, IRC, ss 381, 382, 383, and 384.
246. United States, IRC, s. 382.

apply generally whenever there is a significant change in the share ownership of the loss corporation, even if the situation does not involve the transfer of tax attributes. In general, if there is a more than 50% change in share ownership, the losses of the corporation experiencing the change in ownership will be limited. Thus, if there is a sale of over 50% of the stock of the loss corporation, the carryovers will be subject to the limitations. Similarly, if there is a change of over 50% of the ownership of the loss corporation due to its merger into a profitable corporation, the limitations will apply. The '50% ownership change' test is determined by looking back at changes in the prior three-year period. These rules apply only to ownership changes by shareholders who have at least 5% interests in the corporation, but there are complex rules aggregating less-than-5% shareholders for some purposes.

Where the limitations apply, the loss carryover can offset only income that is subsequently generated by the loss corporation's business. Rather than actually determine that amount of income, an assumed rate of return is applied to the value of the loss corporation at the time the change in ownership takes place, and the loss is allowed to that extent. The basic theory behind the limitation is that the purchasers of the corporation should be able to make no greater use of the losses economically incurred by the selling shareholders than those shareholders would have enjoyed if there had been no change of ownership. Even this limited carryover is not allowed unless the corporation's business is continued or its assets are used in another business. The loss limitations also apply to certain credit carryforwards.[247]

Similar limitations apply to losses that have accrued but are not yet realized for tax purposes at the time of the change in ownership. The deduction of such 'built-in' losses is limited if the losses are realized within five years after the ownership change.

In addition, some broad 'purpose-based' anti-avoidance principles apply to loss situations,[248] but they have largely been supplanted by the more specific statutory provisions dealing with losses.

The *Canadian* rules are somewhat similar, although they are not as extensive. Corporate tax attributes are transferred in the liquidation of a domestic 90%-owned subsidiary into its domestic parent corporation. In addition, in the amalgamation of two or more corporations, the existing tax attributes are preserved. Where control of a corporation changes, any existing capital loss carryforwards are eliminated.[249] Similarly, non-business losses may not be carried forward after an ownership change.[250] With respect to operating loss carryforwards, the business of the loss corporation must be continued and the losses may be used only against the income from that business. In addition, any accrued but unrealized losses are deemed to be realized at the time of the change of control, thus subjecting them to the above limitations.

247. United States, IRC, s. 383.
248. United States, IRC, s. 269.
249. Canada, ITA, s. 111(4).
250. Canada, ITA, s. 111(5).

In *The Netherlands*, a reorganization in the form of a merger under corporate law can result in the carryover of tax attributes, including losses, of the disappearing company at the taxpayer's request if certain conditions set out by the Ministry of Finance are fulfilled.[251] Under the general rules on loss carryovers, the use of losses is restricted if there is a change of at least 30% in share ownership involving those who were shareholders when the business activities ceased. This restriction applies unless (a) the loss was incurred in a taxable year in which for at least nine months the company's passive investments did not represent over 50% of its total assets, or (b) the activities of the companies in the course of the loss-making years did not shrink by more than 70%.[252]

The 2001 tax revisions have also changed the *Japanese* system in this respect. In general, the tax attributes are transferred to a successor corporation in a tax-free reorganization transaction. In addition, in a tax-free merger and certain kinds of tax-free demerger transactions, loss carryovers are generally permitted. Taxable reorganization transactions are regarded as recognition events, and the tax losses may not be transferred from one corporation to another. The 2001 tax revisions introduced an anti-avoidance provision that is generally applicable to any kind of corporate reorganization transaction.[253] This provision is intended to enable the tax authorities to challenge tax-motivated reorganization transactions.

In *Sweden*, corporate tax attributes, normally including loss carryforwards, are transferred in a merger transaction. However, where a change of ownership of the loss corporation occurs, as would typically be the case in an acquisition of shares followed by a liquidation, special limits apply on existing loss carryforwards. First, the existing loss can be used only in an amount equal to twice the purchase price of the shares. In addition, the losses cannot be used against taxable 'group contributions' from other members of the group, the technique by which Sweden allows a consolidation of profits and losses within a group.

While tax attributes in *France* in general are transferred in the case of a merger, loss carryforwards are not transferred except with a special agreement by the fiscal authorities.[254] In addition, if a corporation undergoes a radical change of its business activities, particularly in connection with a change in control, the corporation's existing loss carryforwards will no longer be available.[255]

With minor exceptions, *Australia* permits the transfer of tax attributes (tax cost, losses, imputation credits, and foreign tax credits) only when a 100%-related group of companies consolidates under a new regime introduced in 2002. In a merger, this will generally have the effect of transferring the tax attributes of an acquired company to the head company of a consolidated group, since the acquired company will enter the consolidated group. Elaborate provisions prevent value shifting and the multiple generation of losses among related companies outside

251. Netherlands, CTA, Art. 14b and Decree 19 Dec. 2000, no. CPP2000/3131M, V-N 2001/8.3
252. Netherlands, CTA, Art. 20a.
253. Japan, CTA, s. 132-2.
254. France, CGI, s. 209 II.
255. France, CGI, ss 221-2 and 221 *bis*.

consolidation.[256] The Australian rules limit certain tax attributes of a corporation whose stock ownership undergoes a 50% or greater change unless the corporation continues the 'same business'. The test is interpreted strictly, and the commencement of a new business will result in the loss of carryforwards of operating losses, bad debts not yet written off for tax purposes, realized capital losses, and accrued losses.[257] The general limitations do not apply to imputation credits or foreign tax credits. Much more generous rules for testing continuity of ownership apply to a company's shares listed on the stock exchange.

The pattern in the *United Kingdom* is basically the same. If within a three-year period after a change in ownership (an elaborately defined statutory concept), there is a major change in the nature and conduct of the business, the utilization of pre-change revenue losses is restricted.[258] Historically, these limitations did not apply to capital losses. Due to perceived abuses, however, in 2006 new rules were introduced that may restrict the use of capital losses following a change in ownership.[259] These rules are couched in anti-avoidance language and do not follow those applicable to revenue (operating) losses. The result is somewhat disjointed.

In *Germany*, the carryover of tax losses in merger and demerger situations, which was introduced in 1994, has been dramatically restricted by recent legislation. In a widely criticized move, German legislation in 2007 abolished the option to carry over tax loss positions from the merged company to the acquiring company.[260] This was due to fears that emerging ECJ jurisprudence might force Germany to recognize foreign losses incurred by foreign companies merging with domestic companies. Although it is debatable whether this point was justified, the current law has created a substantial obstacle to business reorganizations in times of economic crisis. In addition, in the case of a demerger, the recent legislation has abolished the option to transfer tax losses to another entity.

Originally, German case law refused to disallow losses where there was a change in share ownership or business as long as there was no formal change in the legal existence of the corporation. A statutory provision implemented in 1988 required that the corporation that is utilizing the losses must not only be 'legally' but also 'economically' identical with the corporation that suffered the losses. The legislation expressly provided that the corporation would not be considered to be the same legal and economic entity if more than three-quarters of the shares of the corporation were transferred, if it has recommenced business (in the same field or a different field), and if the fair market value of newly acquired assets exceeds the value of existing assets.

The 2007 Business Tax Reform has changed this rule.[261] Now, the pure change in ownership defined as 'harmful acquisition of shares' can restrict the use

256. Australia, ITAA 1997, Divs 165-CD, 170-D, 725, 727.
257. Australia, ITAA 1997, Divs 165-175. See Ruling TR 1999/9 on the same business test.
258. United Kingdom, Income and Corporation Taxes Act 1988, s. 768.
259. United Kingdom, Taxation of Chargeable Gains Act 1992, ss 16A and 184A-184I.
260. Germany, RTA, s. 12 para. 3 (mergers) and RTA, s. 15 para. 1 sent. 2 (demergers) with reference to RTA, s. 4 para. 2 sent. 2.
261. Germany, CITA, s. 8c.

of losses at the corporate level. If more than 25% of the shares are transferred to one person or a related party within five years, the accrued losses of the corporation can be used only to the extent that the shares have not been alienated. This leads to arbitrary results, as the sequence of sales may significantly impact the carryforward of losses. If more than 50% of the shares are transferred to one person or a related party within the same period, the utilization of the full amount of losses is disallowed. In a provision that appears to be substantially overreaching, even in alienations of shares between group companies (i.e., in situations where the ultimate 'owner' remains identical), loss carryforwards can be completely lost. The compatibility of this 'anti-avoidance' provision with the Constitution is widely in doubt.

9. CONSOLIDATED CORPORATE TAXATION

Even though corporations are generally treated as separate taxpayers, most systems have special provisions under which affiliated corporations can be combined for tax purposes. These rules allow the overall economic results of the group operation to be taken into account despite the existence of formally separate corporate entities. The requirements for consolidation differ substantially, as do the techniques for treating the consolidated entity. In some cases, the separate corporate existence of the members of the group is ignored for most purposes, and in effect each corporation is treated as a division of a single company. In contrast, some systems generally treat the corporations as separate taxpayers but have special rules that allow the separate profit or loss so computed to be transferred among members of the group. The differences in technique can have important consequences for the timing and character of the income in the group. In still other situations, there is no formal mechanism for consolidation, but the normal rules of income determination are relaxed in the context of related corporations.

The *United States* has a highly developed system of consolidated taxation. The rules are contained in a complex set of administrative regulations based on a broad statutory authorization.[262] To qualify for consolidated treatment, an 'affiliated group' of corporations must have a domestic parent corporation that owns at least 80% of the stock of another domestic corporation. Lower-tier corporations may be included in the group if their higher-tier shareholder(s) in the group meet the 80%-ownership test with respect to those corporations. Corporations subject to special taxing regime (for example, life insurance companies) may not be included in the group. Under this definition, two brother-sister corporations owned by an individual or a foreign corporation are not entitled to consolidated treatment. If the definitional requirements are met, the group can elect to file a consolidated tax return.

When consolidated filing is elected, 'consolidated' income is calculated by combining the separate incomes of each of the members of the group. The income

262. United States, Treas. Regs., ss 1.1502-1–1.1502-100.

of each member of the group is determined under normal principles, with important modifications to reflect the consolidation. Intercompany transactions are accounted for on a 'deferred' basis. In general, no gain or loss is recognized on intercompany sales transactions until the property is sold outside the group. At that time, the gain or loss that would have been involved in the intercompany sale is accounted for by the member who would have realized that amount in the original sale. If the property is depreciable and is used in the business of the buying member, an increased basis for depreciation purposes is allowed, but the selling member must include a corresponding amount in income as the depreciation deductions are taken. Deferred intercompany transactions also have to be taken into account if the group for some reason stops filing a consolidated return. Intercorporate dividends are eliminated in the calculations of consolidated income. Consolidation allows losses in one member of the group to offset income of other members.

The overall effects of the consolidation are reflected in the 'investment account' with respect to the parent's stock in the subsidiaries in the group. In general terms, earnings in the subsidiary that are included in the consolidated income increase the parent's basis in the subsidiary stock, thus preventing double taxation of the same economic income if the stock of the subsidiary is sold. Correspondingly, actual dividend distributions reduce the basis in the stock, as do losses of the subsidiary that are being used by other members of the group. If the losses exceed the basis of the stock, a so-called 'excess loss account' is established, a kind of 'negative' basis that will cause the loss in effect to be recaptured if the stock is sold or the member leaves the group.

In 2002, *Australia* largely replaced its rules for transfer of assets, losses, and foreign tax credits among members of a 100%-related group with a complete and complex consolidation regime that rivals that of the United States in complexity (already 600 pages of legislation from a dozen different tax bills, and counting).[263] To get these benefits, it is now generally necessary to consolidate for income tax purposes, which is the main incentive for companies to enter the regime. The regime is elective for 100%-related resident companies, partnerships, and fixed trusts, but once elected, all entities with the necessary relationship must enter the consolidated group. The 'head entity' of the group must be a company or a trust or partnership taxed as a company. Most types of company may enter a group, including insurance companies, although some are excluded, such as credit unions.

When consolidation is elected, group income is calculated by the 'single-entity rule' that treats all the subsidiary members of the group as divisions of the head company – that is, the members do not calculate taxable income separately for each member and then eliminate intra-group transactions. Pre-consolidation tax events are preserved by the 'entry history rule', by which everything that happened to the subsidiaries before consolidation is deemed to have occurred to the head company. Hence, on entering consolidation it is necessary to allocate all tax attributes of the members to the head company. In the case of assets, this allocation is generally achieved by pushing down the tax cost of shares and other interests in

263. Australia, ITAA 1997, Part 3-90 comprising Divs 700-721.

group members held by the head company and other group members to the assets (other than shares, etc.), which disappear on consolidation. Liabilities are accounted for in this 'push-down' process, with intra-group liabilities eliminated. In the case of other tax attributes such as losses, imputation, and foreign tax credits, the process involves pushing them up to the head company. Losses are subject to a significant number of special rules, but generally the 'available fraction' approach applies. This approach is designed to ensure that the rate of using losses transferred from a particular member of the group remains approximately the same as it would have been if it had remained in that member (similar to the US rules that apply to losses on mergers). Once these parameters are established for the head company, taxable income, etc., is calculated only at the level of the head company.

When a company leaves a consolidated group, the tax cost of the shares is reconstructed from the net assets of the leaving company. The head company calculates any gain or loss for the consideration received for the shares in the company accordingly. If the reconstructed tax cost is negative, the head company makes a capital gain equal to the deficiency, and the tax cost is set at nil for calculating any gain to the head company on departure. Other tax attributes remain with the head company and are not allocated to the leaving company, so that, for example, it will have no imputation credits in its franking account immediately after departure from the group.

One of the main reasons for adopting consolidation in Australia was to prevent value shifting and multiple losses arising from the flexibility to manipulate the tax cost of shares and assets in a group. Related companies that remain outside consolidation (generally because of less than 100% ownership) are subject to revamped and comprehensive value-shifting provisions and new rules on cost base adjustments in relation to multiplication of losses.

The *Canadian* system takes a very different approach to the taxation of affiliated corporations. No formal provisions allow the consolidation of profits and losses. While proposals for consolidation have been made, they have been opposed by the provinces, whose tax is usually a percentage of the federal tax. There was concern that the provisions would allow an avoidance of provincial taxes through the shifting of profits and losses in the group. Nonetheless, informal consolidation has been recognized both administratively and legislatively. Most of the anti-avoidance and anti-loss-trading rules do not apply to transactions between related corporations; transactions structured to transfer profits and losses among the members of a group are generally effective.

Sweden also does not formally recognize consolidation among group members. However, a special tax rule provides a mechanism that allows for the consolidation of profits and losses. It is possible for corporations connected with at least 90% ownership to a common parent corporation to make 'group contributions' to other members of the group. The group contribution is deductible by the paying corporation and taxable to the recipient corporation. Thus, for example, a profitable parent corporation with a loss subsidiary could make a group contribution to the subsidiary, which would reduce the parent's profit and allow the subsidiary to utilize its losses. Group contributions can also be made between subsidiaries of the same parent corporation. The rules are not, in general, applicable to corporations subject to special tax rules.

The *United Kingdom* similarly does not recognize group reporting of income. However, a number of special rules apply to the taxation of company groups. The most important deals with 'group relief'. If a parent company owns at least 75% of the stock of a domestic subsidiary company, then trading losses, capital allowances, and certain other tax attributes can be 'surrendered' from one company to the other.[264] In this case the whole amount of the loss, etc., can be surrendered even where there is less than 100% ownership. In addition, if a 'consortium' of 5% or more corporate shareholders together own 75% of the stock of a company, group relief is available; however, only a proportionate part of the loss, etc., can be surrendered.[265] Group relief allows, for example, losses in one company to be surrendered and offset against income of the other company.

Special rules apply for capital gains purposes. They allow a tax-free transfer of assets within a 75%-owned group.[266] However, if the corporation receiving the asset on a tax-free basis leaves the group within six years, the transaction is retroactively taxable.[267] In contrast to trading losses, capital losses cannot be transferred among group members.

The Netherlands, in contrast, has a complex system of consolidation. A parent corporation and some or all of its 95%-owned subsidiaries can make an application to the fiscal authorities to be treated as a so-called 'fiscal unity'.[268] While the corporations remain separate for corporate law purposes, for tax purposes the activities, assets and liabilities, and income and losses are deemed to be those of the parent corporation. Generally all of the corporations must be organized under Dutch law or, if organized under the law of an EU Member State or a tax treaty country, they must be similar to Dutch companies. Companies that are not residents of The Netherlands may join a fiscal unity only to the extent that they have a Dutch permanent establishment. Further, the companies must be subject to the same tax rules (e.g., an insurance corporation and a business corporation cannot form a fiscal unity). Finally, the companies must meet a series of further requirements, laid down in regulations that have been issued under the statute (and may be supplemented with requirements geared to the individual case), *inter alia*, to prevent the shifting of value to a subsidiary whose stock could be sold on a tax-free basis and to limit the use of pre- and post-unity losses.

France allows a consolidation of a domestic parent (or French branch of a foreign corporation) and any 95% or more domestic subsidiaries (*intégration fiscale*).[269] The holding can be direct or indirect and must be maintained for the

264. United Kingdom, Income and Corporation Taxes Act 1988, s. 402.
265. United Kingdom, Income and Corporation Taxes Act 1988, s. 403C.
266. United Kingdom, Taxation of Chargeable Gains Act 1992, s. 171.
267. United Kingdom, Taxation of Chargeable Gains Act 1992, s. 179.
268. Netherlands, CTA, Art. 15–15d.
269. France, CGI ss 223 A–223 Q.

entire fiscal period.[270] The election to consolidate is binding for five years, but the parent can decide each year which of the qualifying subsidiaries it wants to include.

The income of each member is calculated separately. Losses (capital losses and operating losses) realized by members may be used to offset income of other members. To the extent so used, they are not available to the subsidiary later should it leave the group. Loss carryforwards arising in years before the consolidation can be used only against income generated by that member. Intra-group financial transactions such as loans, loan forgiveness, bad debt reserves, etc. are eliminated in calculating each member's income. Intercompany sales of fixed assets result in deferred gains or losses that are taken into account when the property is sold outside the group, the member leaves the group, or the group is discontinued. The same is true for deferred intra-group financial transactions. Intercorporate dividends are also eliminated.

Germany has statutory provisions dealing with group taxation that are based on a complex and highly developed case law system of de facto consolidation (*Organschaft*).[271] The consolidation has traditionally been available only between domestic businesses (including the German branch of a foreign corporation and an individual proprietorship). However, a 'foreign' parent company can also qualify if it is a dual resident and has central management and control within Germany, or if it has a registered domestic branch to which the profits and losses of the dependent corporation are attributed. Consolidation is possible only where a 'dominant' entity has a majority of voting shares in the 'dependent' entity. Former legislation that also required economic and organizational integration was repealed in 2000. Moreover, election for group taxation requires a profit-and-loss pooling agreement (prescribed in corporation law) between the parent and the subsidiary. Under this pooling agreement, which must last for at least five years, the profit or loss of the dependent entities calculated on a separate basis are transferred to the dominant entity, which includes that amount in its income calculations. The dominant entity is responsible to make up any loss suffered by the dependent entity and takes over its profits. This transfer of profit is not treated as a distribution. As a result of the transfer, the dependent entity shows no income or loss (the loss being offset by the claim against the dominant entity for reimbursement under the agreement). Losses arising prior to the *Organschaft* may not be used while the *Organschaft* arrangement is in effect.

Despite the *Organschaft* arrangement, the participating companies are treated as independent for tax purposes. Thus, intercompany transactions generate income or loss that is taken into account currently. If transactions are not undertaken on an arm's length basis, a constructive dividend (treated as an advance transfer of profit and not carrying an imputation credit) or constructive contribution to capital may be found. Payments by the subsidiary to outside minority shareholders are treated

---

270. The indirect holding in a domestic sub-subsidiary through a foreign subsidiary, which was initially disregarded, must be taken into account in order to comply with the EC freedom of establishment principle: ECJ, 27 Nov. 2008, C-418/07 (*Société Papillon*).
271. Germany, CITA, ss 14–19.

as regular income of the subsidiary as and dividends in the hands of the shareholders.

Unlike the other systems, *Japan* for a long time did not allow any type of formal or informal consolidation. Each corporation was treated as a separate taxpayer and transactions between related corporations had to be undertaken at arm's length without exceptions. However, after strong demand by corporate management of Japanese companies, the 2002 tax revisions introduced a consolidated corporation tax system. Under this system, the consolidated group may include only direct or indirect wholly owned subsidiaries incorporated in Japan, and a consolidated group filing a consolidated return must include all the qualified subsidiaries in the group. No losses incurred by subsidiaries prior to the adoption of consolidated returns may be used for offsetting the taxable income in the consolidated returns. In addition, all the corporations subject to a consolidated return are jointly and severally liable for the full amount of the corporate income tax for the group, and the allocation of such tax within the group is provided for in the tax law.

When this consolidated corporation tax system was introduced, the corporate income tax rate applicable to corporations that file consolidated returns was 32%, which was 2% higher than the normal tax rate (30%). This 2% additional tax was imposed so that the introduction of the consolidated corporate tax system would be revenue neutral. This additional tax was abolished in 2004 according to the original schedule.

10. SPECIAL TAX REGIMES FOR CLOSELY HELD CORPORATIONS

Whatever the basic structure of the corporate tax system, some countries have special rules for the taxation of closely held corporations. They sometimes reflect the judgment that whatever the appropriate taxing pattern for widely held corporations, modification should be made for closely held corporations that more nearly resemble partnerships. Nonetheless, the technical details of the rules vary substantially. In some cases, those rules allow a single level of pass-through taxation on the partnership model. In other situations, the rules are intended to reinforce the normal pattern of taxation by dealing specifically with issues that typically arise in the closely held context or to prevent income from being shifted from one category to another through the closely held corporation.

In the *United States*, special rules provide for pass-through treatment for corporations that meet certain definitional requirements and elect to be treated on a pass-through basis.[272] The technical requirements for qualification have been strictly interpreted, and the rules are often criticized as being too complex for the relatively unsophisticated taxpayers to whom they are intended to apply.

272. United States, IRC, ss 1361–1378.

In general, the number of shareholders is limited to one hundred resident individuals. Special rules for trusts allow them to be shareholders in certain situations. The corporation can have only a single class of stock that participates in dividends, although voting and non-voting common stock is allowed. The corporation is permitted to have subsidiary corporations. If the corporation elects pass-through status, it may further elect to disregard its wholly owned subsidiaries as separate entities and be treated as though it owns directly the subsidiaries' assets and liabilities.

If the corporation elects pass-through status, each shareholder includes in income his share of the items of income and deduction that arise at the corporate level. Thus, the character of the items passes through and is retained, for example, as a capital gain, at the shareholder level. The income is included in the shareholder's taxable year in which the corporation's year ends, whether or not it is distributed. If the share ownership changes during the year, income is generally prorated over the entire year and attributed to the shareholders accordingly. Income that is included increases the shareholder's tax cost in his shares as if the income had been distributed and then reinvested in the corporation. When an actual distribution is made, the tax cost of the shares is reduced accordingly; any excess over the tax cost is treated as a capital gain.

If the corporation operates at a loss, the loss similarly passes through to the shareholder and reduces the tax cost of the stock accordingly. The shareholder is allowed to take a current deduction for the corporate level loss only to the extent of his actual investment in the corporation, whether in the form of stock or debt. If the taxpayer has insufficient investment to use the loss currently, the loss is suspended until the investment is increased (for example, by additional capital contributions or by the recognition of corporate-level income, which in effect increases the investment). Special 'passive activity loss' rules limit otherwise deductible losses if the stockholder does not participate in the corporation's business.[273]

Special rules apply if the corporation electing pass-through treatment has previously done business as a 'normal' corporation subject to the two-level tax system. The rules are intended to ensure that any previously earned but undistributed corporate income is subject to a second shareholder-level tax when distributed. Thus, complex 'stacking' rules are provided that determine whether distributions are deemed to be from current or prior earnings. Similarly, appreciation that was accrued but unrecognized at the time the corporation became subject to the pass-through regime may be subject to a double-level tax to approximate the pattern of taxation that would have applied if the appreciation had been realized and distributed while the corporation was subject to the two-level tax system.

While the corporate-level income and deduction items are subject to the special pass-through rules, the other normally applicable tax rules continue to apply to the corporation. Thus, for example, a reorganization is possible between a 'normal' corporation and a pass-through corporation.

273. United States, IRC, s. 469.

None of the other countries here under consideration has special pass-through treatment for formally organized corporations. However, in *Canada*, special rules apply to Canadian-controlled 'private' corporations (CCPCs). Private corporations are corporations whose stock is not publicly traded on an exchange and that are not controlled by a public corporation.[274] CCPCs qualify for full imputation relief for their investment income and active business income up to $500,000 annually. The latter income qualifies for a 'small business deduction',[275] which reduces the rate of tax on the income significantly. The small business deduction is not available for income from personal services businesses and investment businesses. The rules for investment income are generally designed to prevent individuals from achieving a better result by holding investments in corporate form rather than directly. In *Australia*, government-sponsored committees twice recommended a pass-through regime similar to the American approach, but no action was taken. In practice, pass-through treatment for taxable profits, but not tax losses with the benefit of limited liability, is achieved by operating most closely held businesses in the form of trading trusts rather than as companies.

Many countries have more restrictive rules dealing with closely held companies. In *Sweden*, rules prevent income from employment from being converted to (more lightly taxed) income from capital.[276] The special situation dealt with is dividends from closely held corporations where the shareholder works on behalf of the corporation. A yield on the shareholder capital invested in the corporation is calculated based on the government borrowing rate plus 9%. Dividends up to this amount are taxed as income from capital. Dividends above this amount are treated as income from employment in the hands of the shareholder. The dividends are not deductible at the corporate level but also are not subject to social security tax at the corporate level. Given the levels of corporate and social security tax, the result is that the total tax burden on actual salary distributions and 'deemed' salary in the form of excess dividends is roughly the same. This form of taxation also applies to capital gains in such a corporation when shares are sold. In recent years, the threshold for taxation of dividends as employment income has been raised considerably for most corporations, since the basis for the calculation now includes not only capital invested but also salaries to employees.

Other countries have similar rules to prevent closely held corporations from taking advantage of possible rate differentials between individual- and corporate-level taxation. In the *United States*, the reduced rates of tax available to corporations with low amounts of income are not available to personal service corporations owned by employees. In addition, undistributed investment income realized by closely held investment companies can be subject to a special penalty tax.

As previously mentioned, in *Germany* additional restrictions apply to arrangements between a controlling shareholder (as defined) and the corporation.

274. Canada, ITA, s. 89(1).
275. Canada, ITA, s. 125.
276. Sweden, ITA, Ch. 57.

In addition to the normal arm's length rule, the agreement must be legally valid, clearly expressed, and concluded in advance of the transaction in question. However, there is no specific regime for closely held companies, as the corporate tax legislation largely treats public and private companies in a similar way.

In *Australia*, in the context of private companies, loans to shareholders and similar benefits (such as payments of shareholder's expenses or forgiveness of shareholder debts) can be treated as dividends, which are not usually entitled to the imputation credit. A similar restriction applies to excess employee benefits. Australia generally adopts a 75/20 rule for determining widely held and closely held status – that is, whether 75% of the company is held by twenty or fewer persons.[277]

The *United Kingdom* also applies restrictive rules to closely held companies, defined as companies where five or fewer 'participators' have control of the company. Special rules apply to directors and creditors who can qualify as participators. If a company that meets the definition of 'close' makes a loan to a participator, the company is liable to make a payment to the tax authorities equal to 25% of the loan, as if the amount due 'were an amount of corporation tax'.[278] The amount paid is refunded if and when the loan is repaid. The definition of 'distribution' is also broader in the case of close companies and will cover most in-kind benefits.[279] The lower corporate tax rates for companies with small profits are not available to close investment-holding companies, which are typically non-trading close companies.[280] Further, if an individual provides personal services through a company where, if the services were provided directly, the individual would be regarded as an employee, the individual may be allocated income received by the company for those services.[281]

11. INTEGRATION OF CORPORATE AND SHAREHOLDER TAXES

11.1. General

It is often stated that the policy goal for the taxation of entities is that income should end up being taxed to the same extent whether it is derived directly by an individual or indirectly through an entity. It is possible, as we have just seen, to achieve this goal reasonably well in the case of closely held corporations, although not every country does so. Partnership taxation, dealt with in Subpart B, below is a case where most countries do achieve this result.

277. Australia, ITAA 1936, Part III Divs 7, 7A.
278. United Kingdom, Income and Corporation Taxes Act 1988, s. 414.
279. United Kingdom, Income and Corporation Taxes Act 1988, s. 418.
280. United Kingdom, Income and Corporation Taxes Act 1988, s. 13A.
281. United Kingdom, Income Tax (Earnings and Pensions) Act 2003, ss 50 and 51.

It is not really feasible to achieve the goal in the case of widely held, especially publicly traded, corporations, for a number of reasons. Listed corporations typically do not distribute all their income, which causes two problems. First, it is not possible to determine currently which shareholders, if any, will ultimately benefit from the income, and second, if a shareholder sells shares before the income is distributed, any benefit of the retained income enjoyed by the shareholder can be captured only by the capital gains tax, and then not easily. Further, most countries have a variety of institutional investment vehicles that are subject to special tax rules (e.g., pension plans, mutual funds, life insurers), and these vehicles are major investors in listed corporations in most countries. It is not easy to put the corporate-shareholder tax regime and these special regimes together to produce the goal of taxing corporate income as if it were derived directly by the individual members of such institutions. Finally, the international tax system complicates the achievement of the goal, as discussed in Part Four.

From 1960 through 2000, many countries, including many of those covered here (Australia, Canada, France, Germany, and the United Kingdom), adopted an imputation system as the preferred way of moving toward a single level of taxation at individual rates on distributed corporate income. Under this system, generally the shareholder grosses up dividends by reference to the underlying corporate tax attributable to the dividend and then is taxed at normal marginal tax rates on the grossed-up amount, with a tax credit equal to the gross up, thus integrating the corporate-level tax paid with the individual-level tax. From the mid-1990s there has been a worldwide move away from imputation, so that only Australia and Canada among the countries covered here will retain the system. This change in approach is attributable to several factors. First, imputation systems must deal with a number of complex structural issues that are not present, or not present to the same degree, in classical systems. The following are the principal structural issues that have been dealt with in different ways in the imputation systems that grew up from 1960 through 2000:

(1) Should tax preferences at the corporate level 'pass through' to the individual shareholders when distributed?
(2) If the answer to question 1 is no, should distributed preferences be taxed only at the shareholder level, or should they be subject to some kind of 'compensatory' tax when distributed, so that all dividends carry with them the imputation credit?
(3) If the shareholder's tax liability is less than the attributed corporate tax, should the excess be refunded to the individual shareholder?
(4) How should income passing through several tiers of corporations before reaching an individual investor be treated?
(5) How should retained earnings, which would have carried with them the credit when distributed, be treated if the shareholder sells his shares prior to distribution?
(6) How should shareholders with different 'tax characteristics' (e.g., pension funds, investment companies) be treated?

The imputation systems in the countries here under consideration dealt with these issues in different ways, often in increasingly complex fashion, as taxpayers probed the systems for weakness and governments responded with ever more detailed anti-abuse rules.

Second, beyond the complexities of operating the imputation system domestically, the introduction of imputation systems raised important international issues, where in general they favoured domestic investment over foreign investment and domestic shareholders over foreign shareholders. These issues are discussed in more detail in Part Four. As a result of domestic complexity and international discrimination (and in the case of EU Member States, the requirements of the European Court of Justice), imputation systems have fallen out of favour and have been increasingly replaced with some sort of 'rough-and-ready' integration relief, typically taking the form of shareholder relief for dividend distributions or some other adjustments in the overall rate applicable to distributed profits.

At the same time, countries that had historically used the classical system began to move to some form of shareholder-level relief for distributed profits, either through a special rate of tax for dividends, or more generally in the context of a 'dual' tax system, which has a special lower rate for capital income generally.

Thus, the new half-inclusion system in France[282] and the modified part-inclusion system in Germany have been designed to produce roughly the same overall tax burden for individuals at the top marginal tax rate on distributed profits and income earned directly. In Canada, approximately the same result is achieved for small privately held companies and, after 2011, for public corporations as well. In the United Kingdom and the United States, the total tax on distributed corporate income for taxpayers subject to the maximum individual tax rate is higher in most cases than if they had derived income directly. The recent change in the United Kingdom, which replaced the partial imputation system with a small tax credit and lower individual tax rates on dividend income, was designed to preserve the same outcome as the imputation system in purely domestic situations. The recent change in the United States has considerably reduced the full double tax on dividends; historically, US corporations have paid low dividend returns so that the double tax was not so significant in practice.

The following table describes some basic features of the 'old' imputation and classical systems and the systems that came to replace them. The international issues that arise in connection with imputation systems are examined in more detail in Part Four.

282. From 2006, the amount included in income as 60% of dividends.

	Dividends	
Country	*Individual Shareholder*	*Company Shareholder*
Australia	Full imputation tax credit at variable rates from 1987, refundable since 2000	Imputation system applies since 2002 (previously usually not taxed via separate tax credit)
Canada	Imputation tax credit produces approximately full dividend relief for small companies and for large companies after 2011; non-refundable	Full dividend received deduction
France	Progressive income tax on 60% of dividend (50% in 2005) or, since 2008, preferential optional 18% flat rate on full dividend; plus, in both cases, 12.1% flat rate additional levies	Taxable if participation >5% exempt but recapture of related expenses up to 5% of dividend
Germany	60% of dividend income taxable at individual progressive rates since 2001; 25% withholding tax for dividends from shares that are private assets	95% exempt
Japan	10% tax credit (without gross-up); 5% for dividends > ¥10m; from 2003, taxpayers may opt not to report dividends with respect to listed shares; in such cases, only the withholding tax of 10% (including 3% local income tax, increasing to 20% in 2012) is imposed on dividends	Exempt if participation >25%; half taxed if < 25%
The Netherlands	Tax on presumed yield of 4% on value of share (average of start and end of year) at 30% rate, effectively 1.2% of value; previously classical system with full taxation of dividends at progressive rates for both categories	Exempt if generally >5% participation; otherwise taxable
Sweden	30% tax under dual income tax system for income from capital, no relief for company tax; 25%	Exempt if shares are unlisted or >10% participation;

Country	Individual Shareholder	Company Shareholder
	for dividends from unlisted corporations; 20% for dividends below threshold in ITA Chapter 57	Otherwise taxable
United Kingdom	Tax credit regime that operates like exemption for other than top marginal rate shareholders; equivalent to 25% tax on net dividend for top marginal rate; previously imputation with compensatory tax, abolished over time in late 1990s	Generally exempt
United States	Tax up to 15% maximum since 2003; previously classical system	Dividends received deduction 70%–100% depending on holding
	Capital Gains on Shares	
Australia	50% exclusion if held > one year	Taxable
Canada	50% exclusion (up from 25% exclusion in 2000)	50% exclusion; private companies can pay the exempt part of the capital gain tax-free to shareholders
France	Taxable at 30.1%; 12.1% for share savings plans (after five years)	Taxable; exempt if participation > 5%, long term (> two years) gain with recapture of expenses up to 5% of gain
Germany	Taxed at individual tax rate if there is a substantial participation (1% of stock) or business property; 25% withholding tax if shares are private assets	Exempt since 2002; previously taxable with some exceptions
Japan	26% (including 6% local income tax) tax for unlisted shares and 20% (including 5% local income tax) for listed shares; reduced tax rate of 10% (including 3% local income tax) is applicable 2003–2011 for listed shares	Taxable; tax at 10%–20% on family companies with statutory capital of more than 100 million yen for certain undistributed profits
The Netherlands	Tax as part of presumed yield of 4% on value of share (average of	Exempt if participation > 5%; otherwise taxable

Country	Individual Shareholder	Company Shareholder
	start and end of year) at 30% rate, effectively 1.2% of value since 2001; if participation > 5%, flat rate of 25% on capital gains from 1997; previously exempt if not participation, 20% flat rate of tax if participation	
Sweden	Tax at 30% under dual income tax system for income from capital	Exempt if participation > 10% since 2003; otherwise taxable
United Kingdom	Tax at 18% with exemption for first £10,000 (approx.)	Exempt if participation in trading companies > 10% and > one year since 2002; otherwise, taxable with indexation relief
United States	Taxable capped at 15% if held > one year	Taxable

11.2. Treatment of Capital Gains on Shares

As the table above indicates, one issue that has received more systematic treatment in the various corporate tax reform proposals is the treatment of capital gains on the sale of shares and its relation to corporate-shareholder taxation generally. Imputation and dividend relief systems do not operate when the income of a corporation is earned and retained, and in the case of the classical system, there is no immediate double taxation. It is effectively left to the capital gains tax on sales of shares to deal with double taxation issues in relation to retained earnings. It is sometimes argued that there is double taxation of retentions if capital gains tax applies to shares, unless an adjustment is made to the gain to reflect the retained income or the tax on it. On the other hand, it has been argued that full capital gains tax on share sales by individuals, combined with a full imputation system, produces the result that corporate income is taxed at the marginal tax rates of the individual shareholders who held the shares when the income was derived whether or not the shareholder receives a distribution of the income or sells the shares. One consequence of the latter argument, if full capital gains tax does apply on the sale of shares by an individual, is that tax preferences enjoyed at the corporate level are likely to be eliminated for retained income, which is a reason for producing the same result if the income is distributed.[283]

283. See generally, Richard J. Vann, General Report, 'Trends in company/shareholder taxation: single or double taxation?' in International Fiscal Association (IFA), *Cahiers de droit fiscal international*, 88a (2003): 35–43.

These arguments depend critically on the extent to which the market price of shares reflects both retained earnings and the tax attributes of the corporation and shareholder. There is no general agreement on what these effects are; hence, it is difficult to properly evaluate arguments about double taxation of retained earnings.

In relation to particular countries, an evident trend is to consider the issue more systematically than in the past and to try to align the capital gains treatment with the treatment of dividends. Thus, in Germany the modified shareholder-relief system applies to those capital gains that are taxed to individuals as well as to dividends,[284] and in Japan and the United States the same reduced rate of tax is applied to dividends and capital gains on shares realized by individuals. In The Netherlands, the 4% presumed yield on shares covers both dividends and capital gains, while in Sweden the same flat rate of tax for income from capital is applied to both.

On the other hand, in Australia, Canada, France, and the United Kingdom, the special treatment of capital gains on shares for individuals is not linked in any systematic way to the tax treatment of dividends but flows from the general treatment of capital gains. Some of the countries that do have consistency of treatment for dividends and capital gains on shares also apply the same treatment to capital gains generally (Sweden and the United States), but it is clear that there is an intended linkage between dividends and capital gains on shares in these countries.

In relation to capital gains realized by corporations on shares, a similar trend of aligning treatment with dividends is evident in Germany (both exempt in all cases), The Netherlands, Sweden, France (both exempt if the participation exemption applies, otherwise taxable in full), and to some extent the United Kingdom (with dividends generally exempt and capital gains exempt for participations in trading corporations). In the other countries, dividends are either exempt or subject to reduced taxation, while capital gains are taxable in full (or with some relief in Canada as intercorporate dividends). Hence, in these countries there is unlikely to be consistency in the extent of integration between dividends and capital gains on shares.

As between individuals and corporations, the result can be complementary tax positions. For example, in Australia individuals are taxable on dividends to a greater extent than on capital gains, and corporations are taxable on capital gains to a greater extent than on dividends. This naturally gives rise to tax planning designed to have dividends received by corporations and capital gains by individuals (dividend stripping), which in turn leads to complex anti-avoidance legislation. Other countries also demonstrate similar complementary positions, although to a lesser degree. Again, tax planning undermines the policy intent of the rules and makes judgments about the level of corporate-shareholder tax integration difficult.

The following **Table III** summarizes some of the features of the corporate tax systems discussed in Subpart A. The notations 'Partial imputation' or 'Full imputation' refer to the degree to which the tax imposed at the corporate level is relieved in the hands of the shareholder on distribution. The amount of unrelieved corporate tax on distributed profits is shown in the column headed 'Residual Corporate Tax'.

---

284. Germany, ITA, ss 3 no. 40, 20 para. 1 no. 1, para. 2 and 32d para. 1.

Some Basic Aspects of Corporate Taxation

	Basic Approach	*Corporate Rate on Retentions*	*Residual Corporate Tax on Distributed Profits*	*Total Tax Burden (corp. tax + max. shareholder tax) on Dividend Distribution*	*Profits Requirement for Taxable Distributions*	*Intercorp. Dividend Relief*	*Corp. Level Tax on Distribution of Apprec. Property*	*Consolidated Taxation Possible*
Australia	Full imputation	30%	0%	45%	Yes	Yes via imputation system	Yes	Yes
Canada	Approximately full imputation	21.5%–35% (depending on province and type of income); lower for Canadian small corps.	21.5%–35% (depending on province and type of income); 0% in some cases for Canadian small corps.	43%–63% depending on province; lower for Canadian small corps.	No	Yes (100% relief)	Yes	No (some equiv. techniques)
France	Shareholder relief system (40% allowance); full imputation before 2005	33.33%	33.33% (partial or full imputation before 2005)	For 2008, 49.34% (61.44% with additional levies)	No	Yes (100% relief) but recapture of related expenses up to 5% of dividend	Yes	Yes
Germany	Shareholder relief system (partial-income method and final withholding tax)	15% (plus ca. 12%–14% trade tax)	15% (plus ca. 12%–14% trade tax)	48%–49%	No	Yes (95% relief)	Yes	Yes
Japan	Very limited imputation (10% credit)	30%	20%	57%	Generally no	Limited (50%–100%)	Yes	Yes

The Netherlands	Classical	34.5%	25.5%	44.175% for substantial participations; otherwise, 25.5% plus deemed rate of return of 4%	No	Yes (5% + shareholding)	Yes	Yes
Sweden	Classical	26.3%	26.3%	48.41% for listed corporations 44.72% for unlisted corporations	No	Yes (10% + shareholding for unlisted corporations)	Yes	No (some equivalent techniques)
United Kingdom	Partial imputation	28% (or lower)	28% (or lower)	46%	no	Yes	Yes	No (some equivalent techniques)
United States	Classical	35%	35%	44.75%	yes	Limited (70%–80%–100%)	Yes	yes

Subpart B. Partnership Taxation

All of the systems considered in this book have rules for the taxation of business activities that allow the income and losses of certain types of commercial organization to be passed directly through to the participants. These organizations are typically formed as partnerships for commercial law purposes, and often the commercial law classification is determinative of the tax regime. In this Subpart, the reference to 'partnership' is to an organization, typically but not necessarily organized as a commercial law partnership, to which pass-through principles of taxation generally apply. Similarly, the reference to 'partner' is to the participant to whom the income and losses are attributed.

The taxing patterns examined here are all based on the principle that the income of the partnership should be taxed directly to the individual partners in much the same way as if they had earned it directly. Within that framework, however, the techniques and mechanisms used to achieve pass-through treatment and the actual results vary considerably, as does the sophistication of the systems.

In some cases (in *Japan*, for example), no specific rules deal with the taxation of partnerships and little administrative guidance is provided. The same is true, to some extent, in *France*, where case-developed principles are important but still leave a number of questions open. In the *United Kingdom*, limited statutory provisions deal with partnerships. In other systems, partnerships have been used frequently, often in connection with tax shelter investments, and the principles are correspondingly more highly developed. *Sweden*, for instance, has introduced a number of special rules to counter the use of partnerships in tax planning schemes. As usual, the *United States* seems to have the most highly articulated set of rules.

All of the systems, although generally using a pass-through model, recognize the partnership and the partner as separate tax subjects for some purposes. Thus, a consistent theme in all of the systems is the tension between 'aggregate' pass-through treatment in some situations and 'entity' treatment in other situations.

For example, in some systems, loans made by a partner to the partnership are treated in the same fashion as loans by third parties; interest payments are taxed to the partner making the loan, and the interest deduction that arises at the partnership level is deducted by the appropriate partners. To the extent that interest income is treated differently from business profits, the characterization of the income as interest controls. In other systems, the partnership-partner loan is disregarded and the 'interest' payments are treated as a distribution of partnership income, with corresponding tax results. The following materials first examine the basic methods of implementing a pass-through taxation system and then look at several situations in which the aggregate-entity issues arise.

The current worldwide trend toward lower corporate tax rates causes important frictions for countries where partnerships play a major role in the economy at large. This is true in *Germany*, where commercial partnerships not only represent a substantial portion of small- and medium-sized enterprises but also represent an important part of large enterprises not listed in the stock market (large family businesses). In order to avoid disadvantageous treatment, the Business Tax Reform of 2007 introduced a low-rate mechanism for profits derived by a non-incorporated enterprise that are not withdrawn but reinvested in the business.[285] Any further withdrawal of such low-taxed reserves will be subject to a further layer of income tax resembling a final withholding tax on dividends and interest payments.

1. QUALIFICATION FOR PASS-THROUGH TAXATION

In most of the systems, entities are treated as partnerships for tax purposes and taxed on a pass-through basis if they are formally organized under commercial partnership statutes. In addition, more informal arrangements for pooling assets and labour in a business activity may be found to be partnerships for tax purposes. Thus, in the *United States*, any cooperative activity aimed at a profit that goes beyond simple co-ownership of property will be treated as a partnership for tax purposes (assuming that it is not classified as a corporation).[286] The *Canadian* rules are similar. There is no definition of partnership for tax purposes, but the typically very broad (provincial) commercial-law definition of a partnership as a business carried on jointly with a view to a profit covers most arrangements that extend beyond co-ownership. This characterization is controlling for tax purposes. The Supreme Court of Canada has held that even an ancillary intention to make a profit is sufficient to support the existence of a partnership.[287]

In *Sweden*, according to civil law, only organizations registered as partnerships are treated as legal persons. Tax rules for partnerships apply to civil law partnerships.

285. Germany, ITA, s. 34a.
286. United States, IRC, s. 761(a).
287. *See Spire Freezers Ltd. v. The Queen* [2001] 2 CTC 40 (SCC).

In *France*, there is no general definition of a partnership for tax purposes. Tax status as a partnership is based on a specific enumeration of types of entities the income of which is taxed directly to the participants.[288] But the characteristic those entities have in common is the limited liability of partners. Since 2008, however, newly created small corporations whose shareholders are mainly individuals may opt for tax treatment as partnerships for up to five years.[289]

The definitional rules in *Australia* go so far as to treat jointly owned property that generates income as a partnership, although the possibility of unincorporated joint ventures that are not classified as partnerships allows certain operations (typically in the natural resource field) to be treated in effect as separate enterprises of each participant.[290] In practice, partnerships arising from joint ownership of property are not generally required to file partnership tax returns. Limited partnerships are excluded from pass-through treatment except in recent times for venture capital activities and foreign hybrids.[291] In the *United Kingdom*, there is no formal definition of partnership as such. The partnership rules apply to joint undertakings that, unlike clubs or associations, are organized to do business. However, income from jointly owned property will not of itself be treated as partnership income.

In *The Netherlands*, there are no specific provisions defining the forms of organization that will be subject to pass-through taxation. Instead, all associations that are not covered by the generic definitions of taxable entities in the corporate tax law are transparent for tax purposes, and the income is taxed directly to the participants. A special rule, which is split into two parts, applies to a limited partnership with transferable shares. The income allocable to the limited interests is subject to the corporate tax structure; income at the partnership level is subject to corporate tax, and distributions are again taxed to the limited partners when distributed. The income allocated to the general partners is directly taxable to them.

In the *German* system, characterization of the organization as a partnership for civil law purposes is a necessary precondition for partnership tax treatment.[292] For a taxpayer to qualify as a 'partner', there are some additional tax requirements.[293] In particular, the partner must participate in any appreciation in the value of the assets, at least on the liquidation of the partnership. Furthermore, he must have an active part in the conduct of the business.

Partnerships organized under the Commercial Code in *Japan* are taxed as corporations. Although it is possible to organize partnerships under the Civil Code, there are no statutory rules for their taxation, except for limited provisions with regard to withholding tax for non-residents. Some administrative guidance indicates that the partnership would be treated as a pass-through entity and its partners

288. See France, CGI, s. 8, 8 *bis*, 8 *ter*, 8 *quater*, 8 *quinquies*, 238 *bis* L, 238 *bis* LA, 239 *ter*, 239 *quater*, 239 *quater* A-D, 239 *quinquies*.
289. France, CGI, s. 239 *bis* AB; see also, CGI, s. 239 *bis* AA.
290. Australia, ITAA 1997, s. 995-1(1) definitions of 'partnership' and 'limited partnership'; see also, the definitions of 'company' and 'non-entity joint venture'.
291. Australia, ITAA 1936, Part III Div 5A.
292. Germany, ITA, s. 15 para. 1 sent. 1 no. 2.
293. Compare Germany, ITA, ss 15 para. 1 sent. 1 no. 2 and 20 para. 1 no. 4.

taxed as if they had received the income directly. Similarly, the contractual relation set up in an 'undisclosed association' (*tokumei-kumiai*) results in the direct taxation of the undisclosed participants' share of the net income or loss in accordance with the contractual arrangement.

2. BASIC STRUCTURE OF PASS-THROUGH TAXATION

In the *United States*, income and deductions arising at the partnership level are either aggregated at the partnership level or are passed through directly to the individual partners to the extent that special computations may be necessary at the partner level.[294] For example, capital gains and losses are separately stated so that they may be aggregated with the individual partner's gains and losses. Most elections (e.g., method of depreciation) are made at the partnership level and are binding on the partners.[295] The partnership income is included in the tax year of the partner in which the partnership's tax year ends, independently of whether it is distributed.[296] There are restrictions to prevent manipulation of the tax years to achieve tax deferral.

The partner's tax cost in his partnership interest is increased by the amount of income attributed to him and decreased by distributions and losses.[297] Distributions are taxable only to the extent that they exceed the partner's tax cost in his interest in the partnership.[298] Tax-exempt income increases the tax cost of the interest and thus avoids an indirect tax on the income on a sale of the interest. Losses incurred at the partnership level can be deducted currently only to the extent of the partner's tax cost in his partnership interest.[299] Special 'passive activity loss rules' may limit the ability of partners who are individuals to deduct otherwise deductible partnership expenses. If individual partners do not materially participate in the partnership's business, they may deduct partnership losses only to the extent of income generated by the partnership or other flow-through activities in which they do not materially participate.[300]

Complex rules deal with the allocation of income and deductions among the partners.[301] In general terms, special allocations of items of income and deductions (i.e., allocations that differ from the normal profit and loss sharing arrangement) will be respected for tax purposes only if they have 'substantial economic effect'. In other words, the allocation for tax purposes must actually affect the economic situation of the partners apart from the tax consequences of the allocation. The economic effect of the allocation is generally determined by the partners'

294. United States, IRC, s. 702.
295. United States, IRC, s. 703(b).
296. United States, IRC, s. 706(a).
297. United States, IRC, s. 705(a).
298. United States, IRC, s. 731.
299. United States, IRC, s. 704(d).
300. United States, IRC, s. 469.
301. United States, IRC, s. 704(b); Treas. Regs., ss 1.704-1–1.704-4.

'capital accounts', which reflect the actual economic relations among the partners. Normally, allocation for tax purposes must be reflected in the capital accounts, and those accounts must control the amounts which the partners would receive on the liquidation of the partnership. If a partner had a negative capital account, for example, as a result of receiving a larger share of partnership losses, that amount typically must be required to be made up on the liquidation of the partnership in order for the special allocation of the losses to be recognized. Since non-recourse debt by definition will not have to be repaid by the partners, additional restrictions apply to deductions based on non-recourse debt.

The special allocation rules are enormously complex and have been criticized as unworkable for unsophisticated partnerships.[302]

The *Canadian* system is in general quite similar, although it is substantially simpler. Partnerships are not taxable entities. Each partner's share of the partnership's income is included in the partner's income in the taxable year in which the partnership's taxable year ends.[303] If a partnership interest is disposed of, the new partner is taxed on his share of the income as if he had been a partner for the entire year, and the former partner is not taxable on his share of the partnership's income for the year. The source and character of the income earned by the partnership flows through to the partners. Distributions are not taxable regardless of whether they are characterized as income or capital distributions. The partnership agreement in general controls the allocation of income and deductions among the partners. Rather than limiting special allocations by detailed regulatory rules, the allocation is subject to an anti-avoidance rule that allows the allocation to be ignored if the 'principal reason' for the disproportionate allocation is the reduction or postponement of tax.[304] A similar rule applies if the partners do not deal at arm's length.

The partner's cost basis in his interest is increased by his share of undistributed income and decreased by distributions and losses.[305] Adjustments are made to ensure that income or losses that are subject to special treatment are appropriately reflected in the partnership basis. Thus, for example, because only one-half of capital gains are included in income, the full amount of the gain increases the partner's basis to ensure that the gain is not in effect taxed when the interest is disposed of. Unlike the situation in the United States, for active partners, the cost in the partnership interest can become 'negative' if losses or distributions in excess of the investment are passed through to the partner. The 'negative' basis will increase the gain on the disposition of the partnership interest. However, for limited and passive partners, a negative basis is deemed to be a capital gain.[306]

302. Alan Gunn & James Repetti, *Partnership Income Taxation*, 4th edn (New York: Foundation Press, 2005), 44.
303. Canada, ITA, s. 96.
304. Canada, ITA, s. 103.
305. Canada, ITA, ss 53(1)(c) and 53(2)(c).
306. Canada, ITA, s. 40(3.1)–(3.19).

The partnership rules in *Sweden* follow the same general pattern. Income is computed at the partnership level and then attributed to the individual partners. The income is normally taxed as business income. The use of losses has been substantially restricted after an explosion of tax-shelter activities in the 1980s. For individual partners, losses from a partnership can be used only against income from the same partnership. Perhaps as a result of this limitation, the rules on special allocations are not well developed. The partner's basis in the partnership interest is increased by capital contributions and retained taxable earnings and reduced by withdrawals and tax-deductible losses.

In the *United Kingdom*, the income is calculated at the partnership level according to the schedular system, and then each partner pays tax with reference to his share.[307] For this purpose, allocations of profit and loss in the partnership agreement are generally respected. For capital gains tax purposes, however, the partnership assets are deemed to be owned and disposed of by the individual partners.[308]

In *The Netherlands*, the system is somewhat different. The character of income is basically determined at the individual level. Thus, for example, income of a limited partner is income from capital in general, since the activities as a limited partner do not constitute a business. On the other hand, if the limited partnership interest is held in a (separate) business, the income is business income. Each general partner is treated in respect of his share in the partnership's business as being involved in his own business undertaking. Consequently, where options such as rate of depreciation and formation of reserves are available, each partner may make his own individual choice. Contractual allocations are, in general, respected, but limited partners may offset losses only to the extent of their actual contributions.

The *Australian* rules on income computation are a mix of partnership and partner-level calculations. In general, gains or losses from the disposition of inventory and business activities are determined at the partnership level and passed through to the individual partners. Partnership agreement allocations are generally respected and based on the accounts at the end of the taxable year. While there is some potential for tax planning through manipulation of the timing of partnership accounts, this has not proved to be a problem (there is a provision intended to prevent income splitting through family partnerships, which is no longer of much relevance in light of the income attribution rules discussed in Part Two). Various tax attributes (e.g., foreign tax credit, imputation credit) also flow through. However, capital gains are taxed at the partner level as if each partner had disposed of his share of the partnership capital assets.[309] This treatment applies whether there is a sale of a partnership asset or of the partnership interest, the admission of a new partner, or a change in the relations of existing partners.

307. United Kingdom, Income Tax (Trading and Other Income) Act 2005, ss 849–851.
308. United Kingdom, Taxation of Chargeable Gains Act 1992, s. 59.
309. Australia, ITAA 1997, s. 106-5.

Under the *German* system, the character of the income for purposes of schedular classification takes place at the partnership level. However, if the only general partner in a limited partnership is a corporation, all of the income in the partnership is treated as business income. If a partnership carries on a business or trade, all other income received by the partnership is deemed to be business income as well.[310] Elections must be made at the partnership level, and income and deductions are determined at that level. In general, no special allocation of income or losses is allowed, and the general ratio laid down in the statute or the partnership's articles for the sharing of profits and losses controls. Thus, for example, it is not possible to allocate foreign income only to foreign partners in a cross-border partnership among lawyers. Payments received by partners from the partnership on a contractual basis (salaries, rents, interest, royalties) are included in the business income of the partnership to ensure that the trade tax on partnership profits will be appropriately applied.[311] Complex rules also restrict the ability of limited partners to deduct losses in excess of their capital contributions.[312] Basically, the losses attributable to the partner cannot exceed his share of the assets of the partnership less the partnership-level liabilities (i.e., the net equity in the partnership).

In *France*, income is initially determined at the partnership level, with options or elections (e.g., method of depreciation) determined by the partnership. For purposes of applying the schedular system, in general, the nature of the activities at the partnership level are determinative. However, in some situations, the partner's status (e.g., as a corporation) will affect the income classification and computation. The partnership agreement in general controls the allocation of income and loss and applies to the net result at the partnership level; no allocation of specific items of income or deduction is allowed. Each partner is taxed on his allocable share of the partnership's results regardless of whether or not it is distributed. In the French system, there is no ongoing adjustment to the partner's basis in his partnership interest for undistributed income or for distributions. Instead, at the time the interest is disposed of, adjustments are made in the acquisition cost, which, according to case law, is then increased by the partner's share of retained earnings and compensated accounting losses and decreased by the profits distributed to him and tax losses deducted by him since the acquisition of that interest.

3. LIABILITIES, TAX COST, AND LOSSES

Two basic patterns emerge in the treatment of liabilities at the entity level and their effect on the tax cost or basis of the partner's interest in the partnership, and the corresponding ability to take current loss deductions. Under the *United States* system, liabilities incurred at the partnership level are reflected in the partner's

310. Germany, ITA, s. 15 para. 3 no. 1.
311. Germany, ITA, s. 15 para. 1 sent. 1 no. 2.
312. Germany, ITA, s. 15a.

tax cost in his partnership interest.[313] The liability is allocated to those partners who ultimately would have to pay the debt if the partnership assets were insufficient to pay the debt in the case of liquidation. This means that in general in a limited partnership, partnership-level debt is allocated to the general partners and increases their tax cost; limited partners, who are not liable beyond their capital contributions, are not allocated any portion of the debt and accordingly cannot share in losses financed out of the liabilities. A special rule applies to 'non-recourse' debt – that is, debt secured only by the property in question and for which no partner is personally liable. In general, such debt is allocated in accordance with the partners' share of partnership profits. Since no partner is responsible for the debt personally, it will be repaid, if at all, out of partnership profits and is so allocated for tax cost purposes.

The *Dutch* system follows essentially the general principle that liabilities incurred at the partnership level are treated at the level of the partners as if they had been incurred directly. However, it does not have the complex set of allocation rules present in the United States.

In contrast, in *Canada*, liabilities incurred at the partnership level do not affect the cost basis of the partner in his partnership interest. However, there is no restriction on the ability of a general partner to deduct his share of losses at the partnership level in excess of his actual investment (capital plus retained earnings) in the partnership. Excess losses are accounted for by allowing a 'negative' basis in the partnership interest, which increases the potential gain on the disposition of the interest. Losses allocated to a limited partner are restricted to the amount of his capital investment by specific statutory rules.[314]

The *German* system is similar. Liabilities incurred at the partnership level do not affect the partner's basis in his partnership interest. Where limited partners are involved, existence of the liability is taken into account in calculating the partner's equity in the partnership and deductions are correspondingly limited. On the other hand, liabilities incurred by a partner in his personal capacity (i.e., liabilities incurred in order to acquire his stake in the partnership) are also treated as liabilities in the context of the assessment of the partnership but are directly allocated to the partner at a second stage.

In *France*, there is no limitation on the pass-through of losses to the investment in the partnership, although other quarantining rules may be applicable. For example, if the partnership's activity consists of holding rental real estate, the deductibility of the loss would be restricted. Similarly, liabilities at the partnership level have no effect on the tax treatment of partnership operations but are relevant when the partnership is liquidated.

In the *United Kingdom*, partners claim revenue losses sustained by the partnership separately in accordance with the allocation under the partnership agreement. If the allocation of losses results in losses for some partners and profits for

313. United States, IRC, s. 752.
314. Canada, ITA, s. 96(2.1)–(2.7).

others, the losses are reduced to the net amount of partnership loss.[315] Limited partners can, generally speaking, deduct losses only to the extent of their contribution to the partnership.

In *Australia*, for partnerships that are treated as such under the general partnership law, losses and profits can be distributed freely as the partners agree, but it is not possible to have some partners with a profit and other partners with a loss.[316] For 'tax law partnerships' arising from joint ownership of property, profits and losses must be strictly distributed in accordance with the interests in the property.[317] Now that limited partnerships have been given pass-through treatment in the venture capital and foreign hybrid areas, rules have been introduced to limit the use of losses to the amount of the partner's contribution less any amounts repaid to the partner, losses allowed to the partner in previous years, and any debt owed by the partner that is secured on the interest in the partnership.[318]

4. TRANSACTIONS BETWEEN PARTNER AND PARTNERSHIP

The systems vary considerably in the extent to which transactions between the partner and the partnership will be given independent significance for tax purposes. Under *United States* rules, if a partner engages in a transaction with the partnership 'other than in his capacity as a partner', the form of the transaction is generally respected.[319] Thus, a partner can receive compensation for services rendered to the partnership or for money loaned to the partnership with a corresponding deduction or capital expense at the partnership level. In addition, the statute recognizes a special form of partner-partnership relation where the partner is guaranteed a payment regardless of partnership profits.[320] Such payments are treated in some respects as payments to third parties for purposes of determining taxation of the recipient partner and the deductibility of the payment at the partnership level.

The rules in *Canada* are generally similar. The partnership is usually treated as a separate entity for purposes of transactions with partners. A partner can lend funds to the partnership or perform services for it. The latter principle is also followed in *The Netherlands*, although its application in the international context is not clear.

In the *United Kingdom*, for income tax purposes the partner can have dealings with the partnership as a third party (other than as an employee); for example, a lease of property to the partnership will result in rental income to the partner and a

315. United Kingdom, Income Tax (Trading and Other Income) Act 2005, s. 850, and Income Tax Act 2007, s. 62.
316. Australia, ITAA 1936, s. 92.
317. *McDonald* (1987) 18 ATR 957.
318. Australia, ITAA 1997, Div 830 in relation to foreign hybrids, ITAA 1936, s. 92(2AA) for venture capital partnerships.
319. United States, IRC, s. 707(a).
320. United States, IRC, s. 707(c).

corresponding deduction to the partnership.[321] The rules are more complex for capital gains tax purposes, as each partner is deemed to own directly his share of the capital assets.[322] Thus, a disposal of an asset by a partner to the partnership will be treated as only a partial disposal since the partner retains an interest in the asset.

In *Sweden*, most transactions between partner and partnership are ignored. This can be important because the treatment of income as income from services, capital, or business may result in different tax treatment at the partner level. Payments by the partnership for partner services or capital are not deductible by the partnership or includable by the partner. The increased partnership income is simply allocated to the partners under normal principles and keeps the character it had in the hands of the partnership.

The *Australian* rules are somewhat similar to the Swedish rules, although they rest on a different principle. Under private law principles, a partner cannot be an employee of the partnership, and any purported 'wages' paid to the partner are treated as partnership distributions. This characterization is followed for tax purposes.[323] Similarly, loans by partners that bear interest but are accounted for as interest-bearing capital or retained profits will not generate interest income or corresponding deductions.[324] Other partner loans and transactions, however, will be respected. Disposals of inventory or depreciable assets from a partner to a partnership may, by election, be subject to a rollover so that the partner's tax cost carries over to the partnership.[325] Other disposals of assets by partners to the partnership are taxable on the basis that the partner has disposed of fractional interests in the asset to the other partners.[326]

Similarly, in *France*, since all the participants are considered to be co-owners of the operation, in general, no employment relation can exist between the partnership and a partner, and everything a partner receives is deemed to be part of the profit allocation on which the parties have agreed. There are some exceptions, however. Rentals of property between partner and partnership are respected; the rental payments are deductible by the partnership and treated as rental income or commercial profits in the hands of the partner, depending on the circumstances. In addition, interest on partner current account loans is deductible, subject to the limitation that the rate does not exceed the average bank lending rate. To the extent that the interest is deductible, it is treated as securities income by the partner; any excess is treated as partnership income allocated to the partner.

Germany reaches somewhat similar results with different techniques.[327] Payments for services, interest on loans, or rental payments on leased property received by a partner from a partnership reduce the profit at the entity level but are accounted for in a separate 'special' balance sheet for the individual partner;

321. For example, see *Heastie v. Veitch & Co Ltd* [1933] 18 TC 305 (CA).
322. United Kingdom, Taxation of Chargeable Gains Act 1992, s. 59.
323. Ruling TR 2005/7.
324. *Beville* (1953) 5 AITR 458.
325. Australia, ITAA 1997, ss 40-295(2), 40-340, and 70-100.
326. Australia, ITAA 1997, s. 106-5.
327. Germany, ITA, s. 15 para. 1 sent. 1 no. 2.

they are, in effect, included in the income of the partnership, which is then allocated to the individual partners. The basic policy basis for this rule is not principally the income tax, but the trade tax. Partners should not be able to reduce the trade tax basis by switching regular profit participations into contractual payments.

5. DISPOSITION OF A PARTNERSHIP INTEREST

While most of the systems in general treat the disposition of a partnership interest as the disposition of a separate asset, thus following an entity approach, some require fragmentation. In the *United States*, a partnership interest is treated as a capital asset and gain or loss is treated accordingly.[328] However, where the partnership holds certain assets the sale of which would generate ordinary income (in particular, appreciated inventory and property subject to depreciation recapture), then the sale of the partnership interest generates ordinary income to that extent.[329] *Sweden* also treats the partnership interest as a separate asset and the gain or loss on the disposition is treated as income from capital (capital gain). In special situations, the gain could be taxed as income from business. That is the case if the taxation of business income in the partnership that is earned prior to the sale is transferred to the purchaser. In general, *Canada* treats the gain or loss on the disposition of a partnership interest as capital gain.

In contrast, in *The Netherlands*, the tax treatment of the gain on disposition depends on the character of the partnership's operating income. If that income is treated as business income in the hands of the individual partner (general partner), then the gain or loss will similarly be business income. However, if the income is treated as income from capital (limited partner), then the gain on the disposition is not subject to tax, since private capital gains of individuals are not generally taxed. If the partner is a corporation, the gain is subject to full corporate tax. The underlying theory is that the partnership, viewed from an aggregate point of view, is simply the sum of the activities of the individual partners. As indicated, the principle extends to allowing, for example, different depreciation methods for different partners for the same asset.

Germany follows the same pattern.[330] The nature of the partnership activities (trade or business, agriculture, etc.) will determine the treatment of the gain or loss on the partnership interest. The distinction between a share in the operating profits and a gain from the disposition essentially relates to the applicability of a reduced tax rate.[331]

The *Australian* approach operates on the theory that there is generally no partnership interest separate from the assets of the partnership. Several questions have been raised concerning the operation of the capital gains rules in the

328. United States, IRC, s. 741.
329. United States, IRC, s. 751(a).
330. Germany, ITA, s. 16 para. 1 no. 2.
331. Germany, ITA, s. 34 paras 1, and 2 no. 1 and 3.

partnership context, which have been resolved as a practical matter by a mix of changes to the law, the Australian Taxation Office's flexible interpretation of the law, and the way in which partnerships (especially large partnerships) are structured. It is common for large professional partnerships to have no tangible assets. All such assets are held in a separate unit trust owned effectively by the partners and made available to the partnership. The partners generally agree that there is no goodwill, so that an incoming partner does not pay to enter the partnership, and conversely, a departing partner does not receive anything on departure (apart from adjustments in relation to work in progress). There was previously a problem that payments for work in progress were taxable to the departing partner but not deductible to the partnership, but this has now been overcome by legislation.[332]

The *United Kingdom* treats any change in ownership interests in a partnership as a disposal of partnership assets. The extent to and manner in which tax law recognizes the allocation of specific assets to specific partners under a partnership agreement is an open question.

Several of the systems allow the 'inside' basis of partnership assets to be adjusted when there is a sale of a partnership interest. In *Germany*, such an adjustment is mandatory. As a result, the 'inside' and 'outside' bases of partnership assets and partnership interests are always the same. The increased tax cost at the partnership level is related only to the purchasing partner's tax calculation and is accounted for in a special 'complementary' balance sheet. For purposes of determining the deductibility of losses by a limited partner, the assets shown on the 'complementary' balance sheet are considered to be part of his equity in the partnership.

The *United States* has similar rules in the case of the sale of a partnership interest.[333] The tax basis of partnership property must be reduced with respect to the buying partner if the value of such property is significantly below its tax basis at the time of the sale. In contrast, if the partnership property has increased in value, the partnership may (but is not required to) elect to increase the property's tax basis with respect to the purchasing partner. The *French* system is different from the others in several respects. During partnership operations, no adjustment to basis in the partnership interest is made for distributions, retained earnings taxed to the partner, or losses that have been passed through and deducted. Instead, adjustments are in effect postponed until the interest is sold. Thus, under case law principles, the acquisition cost is increased by earnings taxed to the partner, and losses are effectively borne by him and decreased by losses deducted by and earnings distributed to him.

As for the gain or loss on the disposition, its treatment depends on a complex set of rules involving in part the status of the partner and in part the nature and extent of activities of the partnership. For instance, regardless of partnership activities, for corporate partners and individual proprietorships holding a partnership interest, a gain or loss is treated as a business capital gain or loss subject to a

332. Australia, ITAA 1997, ss 15–50, 25–95.
333. United States, IRC, s. 743.

preferential rate or to the usual loss limitations if it is a long-term gain or loss. The same result applies where the partnership is involved in a trade or business or professional activity and an individual partner who is involved in the business disposes of the interest. If the partnership is engaged in real estate or securities investment, the gain, unless realized by a corporate or sole proprietorship partner, is treated as falling within the category of private capital gains.

6. LIQUIDATION OF THE PARTNERSHIP

When the partnership is liquidated, potential gain or loss may be present both at the partnership level and the partner level, depending on the relation between the fair market value of the partnership assets, their tax cost in the hands of the partnership, and the tax cost of the partnership interest in the hands of the partners. The systems differ substantially in the treatment of the potential gain or loss involved.

The *United States* system provides the most extensive deferral of gain or loss recognition. As a general rule, if property other than cash is distributed, there is no recognition of gain or loss at either the partnership or partner level, and the partner's tax cost in his partnership interest becomes the tax cost for the property received.[334] If cash is received, it first reduces the tax cost of the partner's interest and may result in gain to the extent that it exceeds that amount. Any additional property received would correspondingly take a zero tax cost. A loss may be recognized if only cash or certain ordinary income assets are distributed.

The situation is more complex if the assets are not distributed pro rata and the partnership holds certain assets the sale of which would have generated ordinary income.[335] In effect, the partners are treated as having made a taxable exchange of the assets to the extent that they receive non-pro rata amounts.

Other systems have more extensive recognition on liquidation. In *Sweden*, the distribution of the property is viewed as a removal of the property from business use. The withdrawal would result in gain recognition under normal principles. In addition, if the value of the property exceeds the partner's basis in his partnership interest (increased for the gain recognized on the withdrawal), the partner may recognize additional gain, since the liquidation is treated as a taxable disposition of the partnership interest. Until 2008 assets could be transferred in and out of partnerships and businesses without taxation, if such transfers were made at prices equal to tax basis. These rules could be manipulated in complex tax avoidance schemes, which created large artificial tax losses at the price of minimum income recognition; these rules were subsequently abolished.

The *Canadian* rules have the same basic structure. However, other possibilities for rollover relief are available. If the partners receive undivided interests in the property, there is no current recognition.[336] In addition, if a single partner

334. United States, IRC, ss 731 and 732(b).
335. United States, IRC, s. 751(b).
336. Canada, ITA, s. 98(3).

continues the business, no gain or loss is recognized as to that partner.[337] Similarly, in the *United Kingdom*, if each partner receives his fractional share of partnership assets, there will be no current recognition of gain for capital gains purposes, which will be deferred through an adjustment to the tax cost of the assets received. If the distributions are non-pro rata, gains will be recognized currently to that extent. As with Australia (below), rollover relief will often be available where inventory or assets for which capital allowances are granted are transferred from a partnership to a partner.[338] By contrast, in *Australia*, which generally disregards the interest in the partnership for tax purposes, each partner will be treated as having disposed of the fractional interest held in the partnership assets, either to the other partners or to third parties, if the liquidation is effected by a sale of assets and distribution of the proceeds. Rollover relief will often be available for inventory and depreciable assets transferred from the partnership to one or more partners.

In *Germany*, the distribution of the partnership's property is viewed as a withdrawal of the property from the business that results in the recognition of gain,[339] although the gain would qualify for preferential rate treatment.[340] In addition, if independent business units or particular business assets are transferred to different partners, the distribution is regarded as a mere separation of assets and treated on a tax-deferred basis.

France also treats the liquidation of the partnership as a recognition event for capital gains arising on the cessation of the business. Retained earnings that have previously been taxed may be received on a tax-free basis.

In *The Netherlands*, the same approach is taken as on the disposition of a partnership interest. The transaction is a taxable event and the character of the gain or loss depends on the character of the partnership interest in the hands of the partner as business or investment.

337. Canada, ITA, s. 98(5).
338. United Kingdom, Income Tax (Trading and Other Income) Act 2005, ss 177 and 179, and Capital Allowances Act 2001, ss 266 and 267.
339. Germany, ITA, s. 16 para. 3.
340. Germany, ITA, s. 34.

Part Four
International Taxation

The patterns of international taxation examined here show a high degree of similarity in structure, despite significant differences in technical detail. This broad consensus stems in large part from early efforts in international cooperation, particularly in the context of the League of Nations. Those efforts both produced and reflected the conceptual framework for allocating taxing rights in an international context, which became the basis of most of the systems here considered. Generally speaking, a right to tax is asserted on the basis of the personal connection of the taxpayer to the taxing jurisdiction. Most typically that claim extends to all income, although some countries do not assert personal taxing jurisdiction over foreign business income of resident corporate taxpayers, and there appears to be a trend in favour of the exemption of dividends from certain foreign corporations. Similarly, all jurisdictions claim the right to tax income that can be said to have its 'source' within the country, regardless of the personal status of the recipient.

The problem of overlapping tax claims that arise from the parallel assertion of personal and source jurisdiction by different states to tax the same item of income is resolved in one of three ways. In some situations the state of personal jurisdiction cedes either the primary or exclusive jurisdiction to tax to the state in which the income arises. In the former situation, the primacy of source country jurisdiction is recognized through the mechanism of a credit for foreign taxes. In the latter, the income arising outside the jurisdiction of personal connection is exempted from tax in that jurisdiction and taxed exclusively in the source jurisdiction. In other situations the source country gives up its right to tax income despite the fact that the income arises in its jurisdiction, and the income is taxed exclusively in the residence country. These broad principles are implemented in both domestic legislation and in bilateral treaty relationships. The following Subpart A examines the issues that arise in the assertion of personal taxing jurisdiction and the mechanisms for the relief of double taxation. Subpart B considers the structure of source-based taxation, and Subpart C examines some selected additional international issues.

Subpart A. Residence Taxation

1. BASES FOR THE ASSERTION OF PERSONAL TAXING JURISDICTION

1.1. Individuals

Personal taxing jurisdiction over individuals is typically asserted on the basis of 'residence' and is often referred to as residence jurisdiction. The determination of residence often rests on a facts-and-circumstances test, which looks at the various social and economic connections the taxpayer has to the taxing jurisdiction, as well as the taxpayer's intent with regard to his stay and his connections to other jurisdictions. This general test is frequently supplemented with a mechanical test based on the number of days of presence in the jurisdiction. Residence for tax purposes may or may not be connected with residence in terms of immigration status.

The *United States* approach combines objective and facts-and-circumstances tests. A person is resident for tax purposes if he possesses the right to permanent entry to the United States under the immigration laws (a so-called 'green card') or if he is physically present in the jurisdiction for 183 days or more during the taxable year. In addition, he may be treated as a resident if he is present in the jurisdiction for thirty-one days or more and meets a cumulative presence test that looks to the days present in the current year and in the past two years. If the total days in the present year and the weighted days for the past two years are 183 or more, the individual will be a resident for tax purposes unless he can establish that his 'tax home', usually his principal place of business, is in another country, and he has a 'closer connection' to that country than to the United States. The factors in establishing the 'closer connection' are those typically used in a residence determination. Special rules apply for students and diplomats, which allow them to be present in the country without triggering the mechanical physical presence tests.[1]

Unlike other jurisdictions, the United States also asserts personal jurisdiction based on citizenship. US citizens are, in principle, taxable on their worldwide income regardless of where they are resident. This basis for personal jurisdiction increases the possibility of overlapping claims for worldwide taxation, an issue that is frequently dealt with in US tax treaties.[2]

In *Canada*, residence is, in general, determined on a case-by-case basis, applying a set of factors developed in case law and including the availability of a dwelling in Canada, the residence of family members, physical presence, and social and economic ties. The most important factors are the presence of a dwelling in Canada (i.e., available for the taxpayer's use) and the presence of immediate family members in Canada. Once residence is established, the intention to return to Canada is relevant in cases where the taxpayer has left the jurisdiction. In addition, a specific statutory provision deems a person to be a resident of Canada if he 'sojourns' there for 183 days or more during the taxable period.[3] The meaning of the term 'sojourn' is not entirely clear, but it is not synonymous with physical presence; for example, if a person is resident in Canada for part of the year, he is not 'sojourning' in Canada. Certain individuals, such as diplomats and members of the armed forces, are deemed to be residents of Canada.[4]

Australia also applies a facts-and-circumstances test. In addition, there is deemed residence if the taxpayer is 'domiciled' in Australia and has no 'permanent place of abode' outside the country or if the taxpayer has physical presence for more than one-half of the tax year and cannot establish that his usual place of abode is abroad and that he does not intend to take up residence in Australia. A special rule treats as residents certain governmental employees who would not normally be taxed under the usual residence rules but typically would be exempt from tax in the foreign jurisdiction to which they are posted.[5]

The *United Kingdom* similarly has no comprehensive definition of residence for individuals, and the issue is decided on a facts-and-circumstances approach.[6] This general test is supplemented by a special provision that treats an individual as resident if he is physically present in the United Kingdom for six months or more in the tax year (6 April to 5 April).[7] As an administrative matter, an individual will be treated as resident if he makes 'substantial and habitual' visits. Visits are habitual if they extend over a four-year period and substantial if they exceed three months.

---

1. United States, Internal Revenue Code (IRC), s. 7701(b) sets forth the various tests.
2. United States, IRC, s. 7701(a)(30)(A).
3. Canada, Income Tax Act (ITA), s. 250(1)(a).
4. Canada, ITA, s. 250(1)(b)-(g).
5. Australia, Income Tax Assessment Act 1936 (ITAA 1936), s. 6(1) definition of 'resident' para. (a).
6. Two leading cases are *Levene v. IRC* [1928] AC 217 (HL) and *IRC v. Lysaght* [1928] AC 234 (HL).
7. United Kingdom, Income Tax Act 2007, s. 831.

In *The Netherlands*, the statute requires residence to be determined 'according to the circumstances',[8] and case law has focused on 'durable ties of a personal nature' to Holland.[9] The principal focus is on the existence of a home in Holland and the abode of the family. Dutch diplomats stationed abroad and similar persons are deemed to be resident in Holland if they are Dutch citizens.[10] Also, individuals who give up their Dutch residence but return within twelve months without having taken up residence in another country are deemed not to have given up their Dutch residence unless the other country is an EU Member State or a treaty country where they have been subject to tax as a resident on income sources similar to the ones for which Dutch residents are subject to Dutch taxation.[11]

In *Sweden*, an individual is regarded as resident if he has a 'real dwelling and home' in Sweden or Sweden is his 'habitual abode'. This latter test has been interpreted as being met if the taxpayer is continuously present in Sweden for six months. As discussed below, Sweden also has a complex set of rules that continue to tax residents who have left the jurisdiction but retain substantial connections to Sweden.

Germany treats an individual as resident for tax purposes only if he has either his residence or habitual place of abode in Germany.[12] EU nationals who receive more than 90% of their income from sources in Germany have an option to be treated as a resident when that could be beneficial for tax purposes.[13] Residence is based on the availability to the taxpayer of a home (house, apartment, etc.) which he intends to retain and use.[14] Highly developed case law applies this facts-and-circumstances test. Some of the factors considered are the period of time during which the home is used and the regularity and frequency of the use. 'Habitual abode' is established by presence in Germany indicating an intention to stay more than temporarily.[15] In practice, a continuous stay of six months (even if spanning two calendar years) will constitute a habitual abode, although there are nuances in the rules.

The *French* system has an extensive statutory definition of residence.[16] Individuals are resident for tax purposes if they have their permanent home in France, or, if their permanent home cannot be determined, they are physically present in the jurisdiction for more than 183 days or substantially longer than in any other country. In addition, professional or employment activity in France will lead to resident treatment unless the taxpayer can establish that the activity is

8. Netherlands, General Act on Taxation (GAT), Art. 4.1
9. See, for example, *Hof Amsterdam*, no. 27 October 1993, m. 92/3106, V-N 1994, 785 (married employee who was working and living in different locations abroad while his family remained in The Netherlands was found to have his tax residence in The Netherlands).
10. Netherlands, Income Tax Act (ITA), Art. 2.2-1.
11. Netherlands, ITA, Art. 2.2-2.
12. Germany, Income Tax Act (ITA), s. 1 para. 1.
13. Germany, ITA, s. 1 para. 3.
14. Germany, General Fiscal Code (GFC) (*Abgabenordnung*), s. 8.
15. Germany, GFC, s. 9.
16. France, *Code général des impôts* (General Tax Code, hereafter CGI), s. 4 B.

secondary to activities performed elsewhere. Finally, if the taxpayer has his 'centre of economic interest' in France, he will be treated as resident regardless of the nature of the activity.

The focus in the *Japanese* statute is on both domicile, defined as the base of personal operations, and more than a year of residence, defined as the place of day-to-day living.[17] An administrative regulation provides that if a person is engaged in a business that ordinarily requires living in the country for one year, he will be treated, unless otherwise provided, as domiciled in Japan for tax purposes when he arrives in the country. However, if personal connections to Japan are significant, domicile will be present even if business activities are conducted outside Japan for significant periods. In this regard the tax law provisions are interpreted in light of the civil law concepts of domicile, and the administrative rule is not the exclusive test for domicile.

Japan also distinguishes between ordinary residents and 'short-term' residents. A short-term resident is one who meets the normal residence test but is not a Japanese national and has not maintained a residence for five years during a ten-year period.[18] Short-term residents are taxed only on domestic-source income and foreign-source income that is remitted to Japan.[19]

1.2. Corporations

Two basic approaches are used in establishing a personal jurisdictional connection for corporations. One is to focus on some formal legal connection to the jurisdiction such as incorporation or registry in the commercial register. The other is to select some economic or commercial connection such as the place of management, principal business location, or less frequently, residence of shareholders. Many jurisdictions combine these approaches, treating a corporation as resident if either test is satisfied. In some cases, the test of place of management becomes in effect a formal test by focusing on easily controlled events such as the place at which the board of directors meets, rather than the situs of day-to-day management decisions.

The *United States* is an example of a jurisdiction that relies on a purely formal test. All corporations organized under the laws of the United States or one of the federal states are treated as 'domestic' – that is, resident – corporations, regardless of any other connection to the jurisdiction.[20] Conversely, all other corporations are 'foreign' – that is, non-resident – corporations, even if all of their commercial and economic activities are linked to the United States.[21] *Japan* also has a formal test, although the technical structure of the rule is somewhat different. Under the statutory definition of resident corporation, a corporation is resident if its

17. Japan, Income Tax Act (ITA), s. 1 para. 1 subpara. 3.
18. Japan, ITA, s. 1 para. 1 subpara. 4.
19. Japan, ITA, s. 7.
20. United States, IRC, s. 7701(a)(4).
21. United States, IRC, s. 7701(a)(5).

'headquarters' or 'principal office' is located in Japan.[22] However, these concepts are derived from civil law and commercial law, and under those provisions, all corporations incorporated in Japan must have either a registered headquarters (Company Law) or a registered principal office (Civil Code) in Japan, thus in effect turning the test into one of incorporation in the case of domestically organized corporations. On the other hand, a corporation organized in a foreign country can have a registered principal office or headquarters in Japan (if that is possible under the laws of the incorporating jurisdiction) and will also be treated by Japan as a resident corporation.

Sweden also has a formal test that turns on formation and registration under Swedish corporate law.

The *Commonwealth* countries, which traditionally focused on the place of central management and control to determine corporate residence, now combine that test with a test based on formal incorporation. Thus, in the *United Kingdom* prior to 1988, the only test was the factual one of central management and control of the company's business, which was generally, although not conclusively, considered to be located where the board of directors met.[23] In 1988, this test was supplemented by an incorporation rule that made companies incorporated in the United Kingdom resident there, but left companies incorporated elsewhere to be liable to UK-resident status under the old rule.[24]

The *Canadian* rules follow the UK pattern. Either incorporation[25] or central management and control in Canada will result in resident treatment. The case law has focused primarily on the place of the meeting of the board of directors (assuming that the board exercises control of the affairs of the corporation), thus giving the test a formal character. In some situations, though, the courts have examined the question of actual day-to-day control.

Australia has a similar approach. Formal incorporation under Australian law will cause the corporation to be treated as resident. In addition, if the corporation is doing business in Australia and has its place of central management and control in Australia, it is likewise resident. The Australian rules also take into consideration the residence of the shareholders. If a corporation is doing business in Australia and a majority of voting power is held by Australian residents, the corporation will be viewed as resident.[26] However, the shareholder test is applied without attributing share ownership through interposed companies or trusts and can be avoided by interposing a non-resident entity between the corporation and the ultimate Australian shareholders.

Both *Germany* and *The Netherlands* combine incorporation and management tests. In Germany, a corporation is resident if it has its 'statutory seat' in

22. Japan, ITA, s. 1 para. 1 subpara. 6.
23. For example, see *De Beers Consolidated Mines v. Howe* [1906] AC 455 (HL) at 458.
24. United Kingdom, Corporation Tax Act 2009, ss 14 and 15.
25. Canada, ITA, s. 250(4).
26. Australia, ITAA 1936, s. 6(1) definition of 'resident' para. (b).

Germany.[27] Since all corporations formed under German corporate law are required to designate a statutory seat in the jurisdiction, they are automatically treated as resident. In addition, if a corporation organized under foreign law has its place of management in Germany, it is treated as a resident taxpayer.[28] The focus is on the activities of day-to-day management and not on the supervisory activities of the legal organ roughly equivalent to the (outside) board of directors.

The Netherlands similarly uses both formal incorporation[29] and, as with individuals, a determination 'according to the circumstances'.[30] Case law gives great weight to the place of effective management – that is, where the day-to-day management takes place.[31] In this regard, factors such as residence of directors and location of board meetings, business, and head office may be considered relevant circumstances. In *France*, a corporation formed under French law and having its registered office in France is treated as a resident. However, because France applies the territorial system to corporations, the law on corporate residence is not highly developed as to, for example, the extent to which a corporation must have its place of actual management in France in connection with its registered office.

2. CHANGE OF STATUS

2.1. Change of Status of Individuals

Changing factual circumstances may cause an individual to establish or terminate resident status in a particular jurisdiction. A number of technical issues arise in connection with a change in personal taxing jurisdiction. From the perspective of the receiving country, the principal question is how to establish the 'tax history' of the new tax subject. Here, there are basically two approaches. One is, in effect, to reconstruct past events as if they had taken place while the taxpayer was subject to the taxing system of the receiving jurisdiction and then use these historical factors in determining current tax liability. Thus, for example, the historical cost of an asset, adjusted for notional depreciation, could be used to determine the gain on the disposition of the asset in the new jurisdiction. Alternatively, a 'fresh start' approach could be taken which focused on market values at the time residence was established.

From the perspective of the departing jurisdiction, the issue is what, if any, attempts should be made to enforce taxing claims on income or gains that arose or accrued while the taxpayer was a resident. One approach – so-called exit or departure taxes – is to treat the departure as a realization event for any income that would

27. Germany, Corporate Income Tax Act (CITA), s. 1 para. 1.
28. Germany, CITA, s. 1 para. 1 sentence (hereafter sent.) 2.
29. Netherlands, Company Income Tax Act 1969 (CITA), Art. 4.1.
30. Netherlands, GAT, Art. 4.1.
31. For an overview see the Opinion of Advocate General Overgaauw for Supreme Court decision 1 Dec. 2004, no. 37.719, BNB 2005/105.

cease to be subject to tax in the hands of the departed (non-resident) taxpayer. Alternatively, modifications may be made to the normal taxing pattern for non-residents to allow the continued taxation of former residents on certain types of income – so-called trailing taxes.

For new residents, the *United States* uses historical cost of assets in principle, although the rules are not well developed. Pursuant to legislation adopted in 2008, the United States treats termination of residence as a realization event for taxpayers who had an average income of more than $138,000 during the prior five years or who have a net worth of more than $2 million. Such taxpayers are treated as selling their assets at fair market value on the day prior to expatriation and must recognize gains in excess of $600,000 that accrued while the taxpayer was a US citizen or permanent resident.[32] *Canada* deals with these issues by giving a new resident a tax cost for property equal to its fair market value at the time the individual becomes a resident.[33] Thus, only appreciation or depreciation that takes place during the period of Canadian residence is taken into account for Canadian tax purposes. Similarly, when an individual ceases to be a resident, he is deemed to have disposed of the property for its fair market value, generating a current gain or loss. This departure or exit tax also applies to corporations and trusts. An exception is made for certain types of property, such as real estate located in Canada, and property of a business carried on in Canada through a permanent establishment. The excepted property is property over which Canada retains source-based taxing rights. Taxpayers can elect to have such property deemed to be disposed of for fair market value. Taxpayers can postpone payment of the departure or exit tax until the property is actually sold if adequate security is provided to the tax authorities. In addition, relieving provisions deal with post-emigration losses and foreign taxes on pre-departure gains to reduce double tax problems.

In some circumstances, Canada extends its taxing right to former residents.[34] If a former resident receives employment income from a Canadian resident, the income remains taxable in Canada unless the taxpayer can establish that the services were rendered abroad and the income is subject to foreign tax.

The *Australian* system is similar, although only for capital gains tax purposes. When a non-resident becomes a resident, he is deemed to have acquired assets at their then-market value. When residence is terminated, gain is deemed to be realized on all assets over which Australia does not retain source-based taxation rights, thus ensuring that all (and only) appreciation that took place during the period of Australian residence is subject to tax. It is also possible to elect to defer the tax until the asset is actually disposed of, although in this case all appreciation is subject to tax.[35] In the 2001 Protocol to the US treaty, problems that arise from the interaction of the US and Australian systems were dealt with by giving the taxpayer a market-value tax basis in the United States if moving from Australia to the United States,

32. United States, IRC, s. 877A.
33. The rules governing immigration and emigration are found in ITA, s. 128.1.
34. Canada, ITA, s. 115(2).
35. Australia, Income Tax Assessment Act 1997 (ITAA 1997), ss 104–160, 104–165, 855–45.

and giving up Australian taxing rights altogether if the taxpayer elects to defer tax on moving to the United States. The 2003 treaty with the United Kingdom contains the latter, but not the former, provision and vice versa with respect to the 2006 French treaty. Australia's most recent treaties do not consistently include such provisions, so it is unclear to what extent they will be a feature of Australia's future treaty policy.

In contrast, as a general rule the *United Kingdom* does not treat change of status as a taxable event and has no special rules for deemed acquisitions when residence status is established. However, a special rule applies to individuals who cease to be resident but then resume residence within five years. In such a case, a capital gain realized when the individual is non-resident may be treated as accruing after residence is resumed.[36]

Sweden uses the historical cost as the basis for taxing capital gains of incoming residents. For business income, the basis could be increased from cost to a higher value if the transfer of assets has been taxed by the state of former residence.[37] With respect to departing residents, a special rule effectively extends the residence concept. If a taxpayer has been resident under the basic statutory definition but is no longer covered by that test, he will continue to be taxed as a resident if he maintains an 'essential connection' to Sweden.[38] A statutory catalogue of factors is considered in determining if an essential connection is present. These factors include Swedish citizenship, the period of former residence in Sweden, the existence of permanent residence abroad, the reason for being abroad, access to a dwelling in Sweden, family and/or business connections in Sweden, and other comparable circumstances. A special evidentiary rule applies if the taxpayer is a Swedish citizen or was a resident of Sweden under the normal rules for at least ten years. For the first five years after departure, the taxpayer is deemed to have an essential connection and has the burden of proof of negating enough of the factors to establish that no essential connection to Sweden is present. Thereafter, the tax authorities have the burden of establishing the essential connection with respect to the same factors.

Sweden also retains the right to tax gain on the disposition of shares and other financial assets in Swedish corporations for ten years after departure of an individual.[39] To prevent a tax planning scheme, this rule was extended in 2007 to shares in foreign corporations. The scheme involved a tax-free transfer of shares in a Swedish corporation to a foreign corporation followed by the sale of the shares of the foreign corporation. This rule has been considered by the European Court of Justice (ECJ) to be a restriction on free movement according to the EC treaty. Sweden in its double taxation treaty negotiations attempts to preserve these taxing rights. In a number of tax treaties Sweden has retained the right to tax gains on

36. United Kingdom, Taxation of Chargeable Gains Act 1992, s. 10A.
37. Sweden, Income Tax Act (ITA), Ch. 20 a.
38. Sweden, ITA, Ch. 3 s. 7.
39. Sweden, ITA, Ch. 3 s. 19.

Swedish shares, but not gains on foreign shares, for periods extending from three to seven years.

Germany likewise uses historical cost in determining the tax consequences of transactions undertaken after an individual establishes residence. But according to recent legislation, the sale of a 'substantial participation' does not give rise to taxation of capital gains insofar as they have accrued before the individual became a resident of Germany, if the other country has taxed this accrued gain on that occasion.[40] The termination of residence is generally not considered a realization event. However, in the case of 'substantial participations' in companies that would have been taxable on disposition, termination of residence will be a realization event for gain (but not loss) purposes, if the individual has been a tax resident for at least ten years previously.[41] When the European Commission claimed a violation of the fundamental freedoms under the EC Treaty, the legislature implemented an unconditional deferment of payment until the disposal of the shares if the taxpayer is an EU national and moves to an EU Member State. In addition, special rules apply to German citizens who have been resident in Germany for an extended period and then transfer residence to a low-tax jurisdiction (or to no jurisdiction) if they maintain 'substantial connections' to Germany. If the provisions apply, the former resident is taxed at the usually applicable domestic rates on income from German sources. The extended tax liability lasts for ten years after the termination of German residence.

The Netherlands has a highly developed system for dealing with the taxation of newly arrived resident companies (i.e., a foreign-incorporated company whose effective management has moved to The Netherlands) and individuals engaged in business who move their residence to The Netherlands. Business assets that were not previously subject to Dutch tax take a fair market value basis. Existing Dutch business assets keep their historical cost. Where residence is transferred abroad, there is a deemed disposition (and recognition of any resulting capital gain) of business assets at the time of the change of residence (for purposes of this deemed disposition rule, the term 'business' includes other gainful activities). Taxable substantial participations take a fair market value basis. As to emigration of individuals, in general, termination of residence does not result in taxation, although The Netherlands retains taxing rights over substantial participations in resident companies and certain annuities (pensions) and insurance policies if premiums have been deducted in Holland.

No special rules have been developed in *France* with respect to the taxation of newly arrived residents. The departing taxpayer is taxed on his worldwide income (subject to tax treaties) received or accrued before departure and not yet taxed.[42] As from 1999, gains on shares received previously in certain tax-deferred exchanges or sales were also immediately taxable, and the termination of residence by those individuals who had been resident for six of the last ten years was a taxable

40. Germany, ITA, s. 17 para. 2 sent. 3.
41. Germany, Foreign Transaction Tax Act (*Aussensteuergesetz*), s. 6.
42. France, CGI, s. 167.

event as far as gains on substantial holdings (i.e., at least 25%) in French or foreign corporations were concerned. In both cases, tax might be deferred on certain conditions until the taxpayer actually disposed of the shares.[43] But these provisions were deleted from the Code in 2005, after they had been ruled incompatible with the EC freedom of establishment.[44]

Japan uses historical cost and has no special rules that extend taxing jurisdiction.

2.2. Change of Status of Corporations

The personal taxing jurisdiction over a corporation can change if the corporation is formally reincorporated or 'continued' into another jurisdiction. In addition, for those countries using a management and control test of corporate residency, residency can change if the requisite management activities are shifted to another country. There are several models as to how change of corporate residence might be treated. One approach would be to treat the original domestic corporation as if it had been liquidated, with the attendant consequences to the corporation and shareholders. The assets received by the shareholder would then be treated as if contributed to the non-resident corporation, with the usual tax results for an outbound transaction in those circumstances. Alternatively, the domestic corporation could be viewed as transferring its assets to the non-resident corporation for its shares, followed by a liquidating distribution of those shares to the shareholders, again with the tax consequences that those transactions would have under normally applicable rules. Only a few of the jurisdictions here under consideration have fully developed rules dealing with this situation.

In the *United States*, the transaction in which a domestic corporation is reincorporated as a foreign corporation would be treated as a reorganization involving an outbound transfer. As a result, the normal non-recognition treatment given reorganization exchanges would not be available automatically, and both the deemed transfer of the assets by the domestic corporation and the deemed share exchange by the shareholders would potentially be taxable events.[45] On the other hand, the 'continuation' of a foreign corporation as a US domestic corporation would in general be treated as a qualifying reorganization. As a result, the new resident corporation would continue the tax cost of the assets received, and the shareholders would similarly transfer the tax cost of their old shares to the shares of the continued corporation.[46]

In *Canada*, the same principles are applied to corporations as are applied to individuals.[47] For a corporation that becomes resident in Canada, there is a 'fresh

43. France, CGI, former s. 167 *bis*.
44. ECJ, 11 Mar. 2004, C-9/02 (*de Lasteyrie du Saillant*).
45. United States, IRC, s. 367(a). The section is implemented by extensive regulations.
46. United States, IRC, s. 367(b). The section is implemented by extensive regulations.
47. Canada, ITA, s. 128.1.

start' fair market value for its assets other than taxable Canadian property and property of a business carried on in Canada. A new taxation year is deemed to commence at the time that the corporation becomes a resident of Canada. Loss carryovers are permitted only to the extent that they relate to businesses carried on in Canada.

In the case of a Canadian corporation that becomes non-resident by reincorporation or continuation into another jurisdiction and that is no longer managed or controlled in Canada, the 'expatriation' is a realization event with respect to most property other than real property in Canada and assets of a business carried on through a permanent establishment in Canada. The corporation's taxation year is deemed to have ended immediately before the emigration, and the corporation is deemed to have disposed of all of its assets for their fair market value immediately before that time. This deemed realization gives rise to capital gains and other tax consequences. In addition, a special departure tax of 25% is imposed on the excess of the fair market value of its property over the aggregate of its paid-up capital and liabilities. This special tax is intended to prevent corporations from avoiding the withholding tax on dividends by shifting their residence to another country. The 25% rate is reduced where the corporation emigrates to a country with which Canada has a tax treaty that provides a reduced rate of withholding on dividends.

The *United Kingdom* also has explicit rules dealing with a change of corporate residence. At one time, it was a criminal offence for a company to cease to be resident of the United Kingdom without the permission of the Treasury, but this rule was repealed in 1990. In the case of a residence change, there is a deemed disposal of, in general, all assets over which the United Kingdom no longer has a source-based taxing claim. The tax can be postponed if the migrating company is a subsidiary of a parent company that remains resident.[48]

Australia does not allow as a matter of company law the continuation of an Australian corporation into a foreign jurisdiction, and outbound changes in place of incorporation are probably treated as liquidations. Foreign corporations can be continued into Australia under special procedures, but the tax consequences are generally unclear. When a non-resident corporation becomes resident in Australia, it is deemed to have acquired its assets at their fair market value at that time for capital gains tax purposes. Conversely, when an Australian-resident corporation ceases to be resident in Australia, it is deemed to have disposed of its assets at fair market value.[49] Reincorporation in Australia means that the company becomes an Australian resident under the place of incorporation rule if it is not already. For companies not incorporated in Australia but carrying on business there, it is possible to move residence to and from Australia by shifting central management and control or the residence of shareholders. In these cases the normal change of residence rules apply. The provisions in the US and UK treaties referred to above in section 2.1, concerning the change of residence of individuals, are not available to corporations.

48. United Kingdom, Taxation of Chargeable Gains Act 1992, ss 185 and 187.
49. Australia, ITAA 1997, ss 104–160 and 855-45.

In *Sweden*, a Swedish corporation cannot under corporate law change its status to become incorporated in a foreign state. If the corporation liquidates in order to reincorporate as a foreign corporation, the transaction will be taxable under normal rules. Where a Swedish corporation has its management abroad and, under the applicable tax treaty, the corporation is deemed to be a resident only of the other country (see section 2.3) – with the result that Sweden cannot tax non-Swedish-source income – the transfer of management is treated as a deemed realization. However, this tax was considered by the Swedish Supreme Administrative Court to contravene the EC treaty, and the rule has been amended to provide the possibility to defer the tax until the assets are sold.

In *Germany*, the introduction of the European Company as a new supranational legal form, which entitles a company to transfer its statutory seat and place of management abroad, has led to a substantive rewriting of the rules for corporate taxpayers generally.[50] If a corporation transfers its seat or its place of effective management to a country outside the European Union, terminating the residence and therefore the unlimited tax liability in Germany, this transfer is generally seen as a liquidation of the corporation and the normal rules on liquidation, which require gain recognition on transferred assets, are applicable.[51] However, if the statutory seat or the place of effective management is transferred to another EU Member State, the hidden reserves are taxed only if Germany otherwise does not maintain jurisdiction to tax the assets at the time of their later disposal.[52] This rule not only applies to the transfer of the place of effective management (this is of particular importance for intangibles) but also to the transfer of an asset to a foreign branch.

The transfer of the head office of a corporation from *France* to another country yields the immediate taxation of all income not yet subject to tax and is a realization event as far as capital gains are concerned, unless there is a treaty between France and the host country providing for the continuation of the legal personality of the moving corporation. No such treaty has been concluded yet. However, as a major exception to this rule, the transfer of a French company to another EU country, with or without loss of legal personality, is now tax-free in order to comply with EC law (i.e., freedom of establishment, the legal status of the European company, and the tax directive on mergers). If, however, assets are actually transferred on such an occasion, the gains realized would be taxable. Although the Code encompasses only the transfer from France, the same rules would probably apply to the transfer of a corporation's head office to France.[53]

In *The Netherlands*, the transfer by a Dutch-incorporated corporation of management abroad will not affect Dutch taxing rights because corporate residence is still deemed to be in Holland by virtue of domestic incorporation. However, if under a treaty tie-breaker rule, the other country has the exclusive right to treat the

50. Germany, CITA, s. 12.
51. Germany, CITA, s. 12 para. 3 sent. 1.
52. Germany, CITA, s. 12 para. 1.
53. France, CGI, ss 221–2 and 3.

corporation as a resident, realization is required with respect to all assets over which Holland no longer has taxing rights.[54] Further, the Supreme Court has ruled, in a much-contested decision, that such a company no longer qualifies as a resident company for purposes of treaties with third countries.[55] *Japan* does not have a rule on Japanese corporations moving into a foreign jurisdiction. Therefore, if a Japanese corporation liquidates in order to reincorporate as a foreign corporation, the transaction will be taxed under normal rules.

2.3. Dual Residence

Problems of dual residence are often dealt with in treaties that contain rules to establish a single residence jurisdiction for treaty purposes, which in turn limits the taxing rights of the other country. Apart from treaty rules, some jurisdictions have special domestic legislation that prevents taxpayers from utilizing corporations that are treated as residents of two or more jurisdictions (so-called 'dual resident' corporations) to deduct losses in both jurisdictions. For example, in the *United States*, special rules restrict the use of losses in the US by a dual-resident company where the losses, generally speaking, can also be used in a foreign consolidated group. On the other hand, the rules do not in general prevent the corporation from using the losses to reduce its own income in both jurisdictions (e.g., through the mechanism of a loss carryover). Because the income is potentially taxable in both jurisdictions, allowance of the loss in these circumstances is not viewed as inappropriate. The perceived problem arises only when the income that is being offset against the loss in the foreign consolidated group is not subject to the US taxing claim.[56]

The United States also has developed a complex set of rules intended to prevent taxpayers from using 'hybrid' entities (entities taxable as a corporation in one nation and as a partnership in another) to avoid paying tax in any jurisdiction.

In *Canada*, a dual-resident person considered to be resident in another country pursuant to the provisions of a tax treaty is deemed not to be a resident of Canada for all purposes.[57] This provision applies to corporations, individuals, and other persons and has been reasonably effective in preventing most of the tax planning advantages of dual residence. Dual-resident companies can still be utilized with respect to non-treaty countries.

Australia has also experienced problems with deductions, principally interest, being claimed by dual-resident companies. The problem arose first in 1984 when

54. Netherlands, CITA, Art. 15c.
55. Netherlands, Supreme Court, 28 Feb. 2001, no. 35.557, BNB 2001/295. This result is consistent with the position in the OECD Commentary on Art. 4, which was added as part of the 2008 update.
56. United States, IRC, s. 1503(c).
57. Canada, ITA, s. 250(5).

the right to transfer losses among 100% related companies was introduced. The response was to deny the right to transfer losses by dual-resident investment companies. The definition of dual-resident investment company[58] effectively eliminated many of the dual-resident financing structures. Like the Canadian system, the controlled foreign corporation (CFC) provisions also have a rule that treats an otherwise dual-resident corporation whose residence the treaty allocates to the other country as a foreign company for CFC purposes.[59] In 1997 this approach was extended for dual-resident companies to certain tax benefits available to residents, such as capital gains tax rollovers and transfers of losses within 100% related groups;[60] in addition, the consolidation regime introduced in 2002 does not permit such companies to be members of the consolidated group.[61] The 2003 review of international taxation recommended that Australia drop these specific rules and adopt a general qualification to the company residence rules for dual residents along the lines of Canada and the United Kingdom. The former government accepted this recommendation but did not enact it. The current government indicated in 2008 that the matter was still under review and in 2009 raised the possibility of extending such an approach to all residents, not just companies.

The *United Kingdom* similarly has rules that restrict the use of losses and other reliefs by dual-resident investment companies.[62] The United Kingdom has a rule similar to the Canadian rule under which a corporation that is considered to be resident in the other country pursuant to the tie-breaker rule in a treaty is considered to be non-resident for all purposes.[63]

France, Germany, The Netherlands, and *Japan* do not have any special statutory rules dealing with dual residence.

In *Germany*, dual-resident companies were formerly not possible due to the 'real seat' theory, which under company law did not recognize a corporation that had its central management and its registered office in different jurisdictions. Because the ECJ has recently forced Germany to accept the legal personality of a foreign company that has, in accordance with its 'home state' law,[64] transferred its place of management to Germany without changing its legal form, there will be many more 'dual-resident' companies in the future. They are deemed to be resident in Germany if either the statutory seat or the 'real seat' is located within Germany. They will be characterized as corporate taxpayers if they are comparable to corporate entities in Germany.[65]

58. Australia, ITAA 1936, s. 6F.
59. Australia, ITAA 1936, s. 317 definition of 'Part X Australian resident'.
60. Australia, ITAA 1936, s. 6(1) definition of 'prescribed dual resident', which also covers cases of dual central management and control.
61. Australia, ITAA 1997, s. 703-15(2) table column 3.
62. United Kingdom, Income and Corporation Taxes Act 1988, s. 404.
63. United Kingdom, Corporation Tax Act 2009, s. 18.
64. ECJ, 5 Nov. 2002, C-208/00 (*Überseering*).
65. Germany, CITA, s. 1 para. 1 no. 1.

2.4. Temporary Residents

Although some countries, such as the *United Kingdom*, have long recognized different categories of residents, in more recent times other countries have begun to enact special regimes for expatriate individual employees who are seconded by their employer for a limited period, say two to four years, to another country but plan to return. Which country should be regarded as the one with which the employees have the closer social and economic connections and so is their real country of residence? Such employees will usually become residents of the country of secondment under both the domestic tax law of that country and an applicable tax treaty. They may qualify, for example, for free health care in that country, which may suggest that they should be taxed there on a residence basis. On the other hand, they will usually retain close links with their country of origin, such as membership of a pension plan there. This may suggest for such longer term issues that they should be regarded as residents of the country of origin. For these kinds of reasons, some countries now try to soften the hard line between the tax treatment of resident and non-resident individuals with special tax regimes for temporary residents.

In *Australia*, rules were introduced in 2006 for more limited taxation of temporary residents, who are defined by reference to their visa and social security status in a way designed to target short-stay expatriate employees (four years generally being the limit). Temporary residents are generally exempt from tax on their non-Australian source income (other than employment income, including share options), are not subject to the CFC and foreign investment fund (FIF) regimes, and are not required to pay interest withholding tax on payments of interest to non-residents (which is mainly, but not only, a problem in cases where the expatriate maintains a home in the other country subject to a mortgage to a bank resident there and makes payments to the bank on the mortgage, including an element of interest).[66]

Canada provides special exemptions from the non-resident trust rules and proposed FIF rules for new residents of Canada for a temporary period of five years.[67] There is also an exception for first-year residents from the requirements to file returns concerning certain foreign information.[68]

Since 2004, *France* has granted special tax benefits to its so-called 'impatriates' (employees, corporate managers and even, since 2008, specially authorized self-employed people) who have become French residents insofar as they did not enjoy such status for the preceding five years.[69] Their annual so-called 'impatriation bonus' and the remuneration of their work abroad, if any, are granted a wide-ranging exemption from taxation. Payments to foreign social security schemes are

66. Australia, ITAA 1997, Subdiv. 768-R.
67. Canada, ITA, s. 94(1)(b).
68. Canada, ITA, s. 233.7.
69. France, CGI, s. 81 B and, for those having become resident after 1 Jan. 2008, s. 155 B.

tax deductible.[70] Only 50% of passive foreign-source income (i.e., dividends, interest, royalties, and gains from the sale of stocks or securities) is taxed when received by individuals who become French residents after 1 January 2008. Such benefits are not subject to any condition as to the subsequent length of stay in France, but are restricted to the first five calendar years following the transfer of the residence of the beneficiaries to France. During the same period their foreign assets are also exempt from the French wealth tax.[71]

The concept of short-term resident in *Japan* is similar in the sense that a short-term resident is taxed only on domestic-source income and foreign-source income that is remitted to Japan. However, its historical background is unique. The predecessor of the current system was first introduced in 1950 as a substitute for the absolute exclusion of non-yen denominated income from taxable income. This exclusion was one of the measures taken by the General Headquarters after World War II. In 1957, this system was changed to the short-term resident system, where short-term residents are taxed only on domestic-source income and foreign-source income remitted to Japan. Until 2006, a short-term resident was defined as a resident of Japan who did not intend to remain permanently in Japan and had not maintained a residence for five years. The 2006 tax revisions replaced the first requirement with foreign nationality, and the second requirement with five-year residence in Japan during the most recent ten years. The purposes of this revision were to deny benefits of short-term residency to Japanese nationals and to combat some abusive practices of foreign nationals who had tried to remain short-term residents by returning to their home countries shortly before the expiration of the five-year period.

The primary relief for temporary residents in the *United Kingdom* is the traditional preferential taxation of residents who are not domiciled in the United Kingdom. While the rules vary depending on type of income, broadly 'non-doms' are taxable on foreign-source income only when (and if) remitted to the United Kingdom. This rule was tightened in 2008 so that if a non-dom wishes to continue this treatment after residence of seven years, he must pay a flat tax of £30,000 per annum.[72]

3. MECHANISMS FOR RELIEF OF DOUBLE TAXATION

All of the countries here under consideration have some domestic law mechanism for the relief of the double taxation that results when residence-based and source-based taxing claims are asserted on the same item of income derived by the same taxpayer. The residence country generally eliminates double taxation either by exempting the item of income from its tax base or by giving a credit against the domestic tax liability for the foreign tax.

---

70. France, CGI, s. 83 1° 0 *bis* and 2° 0 *ter*.
71. France, CGI, s. 885 A 1.
72. United Kingdom, ITA 2007, Part 14 Ch. A1.

Under the foreign tax credit mechanism, foreign income is included in the tax base and the prior right of the source country to tax is recognized by giving a credit for the foreign tax liability that displaces or reduces the normally applicable domestic liability. To the extent that the residence country rate is higher than the foreign rate, a residual domestic tax is collected, but international double taxation has been eliminated. If the foreign rate is higher than the domestic rate, all domestic tax is eliminated, and again, double taxation has been avoided.

Beyond resolving the perceived inequity of subjecting the same taxpayer to conflicting taxing claims on the same income, from an economic point of view, the foreign tax credit system is generally viewed as consistent with an overall policy of capital export neutrality – that is, from the perspective of the residence country investor, the credit system tends to ensure that the choice between domestic or foreign investment will not be influenced by tax considerations. In practical operation, the credit systems here considered fall far short of this result, in particular where the tax rate in the foreign jurisdiction is higher than the domestic rate. In addition, in practice, the interaction of the various provisions dealing with international income often makes it difficult to determine if a particular rule does or does not further capital export neutrality. Nonetheless, especially in the context of portfolio investment, capital export neutrality has historically been an important factor in the decision to adopt or maintain a credit system.

International double taxation can also be avoided by exempting from domestic tax certain classes of foreign-source income, thus ceding exclusive taxing jurisdiction to the country of source. If the foreign income is simply exempt, and does not affect the taxation of other foreign- or domestic-source income that is subject to tax, the result is essentially the same as not asserting jurisdiction to tax the income at all. More typically, the exempt income is taken into account in determining the tax treatment of other income – for example, in determining the applicable rate of tax in a progressive rate structure ('exemption with progression').

While the exemption technique is often contrasted with the credit approach, the actual operation of the two methods for relieving double taxation often yield quite similar results. In the systems here considered, exemption is usually limited to specific categories of foreign income – most typically, active business or employment income – that are likely to be subject to a level of foreign tax comparable to that which would have been applicable in the residence country. Where foreign and domestic rates are roughly comparable, in a credit system the residence country will not collect much, if any, additional tax on the foreign-source income; this result is functionally equivalent to exempting the income. Ancillary differences are reduced still further if an 'exemption with progression' technique is used.

Nonetheless, there may be some important differences in the effects of the two techniques in particular situations. While foreign and domestic rates may be roughly similar in general terms, there may be important variations across industries and with respect to different companies, and the choice of exemption means that residual domestic tax may not be collected in some significant cases. In addition, great pressure is put on the source rules, as the decision that a particular item of income is foreign-source income may mean that it is not taxed anywhere if the source rules of the two jurisdictions are not completely congruent. Similarly, transfer pricing differences have different implications in an exemption system.

Beyond its role as a mechanism for relieving potential double taxation, from a policy point of view, an exemption method is consistent with a policy of capital import or competitive neutrality. It ensures that the income from foreign activities will not be subjected to a higher rate of tax than the rate faced by local competitors. It also ensures that foreign tax holidays or preferences are not 'washed out' by additional residence country tax. These effects have been a factor in the decision of some countries to utilize the exemption technique.

Another aspect of the exemption technique that is often stressed is its relative simplicity. Because the foreign income is simply exempt, there is no need to establish in detail the foreign tax burden on particular items of income. However, this asserted advantage over the credit system can be overstated, especially in the context of business taxation. As discussed below, while the exemption system eliminates some technical issues, it raises others. The level of simplicity or complexity seems less a question of the basic approach than the degree to which rough and simple solutions are accepted for administrative or compliance reasons.

Finally, some countries have adopted exemption systems in recent times to achieve 'conduit' tax treatment – that is, where an entity is resident in a country but the owners of the entity are resident elsewhere – and the income earned by the entity is sourced outside its country of residence. The claim of the residence country of the entity to tax the income, given the tax at source and the tax by the country in which the owners are resident, is not considered to be strong, and the tax is given up through the use of the exemption system. Given this rationale, the exemption is usually limited to legal entities (typically limited to corporations).

Whatever their relative advantages and disadvantages, in practice, no country uses a 'pure' exemption or 'pure' credit approach. All of the countries examined here combine these two methods, exempting certain classes of income and giving credit for foreign taxes imposed on others. The relative 'mix' between exemption and credit varies substantially, however. The *United States* makes most use of the credit approach while the *Continental* systems and Australia have more exemption features. *Canada* falls somewhere in the middle, and the *United Kingdom* is heading in that direction. Although *Japan* and the United Kingdom had generally relied on the credit approach, they introduced exemptions for dividends from foreign corporations in 2009.

With respect to the specific systems, the *United States* employs a foreign tax credit for most foreign income,[73] although there is a limited exemption for foreign-earned income.[74] The taxpayer has the choice between crediting or deducting foreign taxes. The credit is restricted to foreign income taxes that are comparable to US income tax and are imposed on income from foreign sources. The credit cannot exceed the US tax on the foreign income. However, rather than tracing particular taxes to particular items or segments of income, the limitation is

73. United States, IRC, s. 901(a).
74. United States, IRC, s. 911.

expressed in terms of a formula that allows high and low foreign taxes on two classes or 'baskets' of foreign income (passive income and non-passive income) to be averaged.[75] The credit extends to taxes paid by foreign corporations in which a US corporation owns at least 10% of the voting stock (the 'indirect' credit).[76]

In *Japan*, the foreign tax credit system is also used and the taxpayer has the choice between crediting or deducting foreign taxes. Credit is given for all foreign income taxes as well as excess profits taxes and taxes on distributed earnings. The credit cannot exceed the Japanese tax on the foreign-source income. In general, an overall limitation allows averaging of high- and low-taxed foreign income. However, there are certain limitations on averaging. For example, two-thirds of untaxed foreign-source income must be eliminated in calculating the credit.[77] The 2009 revisions have abolished the indirect credit system that had been available for dividends from foreign companies received by 25% or greater Japanese corporate shareholders. Instead, 95% of dividends paid by a foreign company in which a Japanese company holds 25% or more of the shares is excluded from the taxable income of the Japanese company.[78]

Until recently, the *United Kingdom* predominantly used the credit system. The credit is limited to the foreign tax on each particular source of income, thus preventing averaging of foreign rates on directly received income. An indirect credit is allowed with respect to dividends received by resident corporate shareholders who own at least 10% of the voting power of the payer foreign corporation. In the case of the indirect credit, the source-by-source approach is relaxed and some pooling is permitted.[79] In 2009, in response to difficulties with EC Law, the United Kingdom is in the process of introducing a broad exemption for foreign dividends received by UK corporations. The exemption is available for most, although not all, types of payments treated as distributions for tax purposes. In principle, the exemption is available for all dividends irrespective of the level of shareholding of a UK company in the distributing foreign corporation. Interest on associated debt financing of the foreign shares continues to be deductible but is subject to a worldwide debt cap (discussed below).[80] No similar exemption for foreign dividends is available for individual shareholders, although the integration system available for domestic dividends is (since 2009) effectively available for foreign dividends. As noted above, in 2008, the remittance basis for non-domiciled individuals (which effectively provides an exemption for foreign-source income) was limited to seven years after acquiring residence unless a fixed annual fee of £30,000 is paid.

Canada uses both the foreign tax credit method and an exemption system for certain income. Credit is given for 'income or profits' taxes paid by a resident

75. United States, IRC, s. 904(a); 904(d)(2).
76. United States, IRC, s. 902.
77. Japan, ITA, s. 95 and Japan, Corporate Tax Act (CTA), s. 69.
78. Japan, CTA, s. 23-2.
79. Generally, see UK Income and Corporation Taxes Act 1988, Part XVIII.
80. United Kingdom, UK Finance Act 2009, Sch. 14 (to insert Corporation Tax Act 2009 Part 9A) and 15.

taxpayer.[81] This credit is limited to the Canadian tax on the foreign-source income from sources in the particular country, a so-called 'per country' limitation. Separate limitations are provided for business and other income. Taxpayers have the option of deducting non-business foreign tax in computing their income.[82] A form of indirect credit is also available for taxes paid by foreign corporations in which there is a direct or indirect 10% share ownership by a Canadian corporation.[83] The credit takes the form of a grossed-up deduction, which in effect limits the credit to the Canadian tax that would have been payable on the foreign income. In addition to the indirect credit, there is an exemption for dividends paid out of active business income from countries with which Canada has a tax treaty or, since 2008, a tax information exchange agreement.[84] Because the Canadian treaty network includes most countries in which Canadian corporations have substantial foreign direct investment, almost all dividends repatriated to Canadian corporations by their foreign affiliates qualify for the exemption. Dividends that would qualify for the indirect credit are rarely paid because the funds can be repatriated in the form of interest-free loans. A 2008 Advisory Panel recommended that Canada should adopt a full exemption system for dividends received by Canadian corporations from 10%-owned foreign affiliates.

A similar combination of credit and exemption is used in *Germany*. The basic statutory system provides for worldwide taxation with a foreign tax credit for foreign income taxes on income that is determined to be foreign-source income under German source rules.[85] The credit is limited to the amount of the German tax paid, and the limitation is applied on a per-country basis. The taxpayer can also elect to deduct foreign taxes if the foreign income is taxable. A special rule allows taxation of foreign-source income at a reduced flat rate in certain circumstances with the approval of the tax authorities. In addition, foreign losses arising from, broadly speaking, foreign activities that do not amount to an active trade or business cannot be deducted against other categories of income.

In almost all of its treaties, Germany exempts business income (and dividends from subsidiaries) under varying conditions, sometimes requiring an active business in the foreign country or that the income be subject to tax there. In light of Germany's extensive treaty network, it is effectively an exemption country as far as business income is concerned.

However, under the most recent legislation Germany has introduced a 'catch-all' clause[86] dealing with 'white income': All income generally exempt under a treaty is taxable on a worldwide basis if the source state does not exercise its taxing right due to a different interpretation of the treaty or special rules for foreign residents. In light of Germany's strong historic commitment to exemption, this

81. Canada, ITA, s. 126.
82. Canada, ITA, s. 20(12).
83. Canada, ITA, s. 113(1)(b).
84. Canada, ITA, s. 113(1)(a).
85. Germany, ITA, s. 1 para. 1 and 34c; CITA, ss 1 and 26.
86. Germany, ITA, 50d para. 9.

sweeping extension of German taxation has been heavily criticized by academics and business representatives alike. This increased assertion of tax jurisdiction found another expression in the 2008 amendment to the treaty with the United Arab Emirates, where the exemption method was replaced by the credit method.

Sweden allows either a deduction[87] or a credit[88] for foreign income taxes. In the case of a credit, the amount is limited to the Swedish taxes due on all foreign income – an overall or general limitation. The general rule is that qualifying dividends from foreign corporations are exempt from tax. There is also an exemption for foreign employment income if the resident is present outside Sweden for more than six months. With respect to active income (profits arising in a foreign permanent establishment and income from foreign employment) and income from foreign real estate, *The Netherlands* provides for double tax relief in domestic law primarily by the exemption method (effected through a proportional reduction of the tax computed on the basis of the worldwide income)[89] rather than through eliminating the foreign income from the taxable base. This has important consequences in respect of offsetting of foreign losses and preservation of the full effect of a progressive tax rate. In addition, a foreign tax credit is applied with respect to investment income received from certain developing countries, and with respect to income earned by sportsmen and artistes abroad and to profits earned through foreign finance branches in low-tax countries.[90] Dividends received from foreign corporations qualify for the 'participation' exemption on essentially the same terms as dividends from domestic companies, with the additional requirement that the corporation not be subject to tax at a rate of less than 10% of the income as determined under Dutch rules.[91] The taxpayer may also elect to deduct the foreign tax.

The form of double tax relief in *Australia* depends on the type of income. Passive investment-type income is dealt with by a credit system that gives a credit for the foreign (usually withholding) tax.[92] Profits arising from direct activities abroad through a permanent establishment (other than income that would be caught by the CFC regime if a foreign branch were instead a subsidiary) and dividends paid by foreign corporations to 10% or more resident corporate shareholders ('non-portfolio dividends') are exempt from Australian tax. A participation exemption for capital gains on shares in foreign 10% subsidiaries of Australian parent companies was introduced in 2004, as part of an international tax reform that also considerably broadened the existing exemption regimes for resident companies. As a consequence, the previous indirect foreign tax credit for dividends that did not qualify for exemption was removed.[93] Until 2009, foreign employment

87. Sweden, ITA, Ch. 16 ss 18 and 19.
88. Sweden, Foreign Tax Credit Act.
89. Netherlands, Decree Avoidance Double Taxation 2001 (DADT), Art. 10.
90. Netherlands, DADT, Arts 25 and 36–38 (investment income), Arts 13 and 14 (sportsmen, etc.) and Art. 39 (finance branch income).
91. Netherlands, CITA, Art. 13.10.
92. Australia, ITAA, 1997, Div. 770.
93. Australia, ITAA, 1936, s. 23AH, 23AJ, ITAA 1997, Subdiv. 768-G.

income was exempt with progression if the taxpayer was abroad for at least ninety-one days and was subject to tax in the foreign jurisdiction. In 2009, this exemption was limited essentially to employees working on foreign aid and similar projects. In other circumstances, a foreign tax credit is allowed for foreign taxes on foreign employment income.

The *French* system is unique in that, apart from treaties, it does not normally grant relief for double taxation, and foreign taxes are simply deductible from the tax base. There are some important exceptions, however. The principle of territoriality exempts from corporate tax profits arising from a trade or business carried on abroad,[94] and dividends from qualifying foreign subsidiaries are likewise exempt.[95] In addition, it is possible to obtain special permission to file a consolidated tax return including both domestic and foreign operations, in which case foreign taxes are creditable and foreign losses deductible.[96] Around a dozen companies have taken advantage of the election. Wages and/or bonuses for working abroad may be exempt in certain circumstances.[97]

3.1. Issues in the Structure of a Foreign Tax Credit System

3.1.1. Creditable Taxes

All systems that give a credit for foreign taxes paid against the domestic income tax liability must determine which foreign levies will be entitled to credit. Several approaches are possible. One is to list specific foreign taxes that qualify for the credit. Another is to credit foreign taxes that have a general resemblance to the domestic income tax without too much concern for the technical details of the foreign tax law. Finally, it is possible to define the specific characteristics that a foreign tax must have to be creditable as an income tax. In addition, it is common practice in treaties to specify which taxes will qualify for the credit.

Most countries focus on general resemblance. Only the *United States* has detailed regulatory rules setting out the criteria that a foreign income tax must meet. The regulatory structure is based in part on some case law principles developing the concept of an income tax for tax credit purposes. Under the regulatory scheme,[98] the foreign 'levy' must be a tax and not a payment for some kind of economic benefit, and it must be likely to reach net gain in normal circumstances. Taxes imposed by national and sub-national political subdivisions can both qualify for credit.

In determining if the tax is an income tax, the tax must be based on a realization of income, although the regulations permit substantial departures from the

94. France, CGI, s. 209 I.
95. France, CGI, ss 145 and 216.
96. France, CGI, s. 209 *quinquies*.
97. France, CGI, s. 81 A.
98. United States, Treasury Regulations (Treas. Regs.), s. 1.901-2.

realization requirement. The tax also must use gross receipts in the computation of taxable income. Thus, taxes imposed on the basis of artificially 'posted' prices would not qualify. However, a tax based on a likely estimate of gross receipts (e.g., costs plus a reasonable profit mark-up) would qualify. Finally, the tax base must be reduced by reasonable allowances for expenses in order for the foreign tax to fall primarily on net income. Here again, substantial latitude is allowed. A gross-based tax would qualify in circumstances in which it is unlikely that there will be significant expenses and would still leave the taxpayer with a net gain after the payment of the tax. At the other extreme, a subtraction-based consumption tax that allowed a full deduction for what, in an income tax, would be treated as capital expenditures was reportedly determined not to qualify as a creditable tax.

Social-security-type taxes used to fund retirement benefits are generally creditable as long as the payment is not based on age, life expectancy, or other similar characteristics. The payments are not viewed as a charge for a specific economic benefit.

Taxes 'in lieu of' an income tax are also creditable. A gross-based tax such as the withholding tax typically imposed on investment income of non-residents is treated as such a tax as long as it is clear that the tax is substituting for an otherwise generally applicable income tax. No credit is allowed, however, for so-called 'soak-up' taxes – taxes that are imposed only in situations in which they would qualify for the credit in the residence country.

Treaties may expand the category of creditable taxes to cover taxes that would not meet the regulatory definition.

Canada restricts the credit to 'income or profits' taxes, but there is no statutory or regulatory definition and little case law on the question. Certain payments to foreign governments pursuant to oil and gas production sharing agreements are deemed to be income or profits taxes.[99] US social security taxes have been held to be creditable despite the limited tax base and the fact that the payments are loosely tied to specific benefits. Income taxes paid to political subdivisions are also creditable. Soak-up taxes are not creditable, and anti-avoidance rules prevent the creation of foreign tax credits inappropriately.[100]

Sweden similarly limits the credit to 'income taxes' paid to all governmental levels. In addition, credit is allowed for real estate taxes that are similar to the tax Sweden levies on real estate in business and the 'fee' levied on personal dwellings.

The *Australian* rules, which were rewritten with effect from 2008, are somewhat more complex. The statutory definition covers any foreign tax on income, profits, or gains. (Taxes covered by tax treaties are mentioned specifically as being covered.) Under administrative rulings in relation to the former system, which would seem to continue to be applicable, creditable taxes must be imposed on a basis 'substantially equivalent' to the Australian legislation, which includes a net basis tax on income or gains and a final gross basis withholding tax on passive income. The rulings contain now somewhat outdated lists of taxes that

99. Canada, ITA, s. 126(5).
100. Canada, ITA, s. 126(4)–(4.2).

do or do not meet these criteria. Social security taxes generally are not creditable, but credit is given for sub-national income taxes and, since 2008, for supra-national taxes such as EU taxes on EU employees. Special rules exclude credit for unitary taxes, aimed at the taxes of some American states, to the extent that they are not applied on a 'water's edge' basis. In addition, no credit is allowed for a 'soak-up' tax, defined as a tax which would not have been imposed if the taxpayer had not been entitled to credit in Australia.[101]

The *United Kingdom* allows a credit for any tax that 'corresponds' to UK income tax or corporation tax.[102] This limitation has been liberally interpreted, and a tax on 90% of gross receipts has been held by the courts to be creditable.[103] The administrative position is to allow credit for taxes that serve the same function in relation to business profits as an income tax, thus excluding turnover taxes but not necessarily taxes on gross receipts. Taxes paid to sub-national governments are creditable. Social security payments do not qualify.

Germany similarly limits the credit to taxes that are comparable to the German income or corporate tax. The tax authorities have published a detailed list of creditable taxes. Following the recent lowering of the corporate tax rate to 15%, more excess tax credits are showing up for German-based multinational enterprises. As these corporations must pay trade tax to domestic municipalities (at an average of 13%), the problem of crediting foreign income tax against domestic trade tax has become important. So far, German legislation does not allow cross-crediting between different tax categories.

The *Japanese* system has a broad regulatory definition that covers individual and corporate income taxes as well as excess profits taxes, revenue taxes, and distributed earnings taxes. However, social security taxes are not creditable and local income taxes are entitled only to a deduction.

Since the *Dutch* system operates primarily under the exemption method, the issue of creditable taxes is not as significant. While under Dutch domestic law, for the foreign tax to be creditable it must be an income tax, the notion of a creditable income tax has been interpreted quite liberally. The situation is the same in *France*, where the territorial principle controls the taxation of foreign corporate income. Most credits are granted by treaty, which identifies the taxes in question. In the context of elective worldwide consolidation, there is a general definition of creditable tax.[104]

3.1.2. Limitations on the Credit

All systems have limitations on the extent to which foreign tax paid can displace domestic tax liability. While, from a theoretical point of view, an unlimited foreign tax credit is sometimes urged as the structure most consistent with complete capital

101. Australia, ITAA 1997, s. 770-10 and 770-15.
102. United Kingdom, Income and Corporation Taxes Act 1988, s. 790(12).
103. *Yates v. GCA International Ltd* [1991] STC 157.
104. France, CGI, Regulatory schedule II, s. 122.

export neutrality, practical revenue constraints make such a policy impossible. In addition, to the extent that the principal function of the credit is to relieve double taxation on international income, there is no reason to allow the credit to reduce domestic taxes on domestic-source income. Within these broad constraints, however, there is a wide variety in the actual form that a limitation might take. At one extreme, the foreign tax could be traced to a particular item of foreign income and the credit limited to the domestic tax on that item. As an alternative, all foreign income and foreign taxes could be considered together and the credit limited to the corresponding domestic tax. This approach would allow an 'averaging' between high-taxed and low-taxed foreign income and allow the credit in full to the extent that the domestic tax was not exceeded. Any number of intermediate structures are also possible. The credit could be limited to the foreign tax on particular categories of income, such as income from a particular country (a 'per country' limitation) or a particular class or type of income (a 'basket' limitation), or some other similar combination of the two.

The systems here under review all fall somewhere between a per-item and an unlimited overall limitation. In most cases, there are restrictions on the ability to average foreign taxes on active business income and passive income, in particular interest income. For those systems that exempt certain forms of income, averaging possibilities are also limited since the exempt income and the corresponding foreign tax do not enter into the limitation calculations. To some extent, the scope of the limitation is related to the breadth of the definition of creditable taxes.

The *United States*, in part because of its historical role as a capital exporting country, has the most complex and developed set of rules limiting the credit. However, since the system does not exempt any foreign-source business income and, in general terms, allows averaging with respect to such income regardless of the tax rate or source, it may in fact be less restrictive than some of the other systems. Prior to 2007, the United States applied limitations to nine baskets of different types of income.[105] Under the current US approach, a worldwide limitation is applied to two baskets of income – the passive category and the general category.[106] Most active business income falls into the 'general category' basket, and averaging is allowed across businesses and geographical sources. Passive income is placed in a separate basket. If the passive income is itself subject to a tax rate comparable to the US rate, then it is moved to the general basket, thus ensuring that low-taxed passive income cannot be averaged with comparably taxed passive income and will bear some residual US tax. If a foreign corporation is controlled by US persons, rentals, royalties, and interest payments received from it are deemed to be out of the relevant baskets of income determined at the level of the foreign corporation. In addition, dividends from 10% or greater US-owned foreign corporations which bring with them the deemed paid or indirect foreign tax credit (whether or not the foreign corporation is a CFC) are also deemed to be out of

105. United States, IRC, s. 904(d) (prior to amendment).
106. United States, IRC, s. 904(d)(2).

the relevant baskets of income on a pro rata basis. Thus, the character of the foreign corporation's income 'passes through' to the US shareholder.

In *Japan*, the limitation is calculated by multiplying the domestic tax liability by a fraction in which the numerator is the total amount of foreign-source income subject to tax and the denominator is total global taxable income. Two special restrictions, however, were enacted to counteract what was perceived as excess averaging of foreign taxes. First, only one-third of foreign income that is not subject to foreign tax is included in the numerator. Second, the foreign-source income included in the numerator of the fraction cannot exceed 90% of the total income.[107] Income on export sales of inventory is treated as foreign source only if effected through a foreign fixed place of business or in other circumstances that make the income subject to tax in the foreign jurisdiction. Other source rules are the same in general as those applied with respect to the taxation of foreign taxpayers.

In *Canada*, a per-country limit is used as the basic limitation on business income that is not exempt. In addition, a 'basket' limitation for non-business income is also applied on a per-country basis. For individuals, the credit in respect of income from property other than real property is subject to an absolute per-country limitation of 15% of the amount of income sourced in the country. The excess tax can be deducted.[108] The 15% limitation does not apply to real property rental income. The non-business basket is primarily important for reasons of provincial taxation but does have the effect of limiting averaging for federal purposes. While source rules are important to the operation of the Canadian system, they are relatively undeveloped and largely administrative. Foreign taxes are generally attributed to foreign income on a tracing basis.

Germany similarly has a per-country limitation.[109] After 2003, statutory provisions prevent the averaging of taxable and tax-free income within a particular foreign country. While *The Netherlands* tax treaties provide for a per-country limitation, the taxpayer has the right to opt for an overall limitation that applies where relief is granted in the absence of a tax treaty.

The limitation in *Sweden* is a function of the schedular system of taxation. For individuals, business income and employment income are treated together, and capital income is in a separate category in the initial limitation computation. Under that limitation, the tax on each category of income is limited to the Swedish tax on the same category. However, if the foreign tax exceeds the limit in one category because the Swedish tax is lower than the foreign tax, excess taxes in the other category can be used to absorb the additional limitation currently. The foreign source character of the income is determined by its treatment under foreign law. Corporations have only one source of income, so the limitation operates on an overall basis. According to case law, loss in one country is not deducted from positive foreign income in other countries.

107. Japan, ITA, s. 95 and Japan, CTA, s. 69.
108. Canada, ITA, s. 20(11).
109. Germany, ITA, s. 34c para. 1 sent. 1; CITA, s. 26 para. 1.

Australia has a worldwide limitation. It was previously based on four baskets but these were eliminated in 2008; in addition, the application of the limit was removed if taxpayers' total foreign tax is $1,000 or less (i.e., such foreign tax is creditable in full).[110]

Previously, the credit applied only if the income was foreign sourced under Australian tax law. From 2008, foreign source in this sense is no longer relevant for income that has been subject to foreign tax on a basis other than residence. Foreign source is now important only when the calculation of the credit limit includes income that has not been subject to any foreign tax. Australia has few explicit legislative source rules dealing with resident taxpayers. The courts have developed some jurisprudence based on a facts-and-circumstances approach. Some rules are fairly clear. For example, interest is sourced where the funds are made available, which may be the place of the contract or of the advancing of the funds. With respect to treaties, Australia generally includes a source rule in its treaties based on whether a country has a taxing right over the income on a basis other than residence. The treaties usually provide that the source rule applies as well for the purpose of Australian domestic tax law, and so can change the source that otherwise would arise under domestic tax law. The limitation on the foreign tax credit was previously calculated using the average rate of Australian tax on the taxpayer's income. Now the foreign income is effectively treated as the top slice of income in determining the amount of Australian tax on the income, which is more generous for individuals subject to a progressive income tax rate scale.

The *United Kingdom* limitation is, in principle, quite restrictive. Direct credit relief is given on a source-by-source basis, and unused credits cannot be used against the UK tax on other income or carried forward, although excess credits can be deducted in some cases. The strictness of this limitation, however, can be avoided by using a non-resident holding company through which foreign income can be routed. There are no 'pass-through' rules, and the income from the intermediate foreign 'mixer' company is considered to be from one source, allowing a credit for all associated taxes. The use of a 'mixer' company to achieve an averaging of high and low foreign tax rates is a common practice, although some restrictions on the use of such companies were imposed in 2001 (discussed below). As a further result of the 2001 changes, the indirect credit is no longer calculated on a source-by-source (dividend-by-dividend) basis. Dividends from related companies are pooled for purposes of calculating the indirect credit limitation. Dividends from unrelated companies are separately pooled. Dividends from CFCs are separately quarantined.[111] From 2009, these rules will cease to be relevant for UK companies due to the exemption for dividends from foreign corporations.

110. Australia, ITAA 1997, s. 770–75.

111. United Kingdom, Income and Corporation Taxes Act 1988, ss 797, 806A–806J.

3.1.3. Allocation of Expenses to Foreign-Source Income

A crucial element in the determination of the credit limitation is the foreign-source *taxable* income of the taxpayer in the various categories to which the limitations apply. To determine this amount, deductions must be allocated to the appropriate types of positive income (or establish a negative amount in a particular category). Despite the centrality of this issue in applying foreign tax credit limitations, only the United States has any fully developed rules in this area. In other countries, the rules are quite general and leave much to taxpayer choice. To some extent, the rules are influenced by financial accounting practice and generally accepted accounting principles.

Since 1977, the *United States* has had detailed administrative rules dealing with the allocation of expenses between foreign-source and domestic-source income.[112] Under the regulations, deductions are first allocated to general classes of income based on the 'factual relationship' between the income and the expense. Deductions allocated to a particular class may exceed the positive income in the class in a given year. Deductions that are not definitely related to a class of income are ratably allocated to all gross income, but the specificity of the rules leaves little scope for gross-to-gross allocation. Once allocated to a class of gross income, deductions are then apportioned to the relevant categories of income, in this case foreign-source and domestic-source. The regulations deal with the factors to be considered in the apportionment and include units sold, gross receipts, cost of goods sold, and the like. Special rules are applied to interest and to research and development costs.

In the case of interest, the interest cost is apportioned on an asset method based on the tax cost of assets generating foreign-source and domestic-source income.[113] The tax basis of stock in foreign corporations is adjusted to reflect retained earnings or deficits in earnings, thus in effect accounting for the current operations of the foreign corporations. The taxpayer can elect to use market values to allocate the interest expense among assets if those values can be adequately established.

This method is based on a 'fungibility' approach and assumes that borrowing costs relate to all productive assets. However, a special rule requires the allocation of interest expense directly to foreign-source income if there is 'excess' borrowing in the United States that has been loaned to foreign subsidiaries. A portion of the domestic interest expense is in effect treated as if it had been incurred abroad in a related subsidiary and was thus directly allocable to foreign-source income.[114]

In the case of a domestic consolidated group of companies, interest expense and associated income must be computed on a consolidated basis. Prior to a

112. United States, Treas. Regs., s. 1.861-8.
113. United States, Treas. Regs., s. 1.861-9T-13T.
114. United States, Treas. Regs., s, 1.861-10T. An elective method of allocation that takes into account interest expense of foreign affiliates can also be available. Unites States, IRC, s. 864(f)(1).

statutory change, it was common practice to isolate interest expense in members of a consolidated group that did not have significant foreign-source income.[115]

The approach to research and development costs has been constantly changed since the introduction of the 1977 regulations. Under the original regulations, the research costs were first allocated to the appropriate product categories in broad classifications. Amounts within those categories were then apportioned to different sources of income based, in part, on where the research was performed and in part on the relative amounts of sales or gross income, with appropriate adjustments in royalties and other similar payments, to arrive at amounts comparable to sales figures. Legislative changes suspended the application of the rules for several years and replaced them with a provision allocating all research expenses incurred in the United States to US-source income.

Regulations enacted in 1995 adopt the same general approach as the 1977 regulations but are more generous in reducing the amount of research expenses apportioned to foreign-source income. Under the sales method of apportionment, 50% of the research expenses are assigned to the place of performance and the remaining expenses are apportioned based on the relative amount of domestic and foreign sales. Under the gross income method of apportionment, 25% of the research expenses are assigned to the place of performance and the remaining expenses are apportioned based on relative gross incomes.[116]

In *Canada*, interest and other expenses are ordinarily allocated to foreign-source income on a factual tracing basis. This approach allows taxpayers to plan their affairs to 'stream' their borrowings to Canadian assets or Canadian income to maximize foreign tax credits. If tracing is impossible, the Canada Revenue Agency (CRA) permits expenses to be allocated in accordance with a reasonable formula based on asset values or gross income. There are no specific statutory rules or case law dealing with the allocation of expenses to foreign-source income. In addition, the CRA's administrative positions are very general.

In *Australia*, expenses must be allocated in a manner that is reasonable, although there is little guidance in the published material. Since 2001, interest expense receives special treatment as a result of a new thin capitalization regime, which is outlined below in Subpart B, section 1.3 in relation to source taxation.

The *Japanese* system provides in its regulations that expenses are to be allocated on a 'rational' basis, with substantial taxpayer choice. The regulations give as examples allocation based on income, capital investment, or workforce size.

In *Sweden*, there are no statutory rules dealing with expense allocation, although it is clear that the foreign tax credit limitations must be applied on a net basis. Some principles developed in the context of allocation between domestic and foreign branches may have some application but, in general, the area is undeveloped.

Historically, the *United Kingdom* had few rules in this area. The domestic law simply referred to the relevant foreign income, and this was viewed as largely a

115. United States, IRC, s. 864(e)(1).

116. United States, Treas. Regs. s. 1.861-17.

reference to the domestic schedular system. Trading income caused a problem, and the tax administration lost a case in which an insurance company successfully argued that the limitation on the foreign tax credit was calculated by reference to its whole trading profits (including UK profits) and not just that part of the profits pertaining to the foreign income.[117] As a result, in 2005 the concept of 'relevant income' was narrowed for the purposes of calculating the limitation on the credit where foreign income is earned as part of a trade.[118] For the purpose of calculating the limitation, the relevant income is such income 'accruing out of the transaction, arrangement or asset in connection with which the credit for foreign tax arises'. That income is to be reduced by any deductible expenses directly relating to it and by a 'reasonable apportionment' of indirect expenses (e.g., general overheads) relating to the income.

In *Germany*, case law principles require that 'directly or indirectly connected' expenses be attributed to foreign-source income under a tracing approach. There is no allocation of general expenses. In the case of foreign tax-free dividends, German tax law follows the Parent-Subsidiary Directive, which enables Member States of the EU to introduce a general rule that 5% of the dividends are deemed to constitute non-deductible expenses.[119]

In *The Netherlands* the foreign tax credit limitation under tax treaties is computed on the basis of a full allocation of expenses (i.e., both the directly attributable expenses and a proportional share of the general expenses). In the absence of a treaty, the unilateral relief rules allow attribution of only the directly allocable costs to royalties (but require full allocation where other items of income are concerned).

With respect to foreign tax-free dividends, *France* has for a long time applied the rule, which was adopted in the Parent-Subsidiary Directive, according to which 5% of the dividends (plus foreign tax credit, if any) are deemed to be referable to non-deductible expenses. Such percentage cannot, however, exceed the total of expenses of all kinds incurred by the corporation during the tax year in question.[120]

3.1.4. Treatment of Losses in the Credit Computation

Where the expenses in a particular credit category exceed the income, the resulting loss may have an impact on the remaining credit calculations. Several situations must be distinguished. First, if expenses allocated to a given foreign income category exceed the income, the excess could be (a) allocated to domestic income, thus not affecting the other credit calculations; (b) allocated on some basis to the other foreign income baskets only, potentially reducing the amount of credit available in those baskets; or (c) allocated pro rata to foreign as well as domestic

117. *Legal & General Assurance Society Ltd v. Revenue and Customs Commissioners* [2006] EWHC 1770.
118. United Kingdom, Income and Corporation Taxes Act 1988, s. 798A.
119. Germany, CITA, s. 8b para. 5.
120. France, CGI, s. 216.

income, having a more limited effect on the credit calculation. Second, assuming that some allocation rule has been established, an ancillary principle must determine what, if any, effect a later positive amount in a basket whose loss had been allocated to other baskets (or to domestic-source income) will have. Finally, if the overall results are negative, so there is an overall net operating loss that may be carried forward, rules must be provided to deal with the effect of the carryover on the credit computation in later years. The systems here under consideration have taken a variety of approaches. Where active business income is exempt when subject to significant foreign taxation, the issues are generally not of great significance because the credit will be applied in respect of categories of foreign income in which losses are unlikely.

Again, the *United States* has the most complex rules for dealing with losses.[121] The complexity is traceable to the prior extensive use of the basket system and the policy decision that foreign losses in a particular basket should not be allowed to reduce domestic-source income in any situation in which there is positive foreign-source income in another basket. Thus, foreign losses in one basket must first reduce proportionally foreign income in the other baskets, with any excess reducing US-source income. When foreign income is subsequently generated in the basket that initially incurred the loss, that income is re-characterized for basket purposes in the same fashion in which the loss was used. However, any foreign taxes imposed on the income are not reattributed to the other basket. If the foreign loss exceeds foreign-source income and reduces US income, so that the taxpayer experiences an 'overall' foreign loss, subsequently arising foreign-source income is recharacterized as US-source income for credit limitation purposes. Similarly, in the reverse situation, where domestic losses reduce foreign income, subsequently arising domestic-source income is re-characterized as foreign-source income.

Until 2008, the *Australian* rule for losses was the strictest. If the deductions allocated to foreign-source income exceeded the income, the loss could not be used against domestic-source income in the current year but was carried forward indefinitely for use against future foreign income. In 2008, this limitation was abolished, and foreign losses can now offset domestic-source income; previously quarantined foreign losses may be similarly used, but with transitional limits in the first four years of the new regime. Special rules apply with respect to interest.[122]

In *Canada*, the limitation is calculated on a country-by-country basis and, in general, losses in one foreign jurisdiction do not affect the credit calculation for other jurisdictions but reduce domestic-source income. Domestic income that arises subsequently is not re-characterized as foreign income for credit purposes. Where domestic losses exceed domestic income and reduce foreign-source income, the credit will be limited to the amount of Canadian tax payable. An overall net operating loss for a year does not have any impact on the foreign tax credit calculations for subsequent years except to the extent that the amount of

121. United States, IRC, s. 904(f).
122. Australia, ITAA 1997, ss 770–75(4).

foreign or Canadian tax payable in those subsequent years is reduced as a result of the loss carryforward.

In principle, the *United Kingdom* source approach does not take losses from other sources into account. However, where foreign activities are part of a domestic trade, the 'source' is the whole trade, with the result that a loss on the foreign activities reduces profits of the trade and so indirectly any profits from the domestic activities.[123] Foreign tax credits are calculated on income 'arising' in a foreign country from the trade.[124] If the foreign activities create an overall loss for the trade, that loss may be used in the same manner as any other loss from a UK trade – that is, against profits from any other source for the current year (with a one-year carryback) and carried forward against profits of that trade, including domestic profits.[125] Because in this common scenario the foreign tax credit limitation is calculated separately from the charge on the profits of the trade, the use of any loss has no impact on the future calculation of foreign tax credits.

Germany, in applying its per-country limitation, does not reduce the positive income from one country with losses incurred in another country. On the other hand, when several different types of income are earned in one country, gains and losses are combined. Moreover, as far as worldwide income taxation applies, in principle, foreign losses reduce domestic or other income in the final calculation of a taxpayer's income. To limit the deductibility of certain foreign losses (arising principally in passive activities likely to create tax shelters), these losses can be deducted only from income from the same source in the same country.[126] For source countries located within the EU/EEA, recent tax legislation has abolished this limitation on loss relief following an ECJ judgment on foreign participations.[127] Those losses do not affect the credit calculation with respect to other income arising in the same country. An overall foreign loss that reduces domestic-source income has no effect on the calculation of the credit in subsequent years.

The question of losses in the *Japanese* system is of relatively minor significance because the overall limitation is used and there is no problem of the allocation of losses among income baskets. Where foreign losses reduce domestic income, there is no provision for later re-characterization of foreign income as domestic.

3.1.5. Carryover of Excess Credits or Limitation

Where limitations on the credit are applicable and excess foreign tax credits are generated, all systems must deal with the structural question of how such excess credits should be treated. Strict adherence to annual accounting principles would

123. United Kingdom, Corporation Tax Act 2009, s. 35.
124. United Kingdom, Income and Corporation Taxes Act 1988, s. 790(4).
125. United Kingdom, Income and Corporation Taxes Act 1988, ss 393 and 393A.
126. Germany, ITA, s. 2a.
127. ECJ, 29 Mar. 2007, C-347/07 (*Rewe Zentralfinanz*).

require each computation to be made on an annual basis, and if credits could not be used in the years in which the foreign taxes were incurred, they would be lost. The most appealing case for some kind of relief from strict annual accounting is where the inclusion of the foreign income in the domestic system differs from the inclusion in the foreign system because of differences in accounting rules. Here, the timing rules can cause the foreign tax and the corresponding domestic tax on the same income to fall in different accounting periods. Other timing differences can arise because of differences in the principles governing the allowance of deductions and the recognition of income. Beyond timing issues, a broader policy question is the extent to which temporal averaging between high- and low-taxed foreign-source income should be allowed as a general matter.

Assuming that some type of temporal averaging is desirable, the question with respect to technical structure is whether the excess taxes themselves should be carried to other periods in which there is an 'excess limitation' or whether the excess limitation should be allowed in the year the taxes were incurred. Most of the systems use the tax carryover method and allow varying degrees of temporal averaging. The structure of the rules is generally the same, although the (essentially arbitrary) periods of carryover differ. The carryover periods may sometimes relate to statute of limitations periods.

In the *United States*, excess credits can be carried back one year and forward ten years, subject to the availability of excess limitation in the appropriate basket.[128]

In *Canada*, excess foreign business taxes can be carried back for three years and forward for ten years.[129] No carryforward is allowed for excess taxes arising in connection with non-business income, but the excess can be deducted in the year incurred.

In the context of the overall limitation system in *Japan*, excess credits can be carried forward three years. In addition, any excess limitation from the preceding three years can be carried forward, and excess credits can be absorbed in the current year to that extent.[130] Any remaining excess credit is then carried forward.

Sweden similarly allows a four-year carryforward, but no carryback.

Australia previously allowed a five-year carryforward of excess credits, but this was abolished in the simplification of the regime in 2008 as a counterbalance to the removal of the previous four baskets, with transitional relief for excess foreign tax credits of the previous five years. Under the current worldwide limitation, no carryover of excess credits is permitted. Timing differences are dealt with by moving the foreign tax for credit purposes to the year in which Australia taxed the equivalent income, even if the foreign tax is paid in a different (earlier or later) year.[131] The permitted period for amendment of the credit calculation is four years from the date of payment of the foreign tax, rather than from the year for which the

128. United States, IRC, s. 904(c).
129. Canada, ITA, s. 126(2).
130. Japan, ITA, s. 95, para. 2 and Japan, CTA, s. 69, para. 2.
131. Australia, ITAA 1997, s. 770-10, Note 1.

credit is claimed, so that foreign tax paid later can be credited even if the payment is made many years later.

In *The Netherlands*, an unlimited carryforward applies. In contrast, no carryover at all is allowed in the *United Kingdom* direct foreign tax credit system. However, since 2001 excess credits attributable to a foreign permanent establishment of a UK-resident company may be carried back three years and forward indefinitely.[132] *Germany* also has a restrictive system, not allowing any carryforward or carryback for excess credits. As a partial response to the problem, the taxpayer can elect (on a country-by-country basis) to deduct rather than credit the foreign taxes.

3.1.6. Indirect Credit for Foreign Taxes Paid by Foreign Subsidiaries

In all of the systems, there is some mechanism for eliminating or reducing multiple burdens of corporate-level tax when corporate profits are distributed by domestic corporations to domestic corporate shareholders. Similarly, all of the systems have some form of relief when the distributing corporation is a foreign corporation. This relief can be seen as performing two functions. First, as in the domestic context, it avoids a cascading of corporate-level taxes. At the same time, it relieves the potential international double taxation that would result from the taxation of the profits in the state where they are earned as well as in the state of the residence of the shareholder. This latter effect also makes more comparable the treatment of foreign operations carried out through foreign branches and foreign subsidiaries.

Several of the countries here considered deal with this problem generally by exempting most intercorporate dividends from the tax base. *Canada, France*, and *Sweden* use or have used an indirect credit system in some situations, but the exemption of foreign corporate dividends is much more common in practice. In *Germany*, the complete abolition of taxes on dividends from domestic or foreign companies has rendered the application of an indirect tax credit superfluous and so it has been repealed. Similarly, when *Australia, Japan*, and the *United Kingdom* adopted an exemption system for dividends received by a resident company, the indirect credit was eliminated. *The Netherlands* uses an exemption method exclusively. The issues the exemption system raises will be considered below.

3.1.6.1. Share Ownership Requirements

As is usually the case in the relief from domestic multiple taxation, all of the systems require some minimum level of shareholding before an 'indirect' foreign tax credit will be given for foreign taxes paid by the distributing corporation. The requirements are based in part on considerations of administrative simplicity and in part on the more basic notion that the function of the credit is to relieve

132. United Kingdom, Income and Corporation Taxes Act 1988, s. 806L.

international double taxation on 'direct' foreign investment rather than on portfolio investment.

The basic requirement in the *United States* is that the US corporate shareholder own directly a 10% or greater interest in the voting stock of the distributing foreign corporation.[133] To the extent that the *United Kingdom* continues to apply an indirect foreign tax credit system (most dividends from foreign subsidiaries are exempt from 2009), it also has a 10% voting stock threshold,[134] and *Australia* had a similar requirement until the repeal of the indirect credit in 2004. The *Canadian* test is more liberal, allowing the credit where a 10% or greater interest in any class of shares is present and is held directly or indirectly. Moreover, the ownership threshold is determined merely by reference to the number of shares of the class owned by the Canadian corporation, not by reference to votes or value. *Japan* had required 25% ownership of an equity interest in the foreign corporation to be eligible for the indirect tax credit. This 25% requirement has been maintained for the newly introduced exemption system.

3.1.6.2. Tier Limitations

The problem of multiple layers of corporate tax also exists if the first-tier foreign corporation itself receives distributions from lower-tier corporations. *Canada* allows the credit without restriction as to the corporate tier at which the tax was paid, as long as the ultimate domestic shareholder owns, directly or indirectly, the requisite 10% stock interest. Similarly, under the *United Kingdom* and the former *Australian* systems, indirect credits were available with no limits on the number of tiers.[135]

The *United States* rules are more restrictive. The credit extends only for six tiers. At each level there must be at least a 10% voting stock interest held by the higher-tier corporation and an indirect 5% interest by the ultimate domestic parent; for tiers below the third tier, the foreign corporation must be a controlled corporation.[136] The tier limits are viewed as a matter of administrative convenience. The former *Japanese* indirect credit was limited to two tiers and required a 25% shareholding at each tier.

3.1.6.3. Computation of the Indirect Credit

The computation of the indirect credit involves several structural issues. The profits distributions must be related to particular profits of the foreign corporation, and foreign taxes must be attributed to the profits distributions. In addition, since the income inclusion of the actual dividend distribution brings with it the

133. United States, IRC, s. 902(a).
134. United Kingdom, Income and Corporation Taxes Act 1988, s. 790(6).
135. United Kingdom, Income and Corporation Taxes Act 1988, s. 801.
136. United States, IRC, s. 904(b)(2).

indirect credit, the amount of the dividend should in principle be 'grossed up' so that the foreign tax itself is included in the domestic tax base.

In the *United States*, profits and associated taxes were initially computed on an annual, last-in, first-out basis. That approach encouraged tax planning to artificially increase taxes from which distributions were made and also created technical difficulties where years with deficits in earnings occurred. In 1986, the system was replaced with a 'cumulative pooling' approach, which pools all earnings and foreign taxes (on a prospective basis) and treats all distributions as bringing back the appropriate portion of the total pool.[137] Indirect credits are 'grossed up' in the computation of the domestic parent's income.[138]

The *Canadian* system is complicated by the fact that profits distributions from 'taxable surplus' bring with them the functional equivalent of a credit, and distributions from 'exempt surplus' are exempt. In general, foreign taxes are allocated between the two categories on a 'reasonable in the circumstances' basis. Distributions are deemed to be first out of the 'pool' of exempt surplus and thereafter out of taxable surplus, where the calculation of the credit-equivalent deduction is made.

3.1.7. Interaction between Indirect Credit and Limitation System

Where the ability to average is limited by some kind of basket system, that limitation must be coordinated with the indirect credit. 'Passing through' the various basket limitations is necessarily complex and is a function of the underlying complexity of the basket system itself. It involves both the treatment of profits distributions in the form of dividends and also deductible payments, such as interest and royalties, which can be viewed as being paid 'out of' the various basket categories.

The problem is most acute in the *United States* because of the extensive use of the credit system and the complex basket structure in its limitation rules, although the complexity has been reduced as a result of the move to only two baskets. In general terms, dividends from a foreign corporation are deemed for foreign tax credit purposes to be out of the appropriate baskets of earnings of the foreign corporation on a pro rata basis regardless of whether or not the foreign corporation is controlled by US persons.[139] In the case of a foreign corporation controlled by US persons, interest, rents, or royalty payments are allocated to the category of income from which they are deemed to be paid under the usual deduction allocation rules and take their character for basket purposes based on that allocation. Interest payments are allocated first to any passive income of the foreign corporation and then allocated to the remaining basket. Complex ordering rules determine which payments are deemed to be made first.[140] The result of these rules

137. United States, IRC, s. 904(c).
138. United States, IRC, s. 78.
139. United States, IRC, s. 904(d)(4).
140. United States, IRC, s. 904(d)(3).

is that income which has borne little or no foreign tax can be put into the overall basket and can be used to 'average down' the effective foreign tax rate for credit purposes.

In *Canada*, while a distinction is made between distributions out of exempt surplus and taxable surplus, no attempt is made to pass through the normal per-country limitation in the case of taxable dividends that qualify for the indirect credit. Thus, it is possible for high and low foreign taxes to be averaged. However, the effective credit is limited on an overall basis with respect to the foreign affiliate paying the dividend to the amount of Canadian tax on the dividend.

3.2. Issues in the Structure of an Exemption for Foreign Income

3.2.1. Structure of the Exemption

Where foreign income of a resident taxpayer is exempted from tax, the structure of the exemption can take several forms. The most extensive is to exclude the income from the coverage of the tax system altogether simply by not asserting jurisdiction to tax the income. Thus, for example, in *France*, the tax base for resident corporations in the case of business income is limited to income arising in France; business income attributable to a foreign trade or business is not in principle subject to tax. Alternatively, as in *Canada*, the foreign income can be included for certain purposes although ultimately relieved from tax liability. One approach ('exemption with progression') is to calculate the tax liability that would have resulted if the income had been included and then apply the resulting rate of tax only to the included income. This is the approach taken, for example, in *Germany*, when foreign income of a resident individual is exempt under a tax treaty. Another approach is to 'stack' the excluded income in the lower progressive rates in calculating the rates applicable to the taxable income. This approach has been used in the past in the *United States* and *Australia* in connection with the exemption for foreign-earned income.

3.2.2. Classes of Exempt Income

As indicated above, none of the systems exempts all foreign-source income of resident taxpayers. Thus, rules must be provided to classify exempt foreign income and includable income, with a credit for foreign taxes typically given in the latter case. The distinction is usually between active income such as business income, either earned directly in a foreign branch or as a dividend from a qualifying foreign subsidiary, and portfolio income in the form of interest, royalties, and other passive income. Sometimes there is a requirement that the exempt income be either actually or, in principle, subject to tax in the foreign jurisdiction. In other cases, the exemption is restricted to income from certain countries (e.g., those with which the domestic country has a tax treaty).

Thus, in *Canada*, which generally uses a foreign tax credit system, exemption is provided for dividends received out of the 'exempt surplus' of foreign subsidiaries ('foreign affiliates') in which the Canadian corporate shareholder holds a 10% or greater stock interest.[141] Exempt surplus is defined as active business income earned in countries with which Canada has a tax treaty or tax information exchange agreement, along with certain capital gains. The definition of active business income is quite complex and excludes certain real estate rental, licensing, financing, and investment businesses.[142] Pass-through rules apply that treat certain interest, royalties, and other deductible payments made out of the active business of one foreign affiliate to another as active business income to the recipient. In addition, dividends received by one foreign affiliate from another are added either to exempt surplus or taxable surplus, depending on from which surplus account of the payer the dividend is paid. An exemption is also provided for a limited amount of foreign employment income earned in qualifying activities and for certain income from offshore banking centers.[143]

The *French* system exempts all income derived by French corporations from a trade or business carried on abroad, including passive income effectively connected to the trade or business. The level of activities qualifying as a trade or business is roughly equivalent to the treaty concept of permanent establishment.[144] In addition, an exclusion is granted for intercorporate dividends received from foreign subsidiary corporations on the same conditions as for investments in the domestic context – that is, in general if there is a 5% or greater stock interest.[145] In both cases, the exemption is available whether or not any foreign tax is paid abroad.

As for individuals, bonuses and special payments for working abroad are generally exempt (with progression). In general, wages for working abroad are granted the same exemption if they bear a foreign income tax equal to two-thirds of the French tax otherwise due or if earned by workers involved in foreign construction, extraction, or commercial canvassing activities.[146]

In contrast, *Sweden* limits its exemption to dividends received from foreign corporations that are similar to Swedish limited corporations or cooperative associations in circumstances where the dividend would have been exempt under the domestic intercorporate dividends regime. An exemption is also given to foreign source employment income if the Swedish resident is abroad for six months and the income is subject to tax in the foreign country.

Australia also exempts foreign business income of corporations. The exemption extends to profits and capital gains earned directly in branch form (unless the income would be taxed under the CFC regime if the foreign branch were a CFC) or

141. Canada, ITA, s. 113(1)(a).
142. Canada, ITA, s. 95(1). The same definitions that apply for purposes of the controlled foreign corporation rules also apply for purposes of the dividend exemption.
143. Canada, ITA, ss 122.3 and 33.1.
144. France, CGI, s. 209 I.
145. France, CGI, ss 145 and 216.
146. France, CGI, s. 81 A.

dividends received by Australian corporate shareholders from non-portfolio (10% or greater voting interest) foreign investments.[147] In the case of foreign companies, as opposed to branches, the CFC regime can apply if its threshold tests are satisfied, thus subjecting the income to current taxation in the hands of shareholders, whereas for branches such income is taxed directly to the company on a similar basis. If income is taxed under the CFC regime, it qualifies for a different exemption when distributed as dividends, whether or not it would meet the requirements of the general dividend exemption. The main difference is that any withholding tax on such dividends is creditable under the foreign tax credit, which is not the case for dividend withholding tax on dividends that qualify for the general exemption.[148] The theory underlying this different treatment is that the exemption for dividends out of previously taxed CFC income is to remove double counting of the income; through a combination of the CFC regime and special dividend exemption, effectively all the income is taxed, with credit for both corporate and dividend withholding tax. A number of these rules are being reconsidered as part of the current reform of the Australian CFC and related rules, discussed below.

Foreign employment income also qualified for exemption up to 2009 if the Australian resident was abroad for three months and the income was subject to tax (with some exceptions) in the foreign jurisdiction. An 'exemption with progression' feature affects the taxation of other income based on average rates. From 2009 this exemption is limited to employees working on foreign aid and similar projects.[149]

The *Dutch* system is structured somewhat differently and is not formally an exemption system, although in operation it has that result. Rather than technically exempting foreign income, initially, all income, both taxable and exempt, is included in the tax base and the tax calculated. The tax is then reduced by the percentage of the tax that the income qualifying for exemption is of the total income.

The exemption under domestic law applies to foreign income that is derived directly as business income from a foreign permanent establishment, income from real property, and income from employment abroad if the income is 'subject to tax' under an income tax in a foreign jurisdiction.[150] The latter requirement has been interpreted as requiring only that the income be 'objectively' subject to tax; whether the particular taxpayer effectively pays tax on the income is not relevant.[151] In the case of employment income, the requirement is deemed to be met if the taxpayer is employed by a Dutch company and is employed abroad for a period of at least three months,[152] while in respect of employment abroad for less than thirty consecutive days a stricter requirement applies: the income must have

147. Australia, ITAA 1936, ss 23AH, 23AJ, ITAA 1997, Subdiv. 768-G.
148. Australia, ITAA 1936, s. 23AI, ITAA 1997, s. 770-10(2).
149. Australia, ITAA 1936, s. 23AG.
150. Netherlands, DADT, Art. 9.1.
151. Netherlands, see e.g., *Hof's-Gravenhage*, 13 Nov. 1995, no. 94/0888, V-N 1996, 2876.
152. Netherlands, GAT, Art. 38.2.

been taxed effectively in the foreign country.[153] Under tax treaties, no 'subject-to-tax' requirement applies.

The most important part of the Dutch exemption system is the extension of the domestic participation exemption to investments in foreign corporations. Dividends received by a 5% or greater domestic corporate shareholder from a foreign corporation will be exempt from tax (completely and not proportionately) if the shares are not held as a 'portfolio' investment, which requires some connection with the business of the domestic company but includes acting as a holding or coordinating company. (The 'no portfolio investment' requirement does not apply with respect to EU subsidiaries.) In addition, the foreign corporation must be subject to a national foreign profits tax.

Because foreign participation dividends are exempt, no credit as such is given for foreign withholding taxes imposed on foreign dividends. However, if certain conditions are met, a portion of the withholding tax on the 'inbound' dividend is allowed to reduce the tax which the Dutch company must remit on the payment of 'outbound' dividends.

While the *German* domestic system utilizes a foreign tax credit mechanism for unilateral relief, German tax treaties provide exemption for income that arises in a foreign permanent establishment and for dividends from foreign subsidiaries. Even in treaties, however, exemption is generally not provided for investment or portfolio income, employment income, or real estate income.

The circumstances in which exemption is available vary substantially, with earlier treaties being less restrictive and newer ones typically restricting exemption to income from an active business or income that is subject to tax in the foreign jurisdiction. Foreign dividends are tax-free by virtue of a domestic statute. The only case in which income from foreign subsidiaries is subject to tax is where the CFC rules apply. As mentioned above, a recently enacted provision of the Income Tax Act functions as a 'catch-all' switchover clause for exempted income that is not taxed in the other country due to a conflict in characterization or special rules in the source country.

The *United States* provides a limited exemption for foreign-earned income when the recipient is a foreign resident or is abroad for a substantial portion of the tax year.[154] The exemption is limited to $80,000, adjusted for inflation after 2004 ($87,600 in 2008) and does not involve 'exemption with progression'; the exempt income reduces the applicable tax rate on the other items of taxable income.

The *United Kingdom* predominantly uses the foreign tax credit system. However, as noted above, from 2009 there is a broad exemption for UK corporations in receipt of dividends from foreign corporations. This exemption extends to all dividends; it is not restricted to non-portfolio dividends, as in most of the other countries.[155]

153. Netherlands, DADT, Art. 9.4.
154. United States, IRC, s. 911.
155. For example, see proposed United Kingdom Corporation Tax Act 2009, s. 931D.

As discussed above, in 2009 *Japan*, which until then had relied solely on a tax credit system, introduced an exemption system for certain foreign dividends, replacing the indirect credit system. The exemption applies to dividends from a foreign company in which a Japanese company holds 25% or more of the equity ownership.[156]

3.2.3. Allocation of Deductions to Tax-Exempt Income

Where an exemption system is used to relieve international double taxation, in principle the exemption should extend only to net foreign income. Accordingly, deductions related to the exempt foreign-source income should not be deductible against taxable domestic or foreign-source income. The issue of allocation of deductions to exempt income is functionally the same as the allocation of deductions to foreign-source income for limitation purposes in a credit system. Until recently, many of the countries ignored the issue or restricted the deduction of interest on a tracing basis, making it relatively easy to avoid the allocation of interest expense to exempt income. Recently, however, some countries have become very concerned about the issue, especially the deduction of interest expense to earn exempt foreign income such as dividends.

Thus, in *Canada*, although expenses incurred to earn exempt income are not deductible as a general principle, there are no specific rules for allocation of deductions to exempt income and, in general, a tracing approach is used. The deduction of interest expense by Canadian companies in relation to exempt dividends received from foreign affiliates is not prohibited because dividends are expressly excluded from the definition of exempt income. The deduction of such interest expense is recognized as a problem by critics of the present system but is justified as important with respect to the international competitiveness of Canadian companies. A recent Advisory Panel recommended that Canada should not adopt any restrictions on the deduction of interest, even though at the same time it recommended that the exemption for foreign dividends be broadened.

While *Sweden* has a relatively sophisticated mechanism for allocating interest expenses of individuals between business and capital income, the rules in the international area are quite rudimentary.[157] *The Netherlands*, too, has no specific rules on the general allocation of deductions to exempt branch or participation income, although under the case law some sort of tracing approach is taken. For participation income, however, there is a specific rule with respect to interest paid on acquisition debt. The interest expense is not deductible unless bona fide commercial reasons apply or the parent is effectively taxed (i.e., not reduced by existing or foreseeable loss carryovers, foreign tax credits, etc.) at a rate of 10% (and the tax inspector cannot demonstrate that the debt or the underlying

156. Japan, CTA, s. 23-2.
157. See the discussion of the Swedish restrictions on the deduction of interest in s. 4 'Limitations on Base Eroding Payments to Non-residents' below.

commercial transaction was not predominantly entered into for valid business reasons).

Australia uses allocation rules for exempt income similar to those used in the context of the foreign tax credit limitation discussed above. Expenses allocable exclusively to exempt foreign income are non-deductible in their entirety. Expenses allocable to both foreign and domestic income may be allocated under case law in a manner that is reasonable. Deductions allocable to no particular income, such as charitable donations, are not prorated. Interest expense used to be allocated on a tracing basis generally, and this is still the case for the exempt income of a foreign branch of an Australian-resident company. From 2001, interest is deductible even if it relates to exempt foreign dividend income on a tracing basis as long as the interest does not fall foul of the new outbound thin capitalization regime, outlined below, in relation to source taxation.[158]

In *Germany*, deductions related to foreign-source income that qualifies for an exemption are disallowed under the general statutory provision that treats the issue of expenses and tax-exempt income generally. The statute requires that the expenses be incurred in 'direct economic connection' with the income, and the provision has been quite restrictively interpreted. In the case of expenses in connection with participation dividends that are exempt under treaties, the provision has generally been interpreted to apply only to the extent that dividends are received in the year the expense is incurred. Thus, where a foreign stock investment is debt-financed, the interest expense incurred in connection with the investment has been held to be deductible in full if no dividends are paid in the current year. Following the EC Parent Subsidiary Directive, recent statutory law has introduced the rule that 5% of a foreign dividend is deemed to represent non-deductible expenses. The remaining amount actually incurred, however, is in principle fully deductible.[159] Nevertheless, it should be borne in mind that additional limitations can arise out of the newly introduced general rules on deductibility of interest payments in the context of 'base erosion'.[160]

France has no statutory rules with respect to allocation of expenses, but under general principles treats expenses directly related to exempt foreign income as non-deductible while allocating expenses that relate to both taxable and tax-exempt income. However, interest related to exempt intercorporate dividends from foreign corporations remains deductible. The allocation of expenses to exempt branch income follows in general the approach taken in the Organisation for Economic Co-operation and Development (OECD) Model Convention article dealing with business profits.

In the *United Kingdom*, expenses continue to be deductible for corporations even when, after 2009, they receive exempt foreign dividends. The only substantial limitation is general; the deductibility of interest incurred by a UK corporation is

158. Australia, ITAA 1997, ss 25–90.
159. Germany, CITA, s. 8b para. 5.
160. See below s. 4 'Limitations on Base Eroding Payments to Non-residents'.

limited to the total amount of interest incurred by the corporation's worldwide group on borrowings from non-related parties.[161]

3.2.4. Treatment of Foreign Losses

The treatment of foreign losses – that is, the excess of deductions allocated to foreign income over gross foreign income – also raises some special problems. In principle, the overall foreign loss arising in a situation that would be entitled to exemption should not reduce otherwise taxable domestic or foreign-source income. The exemption is for the net foreign income, and the existence of a foreign loss simply indicates that there is no net income to exempt. In systems that use an 'exemption with progression' approach, however, a foreign loss may affect the rate of tax on domestic income ('negative' progression). Nonetheless, several of the jurisdictions have special rules for foreign losses that allow current deductions.

In *The Netherlands*, foreign losses are deductible against domestic income on a per-country basis – that is, even if other foreign income is positive. There is a recapture of the deducted loss in later years when the operations in the country that generated the loss become positive.[162] The per-country limitation was introduced in 1995. Prior to that time, foreign income and losses from non-treaty countries and under pre-1980 treaties were combined, and the resulting loss reduced domestic-source income, with subsequent re-characterization as taxable income when any foreign-source income was realized. In addition, if foreign losses in a branch have reduced taxable income, such losses have not yet been recaptured, and the branch is incorporated, the participation exemption is not available until the losses have been compensated for by additional taxable income.[163]

Where *Germany* exempts income under a treaty, in principle, foreign losses have no impact on German income except for the possible effect of 'exemption with progression' – that is, the foreign loss is taken into account in determining the rate of personal income tax on positive income. Compensation of foreign losses had been previously accepted by German legislation even if corresponding profits were exempt, but this beneficial treatment was abolished in 1999. In a landmark decision, the ECJ accepted the compatibility of this provision with the freedom of establishment for permanent establishments located in other EC Member States.[164] Recent legislation has abolished 'exemption with progression' with reference to some activities (e.g., rental income).[165] The ECJ has approved as a general rule such disadvantageous treatment of foreign losses on condition that they can be carried forward in the other state.

In the *French* exemption system, foreign losses are in general not deductible against domestic income. As from 2009, however, losses of foreign branches (or

161. United Kingdom, Finance Act 2009, Sch. 15.
162. Netherlands, DADT, Art. 12.
163. Netherlands, CITA, Art. 13c.
164. ECJ, 15 May 2008, C-414/06 (*Lidl Belgium*).
165. Germany, ITA, s. 2a.

more than 95% directly held subsidiaries) can be deducted currently against domestic income, subject to recapture over a five-year period. But the decrease in tax resulting from such a deduction, which can be viewed as an incentive to foreign investment, is capped to comply with EC law on State aids (*de minimis* rule).[166] In addition, according to case law, losses of foreign branches or subsidiaries can indirectly be taken into account in France through the deduction of the relief (e.g., cancellation of indebtedness) granted to them, provided the business of such branch is directly related to the business activity of the corporation in France (e.g., sale of goods produced in France).[167]

Australia generally does not allow losses where foreign income is exempt, but recently this has been modified in the new thin capitalization regime to allow interest deductions relating to exempt foreign dividend income. As discussed above, the *United Kingdom* now adopts a similar approach with respect to expenses incurred by a UK corporation in deriving exempt foreign dividends.

4. LIMITATIONS ON EXEMPTION OR DEFERRAL OF INCOME OF FOREIGN CORPORATIONS

Under the basic jurisdictional principles discussed previously, the foreign-source income of a foreign corporation is not taxed to the domestic shareholder when earned by the foreign corporation. Taxation occurs, if at all, when the income is distributed; and in the case of countries that use the exemption system to relieve international double taxation, even distributed income may not be subject to tax. In the systems here under consideration, the deferral of or exemption from tax for distributed income usually arose without much consideration of the tax policy implications of that result. Deferral seemed the natural consequence of the recognition of the separate existence of the foreign corporation, and the exemption of the distributed income when received by domestic shareholders was often consistent with the treatment of dividends received from domestic corporations.

All of the systems, however, have recognized that the mechanical application of the basic rules can lead to tax results that are inappropriate in light of other aspects of the country's tax system. Thus, for example, if as a general rule dividends from a substantial participation in a foreign subsidiary are exempt from domestic tax but passive foreign income earned directly is taxed currently, it is questionable whether passive income earned by a foreign corporation and distributed to a domestic shareholder as a dividend should fall under the basic rule that foreign dividend income is exempt. Similarly, even if deferred taxation is taken as

166. France, CGI, s. 209 C.

167. France, Conseil d'État, 16 May 2003, no. 222956, *Société Télécoise*. In the absence of such a link, deduction of aids to foreign subsidiaries is also possible under the unique condition that such aids be granted in the interest of the parent corporation (Conseil d'État, 30 Mar. 1987, no. 52754, *Société Labo Industries*, and 11 Feb. 1994, no. 119726, *SA Editions Jean-Claude Lattès*).

a basic principle, the avoidance of current domestic taxation on portfolio investment income by lodging investment assets in a foreign corporation formed in a tax haven jurisdiction would cause concern.

More generally, all of the countries examined here have been forced, in varying degrees and at varying times, to re-examine the economic and commercial consequences that flow from the application of the historically accepted principles of taxing jurisdiction and methods of double tax relief. This process has produced a more explicit consideration of when and whether deferral or exemption is appropriate and has led to the introduction of special tax regimes that limit the tax advantages flowing from the normally applicable rules. Although the results of these changes differ in many respects, some basic themes recur and there has been much 'borrowing' between systems in terms both of concepts and technical rules.

All systems here considered make some distinction between types or classes of income earned by foreign corporations with domestic shareholders. Active foreign business income is more likely to be entitled to deferral or exemption than passive portfolio or investment income. This distinction is sometimes based on considerations of capital import (or competitive) neutrality. Foreign business activities carried on in a foreign subsidiary must compete with local businesses, which face only the local tax rate; competitive considerations, it is argued, require exemption from, or at least deferral of, any additional domestic tax. These considerations are not present in the case of passive income. The distinction can also be seen as necessary to protect the domestic tax base in the case of 'mobile' types of business income.

Most of the systems are also concerned with the level of foreign tax that the income arising in the foreign corporation bears. This may be tested either by an explicit comparison of foreign and domestic rates on income earned, by some sort of minimum-rate benchmark, or by the mere fact that the corporation is organized in a particular jurisdiction with a high or low tax rate.

Finally, many systems apply the limitations on deferral or exemption only in the case of a significant level of shareholder ownership by domestic shareholders. In some cases, the foreign corporation must be controlled by domestic shareholders, while in others a significant but non-controlling interest is sufficient. Where a significant level of domestic ownership is not present, other mechanisms are often employed to discourage domestic portfolio investors from transferring funds offshore to foreign-owned investment companies.

In the elaboration of these basic concepts, there is a wide variation in the lines drawn and the structure of the tax rules in each country. These differences result in part from different policy judgments and in part because of the choice of different techniques to implement similar policy decisions. In some countries, the issues arose only when exchange controls were eliminated, which made foreign investment possible, while in others they have been present in the system for a considerable period. Thus, some rules have grown 'organically' while others have been enacted in a relatively short period. The following material will first examine limitations used by exemption countries and deferral countries where there is a significant level of domestic share ownership. The subsequent section will consider the response to domestic portfolio investment in foreign investment companies.

4.1. Limitations on Exemption for Shareholders in Foreign Corporations with Significant Domestic Share Ownership

From a structural point of view, limitations on the exemption of foreign-source income have arisen in several ways. In the first place, as discussed above, the definition of the situations in which exemption is permitted itself typically restricts exemption to certain classes or categories of income. In addition, the general exemption rules are often limited by special provisions – typically enacted after the more general rules – that eliminate exemption in certain circumstances (e.g., where operations in tax havens are involved or where the foreign income is of a certain type). The two approaches can obviously reach the same functional results, and it is in part a matter of historical accident as to which features appear as part of the 'general' exemption definition and which take the form of special limitations.

In addition, most of the countries examined here that exempt dividends from foreign corporations have adopted CFC rules, under which certain income of certain foreign corporations controlled by residents or in which residents have a substantial interest is subject to domestic tax currently as the income is earned by the foreign corporation. CFC rules are discussed in the next section. There is obviously a close relationship between an exemption for dividends from foreign companies and CFC rules. CFC rules operate in part to protect the domestic tax base from the diversion of domestic income to a CFC. If dividends from foreign companies are exempt, such income can be distributed by the CFC back to its residence country shareholders and received by them exempt from residence country tax. CFC rules restrict this result by taxing certain income of the CFC (primarily passive income that is easily shifted) to the resident shareholders currently. Notably, however, in most countries the CFC rules and the exemption for dividends from foreign companies are not co-extensive. Often the dividends or participation exemption applies to non-portfolio dividends (defined as dividends received by resident corporations owning a minimum percentage of the shares of the foreign corporation), whereas the CFC rules typically apply only to foreign corporations controlled (usually defined as the ownership of more than 50% of the voting shares) by residents.

Originally in both *Canada* and *Australia*, the exemption for dividends from foreign corporations was limited to distributions out of active business income earned in countries where it was likely that the income would have borne significant foreign tax. In structural terms, this result was reached by the definition of income that qualified for exemption and the residence of the foreign corporation earning the income, rather than as a limitation on a broader class of exempt income. The Canadian approach causes enormous compliance and administrative problems because it requires foreign corporations to keep detailed surplus accounts in respect of the various types of income earned in accordance with Canadian tax rules.

In contrast, in *France*, intercorporate dividends distributed by foreign subsidiaries qualify for the intercorporate dividends exemption in the same way as domestic dividends and, under the territoriality principle, as a general matter, profits and losses arising in a foreign trade or business are not taken into account in determining the base for the French corporate income tax. However, this treatment is limited if the corporate taxpayer is subject to section 209B of the tax code, the CFC rules that were enacted in 1980 and modified in 2005 in order to comply with EC case law relating to the compatibility of anti-avoidance domestic provisions with the freedom of establishment principle.

All of the countries providing participation exemptions for dividends, except *The Netherlands*, do not limit the exemption for foreign dividends but instead impose CFC rules on certain foreign companies.

4.2. Controlled Foreign Corporation (CFC) Rules

Under CFC rules, the resident shareholders of a CFC are subject to residence country tax on their share of certain income of the CFC as it is earned without waiting for the shareholders to receive dividends. These rules are used both by countries that exempt dividends from foreign companies and by countries that tax such dividends subject to direct and indirect foreign tax credits. In the case of countries using the exemption method, the CFC rules provide protection for the domestic tax base by effectively nullifying the exemption for foreign dividends. In the case of countries using the credit method, the CFC rules limit the benefit of the deferral of residence country tax from earning income through a CFC because otherwise there would be no residence country tax until the resident shareholders received dividends from the CFC or disposed of their shares in the CFC.

Of the nine countries considered in this book, only *The Netherlands* does not have CFC rules.

The *United States* has extensive and complex rules limiting deferral. Historically, limits on deferral for portfolio income of individuals were imposed in 1937 in the foreign personal holding company provisions. Those rules, which were repealed in 2004, restricted deferral for closely held, individually owned foreign corporations that had predominantly investment-type income.

In 1962, a comprehensive set of rules restricting deferral was enacted and became the predecessor of similar legislation in several of the other countries here under consideration. The 'Subpart F' rules, as they came to be known internationally, were the outcome of a complex legislative compromise between those favouring the complete elimination of deferral for the income of CFCs in all circumstances and those who argued for a more limited approach.

Broadly speaking, those supporting elimination of deferral were arguing in terms of capital export neutrality and the need to eliminate the incentive that deferral gave for foreign investment. The justifications for continuing deferral were based on the asserted need to preserve the competitive position of US enterprises in foreign markets. The resulting compromise eliminated deferral for passive income, about which there could be no argument based on competitive considerations, and so-called 'base company' income resulting from transactions between related parties, where income can be said to have been diverted through a related company. In those situations, the undistributed income of the foreign corporation must be included currently by the US shareholder. The appropriate scope of the Subpart F rules in the US is currently under discussion, with some urging greater limitations on deferral and others arguing for its limitation to passive income only, with all active business income, even income from financial activities only, taxable on distribution.

More technically, deferral is eliminated for the 'Subpart F income'[168] earned by a CFC.[169] While the definition of Subpart F income is extremely complex, two basic strands run through the provisions. One is the attempt to distinguish between passive investment-type income and business income. Thus, for example, rents and royalties are normally included in Subpart F income but are excluded if they are derived in the active conduct of a trade or business.[170] Similarly, income from dealings in commodity transactions is generally covered but is excluded if it arises from a hedging transaction carried out in the normal course of the business of a producer or processor. Second, the provisions attempt to define those situations where the foreign corporation is being used as a 'base company'. This branch of the provision is aimed at transactions with related parties that have no significant economic connection with the 'base' country jurisdiction. A typical situation covered by the provisions is the purchase of goods manufactured by a related party and the sale of the goods outside the country of incorporation of the selling 'base' company. On the other hand, if the goods are sold in the country of incorporation or are manufactured there and sold to related parties in other jurisdictions, no Subpart F income would arise.[171]

These basic rules are hedged with a number of exceedingly complex refinements. For example, transactions carried out through branches rather than separately incorporated corporations can generate base company income if the overall result has the same economic effect as a related company transaction.[172] An overall relief provision excludes from the definition of base company income any item of income that bears a rate of tax equal to 90% of the maximum US corporate rate, and a *de minimis* rule exempts the lesser of 5% of the foreign corporation's gross income or $1 million.

In addition to covering passive and base company income, the provisions deal with a number of other situations where, for various reasons, the legislative decision was made that deferral was inappropriate. Thus, deferral is denied for income arising in connection with an international boycott, for certain bribes or

168. United States, IRC, s. 952.
169. United States, IRC, s. 957(a).
170. United States, IRC, s. 954(c)(2).
171. United States, IRC, s. 954(d).
172. United States, IRC, s. 954(d)(2).

illegal payments, and for income attributable to countries the United States does not recognize diplomatically.

The overall impact of the Subpart F rules was substantially weakened in 2006 with the introduction of a new provision that made it possible, in effect, to transfer profits between CFCs without incurring current US tax. Deductible payments such as interest, rents, and royalties can be made between related parties without the receipt of the payments being treated as Subpart F income in the hands of the recipient CFC. Thus, payments can be channelled from one operating company through a tax haven to another operating company without running afoul of Subpart F.[173]

Current taxation of undistributed income occurs only if the income is earned by a CFC. CFC status, in turn, requires that over 50% of the stock (either in terms of voting power or value) is owned by 'United States shareholders' – that is, US persons who own, either directly or by attribution through foreign entities, at least 10% of the voting stock of the foreign corporation. The focus is thus on control lodged in concentrated US ownership.[174] CFC status is avoided, for example, if eleven unrelated persons own ratably 100% of the voting stock of a foreign corporation or if exactly 50% voting stock is owned by one US person with the remainder held by foreign persons.

In general, the rules limiting deferral in other jurisdictions are more restricted in scope. Their focus is primarily on passive income and income that could be said to have been diverted from domestic taxation without any 'real' activity by the foreign corporation in a 'real' foreign jurisdiction.

Thus, in *Canadian* legislation, deferral is eliminated only for passive income, known as foreign accrual property income (FAPI), which is directly taxable regardless of the level of foreign tax imposed on the income.[175] There is a limited concept of base company income, and the use of tax haven subsidiaries for sales and services transactions is accepted as necessary to support the international competitiveness of Canadian corporations. Thus, the scope of the Canadian rules is limited to passive income and business income derived from transactions with Canada that erode the Canadian tax base. The basic pattern of taxation, however, is quite similar to that found in Subpart F.

Elimination of deferral is restricted to the FAPI of a 'controlled foreign affiliate', defined as a foreign corporation that is controlled directly or indirectly by five or fewer Canadian residents. Unlike the United States, there is no minimum shareholding requirement for determining control. FAPI over an insignificant *de minimis* amount of $5,000 is included directly in the income of 10% or greater shareholders. FAPI of lower-tier corporations is attributed directly to the Canadian shareholders. A credit is allowed for the Canadian shareholders' portion of the foreign taxes imposed on the FAPI of the controlled foreign affiliate. The basis of the shares is increased by the amount of the income inclusion. Subsequent

173. United States, IRC, s. 954(c)(6).
174. United States, IRC, s. 957(a).
175. The Canadian CFC rules are found basically in ITA, ss 91–95.

distribution of the income as a dividend is tax-free, and a credit is allowed for withholding tax on the dividend if the distribution is made within five years of the inclusion.

The *Japanese* approach to limits on deferral is quite different.[176] Rather than focusing on transactions, the Japanese legislation looks to the location of the principal office or headquarters of the controlled foreign subsidiary. If the operations are located in a jurisdiction that has no corporate tax or an effective tax rate of 25% or less, then all of the undistributed income, passive and active, is taxed currently to the Japanese shareholders. The legislation is directed at the use of tax havens for activities that have no connection with the jurisdiction. To carry out this policy, several exceptions allow continued deferral. Deferral is permitted for an active business that has fixed assets in the jurisdiction, carries out local managerial activities there, and operates its principal business in that location. This exception would cover, for example, the operation of a resort hotel in a tax haven. Another exception allows deferral for financial or transportation activities that do not meet the location-of-business test but generate more than 50% of gross income from dealings with unrelated parties.

The restrictions on deferral apply to 'affiliated foreign corporations'. These are foreign corporations where more than 50% of the stock is owned by Japanese residents or corporations. There is no minimum shareholding requirement for testing control. However, only those shareholders who own 5% of the shares or are part of an affiliated corporate group that owns 5% are subject to direct taxation on the undistributed earnings of the CFC. A foreign tax credit is allowed for the corporate taxes paid on the directly included income.

Sweden takes yet another approach. Prior to 1990 there were no restrictions on the deferral of foreign income earned in foreign corporations. The matter was not regarded as a problem, because exchange controls effectively prevented the use of foreign corporations for portfolio investments and deferral was deemed appropriate for usual corporate activities. When exchange controls were eliminated, restrictions were imposed on deferral through the use of CFCs.[177] This legislation was substantially amended in 2003 and 2007. Under the Swedish legislation, a Swedish shareholder with a 25% or greater interest (votes or value) directly or indirectly in a foreign corporation is taxed currently on the income of a foreign corporation if the corporation tax paid abroad is less than 55% of the Swedish rate, currently 15.4%. In addition, the legislation is accompanied by a 'white list' of countries where the CFC rules do not apply if the foreign corporation is subject to 'normal' taxation there. For countries not on the 'white' list, which includes uncooperative tax havens under the OECD Harmful Tax Competition project, or special regimes, the CFC rules tax the income directly to the Swedish shareholder with a corresponding credit for any foreign tax paid. Under the 2007 amendments, which were made to adapt the rules to the decision of the ECJ in *Cadbury Schweppes*, income of foreign corporations within the European Economic Area is exempt

176. Japan, Special Taxation Measures Act (STMA), ss 40–4 and 66–6.
177. Sweden, ITA, Ch. 39 a.

from the Swedish CFC rules if the foreign corporation is genuinely established in the foreign state. Several factors are mentioned in the rule for the purpose of deciding whether there is a genuine establishment. The rule has been criticized for being more restrictive than required by the ECJ's decision.

Where income is subject to current tax, there is intentionally no basis adjustment in the shares, so the same income could be taxed again on the sale of the shares. Subsequent dividends, however, are exempt from tax and the capital gain can be avoided by timely distributions.

The *United Kingdom* legislation is focused on corporations resident outside the United Kingdom and controlled by UK residents where the corporation is subject to a 'lower level of taxation' in the residence country, defined as less than three-quarters of the taxes the foreign corporation would have paid if it had been resident in the United Kingdom. Control is defined as a more than 50% interest in the shares, the voting power, the profits, or the assets of the company (but the level can be as low as 40% if no other person has a 55% interest); there is no minimum shareholding level in making this determination. However, only UK-resident companies with at least a 25% interest in the foreign company will be attributed the undistributed profits.[178]

Several exceptions to income attribution substantially restrict the reach of the rules.[179] If the company follows an 'acceptable distribution policy' and distributes at least 90% of its profits, there will be no attribution of the undistributed amounts. This distribution exemption is being eliminated as a consequence of the adoption of complete exemption for dividends from foreign companies. In addition, if the foreign company has a business locus in the country in which it is resident and engages in activities other than investment or the dealing in goods involving the United Kingdom or related parties ('exempt activities'), the provisions will not apply. A 'motive' exception is applicable if the transactions generating the profits were carried out for reasons other than reducing UK tax. This exception famously did not save the UK CFC rules when challenged under EC law.[180] As an aid in the administration of the provisions, the fiscal authorities have published a 'white list' of countries. For companies resident in such countries and deriving at least 90% of their income locally, the attribution provision will not apply. In 2008, the UK tax administration released a proposal to replace this approach with a US/Canadian-style tainted income approach. The reasoning was that such an approach might be more compliant with EC law, but doubts have arisen and, as of mid-2009, the reform had stalled.

In addition to the above regime, other provisions attribute the capital gains of a non-resident company to its 'members' if the company would have been classified as 'closely held' had it been a UK resident.[181]

178. United Kingdom, Income and Corporation Taxes Act 1988, s. 747.
179. United Kingdom, Income and Corporation Taxes Act 1988, s. 748.
180. ECJ, 12 Sep. 2006, C-196/04 (*Cadbury Schweppes plc v. IRC*).
181. United Kingdom, Taxable of Chargeable Gains Act 1992, s. 13.

The *German* provisions[182] are focused on 'tainted' income realized by a German CFC in a low-tax jurisdiction. Under the new corporate tax rules, which provide for tax-free dividends in the hands of a corporate shareholder and the application of the 'modified part-income method' if the shareholder is an individual taxpayer, CFC rules have become even more important from the perspective of the tax administration. However, the compatibility of CFC rules with EC law is highly disputed. Following the ECJ decision in *Cadbury Schweppes*, German rules have been restricted to CFCs lacking economic substance (although borderline cases are still highly debated).

Where the income is attributed to the German shareholder, it is characterized as capital income. The attribution of income takes place even where treaty rules provide for a 'participation exemption' for dividends. This aspect of the revised CFC legislation has been subject to criticism as an implicit 'treaty override'.

As to the requirements of the application of German CFC rules, 'tainted' income is defined indirectly by excluding from the definition most active business income, including manufacturing, agriculture, processing, banking and insurance, local distribution, and processing. Income from trading and services will generally be active if the foreign corporation conducts its business operations without assistance from the German shareholder and deals with the public even if the goods are purchased from related parties. Thus, many situations that would be treated as base company sales or services income under the United States Subpart F rules would not be covered by the German provisions.

The foreign corporation will be subject to low tax if it pays tax on a residence basis at a rate of less than 25%. This is astonishing as the German corporate tax rate has been reduced to 15% from 2008. German tax authorities defend this approach by referring to the additional layer of trade tax on the profits of German corporations. In this calculation, operating losses that might reduce tax and foreign tax credits are ignored. Control is defined as more than 50% of the votes or number of shares held by German residents with the attribution of ownership through other corporations or partnerships. The rules also include former German residents who have moved to low-tax jurisdictions. In contrast to the US Subpart F rules, there is no minimum ownership test.

If the foreign corporation has significant amounts of portfolio investment income, that income will be attributed directly to German shareholders owning at least 1% of the shares even if the foreign corporation is not German-controlled. In some cases even shareholdings of less than 1% can qualify for CFC treatment.

Where income is attributed, foreign taxes can be deducted or credited and subsequent distributions of the previously taxed income can be made on a tax-free basis for a four-year period.

The *Australian* approach to restrictions on deferral and exemption has undergone significant change over the past twenty years so as to have come almost full circle. Exchange controls were abolished in 1983, which opened the way for Australian residents to have offshore passive investments that were subject to the

182. See Germany, Foreign Transaction Tax Act (*Aussensteuergesetz*), ss 7–14.

then-broad exemption system. Accordingly, the government announced replacement of the exemption system by a foreign tax credit in 1985 (except for employment income), which commenced in 1987. Even as this system was being developed, it was realized that passive income could go untaxed simply by moving the income offshore into a non-resident Australian-controlled company. Accordingly, a broad CFC-style anti-deferral regime was announced in 1988 and commenced in 1990. In the process of consultation that occurred after the announcement, the CFC regime was considerably narrowed so that it applied only to passive and related-party income of CFCs from low-tax countries (there being a list of more than 60 'white' countries for which attribution occurred only in relation to certain income listed in regulations that was subject to tax concessions or preferences in those countries). The control test was a 50%-or-more rule rather than the more common more-than-50% rule. The passive and related-party income rules were similar to the US rules. In addition, an active income test prevented attribution of passive or related-party income if less than 5% of the CFC's gross income was passive.

At the same time, an exemption system for dividends paid out of comparably taxed active foreign income of CFCs was introduced along with a branch exemption for similar income. These exemptions were functionally equivalent to a foreign tax credit, since they applied only to high-taxed income. It was said to be difficult to maintain the list of over sixty countries and their concessional elements, and so in 1997 the list was reduced to only seven countries (the seven other countries that had CFC regimes at that time). Some commentators were not convinced of the rationale and felt that it was simply a pretext to broaden the CFC regime. The 1988 announcement also foreshadowed a complementary regime for passive income accumulated in foreign companies that were not controlled; consequently, after the CFC regime had been completed, a FIF regime was consulted on and introduced in 1993. It is described in more detail below. Thus, by the later 1990s Australia had extensive regimes designed to remove deferral for passive and related-party income.[183]

As Australian direct and portfolio overseas investment dramatically expanded from the late 1990s (partly driven by the large surpluses accumulating in pension plans as a result of changes to the regime described in Part One), business and investors increasingly complained about Australia's international tax rules in general and the anti-deferral rules in particular. Accordingly, a review of the international tax regime occurred in 2002–2003. As a result, from 2004, two major changes to the regime occurred that were relevant to deferral: first, all non-portfolio dividends became exempt (with comparable changes to the taxation of foreign branches of Australian companies) so that the regime became a genuine exemption rather than a de facto foreign tax credit regime; and second, the application of the CFC rules to designated concession income in listed countries was

183. The regimes are currently found in Australia, ITAA 1936, Parts X and XI. As a result of 2009 announcements described below, in the near future both of these will be repealed and a much stripped-down CFC regime enacted into the ITAA 1997.

narrowed. These changes greatly simplified the treatment of dividends (see above) and significantly reduced the need to dissect countries' tax systems in order to segregate concessional elements. In addition, the 2004 exemption for capital gains on non-portfolio interests in foreign companies involved in active business, along with the extension of this treatment to the disposal of non-portfolio interests of one CFC in another CFC, removed problems in offshore restructuring under Australia's CFC regime and extended the participation exemption for dividends to most capital gains on shares.

The 2002–2003 review indicated that the accruals regimes – in particular, the FIF regime – required further consideration, and as a result a further review was announced in 2006. The government received the report of this review in 2008 and announced significant changes in 2009. The FIF regime is to be repealed with a possible narrow replacement directed at interest income rolled up in passive offshore funds. The CFC regime is to be considerably narrowed. It will no longer apply to related-party (base company) income and the passive income category is to be considerably narrowed. The means to achieve this narrowing are currently being developed. The CFC regime will no longer apply to pension funds as offshore investors. This may seem to be a minor change, but in recent years the most significant operation of the CFC regime has been with respect to offshore investment of pension funds by Australian fund managers (Australia having the fourth-largest amount of funds under management in the world). If the government had accepted another recommendation to remove the application of the CFC regime for Australian stock-exchange listed companies (subject to some minor safeguards), the regime would have become largely an irrelevance. Many other technical changes to the CFC regime will flow from this review and the current consultation.

Although the public debate originally centred on deferral and the competitiveness of Australian business overseas, now the overall regime is probably best regarded as protecting Australia's domestic tax base because it focuses on income of residents that is easily shifted from Australia to a low-taxed foreign entity. As a result of the recent changes, the CFC regime is in effect an anti-avoidance regime for egregious cases.

The changes have also been influenced by Australia's imputation system, under which all profits that have not borne Australian company tax are subject to tax at the resident shareholder level. Hence, it is unnecessary to levy tax at the company level, and Australian companies have a considerable incentive to pay Australian company tax rather than foreign company tax.

The *French* CFC rules are contained in Article 209B of the general tax code, which was enacted in 1980 and modified in 2005 to comply with EC case law relating to the compatibility of domestic anti-avoidance provisions with the freedom of establishment principle. In general terms, Article 209B is applicable to investments in tax haven jurisdictions where the taxpayer is not actively involved in the local market. More technically, a French corporation is subject to tax currently on foreign income that arises in a foreign branch operation or with respect to a more-than-50% (or 5% if more than 50% is held through controlled or non-arm's length entities) investment in the share capital, voting rights, or financial rights in any foreign entity if the foreign branch or entity is not subject locally to an income tax or is subject to an effective rate that is less than 50% of the French rate.

For purposes of such taxation, the tax results of the foreign branch or entity are recalculated under French tax rules. The profits are deemed to be realized by (in the case of a branch) or distributed to (in the case of an entity) the French corporate taxpayer on the first day of the month following the end of the foreign branch's or entity's tax year. Conversely, the losses of the foreign branch or entity are not taken into account in determining the tax on domestic income. Article 209B seems to be compatible with most French tax treaties when applied to foreign entities because of the characterization of the profits of the CFC as distributed income; however, the business profits treaty article seems to forbid its application to branches.[184] In the case of litigation, the burden of proof as to the low-tax status of the foreign branch or entity lies on the government.

Tax paid locally is creditable against the corresponding French separate corporate income tax provided that the foreign tax is of a comparable nature. Withholding taxes on actual distributed dividends also entitle the taxpayer to a credit against such separate tax if the subsidiary is based in a tax treaty country. This credit applies only if the distributions exceed the profits of the same entity that were previously taxed in accordance with Article 209B and were actually taxed (i.e., did not qualify for the intercorporate dividend exemption). A credit is also granted for that part of the profits taxed in France that corresponds to dividends, interest, and royalties subject to withholding tax in third countries if the branch or entity is based in a country with a tax treaty that includes an OECD-type exchange-of-information clause.

Current taxation can be avoided if the French corporate taxpayer can establish that the foreign branch or entity is engaged in actual industrial or commercial activities performed in the local market or, if passive income represents more than 20% of the profits (50% when added to intra-group services income), that the activities of the foreign branch or entity do not have the effect of the 'localization' of profits in the low-tax jurisdiction. Thus, the provision is aimed principally at the isolation of passive investment-type income in a foreign corporation. It also covers some base company transactions where the activities are not principally undertaken in the local market.

Most importantly, Article 209B is inapplicable when the branch or entity is established in another EU country and its operation or the holding of an interest in it cannot be considered to be an 'artificial arrangement'[185] intended to escape the French tax normally payable.

---

184. See Conseil d'État, 28 Jun. 2002, no. 232276, *Société Schneider Electric*.

185. Within the meaning of the term 'wholly artificial arrangement' as used by ECJ in its *ICI* (16 Jul. 1998, C-264/96) and *Cadbury Schweppes* (12 Sep. 2006, C-196/04) decisions.

4.3. SPECIAL PROVISIONS DEALING WITH DOMESTIC PORTFOLIO INVESTMENT IN FOREIGN INVESTMENT COMPANIES

Initially, limitations on exemption or deferral were typically focused on situations in which there was a significant level of domestic investment in the foreign corporation and were often restricted to cases in which there was actual control of the foreign corporation by domestic shareholders. However, as intermediated investment in foreign corporations became more common, the failure to impose current tax on undistributed earnings of portfolio investment in foreign investment funds (FIFs) began to be recognized as a significant problem. Where the level of domestic investment was not substantial, there was some reluctance to require direct inclusion of foreign earnings because the domestic shareholder was unlikely to have access to information or any influence on the distribution policies of the foreign corporation. As a result, various surrogate taxing techniques were employed, ranging from taxation on a mark-to-market basis to the taxation of an assumed notional return on the investment.

In the *United States*, when the Subpart F provisions were introduced in 1962, a provision was included to deny preferential capital gains treatment to gains realized by domestic investors on portfolio investment in the stock of foreign investment companies. The provision was intended to reduce the incentive for US investors to invest in foreign mutual funds where the undistributed earnings would not be subject to current US taxation and would not be reached by the foreign personal holding company rules or the Subpart F rules because of the absence of concentrated US ownership. However, the temporary elimination of the capital gains preference in 1986 made this provision ineffective in discouraging US investment in foreign investment companies. The legislative response was a rule aimed more directly at the deferral of US tax on passive income earned abroad.

Under the passive foreign investment company (PFIC) rules enacted in 1986,[186] an interest charge is imposed on foreign earnings that are accumulated and then subsequently distributed to US shareholders. The distribution is treated as having been received ratably over the period that the US shareholder has held the stock, and an interest charge is imposed on the taxes (calculated at the highest marginal rate for the year in question) that would have been due on the hypothetical distributions. Similarly, if the stock is disposed of at a gain, the gain is attributed ratably to the period that the stock has been held and an interest charge calculated accordingly. The interest charge mechanism was chosen because of perceived disadvantages in requiring current taxation where US interests were not substantial. In some circumstances, it is possible for US shareholders to avoid the interest charge regime by electing to include in income currently the undistributed income of the foreign corporation.

While the provision is aimed primarily at investment in foreign investment companies, the definitional scope is substantially broader. A foreign corporation is classified as a PFIC if (1) 75% or more of its income is passive or (2) 50% or more of the fair market value or adjusted bases of its assets generates passive income.

186. United States, IRC, s. 1291.

Unlike Subpart F, there is no minimum shareholding requirement and no required overall level of US investment.[187]

Similarly, in *Canada*, in addition to the FAPI rules applicable to CFCs, a special provision was enacted in 1984 aimed at foreign investment vehicles. If a resident taxpayer invested in 'offshore investment fund property', defined broadly as an interest that derived its value primarily from investments in portfolio investments, the investment was deemed to generate a notional return that was currently taxable. The rule only applied, however, if one of the main reasons for the investment was a tax advantage in comparison with a direct holding of the investment.

This rule was found to be crude and ineffective and in 1999 was proposed to be replaced by detailed 'foreign investment entity' (FIE) rules for taxation years beginning after 2002. These proposed rules have gone through various iterations and as of mid-2009 have still not been enacted. In general terms, under the proposed new rules, taxpayers must include in income a notional return in respect of any interest owned in a FIE. A FIE is an entity whose principal business is investment or more than 50% of whose assets are investment-type property. In certain circumstances a mark-to-market approach is used to determine the amount included in income. The proposed new FIE rules are complex, and it will be extremely difficult for taxpayers to comply with the rules and for the CRA to administer them.

In *The Netherlands*, as a result of the taxation of passive investment income on a deemed return basis (return deemed to be 4% of the fair market value), there is no need for special provisions in respect of foreign investment income. In these cases the tax paid by the foreign corporation is not relevant, and the treatment is not restricted to tax haven operations. Where the investment amounts to a substantial participation (interest of at least 5%), the general deemed return rules apply only to shares in a foreign investment company. For corporate shareholders who hold 25% or more of the shares of a foreign investment company, the investment is taxed on a mark-to-market basis unless the participation in the foreign investment company qualifies for the participation exemption.[188]

In *Australia*, a separate FIF regime applies to non-CFCs with primarily passive income but, as noted above, it is due to be repealed in the near future and accordingly is not described here. The detailed FIF rules may be replaced by a narrow anti-avoidance rule. *Germany* has detailed rules on foreign-based investment funds and investment companies that have been reformulated in the Investment Tax Law (*Investment-steuergesetz*) that came into force in 2004. According to this law, investments in domestic or foreign investment funds or investment companies are subject to a 'transparent' tax regime. Moreover, the CFC rules are not applicable if the Investment Tax Law applies.[189] Nevertheless, the CFC rules contain provisions dealing with foreign corporations realizing 'passive income with an investment character' that are also responsive to the problem of foreign investment companies, although they are applicable only when a 10% or greater domestic shareholding is present.

187. United States, IRC, s. 1297.
188. Netherlands, CITA, Art. 13a.
189. Germany, Investment Tax Law (FTTA), s. 7 para. 1.

Since 1999, a *French*-resident individual has been subject to tax on foreign undistributed income that arises with respect to a 10% or more direct or indirect interest held in any foreign entity the assets of which principally consist of stocks and securities, deposits, or current accounts. The tax applies if the foreign entity is not subject locally to an income tax or is subject to an effective rate significantly lower than that which would have been levied in France.[190] For purposes of such taxation, the results of the foreign entity are recalculated under French tax rules, and the profits are deemed to pass through to the French taxpayer on the first day of the month following the end of the foreign entity's tax year. Tax paid locally is deductible. Where no exchange of information clause exists between France and the entity's country, the taxable income cannot be lower than a notional return equal to the average bank business lending rate applied to the investment. Earnings actually distributed are exempt as long as they do not exceed the undistributed profits previously taxed in the hands of the taxpayer. The compatibility of this provision with the principle of free movement of capital within the EU is questionable.

The *United Kingdom* has no provisions that seek to tax non-portfolio investors in FIFs or companies on a current (whether actual or deemed) basis. However, under anti-abuse rules, where a resident individual transfers assets out of the United Kingdom so that income from the assets would otherwise arise to a non-resident, the individual may be treated as having derived the income directly.[191] The attribution occurs only where the individual can enjoy the income or is entitled to receive a capital sum connected with the transfer and the taxpayer cannot demonstrate the lack of a tax avoidance purpose. Under different rules, where a person disposes of an interest in an offshore investment fund that does not distribute a substantial portion of its income, the person may be subject to income tax treatment on any gain rather than preferential capital gains treatment.[192]

Japan and *Sweden* do not have any rules to deal with residents investing in FIFs or companies.

5. OUTBOUND TRANSFERS TO FOREIGN BRANCHES OR SUBSIDIARIES

Transfers of assets outside the taxing jurisdiction raise issues in both a credit system and an exemption system. From the point of view of an exemption system, any appreciation in the value of an asset transferred to a foreign business operation whose income qualifies for exemption will not be taxed by the residence country. Similarly, assets transferred to a foreign corporation will not generate tax if the dividends from the direct investment are exempt. Several of the systems have provisions ensuring that tax will be collected in these situations, either by accelerating the income recognition to the time of the transfer or by retaining a tax claim on the income when it is later realized.

190. France, CGI, s. 123 *bis*.
191. United Kingdom, Income Tax Act 2007, Part 13 Ch. 2 (ss 714–751).
192. United Kingdom, Income and Corporation Taxes Act 1988, Part XVII Ch. V (ss 756A–763).

From the perspective of a credit system, the transfer of the asset to a foreign branch does not terminate the claim of the taxing jurisdiction. However, the existence of the credit gives the primary tax claim to the country of source and, if the rates are similar, has the same effect as an exemption system from the government's point of view. Transfers to foreign corporations raise the same issues where the indirect credit is available and involve the problem of deferral because whatever domestic tax may be due will be deferred until repatriation. Specific rules address these problems.

Several countries treat the transfer of an appreciated asset to a foreign branch as a realization event. Thus, in *Sweden* the transfer of assets is deemed to be a withdrawal of the assets from domestic business operations and is a realization event if the transfer is to a foreign branch where Sweden has given up the right to tax in a tax treaty. In the case of a transfer to a foreign subsidiary, the transfer will normally be treated as a realization event. *Germany* completely revamped its rules on cross-border transfers of assets when the EU introduced the European Company. Under the new law that entered into force in 2007, the transfer of an asset from the head office to a foreign branch is treated as a realization event in principle, but the taxpayer may elect deferred taxation of the gain (through the use of a reserve) over a period of five years if the asset is transferred to a branch within the EU.[193] The taxpayer must dissolve the reserve immediately in case of a disposal or a transfer of the asset to a third country. Moreover, this privilege is not granted if the taxpayer ceases to be subject to unlimited tax liability in Germany in the course of this reorganization. Where depreciable assets (which are not likely to be sold) are involved, the deferred income must be taken into account over the remaining useful life of the asset. The taxpayer can, at its option, treat the original transfer as a realization event. Although the Federal Tax Court ruled in 2008 that the transfer of assets between different jurisdictions did not constitute a realization event at all,[194] this ruling referred only to the pre-2007 legislation.

The *Dutch* rules are somewhat more complex. In principle, the transfer of an asset to a foreign branch is not a realization event. However, in calculating foreign exempt income, case law requires that the fair market value of the asset be considered as the cost basis for computing depreciation of the asset in the foreign branch. Historical cost, however, is used in computing worldwide income. Thus, over the life of the asset, the appreciation is included in the tax base by, in effect, reducing the amount of foreign-source income that qualifies for exemption. Similar principles apply to inventory.

France treats the transfer to a foreign branch or subsidiary as a realization event. A tax-free transfer of assets to a foreign subsidiary, however, can be done in exchange for shares, provided the usual statutory requirements are met and prior administrative approval is obtained.[195]

The approach in the *United States* is similar. Transfers to a foreign branch are, in general, not taxable. The US Internal Revenue Service (IRS) has authority, however, to promulgate regulations that will tax the appreciation in assets

193. Germany, ITA, s. 4 para. 1 sent. 3, CITA, s. 4g, sent. 12 para. 1.
194. Federal Tax Court (*Bundesfinanzhof*), judgment of 17 Jul. 2008 I R 77/06.
195. France, CGI, s. 210 C-2.

transferred to a foreign partnership that operates the branch. The concern is that the income may not be subject to later US tax if it can be allocated to a foreign partner. Such an allocation is unlikely, however, given the restrictions on partnership allocations and, as a result, the IRS has not issued regulations.

In the case of transfers to a foreign corporation, the transfer may be taxable or tax-free, depending on the nature of the assets. In general, the transfer of property that is to be used in an active business and that is not likely to be sold can be transferred to a foreign corporation on a tax-deferred basis under the same conditions as the transfer to a domestic corporation. Thus, for example, machinery and buildings can be transferred without immediate recognition of gain, but inventory does not qualify. There are extensive restrictions on transfers of stock or securities, in light of the ease of resale, although a tax-deferred transfer is available in some circumstances if the taxpayer enters into an agreement to pay tax if the stock is in fact later sold or disposed of by the transferee corporation. A special rule applies to the transfer of intangibles in the form of patents, know-how, and the like. The US taxpayer is required to include in income a deemed royalty payment (treated as US-source income) from the transferee foreign corporation over the life of the intangible, which reflects the amounts commensurate with the income generated by the intangible. The deemed royalty rule is aimed at preventing the deduction of research costs in the United States and then a transfer of the resulting income stream from the intangible abroad, but it has a much broader scope. In addition, if the branch operations have been operating at a loss and are then transferred to a foreign corporation, gain must be recognized to the extent of the loss up to the amount of appreciation in the assets transferred.

Japan, on the other hand, allows the transfer to a branch operation to proceed without recognition of income, while the transfer of assets located in Japan to a foreign subsidiary is generally regarded as a recognition event. The *Canadian* rules regard both transfers of assets to a foreign branch and to a foreign corporation as realization events. However, a tax-deferred rollover is allowed for transfers of shares of a foreign affiliate (a foreign company in which the Canadian corporation owns at least 10% of the shares of any class) to another foreign affiliate of the taxpayer in exchange for its shares.[196] This rollover is denied if the transfer is part of a series of transactions whereby the shares are transferred to an arm's length party.[197]

Australia generally takes a strict view (outside the finance industry) that there can be no income realization or deductions in transactions between the head office and branch, whether outbound or inbound. The realization event is the disposal of the asset by the taxpayer to a third party. For inventory, income and deductions are then allocated among the countries and taxed or exempted on the basis of source-of-income and apportionment-of-deductions rules (with arm's length transfer pricing principles being used to allocate income and deductions where the books are not in conformity with this principle). Thus, in the case of inventory manufactured in Australia and shipped to an overseas branch that sells it, the sale price will be allocated partly to Australia and partly to the country of the branch; the latter part will generally be exempted, as discussed above, if the income would not be

196. Canada, ITA, s. 85.1(3).
197. Canada, ITA, s. 85.1(4).

attributable (i.e., not subject to the CFC rules) if the foreign branch were a CFC. The expenses allocated to the Australian income will be deductible, and those allocated to the branch, including interest, will not be deductible.

In the capital gains area, these principles are similarly reflected. If the asset is a building or land, the branch exemption is available for any capital gain as long as the asset would not be a tainted asset under the CFC regime if the branch were a CFC. Land and buildings, of course, cannot be subject to outbound transfers. If a piece of equipment is used in Australia for producing assessable income and is then shipped to a branch where it is used to produce exempt income, it will give rise to depreciation deductions while used in Australia, but not when used in the branch. If it is then sold for more than the depreciated value (which includes notional depreciation for the period of use by the branch), any recapture is apportioned between the head office (taxable) and the branch (exempt from depreciation recapture). Further, there will be a taxable gain equivalent to the proportion of the gain that reflects the taxable proportion of use of the asset and if the asset is a tainted asset under the CFC regime, a capital gain so far as the gain reflects the exempt proportion of use. Capital gains on other assets of a foreign branch are not taxable unless the asset is a tainted asset under the CFC regime.

In the case of the transfer of assets to foreign subsidiaries, the transfer is a realization event and gives rise to income or capital gain. For most capital assets, a rollover will be available if the subsidiary is 100% owned and the asset transferred is a taxable Australian asset in the hands of the transferor and the transferee. Since in this case the rollover is limited to taxable Australian assets, there is no escape from the capital gains net because the subsidiary will be subject to capital gains tax on disposal. Following changes to the definition of taxable Australian assets in 2006, the rollover is limited to land in Australia, non-portfolio interests in land-rich entities, and assets held at some stage by a permanent establishment in Australia. Australia's tax treaties preserve Australia's right to tax gains in respect of these types of assets, so treaties are unlikely to have any impact in preventing Australian taxation on disposal by the subsidiary.

In the *United Kingdom*, transfers to a foreign branch have no tax consequences because the income remains subject to UK tax. As a general matter, the transfer of assets outside the United Kingdom by a resident company to a related foreign company would be a disposition triggering capital gains taxation and the recapture of previously deducted capital allowances in excess of market value of the asset at the time of transfer. However, current taxation can be avoided if the business is transferred to a foreign branch first and then the business is exchanged solely for shares in a non-resident company and the resulting interest amounts to at least 25%.[198]

The following **Table IV-1** summarizes the rules dealing with residence-based taxation of foreign-source income. The column 'CFC Legislation' refers to provisions aimed at foreign corporations with concentrated domestic ownership while the column 'Foreign Investment Company Legislation' is focused on portfolio investment in foreign entities with predominantly passive income.

198. United Kingdom, Taxation of Chargeable Gains Act 1992, s. 140.

Table IV-1. Taxation of Foreign-Source Income of Resident Taxpayers

	Double Tax Relief: Business Income	*Double Tax Relief: Subsidiary Dividends*	*Double Tax Relief: Portfolio Income*	*Controlled Foreign Corporation (CFC) Legislation*	*CFC Basic Approach*	*Foreign Investment Company Legislation (FIC)*	*FIC Basic Approach*
Australia	Mainly exemption; otherwise credit	Exemption	Foreign tax credit	Yes	Jurisdictional and transactional but to be narrowed in the near term	Yes but repeal has been announced	Simplified actual calculation; mark-to-market; deemed return
Canada	Foreign tax credit	Exemption and deemed foreign tax credit	Foreign tax credit and deduction	Yes	Transactional	Yes	Deemed return
France	Exemption (territorial system)	Exemption	No domestic relief (only in treaty)	Yes	Jurisdictional and transactional	Yes	Actual income and deemed return
Germany	Exemption for active PE income (treaty)	Exemption	Foreign tax credit and modified half-income method for dividends	Yes	Jurisdictional and transactional	Yes – part of CFC rules	Allocation of foreign investment income to shareholder
Japan	Foreign tax credit	Deemed foreign tax credit until March 2009; exemption from April 2009	Foreign tax credit	Yes	Jurisdictional	No	N.a.

Table IV-1. (cont'd)

	Double Tax Relief: Business Income	*Double Tax Relief: Subsidiary Dividends*	*Double Tax Relief: Portfolio Income*	*Controlled Foreign Corporation (CFC) Legislation*	*CFC Basic Approach*	*Foreign Investment Company Legislation (FIC)*	*FIC Basic Approach*
The Netherlands	Exemption	Exemption	Foreign tax credit	No	N.a.	Yes	Deemed return
Sweden	Foreign tax credit	Exemption	Foreign tax credit	Yes	Jurisdictional	No	N.a.
United Kingdom	Mainly foreign tax credit, some exemption	Deemed foreign tax credit until 2009, then exemption for all dividends	Foreign tax credit/ exemption for dividends received by UK companies	Yes	Jurisdictional and transactional	Yes	Ordinary income on disposal
United States	Foreign tax credit	Deemed foreign tax credit	Foreign tax credit	Yes	Principally transactional	Yes	Interest charge on deferred distribution or gain on sale

Subpart B. Source Taxation

Regardless of their approach to residence-based taxation, all the countries under consideration in this book assert the right to tax income that, broadly speaking, can be said to 'arise' in the country. This source-based, or *in rem*, jurisdiction focuses on the connection that the particular item of income has to the taxing jurisdiction. The pattern of taxation applied to such income is similar in all of the countries. A distinction is generally made between 'business'-type income that is taxed on a net basis with the allowance of deductions, and 'investment'-type income that is taxed on a gross basis, often collected through the mechanism of a withholding tax. The withholding tax often applies regardless of the status of the recipient of the income, but in the case of taxpayers without a residence connection, it represents a final tax; in other words, the taxpayer does not have an opportunity to file a return and compute tax payable on a net basis. The following materials first analyze the issues arising in the structure of net basis taxation of business and employment income and then consider the treatment of investment income. In this area in particular, the normally applicable domestic rules are often modified by treaties limiting the scope of source-based taxation, and the domestic rules should be viewed with these qualifications in mind.

1. ISSUES IN THE STRUCTURE OF NET BASIS TAXATION OF BUSINESS INCOME

1.1. Threshold of Activity

Income from business operations is typically taxed only if the activities that take place in the country reach a certain level. This approach is based in part on practical and administrative considerations. If the activities are not significant, it may often be difficult to collect the tax, as it is usually not possible to use withholding techniques and the tax must be directly assessed. In addition, if the local activities are not substantial, the compliance burden imposed on the taxpayer to file a return and keep appropriate records may discourage non-residents from carrying on limited temporary income-earning activities in a country.

The degree of commercial penetration required varies, as does the formulation of the applicable test. Some jurisdictions impose net basis taxation if the taxpayer carries on any business activities within the jurisdiction, although the contours of what constitutes a 'business' can be different. Other jurisdictions impose tax only if the non-resident taxpayer has a 'permanent establishment' in the jurisdiction, which represents a more extensive presence in a country than simply carrying on business activities there. The permanent establishment concept is often similar to, but not identical to, the concept used in tax treaties. It involves either the presence of some sort of fixed business location, such as a store or an office, within the country, or the presence of agents in the country with certain types of legal authority.

In the *United States*, the basic threshold for net basis taxation is engaging in a trade or business in the United States. The concept has been developed by case law, which in general focuses on the continuous and regular nature of the activities, although results of the cases and rulings are hard to rationalize.[199] In addition, there are some specific statutory rules. In most circumstances, the performance of personal services in the United States constitutes a trade or business. Specific statutory exclusions apply for certain financial activities, such as trading in stock or securities with a resident broker for the foreign taxpayer's own account.[200] An election is permitted with respect to real estate activities that allow the taxpayer to be taxed on a net basis even where the level of actual activities does not constitute a trade or business.[201]

Canada also uses a business activities test. There is no statutory definition of what constitutes carrying on a business in Canada. The case law focuses on where contracts are entered into and where activities 'essential' to the making of the business profits are performed. Under a special statutory rule, soliciting orders or offering goods for sale in Canada constitutes carrying on business in Canada, as does any processing, construction, or manufacturing activity in Canada.[202] Non-residents who engage Canadian residents to provide investment management services are not considered to be carrying on business in Canada by reason of those activities alone if certain conditions are met.[203] In addition, the disposition of 'taxable Canadian property', such as real property or natural resource property

199. See, e.g., *Chang Hsiao Ling v. CIR*, 23 TC 1040 (1955).
200. United States, IRC, s. 864(b)(2).
201. United States, IRC, s. 871(d).
202. Canada, ITA, s. 253. The mere holding of a limited partnership interest is not sufficient to consider the partner to be carrying on business in Canada (s. 253.1).
203. Canada, ITA, s. 115.2.

by a non-resident, is subject to Canadian tax.[204] Special rules impose net basis taxation on income from employment activities performed in Canada.[205]

In the *United Kingdom*, income derived by non-residents is categorized into the same schedules or cases applicable to domestic taxpayers. With respect to business income, the jurisdictional question is whether the business is being carried on *in* (as opposed to *with*) the United Kingdom, and the question is determined on a facts-and-circumstances basis. In this connection, the place where contracts are entered into is an important factor.[206] From 2003, the test for the taxation of non-resident corporations is based on the existence of a permanent establishment (defined in a manner similar to that in the OECD Model Convention) in the United Kingdom.[207]

In general, *Japan* uses a permanent establishment test as the threshold for net basis taxation.[208] The domestic law concept follows the treaty definition of permanent establishment, although of course, there are differences in detail as each treaty definition may be different. Some categories of income are taxed on a net basis even in the absence of a permanent establishment. These include income from the sale of domestic real estate, income from the 'use or holding' of certain assets in Japan, and gain on certain stock sales.

Although capital gains on stock sales are generally untaxed in the absence of a permanent establishment, such gains are taxed on a net basis if a non-resident together with its affiliates holds 25% or more of the total number of outstanding shares and sells 5% or more of the shares in a tax year. Capital gains on stock sales of a 'real estate company' are also taxed on a net basis irrespective of the absence of a permanent establishment. A real estate company is a company the majority of whose assets consists of real estate in Japan.

The Netherlands also, in general, uses a permanent establishment approach. Although the term is not defined in the statute, the case law has in general followed the definition in the OECD Model Convention. In addition, a statutory rule treats real property held as a business asset as a permanent establishment.[209]

Sweden likewise bases business taxation on the presence of a permanent establishment in Sweden. The domestic law concept of permanent establishment is interpreted in the light of Swedish treaty practice, which in general follows the OECD Model Convention with respect to the definition of a permanent establishment.

Under *German* domestic law, business income derived by non-residents is subject to tax only if it arises in a permanent establishment in Germany or from the presence of a permanent representative in Germany.[210] Both terms are defined

204. Canada, ITA, s. 2(3).
205. Canada, ITA, s. 115(1) and (2).
206. For a famous case in this regard, see *Grainger & Son v. Gough* [1896] AC 325 (HL).
207. United Kingdom, Corporation Tax Act 2009, s. 19.
208. Japan, ITA, s. 164 and Japan, CTA, s. 141.
209. Netherlands, CITA, Art. 17a.-1.a; ITA, Art. 7.2-6.
210. Germany, ITA, s. 1 para. 4, ITA, s. 49 para. 1 no. 2 lit. a.

in some detail in the legislation[211] and are broader than the corresponding treaty concepts. Thus, a permanent establishment is present if a stock of goods is available and a permanent representative does not have to have authority to conclude contracts on behalf of his principal. Income from cultural, sporting, and other events can be taxed even in the absence of a permanent establishment.[212] Gain on the disposition of a greater than 1% interest in a German corporation is subject to tax without further connection to the jurisdiction.[213]

The *Australian* regime revolves around source rules rather than an explicit threshold test. Basically, all assessable income with an Australian source is potentially taxable, and the derivation of taxable income (assessable income less deductions) gives rise to an obligation to file a tax return. Assessable income does not include certain dividends, interest, royalties, and, from 2009, other income from Australian collective investment vehicles (called 'fund payments') payable to non-residents that are subject to a final withholding tax regime. In addition, there are various regimes of greater or lesser specificity mixing assessment and withholding elements for certain types of income and a broad discretionary power in the tax authorities to require withholding on non-residents' income on a case-by-case basis. Provisions were enacted in 2003 to allow regulations to be made for withholding in relation to non-residents; to date these regulations cover gaming junkets, construction, and activities related to entertainment and sports. These provisions function only as collection devices; they are not the basis for determining substantive liability to tax.

Foreign corporations are taxed in *France* on the business income they realize through what the tax code calls 'a trade or business carried on in France' (*entreprise exploitée en France*).[214] As construed in case law, this concept resembles the permanent establishment concept in the OECD Model Convention. It is, however, somewhat broader because no exclusion exists for activities of a preparatory or auxiliary nature and because, in addition to fixed places of business and dependent agents, it includes the performing in France of a 'complete commercial cycle' on a customary basis, such as several purchases followed by sales, or even a one-shot but large purchase-and-sale transaction.

1.2. Attribution of Business Income for Net Basis Taxation

Whatever the threshold for net basis taxation, rules are necessary to determine which items of income are sufficiently associated with the domestic branch[215] to subject them to tax. The approaches used by the countries differ substantially.

211. Germany, General Fiscal Code (GFC), ss 12 and 13.
212. Germany, ITA, s. 49 para. 1 no. 2 lit. d.
213. Germany, ITA, s. 49 para. 1 no. 2 lit. e.
214. France, CGI, s. 209 I.
215. In the subsequent material, the term 'branch' is used to refer to the applicable domestic threshold for taxation – that is, business activity, 'trade or business', permanent establishment, etc.

One approach focuses on the actual economic connection between a particular item of income and the branch. All income with such a connection is subject to net basis taxation, and all other income is either not subject to tax or subject to the withholding regime. Such an approach typically does not use independent source rules with respect to business income.

Another approach treats all income with a domestic source as attributable to the branch and thus subject to net basis taxation even when there is no actual economic connection between the item of income and the branch. This 'force-of-attraction' approach usually involves an independent set of source rules because whether an item of income is subject to net basis taxation depends on whether it has a domestic source. Between these extremes, a number of variations are possible. Under a 'limited' force-of-attraction approach, only certain types of income are subject to net basis taxation without regard to their actual economic connection to the branch. In some cases, income that technically has a foreign source may be subject to net basis tax if it has an economic connection with the domestic activities.

These 'direct' methods attempt to allocate a particular item of *gross* income to the branch operations. A conceptually distinct 'indirect' approach is used to determine the *net* income of the entire enterprise and then allocate that profit to the various geographic locations on some basis. The allocation may be made on the basis of turnover, assets, payroll, or other similar factors. This approach is often used in special industries such as banking, insurance, and transportation, while the direct approach is used for sales and manufacturing operations. The results of the two approaches can be quite different. A branch operation can show a profit on the direct method but have no allocable net income on the indirect method if the overall operations resulted in a loss.

While the general outlines of the various approaches are fairly clear, in practice, the details tend to be relatively undeveloped. This result is attributable partly to the fact that cross-border operations, in general, tend to be conducted in subsidiary form, except in the case of special industries such as banking, real estate, and natural resources.

In addition, special problems arise in determining the income attributable to transactions that involve dealings between the domestic branch and the foreign head office or other foreign branches. Those issues, which arise both in connection with income attribution and with the determination of appropriate deductions for the branch, are discussed in the following section.

The *United States* combines a 'limited' force-of-attraction approach with a focus on the economic connection of the income with the domestic activities. The rules for establishing the tax base are related to the complex set of rules for establishing the source of income that apply to both resident and non-resident taxpayers. With respect to investment-type income such as dividends and interest from US sources, the income is subject to net basis taxation if it is 'effectively connected' with the US business activities. The focus is on the function that the asset generating the income plays in the business and the business activities with respect to the asset. The same rules apply to determine whether capital gains from the disposition of assets are effectively connected with the US business and thus subject to net basis taxation. (Income in these categories that is not effectively connected to the US business is either taxed on a gross basis or not taxed at all.[216])

With respect to other items of income from US sources, the income is treated as effectively connected even if there is no factual connection between the item of income and the US business activities. Thus, for example, sales of inventory property in the United States that are made directly from the foreign head office, with no involvement of the US branch, would nonetheless be treated as effectively connected income.[217]

In *Australia*, as noted above, the regime for taxing non-residents starts with the basic assumption that all Australian-source income is assessable and taxed on a net basis. This applies generally to business income. The source rules for business income come mainly from judge-made law and operate on a facts-and-circumstances basis. In the case of income derived from the sale of goods, there have been suggestions that the sales profit is sourced where the contract is made. The tax administration has the power to determine the source of income for branches and separate entities when making an adjustment under transfer pricing rules. Australia does not generally recognize 'deemed' transactions and payments in the case of branches, and so brings to account only actual income derived, but achieves similar results by using notional transfer prices to source income between different parts (branches) of a taxpayer.

A few special regimes for certain types of business income mix assessment and withholding elements and may be regarded as examples of the indirect approach. For example, in the case of non-resident insurers and overseas ships, a certain percentage of receipts is deemed to be Australian-source taxable income, and an assessment, which effectively operates as a kind of withholding mechanism, is raised against a convenient local deemed agent (e.g., master of a ship, insurer's agent). In practice, tax treaties govern most of the business income derived in Australia by non-residents (although the domestic insurance and shipping rules are generally preserved in whole or in part) and the source rules for business income (profits attributable to a permanent establishment) effectively govern, since Australia's tax treaties provide that the source rule in the treaty becomes the rule for all purposes of Australian tax law.

Canada does not use the force-of-attraction principle in general, although certain items of Canadian-source income become subject to tax if the taxpayer is otherwise subject to net basis taxation. No detailed statutory source rules specify the geographic source of income. In the case of a non-resident's Canadian branch operations, income that may be allocated in a 'reasonable manner' to the Canadian branch is treated as domestic-source income and is taxed on a net basis to the non-resident. A non-resident's Canadian branch income must be computed on the assumption that the non-resident's only income is from carrying on business in

216. United States, IRC, s. 864(c).
217. United States, IRC, s. 864 (c)(3).

Canada.[218] Moreover, the non-resident is entitled only to those deductions that are reasonably attributable to the Canadian business. If inventory, intangible property, or depreciable property is transferred to, or withdrawn from, a Canadian branch by a non-resident, the branch is considered to have acquired the property at a cost equal to its fair market value at that time or disposed of the property for proceeds equal to its fair market value at that time.[219] Although there are no further statutory rules or administrative guidance as to the allocation of profits to a Canadian branch, the matter is likely to be governed by the provisions of a tax treaty because of Canada's broad treaty network.

The *Dutch* rules likewise do not apply a force-of-attraction approach and are similarly open ended. Income 'realized' by a Dutch branch is treated as domestic-source income and is subject to net basis taxation. Income and expenses, as well as assets and liabilities, are attributed to a branch if they are functionally related to the branch activities. For this purpose the Dutch tax administration generally applies the 2008 OECD rules on income attribution to branches. In case law, a payment attributable to branch activities but received after the branch activities had ceased was still considered to be attributable to the branch. Investment-type income such as dividends and interest are taxed to the branch only if the assets that generate the income are part of the business assets of the branch. The manner in which the assets are carried on the books of the branch may provide evidence as to the business character of the assets but is not controlling.

In *Germany*, income is generally attributed to a permanent establishment in accordance with a 'direct' method, focusing on the activities in Germany; the force-of-attraction principle is not used.

Sweden attributes income based on a 'true and fair' calculation of the economic results of the operations in Sweden, based to some extent on the accounting principles used to allocate income between the divisions of a single company.

The *United Kingdom* does not adopt any form of force-of-attraction rule. Income is attributed to the UK business activity on a factual connection basis. If the income can be said to 'arise' in the business, it is subject to net basis taxation. In addition, income from rights or property used or held in the business is subject to tax, as is gain on the disposition of business assets.[220] In the case of non-resident corporations, these types of income are calculated under a provision that is broadly consistent with Article 7 of the OECD Model Convention.

Because, in principle, a branch is assimilated to an independent enterprise, *France* does not follow the force-of-attraction approach, and the indirect or unitary method is used only in exceptional circumstances. Emphasis is generally placed on the branch's books, and the branch is taxed only on the active income attributable to it and to passive income effectively connected with it. No special source rules apply to business income because the existence of a 'trade or business carried on in France' is the criterion for both taxability and source.

218. Canada, ITA, s. 4.
219. Canada, ITA, ss 10(12), (13), 13(9), 14(14), and 14(15).
220. United Kingdom, Corporation Tax Act 2009, s. 19.

Japan has developed a system that relies to a large extent on source rules, income classes, and types of activity in determining the income taxable to Japanese branch activities. Foreign corporations are divided into categories depending on the type of branch activity they conduct. There are eleven (or fourteen for some purposes) types of domestic-source income and four types of corporate activities. Two basic patterns emerge from these rules. For some categories of operations, most importantly those with offices, warehouses, or other fixed operations that would constitute a permanent establishment under general international rules, an extensive force-of-attraction principle operates. For such operations, all income deemed to be from Japanese sources under the source rules (and only such income) is taxed on a net basis. If some of the 'attracted' items are subject to a withholding tax, that tax is credited against the final tax liability. Thus, if the sales branch of a foreign company also has interest income from Japanese sources that is unconnected in fact with the branch activities, that income would nonetheless be attributed to the branch and subjected to net basis taxation. On the other hand, if the sales branch had sales income that, under the source rules did not have a Japanese source, the income would not be subject to tax, even if the branch activities were important in the generation of the income and the income could be said to be 'attributable' to the Japanese branch operations.[221] The overall pattern of the rules resembles that of the United States prior to 1986.

A different approach is taken where the Japanese permanent establishment is not a fixed location but a construction site or trading agent. In this situation all domestic-source business income (and only such income) is taxable. Other types of income, however, are subject to tax only if they are in fact 'attributable' to the activities of the permanent establishment; the force-of-attraction principle does not apply.

There are two important modifications to the above pattern. In some treaties, the source rules are modified to provide that income attributable to the activities of a domestic branch are domestic-source income, thus allowing the taxation of income that would otherwise be technically exempt under the domestic-source rules. In addition, administrative regulations have attempted to extend the definition of domestic-source income to investment-type income, normally foreign-source income, which is generated by investments made by the Japanese branch.

1.3. Determination of Deductions in the Net Basis Taxation of Business Income

The rules for determining the deductions attributable to business income arising in a branch generally focus on the factual or 'causal' connection between the expenditure and the income. Following treaty practices, some of the domestic rules give considerable weight to the manner in which the expense is accounted for in the books of the branch or head office. Some expenses are allocated on a formulary

221. Japan, ITA, ss 161 and 164; Japan, CTA, ss 138 and 141.

basis that takes into account factors such as the ratio of the branch assets to total assets of the enterprise or relative sales volume.

Also following treaty practices, in general none of the jurisdictions in their domestic rules recognize 'self-charged' expenses for payments or transfers made between the branch and the head office. Thus, internally computed 'interest' or 'royalty' charges do not affect the income of the branch or head office. Only expenses that are actually paid or accrued to third parties support deductions, determined either on a 'direct' or formulary basis. It remains to be seen whether the proposed new Article 7 of the OECD Model Convention, which allows the deduction of notional expenses in some circumstances, will have an impact on domestic law. In the case of individuals, deductions for personal allowances and other personal costs are generally quite limited or not allowed at all.

In the *United States*, the same allocation-of-deduction rules applicable to domestic taxpayers for purposes of the foreign tax credit limitation are used to determine the net income of foreign business operations.[222] No deduction is allowed for self-charged expenses, and no income results from transactions between the head office and the branch operations. The focus is on expenses that are 'definitely related' to the income generated by the US business activities. In addition, a formulary approach is allowed for certain expenses. Thus, general and administrative expenses can be allocated on a sales or gross income basis between US and foreign-source income.

A special rule applies to the allocation of interest expense to US business operations.[223] The basic approach is to look to the overall capital structure of the foreign taxpayer and the relation of that structure to the assets used in the United States. It combines what is in effect a tracing rule with a residual allocation rule. In determining the relation between US assets and related liabilities, the taxpayer may use either the actual ratio of assets to liabilities or a fixed arbitrary percentage. Actual and 'allocated' interest expenses deducted by the branch may be subject to gross basis taxation. The special allocation rules are of principal importance to foreign banks that typically operate in the United States in branch form for regulatory reasons.

In *Canada*, expenses are generally allocated on a factual tracing basis, although a formulary apportionment of interest and overhead expense is allowed in certain circumstances. However, the deductible interest expense of a Canadian branch of an authorized foreign bank is determined by a formula that makes allowance for notional interest on funds advanced to the branch by the bank.[224] If all or substantially all of a non-resident's income is earned in Canada, the non-resident is, in effect, assimilated to resident status and other deductions are available to the extent that they can be considered applicable to the income earned in Canada.[225]

---

222. United States, Treas. Regs., s. 881-6.
223. United States, Treas. Regs., s. 882-5.
224. Canada, ITA, s. 20.2.
225. Canada, ITA, s. 115(1)(f).

The *Japanese* approach also combines elements of direct and indirect allocation of costs. Costs must be allocated on a 'rational' basis. For assets located in Japan, this generally means a direct determination of the relevant deductions (e.g., for depreciation). Other expenses may be deducted if they have a factual connection to the domestic-source income regardless of where they are incurred. However, there are strict rules of documentation for claiming deductions for expenses incurred abroad. For expenses related to both domestic-source and foreign-source income, a formulary approach is used to allocate the expenses on the basis of revenues, assets, etc., depending on the nature of the expense. Interest expense may be deducted directly if it can be traced to domestic activities; otherwise, it is allocated on a formulary basis.

The *Swedish* rules on allocation of deductions are quite undeveloped. For clearly identifiable costs incurred in the branch, such as salaries of local employees, the expenses are directly deductible. In other situations, a formulary approach – based on gross sales or a standardized head office charge, for example – may be used. In the *United Kingdom*, the deduction of expenses of a branch is a factual determination. For non-resident corporations, this determination is expressly to be performed according to provisions consistent with Article 7 of the OECD Model Convention. In particular, expenses are allowable if 'incurred for the purposes of the permanent establishment'. 'Royalties' paid by a permanent establishment to the non-resident company are expressly not deductible. However, interest paid by a permanent establishment to the non-resident company may be deducted where incurred in the ordinary course of a financial business.[226]

Germany in general focuses on the economic connection between the expense and the German activities under a tracing approach,[227] although there is no requirement that the expense be incurred in Germany. In the case of management and general expenses, an allocation of the headquarters costs of the enterprise is permitted as long as the connection between the cost and the German activity can be established. Although interest attributable to debt directly allocated to the branch would be deductible, it is unclear how the overall interest expense of the enterprise would be attributable to the branch. Because the branch is a dependent part of the business, contractual arrangements between the branch and the head office generally are not accepted (with some exceptions in the banking and insurance industries). Thus, usually only an allocated portion of costs paid to third parties can be deducted. A 'cost-plus' charge for control and coordination centres has been accepted in practice. It remains to be seen what impact the 'authorized approach' laid out in the OECD report on profit attribution, including the notion of 'dealings', will have on German practice in this area.

In *The Netherlands*, the same 'functional' approach as is taken with income attribution is applied to deductions. There are no statutory rules, and Dutch case law concerning the deduction of self-charged expenses has generally followed the approach in the OECD Commentary on Article 7.

---

226. United Kingdom, Corporation Tax Act 2009, ss 21–32.
227. See in general Germany, ITA, s. 4 para. 4 (not limited to international allocation).

All expenses effectively connected with and borne by the *French* branch of a foreign corporation, whether incurred by it or on behalf of it and wherever incurred, are deductible from taxable income. An expense incurred for the purposes of several branches must be allocated among them according to appropriate criteria. The general administrative expenses of the head office are usually allocable on the ratio that the branch's turnover bears to that of the corporation as a whole. No allowance is normally made for payments by the branch to the head office in return for money loaned, or patent rights conceded by the latter to the former when they do not constitute the reimbursement of expenses paid or accrued to third parties. Non-resident individuals are denied the personal deductions from global net income and tax credits to which residents are entitled unless these are expressly permitted by statute.[228]

In *Australia*, the normal allocation rules for deductions apply in this area as they do in others. Dividends, interest, royalties, and fund payments subject to the non-resident withholding regime are exempt, and accordingly, expenses that relate to these classes of income are not deductible. Generally, though, the withholding taxes (and consequent exemption) do not apply if such income is attributable to a non-resident's permanent establishment in Australia, with the result that such income becomes assessable and expenses related to it deductible. The way in which this is achieved and the application to both treaty and non-treaty countries vary across the different types of income subject to withholding. The special regimes that apply to overseas ships and non-resident insurers deem a certain percentage of freight charges (5%) or premiums (10%) to be taxable income to which the normal tax rates are applied, and thus amount to formulary measures allowing deductions for expenses of 95% and 90% of income respectively. In some cases, the local agent of the taxpayer can elect out of the special regime into net basis taxation.

When the operation of branches of foreign banks became possible in Australia in 1994, a special regime was enacted for the calculation of their income, which was recently superseded in part by another special regime in the new thin capitalization rules (see below). By way of exception to the generally strict single-entity approach in Australia, branches of foreign banks are treated as separate entities for certain purposes of Australian tax law. Most importantly, 4% of the branch's liabilities are treated as equity and 50% of the rest multiplied by the LIBOR interest rate is subject to interest withholding tax (in effect, a one-half reduction in the normal 10% interest withholding tax rate, recognizing the problem of applying full interest withholding tax rates to banks). In most cases, foreign banks can utilize interest withholding tax exemptions in domestic law; as a result, the interest withholding tax often does not apply. A branch of a foreign bank may elect to be taxed under tax treaty rules where a treaty is applicable and more generous to ensure that the statutory regime is not in breach of treaty obligations.

228. France, CGI, s. 164 A.

1.4. Taxation of Employment Income

Most jurisdictions tax employment income earned by non-residents on a net basis, typically with an exemption where the contacts with the jurisdiction are not extensive. Two basic approaches are used in determining the source of employment income. One focuses on the place where the services are performed, taking into account the days of physical presence of the employee in the country. The other is based on the place where the services are 'utilized' – that is, the locus of the benefit from the services. In general, expenses incurred in earning domestic-source employment income are deductible, but personal allowances or preferential rate schedules are not available or are limited.

The *United States* considers services income to have its source where the services are performed. The provision of personal services is treated as a trade or business, thus satisfying the threshold for net basis taxation. A *de minimis* rule exempts the income where both the presence in the jurisdiction and the amount of income are minimal and the payer is a foreign person.[229]

In *Japan*, income from personal services likewise has a domestic source if the services are performed in Japan and there is no further requirement for the income to be subject to net basis taxation. In the case of employees, domestic law allows only limited deductions. A special rule treats director's fees paid by a domestic corporation as Japanese-source income regardless of where the services are performed, thus assimilating such payments to corporate distributions.[230]

The *Canadian* rules also focus on employment performed in Canada. Income from such employment is taxed on a net basis, although the deductions in respect of such income are limited for both resident and non-resident employees.[231] Under a special provision, if a non-resident was formerly a resident of Canada, his entire employment income received from a Canadian payer is subject to Canadian tax except to the extent that the amount received for employment outside Canada is subject to tax in a foreign jurisdiction.[232]

The Netherlands taxes income from employment in the country on a net basis.[233] Director's fees paid by domestic corporations to non-resident directors are taxed even if the services are performed abroad.[234]

In *Australia*, apart from treaties, the source rule for employment income is a mixture of place of performance, place of contract, and place of payment. The original cases establishing these rules concerned seamen based in Australia in the days when tax was levied on a source basis only. In those cases, no jurisdiction would have taxed the sailors on their income earned on the high seas if Australia did not, which partly explains the emphasis on place of contract

229. United States, IRC, s. 861(a)(3).
230. Japan, ITA, s. 161 para. 8.
231. Canada, ITA, s. 8(2).
232. Canada, ITA, s. 115(2).
233. Netherlands, ITA, Art. 7.2-2.b.
234. Netherlands, ITA, Art. 7.2-7.

and payment. Nonetheless, the mix of factors continues to apply. It was held that the income derived by Robert Mitchum for acting in the movie *The Sundowners*, filmed on location in Australia, was not necessarily sourced in Australia.[235] Conversely, the salary paid by an Australian university to a resident academic on sabbatical leave overseas was sourced in Australia.[236]

The normal deduction, assessment, and withholding collection rules apply to non-resident employees, although a different rate scale is in operation for the first $30,000 of taxable income and the personal tax rebates (credits) are not available. Treaties are the only means of providing a liability threshold if the income is Australian-source income, although in practice non-residents with limited contacts with Australia may avoid the net basis tax. The international jurisdictional rules for the fringe benefits tax effectively track those used for employment income. Thus, liability arises in respect of benefits provided to a non-resident employee whose salary is sourced in Australia. However, non-resident employers will often not be aware of this liability, which usually cannot be enforced apart from voluntary compliance (or, more recently, through collection assistance provisions in tax treaties). In two of its tax treaties (with New Zealand and the United Kingdom), Australia has dealt with the fringe benefits tax by giving the exclusive right to tax fringe benefits to the country that has the primary right to tax the salary of the employee (the source country if the conditions in the equivalent of paragraph 2 of Article 15 of the OECD Model Convention are not satisfied, otherwise the residence country). In addition, the introduction of special rules for temporary residents in 2006 means that employees who previously would try to plan to avoid Australian residence may now be more willing to be categorized as residents. As well as the beneficial treatment outlined above, such persons also get the more favourable tax rate scale and tax credits available only to resident individuals.

The *United Kingdom* taxes all compensation for services rendered within the United Kingdom. Where duties are performed partly within and partly outside the United Kingdom, the income is generally apportioned on a time basis. Taxation is levied on a net basis, but certain personal deductions are not available.[237]

Germany taxes employment income if the services are carried out in Germany or 'utilized' by a German-resident employer. The same rule applies to income from self-employment. Taxation is levied on a net basis, but in the case of employment income some deductions are limited. Special rules apply to cross-border workers.

France levies a progressive (0%, 12%, and 20%) withholding tax, which does not exist for French residents, on employment income of non-resident individuals performing their activity in France. The tax is assessed on a net basis in that the salary is reduced by the standard 10% professional expense deduction, but the election to deduct actual expenses open to residents is not then available. The 12% tax is final. However, the income taxed in the upper bracket is included in the global annual income and therefore is subject to progressive individual income tax

235. *Mitchum* (1965) 113 CLR 401.
236. *Evans* 81 ATC 4512.
237. United Kingdom, Income Tax (Earnings and Pensions) Act 2003, ss 9, 11, and 27.

according to the same rules that apply to wages earned by French residents. The 20% withholding tax is then creditable against such income tax. A refund of an excess of both the 12% and 20% withholding taxes is possible under certain conditions. Special rules apply to sportsmen (15% withholding tax on gross income)[238] and artists (15% on net income, creditable and refundable).[239]

1.5. Other Situations Involving Net Basis Taxation

Other types of income are often taxed on a net basis, although there is considerable variation in approach. Most often, the income has substantial associated deductions or deduction levels that vary from situation to situation so that gross taxation, even at a low level, would yield inappropriate results. Often, net basis treatment is available for real estate income, where depreciation and interest deductions can be substantial. Gains from the disposition of substantial investments in domestic corporations are also often taxed on a net basis, with the underlying domestic business activity of the corporation, in effect, attributed to the non-resident shareholder for purposes of taxing the gain.

The *United States* allows an election for net basis taxation in the case of real estate. If the real estate activities constitute a trade or business, the income would be subject to net basis taxation even without a special rule. However, in other cases, the rental income would be subject to gross withholding tax. A special election allows the taxpayer to elect to have all real estate income taxed on a net basis.[240] In addition, gain on the sale of domestic real estate is also taxed on a net basis, and that treatment is extended to gain on the shares of domestic corporations that have substantial domestic real estate holdings.[241]

Canada similarly has an election to have real estate rental income, timber, royalties, pension and related benefits, and income from acting services taxed on a net basis.[242] In the absence of an election, these types of income are subject to gross basis withholding tax at 25%, or 23% in the case of acting services. Also, gains from the disposition of 'taxable Canadian property' by non-residents are subject to Canadian tax on a net basis. Taxable Canadian property includes unlisted shares of a Canadian-resident corporation; unlisted shares of non-resident corporations and interests in partnerships or non-resident trusts that derive their value principally from real property and resource property situated in Canada; and listed shares of a corporation if the non-resident and non-arm's length persons own 25% or more of the shares.[243]

238. France, CGI, s. 182 B.
239. France, CGI, s. 182 A *bis* (same rules as those for sportsmen before 2009).
240. United States, IRC, ss 871(d) and 881(d).
241. United States, IRC, s. 897(a).
242. Canada, ITA, ss 216, 216.1, and 217.
243. Canada, ITA, s. 248(1).

Most other jurisdictions tax real estate income on a net basis regardless of the level of activity or whether the real estate activities would otherwise qualify as a business. In *Germany*, special legislation makes it clear that real estate activities of foreign corporations can be taxed even in the absence of a permanent establishment; individuals, however, are taxed only if the activities amount to a business. The same is generally true for *The Netherlands*. In *Australia* a hybrid system often applies. If rent is derived through a collective investment vehicle (property trust) by a non-resident, a gross final withholding tax is applied to the rent component of the distribution, although normal deductions for property investment are available at the level of the vehicle in calculating the amount of rental income subject to the withholding tax.[244]

Results are more varied with respect to gains from the disposal by non-residents of substantial shareholdings in domestic corporations. The *United States, Sweden*, the *United Kingdom*, and from 2006 *Australia* in general do not impose tax on this category of income. In contrast, *Germany, The Netherlands, Canada*, and *Japan*, under varying conditions, include such gain in domestic-source income and impose a net basis tax. Thus, in Germany, for example, non-residents are subject to tax on gains from the disposition of a greater than 1% interest in a German corporation but do not pay taxes for capital gains from shares under the 1% threshold.[245] Under Dutch tax law, dividend and interest payments received from and capital gains realized on the disposal of shares in a domestic company are subject to tax on a net basis if the non-resident person owns at least 5% of the shares and these shares are not an active business asset of the non-resident person. Under tax treaties, however, the Netherlands typically cannot apply this domestic taxing rule.

Other miscellaneous types of income are often subject to tax on a net basis independent of the general classification of the activity generating the income as a business or permanent establishment. For example, *Australia* levies a withholding tax on natural resource payments to non-residents, but the rate is negotiated with the tax administration and is meant to reflect expenses; the taxpayer can file returns for refunds or be assessed on a net basis if it turns out that the estimated expenses are incorrect.[246] Under the Japanese system, income from the 'use or holding' of assets in Japan is taxed on a net basis, even in the absence of a permanent establishment. This category of income virtually functions as a catch-all provision to cover types of income that, in the belief of the Japanese tax authority, should be regarded as Japanese-source income but that do not seem to fall in other categories of Japanese-source income.[247]

244. Australia, ITAA 1997, Div 840-M, Income Tax (Managed Investment Trust Withholding Tax) Act 2008, Taxation Administration Act 1953, Sch. 1 Div 12-H.
245. Germany, ITA, s. 49 para. 1 no. 2 lit. e.
246. Australia, ITAA, 1936, s. 6CA, Taxation Administration Act 1953, Sch. 1 Div 12-G.
247. Japan, ITA, s. 161 para. 1; Japan, CTA, s. 138 para. 1.

2. ISSUES IN THE STRUCTURE OF GROSS BASIS TAXATION

All of the systems here under consideration impose a gross-based withholding tax on certain categories of income. Sometimes the withholding tax is part of the domestic system and is applied to residents and non-residents alike, although for non-residents it represents a final tax. In other cases, the withholding tax is aimed only at foreign persons. The income subject to withholding is typically investment-type income that is not connected with a business activity and that is deemed to have a domestic source. Thus, the structural rules involve issues as to classification of the income by type as well as by source. In some cases, the source rules are the same as those used in determining the income entitled to domestic double tax relief; in some cases, there are special source rules for income accruing to foreign persons.

The *United States* rules imposing gross basis taxation on foreign persons apply to 'fixed or determinable annual or periodic' income from domestic sources.[248] The taxable category has been broadly interpreted and applies essentially to all income that does not involve the sale of property. The rate of tax is 30% regardless of the type of income. However, statutory exceptions exempt interest on domestic bank deposits and most interest paid by US corporations or the US government on publicly traded debt.[249]

Detailed statutory source rules deal with commonly recurring types of income such as dividends, interest, and royalties.[250] In general, the same source rules that apply to domestic persons apply to foreign persons. The source rules focus in part on economic connections and in part on formal legal relations. For example, royalties are sourced where the property is used while interest, in general, is sourced where the payer is resident. Special rules apply to interest paid by a US trade or business. The interest is treated as if paid by a US corporation and, as such, is subject to tax in the hands of a foreign recipient. In addition, if, under the rules allocating interest expense to the US branch, more interest has been deducted than paid directly, the branch is subject to the usually applicable gross basis tax on that excess.[251]

Domestic-source income is subject to withholding by the payer, and the withheld amount functions as a final tax. No withholding is required if the income is part of the business income of the foreign taxpayer. If for some reason the appropriate tax is not withheld, both the foreign person and the domestic withholding agent are liable for the tax. Special withholding rules also apply to partnerships with non-resident partners and to dispositions of US real estate.[252]

---

248. United States, IRC, ss 771(a) and 881(a).
249. United States, IRC, s. 871(h).
250. United States, IRC, s. 871(a).
251. United States, IRC, s. 884(f).
252. United States, IRC, ss 1441–45.

Japan takes a somewhat similar approach. Source rules deal with rentals, interest, dividends, royalties, prizes, annuities, income from certain financial instruments, and 'silent partnership' income. All such income is subject to withholding even if it arises in connection with a business that is taxed on a net basis.[253] (The corporation can request non-withholding treatment in certain circumstances.) The withheld tax is credited against the net basis tax liability. The source rules are generally the same for both inbound and outbound transactions.

The *Swedish*[254] system does not have extensive source rules and simply defines certain categories of income that are subject to withholding as a final tax. Unlike other systems, Sweden taxes employment income from services performed in Sweden on a gross basis. Withholding is imposed on the following types of income at the given rates: employment income, director's fees, and pensions at 25%; dividends at 30%; and artists and entertainers at 15%. The rates of withholding were set at a level intended roughly to take into account the costs associated with the income. The Swedish 'special income tax' (*Särskild Inkomstskatt*) is a 25% tax on gross income earned by non-residents. The taxation applies mainly to income from employment by a Swedish employer (or by a foreign employer if the employee stays for more than 183 days per year in Sweden) and to pensions paid by the Swedish government or in respect of private employment carried out in Sweden. As the 25% tax on gross income may result in a harsher taxation than taxation according to normal rules, an election has been introduced as a result of criticism from the ECJ. This election is available only for persons whose employment income is earned wholly or almost wholly in Sweden.

Canada imposes a 25% withholding tax on a statutory catalogue of income categories when paid by Canadian residents to a non-resident.[255] The statute is not structured in terms of source rules, but the operative taxing provisions function in that manner. Thus, in general, interest payable by a Canadian resident is subject to the withholding tax. This is functionally the same result as in the United States, which relies on explicit source rules.

Withholding is required on many types of interest, including participating interest, but exceptions are made for interest on governmental obligations and mortgage interest on real property located outside Canada.[256] Estate and trust income is generally subject to withholding when paid to a non-resident. Amounts paid by a resident for the use of, or the right to use, property in Canada, including intangibles, are subject to tax, with the charging provision in effect functioning as a source rule. Dividends paid by Canadian corporations, including constructive dividends, are subject to tax, as are management fees, alimony, pensions and other deferred compensation, the interest element in annuities, and a wide variety of other payments.

---

253. Japan, ITA, s. 212.
254. Sweden, Act on Special Income Tax for Foreign Residents.
255. Canada, ITA, Part XIII.
256. Canada, ITA, s. 212(1)(b) and (3).

The scope of the withholding regime is extended substantially by rules deeming certain payers to be Canadian residents (and thus subject to withholding obligations) and by parallel rules deeming recipients to be non-residents, again triggering a withholding tax liability.[257] Thus, payments by a non-resident that are deductible in computing Canadian business or real estate profits are deemed to be made by a Canadian resident and thus subject to withholding when paid to a non-resident. Specific rules apply to partnerships to treat them as residents for amounts paid to non-residents that are deductible in Canada and as non-residents for amounts received from Canadian-resident payers.[258]

A special regime applies to non-resident actors and their companies. Such non-residents are subject to a flat rate final withholding tax of 23% of the income from acting services performed in Canada.[259] As noted above, the non-resident actor has the option of filing a tax return and paying tax on net income.[260]

The *United Kingdom* requires withholding at the basic rate of 20% on a wide range of investment income.[261] In the case of rent from land, the withholding applies only to payments to non-residents. The withholding is not a final tax and is credited against any tax liability declared by the non-resident. By contrast, interest is subject to withholding but there are many exceptions to its application. In particular, withholding does not apply to payments of interest to a resident company. Annuities and certain other annual payments (including royalties) are subject to withholding at the basic rate of 20%. Dividends are not subject to any withholding tax. Where any of these types of payment (other than rent from land) is received by a non-resident that has no UK representative, UK tax is limited to any withholding tax.

In *Germany*, withholding taxes are imposed on some categories of income regardless of the status of the recipient and are also imposed specifically on certain income paid to non-residents. With respect to capital income (e.g., dividends, certain types of interest, income of silent partners), the withholding tax represents a final tax for non-residents.[262] The tax is imposed at a 25% rate. In addition, a final 20% withholding tax is imposed on income from artistic, sporting, or cultural activities, royalties for the use of intangibles, and rentals for personal property.[263] In 2003, the ECJ declared this 'gross basis' taxation to be an infringement of the freedom of services in the European Union.[264] Therefore, Germany has broadened the deductions available to non-resident taxpayers. A final 30% withholding tax is imposed on the fees of members of the supervisory board of a corporation.[265]

257. Canada, ITA, s. 212(13) and (13.2).
258. Canada, ITA, s. 212(13.1).
259. Canada, ITA, ss 212(5.1) and 215(1).
260. Canada, ITA, s. 216.1.
261. Generally, see United Kingdom, Income Tax Act 2007, Part 15 and regulations made under that Part.
262. Germany, ITA, ss 43–45e.
263. Germany, ITA, s. 50a para. 4.
264. ECJ, 12 Jun. 2003, C-234/01 (*Gerritse*).
265. Germany, ITA, s. 50a paras 1–3.

Under a court-developed principle later incorporated into the statute, the usual rule that all the income of a corporation is treated as business income is not applied in the case of non-resident corporations.[266] Thus, they can be taxed on, for example, royalty or dividend income from German sources even in the absence of a permanent establishment.

The interaction of net basis and gross basis rules in *Australia* is quite complex. The Australian non-resident final withholding tax on dividends, interest, and royalties is levied at rates of 30%, 10%, and 30%, respectively.[267] The interest withholding tax has an important exemption for widely held offshore fund-raisings that extends to all cases where the loan is open to public bidding, even if one lender takes the whole loan. There is also an exemption for interest payments to tax-exempt foreign pension funds and, under treaties since 2001, to foreign financial institutions. The implicit source rule in each case is payment by a resident to a non-resident, which in many cases will differ from the judge-made source rules in these areas. Thus, the theoretical possibility is opened up of a payment derived by a non-resident that is not subject to the withholding regime but is sourced in Australia and thus taxable on an assessment basis. This issue is not solved by the Other Income article in tax treaties, because that article in Australian treaties follows the UN Model and permits source-based taxation; nonetheless, such cases seem to be ignored in practice.

The interest withholding rule also reflects the emphasis on the concept of permanent establishment in tax treaties in the sense that the tax applies to payments of interest *by* non-residents with Australian permanent establishments and payments *to* Australian residents with offshore permanent establishments. The basic criterion is the use of the borrowed funds in an Australian business. In the case of payments to an offshore permanent establishment of a resident, the interest income is still included in assessable income (unlike all other payments subject to the non-resident withholding tax) unless the branch exemption applies, which depends on domestic source rules in some cases and on treaty source rules in other cases. But no credit is given for the tax withheld, which in this case operates as a surrogate tax on interest payments made by the offshore permanent establishment to third parties. In contrast, the royalty rule originally extended only to the case of payments by an Australian permanent establishment of a non-resident; however, as a result of avoidance schemes based on this omission, the royalty rule was aligned with the interest rule.

Dividends are in a special position because of the imputation system. The franked part of dividends is not subject to withholding tax when paid to non-residents but is subject to the net basis regime if there is an Australian permanent establishment to which the dividend is attributable. The non-resident in this case is entitled to the imputation credit, contrary to the normal rule that the imputation credit is not extended to non-residents; but the credit is non-refundable,

---

266. Germany, ITA, s. 49 para. 2.
267. Australia, ITAA 1936, Part III Div 11A, Income Tax (Dividends, Interest and Royalties Withholding Tax) Act 1974, Taxation Administration Act 1953, Sch. 1 Div 12-F.

unlike in the case of certain residents.[268] Normally, the unfranked part of dividends received by a non-resident other than through a permanent establishment is subject to the treaty-reduced withholding tax of 15%.

Where an Australian-resident company receives foreign income, it may be exempt or assessable depending on the kind of income, as discussed above. When the company pays out such income, it will emerge as an unfranked dividend to the extent that no Australian company tax was paid on the income as a result of the foreign income exemption or foreign tax credit systems. The company may track such 'conduit foreign income' and match it with dividends paid that will not be subject to non-resident dividend withholding tax to that extent.[269] Although this benefit is in theory available to Australian multinational companies with non-resident subsidiaries and non-resident shareholders, strict rules to prevent streaming of dividends under the imputation and conduit foreign income systems mean that the benefit will generally have greatest relevance to headquarters companies. More recently, Australia has switched to a policy of negotiating zero withholding tax on dividends paid to non-residents who have an 80% interest in an Australian subsidiary for more than a year and meet anti-treaty shopping rules (starting with the 2001 Protocol to the US treaty). In these cases it is not necessary to rely on the conduit foreign income regime to remove withholding tax on the unfranked part of dividends. As a result of these changes, Australia generally has full conduit treatment for dividends flowing through Australia. In relation to capital gains, the government introduced the participation exemption for capital gains on non-portfolio interests in foreign subsidiaries in 2004 and removed the tax on sales by non-residents of non-portfolio interests in Australian-resident companies in 2006 (apart from land-rich companies) so that Australia now effectively has a full conduit regime for dividends and capital gains.[270]

The *French* tax code contains a list of French-source income; foreign-source income is defined as anything else. Source is determined, according to the categories, on the basis of economic connections or formal legal relations, or a combination of both. Some categories of income are subject to withholding taxes. These are assessed to some extent on a net basis (i.e., salaries, compensation of artists, gains on the sale of real property)[271] and are final[272] or creditable against income tax.[273] In other cases (i.e., income from independent personal services, copyrights, industrial property rights, remuneration for services of any kind supplied or used in France, remuneration of artists and athletes),[274] the withholding tax is assessed on a gross basis but is creditable against income tax levied on a net basis. The only withholding taxes that are both final and levied on gross income are

268. Australia, ITAA 1936, s. 44(1), ITAA 1997, s. 67-25(1DA).
269. Australia, ITAA 1997, Div 802-A.
270. Australia, ITAA, Divs 768-G and 855.
271. France, CGI, respectively ss 182 A, 182 A *bis*, 244 *bis*, and 244 *bis* A.
272. France, CGI, ss 182 A (12% tax), 244 *bis*, and 244 *bis* A (both for individuals).
273. France, CGI, ss 182 A (20% tax), 244 *bis*, and 244 *bis* A (both for corporate taxpayers).
274. France, CGI, s. 182 B.

the 25% tax on distributed income,[275] 18% on interest (subject to many exemptions),[276] and 16% on gains from the disposition of substantial interests in French corporations.[277] Some creditable withholding taxes have been transformed from non-refundable to refundable[278] or from gross to net income[279] to comply with EC case law.[280] Moreover, the withholding tax on dividends paid to an EU parent corporation, even if authorized by treaty, is not applicable or is refundable insofar as the parent is not able to neutralize such tax in its own country (e.g., by a tax credit) because of EU case law. The ECJ ruled that France is not allowed to tax such dividends because profits distributed to a French parent are tax-free according to the intercorporate dividend exemption.[281]

Of all the jurisdictions here considered, *The Netherlands* has the least extensive gross basis source taxation. Historically, this appears to reflect a conscious policy – relinquished at the end of the last century as a result of EU and OECD pressure – to encourage the use of The Netherlands as the location for holding and intermediate companies, often engaged in treaty-shopping activities. Still, dividends paid by Dutch companies are subject to withholding tax at the rate of 15%. For non-residents, this tax is a final tax unless the dividends are attributed to a permanent establishment, in which case the tax is credited against the net basis tax liability. Interest based on profits is treated as a dividend for these purposes. Other interest, royalties, and like payments are in general not subject to any gross or net basis taxation when paid to non-residents.

3. BRANCH PROFITS TAX

Absent special rules, the remittance of profits from a branch activity would not be subject to any further source-based taxation. In contrast, dividends paid by a domestic corporation would typically be subject to a withholding tax. This difference in treatment of alternative investment structures has led some countries to impose a second 'level' of tax on branch income of foreign corporations. Although the technical rules differ in many respects, the basic impact of the tax is to subject the net after-tax profits of the branch to a tax roughly equivalent to the tax that would have been applicable to a profits distribution by a domestic subsidiary.

---

275. France, CGI, s. 119 *bis*-2.
276. France, CGI, ss 119 *bis*-1, 125 A-III, 131 *quater*, etc.
277. France, CGI, s. 244 *bis* B.
278. France, CGI, ss 244 *bis* and 244 *bis* A.
279. France, CGI, s. 182 A *bis*.
280. See ECJ, 12 Jun. 2003, C-234/01 (*Gerritse*).
281. ECJ, 14 Dec. 2008, C-170/05, (*Denkavit International* – distribution by a French subsidiary to a Dutch parent). But the compatibility with EC law of these provisions is itself questionable, since later EC case law seems to require that the neutralization be provided by the treaty itself (e.g., by a full tax credit clause): ECJ, 8 Nov. 2007, C-379/05 (*Amurta* – Dutch subsidiary, Portuguese parent).

Until 1986, the *United States* attempted to impose a second 'level' of tax when a foreign corporation with US branch activities made a dividend distribution to its shareholders. The tax was difficult to enforce and was resented by other countries as an attempt at 'extraterritorial' taxation, involving as it did the taxation of a distribution by a foreign corporation to a foreign shareholder. In 1986, this second-level withholding tax was replaced in most situations by a branch profits tax imposed on the net after-tax income of the branch.[282] After-tax profits that are not reinvested in the US business are subject to the same 30% tax that a dividend distribution by a US corporation would attract. If the tax is avoided currently by reinvesting profits, subsequent decreases in investment trigger a 'recapture' of the tax. If branch activities are terminated, there is no recapture of the tax previously not paid through reinvestment. If the assets are transferred to a US corporation, the taxpayer can defer current tax by agreeing that a subsequent sale of the stock will result in recognition of the deferred branch tax. The treatment is based on the model of a liquidating distribution by a domestic subsidiary that similarly would not have attracted a dividend withholding tax. As discussed above, a somewhat similar 'branch interest' tax is imposed on interest expense that has been allocated to US branch activities. Where tax rates on dividends on direct investments and interest are reduced or eliminated by treaties, the treaty rate applies for the branch profits tax.

Canada has a similar branch profits tax that antedated the US tax. It is imposed at a 25% rate, the normal withholding rate on dividends, on the after-tax profits of a Canadian business operated by a foreign corporation that are not reinvested in the Canadian operations.[283] Any amount claimed by a non-resident corporation as reinvested profits in computing the branch tax payable for a particular year must be included in computing the base for the branch tax for the succeeding year. Accordingly, as in the US system, if a non-resident corporation decreases its branch investment in subsequent years, the prior reduction of the branch tax will be recaptured. A similar result occurs if a branch operation is terminated. However, where a non-resident corporation forms a Canadian corporation and transfers to the corporation the assets of the Canadian branch, the recapture is effectively deferred. In effect, a non-resident corporation may transfer the assets of a branch operation to a wholly owned Canadian subsidiary on a rollover basis.

An authorized foreign bank operating through a branch in Canada is required to pay a special 25% tax on its 'taxable interest expense', which is defined to be 15% of the amount of notional interest deductible in computing the Canadian branch profits.[284] This tax does not apply to banks resident in a country with which Canada has a tax treaty if that country does not impose a tax similar to the Canadian tax on Canadian banks operating in the country. Even if this exemption does not apply, the rate of the tax may be reduced if an applicable tax treaty provides a lower rate on interest payments to related residents of that country.

---

282. United States, IRC, s. 884.
283. Canada, ITA, s. 219.
284. Canada, ITA, s. 218.2.

France has a related method of imposing a second level of source-country tax on foreign corporate operations.[285] France levies its 25% withholding tax normally applicable to distributed income on the net after-tax profits of foreign corporations operating in France. In effect, those profits are deemed to be distributed to non-resident shareholders, and the tax is equivalent to the withholding tax that would have been imposed on distributions by a resident company. However, this second-level tax can be refunded if the foreign corporation can prove that, in the year following the realization of the income, it has distributed no dividends or that all shareholders are French residents. It is partially refunded when the corporation can demonstrate that it has distributed less money than its earnings in France and/or in proportion to the percentage of French residents among its shareholders. Corporations having their place of effective management in other EU States are no longer subject to this tax (because of its probable incompatibility with the EU freedom of establishment principle). Moreover, it has been judged incompatible with tax treaties containing provisions equivalent to the definition of dividends and the Other Income article in the OECD Model Convention.

Australia previously had a branch profits tax, but it was eliminated when, in connection with the introduction of the imputation system, the corporate and maximum individual tax rates were aligned and the non-resident dividend withholding tax on the franked part of dividends was abolished. Although the corporate rate is now significantly below the maximum individual rate, which would provide some justification for both a non-resident dividend withholding tax and a branch profits tax, neither has been reintroduced (perhaps originally to forestall efforts by the United States to obtain imputation benefits by treaty). Australia has progressively lowered its company tax rate to 30% on the grounds of international competitiveness and, as discussed above, is now reciprocally eliminating dividend withholding tax by treaty on holdings of 80% or more in Australian subsidiaries. In that case, there is no need for a branch profits tax, which is the position recently achieved in the Protocol to the treaty with the United States in respect of the US branch profits tax.

Sweden, The Netherlands, Japan, the *United Kingdom*, and *Germany* do not have a branch profits tax.

4. LIMITATIONS ON BASE-ERODING PAYMENTS TO NON-RESIDENTS

Where, as is usually the case, rates on business income taxed on a net basis are higher than rates on deductible gross basis taxed payments, taxpayers have an incentive to reduce the net basis tax base as much as possible. This is particularly true where treaties reduce or even eliminate the gross basis taxation. In response, a number of countries have imposed restrictions on the deductibility of such base-eroding payments. The focus here is on restrictions that are exclusively or

285. France, CGI, s. 115 *quinquies*.

primarily aimed at non-resident-owned domestic operations.[286] The most common problem is debt financing of domestic subsidiary operations by non-residents with the attendant interest deduction reducing the income of the domestic subsidiary. Here, special debt-equity rules are sometimes applied to non-resident-owned domestic corporations. Other provisions limit the extent of the interest deduction if interest payments are deemed excessive in relation to the domestic income. These 'earnings stripping' rules are also typically focused on payments to non-residents.

In the *United States*, there are no special debt-equity rules applicable to non-residents. However, 'earnings stripping' restrictions do limit the deductibility of certain interest payments.[287] The rules are applicable to payments of interest to related parties who are tax-exempt and thus cover loans by domestic tax-exempt organizations, although the thrust of the provisions is clearly at non-resident investors who are often exempt by treaty from withholding tax on outbound interest payments. Originally limited to loans made directly by related tax-exempt persons, the provision was expanded to cover loans by third parties that are guaranteed by foreign persons. For the interest deduction to be limited, the corporation's debt-equity ratio must exceed 1.5:1, and the corporation must have 'excess' interest expense, defined as interest in excess of 50% of the corporation's adjusted taxable income for the period. In that case, any excess interest paid to related tax-exempt persons is not deducted currently but can be carried forward and deducted in a later year, subject to the 50% limitation in that year. In addition, any 'excess' limitation can be carried forward and used to increase the amount of deductible interest in a future year. Where the interest paid to a foreign person is subject to some tax, but the tax is reduced under a treaty, the amount of the disallowed interest expense is determined by treating a proportionate part of the interest as being tax-exempt. Thus, if the treaty reduced the normal 30% rate to 10%, two-thirds of the interest expense would be treated as payable to a tax-exempt person and potentially subject to disallowance.

In addition, the interest deduction can be disallowed if the interest is paid to a third-party lender who is not subject to a gross basis tax and the obligation is guaranteed (formally or informally) by a related foreign person. In this case, the interest deduction can be disallowed even if it is subject to net basis taxation in the hands of the recipient – that is, when received by a US bank.

Canada has statutory thin capitalization rules that apply to loans by non-resident shareholders to Canadian corporations. These rules apply to foreign shareholders of a Canadian corporation who own at least 25%, by votes or value, of the shares of that corporation. Constructive ownership rules apply for this purpose. The rules also apply to debt of the Canadian corporation held by a non-resident

286. The limitations are sometimes applied to all 'tax-exempt' recipients, thus covering domestic tax-exempt organizations as well as foreign taxpayers, but the main impact of the rules usually is, and is intended to be, on foreigners, with the extension to tax-exempt organizations aimed at avoiding treaty-based complaints of discrimination.

287. United States, IRC, s. 163(j).

who does not deal at arm's length with such shareholders. A 2:1 debt-equity ratio is required and is calculated on the basis of the average of the greatest amount of debt outstanding at any time in each month to the specified shareholders and persons not dealing at arm's length with them. The equity of the corporation is defined as the aggregate of its retained earnings, any surplus contributed by the specified non-resident shareholders, and the average of the monthly paid-up capital of the shares owned by such shareholders. Equity is computed on a non-consolidated basis. A special anti-avoidance rule prevents the circumvention of the thin capitalization rules through the use of back-to-back loans. The Canadian thin capitalization rules do not apply to partnerships, trusts, or branches. The rules, first introduced in 1972 and revised in 2000 to reduce the ratio to 2:1, are generally thought to be ineffective. A recent Advisory Panel recommended that the debt-equity ratio be reduced to 1.5:1 and that the rules be extended to partnerships, trusts, and branches.

Australia changed its thin capitalization rules in 2001 so that they deal with base-eroding payments with respect to both inbound and outbound investment. Just as it is possible for a non-resident to erode the source-country tax base by interest deductions, so a resident can erode the residence country tax base by keeping its interest deductions onshore (especially where an exemption regime applies to most foreign business income, as in Australia). As noted previously, the United States has rules in its foreign tax credit system to deal with the latter possibility, but these are quite distinct from the US rules just described dealing with non-residents. Australia deals with both inbound and outbound investment with similar sets of rules, so that in effect the rules isolate the debt that finances the Australian operations of residents and non-residents alike and then apply limitations to interest deductions.[288]

The rules use a 50% or more share ownership threshold for control (compared to 15% under the previous rules for inbound investment) and apply a 3:1 debt-to-equity ratio to all debt, not just related-party debt (expressed in the legislation as a debt-to-assets ratio of 0.75:1). The previous 2:1 ratio applied only to related-party debt and for that reason could be easily circumvented by allocating unrelated party debt to Australian operations. It is possible to exceed this ratio under an arm's length test (i.e., if the borrower can show that it could borrow more from unrelated parties). In the case of outbound investment, there is a further safe harbour based on the worldwide debt-to-equity ratio of the group. This is not allowed for inbound investment because of the difficulty of establishing the actual ratio in the case of non-residents. Banks and other financial institutions are subject to special rules. For banks, reliance is placed on the prudential capital regime that operates internationally (under which the home country sets and regulates capital requirements), and for other financiers there is a choice of a 3:1 ratio (with borrowings matched by on-lending eliminated), or a 20:1 ratio. The rules also apply to partnerships, trusts, and branches.

The *United Kingdom* also has a complex set of thin capitalization rules. Since 2004, these apply domestically as well as internationally. The primary approach is

288. Australia, ITAA 1997, Div 820.

to rely on transfer pricing rules, which are broadly consistent with the approach under the OECD Model Convention and so incorporate the arm's length principle.[289] Under these rules, a deduction for interest may be denied if the interest paid by a resident company to a related non-resident company is not an arm's length amount. Further, a deduction will be denied for interest paid on any part of a loan that could not have been borrowed under arm's length conditions. The interest will be classified as a distribution only where it represents more than a reasonable return on the amount borrowed.[290] As mentioned above, from 2009 the total amount of interest that can be deducted by a corporation for UK tax purposes cannot exceed the total interest incurred by the group of which the corporation is a member on borrowings from unrelated parties.

Japan has thin capitalization rules that restrict the deduction of interest paid by domestic corporations to foreign shareholders under certain conditions. The legislation, enacted in 1992, provides that the interest deduction on loans to Japanese corporations by controlling foreign shareholders is limited if the debt-equity ratio of both related-party and overall borrowing exceeds 3:1. If the taxpayer can establish that comparable Japanese companies have higher ratios, those ratios will be used. Where the provision applies, it disallows a deduction for interest on that portion of the debt that exceeds the relevant ratio. The rule also applies to branch operations.[291]

The *German* thin capitalization rules, which previously applied both to non-residents and resident corporations, have been replaced by an interest-stripping rule that also applies to non-resident shareholders.[292] The new rules provide a strange mixture of traditional thin-capitalization legislation and a broad-based limitation on deductibility of interest payments. Under general income tax law, all owners of a 'business' (incorporated or not) face a disallowance of the deduction of interest payments exceeding 30% of the earnings before the deduction of interest, taxes, depreciation, and amortization (EBITDA). This general rule does not apply to interest of less than €1,000,000 or to single enterprises not belonging to a 'group' of companies. In the case of a group company, the interest limitation applies unless the taxpayer can show that its leverage does not exceed the overall leverage of the group. Apparently, the 'true aim' of the new provision is to fight against strategic allocation of interest expenditure within corporate groups. But the exceptions (for single enterprises and for uniformly leveraged groups) do not apply when more than 10% of the overall interest expenditure flows to a shareholder owning more than 25% of the company's shares.[293] In this case, not only the interest on the shareholder loan, but the interest on all loans, will fall under the harsh 30% rule laid out above.

289. United Kingdom, Income and Corporation Taxes Act 1988, Sch. 28AA.
290. United Kingdom, Income and Corporation Taxes Act 1988, s. 209(2)(d).
291. Japan, STMA, s. 66-5.
292. Germany, ITA, s. 4h.
293. Germany, CITA, s. 8a.

In *The Netherlands*, there have been case law restrictions on the deduction of interest paid on hybrid loans since the late 1980s. In addition, in the late 1990s and the first decade of this century, the government introduced anti-base-erosion rules to consolidate and restrict earlier case law regarding interest paid on related-party debt. Under the statutory rules, interest is not deductible on tax-driven loans between group companies unless the taxpayer demonstrates that the transactions were effected primarily for valid business purposes or that the interest has been effectively taxed (e.g., not reduced by existing or foreseeable loss carryovers or foreign tax credits) at a rate of at least 10% in the hands of the recipient.[294] Further, as a result of the *Bosal* decision of the ECJ, thin capitalization rules were introduced restricting the deductibility of interest in cases where there is an 'excess debt'.[295] These rules apply to both foreign and domestic situations.

For many years *Sweden* had no special provisions dealing with base-eroding payments to non-residents. However, in 2008 a special limitation on the deduction of interest payments was introduced.[296] These rules were a reaction to a tax planning scheme that took advantage of the lack of Swedish rules for thin capitalization and withholding tax on interest payments. The rules basically cover interest on debt created by inter-group sales of shares if the interest is not taxed at a rate of at least 10% to the recipient.

5. RESTRICTIONS ON SOURCE-BASED TAXATION OF NON-RESIDENTS WITHIN THE EUROPEAN UNION

The differential treatment of residents and non-residents reflected in source-based taxation has recently raised some important issues in the European Union. The provisions on freedom of movement of employees, business, services, and capital date back to 1957 when the EC Treaty was concluded and it was not until 1986, that the ECJ ruled that these provisions were applicable to differential taxation by one Member State of resident taxpayers of another Member State. To the extent that taxes have not been harmonized – individual income tax has not been harmonized in any respect, and in the corporate tax field, harmonization has remained limited to the Parent-Subsidiary and Merger Directives – the Court has ruled that the application of the domestic tax laws may not interfere with intra-Community movements of individuals and businesses. While these freedom-of-movement provisions forbid Member States to discriminate on the basis of nationality, the Court has ruled that since non-residents typically have a foreign nationality, discrimination in the treatment of non-resident taxpayers as compared to resident taxpayers is forbidden by these rules. A substantial jurisprudence has developed significant limitations

294. Netherlands, CITA, Art. 10a.
295. Netherlands, CITA, Art. 10d.
296. Sweden, ITA, Ch. 24 s. 10a–10e.

on source country taxation of non-residents. As of 2009, the Court had decided several cases dealing with various aspects of the problem. Forms of differential taxation that the Court declared as violating the Treaty include:

- individual income tax rates (the *Asscher* case[297] on the Netherlands 25% tax rate in first bracket for non-residents in contrast to the 6.5% for resident taxpayers);
- the right to file for a refund (the *Biehl*[298] and *Schumacker*[299] decisions);
- the right to personal deductions (e.g., medical expenses, alimony) and income splitting (*Schumacker*), provided the non-resident taxpayer derives virtually all of his income from the source state;
- the right to the imputation credit (*avoir fiscal*),[300] where shares of a French company were held in a French branch of a non-resident taxpayer;
- the application of CFC rules to a subsidiary established in another EU country (*Cadbury Schweppes*[301]);
- the imposition of a higher tax rate on the profits of a branch of a corporation with its seat in another EU country than on domestic companies (*Royal Bank of Scotland*[302]);
- thin capitalization rules (*Lankhorst-Hohorst*[303] and *Test Claimants in the Thin Cap Group Litigation*[304]);
- the taxation of the services income of self-employed non-residents on a gross basis but residents on a net basis (*Gerritse*[305]);
- the denial of the deduction of interest and other expenses in connection with the acquisition and holding of shares in a company established in another EU country (*Bosal*[306]); and
- the recharacterization of interest paid to a non-resident parent company as a dividend (*NV Lammers & Van Cleef*[307]).

In developing the restrictions on the taxation of non-residents, the Court does not always seem to be fully aware of the extensive impact of its decisions in the highly technical area of international taxation. Apparently animated by a desire to do away with all potentially discriminatory national restrictions, whatever form they take, the Court has increasingly limited the right of source countries to apply traditionally accepted methods of taxing non-residents. The governments of the Member States have become more and more aware of the vast number of

297. ECJ, 27 Jun. 1996, C-279/93.
298. ECJ, 8 May 1990, 175/88, and 26 Oct. 1995, 151/94.
299. ECJ, 14 Feb. 1995, C-279/93.
300. ECJ, 28 Jan. 1986, 270/83 (*Com'r v. French Republic*).
301. ECJ, 12 Sep. 2006, C-196/04.
302. ECJ, 29 Apr. 1999, C-311/97.
303. ECJ, 12 Dec. 2002, C-324/00.
304. ECJ, 13 Mar. 2007, C-524/04.
305. ECJ, 12 Jun. 2003, C-234/01.
306. ECJ, 18 Sep. 2003, C-168/01.
307. ECJ, 17 Jan. 2008, C-105/07.

longstanding rules that may not withstand the scrutiny of the Court. In addition, the 1992 Maastricht Treaty expanded the scope of the EC Treaty beyond restrictions of an economic nature. As a result, the prospect is that cases in which the Court in the past has denied the applicability of the Treaty because only personal matters were involved will in the future be found to be within the scope of the EC Treaty as amended by the EU Treaty. This development may trigger further voluntary harmonization of the taxation of non-residents by the Member States. On the other hand, it may lead the Member States to attempt to restrict the power of the Court through amendments to the EC Treaty.

The following **Table IV-2** summarizes the rules dealing with the taxation of various types of domestic-source income received by non-resident taxpayers. The typically applicable treaty rates are indicated, although there can be substantial variations in individual treaties. The column 'Sale of Stock' deals with source-based tax on gains derived from the sale of stock in a domestic corporation by a foreign shareholder who has no other contact with the source country. Likewise, the column 'Financial Product Income' is focused on source-based taxation of income from derivative financial instruments where there is no other jurisdictional connection.

Table IV-2. Taxation of Domestic-Source Income of Non-Resident Taxpayers

	Dividends	*Interest*	*Royalties*	*Business Income Threshold*	*Employment Income Threshold*	*Sale of Stock of Domestic Corporation*	*Financial Product Income (No Domestic PE/Business)*
Australia	0% if corp. tax paid; 30% gross withholding if not; treaty 0%–15%	10% gross withholding (publicly offered debt, foreign pension funds exempt); treaty 10% except bank interest	30% gross; treaty 5%–10%	Any Australian-source income	Australian source (place of performance in general)	10% + interest in land-rich companies	Generally exempt but Australian-source income taxed
Canada	25% gross withholding; treaty 5%–15%	25% gross withholding (government and arm's length debt exempt); treaty 0%–10%	25% gross withholding; treaty 10%, 0% for technology royalties	Carrying on business	Any employment in Canada	Any private company shares, 25% of public company or real estate in Canada taxable	Generally exempt
France	25% gross withholding; treaty 5%–15%	18% gross withholding (many important exceptions); treaty 0%–10%	33.33% withholding (creditable against net basis tax); treaty 0%–10%	Permanent establishment (some differences from treaty rule)	Any services performed in France	25% + interest in domestic company taxable (real estate no minimum shareholding)	Generally exempt
Germany	25% gross withholding tax; treaty	25% withholding tax;	20% withholding tax; treaty	Permanent establishment/ permanent	Services 'utilized' in Germany	25% withholding tax	Limited inclusion

Table IV-2. (cont'd)

	Dividends	*Interest*	*Royalties*	*Business Income Threshold*	*Employment Income Threshold*	*Sale of Stock of Domestic Corporation*	*Financial Product Income (No Domestic PE/Business)*
Japan	20% gross withholding; treaty 10%–15%	15% gross withholding; treaty 10%	20% gross withholding; treaty 10%	Permanent establishment	Any services performed in Japan over *de minimis*	25% shareholding + sale of 5% taxable (all interests in real estate companies)	Generally exempt
The Netherlands	15% gross withholding; treaty 5%–15%	Exempt	Exempt	Permanent establishment/ permanent representative	Any services performed in The Netherlands	Substantial interest (5%+) taxable	Generally exempt
Sweden	30% gross withholding; treaty 5%–15%	Generally exempt	Taxed as business income; treaty exempt	Permanent establishment	Services performed in Sweden	Generally exempt	Generally exempt
United Kingdom	Effectively exempt	20% withholding; treaty 0%–15%	20% withholding; treaty 0%–15%	Permanent establishment	Any services performed in UK	Exempt	Generally exempt
United States	30% gross withholding; treaty 5%–15%	30% gross withholding (portfolio exempt); treaty 0%	30% gross withholding; treaty 0%	Trade or business	Any services performed in US over *de minimis*	Generally exempt; interest in domestic real estate corporation taxed	Generally exempt

Subpart C. Additional International Topics

1. SPECIAL INTERNATIONAL AVOIDANCE RULES

The general approach of the jurisdictions examined here to tax avoidance schemes is discussed in the material in Part One. Beyond these generally applicable principles and rules, several countries have provisions that are aimed specifically at certain international transactions. In some cases, the same results might have been reached under normally applicable principles, and the international rule only clarifies the situation. In others, the rules are unique to the international area.

In the *United States*, general substance-over-form and 'step-transactions' principles have allowed interrelated financing arrangements to be re-characterized where the particular structure was tax motivated. However, questions about the extent to which the rules would be applied and their limits gave room for substantial aggressive tax planning in the international area. Congress responded by authorizing regulations to re-characterize 'multiple-party financing transactions' as occurring directly between participants, ignoring intermediate parties.[308] Regulations issued under this provision deal with international 'back-to-back' arrangements designed to take advantage of reduced treaty rates available to the intermediate entity. Interest paid to the intermediary is treated as paid directly to the ultimate source of the financing and taxed as such. The re-characterization occurs only if the financing transaction is part of a 'tax avoidance plan' one of the principal purposes of which is the avoidance of US tax. The regulations list a number of factors to be taken into account in making this determination.[309]

308. United States, IRC, s. 7701(l).
309. United States, Treas. Regs., s. 1.881-3.

The *Canadian* general anti-avoidance rule applies to abusive international transactions and to treaty abuses. Special Canadian rules are aimed at the use of non-resident trusts[310] and attempts to convert tax-free capital gains realized by non-residents on the sale of shares in Canadian-resident corporations into paid-up capital of a purchasing Canadian corporation.[311] The sales amount is re-characterized as a dividend (or reduction in the paid-up capital of the transferred corporation), which defeats the benefit that would otherwise be available. Other rules target weak-currency borrowings.[312] In 2007 rules were introduced attacking certain double-dip financing arrangements.[313] These rules were not slated to become effective until 2012. They were repealed in 2009 before ever becoming effective.

In *Germany*, there is a general anti-avoidance provision under domestic law,[314] but it is controversial whether general concepts of tax avoidance can be invoked by the authorities in treaty cases. The tax administration is of the opinion that tax avoidance doctrines are used to assess the facts. Accordingly, the tax administration applies tax avoidance doctrines even if there seems to be a treaty override.

Special domestic rules target tax advantages from abusive cross-border structures in tax treaty situations.[315] Under a recently enacted 'catch-all' provision, a switchover to worldwide taxation has been put in place to cover situations of 'white income' (i.e., income exempt under a treaty), but the treaty exemption does not correspond with effective taxation by the source state due to diverging characterization of the income or the absence of tax liability in the source country.[316]

The *French* anti-avoidance theories of abuse of law (*abus de droit*) and abnormal management decision (*acte anormal de gestion*) apply both to international and domestic tax matters. But some statutory provisions specifically embody these theories to combat more effectively certain types of international tax avoidance, especially by placing the burden of proof on the taxpayer.

Thus, according to the so-called 'rent-a-star company' provision, compensation for services rendered by an individual or a corporation in France, or rendered abroad if such person is resident or has an establishment in France, is taxed to such person if it is received by a person residing or established abroad who is either based in a low-tax jurisdiction or controlled by the person providing the services or who is not shown to be predominantly engaged in an industrial or commercial business other than supplying services.[317]

Similarly, interest, royalties, and remuneration for services paid to individuals or legal entities residing or established in a low-tax jurisdiction and payments of

310. Canada, ITA, s. 94.
311. Canada, ITA, s. 212.1.
312. Canada, ITA, s. 20.3.
313. Canada, ITA, s. 18.2.
314. Germany, GFC, s. 42.
315. Germany, ITA, s. 50d para. 3.
316. Germany, ITA, s. 50d para. 9.
317. France, CGI, s. 155 A.

any kind to an account in a financial institution established in such jurisdiction, are not deductible unless the French taxpayer can prove that the transaction is bona fide and that the amount paid is not exaggerated.[318] Finally, a French corporation is taxed on income arising from assets it had previously transferred, directly or indirectly, to a foreign person or trust without any immediate consideration in order for the transferee to manage such assets or pay interest and capital on a debt on behalf of the transferor.[319]

Similarly, the *United Kingdom* 'settlement' rules may attribute income to certain persons, typically the transferor.[320] These rules are broad and potentially apply to 'any disposition, trust, covenant, agreement, arrangement or transfer of assets' where there is an element of gift or value shifting. The rules are primarily targeted at sheltering income from tax in various types of entities (especially companies), income splitting (e.g., between family members), and income assignment. These rules apply only for income tax, not corporation tax, purposes and so affect only individuals and trusts. In this context, the rules impose substantial limitations on tax planning with respect to international transactions.

Australia has similar rules for transferor trusts used to move foreign-source income into foreign trusts.[321] It also has rules in relation to its corporate tax system designed to remove dividend and capital streaming, which are particularly relevant for non-residents.[322]

Under *Netherlands* case law, anti-avoidance rules do not apply in international cases where a tax treaty applies. Therefore in 2001, statutory rules were introduced to stop dividend stripping and other transactions where, as a result of a share transaction (such as stock lending or usufruct), the amount of the dividend would be effectively received tax-free by the resident or non-resident shareholder.[323]

Japan and *Sweden* do not have any special anti-avoidance rules in the international area.

2. SELECTED INTERCOMPANY PRICING ISSUES

All of the systems recognize as a general principle that dealings between related parties must be undertaken at arm's length, although the specific formulation takes different forms. The arm's length principle usually is applied on a transactional basis and formulary rules are not used. Some countries have detailed administrative rules, while others take a more 'facts-and-circumstances' approach.

318. France, CGI, s. 238 A. See also ss 4.1 and 4.3 above.
319. France, CGI, s. 238 *bis*-0 1.
320. United Kingdom, Income Tax (Trading and Other Income) Act 2005, Part 5 Ch. 5 (ss 619–648).
321. Australia, ITAA 1936, Part III Div 6AAA.
322. Australia, ITAA 1936, ss 45, 45A, 45B, 177EA, ITAA 1997, Div 204.
323. Netherlands, Dividend Tax Act (DivTA), Art. 4.3.

The general framework for analyzing intercompany pricing issues in the OECD Transfer Pricing Guidelines[324] seems to be widely followed. The terminology and methodology of comparable uncontrolled price (CUP), resale price, cost-plus, and other methods are thus present in most of the systems. Profit-based methodologies, such as profit-split and transactional net margin methods, are becoming increasingly acceptable. The following discussion is limited to the general approach taken by the countries and any special or distinguishing features that might be of interest.

The *United States* has historically been a leader in the development of transfer pricing rules, and its system is still the most highly developed. Rather than establishing an order of preference for a particular transfer pricing technique, the transfer pricing regulations instruct the taxpayer to use the 'best method' – that is, the method that provides the most reliable measure of an arm's length price under the circumstances.[325] Taxpayers may use transactions that involve 'inexact' comparables if adjustments can be made to improve the reliability of the comparison between the controlled and uncontrolled transactions. The factors involved in determining comparability include the functions performed by each party, the contractual terms involved, and the allocation of risks. The focus is on arriving at a range of possible arm's length prices using statistical techniques to establish the limits of the appropriate range.

The regulations provide various methods that can be used in the absence of reliable data establishing comparability. They permit a profit-split method in which the aggregate profit is allocated between the controlled parties in light of the functions performed, risks assumed, and resources provided by each party.[326]

The regulations also allow the 'comparable profits method' (CPM) of price determination.[327] Under the CPM approach, the determination of an arm's length price is based on comparable profit level indicators that measure the relationship between profits and costs involved and resources employed. The price charged the controlled taxpayer with respect to particular transactions must result in appropriate profit levels from those transactions as determined by the profit level indicators of comparable but unrelated parties. Unlike previous proposed regulations, which stressed the importance of a profit-based methodology as a check on other methods, the final regulations state that the CPM is simply another possible method and subject to the 'best method' principle. Thus, where better information with respect to some of the traditional methods exists, those approaches are to be used. Only where the information used to establish the appropriate profit margins is more reliable than that needed for one of the other methods will the CPM be the method of choice.

---

324. OECD, *Transfer Pricing Guidelines for Multinational Enterprises and Tax Administrations* (Paris: OECD, 1995) (looseleaf).
325. United States, Treas. Regs., s. 1.482-1 (c)(1).
326. United States, Treas. Regs., s. 1.482-6(a).
327. United States, Treas. Regs., s. 1.482-5.

Beyond the substantive rules, important procedural requirements must be followed to avoid significant penalties in case of a subsequent transfer price adjustment. The penalties can be avoided only if the taxpayer has followed one of the prescribed methods of price determination and has contemporaneous documentation establishing how the price was determined. Thus, the new regulations offer a substantial degree of flexibility in the choice of the method, but taxpayers must be prepared to demonstrate in detail how they arrived at their pricing.[328]

In addition, the United States has encouraged the use of Advance Pricing Agreements (APAs) through which taxpayers can obtain a binding commitment in advance from the fiscal authorities as to the appropriateness of the methodology to be used in establishing the transfer price. In many cases, these agreements involve both the United States and the other countries affected by the business activities in question.

The application of the arm's length principle has two foundations under *German* law. On the one hand, the general rule that there is a 'constructive dividend' where a company provides value to a shareholder without adequate consideration also is applied in the cross-border situation. Moreover, section 1 of the *Aussensteuergesetz* (Foreign Tax Act) provides that all economic or financial relationships between related parties must be scrutinized according to the arm's length standard. This is especially important if there is a hidden shift of profits from the shareholder (parent company) to the company (subsidiary), a case not covered by the rules on constructive dividends. This additional burden on cross-border relationships may constitute an infringement of the EC Treaty rules.

Germany has laid down specific provisions for international intercompany dealings,[329] but in most cases the general rules on constructive dividends[330] and constructive contributions are applied. In a widely discussed move, in 2007 Germany introduced a provision on 'business restructurings', which tries to emulate the outcome of a 'third party transaction' at 'arm's length' when a function is relocated within a multinational group.[331] This provision has been criticized heavily for overreaching, as it seems to tax the mere shift of 'profit potential' to other countries because it includes location benefits of that other country in the 'transfer price' and because it provides for retrospective adjustments in cases of unexpectedly high profits after relocation. The details have been laid out in an additional regulation.

For the details of transfer pricing in general, the administration has provided 'administrative principles' on transfer pricing. While not binding on taxpayers, they are followed in practice. They are based in part on the OECD Guidelines and in part on prior German judicial and administrative practises. The Finance Ministry has recently repeated the position taken in the administrative principles that only 'transactional' methods of price determination are acceptable, expressly rejecting

328. United States, IRC, s. 6662(e).
329. Germany, FTTA, s. 1.
330. Germany CITA, s. 8 para. 3 s. 2.
331. Germany, FTTA, s. 1 para. 3.

profit-based methods such as the profit-split or CPM. In 2003 the law was changed to formally authorize the tax administration to require extensive documentation of cross-border relationships with related parties. This new statutory provision will greatly raise the 'compliance burden' for transfer pricing.

In 1986, *Japan* adopted legislation dealing with transfer pricing. The provision applies to transactions between affiliated corporations where one party is Japanese (or a foreign corporation subject to corporate tax in Japan) and the other is foreign. It allows the tax authorities to make an assessment based on arm's length prices. The statutory provision is quite extensive and sets out at length the details of comparable price, resale price, and cost-plus methods. There is no priority as to the particular method that must be used. If none of the 'basic' methods can be applied, then 'alternative' methods can be used; profit-split may be used, although the tax authorities clearly favour the use of the 'basic' methods if possible. APAs have been available since shortly after the legislation was enacted.[332]

In *Canada*, statutory provisions require that transactions between resident and non-resident related parties occur at prices that would have applied in similar transactions between arm's length parties.[333] While there are no detailed regulations interpreting the statute, the tax authorities have issued various information circulars setting forth their approach to transfer pricing.[334] The positions taken are clearly based on, and consistent with, the approach of the OECD Transfer Pricing Guidelines. There is little case law, however, and it is unclear how the positions taken in the circular would be dealt with by a court. In a 2008 transfer pricing case under the old law, the Tax Court approved the OECD Transfer Pricing Guidelines and applied the CUP method.[335] Serious penalties apply if transfer prices are adjusted unless the taxpayer has made reasonable efforts to determine the arm's length price and has contemporaneous documentation to prove those efforts. The tax administration has significantly increased its resources devoted to transfer pricing over the past several years. Transfer pricing issues are often raised on audit but are usually resolved by negotiation without the need for litigation. There is a special procedure for APAs, both unilateral and bilateral, and several of these APAs are concluded every year.

In the past, Canada has indicated that it will not in principle follow a comparable profit method and will not make corresponding adjustments based on that approach. On the other hand, the acceptance of a profit-based approach in the OECD Guidelines as a 'last resort' may change that view, given the respect that Canada has historically given to the OECD positions.

Australia replaced its original defective provisions on transfer pricing in 1981[336] with fairly elaborate provisions that focus on when adjustments may be

332. Japan, STMA, s. 66-4.
333. Canada, ITA, s. 247.
334. Canada Revenue Agency, Information Circulars 87-2R, 94-4R (advance pricing arrangements) and 06-1 (transfer pricing and customs valuation).
335. *GlaxoSmithKline v. The Queen* [2008] TCC 324 (TCC).
336. Australia, ITAA 1936, Part III Div 13.

made and the mechanics of doing so (including adjustments to other taxpayers' positions) rather than on the pricing methodologies to be used. The 'arm's-length consideration' is the only guide provided and where this cannot be determined because of lack of information, the tax administration has power to determine the amount it considers to be appropriate. The provisions apply to supply or acquisition of property or services under international agreements, defined as the supply or acquisition by a non-resident otherwise than in connection with a business of an onshore permanent establishment of the non-resident or by a resident carrying on a business outside Australia. There is no requirement that the parties to the transaction be related. Thus, the provision deals with situations where unrelated parties enter into two transactions that together may be arm's length, but the one that affects Australia may not have an arm's length price because it is compensated for in the pricing of the other agreement that does not affect Australia. The rules also cover the case of branches where, instead of adjustment through an arm's length pricing of the transaction, the tax administration is given power to adjust the source of income and related expenses on the basis of criteria that include the separate-entity and arm's length pricing hypotheses found in the Business Profits article of tax treaties. The rules are activated only if Australia experiences a loss of revenue. There is no time limit on transfer pricing adjustments, although a time limit of eight years is under consideration and recent treaties impose a time limit of seven years.

The tax administration has released several rulings on transfer pricing that amount to many hundreds of pages. Generally, these rulings follow the OECD Guidelines and, like the United States, look favourably on profit-based 'fourth' methods. APAs are available; indeed, Australia was the first country to enter into a bilateral APA with the United States, in relation to Apple Computer's operations in Australia. The APA procedure is similar to that in the United States. Penalties in the transfer pricing area distinguish between tax avoidance schemes and other situations resulting in income understatement.

The *United Kingdom* replaced its transfer pricing rules in 1998 so that they apply automatically (previously the rules required action by the tax administration). This was necessary in the new self-assessment environment. The new rules are consistent with Article 9 of the OECD Model Convention and the law expressly provides for the rules to be construed in accordance with OECD principles, including its transfer pricing guidelines. The rules apply only if there is a potential benefit for resident taxpayers.[337] The UK tax administration has statutory power to enter into APAs. The power is quite broad and extends to cover the issue of whether income arises outside the United Kingdom.[338]

While *Sweden* has a statutory provision that requires arm's length dealings where an 'economic community' exists between the parties,[339] there are no administrative regulations interpreting the provision and the case law is also quite sparse. In an important case, the Supreme Administrative Court indicated that the

337. United Kingdom, Income and Corporation Taxes Act 1988, Sch. 28AA.
338. United Kingdom, Finance Act 1999, ss 85–88.
339. Sweden, ITA, Ch. 14. s. 19.

principles set out in the OECD Transfer Pricing Guidelines would be considered as 'guidelines' in establishing an arm's length price. That case also stressed that the commercial situation should be judged as it was at the time the parties entered into the agreements. The court seemed to indicate that price adjustments required under the US 'commensurate-with-income' standard would not be accepted. From a procedural point of view, the burden of proof is initially on the government to show that a deviation from an arm's length price has taken place, resulting in lower taxable income in Sweden. Thereafter, the taxpayer has the burden to show that the reduced income was compensated for in other ways, by offsetting transactions or by other commercial factors. The offset rules are quite liberal. Thus, in some cases, failure to charge an arm's length price for services provided by a Swedish company can be justified by the benefit that the Swedish company could be expected to have from future sales to the foreign company. In 2006 new rules were introduced concerning requirements for documentation based on the OECD Transfer Pricing Guidelines.[340] A report has been submitted to the government for the introduction of APAs, but no rules have yet been enacted.

In *France*, the requirement to deal at arm's length to determine transfer prices results from the abnormal management decision theory (a decision that is not in the interest of the enterprise) that has, since 1933, been embodied in section 57 of the tax code as far as international matters are concerned. There are few formal administrative guidelines, and the approach has always been based on the facts and circumstances of each case.

The tax service must show that a deviation from an arm's length price has taken place and, except when the foreign person is resident in or established in a low-tax jurisdiction, that the parties to the transaction are related to each other. Such transferred income is then added back to the tax base and is treated as a deemed distribution of income to a foreign resident, subject to a 25% withholding tax, unless the taxpayer can prove that the price was normal, that failure to charge an arm's length price is justified according to the particular economic circumstances, or that the price has, or could have, resulted in an equivalent increase in French-source income (e.g., because of subsequent sales). Case law is quite liberal in these matters.

Appropriate correlative adjustments are now available through the 1990 European Union arbitration mechanism,[341] which may apply after the mutual agreement procedure has failed to arrive at a satisfactory solution. The first decision arising from this procedure was issued in 2003 and involved two subsidiaries (French and Italian) of a Swedish parent.

A bilateral APA procedure was introduced in 1999; a unilateral procedure has also been available since 2005 where no bilateral APA procedure exists in the other country or the transactions involve many countries, a small business, or a specific

340. Sweden, Act on Income Tax Returns and Statements of Earnings and Tax Deductions, Ch. 19 s. 2a and 2b.

341. 90/436/EEC: Convention on the elimination of double taxation in connection with the adjustment of profits of associated enterprises.

issue.[342] The powers of tax auditors to make requests for clarification about relationships of French businesses with foreign persons and for documentation substantiating transfer prices were increased in 1996. When, in the course of an audit, the authorities have gathered information that leads them to believe there has been an indirect transfer of profits to an associated foreign enterprise, they may require the French enterprise to produce appropriate documents and information specifying the nature of the transactions and the methods used in determining the intercompany pricing for those transactions. Failure to comply entails a fine and entitles the tax authorities to assess the income on the basis of the available data. In addition, the statute of limitations is extended when French tax authorities request international administrative assistance in connection with transfer pricing issues.[343] Beginning in January 2010, major French corporations will have to comply with a new set of rules relating to transfer pricing documentation (general to the group and specific to each corporation) derived from the 2006 EU Code of Conduct in this field.[344]

Although *The Netherlands* has no specific statutory provision requiring arm's length pricing between related parties, the principle that profits can be 'corrected' in transactions between a corporation and its shareholders is firmly established in the case law pursuant to the statutory rule that business profits comprise 'all benefits, under whatever name and in whatever form, derived from business'. On the basis of this provision, the OECD Transfer Pricing Guidelines are considered to be generally applicable. In 2001 and 2004 the revenue authorities issued ten decrees outlining instances where the taxpayer may obtain an APA or an Advance Tax Ruling.

3. CORPORATE-SHAREHOLDER TAXATION IN THE INTERNATIONAL CONTEXT

3.1. General

In the case of cross-border investment by corporations, relieving double taxation has two aspects: the taxation of the earnings of a corporation by more than one country and the taxation of the earnings of a corporation at both the corporate and shareholder levels. Corporate tax integration issues in a domestic context are discussed in Part Three, which notes that international considerations have been one of the driving forces in the abandonment of imputation systems for relieving the double taxation of dividends.

Most imputation systems operated by giving a tax credit only to *resident* shareholders in *resident* companies in respect of *domestic* corporate tax (not foreign corporate tax). As a result, if any one of these elements was lacking,

342. France, *Livre des procédures fiscales* (Book of Tax Proceedings, hereafter 'LPF'), s. L 80 B-7.
343. France, LPF, s. L 13 B.
344. France, LPF, s. L 13 AA.

imputation did not apply: foreign companies, foreign shareholders, and foreign tax did not benefit from the imputation system. As a result of these features, imputation systems discriminated in an economic sense against cross-border investment through corporations and also in a legal sense within the EU because of the four freedoms. Several ECJ decisions concerning imputation systems are generally regarded as having decided implicitly that such systems were not consistent with EU law. These decisions were the main immediate reason for the abandonment of imputation within the EU; most imputation systems had been abandoned by 2005. At the end of 2004 the ECJ finally directly affirmed that the standard imputation system was indeed contrary to EU law.[345]

Within the EU before the abandonment of imputation and outside the EU currently, countries have grappled with the economic side of the issue. Both *France* and the *United Kingdom* regularly extended imputation benefits to foreign shareholders in resident companies, typically through treaties, although the entitled shareholders, mechanisms, and extent of relief varied. *Australia* maintains an imputation system limited to resident shareholders in resident companies in respect of domestic tax paid (which is extended to dividends received by permanent establishments of non-residents in Australia). However, in its recent tax reform Australia considered adopting a system similar to the UK and French systems but did not proceed because analysis suggested that it would have little impact on investment by foreigners in Australian companies.

Australia is still considering whether to grant imputation benefits in respect of foreign tax paid by Australian companies. *Canada*, by contrast, does not require that imputation credits be supported by domestic tax payments and so effectively grants imputation relief in respect of foreign income and foreign tax. For a time, the *United Kingdom* gave separate non-refundable tax credits for dividends received by resident shareholders from resident corporations out of foreign income in respect of foreign tax on that income. As noted earlier, the United Kingdom now operates a reduced non-refundable tax credit on dividends together with lower rates of tax on dividend income of individuals. Domestically, this system is equivalent to no tax on dividends received by individual taxpayers taxable at the basic or lower rate of tax, and a 25% rate of tax on dividends received by higher-rate (40%) taxpayers – which was exactly the outcome of the previous imputation system. One major difference is that the credit is available whether or not UK corporation tax has been paid in respect of the profits, so that the UK system is now like the Canadian system in that regard. The odd combination of reduced credit and reduced rates of tax on dividends was maintained purely for tax treaty reasons; otherwise, under the treaty then in existence, dividends received by all UK shareholders from US corporations would have been subject to 15% withholding tax, which would have been particularly detrimental to UK corporations with US subsidiaries. The new treaty between the countries has solved this problem.

345. ECJ, 23 Oct. 2004, C-319/02 (*Manninen*), 4.

In the case of foreign corporations, *Australia* and *New Zealand* have both recently enacted complementary legislation to pass through imputation credits.[346] Australian shareholders in New Zealand corporations will get imputation benefits for Australian tax paid directly or indirectly by the corporation, and vice versa. Both countries have similar imputation systems, which makes this system feasible, although New Zealand already has had to amend its system to prevent tax avoidance schemes.

The dividend tax relief systems recently introduced in several countries are more able to deal with corporate tax integration issues in an international setting and are thus more neutral with respect to foreign and domestic investment. In particular the *French* (from 2005), *German, United Kingdom* (from 2009), and *United States* systems give the same treatment to most dividends from foreign corporations received by resident individual shareholders as they do to dividends received from domestic corporations. Thus, only 60% of dividends received by German individual shareholders from foreign corporations are included in income.[347] If the shares are held as private assets, the foreign dividend income can also qualify for the 25% final withholding tax.[348] A similar result applies for French individual shareholders (only one-half of the dividend is included in income) if the company is resident in another EU member or a country with which France has a tax treaty.[349] For US individual shareholders, such dividends are subject to a maximum tax of 15% if received from a corporation resident in a country with which the United States has a tax treaty providing for adequate exchange of information or from a corporation whose shares are traded on a US stock exchange. A dividend from a foreign corporation does not qualify for this treatment in the United States if it is a foreign investment company or a PFIC because in these cases it is likely that the foreign corporation will not have paid a significant level of foreign tax. In the United Kingdom, individuals are entitled to both the reduced rate and the dividend tax credit when receiving foreign dividends.[350]

With respect to international double taxation and dividends, it is often said that the standard tax treaty arrangements are premised on a classical system. Two typical cases of cross-border corporate investment can be used to explain why this is the case. If an individual shareholder resident in country A invests in a corporation resident in country B, country B will levy its corporate tax on the corporation and, as usually limited by treaty, a 15% dividend withholding tax on dividends paid to shareholders resident in country A. Country A will then tax the dividend in full and give a foreign tax credit for the country B tax on the dividend. Hence, there is both corporate and individual tax on the income without any integration relief. *Australia, Canada, The Netherlands, Sweden* and *Japan* follow this pattern as the

346. Australia, ITAA 1997, Div 220.
347. Australia, ITAA 1997, s. 3 no. 40 ITA.
348. Australia, ITAA 1997, s. 32 para. 1 ITA.
349. France, CGI, s. 158 3-2.
350. United Kingdom Income Tax (Trading and Other Income) Act 2005, ss 13 and 397A.

residence country of the shareholder. As noted above, *France, Germany, the United Kingdom*, and the *United States* have departed from this pattern and give integration relief to dividends from foreign corporations. All countries except *Australia* (in respect of franked dividends) and the *United Kingdom* also follow this pattern when they are the source country and collect withholding tax on the dividends.

Alternatively, and more commonly, an individual shareholder may invest in a resident parent corporation in country A, which then invests in a subsidiary in country B. In this case, country B will collect corporate tax from the subsidiary but little or no withholding tax on dividends paid to the parent company. As a result of the Parent-Subsidiary Directive within the EU and as a result of recent treaties entered into by *Australia, Japan*, and the *United States*, there is no source withholding tax on direct investment dividends. Under most other treaties that follow the OECD Model Convention, the tax rate on the dividends is limited to 5%. As noted above, all countries except Australia (with respect to franked dividends) and the United Kingdom collect this withholding tax as permitted by the treaty. The elimination or reduction of the withholding tax effectively does away with a potential source of double taxation of corporate income in an international setting.

In addition, country A will give the country A parent corporation either a participation exemption or (in the United Sates) an underlying foreign tax credit so that there is little or no tax on the parent in country A, thus reducing or eliminating double corporate-level taxation on the corporate income. This relief may arise under domestic law (typically in *Australia*, *Canada*, and *Japan*), under treaty, or under domestic law reinforced by treaty (typically in *France, The Netherlands, Sweden*, the *United Kingdom*, and the *United States*). Country A will then tax the dividend received by the individual shareholder from the parent company. Until recently, such dividends were taxable in full without either international or integration double tax relief in *Australia, France, Germany, The Netherlands, Sweden*, the *United Kingdom*, and the *United States*. The foreign corporate-level tax was not taken into account in the domestic imputation system, and there were thus effectively two levels of full taxation (typical of the classical system), one on the corporation in country B and one on the individual shareholder in country A. One of the major recent changes has been to give integration relief in such cases so that the general type of integration relief available in a country now applies in *France* (from 2005), *Germany, Japan*, the *United Kingdom*, and the *United States*. Thus, as these developments show, the 'classical' double tax model for international corporate investment is increasingly being replaced by a variety of integration models that provide more neutral treatment of foreign and domestic investment than has proven to be possible under most imputation systems.

3.2. International Aspects of Capital Gains

The discussion of corporate tax integration in Part Three also considered the position of capital gains. Again, similar issues arise internationally as well as domestically with respect to the effect of the capital gains tax on the retained income of corporations. Putting aside the case of companies holding substantial real estate investments, most countries generally accept the international treaty norm that capital gains on shares are taxable only in the residence country of the shareholder. *Canada, France, Japan*, and *The Netherlands* continue to seek in their treaties to preserve their capital gains tax in respect of certain shares in domestic corporations. A recent proposal in Canada would exempt capital gains in respect of the shares of foreign affiliates of Canadian corporations.

In relation to direct investment in foreign companies (parent/subsidiary cases), the effect in most countries is that there is no tax at source on the sale of shares in a foreign subsidiary and so no tax on retained income there. If the residence country of the parent grants a participation exemption in such cases (*Australia* from 2004, *Germany*,[351] *The Netherlands, Sweden* from 2003, *France* from 2007, and the *United Kingdom* from 2002), there is no double taxation at the level of the parent. In the case where capital gains tax is levied on the sale of the shares in the subsidiary by the country of the parent, similar issues for corporate tax integration are raised, as in the purely domestic case discussed in Part 3. All countries except Australia treat the domestic and international cases of parents selling shares in subsidiaries in the same way, so that neutrality between the domestic and international situation is achieved, with one exception: So far as individual shareholders in the parent corporation are concerned, the domestic capital gains tax rules apply, and consequently the discussion of the issue in Part 3 is relevant.

If an individual shareholder makes a portfolio investment in a foreign corporation, no country seeks to tax the capital gain at source. All countries apply the same capital gains tax rules in this case as apply to an individual selling shares in a purely domestic case (putting aside foreign investment-type regimes). Hence, there is neutrality between domestic and international investment. Consequently, the degree of corporate tax integration achieved for retained earnings is the same as in the domestic case. As noted in Part Three, only *Germany, Sweden*, and the *United States* provide consistent treatment of dividends and capital gains in the context of corporate tax integration. The noticeable difference between dividends and capital gains received by individual portfolio shareholders in the international setting is the levy of a significant withholding tax at source on dividends (15% under the usual treaty limits) but not on capital gains. It is not clear what the continuing justification for this difference is. As already noted, neither the *United Kingdom* nor *Australia* (on franked dividends) levies the tax at source. The appropriate treatment of capital gains and its relation to the taxation of dividends is thus still evolving.

351. Apart from a corporate tax of 15% on 5% of the capital gain, which is deemed to represent non-deductible expenses.

4. SELECTED TREATY ISSUES

All of the countries considered here have treaties broadly based on the OECD Model Convention. Canada and Australia generally insist on greater recognition of source-based taxation than the other countries; however, as a result of the 2003 international tax review, Australia has started to give up an increasing number of source taxing rights and is moving closer to positions in the OECD Model Convention. The following materials consider several topics that have been important in treaty policy discussions.

4.1. Relation between Domestic Law and Treaties; Treaty Override

Under constitutional principles in the *United States*, statutory law and treaties are of equal status.[352] As a consequence, in the case of conflict between domestic legislation and treaty provisions, the provision that is later in time prevails. Thus, in principle, treaty obligations can be overridden by later, inconsistent domestic legislation. Nonetheless, the courts have required that the legislative intent to override a treaty obligation must be 'clearly expressed'. Historically there have been relatively few examples of treaty overrides, although the introduction of the taxation of foreign-owned real estate in 1980 is an important exception. In addition, Congress enacted several technical provisions in connection with the extensive tax reform in 1986 that explicitly overrode treaty obligations. In addition, the Internal Revenue Code was amended to make explicit that treaties have no 'preferential status' in relation to domestic law.[353]

In *Canada*, treaties are put into force by an implementing act that typically provides that the treaty will prevail over domestic law in the case of conflict. In principle, treaties can be overridden by subsequent legislation. However, treaty overrides occur infrequently, are often simply clarifying in nature, and are intended to bring Canadian treaty practice into conformity with that of its treaty partners. For example, domestic legislation overrules the position taken by a domestic court with respect to the static interpretation of a treaty. In addition, a number of terms, such as 'annuity', 'Canada', 'immovable property', 'real property', and 'periodic pension payment', have been defined by statute for purposes of Canada's tax treaties despite the absence of any definition in the treaties. The treaty 'overrides' are all found in one statute: the *Income Tax Conventions Interpretation Act*.[354]

Sweden in general did not allow subsequent legislation to increase the tax liability that would have been established using treaty rules. However, in a recent case the Swedish Supreme Administrative Court decided that subsequent

352. United States, Constitution, Art. VI, s. 2.
353. United States, IRC, s. 7852(d)(1).
354. RSC 1985, c. I-4 as amended.

legislation took precedence over treaty rules.[355] The Swedish CFC rules, enacted after the Swiss–Swedish double taxation treaty was concluded, were applied irrespective of whether they contravened the treaty. This decision has been strongly criticized by academics and practitioners.

In one situation, legislation was passed with the intention to clarify that a certain tax holiday regime was not covered by a treaty; this legislation could be viewed in a sense as a treaty override. However, the position taken in the legislation is also a plausible reading of the treaty without the legislative gloss.

It is now clear in *French* case law that, according to the Constitution, duly ratified and published treaties take precedence over prior or subsequent conflicting domestic law. The French situation is special in that, pursuant to a domestic provision, any income that France is given the right to tax by treaty is taxable, even though it would not be subject to tax under tax code provisions defining the territorial scope of French taxes.[356]

Japan as well does not allow domestic legislation to override treaty obligations. A Japanese constitutional article states that treaty obligations should be 'faithfully observed'.[357] This article has been interpreted as establishing the superiority of international rules over domestic rules, even if the latter are later in time. Thus, under this approach, treaty overrides through domestic law are not possible. Treaty rules can be displaced only if the treaty itself contains a 'saving' clause that, within the context of the treaty, preserves the application of domestic legislation.

Some Japanese treaties provide specific source rules for certain categories of income, often giving a domestic source to income that would have had a foreign source under domestic law rules. It seems accepted that the change in source rules can result in income being subject to Japanese taxation in the hands of a foreign taxpayer, even though the income would not have been taxed under the normally applicable domestic-source principles.

Australia gives effect to treaties by enacting them through the normal parliamentary process as Schedules to the *International Tax Agreements Act* of 1953. This Act states that its provisions have effect notwithstanding anything inconsistent in the basic domestic tax law, with the conspicuous exception of the general anti-avoidance rule. Under normal interpretation rules this Act could be overridden by later inconsistent legislation, but generally Australia is at pains to avoid treaty overrides and courts would be reluctant to reach such a conclusion. The closest things to treaty overrides are provisions enacted in the Agreements Act itself as interpretative measures (generally after consulting with treaty partners). For example, a provision was enacted in 1985 that unit-holders in a unit trust with a permanent establishment in Australia would also be deemed to have a permanent establishment, in order to forestall arguments that Australian taxation of the unit-holders was not permitted under the Business Profits article of tax treaties. A provision to similar effect has been included in subsequently negotiated

355. RA 2008, ref. 24 (Supreme Administrative Court).
356. France, CGI, ss 4 *bis* and 165 *bis* (individual income tax) and 209 I (corporate income tax).
357. Japan, Constitution, Art. 98.

treaties. More recently and controversially, a court decision that land-rich company provisions in the capital gains article of Australia's treaties did not extend beyond one tier was overruled in legislation that provides for the look-through of multiple tiers of companies.[358] The exclusion of the general anti-avoidance rule from the general rule that treaties prevail over domestic law is presumably justified on the basis that it is a domestic recognition of an abuse-of-treaties doctrine in international law, or the OECD view (expressed in the 2003 amendments to the Commentary on Article 1) that tax treaties are generally subject to domestic anti-avoidance rules. The sourcing rule commonly found in Australian treaties probably interacts with domestic law to make income taxable that would not otherwise be taxable under domestic law.

In the *United Kingdom*, treaties come into effect through a special legislative mechanism; it is that version of the treaty relief, and not the treaty itself, that is controlling. As a result, what is in effect a treaty override would be possible but has happened only rarely in practice. In one case, a legislative grant of authority to the tax authorities to deny tax credits in connection with jurisdictions that use unitary taxation would have amounted to a treaty override. On a number of occasions the United Kingdom has been found to be in breach of a treaty but not liable to refund tax to the taxpayer because the relevant treaty was not fully implemented into domestic law (sometimes referred to as a treaty 'underride').[359]

Under the *Dutch* constitution, the application of domestic law is restricted by directly applicable treaty provisions. This may lead occasionally to an increase in the amount of tax to be paid. For example, if a dual-resident business taxpayer is a treaty resident only of the other state, The Netherlands is restricted to taxing only the income attributable to the permanent establishment. However, if the taxpayer were taxed as a resident, the (domestic) business income might be offset by losses from foreign business activities.

German constitutional law distinguishes clearly between the tax treaty binding on the State according to the rules of international public law and the internal legislation where enactments of tax treaty rules enjoy a preference[360] that can easily be overridden by subsequent legislation. The question of whether a treaty override is a breach of customary international law is controversial, but the courts have not in the past interfered with these legislative actions. In two recent cases involving Germany, the ECJ declined to interfere, because any possible breach of an international treaty would not necessarily involve an infringement of European Community law.[361]

358. *Lamesa Holdings BV* (1997) 35 ATR 239, International Tax Agreements Act 1953 s. 3A.
359. For example, *R v. IRC ex parte Commerzbank* (1993) 68 TC 252 (HC), *Boake Allen Ltd & Ors v. Revenue & Customs Commissioners* [2007] UKHL 25 (HL), and *Sun Life Assurance Co of Canada v. Pearson* [1984] 59 TC 250 (CA) involved tax treaty underride.
360. Germany, General Order of Levies (GOL), s. 2.
361. ECJ, 6 Jun. 2007, C-298/05 (*Columbus Container*); 12 Feb. 2009, C-67/08 (*Block*).

4.2. Approach to Treaty Interpretation

The *United States* has signed, but not ratified, the Vienna Convention, and there is no consensus as to whether or to what extent the positions in the Convention are reflective of customary international law. The interpretive methods used by US courts are often consistent with the Vienna Convention approach, although there is generally more of a tendency to look beyond the 'ordinary meaning' of the treaty language to the purposes and objects of the treaty in general and the treaty article in particular. 'Context' is thus given a broader interpretation than the Vienna Convention would seem to allow. On the other hand, recent cases have shown more of a tendency to reject the use of unilateral material such as the Treasury's Technical Explanation of the treaty or the legislative history of the treaty's consideration by the Senate.[362]

Canada has ratified the Vienna Convention and its courts frequently refer to its provisions in the interpretation of tax treaties. Commentaries on the various articles of the OECD Model Convention are also often relied on (the Supreme Court has said that the Commentary is 'of high persuasive value'),[363] although the theory of how such material is available under the Vienna Convention's restrictions on the use of extrinsic material is not entirely clear. Canada has a specific statute dealing with tax treaty interpretation (the *Income Tax Conventions Interpretation Act*). The legislation makes clear that treaty references to domestic law concepts are to be interpreted in an 'ambulatory' fashion, reflecting domestic law changes that occur subsequent to the ratification of the treaty. In general, Canadian courts purport to interpret treaties more liberally than domestic legislation, although this result is difficult to see in practice. Typically, the courts will consider a wide range of extrinsic materials such as other treaties, foreign cases, and scholarly writings, when interpreting a treaty.

Sweden has also ratified the Vienna Convention, and tax treaties are interpreted in accordance with its principles. Following the Vienna Convention reference in Article 31(3) to the subsequent administrative practices of the parties, an important case held that a treaty term should be interpreted in the light of those practices rather than using the domestic law concept.[364] While the Swedish text is the starting point for interpretation, the English version will also be given special weight when, as is often the case, the treaty was negotiated in English. The Commentary on the OECD Model Convention is given special consideration.

Although *Japan* is a signatory of the Vienna Convention, it seems to have had little impact on treaty interpretation practice in Japanese courts. Courts have not referred to the Convention in connection with tax treaties, and the topic is not dealt with extensively in academic writing. On the other hand, the actual results of what sparse case law there is can be said to be consistent with the result that would have occurred under the Convention.

---

362. *Xerox Corp. v. United States*, 41 F.3rd 647 (Fed. Cir. 1994).
363. *The Queen v. Crown Forest Industries Ltd.* [1995] 2 CTC 64 (SCC).
364. RÅ 1987, ref. 162.

In *The Netherlands*, treaty interpretation and the role of the OECD Model Convention Commentary are the subject of lively discussions among commentators. The Supreme Court has occasionally referred to the Vienna Convention and over the past two decades has increasingly shown an awareness of treaty interpretation issues. In the past decade, the Supreme Court seems to have been moving away from a strict grammatical interpretation of tax treaties and appears more inclined to arrive at a reasonable result through broad references to the (assumed) object and purpose of tax treaties.

Australia is a party to the Vienna Convention and in an important 1990 case, the highest court used it to interpret a tax treaty on the basis of the OECD Commentaries.[365] In this case, the court's approach to the Vienna Convention was more in the spirit of international law, which regards the interpretive provisions of the Convention as a codification of a fairly diffuse tradition, rather than as detailed provisions of a tax statute. This approach is in line with the recent relaxation that has occurred in Australia in the use of extrinsic materials in the interpretation of tax law in general.

The *United Kingdom* is also a party to the Vienna Convention. Its courts have referred to OECD Commentaries for interpretive assistance and have approached treaty interpretation in a different manner than statutory interpretation, with more focus on purpose and intent.[366]

Since the *French* Administrative Supreme Court in 1990 reversed its prior policy of referring to the Ministry of Foreign Affairs for the interpretation to be given to ambiguous treaty wording, French tax judges are fully competent in the field of treaty interpretation. Courts do not explicitly specify the construction methods and rules they apply and there is little academic writing on the subject. But the practice of the courts seems mainly based on a principle of narrow, literal construction and, when necessary, on examining the context in its narrowest sense, with no reference to the interpretation given in the other contracting state; very few references to the OECD Commentary, which is not binding as such; and wide recourse to the meaning of corresponding terms in domestic tax law. France is not a party to the Vienna Convention; this does not mean, however, that the principles contained therein are systematically disregarded in practice. French courts consider the principles to be a codification of pre-existing customary rules or even sometimes to qualify as principles of international public law.

In *Germany*, which is a signatory to the Vienna Convention, the courts tend to follow an 'autonomous' interpretation, focusing on the wording of the treaty and the treaty context. The courts have stressed the need to come to a uniform interpretation by both parties, which is facilitated by an 'objective' approach. The Vienna Convention has had some impact on German interpretive practice, moving it in an 'objective' direction. There is still a penchant in German tax jurisprudence to interpret the language of treaties in line with similar concepts

365. *Thiel* (1990) 171 CLR 338.

366. For a classic statement, see *R v. IRC ex parte Commerzbank* (1993) 68 TC 252 (HC) at 297–98.

under domestic law, relying on the equivalent to Article 3(2) of the OECD Model Convention.

4.3. Anti-treaty Shopping Policy

United States treaty policy for the last twenty years has been to insist on a limitation-on-benefits, or anti-treaty-shopping, article in its treaties, and all treaties approved by the Senate since 1981 have contained such an article. While the details of the articles differ, they have in common the focus on the lack of economic connection between the 'resident' corporation claiming treaty benefits and the foreign jurisdiction. While the provisions originated in connection with jurisdictions with relatively low effective tax burdens, they are now present even in treaties involving high-tax jurisdictions. Thus, the treaty with Germany, a traditionally high-tax country, contains a complex limitation-on-benefits article.[367] Companies that are otherwise resident for treaty purposes are entitled to treaty benefits only if they meet certain share ownership and base erosion tests, are engaged in the active conduct of a trade or business, are publicly traded, or can obtain a competent authority agreement permitting treaty benefits.

Other countries have seemed less concerned with insisting in all cases on detailed treaty shopping rules. The reasons for this difference in attitude are varied. In the case of *Canada*, until recently treaty shopping was not viewed as a problem since Canada had a fairly uniform policy concerning the level to which it will agree to a reduction of source-based taxation. As a result, there was typically no advantage for a third-country resident to enter Canada from a particular jurisdiction. Only in the case of residents from countries that have no treaty at all could treaty shopping be a problem, and Canada's extensive treaty network made these situations fairly uncommon.

This difference in approach was reflected in the Third Protocol to the United States–Canada treaty. There, the anti-treaty-shopping article applied only when the United States was applying the treaty to investments from Canada. Canada did not feel it needed an anti-treaty-shopping provision to deal with third-country investment into Canada from the United States. However, the protocol explicitly stated that either state could deny benefits under the treaty if the granting of such benefits would result in an 'abuse' of the treaty. This made it clear that Canada could apply its domestic anti-abuse provisions in appropriate cases of inward investment from the United States, which was apparently all the protection Canada thought it needed.

Canada's attitude to treaty shopping seems to have changed recently. In the 2007 Fifth Protocol to the United States – Canada treaty, the limitation-on-benefits article became applicable bilaterally. It is not clear yet whether Canada will seek to include such comprehensive anti-treaty-shopping provisions in treaties with other countries. Several treaties already include a limited anti-avoidance rule dealing

367. United States – Germany tax treaty, Art. 28.

with treaty shopping concerning dividends, interest, and royalties. These provisions are similar to the anti-abuse rule (see below) included in many UK treaties. Further, several (35) recent treaties contain a provision that denies treaty benefits to a resident entity that is beneficially owned or controlled by the residents of a third country if the tax on the entity is substantially lower than it would have been if the entity were beneficially owned or controlled by residents of the same country in which the entity is resident. A similar provision is included in the Commentary on Article 1 of the OECD Model Convention. Finally, the Canada Revenue Agency (CRA) has aggressively (although unsuccessfully) attacked treaty shopping arrangements on the basis of the beneficial ownership requirement and domestic anti-avoidance rules.[368]

Australia until recently was in a similar position to Canada. Its treaties reflected a strict adherence to withholding rates of 15%/10%/10% for dividends, interest, and royalties respectively, and so the major scope for treaty shopping related to the use of treaties by residents of non-treaty countries. The one major example of the opportunity for treaty shopping that has come to light was quickly fixed by a rapid renegotiation of the offending provision. Since the 2001 Protocol to the Australia–United States treaty, Australia has reduced the royalty withholding rate to 5%, removed equipment leasing from the royalty article, removed withholding tax on interest on bank loans, and reduced withholding tax on dividends, in some cases to zero. Hence, there are significant opportunities for treaty shopping as a result of post-2000 treaties. Correspondingly, protocols and treaties since 2000 have included more detailed provisions on treaty shopping, but these emanate mainly from the other country. Australia would seem to prefer to use its general anti-avoidance rule against treaty shopping, since this rule is not overridden by tax treaties, although to date there have been no explicit cases in which the general anti-avoidance rule has been applied to treaty shopping.

The Netherlands, until recently, did not pursue an anti-treaty-shopping policy and has historically been a base for treaty-shopping activities. Under pressure from the United States and some of its other treaty partners and the OECD and EU policies on harmful tax competition, it has agreed on occasion to a limitation-on-benefits article and other treaty provisions against abuse of its tax treaties. Further, by statutory elimination from income of receipts from abroad that merely pass through a Dutch corporation, no treaty benefits in respect of such receipts can be claimed any longer.

Swedish treaty policy has been guided very much by the OECD Model Convention. Swedish treaties generally have not had anti-treaty-shopping articles unless the treaty partner insisted upon such articles. Even after the changes to the OECD Commentary in 1992 and 1994 recognizing the problem of treaty shopping and the possibility of requiring shareholders to be residents of the contracting states, Sweden's policy has remained unchanged. With respect to the relationship between Swedish CFC rules and treaties, prior to 1992 the white list of countries

368. *The Queen v. ML Investments SA* [2007] 4 CTC 235 (FCA) and *Prévost Car Inc. v. The Queen* [2008] 5 CTC 2306, aff'd 2009 FCA 57.

for purposes of the CFC rules included all treaty countries. However, Sweden has altered its practice, and occasionally treaty countries are excluded from the CFC white list.

Until recently *Japan* has taken no serious measures to deal with treaty-shopping problems. However, Japan is trying to add a US-style anti-treaty-shopping article to its tax treaties, including the treaties with the United Kingdom, France, and Australia.

French tax treaties rarely contain anti-treaty-shopping clauses other than those in the OECD Model Convention, in spite of the fact that France has an extensive treaty network (about 118 treaties as of 1 January 2009, including treaties with Eastern Europe, African, and South American countries), which third-country residents would perhaps like to utilize. In addition to the limitation-on-benefits clause in the 1994 French–US convention, some specific exclusions can be found in treaties with countries whose tax law could provide some incentive for tax avoidance (e.g., Switzerland or Luxembourg).

The *United Kingdom* as a general matter has been opposed to broad anti-treaty-shopping articles. Concern has been expressed with the uncertainty such articles generate, the administrative problems they entail, and the difficulty in distinguishing between abusive and non-abusive cases. A more targeted approach to treaty shopping is preferred, and the United Kingdom often negotiates an anti-abuse rule with respect to the dividend, interest, royalty, and other income articles. The rule typically denies the benefit of the article where one of the main purposes of creating the rights giving rise to the income in question is to take advantage of the treaty.[369] The major exception to this approach is the treaty with the United States, which contains a broad limitation-on-benefits clause.[370] *Germany* does not typically include anti-treaty-shopping rules in its treaties, although such rules exist in the United States and Swiss treaties. The general domestic anti-avoidance rule can be used in some treaty shopping situations unless it is clear that the case in question has been dealt with in the treaty itself.

In addition, a special legislative provision aims mainly at 'letterbox' companies claiming treaty benefits, in particular the reduction or waiver of withholding taxes.[371] The provision denies treaty-based claims for tax relief where third-country shareholders who would not be entitled to treaty relief on directly received income interpose a treaty country company that does not itself engage in significant economic activities and there is no economic or other significant reason for the use of the foreign company.

369. For example, see Australia–United Kingdom tax treaty, Art. 10(7).
370. United Kingdom–United States tax treaty, Art. 23.
371. Germany, ITA, s. 50d para. 3.

4.4. Non-discrimination

While most of the countries here considered usually have non-discrimination articles in their treaties, there are some important exceptions and restrictions. Most striking is the case of *Australia*, which until 2008 reserved its position on the non-discrimination article in the OECD Model Convention. Until 2003, Australia had a non-discrimination article only in its treaties with the United States. Since then, Australia has included non-discrimination articles in most of its treaties. The article in the US treaty is itself quite limited. While its formal coverage follows the general outline of the OECD Model Convention article, the range of situations treated is more limited. More significant, the article is framed in terms of the state's duty to ensure non-discrimination. It does not give any right to individual taxpayers to complain about possible discrimination in domestic courts. The discriminating state is required only to 'consult' in an endeavor to remove the discrimination. Finally, the provision was never included in implementing legislation applicable to the other articles of the treaty.

The 2003 treaty with the United Kingdom, however, represents a shift in Australia's treaty policy, so that non-discrimination articles will be included as a matter of course in future treaties. The UK treaty has triggered several most-favoured-nation protocols in this regard, and there is an active program underway of renegotiating Australia's treaties, especially with European countries. The UK treaty provision is, however, still subject to a number of restrictions. Specific features of Australian tax law shielded from the provision include the imputation system, research and development deductions, and limitations on rollover relief designed to prevent assets from being rolled outside Australia's jurisdictional net, and there is general protection in relation to the whole treaty for rules directed to tax avoidance or evasion (among which are specified thin capitalization, CFC, FIF, and grantor trust regimes). At least one country, France, has not been willing to accept this list of exclusions, with the result that the new treaty between Australia and France, signed in 2006, does not include a non-discrimination article.

Canada's approach to non-discrimination articles also contrasts with the other countries here considered. While the scope of non-discrimination clauses in Canadian treaties varies slightly, they typically do not grant to non-residents the usual protections against non-discrimination found in the OECD Model Convention. Thus, Canadian treaties do not contain an article guaranteeing national treatment of domestic corporations owned by non-resident shareholders. Instead, such investments are entitled only to a kind of 'most-favoured-nation' treatment according to which they will not be treated in a less favourable fashion than comparable investments held by third-country residents. In addition, the provision ensuring non-resident enterprises the right to deduct expenses on the same terms as residents is usually not present. Thus, Canada takes the position that it is entitled to apply its thin capitalization rules to interest paid by Canadian corporations to non-residents. As is the case in Australia, in Canada the desire to implement certain domestic tax policies that might be viewed as contravening traditional concepts of non-discrimination has led to a much more limited acceptance of treaty limitations on domestic action. Canada has reserved its position on the non-discrimination article in the OECD Model Convention.

In contrast, *Sweden* has followed the non-discrimination article in the OECD Model Convention in its treaty practice. The Swedish courts have given the article a fairly broad interpretation. Thus, a domestic provision allowing the deduction of an intra-group contribution only where the members of the group were all domestic corporations was found to be discriminatory when applied to two Swedish subsidiaries owned by a parent company resident in a treaty country. Similarly, where a foreign company with Swedish branch operations was merged into another foreign company, losses accruing in the branch operations were held to carry over to the merged company in the same way they would have if the merger had been between two Swedish companies.

French courts have liberally applied treaty non-discrimination clauses, under which they have, for instance, granted French permanent establishments of treaty-country corporations the exemption from withholding tax on French-source dividends and the intercorporate dividends exemption. In 2003, the Conseil d'État ruled that a limitation on the deductibility of interest paid to a parent company in the other contracting state was discriminatory because interest paid to a French parent would have been deductible.[372]

French treaty practice generally follows the OECD pattern. But with respect to the non-discrimination article, France has entered two reservations that it tries to incorporate in its bilateral tax conventions.[373] First, France is willing to apply the general non-discrimination provision contained in paragraph 1 of the OECD article solely to individuals, given French case law that equates the nationality of corporations with their residence. The second reservation – limiting the deductibility of interest paid to shareholders even when such limitation does not affect French parents – should have been deleted because it has become irrelevant under the new thin capitalization rules.

The other jurisdictions generally follow the pattern in the OECD Model Convention, with some differences in detail. In *The Netherlands*, there has been a rapid increase in the number of cases where the taxpayer has invoked the non-discrimination rules of a tax treaty (along with the non-discrimination provisions in the EC Treaty), and in many important instances the courts have decided these cases in favour of the taxpayer. In the *United Kingdom*, the non-discrimination article reached the House of Lords in the *Boake Allen* case in 2007.[374] While adopting a broad approach to the necessary comparator, the House of Lords interpreted the article in a fashion not wholly consistent with the 2008 OECD amendments to the Commentary.

Germany follows the OECD pattern. In recent years several judgments by the Federal Tax Court have increased the relevance of the non-discrimination article for tax practice.

372. Conseil d'État, 30 Dec. 2003, no. 233894 (*SA Andritz*).
373. OECD Model Tax Convention, Commentary on Art. 24, paras 88 and 91.
374. *Boake Allen Ltd v. IRC* [2007] UKHL 25 (HL).

4.5. 'Model' Tax Treaties

A number of countries have published, formally or informally, 'model' tax treaties that set forth the basic positions that their treaty negotiators take in the opening round of treaty discussions.

The *United States* Model Convention, first published in draft form in 1977, was modified in 1981, 1996, and 2006. The Model Convention provides for a 15% withholding rate for portfolio dividends and a 5% rate for dividends paid to 10% stockholders. Royalties attributable to computer software are taxable in the recipient's country of residence unless the royalties are attributable to a permanent establishment in the other country. The Model Convention also includes a provision for determining the residence of fiscally transparent entities. The 2006 Model Convention denies treaty benefits to partnerships and other pass-through entities unless their partners or members are subject to tax as residents. Thus, for treaty benefits to apply, the income must be taxable either to the entity or the entity's owners in the treaty country. The US Model is intended to apply only to relations between developed countries. In treaties with developing countries, the United States in the past has been willing to accept substantially more source-based taxation than is contemplated in its model treaty.

Canada does not have a public model treaty. Canada's treaty policy differs from the OECD Model Convention in several respects. For example, Canada insists on the right to impose a 10% withholding tax on certain royalties, a branch tax, and tax on other income arising in Canada. In addition, as noted above, Canada does not follow the non-discrimination article in the OECD Model Convention. In the treaty with the United States, Canada has recently agreed to zero withholding on interest paid by a Canadian resident to a related US resident. It is unclear whether this position will be extended to treaties with other countries.

Sweden has a model treaty that is accessible to the public, although it has not been officially published; nevertheless, some of its negotiating positions are well known. It favours the lowest withholding taxes possible on dividends, interest, and royalties in the direct investment context. Sweden also attempts to establish the principle of source-based taxation of pension income with a credit in the residence country for the source tax. This position is a result of the large number of Swedes who retire to countries with warmer climates. The permanent establishment provision generally follows the OECD Model Convention.

Japan has not published a model treaty and in general follows the OECD Model Convention, although it typically seeks a 10% withholding tax on royalties. *Germany* follows the OECD Model Convention as well, although there has been debate in recent years on a new and consolidated approach to tax treaty policy.

In *The Netherlands* more than two decades ago (1987), a standard treaty was published that in general follows the OECD pattern. The 1987 standard treaty is accompanied by a detailed explanation that has been updated. It has been decided that no further updates of the standard treaty will be published in the light of varying standards employed to negotiate tax treaties with many different treaty partners. Since dividends on direct investments are exempt from Dutch tax and, consequently, no credit is available for foreign withholding tax, Holland tries to reduce dividend withholding tax in such cases to zero. Under Dutch treaty policy there is also no source taxation on interest payments.

The *United Kingdom* has no published model treaty and generally follows the OECD Model Convention. Likewise, *France* has no formal model, and its treaties generally follow the OECD pattern. Its modern treaty practice is, however, characterized, by the following specific features: a wide definition of dividends encompassing all kinds of deemed distributions under French law; a 10% minimum shareholding as a prerequisite for the benefit of the reduced rate of withholding tax on intercorporate dividends; exemption of interest from withholding tax; the right of the source country to tax income and gains from shares in real property companies and gains from the sale of large shareholdings in local corporations; a definition of treaty-country residents, including French partnerships; provisions expressly enabling France to use its domestic anti-avoidance devices in the treaty context; certain exceptions to the non-discrimination principle (see section 4.4 above); special clauses in favour of developing countries; and clauses extending (in one-third of the French conventions) the benefit of the imputation credit to residents of the other contracting state.[375]

Although the *Australian* tax administration has been considering the publication of the Australian Model on and off for at least a decade, the government announced in 2003 that the model would not be published to preserve flexibility in treaty policy and negotiation.

On substantive matters, until recently Australia gave greater emphasis to source taxation than does the OECD Model Convention because it was a substantial net capital importer. Recent tax reform has included a reconsideration of treaty policy with a shift to greater emphasis on Australia's interests as a residence country. At this stage Australia has not fully resolved its new treaty position and seems to waver between source and residence preferences. Thus, the definition of permanent establishment is still wider than the OECD's, but the 10% minimum tax rate on royalties previously insisted on has been reduced to 5%. As well, the changes to the interest and dividend articles outlined above may be considered to go further than the OECD's. Although Australia initially maintained its insistence in 2001–2003 treaties of levying capital gains tax in accordance with its domestic law, it changed tack in 2005, when significant changes to domestic law that were generally in line with international norms were announced and enacted in 2006. Since then Australia has more or less followed the OECD Model Convention on capital gains in its treaty policy.

Despite the reintroduction of an exemption system for most direct investment overseas by Australian companies in 1990, which was turned into a full participation exemption in 2004, Australia continues to rely exclusively on a credit

375. Since the abolition of the imputation credit in 2005, the only effect of such clauses has been to grant non-resident individual shareholders a residual credit (50% of the dividend, but capped at €115, or €230 for married persons or civil partners).

provision in its tax treaties, on the theory that there is no double taxation to relieve in cases where a domestic exemption provision applies.

4.6. Tax Sparing by Treaty

Tax sparing, or the crediting of taxes not actually paid, has been an important issue in treaty relations with developing countries. Where the developed country uses the foreign tax credit method to relieve double taxation, any tax reductions or exemptions that developing countries may enact usually benefit the treasury of the developed country rather than the treaty investor. The issue comes up both with respect to net basis taxes on business profits and withholding taxes on investment income.

The *United States* has historically rejected tax sparing as a matter of treaty policy, viewing tax treaties as an inappropriate vehicle to administer what is in effect a program of assistance to foreign investment. Other countries, however, have included tax sparing credits in their treaties with developing countries, both for foregone business taxes and for reduced withholding taxes.

For example, *The Netherlands* uses an exemption method for foreign business profits but has a credit method for payments of dividends, interest, and royalties. It has granted tax sparing credits with respect to such payments in some fifteen treaties. In more recent treaties, the credits are typically limited to payments of dividends, interest, and royalties made within ten or fifteen years from the entry into effect of the treaty.

Canada, in contrast, does not generally give tax sparing credits for investment income but does accept such credits for business income. Canada gives credits for spared taxes on business income for a limited period, usually ten years. A few older treaties also provide for tax sparing in respect of certain dividends, interest, and royalties. Where a Canadian corporation receives dividends out of the exempt surplus of a foreign corporation, the dividends are not taxable in Canada and tax sparing credits are irrelevant. Therefore, the only dividends that give rise to tax sparing credits are dividends that are taxable in Canada (i.e., dividends received out of the taxable surplus of foreign affiliates and dividends received from foreign corporations that are not foreign affiliates).

Japan gives tax sparing credits for both business income and withholding taxes, as do *Sweden* and *Germany*, although in 2003 the Japanese government announced its policy to reduce tax sparing credits.

The *United Kingdom* has granted tax sparing credits in a limited number of treaties, typically involving former colonies. The use of such credits has been heavily criticized, primarily on the ground that it is inconsistent with the neutrality of treatment between domestic and foreign investment that underlies the granting of the basic foreign tax credit.

Australia was happy to grant tax sparing for both tax holidays and withholding tax reliefs in developing countries and included such provisions in many of its treaties, especially with Asian countries. The conditions for tax sparing are usually specified in some detail and are limited in duration, with the possibility of extension by mutual agreement.[376] Extension was routinely agreed upon. A change of policy was announced in 1997 in line with an OECD review of the issue[377] to the effect that in the future Australia would not grant tax sparing relief by treaty and existing provisions would not be extended. Since 2004 Australia has used a comprehensive participation exemption for dividends from foreign subsidiaries; therefore, the change in policy has little impact, except in relation to withholding taxes.

In *France*, traditional tax treaty policy used the tax sparing credit technique as well as a wide definition of the permanent establishment concept as a way to support the fiscal revenues of developing countries. Many treaties with Asian, South American, and African countries provide for tax sparing credits for passive income (i.e., dividends, interest, royalties). A special technique *(la décote africaine)* grants French investors tax credits inversely proportional to local withholding taxes on dividends distributed by corporations based in French-speaking Africa or deemed to have been distributed from benefits of permanent establishments (extraterritorial taxation) in those countries. These special clauses have become rare in recent treaties, and some have been removed from existing conventions. These tax sparing mechanisms are of less interest today because the rate of withholding taxes in developing countries has often greatly increased, and many statutory incentives to local investment have been eliminated, thus eliminating the need for tax sparing credits.

376. For example, Australia–Vietnam tax treaty, Art. 23, International Tax Agreements Act 1953, Sch. 38.
377. OECD, *Tax Sparing: A Reconsideration* (Paris: OECD, 1997).

Index

www.ingramcontent.com/pod-product-compliance
Lightning Source LLC
LaVergne TN
LVHW020003031026
849161LV00023B/862